CW00487209

CIVIL WAR AND RECONSTRUCTION
IN ALABAMA

CIVIL WAR AND RECONSTRUCTION

IN

ALABAMA

BY

WALTER L. FLEMING, Ph.D.

PROFESSOR OF HISTORY IN WEST VIRGINIA UNIVERSITY

New York

THE COLUMBIA UNIVERSITY PRESS

THE MACMILLAN COMPANY, Agents

LONDON: MACMILLAN & CO., Ltd.

1905

Norwood Press
J. S. Cushing & Co. — Berwick & Smith Co.
Norwood, Mass., U.S.A.

TO

MY WIFE

MARY BOYD FLEMING

PREFACE

THIS work was begun some five years ago as a study of Reconstruction in Alabama. As the field opened it seemed to me that an account of ante-bellum conditions, social, economic, and political, and of the effect of the Civil War upon ante-bellum institutions would be indispensable to any just and comprehensive treatment of the later period. Consequently I have endeavored to describe briefly the society and the institutions that went down during Civil War and Reconstruction. Internal conditions in Alabama during the war period are discussed at length; they are important, because they influenced seriously the course of Reconstruction. Throughout the work I have sought to emphasize the social and economic problems in the general situation, and accordingly in addition to a sketch of the politics I have dwelt at some length upon the educational, religious, and industrial aspects of the period. One point in particular has been stressed throughout the whole work, viz. the fact of the segregation of the races within the state — the blacks mainly in the central counties, and the whites in the northern and the southern counties. This division of the state into "white" counties and "black" counties has almost from the beginning exercised the strongest influence upon the history of its people. The problems of white and black in the Black Belt are not always the problems of the whites and blacks of the white counties. It is hoped that the maps inserted in the text will assist in making clear this point. Perhaps it may be thought that undue space is devoted to the history of the negro during War and Reconstruction, but after all the negro, whether passive or active, was the central figure of the period.

Believing that the political problems of War and Reconstruction are of less permanent importance than the forces which have shaped and are shaping the social and industrial life of the people, I have confined the discussion of politics to certain chapters chronologically arranged, while for the remainder of the book the topi-

cal method of presentation has been adopted. In describing
the political events of Reconstruction I have in most cases endeavored to show the relation between national affairs and local
conditions within the state. To such an extent has this been done
that in some parts it may perhaps be called a general history with
especial reference to local conditions in Alabama. Never before
and never since Reconstruction have there been closer practical
relations between the United States and the state, between Washington and Montgomery.

As to the authorities examined in the preparation of the work it
may be stated that practically all material now available — whether
in print or in manuscript — has been used. In working with newspapers an effort was made to check up in two or more newspapers
each fact used. Most of the references to newspapers — practically all of those to the less reputable papers — are to signed
articles. I have had to reject much material as unreliable, and it
is not possible that I have been able to sift out all the errors.
Whatever remain will prove to be, as I hope and believe, of only
minor consequence.

Thanks for assistance given are due to friends too numerous to
mention all of them by name. For special favors I am indebted
to Professor L. D. Miller, Jacksonville, Alabama; Mr. W. O.
Scroggs of Harvard University; Professor G. W. Duncan, Auburn,
Alabama; Major W. W. Screws of the *Montgomery Advertiser;*
Colonel John W. DuBose, Montgomery, Alabama; Mrs. J. L.
Dean, Opelika, Alabama; Major S. A. Cunningham of the *Confederate Veteran*, Nashville, Tennessee; and Major James R.
Crowe, of Sheffield, Alabama. I am indebted to Mr. L. S. Boyd,
Washington, D.C., for numerous favors, among them, for calling
my attention to the scrap-book collection of Edward McPherson,
then shelved in the library of Congress along with Fiction. On
many points where documents were lacking, I was materially
assisted by the written reminiscences of people familiar with conditions of the time, among them my mother and father, the late
Professor O. D. Smith of Auburn, Alabama, and the late Ryland
Randolph, Esq., of Birmingham. Many old negroes have related
their experiences to me. Hon. Junius M. Riggs of the Alabama
Supreme Court Library, by the loan of documents, assisted me
materially in working up the financial history of the Reconstruc-

tion; Dr. David Y. Thomas of the University of Florida read and criticised the entire manuscript; Dr. Thomas M. Owen, Director of the Alabama Department of Archives and History, has given me valuable assistance from the beginning to the close of the work by reading the manuscript, by making available to me not only the public archives, but also his large private collection, and by securing illustrations. But above all I have been aided by Professor William A. Dunning of Columbia University, at whose instance the work was begun, who gave me many helpful suggestions, read the manuscript, and saved me from numerous pitfalls, and by my wife, who read and criticised both manuscript and proof, and made the maps and the index and prepared some of the illustrations.

WALTER L. FLEMING.

New York City,
August, 1905.

CONTENTS

PART I

INTRODUCTION

CHAPTER I

PERIOD OF SECTIONAL CONTROVERSY

CHAPTER II

SECESSION FROM THE UNION

PART II

WAR TIMES IN ALABAMA

CHAPTER III

MILITARY AND POLITICAL EVENTS

CHAPTER IV

ECONOMIC AND SOCIAL CONDITIONS

PART III

THE AFTERMATH OF WAR

CHAPTER V

SOCIAL AND ECONOMIC DISORDER

                     PART IV

              PRESIDENTIAL RESTORATION

                    CHAPTER VIII

            FIRST PROVISIONAL ADMINISTRATION

CHAPTER IX

SECOND PROVISIONAL ADMINISTRATION

CHAPTER X

MILITARY GOVERNMENT, 1865–1866

CHAPTER XI

THE WARDS OF THE NATION

PART V

CONGRESSIONAL RECONSTRUCTION

CHAPTER XII

MILITARY GOVERNMENT UNDER THE RECONSTRUCTION ACTS

CHAPTER XIII

THE CAMPAIGN OF 1867

CHAPTER XIV

THE "RECONSTRUCTION" CONVENTION

CHAPTER XV

THE "RECONSTRUCTION" COMPLETED

CHAPTER XVI

THE UNION LEAGUE OF AMERICA

PART VI

CARPET-BAG AND NEGRO RULE

CHAPTER XVII

TAXATION AND THE PUBLIC DEBT

CHAPTER XVIII

RAILROAD LEGISLATION AND FRAUDS

CHAPTER XIX

RECONSTRUCTION IN THE SCHOOLS

CHAPTER XX

RECONSTRUCTION IN THE CHURCHES

CHAPTER XXI

THE KU KLUX REVOLUTION

CHAPTER XXII

REORGANIZATION OF THE INDUSTRIAL SYSTEM

CHAPTER XXIII

POLITICAL AND SOCIAL CONDITIONS DURING RECONSTRUCTION

CHAPTER XXIV

THE OVERTHROW OF RECONSTRUCTION

LIST OF ILLUSTRATIONS

LIST OF MAPS

PART I

INTRODUCTION

CIVIL WAR AND RECONSTRUCTION IN ALABAMA

CHAPTER I

THE PERIOD OF SECTIONAL CONTROVERSY

WHEN Alabama seceded in 1861, it had been in existence as a political organization less than half a century, but in many respects its institutions and customs were as old as European America. The white population was almost purely Anglo-American. The early settlements had been made on the coast near Mobile, and from thence had extended up the Alabama, Tombigbee, and Warrior rivers. In the northern part the Tennessee valley was early settled, and later, in the eastern part, the Coosa valley. After the river valleys, the prairie lands in central Alabama were peopled, and finally the poorer lands of the southeast and the hills south of the Tennessee valley. The bulk of the population before 1861 was of Georgian birth or descent, the settlers having come from middle Georgia, which had been peopled from the hills of Virginia. Georgians came into the Tennessee valley early in the nineteenth century. The Creek reservation prevented immigration into eastern Alabama before the thirties, but the Georgians went around and settled southeast Alabama along the line of the old "Federal road." When the Creek Indians consented to migrate, it was found that the Georgians were already in possession of the country, — more than 20,000 strong, and a government was at once erected over the Indian counties. People from Georgia also came down the Coosa valley to central Alabama. The Virginians went to the western Black Belt, to the Tennessee valley, and to central Alabama. North Carolina sent thousands of her citizens down through the Tennessee valley and thence across country to the Tombigbee valley and western Alabama; others came through Georgia and followed the routes of Georgia migration.

3

South Carolinians swarmed into the southern, central, and western counties, and a goodly number settled in the Tennessee valley. Tennessee furnished a large proportion of the settlers to the Tennessee valley, to the hill counties south of the Tennessee, and to the valleys in central and western Alabama. Among the immigrants from Virginia, North and South Carolina, and Tennessee was a large

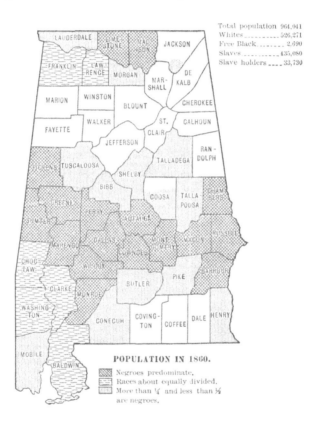

Total population 964,041
Whites _____ 526,271
Free Black _____ 2,690
Slaves _____ 435,080
Slave holders ____ 33,730

POPULATION IN 1860.

Negroes predominate.
Races about equally divided.
More than ¼ and less than ½ are negroes.

Scotch-Irish element, and with the Tennesseeans came a sprinkling of Kentuckians. In western Alabama were a few thousand Mississippians, and into southeast Alabama a few hundred settlers came from Florida. From the northern states came several thousand, principally New England business men. The foreign element was insignificant — the Irish being most numerous, with a few hundred each of Germans, English, French, and Scotch. In Mobile and

Marengo counties there was a slight admixture of French blood in the population.[1]

In regard to the character of the settlers it has been said that the Virginians were the least practical and the Georgians the most so, while the North Carolinians were a happy medium. The Georgians were noted for their stubborn persistence, and they usually succeeded in whatever they undertook. The Virginians liked a leisurely planter's life with abundant social pleasures. The Tennesseeans and Kentuckians were hardly distinguishable from the Virginians and Carolinians, to whom they were closely related. The northern professional and business men exercised an influence more than commensurate with their numbers, being, in a way, picked men. Neither the Georgians nor the Virginians were assertive office-seekers, but the Carolinians liked to hold office, and the politics of the state were moulded by the South Carolinians and Georgians. All were naturally inclined to favor a weak federal administration and a strong state government with much liberty of the individual. The theories

[1] NATIVITIES OF THE FREE POPULATION

STATE OR COUNTRY	1850	1860	STATE OR COUNTRY	1850	1860
Alabama	237,542	320,026	Ohio	276	265
Connecticut	91	343	Pennsylvania	876	989
Florida	1,060	1,644	South Carolina	48,663	45,185
Georgia	58,997	83,517	Tennessee	22,541	19,139
Kentucky	2,694	1,966	Virginia	10,387	7,598
Louisiana	628	1,149	England	941	1,174
Maine	215	272	France	503	359
Maryland	757	683	Germany	1,068	2,601
Massachusetts	654	753	Ireland	2,639	5,664
Mississippi	2,852	4,848	Scotland	584	696
New York	1,443	1,848	Spain	163	157
North Carolina	28,521	23,504	Switzerland	113	138

TOTALS	1850	1860
Native	420,032	526,769
Foreign	7,638	12,352

The total population from 1820 to 1860 was as follows : —

	WHITE	BLACK
1820	85,451	41,879
1830	190,406	117,549
1840	335,185	253,532
1850	426,514	342,844
1860	526,271	435,080

of Patrick Henry, Jefferson, and Calhoun, not those of Washington and John Marshall, formed the political creed of the Alabamians.

The wealthy people were found in the Tennessee valley, in the Black Belt extending across the centre of the state, and in Mobile, the one large town. They were (except a few of the Mobilians) all slave-holders. The poorer white people went to the less fertile districts of north and southeast Alabama, where land was cheap, preferring to work their own poor farms rather than to work for some one else on better land. But nearly every slave county had its colony of poorer whites, who were invariably settled on the least fertile soils. Among these settlers there was a certain dislike of slavery, because they believed that, were it not for the negro, the whites might themselves live on the fertile lands. Yet they were not in favor of emancipation in any form, unless the negro could be gotten entirely out of the way — a free negro being to them an abomination. If the negro must stay, then they preferred slavery to continue.

NATIVITY OF PUBLIC MEN

Virginia _____1
Georgia _____2
South Carolina _____3
North Carolina _____4
Kentucky _____5
Tennessee _____6
Miss. and other So. states __7
Middle States and West __8
New England _____9
Foreign _____10
Indian _____11
a = Location of Anti-Slavery Society before 1835

Each figure represents some person who became prominent before 1865, and indicates his native state. The location of the figure on the map indicates his place of residence. Note the segregation along the rivers and in the Black Belt.

Over the greater part of Alabama there were no class distinctions before 1860; the state was too young. In the wilderness classes had fused and the successful men were often those never heard of in the older states. A candidate of "the plain people" was always elected, because all were frontier people. This does not mean that in Huntsville, Montgomery, Greensboro, and Mobile there were not the beginnings of an aristocracy based on education, wealth, and family descent. But these were very small spots on the map of Alabama, and there were no heartburnings over social inequalities.[1]

Such was the composition of the white population of Alabama before 1860. No matter what might be their political affiliations, in practice nearly all were Democrats of the Jeffersonian school, believing in the largest possible liberty for the individual and in local management of all local affairs, and to the frontier Democrat nearly all questions that concerned him were local. The political leaders excepted, the majority of the population knew little and cared less about the Federal government except when it endeavored to restrain or check them in their course of conquest and expansion in the wilderness. The relations of the people of Alabama with the Federal government were such as to confirm and strengthen them in their local attachments and sectional politics. The controversies that arose in regard to the removal of the Indians, and over the public lands, nullification, slavery, and western expansion, prevented the growth of attachment to the Federal government, and tended to develop a southern rather than a "continental" nationality. The state came into the Union when the sections were engaged in angry debate over the Missouri Compromise measures, and its attitude in Federal politics was determined from the beginning. The next most serious controversy with the Federal government and with the North was in regard to the removal of the Indians from the southern states. The southwestern frontiersmen, like all other Anglo-Americans, had no place in their economy for the Indian, and they were determined that he should not stand in their way.

[1] Hundly, "Social Relations"; Hodgson, "Cradle of the Confederacy," Ch. I; Garrett, "Reminiscences," Ch. I; Miller's and Brown's "Histories of Alabama," *passim;* Saunders, "Early Settlers," *passim.* From 1840 to 1860 there was a slight sectional and political division between the counties of north Alabama and those of central and south Alabama, owing to the conflicting interests of the two sections and to the lack of communication. By 1860 this was tending to become a social division between the white counties and the black counties. The division to some extent still exists.

Indians and Nullification

For half a century, throughout the Gulf states, the struggle with the Indian tribes for the possession of the fertile lands continued, and in this struggle the Federal government was always against the settlers. Before the removal of the Indians, in 1836, the settlers of Alabama were in almost continual dispute with the Washington administration on this subject.[1] The trouble began in Georgia, and thousands of Georgians brought to Alabama a spirit of jealousy and hostility to the United States government, and a growing dislike of New England and the North on account of their stand in regard to the Indians. For when troubles, legal and otherwise, arose with the Indians, their advisers were found to be missionaries and land agents from New England. The United States wanted the Indians to remain as states within states; the Georgia and Alabama settlers felt that the Indians must go. The attitude of the Federal government drove the settlers into extreme assertions of state rights. In Georgia it came almost to war between the state and United States troops during the administration of John Quincy Adams, a New Englander, who was disliked by the settlers for his support of the Indian cause; and the whole South was made jealous by the decisions of the Supreme Court in the Indian cases. Had Adams been elected to a second term, there would probably have been armed resistance to the policy of the United States. Jackson, a southern and western man, had the feeling of a frontiersman toward the Indians; and his attitude gained him the support of the frontier southern states in the trouble with South Carolina over nullification.

Immediately after the nullification troubles, the general government attempted to remove the white settlers from the Indian lands in east Alabama. The lands had been ceded by the Indians in 1832, and the legislature of Alabama at once extended the state administration over the territory. Settlers rushed in; some were already there. But by the treaty the Indians were entitled to remain on their land until they chose to move; and now the United States marshals, supported by the army, were ordered to remove the 30,000 whites

---

[1] In all studies of the sectional spirit it should be remembered that the Southwest was settled somewhat in spite of the Washington government and without the protection of the United States army ; the reverse is true of the Northwest.

GAINESWOOD.

A Marengo County Plantation Home. Abandoned since the War.

who had settled in the nine Indian counties. Governor Gayle, who had been elected as an opponent of nullification, informed the Secretary of War that the proposed action of the central government meant nothing less than the destruction of the state administration, and declared that he would, at all costs, sustain the jurisdiction of the state government. The troops killed a citizen who resisted removal, and the Federal authorities refused to allow the slayers to be tried by state courts. There was great excitement in the state, and public meetings were everywhere held to organize resistance. The legislature authorized the governor to persist in maintaining the state administration in the nine Indian counties. A collision with the United States troops was expected, and offers of volunteers were made to the governor, — even from New York. Finally the United States government yielded, the whites remained on the Indian lands, the state authority was upheld in the Indian counties, the soldiers were tried before state courts, and the Indians were removed to the West. The governor proclaimed a victory for the state, and the 30,000 angry Alabamians rejoiced over what they considered the defeat of the unjust Federal government.[1]

Thus in Alabama nullification of Federal law was successfully carried out. And it was done by a state administration and a people that a year before had refused to approve the course of South Carolina. But South Carolina was regarded in Alabama, as in the rest of the South, somewhat as an erratic member that ought to be disciplined once in a while. A strong and able minority in Alabama accepted the basis of the nullification doctrine, *i.e.* the sovereignty of the states, and after this time this political element was usually known as the State Rights party. They had no separate organization, but voted with Whigs or Democrats, as best served their purpose. Secession was little talked of, for affairs might yet go well, they thought, within the Union. A majority of the Democrats, for several years after 1832, were probably opposed in theory to nullification and secession when South Carolina was an actor, but in practice they acted as they had done in the Indian disputes which concerned them more closely.

[1] Hodgson, " Cradle of the Confederacy," Chs. 2, 4, 6, 8 ; DuBose, " Life of William L. Yancey " ; Phillips, " Georgia and State Rights," Chs. 2, 3 ; Pickett, " Alabama," Owen's edition.

The Slavery Controversy and Political Divisions

It was at the height of the irritation of the Indian controversy that the agitation by the abolitionists of the North began. The question which more than any other alienated the southern people from the Union was that concerning negro slavery. From 1819 to 1860 the majority of the white people of Alabama were not friendly to slavery as an institution. This was not from any special liking for the negro or belief that slavery was bad for him, but because it was believed that the presence of the negro, slave or free, was not good for the white race. To most of the people slavery was merely a device for making the best of a bad state of affairs. The constitution of 1819 was liberal in its slavery provisions, and the legislature soon enacted (1827) a law prohibiting the importation, for sale, hire, or barter, of slaves from other states. For a decade there was strong influence at each session of the state legislature in favor of gradual emancipation; agents of the Quakers worked in the state, buying and paying a higher price for cotton that was not produced by slave labor; and in north Alabama, during the twenties and early thirties, there was a number of emancipation societies.[1] An emancipation newspaper, *The Huntsville Democrat*, was published in Huntsville, and edited by James G. Birney, afterwards a noted abolitionist. The northern section of the state, embracing the strong Democratic white counties, was distinctly unfriendly to slavery, or rather to the negro, and controlled the politics of the state.[2] The effect of the abolition movement in the North was the destruction of the emancipation organizations in the South, and both friends and foes of the institution united on the defensive. The non-slaveholders were not deluded followers of the slave owners. After the slavery question became an issue in politics, the non-slaveholders in Alabama were rather more aggressive, and were even more firmly determined to maintain negro slavery than were the slaveholders. To the rich

[1] In 1832 there were eight emancipation societies in north Alabama: The State Society, Courtland, Lagrange, Tuscumbia, Florence, Madison County, Athens, and Lincoln. Publications, Southern History Association, Vol. II, pp. 92, 93.

[2] See Hodgson, p. 7. In 1842 representation in the legislature was changed from the "federal" basis and based on white population alone. This change was made by the Democrats and was opposed by the Whigs. The latter predominated in the Black Belt.

hereditary slaveholders, who were relatively few in number, it was more or less a question of property, and that was enough to fight about at any time. But to the average white man who owned no negroes and who worked for his living at manual labor, the question was a vital social one. The negro slave was bad enough; but he thought that the negro freed by outside interference and turned loose on society was much more to be feared.[1] The large majorities for extreme measures came from the white counties; the secession vote in 1860 was largely a white county vote. But when secession came, the Whiggish Black Belt which had been opposed to secession was astonished not to receive, in the war that followed, the hearty support of the Democratic white counties.

Before the nullification troubles in 1832 there was no distinct political division among the people of Alabama; all were Democrats. Those of the white counties were of the Jacksonian type, those of the black counties were rather of the Jeffersonian faith; but all were strict constructionists, especially on questions concerning the tariff, the Indians, the central government, and slavery. The question of nullification caused a division in the ranks of the Democratic party — one wing supporting Jackson, the other accepting Calhoun as leader. For several years later, however, the Democratic candidates had no opposition in the elections, though within the party there were contests between the Jacksonians and the growing State Rights (Calhoun) wing. But with the settling of the country, the growth of the power of the Black Belt, and the differentiation of interests within the state, there appeared a second party, the Whigs. Its strength lay among the large planters and slaveholders of the central Black Belt, though it often took its leaders from the black counties of the Tennessee valley. This party was able to elect a governor but once, and then only because of a division in the Democratic ranks. After 1835 it secured one-third of the representation in Congress and the same proportion in the legislature. It was the "broadcloth" party, of the wealthier and more cultivated people. It did not appeal to the "plain people" with much success; but it was always a respectable party, and there was no jealousy of it then, and now "there are no bitter memories against it."[2]

---

[1] Hodgson, Ch. 1 ; Debates of Convention of 1861, *passim.*
[2] Miller, "Alabama," p. 123.

Numerically, the Whigs were about as strong as the anti-nullification wing of the Democratic party, so that the balance of power was held by the constantly increasing State Rights (Calhoun) element. When Van Buren became leader of the national Democracy, the State Rights people in Alabama united with the regular Democrats and voted with them for about ten years. The State Rights men were devoted followers of Calhoun, but in political theories they soon went beyond him. For a while they were believers in nullification as a constitutional right, but soon began to talk of secession as a sovereign right. They were in favor of no compromise where the rights of the South were concerned. They were logical, extreme, doctrinaire; they demanded absolute right, and viewed every action of the central government with suspicion. A single idea firmly held through many years gave to them a power not justified by their numerical strength.

The Whigs did not stand still on political questions; as the Democrats and the State Rights men abandoned one position for another more advanced, the Whigs moved up to the one abandoned. Thus they were always only about one election behind. It was the constant agitation of the slavery question that drove the Whigs along in the wake of the more advanced party. Both parties were in favor of expansion in the Southwest. They were indignant at the New England position on the Texas question, and talked much of disunion if such a policy of obstruction was persisted in. Again, after the Mexican War all parties were furious at the opposition shown to the annexation of the territory from Mexico. It was now the spirit of expansion, the lust for territory, that rose in opposition to the obstructive policy of northern leaders; and a new element was added when an attempt was made to shut out southerners from the territory won mainly by the South by forbidding the entrance of slavery.

The number of those in favor of resisting at every point the growing desire of the North to restrict slavery was increasing steadily. The leader of the State Rights men was William L. Yancey. He opposed all compromises, for, as he said, compromise meant that the system was evil and was an acknowledgment of wrong, and no right, however abstract, must be denied to the South. He was a firm believer in slavery as the only method of solving the race question, and saw clearly the dangers that would result from the abolition programme if the North and South remained united. So to prevent worse calamities he was in favor of disunion. He was the greatest orator ever heard in the South. He was in no sense a demagogue; he had none of the arts of the popular politician. Sent to Congress in the heat of the fight between the sections, he resigned because he thought the battle was to be fought elsewhere. For twenty years he stood before the people of Alabama, telling them that slavery could not be preserved within the Union; that before any effective settlement of controversies could be made, Alabama and the other southern states must withdraw and make terms from the outside, or stay out of the Union and have done with agitation and interference. Secession was self-preservation, he told a people who believed that the destruction of slavery meant the destruction of society. For twenty years he and his followers, heralds of the storm, were ostracized by all political parties, which accepted his theories, but denied the necessity for putting them into practice. When at last the people came to follow him, he told them that they had probably waited too late, and that they were seceding on a weaker cause than any of those he had presented for twenty years.

Yancey was a leader of State Rights men but never a leader in the Democratic party. Once, in 1848, when all were angry on account of the opposition on the Mexican question, Yancey was called to the front in the Democratic state convention. He offered resolutions, which were adopted,[1] to the effect (1) that the people of a territory could not prevent the holding of slaves before the formation of a state constitution, and that Congress had no power whatever to restrict slavery in the territories; (2) that those who held the opposite opinion were not Democrats, and that the Democratic party of Alabama would not support for President any candidate who held such views. The delegates to the National Democratic Convention at Baltimore were instructed to withdraw if the Alabama resolutions were rejected. By a vote of two hundred and sixteen to thirty-six they were rejected; yet none of the delegates except Yancey withdrew. Refusing to support Cass for the presidency because he believed in "squatter sovereignty," Yancey was again ostracized

---

[1] Known as the "Alabama Platform" of 1848.

by the Democratic leaders.[1] Now the State Rights men became
more aggressive, for they said this was the time to settle the slavery
question, before it was too late. The North, it was thought, would
not be averse to separation from the South. The Whigs began to
advance non-intervention theories, and but for the death of President
Taylor, who adhered to the free-soil Whigs, political parties in
Alabama would probably have broken up in 1850 and fused into
one on the slavery question.

Growth of Secession Sentiment

The compromise measures of 1850 pleased few people in Alabama,
and there was talk of resistance and of assisting Texas by force, if
necessary, against the appropriation of her territory by the central
government. The moderates condemned the Compromise and said
they would not yield again. The more advanced demanded a repeal
of the Compromise or immediate secession. Yancey said there was
no hope of a settlement and that it was time to set the house in order.
In 1850-1851 there was a widespread movement toward a rejection
of the Compromise and a secession of the lower South, but the political
leaders were disposed to give the Compromise a trial. To the Nashville convention, held in June, 1850, to discuss measures to secure
redress of grievances, the Alabama legislature at an unofficial meeting chose the following delegates: Benjamin Fitzpatrick, William
Cooper, John A. Campbell, Thomas J. Judge, John A. Winston,
Leroy P. Walker, William M. Murphy, Nicholas Davis, R. C. Shorter,
Thomas A. Walker, Reuben Chapman, James Abercrombie, and
William M. Byrd — all Whigs or Conservative Democrats. The
resolutions passed by the convention were cautious and prudent,
and were generally supported by the Whigs and opposed by the
Democrats. In Montgomery, upon the return of the Alabama delegation, a public meeting, held to ratify the action of the Nashville
convention, condemned it instead, and approved the programme of
Yancey who again declared that it was "time to set the house in
order." The contest in Alabama was simply between the Compromise, with maintenance of the Union, and rejection of the Com-

---

[1] Benjamin Fitzpatrick led the conservative element of the Democratic party and
opposed Yancey.

promise to be followed by secession. It was not a campaign between Whig and Democrat, but between Union and Secession. The old party lines were not drawn. Associations were formed all over the state to oppose the Compromise and to advocate secession. The Unionists drew together, but less heartily. The compact State Rights element lost influence on account of a division that now showed in its ranks. One section, led by William L. Yancey, was for separate and unconditional secession; another, led by J. J. Seibels, favored coöperation of the southern states within the Union and united deliberation before secession.[1] The State Rights Convention met in Montgomery, February 10, 1851, and recommended a southern congress to decide the questions at issue and declared that if any other state would secede, Alabama should go also.[2] The action of the convention pleased few and was repudiated by the "separate secessionist" element. The candidates of the State Rights — now called the "Southern Rights" — party were supported by a majority of the Democrats. They demanded the repeal of the Compromise, and resistance to future encroachments; they demanded southern ministers and southern churches, southern books and papers, and southern pleasure resorts.

The "Union" leaders were Judge Benajah S. Bibb, James Abercrombie, Thomas J. Judge, Henry W. Hilliard, Thomas H. Watts, Senator William R. King, — nearly all Virginians or North Carolinians by birth or descent. At the State "Union" Convention held in Montgomery, January 19, 1851, among the more prominent delegates were: Thomas B. Cooper, R. M. Patton, W. M. Byrd, B. S. Bibb, J. M. Tarleton, W. B. Moss, James H. Clanton, L. E. Parsons, Robert J. Jamison, Henry W. Hilliard, R. W. Walker, Thomas H. Watts, Nicholas Davis, Jr., and C. M. Wilcox, — all were Whigs, and were Virginians, North Carolinians, and men of northern birth. This meeting denied the "constitutional" right of secession. The Union candidates for Congress were C. C. Langdon, James

[1] This division in the State Rights ranks existed until secession was actually achieved and even after.

[2] Each extreme southern state — Texas, Mississippi, Alabama, and South Carolina — showed a desire to have some more moderate state act first. Some prominent men in this convention were Yancey, Seibels, Thomas Williams, John A. Elmore, B. F. Saffold, Abram Martin, A. P. Bagley, Adam C. Felder, David Clopton, and George Goldthwaite, nearly all South Carolinians by birth.

Abercrombie, Judge Mudd, William R. Smith, W. R. W. Cobb, George S. Houston, and Alexander White, — each of whom denied the "constitutional" right of secession, but said nothing about it as a "sovereign" right.

The "Unionists" — the old Whigs and the Jacksonian Democrats — were successful in the elections, but by accepting, though disapproving, the Compromise measures, and by repudiating the doctrine of secession as a "constitutional" right,[1] they had advanced beyond the position held by Yancey in 1848.

After the success of the "Union" party in 1851-1852, the Southern Rights Associations resolved to suspend for a time the debate on secession. Thereupon the "Union" Democrats resumed their old party allegiance and the "Union" party was left to consist of old Whigs alone. The Whigs wished to continue the "Union" organization, for they no longer found it possible to act with the northern Whigs, and in 1852 several of their prominent leaders in Alabama refused to support the Whig presidential ticket. On the other hand, the extreme "Southern Rights" men broke away from the Democrats in 1852 and declared for immediate secession. They supported Troup and Quitman, who polled, however, only 2174 votes in the state; but the Whigs and the Democrats each lost about 15,000, who refused to vote.

And now came the break-up of old parties. The slavery question was always before the people and was becoming more and more irritating. Compromises had failed to quiet the controversy. The position of the "Union" Whigs in the black counties became intolerable. They had to combat secession at home, and they had to guard against trouble among their slaves caused by the abolitionist propaganda. By 1855 almost all the Alabama Whigs had become "Americans," at the same time searching for a new issue and repudiating the principles upon which the "American" party was founded. Again they were left alone by the antislavery stand taken by the northern wing of this party. Yet in spite of every possible discouragement they held together and controlled the black counties. When the Kansas question arose all the parties in Alabama were united in reference to it. The doctrine of squatter sovereignty was not accepted, but there was an opportunity, both parties thought, to

[1] A dodging of the question.

win Kansas peaceably and stay the threatened separation, but the northern methods of settling Kansas by organized antislavery emigration from New England paralyzed the efforts of the moderate "Union" southerners. Similar methods were attempted by the South, and several colonies of emigrants were sent from Alabama; [1] but by 1857 it was known that Kansas was lost.

The great debate between William L. Yancey and Roger A. Pryor in the Southern Commercial Convention held in Montgomery in May, 1858, showed that the people of Alabama were then in advance of their political leaders and were coming to the position long held by Yancey and the secessionists. Pryor's position in favor of compromise and delay had the support of nearly all the party leaders of Alabama; Yancey, always in disfavor with party leaders, captured the convention with his policy of secession in case of failure of redress of grievances. Secession was no longer a doctrine to be condemned unless on the ground of expediency. Whig leaders were now becoming Southern Rights Democrats. Many Democrats thought it was time to force an issue and come to a settlement; this Yancey proposed to do by demanding a repeal of all the laws against the slave trade because they expressed a disapproval of slavery. If slavery were not wrong, then the slave trade should not be denounced as piracy. Yancey had not the slightest desire to reopen the slave trade, and knew that the North would not consent to a repeal of the laws against it, yet he said the demand should be made. He believed the demand to be legitimate, though sure to be rejected. The national Democratic party would thus be divided and the issue forced. [2]

For any purpose of opposing the Yancey programme the Alabama "Union" men were rendered helpless by the turn politics were taking in the North. The formation out of the wreck of the old Whig party of the distinctly sectional and radical Republican party, the attitude of the leaders of that party, the talk about the "irrepressible

---

[1] For an account of one of these, see the *American Historical Review*, Oct., 1900.

[2] General Pryor informs me that at the convention of 1858 no one understood that there was any desire on the part of Yancey and others to reopen the slave trade. They recognized that the rest of the world was against them on that question and were demanding simply a repeal of what they considered discriminating laws. Yancey compared the question to that of the tea tax in the American colonies. See also Hodgson, p. 371, and Yancey's speeches in Smith's "Debates of 1861."

conflict" and the "Union cannot endure half slave and half free," the indorsement of the "Impending Crisis" with its incendiary teachings, the effect of "Uncle Tom's Cabin" on thousands who before had cared nothing about slavery, and finally the raid of John Brown into Virginia,[1] — these were influences more powerful toward uniting the people to resistance than all the speeches of State Rights leaders on abstract constitutional questions.   After 1856 the people were in advance of their leaders.

On January 11, 1860, the Democratic state convention unanimously adopted resolutions favoring the Dred Scott decision as a settlement of the slavery question.   The delegation to the national nominating convention at Charleston was instructed to withdraw in case these resolutions were not accepted in substance as a part of the platform.   At Charleston the majority report of the committee on the platform sustained the Alabama position.   When the report was laid before the convention, a proposition was made to set it aside for the minority report, which vaguely said nothing.   Yancey in a great speech delivered the ultimatum of the South, the adoption of the majority report.   The vote was taken and the South defeated. L. Pope Walker[2] announced the withdrawal of the Alabama delegation and the delegations from the other southern states followed.[3] Both sections of the convention then adjourned to meet in Baltimore. Influences for and against compromise were working, and it is probable that a majority of the seceders would have harmonized had not the Douglas organization declared the seats of the seceders vacant and admitted delegates irregularly elected by Douglas conventions

---

[1] A branch of the Underground Railway reached from Ohio as far into Alabama as Tallapoosa County.   Kagi, one of Brown's confederates, had marked out a chain of black counties where he had travelled and where the negroes were expected to rise.   He had travelled through South Carolina, Georgia, Alabama, and Mississippi.   Russell County, Alabama, was one of those marked on his map.   The people were greatly alarmed when the map was discovered.   See Seibert's " Underground Railroad," pp. 119, 160, 167, 195; Hinton, "John Brown"; Hague, "Blockaded Family."   As early as 1835 incendiary literature had been scattered among the Alabama slaves, and in that year the grand jury of Tuscaloosa County indicted Robert G. Williams of New York for sending such printed matter among the slaves.   General Gayle demanded that he be sent to Alabama for trial, but Governor Marcy refused to give him up.   See Brown's " Alabama," p. 167, and *Gulf States Hist. Mag.*, July, 1903.

[2] Afterwards Confederate Secretary of War.

[3] Yancey was willing to disregard instructions and not withdraw; the rest of the delegation overruled him.   See paper by Petrie in Transactions Ala. Hist. Soc., Vol. IV.

DALLAS GAZETTE,
EXTRA.

CAHABA, FRIDAY NIGHT, Dec. 2, 1859.

Execution of Old-Brown.

THE DOG IS DEAD!

No Chance for a Rescue!!

Thus perish all the enemies of the South!

Justice has been executed on old JOHN
BROWN, commonly known as OSSAWATO-
MIE BROWN. He is now before the judgment bar to answer for the crime of
murder, and for attempting to incite a
servile war amongst a people who had
never harmed him, and who lived under
the same constitution and government
with himself. To his execution every
right-thinking man will say AMEN!

The following despatch was received,
to-night, from the telegraphic operator
at Montgomery, by Mr. C. I. CURRIE.
We hasten to lay this important news
before the public:

MONTGOMERY, —

JOHN BROWN was hung be-
tween 11 and 12 to-day.
He hung on the gallows a
half hour.

A JOHN BROWN EXTRA.

in the South. After the damage was done, Yancey was pressed to take the vice-presidency on the Douglas ticket.[1] Douglas was known to be in bad health and Yancey was told that he might expect to be President within a few months, if he accepted. But it was too late for further compromise, and Yancey toured the North, speaking for Breckenridge. A State Rights convention in Alabama indorsed the candidates of the seceded convention; a convention of Douglas Democrats in Montgomery declared for Douglas; the "Constitutional Union" party (the old Whigs and "Americans" or "Know-nothings"), for Bell and Everett and old-fashioned conservative respectability. During the campaign Douglas visited the state and was well received, but aroused no enthusiasm, while Yancey was tumultuously welcomed.

As far back as February 24, 1860, the legislature had passed almost unanimously a resolution concurring with South Carolina in regard to the right and necessity of secession, and declaring that Alabama would not submit to the domination of a "foul sectional party." In case of the election of a "Black" Republican President a convention was to be called, and $200,000 was appropriated for its use.[2] A committee was appointed to reorganize the militia system of the state, and so important was the work deemed that the committee was excused from all other duties. The Senate declared that it was expedient to establish an arsenal, a firearms factory, and a powder mill. A bill was passed to encourage the manufacture of firearms in Alabama.[3] At this session seventy-four military companies were incorporated and provision made for military schools.[4] Elections returns were anxiously awaited.[5] It was certain that the election of Lincoln and Hamlin would result in secession.[6] When

---

[1] Hodgson, Ch. 15.

[2] Acts of Alabama (1859–1860), pp. 689–690; Smith's "Debates," pp. 10, 11.

[3] Acts of Alabama (1859–1860), pp. 681–682; Senate Journal (1859–1860), pp. 147, 176, 293, 302.

[4] During this session Judge Sam. Rice, in reply to John Forsyth and others who feared that secession would lead to war, said: "There will be no war. But if there should be, we can whip the Yankees with popguns." After the war, when he had turned "scalawag," he was taken to task for the speech. "You said we could whip the Yankees with popguns." "Yes, — but the damned rascals wouldn't fight that way."

[5] The popular vote in Alabama was: for Breckenridge, 48,831; for Douglas, 13,621; for Bell, 27,875.

[6] Many people believed that Hamlin was a mulatto.

the news came the old "Union" leaders declared for secession and by noon of the next day the "Union" party had gone to pieces. The leaders who had opposed secession to the last — Watts, Clanton, Goldthwaite, Judge, and Hilliard — now took their stand by the side of Yancey and declared that Alabama must withdraw from the Union. Governor Moore, a very moderate man, in a public speech said that no course was left but for the state to secede, and with the other southern states form a confederacy. Public meetings were held in every town and village to declare that Alabama would not submit to the rule of the "Black Republican." A typical meeting held in Mobile, November 15, 1860, arraigned the Republican party because: (1) it had declared for the abolition of slavery in all territories and Federal districts and for the abolition of the interstate slave trade; (2) it had denied the extradition of murderers,

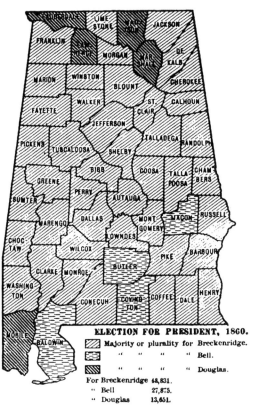

ELECTION FOR PRESIDENT, 1860.

▨ Majority or plurality for Breckenridge.
▤ "   "   "   " Bell.
▧ "   "   "   " Douglas.

For Breckenridge 48,831.
" Bell   27,875.
" Douglas   13,651.

In Lawrence, Coosa, and Mobile Counties the vote was nearly evenly divided.

marauders, and other felons; (3) it had concealed and shielded the murderers of masters who had sought to recover fugitive slaves; (4) it advocated negro equality and made it the basis of legislation hostile to the South; (5) it opposed protection of slave property on the high seas and had justified piracy in the case of the *Creole;* (6) it had invaded Virginia and shed the blood of her citizens on her own soil; and (7) had announced a policy of total abolition.[1]   In December, 1860, the Federal grand jury at Montgomery declared the Federal government "worthless, impotent, and a nuisance," as it had failed to protect the interests of the people of Alabama.   The presentment was signed by C. C. Gunter, foreman, and nineteen others.[2]

Had the governor been willing to call a convention at once, secession would have been almost unanimous; but delay caused the more cautious and timid to reflect and gave the so-called "coöperationists" time to put forth a platform.   The leaders of the party of delay representing north Alabama, the stronghold of radical democracy, were William R. Smith, M. J. Bulger, Nicholas Davis, Jere Clemens, and Robert J. Jemison, all strong men, but none of them possessing the ability of the secessionist leaders or of the former "Union" leaders who had joined the secession party.   But secession was certain, — it was only a question as to how and when.   By law the governor was to call a convention in case the "Black Republican" candidates were elected, and December 24, 1860, was fixed as the time for election of delegates, and January 4, 1861, the time for assembly.

Separation of the Churches

Before the political division in 1861 the religious division had already occurred in the larger and in several of the smaller denominations.   At the close of 1861 every religious body represented in the South, except the Roman Catholic church,[3] had been divided into northern and southern branches.   The political rather than the moral aspects of slavery had finally led to strife in the churches. The southern churches protested against the action of the northern

---

[1] Horace Greeley, "The American Conflict," Vol. I, p. 355.   For a similar meeting in Montgomery, see Hodgson, p. 459 *et seq.*

[2] See Townsend Collection, Columbia University Library, Vol. I, p. 187.   One poor white man in Tallapoosa County welcomed the election of Lincoln, for " now the negroes would be freed and white men could get more work and better pay."   Authorities for the political history of Alabama before 1860: Hodgson's "Cradle of the Confederacy"; Garrett's "Reminiscences of Public Men of Alabama"; Brewer's " Alabama "; Brown's "History of Alabama "; Miller's "History of Alabama "; Pickett's "History of Alabama " (Owen's edition); " Northern Alabama Illustrated "; " Memorial Record of Alabama "; DuBose's " Life and Times of William L. Yancey "; Hilliard's " Politics and Pen Pictures and Speeches ";; Transactions of Ala. Hist. Soc., Vol. IV, papers by Yonge, Cozart, Culver, Scott, and Petrie.

[3] O'Gorman, " History of the Roman Catholic Church in the United States," p. 425.

religious bodies in going into politics on the slavery question and thus causing endless strife between the sections as represented in the churches. The response of the northern societies to such protests resulted in the gradual alienation of the southern members and finally in separation. The first division in Alabama came in 1821, when the Associate Reformed Presbyterian church excluded slaveholders from communion and thereby lost its southern members.[1] Next came the separation of the two strongest Protestant denominations, the Baptists and the Methodists. The southern Baptists were, as slaveholders, excluded from appointment as missionaries, agents, or officers of the Board of Foreign Missions, although they contributed their full share to missions. The Alabama Baptist Convention in 1844 led the way to separation with a protest against this discrimination. The Board stated in reply that under no circumstances would a slaveholder be appointed by them to any position. The Board of the Home Mission Society made a similar declaration. The formal withdrawal of the southern state conventions followed in 1844, and in 1845 the Southern Baptist Convention was formed.[2]

In the Methodist Episcopal church the conflict over slavery had long been smouldering, and in 1844 it broke out in regard to the ownership of slaves by the wife of Bishop Andrew of Alabama. The hostile sections agreed to separate into a northern and a southern church, and a Plan of Separation was adopted. This was disregarded by the northern body and the question of the division of property went to the courts. The United States Supreme Court finally decided in favor of the southern church. From these troubles angry feelings on both sides resulted. The southern church took the name of the Methodist Episcopal Church South; the northern church retained the old name.[3]

In 1858, the northern conferences of the Methodist Protestant

---

[1] Carroll, "Religious Forces of the United States," p. 306; Thompson, "History of the Presbyterian Churches in the United States," pp. 41, 135.

[2] Statistics of Churches, Census of 1890, p. 146; Riley, "History of the Baptists in the Southern States East of the Mississippi," p. 205 *et seq.;* Newman, "History of the Baptists of the United States," pp. 443–454.

[3] See Smith, "Life of James Osgood Andrew"; Buckley, "History of Methodism"; McTyeire, "History of Methodism"; Alexander, "History of the Methodist Episcopal Church South"; Statistics of Churches, p. 581.

Church, having failed to change the constitution of the church in regard to slavery, withdrew, and uniting with a number of Wesleyan Methodists, formed the Methodist Church.[1]

The Southern Aid Society was formed in New York in 1854 for mission work in the South because it was generally believed that the American Home Mission Society was allied with the abolitionists, and because the latter society refused to aid any minister or missionary who was a slaveholder. In Alabama the Southern Aid Society worked principally among the Presbyterians of north Alabama.[2]

The Presbyterians (N.S.) separated in 1858 "on account of politics," and the southern branch formed the United Synod South.[3] The East Alabama Presbytery (O.S.) in 1861 supported the Presbytery of Memphis in a protest against the action of the General Assembly of the church in entering politics. The Presbytery of South Alabama (O.S.) met at Selma in July, 1861, severed its connection with the General Assembly, and recommended a meeting of a Confederate States Assembly. This Assembly was held at Augusta and formed the Presbyterian Church in the Confederate States of America. A long address was published, setting forth the causes of the separation, the future policy of the church, and its attitude towards slavery. It declared that the northern section of the church with its radical policy was playing into the hands of both slaveholders and abolitionists and thus weakening its influence with both. "We," the address stated, "in our ecclesiastical capacity are neither the friends nor foes of slavery." As long as they were connected with the radical northern church the southern Presbyterians felt that they would be excluded from useful work among the slaves by the suspicions of the southern people concerning their real intentions.[4]

The Christian church was divided in 1854. During the war the southern synods of the Evangelical Lutherans withdrew and

[1] Statistics of Churches, p. 566.
[2] Southern Aid Society Reports, 1854-1861.
[3] Statistics of Churches, p. 684; Carroll, "Religious Forces," pp. 281, 306; Thompson, "History of the Presbyterian Churches," p. 135.
[4] Thompson, "History of the Presbyterian Churches," p. 155; Johnson, "History of the Southern Presbyterian Church," pp. 333, 339; McPherson, "History of the Rebellion," p. 508; "Annual Cyclopædia" (1862), p. 707; Statistics of Churches, p. 683.

formed the General Synod South.   There were few members of these churches in Alabama.[1]

The Cumberland Presbyterians, though separated by the war, seem not to have formally established an independent organization in the Confederate States.   A convention was called to meet at Selma in 1864, but nothing resulted.[2]

In May, 1861, the Protestant Episcopal Convention of Alabama declared null and void that part of the constitution of the diocese relating to its connection with the church in the United States.   Instead of the President of the United States, the Governor of Alabama, and later, the President of the Confederate States, was prayed for in the formal prayer.   Bishop Cobbs, a strong opponent of secession, died one hour before the secession of the state was announced.   Rev. R. H. Wilmer, a Confederate sympathizer, was elected to succeed him.[3]   In July the bishops of the southern states met in Montgomery to draft a new constitution and canons.   A resolution was passed stating that the secession of the southern states from the Union and the formation of a new government rendered it expedient that the dioceses within those states should form an independent organization.   The new constitution was adopted in November, 1861, by a general convention, and the Protestant Episcopal Church in the Confederate States was formed.[4]   And thus the religious ties were broken.

Business had also become sectionalized by 1861.   The southern states felt keenly their dependence upon the states of the North for manufactures, water transportation, etc.   For two decades before the war the southern newspapers agitated the question and advocated measures that would tend to secure economic independence of the North.   As an instance of the feeling, many of the educators of the state were in favor of using only those text-books written by southern men and printed in the South.   Professor A. P. Barnard[5] of the University of Alabama was strenuously in favor of such action.   He

[1] Carroll, " Religious Forces," pp. 93, 178.

[2] Annual Cyclopædia (1864), p. 683.

[3] Wilmer, " Recent Past," p. 248.

[4] Perry, " History of the American Episcopal Church," Vol. II, p. 328 *et seq.;* McPherson, " History of the Rebellion," p. 515 ; Whitaker, " Church in Alabama."

[5] President of Columbia College (N.Y.) during and after the war.

declared that nothing ought to be bought from the North. From 1845 to 1861, fifteen "Commercial Conventions" were held in the South, largely attended by the most prominent business men and politicians. The object of these conventions was to discuss means of attaining economic independence.

When Alabama withdrew from the Union in 1861, no bonds were broken. Practically the only bond of Union for most of the people had been in the churches; to the Washington government and to the North they had never become attached. The feelings of the great majority of the people of the state are expressed in the last speech of Senator C. C. Clay of north Alabama in the United States Senate. It had been forty-two years, he said, since Alabama had entered the Union amidst scenes of excitement and violence caused by the hostility of the North against the institution of slavery in the South (referring to the conflict over Missouri). In the churches, southern Christians were denied communion because of what the North styled the "leprosy of slavery." In violation of Constitution and laws southern people were refused permission to pass through the North with their property. The South was refused a share in the lands acquired mainly by her diplomacy, blood, and treasure. The South was robbed of her property and restoration was refused. Criminals who fled North were protected, and southern men who sought to recover their slaves were murdered. Southern homes were burned and southern families murdered. This had been endured for years, and there was no hope of better. The Republican platform was a declaration of war against the South. It was hostile to domestic peace, reproached the South as unchristian and heathenish, and imputed sin and crime to that section. It was a strong incitement to insurrection, arson, and murder among the negroes. The southern whites were denied equality with northern whites or even with free negroes, and were branded as an inferior race. The man nominated for President disregarded the judgment of courts, the obligations of the Constitution, and of his oath by declaring his approval of any measure to prohibit slavery in the territories of the United States. The people of the North branded the people of the South as outlaws, insulted them, consigned them to the execration of posterity and to ultimate destruction. "Is it to be expected that we will or can exercise that Godlike virtue that beareth all things, believeth all things, hopeth all things, endureth all things; which tells us to love our enemies, and bless them that curse us? Are we expected to be denied the sensibilities, the sentiments, the passions, the reason, the instincts of men?" Have we no pride, no honor, no sense of shame, no reverence for ancestors and care for posterity, no love of home, of family, of friends? Are we to confess baseness, discredit the fame of our sires, dishonor ourselves and degrade posterity, abandon our homes and flee the country — all — all — for the sake of the Union? Shall we live under a government administered by those who deny us justice and brand us as inferiors? whose avowed principles and policy must destroy domestic tranquillity, imperil the lives of our wives and children, and ultimately destroy the state? The freemen of Alabama have proclaimed to the world that they will not.[1]

[1] Smith, pp. 448–450, condensed.

CHAPTER II

SECESSION FROM THE UNION

On November 12, 1860, a committee of prominent citizens, appointed by a convention of the people of several counties, asked the governor whether he intended to call the state convention immediately after the choice of presidential electors or to wait until the electors should have chosen the President. They also asked to be informed of the time he intended to order an election of delegates to the convention.[1] Governor Moore replied that a candidate for the presidency was not elected until the electors cast their votes, and until that time he would not call a convention. The electors would vote on December 5, and as he had no doubt that Lincoln would be elected, he would then order an election for December 24, and the convention would assemble in Montgomery on January 7, 1861. The date, he said, was placed far ahead in order that the people might have time to consider the subject. He summed up the situation as follows: Lincoln was the head of a sectional party pledged to the destruction of slavery; the non-slaveholding states had repeatedly resisted the execution of the Fugitive Slave Law, even nullifying the statutes of the United States by their laws intended to prevent the execution of the Fugitive Slave Law; Virginia had been invaded by abolitionists and her citizens murdered; emissaries had burned towns in Texas; and in some instances poison had been given to slaves with which to destroy the whites. With Lincoln as President the abolitionists would soon control the Supreme Court and then slavery would be abolished in the Federal district and in the territories. There would

[1] Smith, " History and Debates of the Convention of Alabama," 1861, p. 12. My account of the convention is condensed almost entirely from Smith's " Debates." Smith was a coöperationist member from Tuscaloosa County. He kept full notes of the proceedings and is impartial in his reports of speeches. Almost the entire edition of the " Debates " was destroyed by fire in 1861. Hodgson, " Cradle of the Confederacy," and DuBose, " Life and Times of William L. Yancey," both give short accounts of the convention.

soon be a majority of free states large enough to alter the Constitution and to destroy slavery in the states. The state of society, with four million negroes turned loose, would be too horrible to contemplate, and the only safety for Alabama lay in secession, which was within her right as a sovereign state. The Federal government was established for the protection and not the destruction of rights; it had only the powers delegated by the states and hence had not the power of coercion. Alabama was devoted to the Union, but could not consent to become a degraded member of it. The state in seceding ought to consult the other southern states; but first she must decide for herself, and coöperate afterwards. The convention, the governor said, would not be a place for the timid or the rash. Men of wisdom and experience were needed, men who could determine what the honor of the state and the security of the people demanded, and who had the moral courage to carry out the dictates of their honest judgment.

The proclamation, ordering an election on Christmas Eve and the assembly of the convention at Montgomery, on January 7, 1861, was issued on December 6, the day after the choice of Lincoln by the electors. On January 7, every one of the one hundred delegates was present. It was a splendid body of men, the best the people could send.

There were the "secessionists," who wanted immediate and separate secession of the state without regard to the action of the other southern states; the "coöperationists," who were divided among themselves, some wanting the coöperation of the southern states within the Union in order to force their rights from the central government, and others wanting the southern states to come to an agreement within the Union and then secede and form a confederacy, while a third class wanted a clear understanding among the cotton states before secession. It was said that there were a few "submissionists," but the votes and speeches fail to show any.

At first both parties claimed a majority, but before the convention opened it was known that the larger number were secessionists. A test vote on the election of a presiding officer showed the relative strength of the parties. William M. Brooks of Perry was elected over Robert Jemison of Tuscaloosa by a vote of 54 to 46, north Alabama voting for Jemison, central and south Alabama for Brooks. And thus the parties voted throughout the convention.

It is probable that the majority of the delegates were formerly Whigs, and a majority of them was still hostile to Yancey, who was the only prominent agitator elected. His colleague, from Montgomery County, was Thomas H. Watts, formerly a Whig. Other prominent secessionists were J. T. Dowdell, John T. Morgan, Thomas H. Herndon, E. S. Dargan, William M. Brooks, and Franklin K. Beck. The opposition leaders were William R. Smith, Robert Jemison, M. J. Bulger, Nicholas Davis, Jeremiah Clemens, Thomas J. McClellan, and David P. Lewis. Yancey, Morgan, and Watts excepted, the opposition had the more able speakers and debaters and the more political experience. The advantage of representation was with the white counties, which sent 70 of the 100 delegates.

When the convention settled down to work, the grievances of the South had no important place in the discussions.

PARTIES IN SECESSION CONVENTION

   Secession at once.
   Coöperation.
+ Majority of population (1860) Negroes.
Contesting delegation from Shelby County.
Delegates from Coosa and Talladega, and Clemens from Madison voted for Secession though elected and acted until final vote as coöperationists.

The little that was said on the subject came from the coöperationists and that only incidentally. There was a genuine fear of social revolution brought about by the Republican programme, but the secessionists had been stating their grievances for twenty years and were now silent.[1] All seemed to agree that the present state of affairs was

[1] Except Yancey, who declared that the disease preying on the vitals of the Federal Union was not due to any defect in the Constitution, but to the heads, hearts, and consciences of the northern people; that no guarantees, no amendments, could reëducate

unbearable, and that secession was the only remedy. The only question was, How to secede? To decide that question the leaders of each party were placed on the Committee on Secession. A majority of the convention was in favor of immediate, separate secession. They held the logical state sovereignty view that the state, while a member of the Union, should not combine with another against the government or the party controlling it. Such a course would be contrary to the Constitution and would be equivalent to breaking up the Union while planning to save it. As a sovereign state, Alabama could withdraw from the Union, and hence immediate, separate secession was the proper method. Then would follow consultation and coöperation with the other seceded southern states in forming a southern confederacy. From the first it was known that the secessionists were strong enough to pass at once a simple ordinance of withdrawal. They said but little because their position was already well understood. The people were now more united than they would be after long debates and outside influence. Yet, for policy's sake, and in deference to the feelings of the minority, the latter were allowed to debate for four days before the question at issue was brought to a vote. In that time they had about argued themselves over to the other side. With the exception of Yancey, the secessionists were silent until the ordinance was passed. The first resolution declared that the people of Alabama would not submit to the administration of Lincoln and Hamlin. Both parties voted unanimously for this resolution.[1]

The coöperationists were determined to resist Republican rule, but did not consider delay dangerous. Some doubtless thought that in some way Lincoln could be held in check and the Union still be preserved, and a number of them were doubtless willing to wait and make another trial. It was known that an ordinance of secession would be passed as soon as the secessionists cared to bring the question to a vote, but for four days the Committee on Secession con-

the northern people on the slavery question, so as to induce a northern majority to withhold the exercise of its power in aid of abolition. Governor Moore, in the commissions given to the ambassadors to the other states, declared that the peace, honor, and security of the southern states were endangered by the election of Lincoln, the candidate of a purely sectional party, whose avowed principles demanded the destruction of slavery.

[1] It would seem that after this vote no one would say that nearly half of the members were "Unionists," yet nearly all accounts make this statement.

sidered the matter while the coöperationists made speeches.[1] On January 10 the committees made two reports. The majority report, presented by Yancey, simply provided for the immediate withdrawal of the state from the Union. The minority report, presented by Clemens, was in substance as follows: We are unable to see in separate state secession the most effectual mode of guarding our honor and securing our rights. This great object can best be attained by concurrent and concentrated action of all the states interested, and such an effort should be made before deciding finally upon our own policy. All the southern states should be requested to meet in convention at Nashville, February 22, 1861, to consider wrongs and appropriate remedies. As a basis of settlement such a convention should consider: (1) the faithful execution of the Fugitive Slave Law and the repeal of all state laws nullifying it; (2) more stringent and explicit provisions for the surrender of criminals escaping into another state; (3) guarantees that slavery should not be abolished in the Federal district or in any other place under the exclusive jurisdiction of Congress; (4) non-interference with the interstate slave trade; (5) protection of slavery in the territories which, when admitted as states, should decide for themselves the question of slavery; (6) right of transit through free states with slave property; (7) the foregoing to be irrepealable amendments to the Constitution. This basis of settlement was not to be regarded as absolute, but simply as the opinion of the Alabama convention, to which its delegates to the proposed convention were expected to conform as nearly as possible. Secession should not be attempted except after the most thorough investigation and discussion.[2]

The secessionists were of one mind in regard to secession and did not debate the subject; the coöperationists — all from north Alabama — were careful to explain their views at length in their speeches of opposition. Bulger (c.)[3] of Tallapoosa thought that separate secession was unwise and impolitic, but that an effort should be made

---

[1] There were many indications that the opposition was more sectional and personal than political. It is safe to state for north Alabama that had the Black Belt declared for the Union, that section would have voted for secession.

[2] This minority report was signed by Clemens of Madison, Lewis of Lawrence, Winston of De Kalb, Kimball of Tallapoosa, Watkins of Franklin, and Jemison of Tuscaloosa, all from north Alabama.

[3] c. = coöperationist ; s. = secessionist ; cs. = coöperationist who voted for secession.

to secure the coöperation of the other southern states before seceding. To this end he proposed a convention of the southern states to consider the grievances of the South and to determine the mode of relief for the present and security for the future, and, should its demands not be complied with, to determine upon a remedy.

Clark (c.) of Lawrence denied the right of separate secession, which would not be a remedy for existing evils. The slavery question would not be settled but would still be a vital and ever present issue. Separate secession would revolutionize the government but not the northern feeling, would not hush the pulpits, nor calm the northern mind, nor purify Black Republicanism. The states would be in a worse condition politically than the colonies were before the Constitution was adopted. The border states would sell their slaves south and become free states; separate secession would be the decree of universal emancipation. A large majority of the people were opposed to separate secession, and besides, the state alone would be weak and at the mercy of foreign powers. The proper policy for Alabama was to remain in a southern union, at least, with the border states for allies. Would secession repeal "personal liberty" laws, return a single fugitive slave, prevent abolition in the Federal district and territories, or the suppression of interstate slave trade? By secession Alabama would relinquish her interest in the Union and leave it in the control of Black Republicans. It would be almost impossible to unite the southern states after separate secession — as difficult as it was to form the original Union. The only hope for peaceable secession was in a united South, and now was the time for it, for southern sentiment, though opposed to separate secession, was ripe for southern union. The "United South" would possess all the requirements of a great nation — territory, resources, wealth, population, and community of interests. Separate secession would result in the deplorable disasters of civil war. He hoped that even yet some policy of reconciliation might succeed, but if the contrary happened, there should be no scruples about state sovereignty; the United South would assert the God-given right of every community to freedom and happiness. Jones (c.) of Lauderdale declared that it was a great mistake to call his constituents submissionists, since time after time they had declared that they would not submit to Black Republican rule. They differed as to the time and manner of secession, believing that hasty secession was not a proper remedy, that it was unwise, impolitic, and discourteous to the border states.

Smith of Tuscaloosa, the leader of the coöperationists,[1] read the platform upon which he was elected to the convention; which, in substance, was to use all honorable exertions to secure rights in the Union, and failing, to maintain them out of the Union. Allegiance, he went on to say, was due first to the state, and support was due her in any course she might adopt. If an ordinance of secession should be passed, it would be the supreme law of the land. Kimball (c.) of Tallapoosa said that his constituents were opposed to secession, but were more opposed to Black Republicanism. Before taking action he desired a solid or united South. He agreed with General Scott that with a certain unanimity of the southern states it would be impolitic and improper to attempt coercion. To secure the coöperation of the southern states and to justify themselves to the world a southern convention should be called. However, rights should be maintained even if Alabama had to withdraw from the Union.

Watkins (c.) of Franklin stated that he would vote against the ordinance of secession in obedience to the will of the people he represented. He believed that separate secession was wrong. Edwards (c.) of Blount said that secession was unwise on the part of Alabama, while Beard (c.) of Marshall thought the best, safest, and wisest course would be to consult and coöperate with the other slave states. He favored resistance to Black Republican rule, and his constituents, though desiring coöperation, would abide by the action of the state.

Bulger (c.) of Tallapoosa stated that he had voted against every proposition leading to immediate and separate secession. Yet he would give to the state, when the ordinance was passed, his whole allegiance; and, if any attempt were made to coerce the state, would join the army.[2] Winston (c.) of De Kalb stated that his constituents were opposed to immediate secession, yet they would, no doubt, acquiesce. He had written to his son, a cadet at West Point, to resign and come home. A convention of the slave states should be called to make an attempt to settle difficulties. Davis (c.) of Madison, who had stoutly

---

[1] It was he who compiled the debates of the convention.

[2] He was the oldest general officer in the Confederate service.

D

opposed separate secession, now declared that since the meeting of the convention serious changes had occurred. Several states had already seceded and others would follow. Consequently Alabama would not be alone. Clemens (cs.) of Madison said he would vote for secession, but would not do so if the result depended upon his vote. He strongly preferred the plan proposed by the minority of the committee on secession.

During the debates there was not a single strong appeal for the Union. There was simply no Union feeling, but an intense dislike for the North as represented by the Republican party. The coöperationists contemplated ultimate secession. They wished to make an attempt at compromise, but they felt sure that it would fail. Their plan of effecting a united South within the Union was clearly unconstitutional and could only be regarded as a proposition to break up the old Union and reconstruct a new one.[1]

Political Theories of the Members

The secessionists held clear, logical views on the question before them. They clearly distinguished the "state" or "people" from "government." No secessionist ever claimed that the right of secession was one derived from or preserved by the Constitution; it was a sovereign right. Granted the sovereignty of the state, the right to secede in any way at any time was, of course, not to be questioned. Consequently, they said but little on that point.

The coöperationists were vague-minded. Most of them were stanch believers in state sovereignty and opposed secession merely on the ground of expediency. A few held a confused theory that while the state was sovereign it had no right to secede unless with the whole South. This view was most strongly advocated by Clark of Lawrence. Separate secession was not a right, he said, though he admitted the sovereignty of the state. To secede alone would be rebellion; not so, if in company with other southern states. Earnest (c.) of Jefferson said that the state was sovereign, and that after secession any acts of the state or of its citizens to protect their rights would not be treason. But unless the state acted in its sovereign capacity, it could not withdraw from the Union, and her citizens

---

[1] Constitution, Article I, Section X: "No state shall without the consent of Congress enter into any agreement or compact with another state," etc.

would be subject to the penalties of treason.[1] Sheffield (c.) of Marshall believed in the right of "secession or revolution." Clemens of Madison, elected as a coöperationist, said that in voting for secession he did it with the full knowledge that in secession they were all about to commit treason, and, if not successful, would suffer the pains and penalties pronounced against the highest political crime. Acting "upon the convictions of a lifetime" he "calmly and deliberately walked into revolution."[2]

The coöperationists were generally disposed to deny the sovereignty of the convention. Most of them were former Whigs, who had never worked out a theory of government. Davis (c.) of Madison repeatedly denied that the convention had sovereign powers; sovereignty, he said, was held by the people. Clark (c.) of Lawrence complained that the convention was encroaching upon the rights of the people whom it should protect, and asserted it did not possess unlimited power, but that its power was conferred by act of the legislature, which created only a general agency for a special purpose; that the convention had no power to do more than pass the ordinance of secession and acts necessary thereto. Smith (c.) said that the convention was the creature of the legislature, not of the people, and that the southern Congress was the creature of the convention. Buford (s.) of Barbour[3] doubted whether the convention possessed legislative powers. According to his views, political or sovereign power was vested in the people; the convention was not above the constitution which created the legislature. Watts (s.) of Montgomery believed that the power of the convention to interfere with the constitution was confined to such changes as were necessary to the perfect accomplishment of secession. Yelverton (s.) of Coffee summed up the theory of the majority: the convention had full power and control over the legislative, executive, and judiciary; the people were present in convention in the persons of their representatives and in them was the sovereignty, the power, and the will of the state. This was the theory upon which the convention acted.

[1] He was here referring indirectly to the action of the state authorities in seizing the forts at Pensacola and Mobile before secession.

[2] Clemens was accused of voting for secession in order to obtain the command of the militia. He had formerly been an army officer, and was now made major-general of militia. It was not long before he deserted and went North.

[3] Who succeeded Yancey in the convention after the latter was sent to Europe.

Passage of the Ordinance of Secession

On January 11, 1861, Yancey spoke at length, closing the debate on the question of secession. Referring to the spirit of fraternity that prevailed, he stated that irritation and suspicion had, in great degree, subsided. The majority had yielded to the minority all the time wanted for deliberation, and every one had been given an opportunity to record his sentiments. The question had not been pressed to a vote before all were ready. Though preferring a simple ordinance of secession, the majority had, for the sake of harmony and fraternal feeling, yielded to amendment by the minority. All, he said, were for resistance to Republican rule, and differed only as to the manner of resistance. Some believed in secession, others in revolution. The ordinance might mean disunion, secession, or revolution, as the members preferred. The mode was organized coöperation, not of states, but of the people of Alabama, in resistance to wrong. Yet the ordinance provided for coöperation with other states upon the basis of the Federal Constitution. Every effort, he said, had been made to find common ground upon which the advocates of resistance might meet, and all parties had been satisfied. This was not a movement of the politicians, but a great popular movement, based upon the widespread, deep-seated conviction that the government had fallen into the hands of a sectional majority who were determined to use it for the destruction of the rights of the South. All were driven by an irresistible tide; the minority had been unable to repress the movement, the majority had not been able to add one particle to its momentum; in northern, not in southern, hands was held the rod that smote the rock from which flowed this flood.

Some, he said, concluded that by dissolving the Union the rich inheritance bequeathed by the fathers was hazarded. But liberties were one thing, the power of government delegated to secure them was another. Liberties were inalienable, and the state governments were formed to secure them; the Federal government was the common agent, and its powers should be withdrawn when it abused them to destroy the rights of the people. This movement was not hostile to liberty nor to the Federal Constitution, but was merely a dismissal of an unfaithful agent. The state now resumed the duties formerly delegated to that agent. The ordinance of secession was a declaration

ALEXANDER HAMILTON STEPHENS.

WILLIAM LOWNDES YANCEY.

GENERAL L. P. WALKER, First Confederate Secretary of War.
President of Convention of 1875.

WILLIAM R. SMITH, Leader of
Coöperationists in 1861.

JERE. CLEMENS.

CIVIL WAR LEADERS.

of this fact and also a proposition to form a new government similar to the old. All were urged to sign the ordinance, not to express approval, but to give notice to their enemies that the people were not divided. "I now ask that the vote may be taken," he said.

The ordinance was called up. It was styled "An Ordinance to dissolve the Union between Alabama and other States united under the Compact styled 'The Constitution of the United States of America.'" The preamble stated that the election of Lincoln and Hamlin by a sectional party avowedly hostile to the domestic institutions, peace, and security of Alabama, preceded by many dangerous infractions of the Constitution by the states and people of the North, was a political wrong of so insulting and menacing a character as to justify the people of Alabama in the adoption of prompt and decided measures for their future peace and security. The ordinance simply stated that Alabama withdrew from the Union and that her people resumed the powers delegated by the Constitution to the Federal government. A coöperationist amendment expressed the desire of the people to form with the other southern states a permanent government, and invited a convention of the states to meet in Montgomery on February 4, 1861, for consultation in regard to the common safety. The ordinance was passed by a vote of 69 to 31, every delegate voting. Fifteen coöperationists voted for secession and 22 signed the ordinance.

In the convention opinions varied as to whether peace or war would follow secession. The great majority of the members, and of the people also, believed that peaceful relations would continue. All truly wished for peace. A number of the coöperationists expressed themselves as fearing war, but this was when opposing secession, and they probably said more than they really believed. Yet in nearly all the speeches made in the convention there seemed to be distinguishable a feeling of fear and dread lest war should follow. However, had war been a certainty, secession would not have been delayed or checked.

There was warm discussion on the question of submitting the ordinance to the people for ratification or rejection. The coöperationists, both before and after the passage of the ordinance, favored its reference to the people in the hope that the measure would be delayed or defeated. No one expected that it would be referred to the people, but this was a good question for obstructive purposes.

The minority report on secession declared that, in a matter of such vital importance, involving the lives and liberties of a whole people, the ordinance should be submitted to them for their discussion, and that secession should be attempted only after ratification by a direct vote of the people on that single issue.

Posey (c.) of Lauderdale said that his constituents expected the question of secession to be referred to the people, and that they would submit more willingly to a decision made by popular vote; that the ordinance was objectionable to them unless they were allowed to vote on it. He further stated that when the convention had refused to submit the ordinance to the popular vote, the first impulse of some of the coöperationists had been to "bolt the convention." However, not being responsible, they preferred to remain and aid in providing for the emergencies of the future. Kimbal (c.) of Tallapoosa said that the people were the interested parties, that sovereignty was in the people, and that they ought to decide the question. Edwards (c.) of Blount said that his constituents expected the ordinance to be referred to them and had instructed him to use his best exertions to secure reference to the people. Bulger (c.) of Tallapoosa voted against all propositions looking toward secession without reference to the people. Davis (c.) of Madison denied the sovereignty of the convention. He said that the vote of the people might be one way and that of the convention another. He believed that the majority in convention represented a minority of the people.

In closing the debate on this subject, Yancey (s.) of Montgomery said that, as a measure of policy, to submit the ordinance to a vote of the people was wrong. The convention was clothed with all the powers of the people; it was the people acting in their sovereign capacity; the government was not a pure democracy, but a government of the people, though not by the people. Historically the convention was the supreme power in American political theory, and submission to the people was a new doctrine. If the ordinance should be submitted to the people, the friends of secession would triumph, but irritation and prejudice would be aroused. Yancey's views prevailed.

Establishing the Confederacy

A number of the coöperationists prefessed to believe that secession would result in disintegration and anarchy in the South. The secessionists were accused of desiring to tear down, not to build up. These assertions were, in fact, unfounded, since, during the entire debate, those favoring immediate secession stated plainly that they expected to reunite with the other southern states after secession. Williamson (s.) of Lowndes said that to declare to the world that they were not ready to unite with the other slave states in a permanent government would be to act in bad faith and subject themselves to contempt and scorn; united action was necessary; financial and commercial affairs were in a deplorable condition; confidence was lost, and in the business world all was gloom and despair — this could be remedied only by a permanent government. Whatley (s.) of Calhoun was unwilling for it to be said by posterity that they tore down the old government and failed to reconstruct a new; the cotton states should establish a government modelled on the Federal Union.

In accordance with these views the ordinance of secession proposed a convention of southern states, and a few days later a resolution was passed approving the suggestion of South Carolina to form a provisional government upon the plan of the old Union and to prepare for a permanent government. Each state was to send as many delegates to the convention on February 4 as it had had senators and representatives in Congress. The Alabama convention (January 16) elected one deputy from each congressional district and two from the state at large, most of them being coöperationists or moderate secessionists.

Yancey, on January 16, read a unanimous report from the Committee on Secession in favor of forming a provisional confederate government at once. The report also stated that the people of Alabama had never been dissatisfied with the Constitution of the United States; that their dissatisfaction had been with the conduct of the northern people in violating the Constitution and in dangerous misinterpretation of it, causing the belief that, while acting through the forms of government, they intended to destroy the rights of the South. The Federal Constitution, the report declared, represented a complete scheme of government, capable of being put into speedy operation, and was so familiar to the people that when properly interpreted they would feel safe under it. A speedy confederation of the seceded states was desirable, and there was no better basis than the United States Constitution. The report recommended the formation, first, of a provisional, and later, of a permanent, government. The secessionists warmly advocated the speedy formation of a new confederacy. The coöperationists renewed their policy of obstruction. Jemison (c.) of Tuscaloosa proposed to strike out the part of the resolution relating to the formation of a permanent government. Another coöperationist wanted delay in order that the border states might have time to take part in forming the proposed government. Others wanted the people to elect a new convention to act on the question. Yancey replied that delay was dangerous, if coercion was intended by the North; that the issue had been before the people and that they had invested their delegates with full power; that the convention then in session had ample authority to settle all questions concerning a provisional or a permanent government; that another election would only cause irritation; that delay, waiting for the secession of the border states, would be suicidal. The proposition for a new convention was lost by a vote of 53 to 36.

The convention decided to continue the work until the end. After choosing delegates (January 16) to the southern convention, which was to meet in Montgomery on February 4, the state convention adjourned until the Confederate provisional government was planned and the permanent constitution written. Then the state convention met again on March 4 to ratify them. The coöperationists now proposed that the new plan of government be submitted to the people. It was right and expedient, they said, to let the people decide. Morgan [1] (s.) of Dallas said that the proposition for ratification by direct vote of the people was absurd. The people would never ratify, for too many unrelated questions would be brought in. Dargan (s.) of Mobile said that the people had conferred upon the convention full powers to act, and that a new election would harass the candidates with new issues such as the slave trade, reconstruction, etc., introduced by the opponents of secession. Stone (s.) of Pickens thought that a new election would cause angry and bitter discussions, wrangling, distrust, and division among the people; that the proposed

[1] The present (1905) senior U. S. senator from Alabama.

constitution was very like the United States Constitution, to which the people were so devoted that they had given up the Union rather than the Constitution; that Lincoln's inaugural address was a declaration of war, and a permanent government was necessary to raise money for armies and fleets. Still the coöperationists obstructed, saying that not to refer to the people was unfair and illiberal; that the convention was usurping the powers of the people, who desired to be heard in the matter; that government by a few was like a house built on the sand; that there was no danger in waiting, for the people would be sure to ratify and then would be better satisfied, etc. Finally most of the coöperationists agreed that it would be better not to refer the question to the people and the permanent Confederate constitution was ratified on March 12 by the vote of 87 to 5.[1]

For the first time Yancey stood at the head of the people of the state. They were ready to give him any office. But the coöperationists and a few secessionist politicians in the convention were jealous of his rising strength and desired to stay his progress. So Earnest (c.) of Jefferson introduced a self-denying resolution making ineligible to election to Congress the members of the state legislature and of the convention. It was a direct attack by the dissatisfied politicians upon the prominent men in the convention, and especially upon Yancey. The measure was supported by Jemison (c.) who said that it was a practice never to elect a member of a legislative body to an office created by the legislature.. Clemens (cs.) thought such a measure unnecessary, as the majority necessary to pass it could defeat any undesirable candidate. Stone (s.) said that such a resolution would cost the state the services of some of her best men when most needed; that the best men were in the convention; and that the southern Confederacy should be intrusted to the friends, not to the enemies, of secession. Morgan (s.) of Dallas thought that, as a matter of policy, the congressmen would be chosen from outside of the convention. Bragg (s.) of Mobile wanted the best men regardless of place; this was no ordinary work and the best men were needed; the people had already made a choice of the members once and would approve them again. Yancey said that in principle he was opposed to such a measure. He declared that he would not be a candidate.

---

[1] Bulger of Tallapoosa, Jones and Wilson of Fayette, and Sheets of Winston voted in the negative.

But he believed that the people had a right to a choice from their entire number, and that the convention had no right to violate the equality of citizenship by disfranchising the 223 members of the convention and the legislature. Yelverton (s.) of Coffee at first favored the resolution, but upon discovering that it was aimed at a few leaders and especially at Yancey, he opposed it. He did not wish the leaders of secession to be proscribed.

The resolution was lost by a vote of 46 to 50, but the delegates sent to the Provisional Congress were, with one exception, taken from outside the convention. A few politicians among the secessionists united with the coöperationists and, passing by the most experienced and able leaders, chose an inexperienced Whiggish delegation.[1]

The African Slave Trade

The Committee on Foreign Relations reported that the power of regulating the slave trade would properly be conferred upon the Confederate government, but, meanwhile, believing that the slave trade should be prohibited until the Confederacy was formed, the committee reported an ordinance forbidding it. Morgan (s.) of Dallas opposed the ordinance because it was silent as to the cause of the prohibition. He was opposed to the slave trade on the ground of public policy. If at liberty to carry out Christian convictions, he would have Africans brought over to be made Christian slaves, the highest condition attainable by the negro. In holding slaves, the South was charged with sin and crime, but the southern people were unable to perceive the wrong and unwilling to cease to do what the North considered evil. The present movement rested, in great measure, upon their assertion of the right to hold the African in slavery. The laws of Congress denouncing the slave trade as piracy had been a shelter to those who assailed the South, and had affected the standing of the South among nations. If the slave trade were wrong, then it was much worse to bring Christian and enlightened negroes from Virginia to Alabama than a heathen savage from Africa to Alabama. Slavery was the only force which had ever been able to elevate the negro. He believed that on grounds of public policy the traffic should be condemned, but it was a question better left to the Confederate

[1] See below, Ch. III, sec. 5.

government, because the various states would not make uniform laws. There were slaves enough for twenty years and, when needed, more could be had. Reopening of the African slave trade should be forbidden by the Confederate government expressly for reasons of public policy.

Smith (c.) of Tuscaloosa said that the question of morality did not arise; the slave trade was not wrong. The heathen African was greatly benefited by the change to Christian Alabama. But no more negroes were needed; they were already increasing too fast and there was no territory for extension. Crowded together, the white and black might degenerate like the Spaniards and natives in Mexico. He supported the ordinance as a measure to disarm foes who charged that one of the reasons for secession was a desire to reopen the African slave trade, which should be denied to the world. The slave trade would lead to war, and "If Cotton is King, his throne is peace," war would destroy him. Jones (c.) of Lauderdale did not want another negro on the soil of Alabama. The people of the border states were afraid that the cotton states would reopen the slave trade, but for the sake of uniformity the question should be left to the Confederate government. Posey (c.) of Lauderdale also thought the border states should be reassured, and said that on the grounds of expediency alone he would vote against the slave trade. There were already too many negroes; already more land was needed, and that for whites. The slave trade should be prohibited as a great evil to the South. Potter (c.) of Cherokee was astonished that the slave trade and slavery were treated as if identical in point of morality. It was a duty to support and perpetuate slavery; the slave trade was immoral in its tendency and effects; the question, however, should be settled on the grounds of policy alone.

Yelverton (s.) of Coffee [1] said that the slave trade should not now be reopened nor forever closed, but that the regulation of it should be left to the legislature. It was said that the world was against the South on the slavery question; then the South should either own all the slaves, or set them all free in deference to unholy prejudice. As the southern people were not ready to surrender the negroes, they should be at liberty to buy them in any market, subject simply to the laws of trade. Slavery was the cause of secession and should not be

[1] Coffee was a white county and had very few slaves.

left in doubt. A slave in Alabama cost eight times as much as one imported from Africa. If the border states entered the Confederacy, they could furnish slaves; if they remained in the Union and thus became foreign country, the South should not be forced to buy from them alone. Slavery was a social, moral, and political blessing. The Bible sanctioned it, and had nothing to say in favor of it in one country and against it in another. To restrict the slave market to the United States would be a blow at states rights and free trade, and with slavery stricken, King Cotton would become a petty tyrant. Slavery had built up the Yankees, socially, politically, and commercially. The English were a calculating people and would not hesitate, on account of slavery, to recognize southern independence, and other nations would do likewise. Expansion of territory would come and would cause an increased demand for slaves. The arguments against the slave trade, he said, were that fanaticism might be angered, that there were too many negroes already, and that those who had slaves to sell might suffer from reduced prices. But the larger part of the people would prefer to purchase in a cheaper market, and non-slave-holders, as they grew wealthier, could become slave owners. The argument against the slave trade, he added, was usually the one of dollars and cents. The great moral effect was lost sight of, and it seemed from some arguments that Christianity did not require the Bible to be taught to the poor slave unless profit followed. The time was not far distant when the reopening of the slave trade would be considered essential to the industrial prosperity of the cotton states.

Stone (s.) of Pickens said that he would not hesitate, from moral reasons, to purchase a slave anywhere. Slavery was sanctioned by the divine law; it was a blessing to the negro. But on grounds of policy he would insist upon the prohibition of the slave trade. Too many slaves would make too much cotton; prices would then fall and weaken the institution. Keep the prices high, and the institution would be strengthened; reduce the value of the slaves, and the interest of the owners in the institution would be reduced, and the border states would listen to plans for general emancipation. There was no territory in which slavery could expand.

Yancey (s.) explained his course in the Southern Commercial Conventions in preceding years when he had advocated the repeal of the laws against the slave trade. He thought that the laws of Congress defining the slave trade as piracy placed a stigma on the institution, condemned it from the point of view of the government, and thus violated the spirit of the Constitution by discriminating against the South. He did not then advocate the reopening of the slave trade, nor would he do so at this time. For two reasons he insisted that the Confederate Congress should prohibit the slave trade: (1) already there were as many slaves as were needed; (2) to induce the border states to enter the Confederacy.

Dowdell (s.) of Chambers proposed an amendment to the ordinance of prohibition, declaring that slavery was a moral, social, and political blessing, and that any attempt to hinder its expansion should be opposed. He opposed reopening the slave trade, though he considered that there was no moral distinction between slavery and the slave trade. The border states, he said, need not be encouraged by declarations of policy; they would join the Confederacy anyway. Slavery might be regulated by Congress, but should not be prohibited by organic law. He expressed a wish that he might never see the day when white immigration would drive out slave labor and take its place, nor did he want social or political inequality among white people whom he believed should be kept free, independent, and equal, recognizing no subordinate except those made as such by God. The legislature, he thought, should be left to deal with the evil of white immigration from the North, so that the southern people might be kept a slaveholding people. But, he asked, can that be done with slaves at $1000 a head? And must the hands of the people be tied because a fantastical outside world says that slavery and the slave trade are morally wrong?

Watts (s.) of Montgomery proposed that the Confederacy be given power to prohibit the importation of slaves from any place. Smith (c.) of Tuscaloosa said that the proposal of Watts was a threat against the border states, which would lose their slave market unless they joined the Confederacy; that the border states must be kept friendly, a bulwark against the North.

A resolution was finally passed to the effect that the people of Alabama were opposed, for reasons of public policy, to reopening the slave trade, and the state's delegates in Congress were instructed to insist on the prohibition.

The debates show clearly the feeling of the delegates that, on the slavery question, the rest of the world was against them, and hence, as a measure of expediency, they were in favor of prohibiting the trade. Some wished to have all the whites finally become slaveholders; others believed that the negroes were the economic and social enemies of the whites, and they wanted no more of them. But all agreed that slavery was a good thing for the negro.

Yancey (s.) introduced a resolution favoring the free navigation of the Mississippi. The North, he said, was uncertain as to the policy of the South and must be assured that the South wished no restrictions upon trade. "Free trade" was its motto. Dowdell (s.) proposed that the navigation should be free only to those states and territories lying on the river and its tributaries, while Smith (c.) thought that all navigation should remain as unrestricted and open to all as before secession. Yancey thought that absolutely unrestricted navigation would tend to undermine secession, for it would tend to reconstruct the late political union into a commercial union. Such a policy would discriminate against European friends in favor of New England enemies. As passed, the resolution expressed the sense of the convention that the navigation of the Mississippi should be free to all the people of those states and territories which were situated on that river or its tributaries.

Commissioners to Other States

As soon as the governor issued writs of election for a convention, fearing that the legislatures of other states then in session might adjourn before calling conventions, he sent a commissioner to each southern state to consult and advise with the governor and legislature in regard to the question of secession and later confederation. These commissioners made frequent reports to the governor and convention and did much to secure the prompt organization of a permanent government.[1]

[1] The commissioners sent to the various states were as follows: *Virginia*, A. F. Hopkins and F. M. Gilmer; *South Carolina*, John A. Elmore; *North Carolina*, I. W. Garrott and Robert H. Smith; *Maryland*, J. L. M. Curry; *Delaware*, David Clopton; *Kentucky*, S. F. Hale; *Missouri*, William Cooper; *Tennessee*, L. Pope Walker; *Arkansas*, David Hubbard; *Louisiana*, John A. Winston; *Texas*, J. M. Calhoun; *Florida*, E. C. Bullock; *Georgia*, John G. Shorter; *Mississippi*, E. W. Pettus. Only one state, South Carolina, sent a delegate to Alabama.

After the ordinance of secession was passed a resolution was adopted to the effect that Alabama, being no longer a member of the Union, was not entitled to representation at Washington and that her representatives there should be instructed to withdraw. A second resolution, authorizing the governor to send two commissioners to Washington to treat with that government, caused some dabate.

Clemens (cs.) said that there was no need of sending commissioners to Washington, because they would not be received. Let Washington send commissioners to Alabama; South Carolina was differently situated; Alabama held her own forts, South Carolina did not. Smith (c.) proposed that only one commissioner be sent. One would do more efficient work and the expense would be less. Watts (s.) said that Alabama as a former member of the Union should inform the old government of her withdrawal and of her policy for the future; that there were many grave and delicate matters to be settled between the two governments; and that commissioners should be sent to propose terms of adjustment and to demand a recognition of the new order.

Webb (s.) of Greene said that Alabama stood in the same attitude toward the United States as toward France. And the fact that the commissioners of South Carolina had been treated with contempt should not influence Alabama. If one was to be in the wrong, let it be the Washington government. To send commissioners would not detract from the dignity of the state, but would show a desire for amicable relations. Whatley (s.) took the same ground, and added that, having seized the forts to prevent their being used against Alabama, the state, as retiring partner, would hold them as assets until a final settlement, especially as its share had not been received. Some members urged that only one commissioner be sent in order to save expenses. All were getting to be very economical. And practically all agreed that it was the duty of the state to show her desire for amicable relations by making advances.

Yancey thought the matter should be left to the Provisional Congress; the United States had made agreements with South Carolina about the military status of the forts and had violated the agreement; the other states also had claims of public property, and negotiations should be carried on by the common agent. Separate action by the state would only complicate matters.

Finally, it was decided to send one commissioner, and the governor appointed Thomas J. Judge, who proceeded to Washington, with authority to negotiate regarding the forts, arsenals, and customhouses in the state, the state's share of the United States debt, and the future relations between the United States and Alabama, and through C. C. Clay, late United States senator from Alabama, applied for an interview with the President. Buchanan refused to receive him in his official capacity, but wrote that he would be glad to see him as a private gentleman. Judge declined to be received except in his official capacity, and said that future negotiations must begin at Washington.

Foreseeing war, Watts (s.) proposed that the general assembly be given power to confiscate the property of alien enemies, and also to suspend the collection of debts due to alien enemies. Shortridge (s.) thought that the measure was not sufficiently emphatic, since war had practically been declared. He said the courts should be closed against the collection of debts due persons in the northern states which had passed personal liberty laws. He stated that Alabama owed New York several million dollars, and that to pay this debt would drain from the country the currency, which should be held to relieve the strain.

Jones (c.) was opposed to every description of robbery. The course proposed, he said, would be a flagrant outrage upon just creditors, as the greater wrong would be done the friends of the South, for nineteen-twentieths of the debt was due to political friends — merchants who had always defended the rights of the South. Those debts should be paid and honor sustained. The legislature, he added, would pass a stay-law, which he regretted, and that would suffice. Smith (c.) said that confiscation was an act of war, and would provoke retaliation. Every action should look toward the preservation of peace.

Clarke (s.) of Marengo saw nothing wrong in the measure. There was no wish or intention of evading payment of the debt; payment would only be suspended or delayed. It was a peace measure. Lewis (cs.) said that only the war-making power would have authority to pass such a measure, and that this power would be lodged in the Confederate Congress. Meanwhile, he proposed to give the power temporarily to the legislature.

Early in the session the secessionists introduced a resolution pledging the state to resist any attempt by the United States to coerce any of the seceded states. Alabama could not stand aside, they said, and see the seceded states coerced by the United States government, which had no authority to use force. All southern states recognized secession as the essence and test of state sovereignty, and would support each other.

Earnest (c.) of Jefferson was of the opinion that this resolution was intended to cover acts of hostility already committed by individuals, such as Governor Moore and other officials, before the state seceded, and to vote for the resolution subjected the voter to the penalties of treason. When a state acted in its sovereign capacity and withdrew from the Union, then those individuals were relieved. But to vote for such a measure before secession was treason.

Morgan (s.) of Dallas said that, whether Alabama were in or out of the Union, she could see no state coerced; the question was not debatable. To attack South Carolina was to attack Alabama. "We are one united people and can never be dissevered." The North was pledging men and money to coerce the southern states, and its action must be answered. Jemison (c.) thought the war alarms were false and that there was no necessity for immediate action, while Smith (c.), his colleague, heartily indorsed the measure. Jones (c.) declared that before the state seceded he would not break the laws of the United States; that he had sworn to support the Constitution, and only the state could absolve him from that oath; that such a measure was not lawful while the state was in the Union.

After secession the resolution was again called up, and all speakers agreed that aid should be extended to seceded states in case of coercion. Some wanted to promise aid to any one of the United States which might take a stand against the other states in behalf of the South. Events moved so rapidly that the measure did not come to a vote before the organization of the Provisional Congress.

Legislation by the Convention

Not only was the old political structure to be torn down, but a new one had to be erected. In organizing the new order the convention performed many duties pertaining usually to the legislature.

E

This was done in order to save time and to prevent confusion in the administration.

Citizenship was defined to include free whites only, except such as were citizens of the United States before January 11, 1861. A person born in a northern state or in a foreign country before January 11, 1861, must take the oath of allegiance to the state of Alabama, and the oath of abjuration, renouncing allegiance to all other sovereignties. The state constitution was amended by omitting all references to the United States; the state officers were absolved from their oath to support the United States Constitution; jurisdiction of the United States over waste and unappropriated lands and navigable waters was rescinded; and navigation was opened to all citizens of Alabama and other states that "may unite with Alabama in a Southern Slaveholding Confederacy." A registration of lands was ordered to be made; the United States land system was adopted, a homestead law was provided for, and a new land office was established at Greenville, in Butler County. The governor was authorized to revoke contracts made under United States laws with commissioners appointed to locate swamps and overflowed lands. The general assembly was authorized to cede to the Confederacy exclusive jurisdiction over a district ten miles square for a seat of government for the Confederate States of America.

Provision was made for the military defence of Alabama, and the United States army regulations were adopted almost in their entirety. The militia was reorganized; all commissions were vacated, and new elections ordered. The governor was placed in charge of all measures for defence. He was authorized to purchase supplies for the use of the state army, to borrow money for the same, and to issue bonds to cover expenses. Later, the convention decreed that all arms and munitions of war taken from the United States should be turned over to the Confederacy; only the small arms belonging to the state were retained. The governor was authorized to transfer to the Confederate States, upon terms to be agreed upon between the governor and the president, all troops raised for state defence. Thus all volunteer companies could be transferred to the Confederate service if the men were willing, otherwise they were discharged. A number of ordinances were passed organizing the state military system, and coöperating with the Confederate government. Jurisdiction over forts, arsenals, and navy yards was conferred upon the Confederate States. This ordinance could only be revoked by a convention of the people.

The port of Mobile was resumed by the state. The collector of the port and his assistants were continued in office as state officials who were to act in the name of the state of Alabama. With a view to future settlement the collector was ordered to retain all funds in his hands belonging to the United States, and the state of Alabama guaranteed his safety, as to oath, bond, etc. As far as possible, the United States customs and port regulations were adopted. Vessels built anywhere, provided that one-third was owned by citizens of the southern states and commanded by southern captains, were entitled to registry as vessels of Alabama. The collector was authorized to take possession in the name of the state of all government customhouses, lighthouses, etc., and to reappoint the officers in charge if they would accept office from the state. The weights and measures off the United States were adopted as the standard; discriminating duties imposed by the United States, and regulations on foreign vessels and merchandise were abolished; Selma and Mobile were continued as ports of entry, and all ordinances relating to Mobile were extended to Selma.

Thaddeus Sanford, the collector of Mobile, reported to the convention that the United States Treasury Department had drawn on him for $26,000 on January 7, 1861, and asked for instructions in regard to paying it. The Committee on Imports reported that the draft was dated before secession and before the ordinance directing the collector to retain all United States funds, that it was drawn to pay parties for services rendered while Alabama was a member of the Union. So it was ordered to be paid.

After the Confederacy was formed, the convention ordered that the custom-houses, marine hospital, lighthouses, buoys, and the revenue cutter, *Lewis Cass*, be turned over to the Confederate authorities; and the collector was directed to transfer all money collected by him to the Confederate authorities, who were to account for all moneys and settle with the United States authorities. The collector was then released from his bond to the state.

Postal contracts and regulations in force prior to January 11, 1861, were permitted to remain for the present. The general assembly was empowered to make postal arrangements until the Confederate government should be established. Meanwhile, the old arrangements with the United States were unchanged.[1] Other ordinances adopted the laws of the United States relating to the value of foreign coins, and directed the division of the state into nine congressional districts.

The judicial powers were resumed by the state and were henceforth to be exercised by the state courts. The circuit and chancery courts and the city court of Mobile were given original jurisdiction in cases formerly arising within the jurisdiction of the Federal courts. Jurisdiction over admiralty cases was vested in the circuit courts and the city court of Mobile. The chancery courts had jurisdiction in all cases of equity. The state supreme court was given original and exclusive jurisdiction over cases concerning ambassadors and public ministers. All admiralty cases, except where the United States was plaintiff, pending in the Federal courts in Alabama were transferred with all records to the state circuit courts; cases in equity in like manner to the state chancery courts; the United States laws relating to admiralty and maritime cases, and to the postal service were adopted temporarily; the forms of proceedings in state courts were to be the same as in former Federal courts; the clerks of the circuit courts were given the custody of all records transferred from Federal courts and were empowered to issue process running into any part of the state and to be executed by any sheriff; United States marshals in whose hands processes were running were ordered to execute them and to make returns to the state courts under penalty of being prosecuted as if defaulting sheriffs; the right was asserted to prosecute marshals who were guilty of misconduct before secession. The United States laws of May 26, 1796, and March 27, 1804, prescribing the method of authentication of public acts, records, or judicial proceedings for use in other courts, were adopted for Alabama. In cases appealed to the United States Supreme Court from the Alabama supreme court, the latter was to act as if no appeal had been taken and execute judgment; cases appealed from inferior Federal courts to the United States

---

[1] It was not until the end of June, 1861, that the United States postal service was withdrawn and final reports made to the United States. The Confederate postal service succeeded. At first, the Confederate Postmaster-General directed the postmasters to continue to report to the United States.

Supreme Court, were to be considered as appealed to the state supreme court which was to proceed as if the cases had been appealed to it from its own lower courts. The United States were not to be allowed to be a party to any suit in the state courts against a citizen of Alabama unless ordered by the convention or by the general assembly. Federal jurisdiction in general was to be resumed by state courts until the Confederate government should act in the matter.

No law of Alabama in force January 11, 1861, consistent with the Constitution and not inconsistent with the ordinances of the convention, was to be affected by secession; no official of the state was to be affected by secession; no offence against the state, and no penalty, no obligation, and no duty to or of state, no process or proceeding in court, no right, title, privilege, or obligation under the state or United States Constitution and laws, was to be affected by the ordinance of secession unless inconsistent with it. No change made by the convention in the constitution of Alabama should have the effect to divest of any right, title, or legal trust existing at the time of making the change. All changes were to have a prospective, not a retrospective, effect unless expressly declared in the change itself.

The general assembly was to have no power to repeal, alter, or amend any ordinance of the convention incorporated in the revised constitution. Other ordinances were to be considered as ordinary legislation and might be amended or repealed by the legislature.[1]

North Alabama in the Convention

All the counties of north Alabama sent coöperation delegates to the convention, and these spoke continually of a peculiar state of feeling on the part of their constituents which required conciliation by the convention. The people of that section, in regard to their grievances, thought as the people of central and south Alabama, but they were not so ready to act in resistance. Moreover, it would seem that they desired all the important measures framed by the convention to be referred to them for approval or disapproval. The coöperationists made much of this state of feeling for purposes of obstruction. There was, and had always been, a slight lack of sympathy between the people of the two sections; but on the present question they were

[1] This account of the work of the convention is compiled from the pamphlet ordinances in the Supreme Court Library in Montgomery.

very nearly agreed, though still opposing from habit. Had the co-operationists been in the majority, secession would have been hardly delayed. Of course, among the mountains and sand-hills of north Alabama was a small element of the population not concerned in any way with the questions before the people, and who would oppose any measure supported by southern Alabama. Sheets of Winston was probably the only representative of this class in the convention. The members of the convention referred to the fact of the local nature of the dissatisfaction. Yancey, angered at the obstructive tactics of the coöperationists, who had no definite policy and nothing to gain by obstruction, made a speech in which he said it was useless to disguise the fact that in some parts of the state there was dissatisfaction in regard to the action of the convention, and warned the members from north Alabama, whom he probably considered responsible for the dissatisfaction, that as soon as passed the ordinance of secession became the supreme law of the land, and it was the duty of all citizens to yield obedience. Those who refused, he said, were traitors and public enemies, and the sovereign state would deal with them as such. Opposition after secession was unlawful and to even speak of it was wrong, and he predicted that the name "tory" would be revived and applied to such people. Jemison of Tuscaloosa, a leading coöperationist, made an angry reply, and said that Yancey would inaugurate a second Reign of Terror and hang people by families, by towns, counties, and districts.

Davis (c.) of Madison declared that the people of north Alabama would stand by the expressed will of the people of the state, and intimated that the action of the convention did not represent the will of the people. If, he added, resistance to revolution gave the name of "tories," it was possible that the people of north Alabama might yet bear the designation; that any invasion of their rights or any attempt to force them to obedience would result in armed resistance; that the invader would be met at the foot of the mountains, and in armed conflict the question of the sovereignty of the people would be settled. Clark (c.) of Lawrence said that north Alabama was more closely connected with Tennessee, and that many of the citizens were talking of secession from Alabama and annexation to Tennessee. He begged for some concession to north Alabama, but did not seem to know exactly what he wanted. He intimated that there would be

JEFFERSON DAVIS.

civil war in north Alabama. Jones (c.) of Lauderdale said that his people were not "submissionists" and would share every toil and danger in support of the state to which was their supreme allegiance. Edwards (c.) of Blount was not prepared to say whether his people would acquiesce or not. He promised to do nothing to excite them to rebellion! Davis of Madison, who a few days before was ready to rebel, now said that he, and perhaps all north Alabama, would cheerfully stand by the state in the coming conflict.

A majority of the coöperationists voted against the ordinance of secession, at the same time stating that they intended to support it when it became law. The ordinance was lithographed, and the delegates were given an opportunity to sign their names to the official copy. Thirty-three of the delegates from north Alabama, two of whom had voted for the ordinance, refused to sign, because, as they said, it might appear as if they approved all that had been done by the secessionists. Their opposition to the policy of the majority was based on the following principles: (1) the fundamental principle that representative bodies should submit their acts for approval to the people; (2) the interests of all demanded that all the southern states be consulted in regard to a plan for united action. The members who refused to sign repeatedly acknowledged the binding force of the ordinance and promised a cheerful obedience, but, at the same time, published far and wide an address to the people, justifying their opposition and refusal to sign, causing the impression that they considered the action of the convention illegal. There was no reason whatever why these men should pursue the policy of obstruction to the very last, yet it was done. Nine of the thirty-three finally signed the ordinance, but twenty-four never signed it, though they promised to support it.

The majority of the members and of the people contemplated secession as a finality; reconstruction was not to be considered. A few of the coöperationists, however, were in favor of secession as a means of bringing the North to terms. Messrs. Pugh and Clay (members of Congress) in a letter to the convention suggested that the border states considered the secession of the cotton states as an indispensable basis for a reconstruction of the Union. Smith of Tuscaloosa, the leading coöperationist, stated his belief that the revolution would teach the North her dependence upon the South, how much she owed that section, bring her to a sense of her duty, and cause her to yield to the sensible demands of the South. He looked forward with fondest hopes to the near future when there would be a reconstruction of the Union with redress of grievances, indemnity for the past, complete and unequivocal guarantees for the future.

Incidents of the Session

The proceedings were dignified, solemn, and at times even sad. During the whole session, good feeling prevailed to a remarkable degree among the individual members, and toward the last the utmost harmony existed between the parties.[1] For this the credit is due the secessionists. At times the coöperationists were suspicious, and pursued a policy of obstruction when nothing was to be gained; but they were given every privilege and shown every courtesy. During the early part of the session an enthusiastic crowd filled the halls and galleries and manifested approval of the course of the secessionist leaders by frequent applause. In order to secure perfect freedom of debate to the minority, it was ordered that no applause be permitted; and this order failing to keep the spectators silent, the galleries were cleared, and thereafter secret sessions were the rule.

Affecting and exciting scenes followed the passage of the ordinance of secession. One by one the strong members of the minority arose and, for the sake of unity at home, surrendered the opinions of a lifetime and forgot the prejudices of years. This was done with no feeling of humiliation. To the last, they were treated with distinguished consideration by their opponents. There was really no difference in the principles of the two parties; the only differences were on local, personal, sectional, and social questions. On the common ground of resistance to a common enemy they were united.

On January 11, 1861, after seven days' debate, it became known that the vote on secession would be taken, and an eager multitude crowded Capitol Hill to hear the announcement of the result. The senate chamber, opposite the convention hall, was crowded with the waiting people, who were addressed by distinguished orators on the topics of the day. As many women as men were present, and, if

---

[1] So Smith, the coöperationist historian, reported.

possible, were more eager for secession. Their minds had long ago been made up. "With them," says the grave historian of the convention, "the love songs of yesterday had swelled into the political hosannas of to-day."

The momentous vote was taken, the doors were flung open, the result announced, and in a moment the tumultuous crowd filled the galleries, lobbies, and aisles of the convention hall. The ladies of Montgomery had made a large state flag, and when the doors were opened this flag was unfurled in the hall so that its folds extended almost across the chamber. Members jumped on desks, chairs, and tables to shake out the floating folds and display the design. There was a perfect frenzy of enthusiasm. Yancey, the secessionist leader and splendid orator, in behalf of the ladies presented the flag to the convention. Smith, the leader of the coöperationists, replied in a speech of acceptance, paying an affecting tribute to the flag that they were leaving — "the Star-Spangled Banner, sacred to memory, baptized in the nation's best blood, consecrated in song and history, and the herald of liberty's grandest victories on land and on sea." In memory of the illustrious men who brought fame to the flag, he said, "Let him who has tears prepare to shed them now as we lower this glorious ensign of our once vaunted victories." Alpheus Baker of Barbour in glowing words expressed to the ladies the thanks of the convention.

Amidst wild enthusiasm in hall and street the convention adjourned. One hundred and one cannon shots announced the result. The flag of the Republic of Alabama floated from windows, steeples, and towers. Party lines were forgotten, and until late in the night every man who would speak was surrounded by eager listeners. The people were united in common sentiment in the face of common danger.

One hour before the signal cannon shot announced that the fateful step had been taken and that Alabama was no longer one of the United States, there died, within sight of the capitol, Bishop Cobb of the Episcopal Church, the one man of character and influence who in all Alabama had opposed secession in any way, at any time, or for any reason.[1]

---

[1] See Smith's "Debates"; Hodgson's "Cradle of the Confederacy"; DuBose's "Yancey"; Wilmer's "Recent Past."

PART II

WAR TIMES IN ALABAMA

CHAPTER III

MILITARY AND POLITICAL EVENTS

SEC. 1. MILITARY OPERATIONS

ON January 4, 1861, the Alabama troops, ordered by Governor Andrew B. Moore, seized the forts which commanded the entrance to the harbor at Mobile, and also the United States arsenal at Mount Vernon, thirty miles distant. A few days later the governor, in a communication addressed to President Buchanan, explained the reason for this step. He was convinced, he said, that the convention would withdraw the state from the Union, and he deemed it his duty to take every precaution to render the secession peaceable. Information had been received which led him to believe that the United States government would attempt to maintain its authority in Alabama by force, even to bloodshed. The President must surely see, the governor wrote, that coercion could not be effectual until capacity for resistance had been exhausted, and it would have been unwise to have permitted the United States government to make preparations which would be resisted to the uttermost by the people. The purpose in taking possession of the forts and arsenal was to avoid, not to provoke, hostilities. Amicable relations with the United States were ardently desired by Alabama; and every patriotic man in the state was praying for peaceful secession. He had ordered an inventory to be taken of public property in the forts and arsenal, which were held subject to the control of the convention.[1] A month later, Governor Moore, in a communication addressed to the Virginia commissioners for mediation, stated that Alabama, in seceding, had no hostile intentions against the United States; that the sole object was to protect her rights, interests, and honor, without disturbing peaceful relations. This would continue to be the policy

[1] Gov. A. B. Moore to President Buchanan, Jan. 4, 1861, in O. R. Ser. I, Vol. I, pp. 327, 328.

of the state unless the Federal government authorized hostile acts. Yet any attempt at coercion would be resisted.   In conclusion, he stated that he had no power to appoint delegates to the proposed convention, but promised to refer the matter to the legislature.   However, he did not believe that there was the least hope that concessions would be made affording such guarantees as the seceding states could accept.[1]

The War in North Alabama

For a year Alabama soil was free from invasion, though the coast was blockaded in the summer of 1861.   In February, 1862, Fort Henry, on the Tennessee River, fell, and on the same day Commodore Phelps with four gunboats sailed up the river to Florence.   Several steamboats with supplies for Johnston's army were destroyed to prevent capture by the Federals.   Phelps destroyed a partly finished gunboat, burned the Confederate supplies in Florence, and then returned to Fort Henry.[2]   The fall of Fort Donelson (February 16) and the retreat of Johnston to Corinth left the Tennessee valley open to the Federals.   A few days after the battle of Shiloh, General O. M. Mitchell entered Huntsville (April 11, 1862) and captured nearly all the rolling stock belonging to the railroads running into Huntsville.   Decatur, Athens, Tuscumbia, and the other towns of the Tennessee valley were occupied within a few days.   To oppose this invasion the Confederates had small bodies of troops widely scattered across north Alabama.   The fighting was almost entirely in the nature of skirmishes and was continual.   Philip D. Roddy, later known as the "Defender of North Alabama," first appears during this summer as commander of a small body of irregular troops, which served as the nucleus of a regiment and later a brigade.   Hostilities in north Alabama at an early date assumed the worst aspects of guerilla warfare.   The Federals were never opposed by large commands of Confederates, and were disposed to regard the detachments who fought them as guerillas and to treat them accordingly.   In spite of the strenuous efforts of General Buell to have his subordinates wage war in civilized manner,[3] they were guilty of infamous

[1] O. R., Ser. IV, Vol. I, p. 89.

[2] Miller, "History of Alabama," p. 158.

[3] See D. C. Buell, "Operations in North Alabama," in "Battles and Leaders of the Civil War," Vol. II, pp. 701–708.

conduct. General Mitchell was charged by the people with brutal conduct toward non-combatants and with being interested in the stealing of cotton and shipping it North. He was finally removed by Buell.[1]

One of Mitchell's subordinates — John Basil Turchin, the Russian colonel of the Nineteenth Illinois regiment — was too brutal even for Mitchell, and the latter tried to keep him within bounds. His worst offence was at Athens, in Limestone County, in May, 1862. Athens was a wealthy place, intensely southern in feeling, and on that account was most heartily disliked by the Federals. Here, for two hours, Turchin retired to his tent and gave over the town to the soldiers to be sacked after the old European custom. Revolting outrages were committed. Robberies were common where Turchin commanded. His Russian ideas of the rules of war were probably responsible for his conduct. Buell characterized it as "a case of undisputed atrocity." For this Athens affair Turchin was court-martialled and sentenced to be dismissed from the service. The facts were notorious and well known at Washington, but the day before Buell ordered his discharge, Turchin was made a brigadier-general.[2]

General Mitchell himself reported (May, 1862) that "the most terrible outrages — robberies, rapes, arson, and plundering — are being committed by lawless brigands and vagabonds connected with the army." He asked for authority to hang them and wrote, "I hear the most deplorable accounts of excesses committed by

---

[1] Miller, p. 160; Brewer, "Alabama," p. 65; Mrs. Clay-Clopton, "A Belle of the Fifties," Chs. 18–22; O. R., Ser. I, Vol. X, Pt. II, pp. 204, 294, 295, *et passim*. Buell stated that "habitual lawlessness prevailed in a portion of General Mitchell's command," and that though authority was granted to punish with death there were no punishments. Discipline was lost. The officers were engaged in cotton speculation, and Mitchell's wagon trains were used to haul the cotton for the speculators. Flagrant crimes, Buell stated, were "condoned or neglected" by Mitchell. "Battles and Leaders," Vol. II, pp. 705, 706. North Alabama was not important to the Federals from a strategic point of view, and only the worst disciplined troops were stationed in that section.

[2] His real name was Ivan Vasilivitch Turchinoff. Several other officers were court-martialled at the same time for similar conduct. Keifer, "Slavery and Four Years of War," Vol. I, p. 277; Miller, p. 160; "Battles and Leaders," II, p. 706. A former "Union" man declared after the war that the barbarities of Turchin crushed out the remaining "Union" sentiment in north Alabama. Ku Klux Rept., Ala. Testimony, p. 850 (Richardson); O. R., Ser. I, Vols. X and XVI, *passim*; Brewer, "Alabama," pp. 319, 348. Accounts of eye-witnesses.

soldiers."[1] About fifty of the citizens of Athens, at the suggestion of Mitchell, filed claims for damages. Thereupon Mitchell informed them that they were laboring under a very serious misapprehension if they expected pay from the United States government unless they had proper vouchers.[2] Buell condemned his action in this matter also. Mitchell asked the War Department for permission to send prominent Confederate sympathizers at Huntsville to northern prisons. He said that General Clemens and Judge Lane advised such a measure. He reported that he held under arrest a few active rebels "who refused to condemn the guerilla warfare." The War Department seems to have been annoyed by the request, but after Mitchell had repeated it, permission was given to send them to the fort in Boston Harbor.[3]

Mitchell was charged at Washington with having failed in his duty of repressing plundering and pillaging. He replied that he had no great sympathy with the citizens of Athens who hated the Union soldiers so intensely.[4]

As the war continued the character of the warfare grew steadily worse. Ex-Governor Chapman's family were turned out of their home to make room for a negro regiment. A four-year-old child of the family wandered back to the house and was cursed and abused by the soldiers. The house was finally burned and the property laid waste. Governor Chapman was imprisoned and at last expelled from the country. Mrs. Robert Patton they threatened to strip in search of money and actually began to do so in the presence of her husband, but she saved herself by giving up the money.[5] Such experiences were common.

The provost marshal at Huntsville — Colonel Harmer — selected a number of men to answer certain political questions, who, if their answers were not satisfactory, were to be expelled from the country. Among these were, George W. Hustoun, Luke Pryor, and —— Malone of Athens, Dr. Fearn of Huntsville, and two ministers — Ross and

---

[1] O. R., Ser. I, Vol. X, Pt. II, pp. 204, 294, 295.

[2] O. R., Ser. I, Vol. X, Pt. II, p. 212.

[3] O. R., Ser. I, Vol. X, Pt. II, pp. 167, 168, 174 (May, 1862) ; for Clemens and Lane, see Ch. III, sec. 4.

[4] O. R., Ser. I, Vol. X, Pt. II, pp. 290–293.

[5] Brewer, p. 485, *et passim ;* Miller, p. 125 ; O. R., Ser. I, Vol. XXXIII, Pt. III, pp. 750–751.

Banister. General Stanley condemned the policy, but General Granger wanted the preachers expelled anyway, although Stanley said they had never taken part in politics.[1] The harsh treatment of non-combatants and Confederate soldiers by Federal soldiers and by the tories resulted in the retaliation of the former when opportunity occurred. Toward the end of the war prisoners were seldom taken by either side. When a man was caught, he was often strung up to a limb of the nearest tree, his captors waiting a few minutes for their halters, and then passing on. The Confederate irregular cavalry became a terror even to the loyal southern people. Stealing, robbery, and murder were common in the debatable land of north Alabama.[2]

Naturally the "tory" element of the population suffered much from the same class of Confederate troops. The Union element, it was said, suffered more from the operation of the impressment law. The Confederate and state governments strictly repressed the tendency of Confederate troops to pillage the "Union" communities in north Alabama.[3]

General Mitchell and his subordinates were accustomed to hold the people of a community responsible for damages in their vicinity to bridges, trestles, and trains caused by the Confederate forces. In August, 1862, General J. D. Morgan, in command at Tuscumbia, reported that he "sent out fifty wagons this afternoon to the plantations near where the track was torn up yesterday, for cotton. I want it to pay damages."[4] When Turchin had to abandon Athens, on the advance of Bragg into Tennessee, he set fire to and burned much of the town, but his conduct was denounced by his fellow-officers.[5] Near Gunterville (1862) a Federal force was fired upon by scouts, and the Federals, in retaliation, shelled the town. This was done a second time during the war, and finally the town was burned. In Jackson County four citizens were arrested (1862) because the pickets at Woodville, several miles away, had been fired upon.[6]

In a skirmish in north Alabama, General R. L. McCook was

[1] Gen. D. S. Stanley to Gen. William D. Whipple, Feb., 1865; O. R., Ser. I, Vol. XLIX, Pt. I, p. 718.

[2] Clanton's report, March, 1864; O. R., Ser. I, Vol. XXXIII, Pt. III, p. 718.

[3] Miller, "Alabama."   [4] Miller, p. 165.

[5] Miller, "Alabama"; Brewer, pp. 318, 348.   [6] Brewer, pp. 284, 383.

F

shot by Captain Gurley of Russell's Fourth Alabama Cavalry. The Federals spread the report among the soldiers that he had been murdered, and as the Federal commander reported, "Many of the soldiers spread themselves over the country and burned all the property of the rebels in the vicinity, and shot a rebel lieutenant who was on furlough." Even the house of the family who had ministered to General McCook in his last moments was burned to the ground. The old men and boys for miles around were arrested. The officer who was shot was at home on furlough and sick. General Dodge's command committed many depredations in retaliation for the death of McCook. A year later Captain Gurley was captured and sentenced to be hanged. The Confederate authorities threatened retaliation, and he was then treated as a prisoner of war. After the close of the war he was again arrested and kept in jail and in irons for many months at Nashville and Huntsville. At last he was liberated.[1]

Later in the war (1864), General M. L. Smith ordered the arrest of "five of the best rebels" in the vicinity of a Confederate attack on one of his companies, and again five were arrested near the place where a Union man had been attacked.[2] These are examples of what often happened. It became a rule to hold a community responsible for all attacks made by the Confederate soldiers.

The people suffered fearfully. Many of them had to leave the country in order to live. John E. Moore wrote to the Confederate Secretary of War from Florence, in December, 1862, that the people of north Alabama "have been ground into the dust by the tyrants and thieves."[3] The citizens of Florence (January, 1863) petitioned the Secretary of War for protection. They said that they had been greatly oppressed by the Federal army in 1862. Property had been destroyed most wantonly and vindictively, the privacy of the homes invaded, citizens carried off and ill treated, and slaves carried off and refused the liberty of returning when they desired to do so. The harshness of the Federals had made many people submissive for fear of worse things. No men, except the aged and infirm, were left in the country; the population was composed chiefly of women and

---

[1] O. R., Ser. I, Vol. XVI, Pt. I, pp. 841, 839 ; Wyeth, "Life of Forrest," pp. 111-113.

[2] O. R., Ser. I, Vol. XXXII, Pt. I, p. 394.

[3] O. R., Ser. I, Vol. XX, Pt. II, p. 442.

children.[1] It was in response to this appeal that Roddy's command was raised to a brigade. But the retreat of Bragg left north Alabama to the Federals until the close of the war, except for a short period during Hood's invasion of Tennessee.

The Streight Raid

April 19, 1863, Colonel A. D. Streight of the Federal army, with 2000 picked troops, disembarked at Eastport and started on a daring raid through the mountain region of north Alabama. The object of the raid was to cut the railroads from Chattanooga to Atlanta and to Knoxville, which supplied Bragg and to destroy the Confederate stores at Rome. To cover Streight's movements General Dodge was making demonstrations in the Tennessee valley and Forrest was sent to meet him. Hearing by accident of Streight's movements, Forrest left a small force under Roddy to hold Dodge in check and set out after the raider. The chase began on April 29. Streight had sixteen miles the start with a force reduced to 1500 men, mounted on mules. As his mounts were worn out, he seized fresh horses on the route. The chase led through the counties of Morgan, Blount, St. Clair, De Kalb, and Cherokee — counties in which there was a strong tory element, and the Federals were guided by two companies of Union cavalry raised in north Alabama. Streight had asked for permission to dress some of his men "after the promiscuous southern style," but, fortunately for them, was not allowed to do so.[2]

On May 1 occurred the famous crossing of Black Creek, where Miss Emma Sansom guided the Confederates across in the face of a heavy fire. Forrest now had less than 600 men, the others having been left behind exhausted or with broken-down horses. The best men and horses were kept in front, and Streight was not allowed a moment's rest. At last, tired out, the Federals halted on the morning of May 3. Soon the men were asleep on their arms, and when Forrest appeared, some of them could not be awakened. Men were asleep in line of battle, under fire. Forrest placed his small force so as to magnify his numbers, and Streight was persuaded by his officers to surrender — 1466 men to less than 600. The running

[1] O. R., Ser. I, Vol. XX, Pt. II, p. 443.
[2] The Andrews raiders in Georgia were hanged as spies for being dressed "in the promiscuous southern style."

fight had lasted four days, over a distance of 150 miles, through rough and broken country filled with unfriendly natives. Forrest could not get fresh mounts, the Federals could; the Federals had been preparing for the raid a month; Forrest had a few hours to prepare for the pursuit, and his whole force with Roddy's did not equal half of the entire Federal force of 9500.[1]

During the summer and fall there were many small fights between the cavalry scouts of Roddy and Wheeler and the Federal foraging parties. In October General S. D. Lee from Mississippi entered the northwestern part of the state, and for two or three weeks fought the Federals and tore up the Memphis and Charleston Railroad. The First Alabama Union Cavalry started on a raid for Selma, but was routed by the Second Alabama Cavalry. The Tennessee valley was the highway along which passed and repassed the Federal armies during the remainder of the war.

During the months of January, February, March, and April, 1864, scouting, skirmishing, and fighting in north Alabama by Forrest, Roddy, Wheeler, Johnson, Patterson, and Mead were almost continuous; and Federal raids were frequent. The Federals called all Confederate soldiers in north Alabama "guerillas," and treated prisoners as such. The Tennessee valley had been stripped of troops to send to Johnston's army. In May, 1864, the Federal General Blair marched through northeast Alabama to Rome, Georgia, with 10,500 men. Federal gunboats patrolled the river, landing companies for short raids and shelling the towns. In August there were many raids and skirmishes in the Tennessee valley. On September 23, Forrest with 4000 men, on a raid to Pulaski, persuaded the Federal commander at Athens that he had 10,000 men, and the latter surrendered, though in a strong fort with a thousand men.

Rousseau's Raid

July 10, 1864, General Rousseau started from Decatur, Morgan County, with 2300 men on a raid toward southeast Alabama to destroy the Montgomery and West Point Railway below Opelika, and thus cut off the supplies coming from the Black Belt for Johnston's army. General Clanton, who opposed him with a small force,

---

[1] Wyeth, "Life of Forrest," pp. 185-222; Mathes, "General Forrest," pp. 109-127; Miller, Ch. 32.

was defeated at the crossing of the Coosa on July 14; the iron works in Calhoun County were burned, and the Confederate stores at Talladega were destroyed. The railroad was reached near Loachapoka in what is now Lee County, and miles of the track there and above Opelika were destroyed, and the depots at Opelika, Auburn, Loachapoka, and Notasulga, all with quantities of supplies, were burned. This was the first time that central Alabama had suffered from invasion.[1]

In October General Hood marched *via* Cedartown, Georgia, into Alabama to Gadsden, thence to Somerville and Decatur, crossing the river near Tuscumbia on his way to the fatal fields of Franklin and Nashville. "Most of the fields they passed were covered with briers and weeds, the fences burned or broken down. The chimneys in every direction stood like quiet sentinels and marked the site of once prosperous and happy homes, long since reduced to heaps of ashes. No cattle, hogs, horses, mules, or domestic fowls were in sight. Only the birds seemed unconscious of the ruin and desolation which reigned supreme. No wonder that Hood pointed to the devastation wrought by the invader to nerve his heroes for one more desperate struggle against immense odds for southern independence."[2] A few weeks later the wreck of Hood's army was straggling back into north Alabama, which now swarmed with Federals. Bushwhackers, guerillas, tories, deserters, "mossbacks," harried the defenceless people of north Alabama until the end of the war and even after. A few scattered bands of Confederates made a weak resistance.

The War in South Alabama

To return to south Alabama. During the years 1861 and 1862 the defences of Mobile were made almost impregnable. They were commanded in turn by Generals Withers, Bragg, Forney, Buckner, and Maury. The port was blockaded in 1861, but no attacks were made on the defences until August, 1864, when 15,000 men were landed to besiege Fort Gaines. Eighteen war vessels under Farragut passed the forts into the bay and there fought the fiercest naval battle of the war. Admiral Buchanan commanded the Confederate fleet of four vessels — the *Morgan*, the *Selma*, the *Gaines*, and the *Ten-*

---

[1] Brewer, p. 339. [2] Miller, p. 213.

nessee.[1] The *Tecumseh* was sunk by a torpedo in the bay, and Farragut had left 17 vessels, 199 guns, and 700 men against the Confederates' 22 guns and 450 men. The three smaller Confederate vessels, after desperate fighting, were riddled with shot; one was captured, one beached, and one withdrew to the shelter of the forts. The *Tennessee* was left, 1 against 17, 6 guns against 200. After four hours' cannonade from nearly 200 guns, her smoke-stack and steering gear shot away, her commander (Admiral Buchanan) wounded, one hour after her last gun had been disabled, the *Tennessee* surrendered. The Federals lost 52 killed, and 17 wounded, besides 120 lost on the *Tecumseh*. The *Tennessee* lost only 2 killed and 9 wounded, the *Selma* 8 killed and 17 wounded, the *Gaines* about the same.[2] The fleet now turned its attention to the forts. Fort Gaines surrendered at once; Fort Morgan held out. A siege train of 41 guns was placed in position and on August 22 these and the 200 guns of the fleet opened fire. The fort was unable to return the fire of the fleet, and the sharpshooters of the enemy soon prevented the use of guns against the shore batteries of the Federals. The firing was furious; every shell seemed to take effect; fire broke out, and the garrison threw 90,000 pounds of powder into cisterns to prevent explosion; the defending force was decimated; the interior of the fort was a mass of smouldering ruins; there was not a place five feet square not struck by shells; many of the guns were dismounted. For twenty-four hours the bombardment continued, the garrison not being able to return the fire of the besiegers, yet the enemy reported that the garrison was not "moved by any weak fears." On the morning of August 23, 1864, the fort was surrendered.[3] Though the outer defences had fallen, the city could not be taken. The inner defences were strengthened, and were manned with "reserves," — boys and old men, fourteen to sixteen, and forty-five to sixty years of age.

[1] After completion at Selma the *Tennessee* was taken down the river to defend Mobile. It was found, even after removing her armament, that the vessel could not pass the Dog River bar, and timber was cut from the forests up the river and " camels " made with which to buoy up the heavy vessel. By accident these camels were burned and more had to be made. At last the heavy ram was floated over the bar. Of course the newspapers harshly criticised those in charge of the *Tennessee*. Maclay, " History of the United States Navy," Vol. II, p. 448.

[2] Brewer, p. 389; Scharf, "Confederate Navy," Ch. 18; Miller, pp. 205–206.

[3] Brewer, p. 120; Miller, p. 207.

In March, 1865, General Steele advanced from Pensacola to Pollard with 15,000 men, while General Canby with 32,000 moved up the east side of Mobile Bay and invested Spanish Fort. He sent 12,000 men to Steele, who began the siege of Blakely on April 2. Spanish Fort was defended by 3400 men, later reduced to 2321, against Canby's 20,000. The Confederate lines were two miles long. After a twelve days' siege a part of the Confederate works was captured, and during the next night (April 8), the greater part of the garrison escaped in boats or by wading through the marshes. Blakely was defended by 3500 men against Steele's 25,000. After a siege of eight days the Federal works were pushed near the Confederate lines, and a charge along the whole three miles of line captured the works with the garrison (April 9). Three days later batteries Huger and Tracy, defending the river entrance, were evacuated, and on April 12 the city surrendered.[1] The state was then overrun from all sides.[2]

Wilson's Raid and the End of the War

During the winter of 1864-1865, General J. H. Wilson gathered a picked force of 13,500 cavalry, at Gravelly Springs in northwestern Alabama, in preparation for a raid through central Alabama, the purpose of which was to destroy the Confederate stores, the factories, mines, and iron works in that section, and also to create a diversion in favor of Canby at Mobile.[3] On March 22 he left for the South. There was not a Confederate soldier within 120 miles; the country was stripped of its defenders. The Federal army under Wilson foraged for provisions in north Alabama when they themselves reported people to be starving.[4] To confuse the Confederates, Wilson moved his corps in three divisions along different routes. On March 29, near Elyton, the divisions united, and General Croxton

---

[1] Some of the Confederate gunboats were sunk (*Huntsville* and *Tuscaloosa*), and Commander Farrand surrendered twelve gunboats in the Tombigbee. All of these had been built at Mobile, Selma, and in the Tombigbee.

[2] Miller, pp. 208, 217-221.

[3] It was intended that Wilson should raid to and fro all through central Alabama. His men were armed with repeating carbines; his train of 250 wagons was escorted by 1500 unmounted men who secured mounts as they went farther into the interior. Greeley, Vol. II, p. 716.

[4] *N. Y. Herald*, April 6, 1865.

was again detached and sent to burn the University and public buildings at Tuscaloosa. Driving Roddy before him, Wilson, on March 31, burned five iron works near Elyton. Forrest collected a motley force to oppose Wilson. The latter sent a brigade which decoyed one of Forrest's brigades away into the country toward Mississippi,[1] so that this force was not present to assist in the defence when, on April 2, Wilson arrived before Selma with 9000 men. This place, with works three miles long, was defended by Forrest with 3000 men, half of whom were reserves who had never been under fire. They made a gallant fight, but the Federals rushed over the thinly defended works. Forrest and two or three hundred men escaped; the remainder surrendered. When the Federals entered the city, night had fallen, and the soldiers plundered without restraint until morning. Forrest had ordered that all the government whiskey in the city be destroyed, but after the barrels were rolled into the street the Confederates had no time to knock in the heads before the city was captured. The Federals were soon drunk. All the houses in the city were entered and plundered. A newspaper correspondent who was with Wilson's army said that Selma was the worst-sacked town of the war. One woman saved her house from the plunderers by pulling out all the drawers, tearing up the beds, throwing clothes all over the floor along with dishes and overturned tables, chairs, and other things. When the soldiers came to the house, they concluded that others had been there before them and departed. The outrages, robberies, and murders committed by Wilson's men, notwithstanding his stringent order against plundering,[2] are almost incredible. The half cannot be told. The destruction was fearful. The city was wholly given up to the soldiers, the houses sacked, the women robbed of their watches, earrings, rings, and other jewellery.[3] The negroes were pressed into the work of destruction, and when they refused to burn and destroy, they were threatened with death by the soldiers. Every one was robbed who had anything worth taking about his person. Even negro men on the streets

---

[1] April 5 Cahaba was captured by a part of Wilson's force and twenty Federal prisoners released from the military prison at that place. They reported that they had been well treated. — *N. Y. Herald*, April 29, 1865.

[2] Wyeth, "Life of Forrest," pp. 606, 607.

[3] Parsons's Cooper Institute Speech in *N. Y. Times*, Nov. 27, 1865 ; Trowbridge, "The South," pp. 435, 440. Accounts of eye-witnesses.

and negro women in the houses were searched and their little money and trinkets taken.[1]

The next day the public buildings and storehouses with three-fourths of the business part of the town and 150 residences were burned. Three rolling mills, a large naval foundry, and the navy yard, — where the *Tennessee* had been built, — the best arsenal in the Confederacy, powder works, magazines, army stores, 35,000 bales of cotton, a large number of cars, and the railroad bridges were destroyed. Before leaving, Wilson sent men about the town to kill all the horses and mules in Selma, and had 800 of his own worn-out horses shot. The carcasses were left lying in the roads, streets, and dooryards where they were shot. In a few days the stench was fearful, and the citizens had to send to all the country around for teams to drag away the dead animals, which were strewn along the roads for miles.[2]

Nearly every man of Wilson's command had a canteen filled with jewellery gathered on the long raid through the richest section of the state. The valuables of the rich Cane Brake and Black Belt country had been deposited in Selma for safe-keeping, and from Selma the soldiers took everything valuable and profitable. Pianos were made into feeding troughs for horses. The officers were supplied with silver plate stolen while on the raid. In Russell County a general officer stopped at a house for dinner, and had the table set with a splendid service of silver plate taken from Selma. His escort broke open the smoke-house and, taking hams, cut a small piece from each of them and threw the remainder away. Everything that could be was destroyed. Soft soap and syrup were poured together in the cellars. They took everything they could carry and destroyed the rest.

On April 10 Wilson's command started for Montgomery. A negro regiment of 800 men[3] was organized at Selma and accompanied

---

[1] Trowbridge, "The South," p. 435.

[2] Hardy, "History of Selma," p. 51; Miller, "Alabama," pp. 221-226; Parsons, speeches in *N. Y. Times*, Nov. 27, 1865, Apr. 20, 1866; *N. Y. Herald*, May 4, and Apr. 6, 1865; *Montgomery Advertiser*, July 14, 1867; Wilson's Report, June 29, 1865; *Selma Times*, Feb. 13, 1866; "Our Women in War Times," p. 277; Greeley, Vol. II, p. 719; Wyeth, "Life of Forrest," pp. 604-607; "Northern Alabama," p. 655.

[3] Hardy, "History of Selma," p. 52, says four regiments were organized, and the others were driven away.

the army, subsisting on the country. Before reaching Georgia there were several such regiments. On April 12 Montgomery was surrendered by the mayor. The Confederates had burned 97,000[1] bales of cotton to prevent its falling into the hands of the enemy. The captors burned five steamboats, two rolling mills, a small-arms factory, two magazines of stores, all the rolling stock of the railways, and the nitre works, the fire spreading also to the business part of the town.[2] Here, as at Selma, horses, mules, and valuables were taken by the raiders.

The force was then divided into two columns, one destined for West Point and the other for Columbus. The last fights on Alabama soil occurred near West Point on April 16, and at Girard, opposite Columbus, on the same day. At the latter place immense quantities of stores, that had been carried across the river from Alabama, were destroyed.[3]

Croxton's force reached Tuscaloosa April 3, and burned the University buildings, the nitre works, a foundry, a shoe factory, and the Sipsey cotton mills. After burning these he moved eastward across the state, destroying iron works, nitre factories, depots, and cotton factories. Before he reached Georgia, Croxton had destroyed nearly all the iron works and cotton factories that had been missed by Rousseau and Wilson.[4]

Destruction by the Armies

For three years north Alabama was traversed by the contending armies. Each burned and destroyed from military necessity and from malice. General Wilson said that after two years of warfare the valley of the Tennessee was absolutely destitute.[5] From the spring of 1862 to the close of the war the Federals marched to and fro in the valley. There were few Confederate troops for its defence, and the Federals held each community responsible for all attacks made within its vicinity. It became the custom to destroy property

---

[1] 125,000 bales, according to Greeley, Vol. II, p. 719.

[2] The *Advertiser* of April 18, 1865.

[3] *N. Y. World*, May 1 and July 18, 1865; *N. Y. Herald*, May 4 and 15, and June 17, 1865; Brewer, p. 512; Greeley, Vol. II, p. 720.

[4] *N. Y. Daily News*, May 29, 1865; *Century Magazine*, Nov., 1889; Transactions Ala. Hist. Soc., Vol. IV, p. 449.

[5] Report, June 29, 1865.

as a punishment of the people.   Much of the destruction was unnecessary from a military point of view.[1]   Athens and smaller towns were
sacked and burned, Guntersville was shelled and burned; but the
worst destruction was in the country, by raiding parties of Federals
and "tories," or "bushwhackers" dressed as Union soldiers. Huntsville, Florence, Decatur, Athens, Guntersville, and Courtland, all
suffered depredation, robbery, murder, arson, and rapine.[2] The
tories destroyed the railways, telegraph lines, and bridges, and as
long as the Confederates were in north Alabama they had to guard
all of these.[3]

Along the Tennessee River the gunboats landed parties to ravage
the country in retaliation for Confederate attacks.   In the counties
of Lauderdale, Franklin, Morgan, Lawrence, Limestone, Madison,
and Jackson nearly all property was destroyed.[4]

In 1863, a member of Congress from north Alabama tried to get
arms from Bragg for the old men to defend the county against Federal
raiders, but failed, and wrote to Davis that all civilized usages were
being disregarded, women and children turned out and the houses
burned, grain and provisions destroyed, women insulted and outraged, their money, jewellery, and clothing being stolen.

In December, 1863, General Sherman ordered that all the forage
and provisions in the country around Bridgeport and Bellefont "be
collected and stored, and no compensation be allowed rebel owners."
In April, 1864, General Clanton wrote to Governor Watts that the
"Yankees spared neither age, sex, nor condition."   Tories and deserters from the hills made frequent raids on the defenceless population.

General Dodge reported, May, 1863, that his army had destroyed
or carried off in one raid near Town Creek, "fifteen million bushels
of corn, five hundred thousand pounds of bacon, quantities of wheat,
rye, oats, and fodder, one thousand horses and mules, and an equal
number of cattle, sheep, and hogs, besides thousands that the army
consumed in three weeks; we also brought out fifteen hundred
negroes, destroyed five tanyards and six flouring mills, and we left
the country in such a devastated condition that no crop can be raised

---

[1] Somers, "The South Since the War," pp. 134, 135.
[2] Truman in *N. Y. Times*, Nov. 2, 1865.
[3] O. R., Ser. I, Vol. III, pp. 230-233.
[4] See Brewer, " County Notes."

during the year;" and nothing was left that would in the least aid the Confederates. On the night of his retreat Dodge lit up the Tennessee valley from Town Creek to Tuscumbia with the flames of burning dwellings, granaries, stables, and fences. In June Colonel Cornyn reports that in a raid from Corinth to Florence he had destroyed cotton factories, tanyards, all the corn-cribs in sight, searched every house in Florence, burned several residences, and carried off 200 mules and horses.[1] A few days later General Stanley raided from Tennessee to Huntsville and carried off cattle and supplies, but did not lay waste the country. General Buell did all that he could to restrain his subordinates, but often to no avail. After Sherman took charge affairs grew steadily worse. In a remarkable letter giving his views in the matter he says: "The government of the United States has in north Alabama any and all rights which they choose to enforce in war, to take their lives, their houses, their lands, their everything, because they cannot deny that war exists there, and war is simply power unrestrained by constitution or compact. If they want eternal warfare, well and good. We will accept the issue and dispossess them and put our friends in possession. To those who submit to the rightful law and authority all gentleness and forbearance, but to the petulant and persistent secessionists, why, death is mercy and the quicker he or she is disposed of the better. Satan and the rebellious saint of heaven were allowed a continuance of existence in hell merely to swell their just punishment." He referred to the fact that in Europe, whence the principles of war were derived, wars were between the armies, the people remaining practically neutral, so that their property remained unmolested. However, this present war was, he said, between peoples, and the invading army was entitled to all it could get from the people. He cited as a like instance the dispossessing of the people of north Ireland during the reign of William and Mary.[2] After this no restraint on the plundering and persecution of Confederate non-combatants was even attempted, and hundreds of families from north Alabama "refugeed" to south Alabama.

General Sherman wrote to one of his generals, "You may send

---

[1] Brewer, p. 188 *et passim*; Miller, p. 179; O. R., Ser. I, Vol. XXIII, Pt. I, pp. 245–249.

[2] Miller, p. 183; Garrett, " Public Men."

notice to Florence that if Forrest invades Tennessee from that direction, the town will be burned; and if it occurs, you will remove the inhabitants north of the Ohio River and burn the town and Tuscumbia also.[1]" All through this section fences were gone, fields grew up in bushes, and weeds, residences were destroyed, farm stock had disappeared. People who lived in the Black Belt report that Wilson's raiders ate up all the cooked provisions wherever they went, taking all the meat, meal, and flour to their next camping-place, where they would often throw away wagon loads of provisions. Frequently the meal and flour that could not be taken was strewn along the road. The mills were burned, and some families for three months after the close of the war lived on corn cracked in a mortar. All the horses and mules were taken; and only a few oxen were left to work the crops.

Governor Parsons said that Wilson's men were a week in destroying the property around Selma. Three weeks after, as Parsons himself was a witness, it was with difficulty that one could travel from Planterville to Selma on account of the dead horses and mules. The night marches of the enemy in the Black Belt were lighted by the flames of burning houses. Until this raid only the counties of north Alabama had suffered.[2]

Wilson had destroyed during this raid 2 gunboats; 99,000 small arms and much artillery; 10 iron works; 7 foundries; 8 machine shops; 5 rolling mills; the University buildings; many county courthouses and public buildings; 3 arsenals; a naval foundry and navy yard; 5 steamboats; a powder magazine and mills; 35 locomotives and 565 cars; 3 large railroad bridges and many smaller ones; 275,000 bales of cotton; much private property along the line of march, many magazines of stores; and had subsisted his army on the country.[3] Trowbridge, who passed through Alabama in the fall of 1865, said that Wilson's route could be traced by burnt gin-houses dotting the way.[4] Three other armies marched through the state in 1865, burning and destroying.

[1] Miller, p. 301.
[2] Speech at Cooper Institute, Nov. 13, 1865, in *N. Y. Times*, Nov. 27, 1895.
[3] *N. Y. Herald*, May 4 and 15, 1865; the *World*, May 1, 1865; the *Times*, April 20, and Nov. 2, 1865; *Montgomery Advertiser*, July 14, 1867; *Selma Times*, Feb. 13, 1866; Wilson's Report, June 29, 1865: Hardy, "History of Selma," pp. 46, 51.
[4] "The South," p. 440.

The Federals took horses and mules, cattle and hogs, corn and meat, gold and silver plate, jewellery, and other valuables. Aged citizens were tortured by "bummers" to force them to tell of hidden treasure. Some were swung up by the neck until nearly dead. Straggling bands of Federals committed depredations over the country. Houses were searched, mattresses were cut to pieces, trunks, bureaus, wardrobes, and chests were broken open and their contents turned out. Much furniture was broken and ruined. Families of women and children were left without a meal, and many homes were burned. Cattle and stock were wantonly killed. What could not be carried away was burned and destroyed.[1]

Though two-thirds of the state was untouched by the enemy two months before the close of hostilities, yet when the surrender came Alabama was as thoroughly destroyed as Georgia or South Carolina in Sherman's track.

SEC. 2.   MILITARY ORGANIZATION

Alabama Soldiers: Numbers and Character

The exact number of Confederate soldiers enlisted in Alabama cannot be ascertained. The original records were lost or destroyed, and duplicates were never completed. There were on the rolls infantry regiments numbered from 1 to 65, but the 52d and 64th were never organized. Of the 14 cavalry regiments, numbered from 1 to 12, two organizations were numbered 9. There was one battalion of artillery, afterwards transferred to the regular service, and 18 batteries.

In Alabama, as in the other southern states, local pride has placed the number of troops furnished at a very high figure. Colonel W. H. Fowler, superintendent of army records, who worked mainly in the Army of Northern Virginia, estimated the total number of men from Alabama at about 120,000. Governor Parsons, in his inaugural proclamation, evidently following Fowler's statistics, placed the number at 122,000,[2] while Colonel M. V. Moore placed the number

---

[1] Hague, "Blockaded Family," *passim ;* Riley, "Baptists in Alabama," pp. 304, 305 ; "Our Women in the War," p. 275 *et seq. ;* Riley, "History of Conecuh County," p. 173.

[2] Miller, "History of Alabama," p. 359 ; Brewer, "History of Alabama," pp. 68, 69 ; Transactions Ala. Hist. Soc., Vol. II, p. 188.

at 60,000 to 65,000.[1] General Samuel Cooper, adjutant and inspector-general of the Confederate States Army, estimated that not more than 600,000 men in the Confederacy actually bore arms.[2] This estimate would make the share of Alabama even less than Colonel Moore estimated. The highest estimates have placed the number at 128,000 and 135,000, but the correct figures are evidently somewhere between these extremes.[3]

The Superintendent of the Confederate Bureau of Conscription estimated that according to the census of 1860 there were in Alabama, from 1861 to 1864, 106,000 men between the ages of eighteen and forty-five, and of these, more than 8000 had been regularly exempted during the year 1864, all former exemptions having been revoked by act of Congress, February 17, 1864.[4] Livermore's estimate,[5] based on the census of 1860, was: There were in Alabama (1861) between the ages of eighteen and forty-five, 99,967 men, and in the entire Confederacy there were 265,000 between the ages of thirteen and sixteen. Of the latter, a rough estimate would place Alabama's proportion about one-tenth of the whole, that is, about 26,500. Those men over forty-five who later became liable to military duty he estimates at 20,000, that is, about 2000 in Alabama. Thus there were in Alabama, in 1861, not allowing for deaths, 127,467 persons who would become subject to military service unless exempted. Livermore places the number of boys from ten to twelve years of age and of men from forty-seven to fifty, in the Confederacy in 1861, at 300,000, or about 30,000 in Alabama. These would become liable to service in the state militia before 1865.[6] In 1861 the governor stated that by October 7 there had been 27,000 enlistments in the various organizations. Several of these commands were enrolled for short terms of three months, six months, or one year. Before November, 1862, there had been 60,000 enlistments. Included in this number were several thousand reënlistments and transfers. At the end of 1863, when

---

[1] Miller, "History of Alabama," p. 360 ; Colonel Moore's article in the *Louisville Post*, May 30, 1900.

[2] Miller, p. 359.

[3] For other estimates, see Livermore, "Numbers and Losses," and Curry, "Civil History of the Confederate States," pp. 152, 153.

[4] O. R., Ser. IV, Vol. III, pp. 102, 103.

[5] Livermore, "Numbers and Losses," pp. 20, 21.

[6] Alabama did not succeed in organizing the militia.

enlistment and reorganization had practically ceased, there had been 90,857 enlistments of all kinds from Alabama.[1]   For two years troops were organized in Alabama much faster than they could be supplied with arms.   For months some of the new regiments waited for equipment.   Four thousand men at Huntsville were in service several months before arms could be procured, and several infantry regiments were drilled as artillery for a year before muskets were to be had.[2]

Before the close of 1863, Alabama had placed in the Confederate service about all the men that could be sent.   The organization of new regiments by original enlistment practically ceased with the fall of 1862.   In 1863, only three regiments were thus organized, and two of these were composed of conscripts and men attracted by the special privileges offered.[3]   The other regiments, formed after the summer of 1862, were made by consolidating smaller commands that were already in service.   The few small regiments of reserves called out in 1864 and 1865 and given regular designations saw little or no service.   Those few who were made liable to service by the conscript law and who entered the army at all, as a rule went as volunteers and avoided the conscript camps.   The strength of the Alabama regiments came from central and south Alabama, for the full military strength of north Alabama could not be utilized on account of invasion by the enemy.   At first there were many small commands — companies and battalions — which were raised in a short time and sent at once to the front before a regimental organization could be effected.   Later these were united to form regiments. Nearly all the higher numbered infantry regiments and more than half of the cavalry regiments were formed in this way.   The first regiments raised and the strongest in numbers were sent to Virginia. To these went also the largest number of the recruits secured by the

---

[1] Miller, "Alabama," Appendix; Report of Col. E. D. Blake, Supt. of Special Registration, in O. R., Ser. IV, Vol. III, pp. 102, 103; Brewer, "Alabama," see "Regimental Histories."

[2] O. R., Ser. 1, Vol. III, pp. 440, 445; Brewer, "Alabama." Several commands were equipped at the expense of the commanders; others were equipped by the communities in which they were raised; one old gentleman, Joel E. Matthews of Selma, gave his check for $15,000 to the state, besides paying for the outfitting of several companies of soldiers. "Northern Alabama Illustrated," p. 661.

[3] These regiments were the 57th and 61st Infantry, and 7th Cavalry.

recruiting officers sent out by the regiments.   On an average, about 350 recruits or transfers were secured by each Alabama regiment in Virginia, though some had almost none.   There were numbers of persons who obtained authority to raise new commands for service near their homes, and in order to fill the ranks of their regiments and companies they would offer special inducements of furloughs and home stations.   The cavalry and artillery branches of the service were popular and secured many men needed in the infantry regiments.[1] Each commander of a separate company or battalion desired to raise his force to a regiment, and it was to the interest of the state to have as many organizations as possible in the field as its quota.   A better show was thus made on paper.   Such conditions prevented the recruitment of old regiments, especially those in the armies that surrendered under Johnston and Taylor.   Consequently the regiments in the Western Army were, as a rule, much smaller than the ones in the Army of Northern Virginia, to which recruits were sent instead of new regiments.

In each infantry and cavalry regiment there were ten companies.[2] The original strength of each company was from 64 to 100.   Later the number was fixed at 104 to the company for infantry, 72 for cavalry, and 70 in the artillery.   After the formation of new commands had practically ceased, the number for each company of infantry was raised to 125 men, 150 in the artillery, and 80 in the cavalry.[3] The original strength of each infantry regiment was, therefore, from 640 to 1000, not including officers; of cavalry, 600 to 720.   A battery of artillery seems to have had any number from 70 to 150, though usually the smaller number.   The size of the regiments varied greatly. Colonel Fowler reported that to February 1, 1865, 27,022 men had joined the 20 Alabama regiments in Virginia, an average of 1351 men to the regiment.   Brewer gives the total enrolment of 15 regiments in the Army of Northern Virginia as 21,694, an average of 1446 to the regiment.[4]   Four of these regiments had an enrolment of less than

---

[1] General Lee protested against this practice as preventing the proper recruitment of the armies.   Livermore, "Numbers and Losses in the Civil War," p. 12.

[2] The infantry regiments in Lee's army had 12 companies.

[3] See summary of Confederate legislation on the subject.   Livermore, p. 30.   The purpose of these laws was to discourage the formation of new commands.   It was not effective in Alabama.

[4] These were the infantry regiments numbered 3, 4, 5, 6, 8, 9, 10, 11, 12, 13, 14, 15, 41, 44, 48.

G

1200;[1] so it is evident that the other 5, not given by Brewer, must have averaged about 1265 to the regiment.[2] These numbers include transfers, details, and reënlistments, the exact number of which it is impossible to ascertain. Brewer lists the transfers and discharges from 15 regiments at 4398, an average of 293 each, of which about one-third seem to have been transfers.[3] There were also many reënlistments from disbanded organizations.[4] Both Brewer and Fowler count each enlistment as a different man and arrive at about the same results.[5]

The enrolment of 8 Alabama regiments in Johnston's army, as given by Brewer, amounted to 8300, an average to the regiment of 1037.[6] It was the practice, in 1864 and 1865, to unite two or more weaker regiments into one. No Alabama regiments in Virginia were so united, and of the 8 in the Western Army, whose enrolment is given by Brewer, only 1 was afterward united with another.[7] It would then seem that the enrolment of the strongest regiments is known.[8] The total number of enlistments in the Alabama commands in Virginia was, according to Fowler, about 30,000, and these were in 20 infantry regiments, and a few smaller commands. In the armies surrendered by Johnston and Taylor there were 38 Alabama infantry regiments, and 13 of these had been consolidated on account of their small numbers. Eight of them which remained separate and which must have been stronger than the ones united had enrolled

---

[1] The infantry regiments numbered 9, 11, 44, 48.

[2] The infantry regiments numbered 43, 47, 49, 61.   Brewer, "Regimental Histories."

[3] These were the infantry regiments numbered 3, 4, 5, 6, 8, 9, 10, 11, 12, 13, 14, 15, 41, 44, 48.

[4] When the regiments enlisted for a short time were retained in the service, the men were allowed to change to other regiments if they desired, and many did so. These transfers and reënlistments swelled the total enrolment of popular regiments.

[5] This has since been the method of estimating the number of soldiers furnished by Alabama, — each enlistment counting as one man.

[6] The infantry regiments numbered 20, 23, 28, 31, 34, 37, 42, 55.

[7] The 23d Infantry.

[8] The regiments that were united were : 24, 34, and 28; 33 and 38; 32 and 58; 23 and 46; 7, 39, 22, and 26–50. All were in Johnston's army except the 32d and 58th, which were in Taylor's command. Some of these regiments were consolidated after only one year's service; the others after less than two years. This indicates a low enrolment. Many companies were never recruited to the minimum. Three infantry regiments were disbanded after short service, — 1, 2 and 7, — and the men reënlisted in other organizations.

an average of 1037 (according to Brewer). Thirty-eight regiments of this strength (which is probably too large an estimate) would give a total enrolment of 39,406. This number, added to Fowler's estimate of 27,022 in the Army of Northern Virginia, will give 66,428 enlistments of all kinds, for the infantry arm of the service. Add to this 3000 for the 3 regiments of reserves called out in 1864,[1] and the total is 69,428 enlistments in the infantry.

There were 14 cavalry regiments, 7 of which, and possibly more, were formed by the consolidation of smaller commands already in service. The cavalry regiments did not enter the service as early as the infantry, only 1 regiment being organized in 1861. The original strength of each regiment, as has been said, was from 600 to 720. All these regiments served in the commands surrendered by Johnston and Taylor, where recruits were scarce, so 1000 to the regiment is a very large estimate of total enrolment. However, this would give 14,000 in the cavalry regiments.

Of artillery, there were 19 batteries and 1 battalion of 6 batteries, making 25 batteries in all, with an enrolment ranging from 70 to 150 in each. A total enrolment of 3750, or 150 to each battery, would be a large estimate.

Fowler reported about 3000 enlistments in the various smaller commands from Alabama in the Army of Northern Virginia.[2] An additional 2000 would more than account for all similar scattering commands in the other armies.[3]

The total enrolment may then be estimated: —

Army of Northern Virginia (Fowler report)	27,022
Army of Northern Virginia, scattering (Fowler report)	3,000
Armies of the West — infantry (estimate)	39,406
Armies of the West — cavalry	14,000
Scattering	2,500
Artillery	3,750
	89,678

This total includes many transfers and reënlistments, which can be only roughly estimated. In the Army of Northern Virginia 464 re-

[1] The 62d, 63d, 65th. A thousand to the regiment is a very liberal estimate; 500 is probably more nearly correct, I am told by old soldiers.

[2] Jeff Davis Artillery, Hadaway's Battery, Jeff Davis Legion, 4th Battalion Infantry, 23d Battalion Infantry.

[3] The 1st, 3d, 8th, 10th, and 15th Confederate regiments of cavalry had some companies from Alabama.

signed, 245 were retired, 3639 were discharged, 1815 were transferred to other commands, and 1666 deserted or were unaccounted for. Those who resigned — as a rule to accept higher positions — reëntered the service. Almost all of those who retired or were discharged had to enter the reserves, and many of them again became liable to service. Numbers of soldiers were accustomed to leave one command and go to another without any formality of transfer. Deserters who were driven back to the army nearly always chose to enter other regiments than their own. There were numbers of transfers from the cavalry to the infantry, for each cavalryman had to furnish his own horse, and, should it be killed or die and the soldier be unable to secure another, he was sent to an infantry regiment. There were also smaller infantry organizations, which were mounted and merged into the cavalry regiments. Half of the enlistments in the artillery came from the infantry. One regiment[1] at one time lost 100 men in this way, and it has been estimated that one-fifth of the Alabama soldiers served in more than one command.[2] Counting each name on the rolls as one man, as Brewer and Fowler do,[3] it is difficult to see how more than 90,000 enlistments can be counted, and from this total must be deducted several thousand for transfers and reënlistments. Miller's estimate of a deduction of one-fifth for names counted twice would make the total number of different men about 75,000, which is probably about the correct number. Not only were the same names counted twice, and even oftener in different commands, but sometimes in the same companies and regiments they were counted more than once. It was to the interest of local and state authorities to have each enlistment counted as a different man, and this was invariably done.[4] Five of the early regiments were reorganized and reënlisted, and thus 5000 at least were added to the total enrolment without securing a single recruit. The three-year regiments reënlisted in 1864,[5] and here again were extra thou-

---

[1] The 6th Infantry.   [2] Miller, p. 374.

[3] Brewer evidently follows Fowler, as to the Army of Northern Virginia.

[4] Not that this deceived the Confederate administration, but the large estimates sounded well in the governor's messages, and when there was a dispute with Richmond about the quota of the state.

[5] In 1861 and 1862 some regiments enlisted for short terms, some for three years, some for the war. I have been unable, in more than two or three cases, to find out the exact term, but there could hardly have been more than one reënlistment of an organization.

sands of enlistments to be added to the former total. There were also 19 infantry regiments[1] which were formed by the reorganization of former commands that had already been counted, and upon reënlistment for the war they were again counted. In this same way 7 regiments at least of cavalry were formed.[2] In this way it is possible to count up a total enlistment from Alabama of about 120,000.[3] There is no method which will even approximate correctness by which the total number of enlistments may be reduced to enlistments for a certain term, as three years or four years. The history of every enlistment must first be known.

There were three lieutenant-generals who entered the service in command of Alabama troops — John B. Gordon, Joseph Wheeler,[4] James Longstreet[4]; seven major-generals — H. D. Clayton, Jones M. Withers,[4] E. M. Law, C. M. Wilcox, John H. Forney,[4] W. W. Allen, R. E. Rodes[2]; and thirty-six brigadier generals — Tennent Lomax,[5] P. D. Bowles,[4] S. A. M. Wood, E. A. O'Neal, William H. Forney, J. C. C. Sanders,[4,5] I. W. Garrott,[5] Archibald Gracie,[4,5] B. D. Fry, James Cantey, J. T. Holtzclaw, E. D. Tracy,[5] E. W. Pettus, Z. C. Deas, G. D. Johnston, C. M. Shelly, Y. M. Moody, Wm. F. Perry, John T. Morgan, M. H. Hannon, Alpheus Baker, J. H. Clanton, James Hagan, P. D. Roddy, John Gregg,[5] L. P. Walker, D. Leadbetter,[4,5] J. H. Kelley,[4,5] J. Gorgas, C. A. Battle, John W. Frazer, Alex. W. Campbell, Thomas M. Jones, M. J. Bulger, John C. Reid, James Deshler.[5] Other Alabamians exercised commands in the troops of other states, and several were staff officers of general rank. The naval commanders were Semmes, Randolph, and Glassell, and a few subordinate officers.[6]

[1] The 1st, 2d, 7th, 11th, 21st, 25th, 26th–50th, 27th, 29th, 42d, 46th, 54th, 55th, 56th, 58th, 59th, 60th, 62d, 65th.

[2] The 3d, Russell's 4th, 8th, 9th, 10th, 11th, 12th.

[3] (a) There had been to the end of 1863, 90,857 enlistments in Alabama. Included in these figures were all reënlistments and transfers.

(b) In the summer of 1863 the state took a census of all males from sixteen to sixty years of age, a total of 40,500 names. These included 8835, and later 10,000, exempts, and all the cripples and deadheads in the state. Since this was six months previous to the report of the 90,857 enlistments, there must have been in the latter number many that were on the former list. See O. R., Ser. IV, Vol. III, pp. 101–103, 1101.

[4] West Point graduates, nine.   [5] Killed in battle, ten.

[6] Derry, "Story of the Confederate States"; Southern Hist. Soc. Papers, Vol. VI ; Brewer, "Alabama," "Regimental Histories"; Miller, "History of Alabama," p. 375 ; Brown, "History of Alabama," pp. 238–254.

During the early months of 1865 a movement was started to enroll negroes as Confederate soldiers, and a number of officers, among whom was John T. Morgan, received permission to raise negro troops. The conference of governors at Augusta in 1864 recommended the arming of slaves, but Governor Watts asked the Alabama legislature to disapprove such a movement.[1] An enthusiastic meeting of citizens, held in Mobile, February 19, 1865, declared that the war must be prosecuted "to victory or death," and that 100,000 negroes should be placed in the field.[2] It was too late, however, for success. Wilson, on his raid, picked up the Confederate negro troops at Selma, and took them with him.[3] In 1862, the "Creoles" of Mobile applied for permission to enlist in a body. They were mulattoes, but were free by the treaties with France in 1803 and with Spain in 1819, were property holders, often owning slaves, and were an orderly, respectable class, true to the South and anxious to fight for the Confederacy. The Secretary of War was not friendly to the proposal, but in November, 1862, the legislature of Alabama authorized their enlistment for the defence of Mobile. A year later, at the urgent request of General Maury, they were received into the Confederate service as heavy artillery.[4]

The Alabama troops in the Confederate service made a notably good record. The flower of the Alabama army served with Lee in Virginia, but nearly as good were the Alabama troops in the western armies. Brewer says they moved "high and haughty in the face of death." The regiments of reserves raised late in the war and stationed within the state were not very good. Yet there were instances of regiments, with bad reputation when stationed near home, making splendid records when sent to the front. The spirit of the troops at the front was high to the last. In 1864 an Alabama regiment reënlisted for the war, with the oath that they would "live on bread and go barefoot before they would leave the flag under which they had fought for three years."[5] On the morning of April 9, 1865, the Sixtieth Alabama (Hilliard's Legion), then about 165 strong,

---

[1] Annual Cyclopædia (1864), p. 7.
[2] Annual Cyclopædia (1865), p. 10.
[3] Riley, "Baptists of Alabama," p. 305 ; O. R., Ser. IV, Vol. III, p. 1193.
[4] O. R., Ser. IV, Vol I, p. 1088 ; Vol. II, pp. 94, 197.
[5] *N. Y. World*, March 12, 1864 ; "The Land We Love," Vol. II, p. 296.

captured a Federal battery.[1] Fowler, in his report in 1865, asserts that Alabama sent more troops into the service than any other state; also that she sent more troops in proportion to her population than any other state. "I am certain too," he says, "that when General Lee surrendered his army, the representation from Alabama on the field that day was inferior to no other southern state in numbers, and surely not in gallantry."[2]

Union Troops from Alabama

To the Union army Alabama furnished about 3000 regular enlistments. Of these 2000 were white men. It is not likely that there were many more, since in 1900 there were in Alabama only 3649 persons, northerners, negroes, and all, drawing pensions, and some of these on account of the Indian and Mexican wars.[3] The white Union troops served in the First Alabama Union Cavalry, in the First Alabama and Tennessee Cavalry (the First Vedette), Kennamer's Scouts (Cavalry), and in northern regiments — principally those from Indiana. The report of the Secretary of War for 1864–1865 says that no white regiments were regularly enlisted in Alabama for the Union army. But this is evidently not correct, since the report for 1866 says that there were 2576 enlistments in Alabama for various periods of service.[4]

Of negro regiments in the Union army, there were the First Alabama Volunteers, afterward known as the Fifth United States Colored Infantry, the Second Alabama Volunteers (negroes), and the First Alabama Colored Artillery, afterward known as the Sixth United States Heavy Artillery, which served at Fort Pillow. Late in 1864 General Lorenzo Thomas reported that he had recently organized three regiments of colored infantry in Alabama, and Wilson organized several other negro regiments in the state in 1865. Many

---

[1] Southern Hist. Soc. Papers, Vol. II, p. 61; Shaver, "History of the Sixtieth Alabama," p. 106; Miller, "History of Alabama," pp. 359, 374; Brewer, "Alabama," pp. 586–705; "Confederate Military History"—Alabama; Longstreet, "Manassas to Appomattox"; "Memorial Record of Alabama" (Wheeler's "Military History"); McMorries, "History of the First Alabama Regiment."

[2] Transactions Ala. Hist. Soc., Vol. II, p. 188; also John S. Wise, "End of an Era"; Longstreet, "Manassas to Appomattox."

[3] *Montgomery Advertiser* Almanac (1901), p. 220.

[4] Report of 1866, Appendix, Pt. I, p. 166.

negroes from north Alabama went into various negro organizations, and were credited to the northern states, the official records showing only 4969 negro enlistments credited directly to Alabama. A conservative estimate would be from 2000 to 2500 whites and 10,000 negroes enlisted in Alabama, not counting those who were enrolled in the spring of 1865.[1] The white Union soldiers from Alabama were mostly poor men from the mountain counties of north Alabama. The Union troops from Alabama received no bounty.[2]

The Militia System

The militia system of Alabama in 1861 existed only in the statute books, and in the persons of a few brigadiers and a major-general, whose entire duty had consisted in wearing uniforms at the inauguration of a governor and ever thereafter bearing military titles. A series of Arabic numbers, something more than a hundred, was assigned to the militia regiments that were unorganized, but which, under favorable circumstances, might be enrolled and called out. The county was the unit. To each county was assigned one regiment or more according to the white population. Several counties formed a militia district under a brigadier-general, and over all was a major-general. Bodies of trained volunteers were not connected with the militia system at all, but these went at once, on the outbreak of war, into the state army, which was soon merged into the Confederate army.

In theory the militia consisted of all the male citizens of Alabama of military age. The enlistments for war service soon reduced the material from which militia regiments could be formed, and the system broke down before it was tried. A few regiments may have been enrolled in 1861 and 1862, but if so, they at once entered the Confederate service. The Forty-eighth Alabama Militia regiment was ordered out to defend Mobile in 1861, and $6000 was appropriated to provide pikes and knives with which to arm them, as it was impos-

---

[1] Report of the Secretary of War, 1866, Appendix, Pt. I, p. 69; Report of the Secretary of War (1864–1865), p. 28; Moore, " Rebellion Record," Vol. VII, p. 45; Miller, p. 360; O. R., Ser. III, Vol. III, pp. 1115, 1190, and Vol. IV, pp. 16, 921, 925, 1269, 1270; O. R., Ser. II, Vol. V, pp. 589, 570, 626, 627, 716, 946, 947; " Confederate Military History " — Alabama.

[2] Ku Klux Rept., Ala. Test., p. 592.

sible to get firearms.   On March 1, 1862, Governor Shorter appealed
to the people to give their shotguns, rifles, bowie-knives, pikes, powder,
and lead to state agents, probate judges, sheriffs, and other state
officials for the use of the state militia.[1]   A few days later he ordered
out, for the defence of Mobile and the coast, the militia from the river
counties and the southwestern counties — eighteen counties in all.
But the militia failed to appear.   It seems that the governor expected
a hearty response from the people.   He asked for too much, and got
nothing.   On March 12, 1862, he again ordered out the militia,
this time specifying the regiments by number.[2]   But again the militia
failed to respond.   The fact was, there was no longer any militia;
the officers and men had gone, or were preparing to go, into the Confederate service.   Many of the militia regiments could not have
mustered a dozen men, and it is doubtful if there was a muster-roll
of a militia regiment in all Alabama.[3]   In May, 1862, the governor,
recognizing that the militia system was worthless as a means of raising troops for home defence, issued a proclamation asking the people
to form volunteer organizations.   The response, as he said, "was not
prompt."   The legislature of that year, not seeing the necessity,
refused to reorganize the militia so as to give the governor any effective
control.   The people seem not to have been worried by any fear
of invasion, and many thought that organization into militia companies was merely preliminary to entering the Confederate service.
Some did not wish to go until they had to do so, others preferred
to go at once to the Confederate army.   It appears that all persons,
for various reasons, disliked militia service.

December 22, 1862, the governor issued a proclamation, in which,
after mentioning the tardy response to his May proclamation and the
failure of the legislature to reorganize the system, he again asked
the people to volunteer in companies for home defence.[4]   He begged
the people to drive those who were shirking service to their duty
by the force of public scorn.   He requested that business houses
be closed early in order to give time for drill.   The response to this

---

[1] Moore, " Rebellion Record," Supplement.
[2] The 89th, 94th, 95th, etc.   See Moore, " Rebellion Record," Supplement.   The
highest number of a militia regiment to be found on the records was the 102d, in Sumter
County.
[3] See O. R., Ser. I, Vol. XXVI, Pt. II (Shorter to Johnston).
[4] Moore, " Rebellion Record," Vol. VI ; O. R., Ser. IV, Vol. II, pp. 253–256.

was the same as to his previous proclamation.   There was no longer any material for a militia organization.   Early in 1863, and in some sections even before, the need began to be felt for a militia force to execute the laws.   Under the direction of the governor, small commands were organized here and there of those who were not likely to become subject to service in the Confederate army.   These were state and Confederate officials, young boys, and sometimes old men.   These organizations were later a source of constant conflict between the state authorities and the Confederate enrolling officers, who wanted to take such commands bodily into the Confederate service, and who usually did so with the full consent of most of the men and to the great indignation of the governor.[1]   In August, 1863, the legislature finally passed a law to reorganize the militia system, or rather to establish a new system.   By the law an official in each county, appointed by the governor, was to enroll as first-class militia all males under seventeen and over forty-five years of age, including all state and Confederate civil officials, and those physically disqualified for service in the Confederate army.   The second class was to consist of those not in the first class, that is, of men between seventeen and forty-five years of age.   But men of the second class were subject to enrolment by Confederate conscript officers, and consisted of the few thousand who were specially exempted by the Confederate authorities.   Those of the first class who wished to do so might enroll in the second class.   The governor was given the usual power over the militia, but it was ordered that the first-class militia was not to go beyond the limits of the county to which it belonged.[2]   Presumably the second class might be ordered beyond the county limits, but there were so few in their class that they were not organized.   The first-class militia in each county was under a commandant of reserves, militia now being called reserves.   He had the power to call it out to repel invasion and execute the laws. Jealousy of Confederate authority had caused the legislature to take legal means of making the militia worthless to the Confederacy, and useful only for local defence and for executing the state laws in par-

[1] O. R., Ser. I, Vol. XXXIX, Pts. II and III, pp. 780, 855; Ser. IV, Vol. III, pp. 175, 323.

[2] Act of General Assembly, Aug. 29, 1863, which seems to have followed an act of Congress of similar nature.

ticular localities.[1] Still, the system seems to have been practically useless, and the governor continued to organize small irregular commands to execute the laws and to furnish military escorts to civil officials. As has been stated, such commands were highly approved of by the Confederate enrolling officers, who eagerly persuaded them to join the Confederate army, and thus called forth strong remonstrances from Governor Watts. The War Department reasoned that a state could keep troops of war which were not subject to absorption in the Confederate service, but that the militia were subject to the superior claims of the Confederacy.[2] February 6, 1864, Governor Watts, in an address to the people, declared that a raid into the state was threatened and called upon young and old to volunteer for the defence of the state.[3] The reserve system was now worthless. Few of the regiments had more than fifty men, many had none, and the governor was powerless to use them beyond the limits of their respective counties. The state was at the mercy of any invading force, and Rousseau's Raid, through the heart of the state, showed the woful condition of affairs. On October 7, 1864, the legislature passed an act which prohibited Confederate army officers from commanding the reserves. It was again ordered that the first-class reserves should not serve beyond the limits of the county to which they belonged. At the same time, permission was granted to the harassed citizens of Dale and Henry counties to organize themselves to protect their homes, provided they did so under the direction of the commandant of the first-class militia. Perhaps the legislature was afraid that, if left to themselves, they might cross the county line, or choose a Confederate officer to lead them. In December, 1864, when north Alabama was almost entirely overrun by tories, deserters, and Federals, the citizens of Marion County were authorized to organize into squads and protect themselves.[4] Still the legislature refused to make an effective reorganization of the militia. When the spring campaign in 1865 began, Governor Watts appealed to the people to do what the legislature had failed to do. The first-class militia could not, he said, be ordered beyond the limits of their coun-

---

[1] O. R., Ser. IV, Vol. III, p. 1133.

[2] O. R., Ser. IV, Vol. III, pp. 172–174, 256, 376. The state supreme court held the same view.   [3] Moore, " Rebellion Record," Vol. VIII, p. 378.

[4] Acts of General Assembly, Dec. 12, 1864.

ties, and in three congressional districts in north Alabama it had not been and, by law, could not be, organized. He estimated that 30,000 men were enrolled in the first-class militia, of whom 4000 were boys, and to the latter he made the appeal to defend the state. Evidently the remaining 26,000 men were, in his estimation, not worth much as soldiers. However, he called upon all first-class militia to volunteer as second class.[1]   A few hundred responded to this appeal, and all of them who saw active service were with Forrest in front of Wilson.

The various organizations mentioned in the War Records, the Junior Reserves, Senior Reserves, Mobile Regiment, Home Guards, Local Defence Corps,[2] and others, were, except the reserves, volunteer organizations for local defence, and all that saw active service before 1865, except the Home Guards, were absorbed into the Confederate organization.[3]   The stupid conduct of the legislature during the last two years of the war in failing to provide for the defence of the state cannot be too strongly condemned.   The final result would have been the same, but a strong force of militia would have enabled Governor Watts to execute the laws in all parts of the state, and to protect the families of loyal citizens from outrage by tories and deserters.

SEC. 3.   CONSCRIPTION AND EXEMPTION

Confederate Enrolment Laws

In the spring of 1862, the Confederate Congress passed the Enrolment Act, by which all white men between the ages of eighteen and thirty-five were made liable to military service at the call of the President, and those already in service were retained.   The President was authorized to employ state officials to enroll the men made subject to duty, provided the governor of the state gave his consent; otherwise he was to employ Confederate officials.   The conscripts thus secured were to be assigned to the state commands already in the field until these organizations were recruited to their full strength. Substitutes were allowed under such regulations as the Secretary of

---

[1] *N. Y. Times,* April 16, 1865 ; Annual Cyclopædia (1865), p. 10.

[2] See O. R., General Index.

[3] The 61st, 62d, and 65th regiments were thus formed, the men becoming subject to duty under the conscript act, or by volunteering.

War might prescribe.[1] Five days later, a law was passed exempting certain classes of persons from the operations of the Enrolment Act. These were: Confederate and state officials, mail-carriers, ferrymen on post-office routes, pilots, telegraph operators, miners, printers, ministers, college professors, teachers with twenty pupils or more, teachers of the deaf, dumb, and blind, hospital attendants, one druggist to each drug store, and superintendents and operatives in cotton and wool factories.[2] In the fall of 1862, the Enrolment law was extended to include all white men from thirty-five to forty-five years of age and all who lacked a few months of being eighteen years of age. They were to be enrolled for three years, the oldest, if not needed, being left until the last.[3]

At this time was begun the practice, which virtually amounted to exemption, of making special details from the army to perform certain kinds of skilled labor. The first details thus made were to manufacture shoes for the army.[4] The list of those who might claim exemption, in addition to those named in the act of April 21, 1862, was extended to include the following: state militia officers, state and Confederate clerks in the civil service, railway employees who were not common laborers, steamboat employees, one editor and the necessary printers for each newspaper, those morally opposed to war, provided they furnished a substitute or paid $500 into the treasury, physicians, professors, and teachers who had been engaged in the profession for two years or more, government artisans, mechanics, and other employees, contractors and their employees furnishing arms and supplies to the state or to the Confederacy, factory owners, shoemakers, tanners, blacksmiths, wagon makers, millers, and engineers. The artisans and manufacturers were granted exemption from military service provided the products of their labor were sold at not more than seventy-five per cent profit above the cost of production. On every plantation where there were twenty or more negroes one white man was entitled to exemption as overseer.[5]

---

[1] Act, April 16, 1862, Pub. Laws, C.S.A., 1st Cong., 1st Sess.

[2] Act, April 21, 1862, Pub. Laws, C.S.A., 1st Cong., 1st Sess.

[3] Act, Sept. 27, 1862, Pub. Laws, C.S.A., 1st Cong., 2d Sess.

[4] Act, Oct. 9, 1862, Pub. Laws, C.S.A., 1st Cong., 2d Sess. These details were still carried on the rolls of the company.

[5] Act, Oct. 11, 1862, Pub. Laws, C.S.A., 1st Cong., 2d Sess. The exemption of one white for twenty negroes was called the "twenty-nigger law." One peaceable Black Belt

In the spring of 1863 mail contractors and drivers of post-coaches were exempted;[1] and it was ordered that those exempted under the so-called "twenty-negro" law should pay $500 into the Confederate treasury; also, that such state officials as were exempted by the governor might be also exempted by the Confederate authorities. The law permitting the hiring of substitutes by men liable to service was repealed on December 28, 1863, and a few days later even those who had furnished substitutes were made subject to military duty.[2]

A law of February 17, 1864,[3] provided that all soldiers between the ages of eighteen and forty-five should be retained in service during the war. Those between the ages of seventeen and eighteen, and forty-five and fifty were called into service as a reserve force for the defence of the state. All exemptions were repealed except the following: (1) the members of Congress and of the state legislature, and such Confederate and state officers as the President or the governors might certify to be necessary for the proper administration of government; (2) ministers regularly employed, superintendents, attendants, and physicians of asylums for the deaf, dumb, and blind, insane, and other public hospitals, one editor for each newspaper, public printers, one druggist for each drug store which had been two years in existence, all physicians who had practised seven years, teachers in colleges of at least two years' standing and in schools which had twenty pupils to each teacher; (3) one overseer or agriculturist to each farm upon which were fifteen or more negroes, in case there was no other exempt on the plantation. The object was to leave one white man, and no more, on each plantation, and the owner or overseer was preferred. In return for such exemption, the exempt was bound by bond to deliver to the Confederate authorities, for each slave on the plantation between the ages of sixteen and fifty, one hundred pounds of bacon or its equivalent in produce, which

citizen wished to stay at home, but he possessed only nineteen negroes. His neighbors thought that he ought to go to war, and no one would give, lend, or sell him a slave. Unable to purchase even the smallest negro, he was sadly making preparations to depart, when one morning he was rejoiced by the welcome news that one of the negro women had presented her husband with a fine boy. The tale of twenty negroes was complete, and the master remained at home.

[1] Act of April 14, 1863, Pub. Laws, C.S.A., 1st Cong., 3d Sess.

[2] Acts, Dec. 28, 1863, and Jan. 5, 1864, Pub. Laws, C.S.A., 1st Cong., 4th Sess.

[3] Pub. Laws, C.S.A., 1st Cong., 4th Sess.

was paid for by the government at prices fixed by the impressment commissioners. In addition, the exempt was to sell his surplus produce at prices fixed by the commissioners. The Secretary of War was authorized to make special details, under the above conditions, of overseers, farmers, or planters, if the public good demanded it; also (4) to exempt the higher officials of railroads and not more than one employee for each mile of road; and (5) mail carriers and drivers. The President was authorized to make details of old men for special service.[1] By an act passed the same day free negroes from eighteen to fifty years of age were made liable to service with the army as teamsters. These acts of February 17, 1864, were the last Confederate legislation of importance in regard to conscription and exemption. During the year 1864 the Confederate authorities devoted their energies to construing away all exemptions possible, and to absorbing the state reserve forces into the Confederate army.

Policy of the State in Regard to Conscription

To return to 1861. The state legislature, when providing for the state army, authorized the governor to exempt from militia duty all railway, express, steamboat, and telegraph employees, but even the fire companies had to serve as militia.[2] The operation of the enrolment law stripped the land of men of militia age, and on November 17, 1862, the legislature ordered to duty on the public roads men from sixteen to eighteen years of age, and forty-five to fifty-five, and later all from sixteen to fifty as well as all male slaves and free negroes from fourteen to sixty years of age.[3] Militia officers between the ages of eighteen and forty-five were declared subject to the enrolment acts of Congress,[4] as were also justices of the peace, notaries public, and constables.[5]

Yet, instead of making an effective organization of the militia, the legislature in 1863 proceeded to frame a law of exemptions patterned after that of the Confederacy. It released from militia duty all persons over forty-five years of age, county treasurers, physicians of seven years' practice or who were in the public service, ministers, teachers of three years' standing, one blacksmith in each beat, the

---

[1] Act, Feb. 17, 1864, Pub. Laws, C.S.A., 1st Cong., 4th Sess.
[2] Acts, Jan. 31, 1861, 1st Called Session.
[3] Act, Aug. 29, 1863.   [4] Nov. 25, 1862.   [5] Dec. 6, 1862.

city police and fire companies, penitentiary guards, general administrators who had been in service five years, Confederate agents, millers,
railroad employees, steamboat officials, overseers, managers of foundries, salt makers who made as much as ten bushels a day and who
sold it for not more than $15 per bushel. Besides, the governor could
make special exemptions.[1] In 1864 millers who charged not more
than one-eighth for toll were exempted.[2] It will be seen that in some
respects the state laws go farther in exemption than the Confederate
laws, and thus were in conflict with them. But it must be remembered that the Confederacy had already stripped the country of
nearly all the able-bodied men who did not evade duty. To this
time, however, there was no conflict between the state and Confederate authorities in regard to conscription. An act was also passed
providing for the reorganization of the penitentiary guards, and only
those not subject to conscription were retained.[3] A joint resolution
of August 29, 1863, called upon Congress to decrease the list of exemptions, as many clerks and laborers were doing work that could
be done by negroes. At the end of the year 1863 the legislature
asked that the conscript law be strictly enforced by Congress.[4]

On the part of the state rights people, there was much opposition
to the enrolment or conscription laws on the ground that they were
unconstitutional. Several cases were brought before the state supreme court, and all were decided in favor of the constitutionality
of the laws; furthermore, it was decided that the courts and judicial
officers of the state had no jurisdiction on *habeas corpus* to discharge
from the custody of a Confederate enrolling officer persons who had
been conscripted under the law of Congress.[5] A test case was carried to the state supreme court, which decided that a person who had
conscientious scruples against bearing arms might pay for a substitute in the state militia and claim exemption from state service, but

---

[1] Act, Aug. 29, 1863.

[2] Dec. 13, 1864. This was a measure of obstruction, since the Confederate laws did
not exempt millers. The legislature elected in 1863 contained many obstructionists.

[3] Act, Aug. 29, 1863.   [4] Resolution, Dec. 4, 1863.

[5] *Ex parte* Hill, *In re* Willis *et al. vs.* Confederate States — 38 Alabama Reports
(1863), 429. All over the state at various times men sought to avoid conscription or
some certain service under every pretext, sometimes " even resorting to a *habeas corpus*
before an ignorant justice of the peace, who had no jurisdiction over such cases." See
O. R., Ser. I, Vol. XXVI, Pt. II, p. 139; also Governor Shorter to General Johnston.
Aug., 1863.

THE FIRST CONFEDERATE CAPITOL.
The State Capitol, Montgomery.

MONTGOMERY RESIDENCE OF
PRESIDENT DAVIS.

CONFEDERATE MONUMENT, MONTGOMERY.

THE INAUGURATION OF JEFFERSON DAVIS.
(From an old negative.)

if conscripted he was not exempted from the Confederate service unless he belonged to the religious denominations specially exempted by the act of Congress.[1] The court also declared constitutional the Confederate law which provided that when a substitute became subject to military duty his principal was thereby rendered liable to service.[2] In 1864 the supreme court held that the state had a right to subject to militia service persons exempted by the Confederate authorities as bonded agriculturists under the acts of February 17, 1864, and that only those overseers were granted exemption from militia service under the act of Congress in 1863 who at the time were not subject to militia duty, and not those exempted from Confederate service by the later laws,[3] and that the clause in the act of Congress passed February 17, 1864, repealing and revoking all exemptions, was constitutional.[4] In other cases the court held that a person regularly enrolled and sworn into the Confederate service could not raise any question, on *habeas corpus*, of his assignment to any particular command or duty,[5] but that the state courts could discharge on *habeas corpus* from Confederate enrolling officers persons held as conscripts, who were exempted under Confederate laws;[6] that the Confederacy might reassert its rights to the military service of a citizen who was enrolled as a conscript and, after producing a discharge for physical disability, had enlisted in the state militia service;[7] and finally, that the right of the Confederacy to the military service of a citizen was paramount to the right of the state.[8]

During the year 1864 Governor Watts had much trouble with the Confederate enrolling officers who insisted upon conscripting his volunteer and militia organizations, whether they were subject to duty under the laws or not. The authorities at Richmond held that while a state might keep "troops of war" over which the Confederacy could have no control, yet the state militia was subject to all the laws of Congress. "Troops of war," as the Secretary of War explained, would be troops in active and permanent service,[9] and hence virtually Confederate troops. A state with troops of that description would be very willing to give them up to the Confederacy to save expense.

---

[1] Dunkards, Quakers, Nazarenes. *In re* Stringer — 38 Alabama (1863), 457.
[2] 38 Alabama, 458. [3] 39 Alabama, 367. [4] 39 Alabama, 254.
[5] 39 Alabama, 457. [6] 39 Alabama, 440. [7] 39 Alabama, 611.
[8] 39 Alabama, 609. [9] O. R., Ser. IV, Vol. III, pp. 256, 463, *et passim.*

H

Thus we find the legislature of Alabama asking the President to receive and pay certain irregular organizations which had been used to support the Conscript Bureau.[1] The legislature, now somewhat disaffected, showed its interest in the operations of the enrolling officers by an act providing that conscript officials who forced exempts into the Confederate service should be liable to indictment and punishment by a fine of $1000 to $6000 and imprisonment of from six months to two years.[2] It went a step further and nullified the laws of Congress by declaring that state officials, civil and military, were not subject to conscription by the Confederate authorities.[3]

Effect of the Enrolment Laws

Few good soldiers were obtained by conscription,[4] and the system, as it was organized in Alabama,[5] did more harm than good to the Confederacy. The passage of the first law, however, had one good effect. During the winter of 1861-1862, there had been a reaction from the enthusiastic war feeling of the previous summer. Those who thought it would be only a matter of weeks to overrun the North now saw their mistake.[6] Many of the people still had no doubt that the North would be glad to make peace and end the war if the government at Richmond were willing. Numbers, therefore, saw no need of more fighting, and hence did not volunteer. Thousands left the army and went home. A measure like the enrolment act was necessary to make the people realize the actual situation. Upon the passage of the law all the loyal population liable to service made preparations to go to the front before being conscripted, which was deemed a disgrace, and the close of the year 1862 saw practically all of them in the army. Those who entered after 1862 were boys and old men.[7] Many not subject to service

---

[1] Memorial, Oct. 7, 1864.   [2] Acts, Dec. 12, 1864.   [3] Dec. 13, 1864.

[4] Curry, "Civil History of the Confederate States," p. 151.

[5] The Conscript Bureau had posts at the following places: Decatur, Courtland, Somerville, Guntersville, Tuscumbia, Fayetteville, Pikeville, Camden, Montgomery, Selma, Lebanon, Pollard, Troy, Mobile, West Point (Ga.), Marion, Greensborough, Blountsville, Livingston, Gadsden, Cedar Bluff, Jacksonville, Ashville, Carrollton, Tuscaloosa, Eutaw, Eufaula, Jasper, Newton, Clarksville, Talladega, Elyton. O. R., Ser. IV, Vol. III, pp. 819-821.

[6] See De Leon, "Four Years in Rebel Capitals."

[7] President Davis visited Mobile in October, 1863, and upon reviewing the Alabama troops recently raised, was much moved at seeing the young boys and the old gray-haired

volunteered, so that when the age limit was extended but few more were secured.

Great dissatisfaction was expressed among the people at the enrolment law. Some thought that it was an attack upon the rights of the states, and the irritating manner in which it was enforced aroused, in some localities, intense popular indignation. Conscription being considered disgraceful, many who would have been glad for various good reasons to remain at home a few months longer went at once into service to escape conscription. Yet some loyal and honest citizens found it disastrous to leave their homes and business without definite arrangements for the safety and support of their families. Such men suffered much annoyance from the enrolling officers, in spite of the fact that the law was intended for their protection. The conscript officials, often men of bad character, persecuted those who were easy to find, while neglecting the disloyal and refractory who might make trouble for them. In some sections such weak conduct came near resulting in local insurrections; this was especially the case in Randolph County in 1862.[1] The effect of the law was rather to stop volunteering in the state organizations and reporting to camps of instructions, since all who did either were classed as conscripts. Not wishing to bear the odium of being conscripted, many thousands in 1862 and 1863 went directly into the regular service.[2]

While the conscript law secured few, if any, good soldiers who would not have joined the army without it, it certainly served as a reminder to the people that all were needed, and as a stimulus to volunteering. Three classes of people suffered from its operations: (1) those rightfully exempted, who were constantly annoyed by the enrolling officers; (2) those soon to become liable to service, who were not allowed to volunteer in organizations of their own choice; and (3) "deadheads" and malcontents who did not intend to fight at all if they could keep from it. It was this last class that made nearly all the complaints about conscription, and it was they whom the enrolling officers left alone because they were so troublesome.

men in the ranks before him. See Annual Cyclopædia (1863), p. 8. The A. and I. General of Alabama reported, July 29, 1862, that not more than 10,000 conscripts could be secured from Alabama unless the enemy could be expelled from the Tennessee valley. In that case, 3000 more men might be secured. O. R., Ser. IV, Vol. II, p. 21.

[1] O. R., Ser. IV, Vol. I, p. 1149; Vol. II, pp. 87, 207, 208, 790.
[2] See Curry, "Civil History," p. 151.

The defects in the working of conscription are well set forth in a letter from a correspondent of President Davis in December, 1862. In this letter it was asserted that the conscript law had proven a failure in Mississippi and Alabama, since it had stopped the volunteering. Governor Shorter was reported to have said that the enforcement of it had been "a humbug and a farce." The writer declared that the enrolling officers chosen were frequently of bad character; that inefficient men were making attempts to secure "bomb-proof" offices in order to avoid service in the army; and that the exemption of slave owners by the "twenty-negro law" had a bad influence upon the poorer classes. He also declared that the system of substitutes was bad, for many men were on the hunt for substitutes, and others liable to duty were working to secure exemptions in order to serve as substitutes, while large numbers of men connected with the army managed in this way to keep away from the fighting. He was sure, he said, that there were too many hangers-on about the officers of high rank, and that it was believed that social position, wealth, and influence served to get young men good staff positions.[1] Another evil complained of was that "paroled" men scattered to their homes and never heard of their exchange. To a conscript officer whose duty it was to look after them they said that they were "paroled," and he passed them by. The officers were said to be entirely too lenient with the worthless people and too rigorous with the better classes.[2]

Exemption from Service

After the passage of the enrolment laws, every man with excessive regard for the integrity of his person and for his comfort began to secure exemption from service. In north Alabama men of little courage and patriotism lost confidence after the invasions of the Federals, and resorted to every expedient to escape conscription. Strange and terrible diseases were developed, and in all sections of the state health began to break down.[3] It was the day of certificates, — for old age, rheumatism, fits, blindness, and various physical disabilities.[4] Various other pretexts were given for staying away from the

---

[1] James Phelan to President Davis, O. R., Ser. I, Vol. XVII, Pt. II, p. 790.

[2] O. R., Ser. I, Vol. XVII, Pt. II, p. 790.

[3] C. C. Clay, Jr., to Secretary of War, O. R., Ser. IV, Vol. II, pp. 141, 142.

[4] I know of one man who for two years carried his arm in a sling to deceive the

army, while some men hid out in the woods. The governor asked the people to drive such persons to their duty.[1] There was never so much skilled labor in the South as now. Harness making, shoe making, charcoal burning, carpentering — all these and numerous other occupations supposed to be in support of the cause secured exemption. Running a tanyard was a favorite way of escaping service. A pit was dug in the corner of the back yard, a few hides secured, carefully preserved, and never finished, — for more hides might not be available; then the tanner would be no longer exempt. There were purchasing agents, sub-purchasing agents, and sub-sub-agents, cattle drivers, tithe gatherers, agents of the Nitre Bureau, agents to examine political prisoners,[2] and many other Confederate and state agents of various kinds.[3] The class left at home for the enrolling officers to contend with, especially after 1862, was a source of weakness, not of strength, to the Confederate cause. The best men had gone to the army, and these people formed the public. Their opinion was public opinion, and with few exceptions the home stayers were a sorry lot. From them came the complaint about the favoritism toward the rich. The talk of a "rich man's war and a poor

enrolling officers. It was sound when he put it into the sling. After the war ended he could never regain the use of it.

A draft from the Home Guards of Selma was ordered to go to Mobile. The roll was made out, and opposite his name each man was allowed to write his excuse for not wishing to go. One cripple, John Smith, wrote, "One leg too short," and was at once excused by the Board. The next man had no excuse whatever, but he had seen how Smith's excuse worked, so he wrote, "Both legs too short," but he had to go to Mobile. "The Land We Love," Vol. III, p. 430.

[1] Shorter's Proclamation, Dec. 22, 1862.

[2] M. J. Saffold, afterward a prominent "scalawag," escaped service as an "agent to examine political prisoners." O. R., Ser. II, Vol. VI, p. 432.

[3] The list of pardons given by President Johnson will show a number of the titles assumed by the exempts. The chronic exempts were skilled in all the arts of beating out. If a new way of securing exemption were discovered, the whole fraternity of "deadheads" soon knew of it. In 1864 nearly all the exemptions and details made in order to supply the Quartermaster's Department were revoked, and agents sent through the country to notify the former exempts that they were again subject to duty. Before the enrolling officers reached them nearly all of them had secured a fresh exemption, and from a large district in middle Alabama, I have been informed by the agent who revoked the contracts, not one recruit for the armies was secured. Often the exemption was only a detail, and large numbers of men were carried on the rolls of companies who never saw their commands. Often a man when conscripted would have sufficient influence to be at once detailed, and would never join his company. Little attention was paid to the laws regarding exemption.

man's fight" originated with them, as well as the criticism of the "twenty-negro law." In the minds of the soldiers at the front there was no doubt that the slaveholder and the rich man were doing their full share.[1]

Very few of the slaveholders and wealthy men tried to escape service; but when one did, he attracted more attention and called forth sterner denunciation than ten poor men in similar cases would have done. In fact, few able-bodied men tried to secure exemption under the "twenty-negro law." It would have been better for the Confederacy if more planters had stayed at home to direct the production of supplies, and the fact was recognized in 1864,[2] when a "fifteen-negro law" was passed by the Congress, and other exemptions of planters and overseers were encouraged.[3]

There is no doubt that those who desired to remain quietly at home — to be neutral, so to speak — found it hard to evade the conscript officers. One of these declared that the enrolling officers "burned the woods and sifted the ashes for conscripts." Another who had been caught in the sifting process deserted to the enemy at Huntsville. He was asked, "Do they conscript close over the river?" "Hell, stranger, I should think they do; they take every man who has not been dead more than two days."[4] But the "hill-billy" and "sand-mountain" conscripts were of no service when captured; there were not enough soldiers in the state to keep them in their regiments. The Third Alabama Regiment of Reserves ran away almost in a body. There were fifteen or twenty old men in each county as a supporting force to the Conscript Bureau, and they had old guns, some of which would not shoot, and ammunition that did not fit.[5] Thus the best men went into the army, many of them never to return, and a class of people the country could well have spared survived to assist a second time in the ruin of their country in the darker days of Reconstruction. Often the "fire-eating, die-in-the-last-ditch" radical of 1861 who remained at home "to take care of the ladies" became an exempt, a "bomb-proof" or a conscript officer, and later a "scalawag."

[1] Curry, "Civil History," pp. 142–148. The wealthy young men volunteered, at first as privates or as officers; the older men of wealth nearly all became officers, chosen by their men. One company from Tuskegee owned property worth over $2,000,000. *Opelika Post*, Dec. 4, 1903.

[2] Act of Feb. 17, 1864, Pub. Laws, C. S. A.   [3] Curry, "Civil History," pp. 142–148, 151.
[4] *N. Y. World*, March 28, 1864.   [5] O. R., Ser. IV, Vol. III, p. 881.

Some escaped war service by joining the various small independent and irregular commands formed for frontier service by those officers who found field duty too irksome. Though these irregular bodies were, as we have seen, gradually absorbed by the regular organizations, yet during their day of strength they were most unpleasant defenders. The men sometimes joined in order to have more opportunity for license and plunder, and such were hated alike by friend and foe.

Another kind of irregular organization caused some trouble in another way. Before the extension of the age limits to seventeen and fifty, the governor raised small commands of young boys to assist in the execution of the state laws, no other forces being available. Later, when the Confederate Congress extended its laws to include these, the conscript officers tried to enroll them, but the governor objected. The officers complained that, in order to escape the odium of conscription, the young boys who were subject by law to duty in the reserves evaded that law by going at once into the army, or by joining some command for special duty. They were of the opinion that these boys should be sent to camps of instruction. The governor had ten companies of young men under eighteen years of age raised near Talladega, and really mustered into the Confederate service as irregular troops, before the law of February 17, 1864, was passed. After the passage of the law, the enrolling officers wished to disband these companies and send the men to the reserves. Watts was angered and sharply criticised the whole policy of conscription. He said that much harm was done by the method of the conscript officers; that it was nonsense to take men from the fields and put them in camps of instruction when there were no arms for them, and no active service was intended; they had better stay at home, drill once a week with volunteer organizations, and work the rest of the time; to assemble the farmers in camps for useless drill while the crops were being destroyed was "most egregious folly." The governor also attacked the policy of the Bureau in refusing to allow the enrolment in the same companies of boys under eighteen and men over forty-five.[1] In regard to the attempts to disband his small

[1] The law of Feb. 17, 1864, provided for the separate enrolment of these two classes, and the enrolling officers interpreted it as requiring separate service. Such an interpretation would practically prohibit the formation of volunteer commands and would leave the reserves to the enrolling officers to be organized in camp.

force of militia in active service, the governor used strong language. To Seddon, the Secretary of War, he wrote in May, 1864: "It must not be forgotten that the states have some rights left, and that the right to troops in the time of war is guaranteed by the Constitution. These rights, on the part of Alabama, I am determined shall be respected. Unless you order the Commandant of Conscripts to stop interfering with [certain volunteer companies] there will be a conflict between the Confederate general [Withers] and the state authorities."[1] Watts carried the day and the Confederate authorities yielded.

The enrolment law provided that state officials should be exempt from enrolment upon presenting a certificate from the governor stating that they were necessary to the proper administration of the government. In November, 1864, Governor Watts complained to General Withers, who commanded the Confederate reserve forces in Alabama, that the conscript officers had been enrolling by force state officials who held certificates from the governor and also from the commandant of conscripts, and, he added: "This state of things cannot long last without a conflict between the Confederate and state authorities. I shall be compelled to protect my state officers with all the forces of the state at my command." The enrolling officers referred him to a decision of the Secretary of War in the case of a state official in Lowndes County,—that by the act of February 17, 1864, all men between the ages of seventeen and fifty were taken at once into the Confederate service, and that state officials elected later could not claim exemption. Governor Watts then wrote to Seddon, "Unless you interfere, there will be a conflict between the Confederate and the state authorities." He denied the right of Confederate officers to conscript state officials elected after February 17, 1864: "I deny such right, and will resist it with all the forces of the state."[2] The Secretary of War replied by commending the Confederate officers for the way in which they had done their duty, insisting that it was not a political nor a constitutional question, but one involving private rights, and that it should be left to the courts. This was receding from the confident ruling made in the case of the Lowndes County man. There was no more dispute and it is to be

---

[1] O. R., Ser. IV, Vol. III, pp. 322, 323, 463, 466, 1059, 1060.
[2] O. R., Ser. IV, Vol. III, pp. 817, 819, 920.

presumed that the governor retained his officials.[1] No wonder that
Colonel Preston, the chief of the Bureau of Conscription, wrote to
the Secretary of War that, "from one end of the Confederacy to the
other every constituted authority, every officer, every man, and
woman was engaged in opposing the enrolling officer in the execution of his duties."[2]

But these officers had only themselves to blame. They pursued
a short-sighted, nagging policy, worrying those who were exempt —
the state officials and the militia — because they were easy to reach,
and neglecting the real conscript material.[3] The work was known
to be useless, and the whole system was irritating to the last degree
to all who came in contact with it. It was useless because there was
little good material for conscription, except in the frontier country
where no authority could be exerted. During 1862 and 1863 practically nothing was done by the Bureau in Alabama, and at the end
of the latter year, Colonel E. D. Blake, the Superintendent of Special
Registration, reported that there were 13,000 men in the state between
the ages of seventeen and forty-five, and of these he estimated 4000
were under eighteen years of age, and hence, at that time, beyond
the reach of the enrolling officers. More than 8000[4] were exempt

---

[1] O. R., Ser. IV, Vol. III, pp. 821, 848. At this time there were in the state 1223
officials who had the governor's certificate of exemption. There were 1012 in Georgia,
1422 in Virginia, 14,675 in North Carolina, and much smaller numbers in the other
states. See O. R., Ser. IV, Vol. III, p. 851.

[2] O. R., Ser. IV, Vol. III, p. 224 (March 18, 1864).

[3] An ex-Confederate related to me his experiences with the conscript officers. In
1864 he was at home on furlough and was taken by the "buttermilk" cavalry, carried
to Camp Watts, at Notasulga, and enrolled as a conscript, no attention being paid to his
furlough. To Camp Watts were brought daily squads of conscripts, rounded up by
the "buttermilk" cavalry. They were guarded by conscripts. When rested, the new
recruits would leave, the guards often going with them. Then another squad would
be brought in, who in a day or two would desert.. This soldier came home again with
a discharge for disability. The conscript officials again took him to Camp Watts. He
presented his discharge papers; the commandant tore them up before his face, and a
few days later this soldier with a friend boarded the cowcatcher of a passing train and
rode to Chehaw. The commandant sent guards after the fugitives, who captured the
guards and then went to Tuskegee, where they swore out, as he said, a *habeas corpus*
before the justice of the peace and started for their homes with their papers. They
found the swamps filled with the deserters, who did not molest them after finding that
they too were "deserters."

[4] 8835 to January, 1864. See report of Colonel Preston, April, 1864, in O. R., Ser.
IV, Vol. III, pp. 355, 363. The estimate was based on the census of 1860.

under laws and orders. This left, he said, 1000 subject to enrolment. Nowhere, in any of the estimates, are found allowances for those physically and mentally disqualified. The number then exempted in Alabama by medical boards is unknown. In other states this number was sometimes more and sometimes less than the number exempted by law and by order.

A year later, after all exemptions had been revoked, the number disqualified for physical disability by the examining boards amounted to 3933. Besides these there were the lame, the halt, the blind, and the insane, who were so clearly unfit for service that no enrolling officer ever brought them before the medical board. The 4000 between the ages of seventeen and eighteen, and also the 4600 between sixteen and seventeen, came under the enrolment law of February 17, 1864, as also several thousand who were over forty-five. But it is certain that many of these, especially the younger ones, were already in the general service as volunteers. It is also certain that many hundreds of all ages who were liable to service escaped conscription, especially in north Alabama. In a way, their places in the ranks were filled by those who did not become liable to enrolment until 1864, or even not at all, but who volunteered nevertheless.

From April, 1862, to February, 1865, there had been enrolled at the camps in Alabama 14,875 men who had been classed in the reports as conscripts. This included all men who volunteered at the camps, all of military age that the officers could find or catch before they went into the volunteer service, details made as soon as enrolled, irregular commands formed before the men were liable to duty, and a few hundred genuine conscripts who had to be guarded to keep them from running away. It was reported that for two years not a recruit was sent by the Bureau from Alabama to the army of Tennessee or to the Army of Northern Virginia, but that the men were enrolled in the organizations of the state. This means that much of the enrolment of 14,875 was only nominal, and that this number included the regiments sent to the front from Alabama in 1862, after the passage of the Enrolment Act in April. Eighteen regiments were organized in Alabama after that date, in violation of the Enrolment Act, many of the men evading conscription, as the Bureau reported, by going at once into the general service. The number who left in these regiments was estimated at more than 10,000.[1] There was not a single conscript regiment.

It is possible to ascertain the number exempted by law and by order before 1865. A report by Colonel Preston, dated April, 1864, gives the number of exempts in Alabama as 8835 to January, 1864.[2] A month later, all exemptions were revoked.[3] In February, 1865, a complete report places the total number exempted by law and order in Alabama at 10,218, of whom 3933 were exempted by medical boards. The state officials exempted numbered 1333,[4] and Confederate officials, 21; ministers, 726; editors, 33, and their employees, 155; public printers, 3; druggists, 81; physicians, 796; teachers, 352; overseers and agriculturists, 1447; railway officials and employees, 1090; mail carriers and contractors, 60; foreigners, 167; agriculture details, 38; pilots, telegraphers, shoemakers, tanners, and blacksmiths, 86; government contractors, 44; details of artisans and mechanics, 570; details for government service (not specified), 218. There were 1046 men incapable of field service who were assigned to duty in the above details, chiefly in the Conscript Bureau, Quartermaster's Department, and Commissariat.[5] It is certain that many others were exempted by being detailed from service in the army. The list of those pardoned in 1865 and 1866 by President Johnson shows many occupations not mentioned above.

It is interesting to notice the fate of the conscript officers when captured by the Federals. Bradford Hambrick was tried by a military commission in Nashville, Tennessee, in January, 1864, charged with being a Confederate conscript officer and with forcing "peaceable citizens of the United States" in Madison County, Alabama, to enter the Confederate army. He was convicted and sentenced to imprisonment at hard labor for one year, and to pay a fine of $2000 or serve an additional imprisonment of 1000 days.[6]

To sum up: The early enrolment laws served to stimulate enlistment; the later ones probably had no effect at all except to give

---

[1] O. R., Ser. IV, Vol. III, pp. 101, 103, et passim.

[2] O. R., Ser. IV, Vol. III, pp. 355, 363.   [3] Feb. 17, 1864.

[4] There were 1223 to Nov. 30, 1864.   [5] O. R., Ser. IV, Vol. III, pp. 1, 103-109.

[6] G. O., No. 144, Dept. of the Cumberland, Atlanta, Ga., Oct. 4, 1864, War Department Archives. There were other similar cases, but I found record of no other conviction. The "tories" were sometimes in league with the conscript officers, and sometimes they shot them at sight.

the Bureau something to do, and the law officers something on which to exercise their wits. The conscript service also served as an exemption board. It secured few, if any, enlistments that the state could not have secured, and certainly lost more than it gained by harassing the people. The laws were constantly violated by the state; this is proved by the enlistment of eighteen new regiments contrary to the law. It finally drove the state authorities into an attitude of nullification by its construction of the enrolment laws.

Neither the state nor the Confederate government had an efficient machinery for securing enlistments. If there ever were laws regarded only in the breaking, the Enrolment Acts were such laws. The conscripts and exempts, like the deserters, tories, and Peace Society men, are important, not only because they so weakened the Confederacy, but also because they formed the party that would have carried out, or at least begun, Reconstruction according to the plans of Lincoln and Johnson as first proclaimed. Many of these people became "scalawags" later, probably influenced to some extent by the scorn of their neighbors.

SEC. 4. TORIES AND DESERTERS

In Alabama opposition to the Confederate government took two forms. One was the rebellious opposition of the so-called "unionists" or "tories," who later joined with the deserters from the army; the other was the legal or constitutional opposition of the old coöperation or anti-secession party, which maintained an unfriendly attitude toward the Confederate administration, though the great majority of its members were loyal to the southern cause. From this second class arose a so-called "Peace Party," which desired to end the war on terms favorable to the South; and from this, in turn, when later it was known that such terms could not be secured, sprang the semi-treasonable secret order — the "Peace Society." In 1864, the "tories" and the Peace Society began to work together. Peculiar social and political conditions will in part account for the strength and growth of the opposition in two sections of the state far removed from each other — in north Alabama and in southeast Alabama.

Conditions in North Alabama

To the convention of 1861 forty-four members from north Alabama were elected as coöperationists, that is, in favor of a union of the southern states, within the old Union, for the purpose of securing their rights under the Constitution or of securing safe secession. They professed to be afraid of separate state secession as likely to lead to disintegration and war. Thirty-one of these coöperationists voted against the ordinance of secession, and twenty-four of them (mostly members from the northern hill counties) refused to sign the ordinance, though all expressed the intention to submit to the will of the majority, and to give the state their heartiest support. When war came all espoused the Confederate cause.[1] The coöperationist party as a whole supported the Confederacy faithfully, though nearly always in a more or less disapproving spirit toward the administration, both state and Confederate.

North Alabama differed from other portions of the state in many ways. There was no railroad connecting the country north of the mountains with the southern part of the state, and from the northern counties it was a journey of several days to reach the towns in central and south Alabama. Hence there was little intercourse between the people of the two sections, though the seat of government was in the central part of the state; even to-day the intimacy is not close. For years it had been a favorite scheme of Alabama statesmen to build railroads and highways to connect more closely the two sections.[2] Geographically, this northern section of the state belonged to Tennessee. The people were felt to be slightly different in character and sympathies from those of central and south Alabama, and whatever one section favored in public matters was usually opposed by the other. Even in the northern section the population was more or less divided. The people of the valley more closely resembled the west Tennesseans, the great majority of them being planters, having little in common with the small farmers of the hill and mountain country, who were like the east Tennesseans. Of

---

[1] D. P. Lewis of Lawrence, Jeremiah (or Jere) Clemens of Madison, and C. C. Sheets of Winston deserted later.

[2] T. H. Clark, "Railroads and Highways," in the "Memorial Record of Alabama," Vol. I, pp. 322–323.

the latter the extreme element was the class commonly known as "mountain whites" or "sand-mountain" people. These were the people who gave so much trouble during the war, as "tories," and from whom the loyal southerners of north Alabama suffered greatly when the country was stripped of its men for the armies. Yet it

DISAFFECTION, 1861-1865

Tories, 1861-1865.

Deserters, 1862-1865.

"Reconstruction" sentiment 1861-5 in same localities.

can hardly be said that they exercised much influence on politics before the war. Their only representative in the convention of 1861 was Charles Christopher Sheets, who did not speak on the floor of the convention during the entire session.

On the part of all in the northern counties there was a strong desire for delay in secession, and they were angered at the action of the convention in not submitting the ordinance to a popular vote for ratification or rejection. Many thought the course taken indicated a suspicion of them or fear of their action, and this they resented. Their leaders in the convention expressed the belief that the ordinance would have easily obtained a majority if submitted to the popular vote.[1] Much of the opposition to the ordinance of secession was due to the vague sectional dislike between the two parts of the state. It was felt that the ordinance was a south Alabama measure, and this was sufficient reason for opposition by the northern section. Throughout the entire session a local sectional spirit dictated their

[1] Smith, Clemens, Jemison, and Bulger, in Smith's "History and Debates of the Convention of 1861"; Hodgson, "Cradle of the Confederacy"; Garrett, "Public Men of Alabama."

course of obstruction.[1] In January and February of 1861, there was some talk among the discontented people of seceding from secession, of withdrawing the northern counties of Alabama and uniting with the counties of east Tennessee to form a new state, which should be called Nick-a-Jack, an Indian name common in East Tennessee.[2] Geographically, this proceeding would have been correct, since these two parts of the country are closely connected, the people were alike in character and sentiment, and the means of intercourse were better. The people of the valley and many others, however, had no sympathy with this scheme. Lacking the support of the politicians and no leaders appearing, the plan was abandoned after the proclamation of Lincoln, April 10, 1861. Had the war been deferred a few months, it is almost certain that the discontented element of the population would have taken positive steps to embarrass the administration; many believed that reconstruction would take place. Only after four years of war was there after this any appreciable number of the people willing to listen again to such a proposition. In February, 1861, Jeremiah Clemens wrote that Yancey had been burned in effigy in Limestone County (something that might have happened at any time between 1845 and 1861); that some discontent still existed among the people, but that this was daily growing weaker, and unless something were done to excite it afresh, it would soon die out.[3] Mr. John W. DuBose, a keen observer from the Cotton Belt, travelled on horseback through the northern hill counties during the winter of 1861 and 1862 as a Confederate recruiting officer. Thus he came into close contact with all classes of people, eating at their tables, sleeping in their beds, and in conversation learning their opinions and sentiments on public

[1] See Smith's "History and Debates of the Convention of 1861"; Nicolay and Hay, "Lincoln," Vol. III, p. 186.

[2] A. B. Hendren, mayor of Athens and editor of the *Union Banner*, wrote in 1861 to Secretary Walker, stating that he had strongly opposed secession, but was now convinced that it was right; as mayor, he was committed to reconstruction, which he no longer favored; he did not proclaim his new sentiments through his paper for fear of pecuniary loss, but people were becoming suspicious of his lukewarm reconstruction spirit. O. R., Ser. IV, Vol. I, pp. 181, 182.

[3] "Northern Alabama Illustrated," p. 47; Ku Klux Rept. Ala. Test., pp. 592, 824; Saunders, "Early Settlers"; Brewer, "Alabama," p. 65; Garrett, "Public Men"; Miller, "Alabama"; Nicolay and Hay, Vol. III, p. 186; DuBose, "Life of Yancey," pp. 562, 563.

matters. He saw no man, he says, who was not devoted to the Confederacy. Several of the first and best volunteer regiments came from this section of the state, and in these regiments there were whole companies of men none of whom owned a slave. In order to preserve this spirit of loyalty in those who had been opposed to the policy of secession, Yancey and others, after the outbreak of the war, recommended a prompt invasion of the North.[1]

Unionists, Tories, and Mossbacks

Before secession, the term "unionist" was applied to those who were opposed to secession and who wished to give the Union a longer trial. They were mostly the old Whigs, but many Democrats were among them. Then again the coöperationists, who wanted delay and coöperation among the states before secession, were called "unionists." In short, the term was applied to any one opposed to immediate secession. This fact deceived the people of the North, who believed that the opposition party in the South was unconditionally for the Union, and that it would remain in allegiance to the Union if secession were attempted. But after secession this "union" party disappeared.

---

[1] See DuBose, "Life of Yancey," p. 563.

The non-slaveholders in the Black Belt appear to have been more dissatisfied than those of the white counties at the outbreak of the war. May 13, 1861, William M. Brooks, who had presided over the secession convention, wrote from Perry County to President Davis in regard to the bad effect of the refusal to accept short-time volunteers. He said that though there were 20,000 slaves in Perry County, most of the whites were non-slaveholders. Some of the latter had been made to believe that the war was solely to get more slaves for the rich, and many who had no love for slaveholders were declaring that they would "fight for no rich man's slave." The men who had enlisted were largely of the hill class, poor folks who left their work to go to camp and drill. Here, while their crops wasted, they lost their ardor, and when they heard that their one-year enlistment was not to be accepted, they began to murmur. They were made to believe by traitors that a rich man could enter the army for a year and then quit, while they had to enlist for the war. O. R., Ser. IV, Vol. VIII, pp. 318–319.

Horace Greeley in the *Tribune* was reported to have said: Large slaveholders were not secessionists, they resisted disunion; those who had much at stake hesitated a long while; it was not a "slaveholders' rebellion"; it was really a rebellion of the non-slaveholders resident in the strongholds of slavery, springing from no love of slavery, but from the antagonism of race and the hatred of the idea of equality with the blacks involved in simple emancipation. — Ku Klux Rept., p. 519. There is a basis of truth in this.

The "tories" were those who rebelled against the authority of
the Confederate States. Some of them were true "unionists" or
"loyalists," as they were called at the North. Most of them were
not. The "mossback," who according to popular belief hid himself in the woods until moss grew on his back, might or might not
be a "tory." If he were hostile to the Confederacy, he was a "tory";
if he was simply keeping out of the way of the enrolling officers,
he was not a "tory," but a plain "mossback" or "conscript." When
too closely pressed he would either become a "tory" or enter the
Confederate army, though he did not usually remain in it. The
"deserter" was such from various reasons, and often became a
"tory" as well; that is, he became hostile to the Confederacy. Often
he was not hostile to the government, but was only hiding from
service, and doing no other harm. The true "unionists" always
claimed great numbers, even after the end of the war. The North
listened to them and believed that old Whigs, Know-nothings,
Anti-secessionists, Douglas Democrats, Bell and Everett men, co-
operationists — all were at heart "Union" men. It was also claimed
that the only real disunion element was the Breckenridge Democracy. Such, however, was not the case. Probably fewer of the
old Whig party than of any other were disloyal to the Confederacy.
So far as the "tory" or "loyalist" had any politics, he was probably a Democrat, and the more prominent of them had been Douglas'
Democrats. The others were Douglas and Breckenridge Democrats from the Democratic stronghold — north Alabama.[1] Very
few, if any, Bell and Everett men were among them. The small
lower class had no party affiliations worth mentioning. During
the war, the terms "unionist" and "tories" were very elastic and
covered a multitude of sins against the Union, against the Confederate States, and against local communities. With the exception of
those who entered the Federal army the "tories" were, in a way,
traitors to both sides. North Alabama was not so strongly opposed

---

[1] North Alabama before the war was overwhelmingly Democratic and was called
"The Avalanche" from the way it overran the Whiggish counties of the southern and
central sections. This was shown in the convention, where representation was based on
the white vote. Since the war representation in the conventions is based on population,
and the Black Belt has controlled the white counties. "Northern Alabama Illustrated,"
pp. 251, 756. See also DuBose, "Yancey," p. 562.

I

to secession as was east Tennessee,[1] nor were the Alabama "union-ists" or "loyalists," as they called themselves, "tories" as other people called them, of as good character as the "loyalists" of Tennessee.

The Alabama tory was, as a rule, of the lowest class of the population, chiefly the "mountain whites" and the "sand-mountain" people, who were shut off from the world, a century behind the times, and who knew scarcely anything of the Union or of the questions at issue. There was a certain social antipathy felt by them toward the lowland and valley people, whether in south or in north Alabama, and a blind antagonism to the "nigger lord," as they called the slaveholder, wherever he was found. In this feeling the women were more bitter than the men. Secluded and ignorant, they did not feel it their duty to support a cause in which they were not directly concerned, and most of them would have preferred to remain neutral during the entire war, as there was little for them to gain either way. As long as they did not have to leave their hills, they were quiet, but when the enrolling officers went after them, they became dangerous. To-day those people are represented by the makers of "moonshine" whiskey and those who shoot revenue officers. They were "moon-shiners" then. Colonel S. A. M. Wood, who caught a band of thirty of these "tories," reported to General Bragg, "They are the most miserable, ignorant, poor, ragged devils I ever saw."[2] Many of the "tories" became bushwhackers, preying impartially on friend and foe, and especially on the people of the rich Tennessee valley.[3]

Growth of Disaffection

The invasion of the Tennessee valley had discouraging effects on the weaker element of the population, and caused many to take a rather degrading position in order to secure Federal protection

---

[1] Professor George W. Duncan of Auburn, Ala., and many others have given me information in regard to the people in that section. See also H. Mis. Doc. No. 42, 39th Cong., 1st Sess. ; *N. Y. Tribune*, Nov. 14, 1862.

[2] O. R., Ser. I, Vol. III, p. 249. For much information concerning the conditions in north Alabama during the war, I am indebted to Professor O. D. Smith of the Alabama Polytechnic Institute, a native of Vermont who was then a Confederate Bonded Treasury Agent and travelled extensively over that part of the country.

[3] Reid, "After the War," pp. 348-350 ; Saunders, "Early Settlers," pp. 115, 164; Jones, "A Rebel War Clerk's Diary," Vol. I, pp. 182, 208.

for themselves and their property. To call the tories and those who submitted and took the oath "unionists" would be honoring them too highly. Little true "Union" sentiment or true devotion to the United States existed except on the part of those who enlisted in the Federal armies. In October, 1862, C. C. Clay, Jr., wrote to the Secretary of War at Richmond that the Federal invasion had resulted in open defiance of Confederate authority on the part of some who believed that the Confederacy was too weak to protect or punish. Even loyal southerners were afraid to be active for fear of a return of the Union troops. Some had sold cotton to the Federals during their occupation, bought it for them, acted as agents, spies, and informers; and now these men openly declared for the Union and signed calls for Union meetings. Huntsville, Mr. Clay stated, was the centre of disaffection.[1] But in April, 1863, a northern cotton speculator reported that there were but few "true Union men" at Huntsville or in the vicinity.[2]

Though not fully in sympathy with the secession movement, the majority of the people in the northern counties acquiesced in the action of the state, and many volunteers entered the army. Until late in the war this district sent as many men in proportion to population as any other section, and the men made good soldiers. But with the opening of the Tennessee and the passage of the conscription laws the mountaineers and the hill people became troublesome. To avoid conscription they hid themselves. Their families, with their slender resources, were soon in want of the necessaries of life, which they began to obtain by raids on their more fortunate neighbors in the river valleys. A few entered the Federal army. In July, 1862, small parties came to Decatur, in Morgan County, from the mountains and joined the Federal forces under the command of Colonel Streight. They told him of others who wished to enlist, so Streight made an expedition to Davis Gap, in the mountains south of Decatur, and secured 150 recruits.

These formed the nucleus of the First Alabama Union Cavalry, of which George E. Spencer of Ohio, afterward notorious in Alabama politics, was colonel. At this time C. C. Sheets, who said that he had been in hiding, appeared and made a speech encouraging all to enlist. Streight said that the "unionists" were poor people,

[1] O. R., Ser. IV, Vol. II, pp. 141, 142.   [2] O. R., Ser. I, Vol. X, Pt. II, p. 638.

often destitute. There were, he reported, about three "unionists" to one "secessionist" in parts of Morgan, Blount, St. Clair, Winston, Walker, Marion, Taylor, and Jefferson counties, and he thought two full regiments could be raised near Decatur. Though so few in numbers, the "secessionists" seem to have made it lively for the "unionists," for Streight reported that the "unionists" were much persecuted by them and often had to hide themselves.[1] The Confederate commander at Newberne, in Greene County, reported (January, 1862) that in an adjoining county the "Union" men were secretly organizing, that 300 had met, elected officers, and gone into camp.[2] A month later, Lieutenant-Commander Phelps of the United States navy, after his river raid to Florence (1862), reported that along the Tennessee the "Union" sentiment was strong, and that men, women, and children in crowds welcomed the boats. However, he adds that they were very guarded in their conversation. It may be that he mistook curiosity for "Union" sentiment. Another naval officer reported that the fall of Fort Donelson was beneficial to the Union cause in north Alabama. Neither of these observers landed, and their observations were limited to the river banks.[3] In June, 1862, Governor Shorter said that much dissatisfaction existed in several of the northern counties,[4] and in December, 1862, that Randolph County was defying the enforcement of the conscript law, and armed forces were releasing deserters from jail. Colonel Hannon was at length sent with a regiment and suppressed for a time the disloyal element.[5] September 21, 1862, General Pillow reported to Seddon that there were 8000 to 10,000 deserters and tory conscripts in the mountains of north Alabama, as "vicious as copperheads."[6] In April, 1863, a civilian of influence and position wrote to General Beauregard that the counties of north Alabama were full of tories. During 1862, he stated, a convention had been held in the corner of Winston, Fayette, and Marion counties, in which the people had resolved to remain neutral. He believed that this meant that when the enemy appeared the so-called neutrals would

---

[1] Moore, "Anecdotes, Poetry, and Incidents of the War," p. 215 (Letters from the chaplain of Streight's regiment) ; O. R., Ser. I, Vol. XVI, Pt. I, pp. 124, 785 (Streight's Report) ; Miller, "Alabama" ; Jones, "Diary," Vol. I, pp. 182-208.
[2] O. R., Ser. I, Vol. VII, p. 840.   [3] O. R., Ser. I, Vol. VII, pp. 153-156, 424.
[4] O. R., Ser. IV, Vol. I, p. 1149.   [5] O. R., Ser. IV, Vol. II, p. 258.
[6] O. R., Ser. IV, Vol. II, pp. 819-821.

join them, for they openly carried United States flags.[1] A similar convention was held in north Alabama (apparently in Winston County) in the spring of 1863. A staff officer reported to General Beauregard (May, 1864) that in the counties of Lawrence, Blount, and Winston, Federal recruiting agents for mounted regiments carried on open correspondence with the disaffected citizens,[2] apparently with little success, for although disaffection and hostility to the Confederacy among the people of north Alabama had continued for three years, and there was every opportunity for entering the Federal army, yet the official statistics give the total number of enlistments and reënlistments of whites from Alabama at 2576.[3]

In 1862 deserters from the army began to gather in the more remote districts of the state. Many of them had been enrolled under the conscript law, and had become dissatisfied. As the war went on the number of these deserters increased, until their presence in the state became a menace to government. After the Confederate reverses in the summer of 1863, great numbers of deserters and stragglers from all of the Confederate armies east of the Mississippi River and from the Union armies collected among the hills, mountains, and ravines of north Alabama. A large portion of them became outlaws of the worst character. In August, 1863, the general assembly passed a law directing the state officials and the militia officers to assist the Confederate enrolling officers in enforcing the conscript law, and in returning deserters to their commands. The state and county jails were offered as places to confine the deserters until they could be sent back to the army. To give food and shelter to deserters was declared a felony, and civilians were authorized to arrest them.[4]

The deserters and stragglers of north Alabama were well armed and somewhat organized, and kept the people in terror. General Pillow thought that the temporary suspension of the conscript law had made them bolder. Eleven counties were infested with them. No man was safe in travelling along the roads, for murders, robberies, and burnings were common, and peaceable citizens were shot while

---

[1] O. R., Ser. I, Vol. X, p. 431.   [2] O. R., Ser. I, Vol. XXXIX, Pt. II, p. 57.

[3] The official statement of the War Department. See also "Confederate Military History," Vol. XII, p. 502.

[4] Act of General Assembly, Aug. 29, 1863.

at work in the fields. It was estimated that in July, 1863, there were 8000 to 10,000 tories and deserters in the mountains of north Alabama, and these banded themselves together to kill the officers sent to arrest them. It was impossible to keep a certain class of men in the army when they were encamped near their homes.[1] Even good soldiers, when so stationed, sometimes deserted. Had these same men been in the Army of Northern Virginia, they would have done their duty well. But here, near their home, many influences led them to desert. There was little fighting, and they could see no reason why they should be kept away from their suffering families.

General Pillow, in the fall of 1863, forced several thousand deserters and stragglers from Alabama, Mississippi, and Texas, who were in hiding in north Alabama, to return to their commands. The legislature commended his work and asked that his jurisdiction be extended over a larger area, even over the whole Confederacy.[2] In April, 1864, the Ninth Texas Cavalry was sent against the "unionists" in Marion County. The colonel reported that the number of tories had been greatly exaggerated, though the woods seemed to be swarming with deserters, and he learned that they had a secret organization.[3] The deserters always infested the wildest and most remote parts of the country, and were found wherever disaffection toward the Confederacy had appeared. The Texans, who had no local attachments to interfere with their duty, drove back into the army several thousand "stragglers," as the better class of deserters were called.[4] General Polk reported (April, 1864) that in north Alabama formidable bands were being organized for resistance to the government, and that hostility to the Confederacy was openly proclaimed by them. He sent out detachments which forced more than a thousand men to leave the woods and hills and return to the army.[5] When Alabama soldiers were captured or deserted to the enemy, it was the custom of the Federals to send them north of the Ohio River, and to offer to enlist as many as possible in regiments to fight the Indians in the West. Some took advantage of the offer

---

[1] O. R., Ser. IV, Vol. II, p. 680.   [2] Joint Resolution, Dec. 4, 1863.

[3] O. R., Ser. I, Vol. XXXII, Pt. I, p. 671.

[4] O. R., Ser. I, Vol. XXXII, Pt. I, p. 671, and Vol. XXXIII, Pt. III, pp. 570, 683, 856.

[5] O. R., Ser. I, Vol. XXXIII, Pt. III, pp. 825, 826, 856.

and thus avoided prison life. Such men were called "galvanized Yankees" and were hated by the loyal soldiers. Early in 1865, J. J. Giers, a prominent tory, wrote General Grant that if Alabama deserters were permitted to remain near home their numbers would increase.[1]

Outrages by Tories and Deserters

The tory and the deserter often led squads of Federal soldiers on expeditions of destruction and pillage. When possible, they would burn the county court-houses, jails, and other public buildings, with the books and records of the counties. Sometimes disguised as Union troops, they committed the worst outrages. On one occasion four men, dressed as soldiers, went to the house of an old man named Wilson, three miles from Florence, and searched it for money supposed to be hidden there. As the old man would tell them nothing, they stripped him to the waist, tied him face downward upon a table, tore leaves from a large Bible, and, piling them on him, burned him to death. His nephew, unable to tell about the money, was shot and killed. A grandson was shot and wounded, and left for dead. The overseer, coming up, was shot and killed in spite of the appeals of his wife. Senator R. M. Patton had the wounded boy taken to Florence, where the same band came the next night and demanded him. Upon being refused, they fired repeatedly into the house until they were driven away. They then went to the house of a druggist, and, failing to find money, burned him as they had Wilson. Though fearfully burned, he survived. Two of the band, natives of Florence, were captured, court-martialled by the Federal authorities, and hanged.[2]

Twenty Federals, or disguised tories, led by a tory from Madison County, killed an old man, his son, a nephew and his son, and wounded a fifth person, who was then thrown into the Tennessee River. When he caught the bush on the bank, he was beaten and shot until he turned loose. An enrolling officer was made to wade out into the river, and then was shot from the bank. An overseer who had

[1] O. R., Ser. I, Vol. XLIX, Pt. I, p. 659.
[2] Somers, "The Southern States since the War," p. 135; *Montgomery Advertiser*, Aug. 17, 1902; *N. Y. Tribune*, Feb. 10, 1865; Freemantle, "Three Months in the Southern States."

hidden some stock was hanged. A Confederate officer was robbed of several thousand dollars and driven from the country.[1]

The tories, who were often deserters from the armies, gathered in the hill country and watched for an opportunity to descend into the valley to rob, burn, and murder. One family had the following experience with Federal troops or "unionists": On the first raid six mules, five horses, a wagon, and fifty-two negroes were taken; on the second, the remainder of the mules, a cart, the milch cows, some meat, and the cooking utensils. On the third the wagons were loaded with the last of the meat, and all of the sugar, coffee, molasses, flour, meal, and potatoes. The mother of the family told the officer in charge that they were taking away their only means of subsistence, and that the family would starve. "Starve and be d—d," was the reply. Then the buggy and the carriage harness and cushions were taken, and the carriage cut to pieces. The house was searched for money. Closets and trunks were broken open, the offer of keys being refused. Clothing and bedding, dishes, knives and forks were taken, and whatever could not be carried was broken. The "Destroying Angels," as they called themselves, then burned the gin-house and cotton press with one hundred and twenty-five bales of cotton, seven cribs of corn, stables, and stacks of fodder, a wagon, four negro cabins, the lumber room, $500 worth of thread, axes, hoes, scythe-blades, and other plantation implements. They started to burn the dwelling house, but the woman pleaded that it was the only shelter for her children and herself. "You may thank your good fortune, madam, that we have left you and your d—d brats with your heads to be sheltered," answered one of the "Destroying Angels." Then an officer galloped up, claimed to be much astonished, and ordered away the men.[2]

The tories or "unionists" of the mountains, instead of joining the Federal army, formed bands of "Destroying Angels," "Prowling Brigades," etc., to prey upon their lowland neighbors. All the able-bodied loyal men were in the army, and there were no defenders. During the Federal occupation these marauders harassed the country. When the Confederates temporarily occupied

---

[1] Moore, "Rebellion Record," Vol. VII, p. 45; Freemantle, p. 141.

[2] Freemantle, "Three Months in the Southern States," p. 141, quoted from a local newspaper; accounts of eye-witnesses.

the country, they tried to drive out the brigands, whence arose the "persecution of unionists" that we read about. Thousands of Confederate sympathizers were driven from their homes during the Federal occupation in 1862. When the Union army retreated in 1862, attempts at retaliation were made by those who had suffered, but this was strictly suppressed by the state and Confederate authorities. An officer was dismissed for cruelty to "unionists," and the state troops destroyed a band of deserters and guerillas who were preying upon the "union" people in the mountain districts. Marion, Walker, and Winston counties were especially infested with tories.[1]

In 1864, when there were few Confederate troops in north Alabama, the tories were very troublesome in De Kalb, Marshall, Marion, Winston, Walker, Lawrence, and Fayette counties, and the poor people were largely under their control. Among the hills were deserters from both armies, and these, banded with the tory element, reduced the helpless poor whites to submission. These men were few in comparison with the total population, but most of the able-bodied loyal men were in the army, and the tories and deserters were almost unchecked.[2] Sometimes the Confederate soldiers from north Alabama would get furloughs, come home, and clear the country of tories, who had been terrorizing the people. Short work was made of them when the soldiers found them. Some were shot, others were hanged, and the remainder driven out of the country for a time.[3]

After their occupation of north Alabama, the Federal commanders were embarrassed by the violent clamorings of the "unionists" for revenge, and for superior privileges over the non-unionist population. Material advantage and personal dislikes were too often the basic principles of their unionism. They were extremely vindictive, demanding that all Confederate sympathizers be driven from the country. Thus they made themselves a nuisance to the Federal officers, and especially was this true of the small lowland tory element. Subjugation, banishment, hanging, confiscation, — was the programme planned by the "loyalists." They wanted the country "pacified" and then turned over to themselves. Though they

[1] Miller, *passim*; Somers, "Southern States," p. 135.
[2] Miller, p. 193; Moore, "Rebellion Record," Vol. VII, p. 357.
[3] Saunders, "Early Settlers," pp. 115, 164.

claimed to be numerous, no instance is found where they proposed to do anything for themselves; they seemed to think that the sole duty of the United States army in Alabama was to look after their interests.   The northerners who had dealings with the "loyalist" did not like him, as he was a most unpleasant person, with a grievance which could not be righted to his satisfaction without giving rise to numerous other grievances.

Some qualifications of loyalty seem to have been: a certain mild disapproval of secession, a refusal to enlist in the Confederate army or desertion after enlisting, hiding in the woods to avoid conscript officers.   These qualifications, or any of them, the "loyalist" thought entitled him to the everlasting gratitude and protection of the United States.   But a newspaper correspondent, who was on a sharp lookout for all signs of weakness in the Confederacy, said: "You can tell the southern loyalists as far as you can see them.   They all have black or yellow skins and kinky hair."   Sometimes, he added, there was a white "unionist," but this was rare, and the exceptions in any town in north Alabama could be counted on the fingers of one hand.[1]   As long as the war lasted the lawless element fared well, and when peace should come they hoped for a division of the spoils.[2]

Disaffection in South Alabama

So much for toryism in the northern part of the state.   There were also manifestations of a disloyal spirit in the extreme inaccessible corner of the state next to Florida and Georgia, where the population of the sparsely settled country was almost entirely non-slaveholding.   Though most of the people were Democrats, they were somewhat opposed to secession.   Delegates were elected, however, to the convention of 1861, who voted for secession, and after the war began nearly or quite all of those who had opposed secession heartily supported the Confederacy.   If there were any "union" men, they

[1] This correspondent defined a "unionist" or "loyalist" as one truly devoted to the Union and who had never wavered, thus excluding from consideration those who had gone with the Confederacy and later become disappointed. *Boston Journal*, Nov. 15, 1864; *N. Y. Herald*, April 7, 1864; *The Tribune*, Nov. 14, 1862; *N. Y. Times*, Nov. 23, 1862; Tharin, "The Alabama Refugee."

[2] *The World*, Feb. 15, 1865.

kept very quiet, and for two years there was no trouble.[1] But during the winter of 1862–1863, numerous outrages were committed by outlaws who were called, indiscriminately, tories and deserters. Much trouble was given by an organization called the First Florida Union Cavalry, which for two years committed various outrages while on bushwhacking expeditions under the leadership of one Joseph Sanders. After being soundly beaten one night by the citizens of Newton, in Dale County, these marauders were less troublesome.[2] The country near the Gulf coast was infested with tories, deserters, and runaway slaves, concealed in caves, "tight-eyes,"[3] canebrakes, swamps, and the thick woods of the sparsely settled country. In January, 1863, Governor Shorter wrote to President Davis that nearly all the loyal population of southeast Alabama was in the army, and that the country was suffering from the outrages of tories and deserters. About the same time, Colonel Price "suppressed unionism and treason in Henry County," though only one prisoner was reported as being taken.[4]

In August of the same year (1863) conditions had grown worse. General Howell Cobb reported that there was a disloyal feeling in southeast Alabama, but that there was no way to reach the offenders, as they were guilty of no overt act, and therefore the military courts could not try them. To turn them over to the civil authorities in that district would secure only a farcical trial, and the justices of the peace, though assuming the highest jurisdiction, were ignorant, and there was little chance of conviction. At this time, Governor Shorter said that affairs in lower Henry County were in bad condition; that the deserter element was strong and threatened the security of loyal people; and that the soldiers were afraid to leave their families.[5] A judge could not hold court unless he had a military escort.

During the next year matters grew worse in this section as well as in north Alabama. Some of the best soldiers felt compelled to go home, even without permission, to protect or to support their

[1] Information in regard to affairs in southeast Alabama during the war I have obtained from relatives (all of whom were " Union " men before the war) and from neighbors who were acquainted with the conditions in that section of the country.
[2] Miller, " Alabama." Sanders had been a Confederate officer.
[3] Thickets which the eye could not penetrate.
[4] O. R., Ser. I, Vol. LII, p. 403.
[5] O. R., Ser. I, Vol. XXVIII, Pt. II, p. 273; Ser. IV, Vol. II, p. 1043.

families; and in October, 1864, the legislature recognized this condition of affairs, and asked the Alabama soldiers, then absent without leave, to return to their duty under promise of lenient treatment.[1]

The worst depredations were committed during the winter of 1864–1865, in the counties of Dale, Henry, and Coffee. The loyal people in the thinly settled country were terrorized. The legislature, unable to protect them, authorized them to band themselves together in military form for protection against the outlaws. These bands of self-constituted "Home Guards," composed of boys and old men, captured numbers of the outlaws and straightway hanged them.

Desertions from the regiments raised in the white counties were often caused by denying to recruits or conscripts the privilege of choosing the command in which they should serve. Others deserted because their families were exposed to tory depredations and Federal raids, or were in want of the necessaries of life. These would have returned to the army after providing for their families had they been permitted to join other organizations and not subjected to punishment. Assigned arbitrarily to commands in need of recruits, some became dissatisfied, and deserted. A deserter was an outlaw and found it impossible to remain neutral. Hence many joined the bands of outlaws to pillage, and burn, and steal horses and cattle. Others of better character joined the Federals or became tories, that is, allied themselves with the original tories in order to work against the Confederacy. Numbers of these disaffected people had once been secessionists.[2]

Prominent Tories and Deserters

In view of the fact that the "unionists" were to play an important part in Reconstruction, it will be of interest to examine the records of the most prominent tories and deserters. A few prominent men joined the Federals during the course of the war, though none did so before the Union army occupied the Tennessee valley. Only one of these tried to assume any leadership over the so-called union-

---

[1] Joint Resolution, Oct. 7, 1864. J. J. Seibels proposed to raise a regiment for state defence of men under and over military age. He wanted, also, to get the skulkers who could not otherwise be obtained. O. R., Ser. IV, Vol. II, p. 604.

[2] O. R., Ser. IV, Vol. III, pp. 1042, 1043 (Solicitor James N. Arrington and Attorney-General M. A. Baldwin).

ists. This was William H. Smith, who had come within a few votes
of being elected to the Confederate Congress, and was later the first
Reconstruction governor. He went over to the enemy in 1862, and
did much toward securing the enlistment of the 2576 Union soldiers
from Alabama.

At the same time, a more important character, General Jeremiah
Clemens,[1] who had been in command of the militia of Alabama
with the rank of major-general, became disgruntled and went over
to the enemy. In the secession convention, Clemens had declared
that he "walked deliberately into rebellion" and was prepared for
all its consequences.[2] He first opposed, then voted for, the ordinance
of secession, and afterwards accepted the office of commander of
the militia under the "Republic of Alabama." For a year Clemens
was loyal to the "rebellion," but in 1862 he had seen the light and
wished to go to Washington as the representative of north Alabama
to learn from President Lincoln in what way the controversy might
be ended. The Washington administration, by that time, had little
faith in any following he might have, and when Clemens with John
Bell started to Washington, Stanton advised them to stay at home and
use their influence for the Union.[3]

George W. Lane, also of Madison County, was a prominent man
who cast his lot with the Federals. Lane never recognized secession,
and was an outspoken Unionist from the beginning. He was appointed Federal judge by Lincoln and died in 1864.[4] In April,
1861, Clemens wrote to the Confederate Secretary of War that the
acceptance of a United States judgeship by Lane was treason, and
that the "north Alabama men would gladly hang him."[5] General
O. M. Mitchell seemed to think that the negroes were the only "truly
loyal," but he recommended in May, 1862, that, when a military
government should be established in Alabama, George W. Lane,

---

[1] Clemens was a cousin of "Mark Twain." He was fond of drink, and once when
William L. Yancey asked him not to drink so much, he answered that he was obliged to
drink his genius down to a level with Yancey's.

[2] *N. Y. Tribune*, May 23, 1865. See Smith, "Debates," Index.

[3] O. R., Ser. I, Vol. X, Pt. II, pp. 167, 168, 174, 178. Clemens had been captain,
major, and colonel of the Thirteenth United States Infantry. From 1849 to 1853 he
was United States Senator. He died in Philadelphia a few years after the war. Garrett, "Public Men of Alabama," pp. 176-179.

[4] Brewer, "Alabama," p. 364.   [5] O. R., Ser. I, Vol. LII, Pt. II, p. 35.

the United States district judge appointed by Lincoln, be appointed military governor. Lane's faded United States flag still flew from the staff to which he had nailed it at the beginning of the war, and his appointment as governor, Mitchell thought, would give the greatest satisfaction to Huntsville and to all north Alabama.[1]

Two members of the convention of 1861, besides Clemens, deserted to the Federals. These were C. C. Sheets and D. P. Lewis. Like Clemens, they were elected as coöperationists and opposed immediate secession, though all three voted for the resolution declaring that Alabama would not submit to the rule of Lincoln. Sheets voted against secession and would not sign the ordinance. For a while he remained quietly at home and refused to enter the Confederate army. At length he reappeared from his place of hiding and assisted in recruiting soldiers for the First Alabama Union Cavalry. He was elected to the state legislature, but in 1862 was expelled for disloyalty. After some time in hiding, he was arrested, and imprisoned for treason. General Thomas retaliated by arresting and holding as a hostage General McDowell. Sheets remained in prison until the end of the war.[2]

David P. Lewis of Madison County voted against secession but signed the ordinance, and was elected to the Provisional Congress by the convention, and in 1863 was appointed circuit judge by the governor. This position he held for a few months, and then deserted to the Federals. During the remainder of the war he lived quietly at Nashville.[3]

Another prominent citizen of Madison County, Judge D. C. Humphreys, joined the Federals late in the war. Humphreys had been in the Confederate army and had resigned. He was arrested by General Roddy on the charge of disloyalty. It is not known that he was ever tried or put into prison, but in January, 1865, Hon. C. C. Clay, Sr., and other prominent citizens of Huntsville, of southern sympathies, all old men, were arrested and carried to prison in Nashville as hostages for the safety of Humphreys, who had been released

---

[1] O. R., Ser. I, Vol. X, Pt. II, pp. 161–163.

[2] "Northern Alabama Illustrated," p. 327; Acts of Alabama, 1862, p. 225; Moore, "Anecdotes, Poetry, and Incidents of the War," p. 215.

[3] Lewis became the second "Radical" or scalawag governor of Alabama, serving from 1872 to 1874. Miller, "Alabama," pp. 260, 261 ; Brewer, "Alabama," p. 368.

by order of the Confederate War Department as soon as the rumor of his arrest reached Richmond.[1] In April, 1864, General Clanton, commanding in north Alabama, sent Governor Watts a Nashville paper in which Jeremiah Clemens, "the arch traitor," and that "crazy man," Humphreys, figured as advisers to their fellow-citizens of Alabama in recommending submission.[2] There are indications that several such addresses were issued by Clemens, Humphreys, Lane, and others from the safety of the Federal lines, but the text of none of them has been found except those written and published when the war was nearly ended.

Of the men of position and influence who were found in the ranks of opposition to the Confederate government after 1861, Judge Lane is the only one whose course can command respect. He was faithful to the Union from first to last, while the others were erratic persons who changed sides because of personal spites and disappointments. They had little or no influence over, and nothing in common with, the dissatisfied mountain people and the tories and deserters.[3]

Numbers of the Disaffected

At the surrender the deserters came in in large numbers to be paroled. The reports of the Federal generals who received the surrender of the Confederate armies in the southwest show a surprisingly large number of Confederates paroled. A large proportion of them were deserters, "mossbacks," and tories, who, hated by the Confederate soldiers and fearing that the latter would seek revenge for their misdeeds during the war, felt that it would be some protection to take the oath, be paroled, and secure the certificate. Then, they thought, the United States government would see to their safety. At the surrender of a Confederate command in their vicinity, they flocked in from their retreats and were paroled as Confederate sol-

---

[1] O. R., Ser. II, Vol. VIII, p. 86.

[2] O. R., Ser. I, Vol. XXX, Pt. III, pp. 750-751.

[3] It is a notable fact that among the disaffected persons of prominence there were none of the old Whigs, or Bell and Everett men. Nearly all were Douglas Democrats. The Bell and Everett people so conducted themselves during the war that afterwards they were as completely disfranchised and out of politics as were the Breckenridge Democrats. The work of reconstruction under the Johnson plan fell mainly to the former Douglas Democrats and the lesser Whigs.

diers. To show how large this element in Mississippi and Alabama was, when General Dick Taylor surrendered, May 4, 1865, at Meridian, Mississippi, he had not more than 8000 real soldiers, or men under arms. It is possible, though not probable, that many were absent with leave. Yet of the 42,293 soldiers paroled in the armies of the Southwest[1] about 30,000 of them were at Meridian. Many of these had never been in the army; some had served in both armies; none had been in either for a long time. For weeks they kept coming in at all points where a United States officer was stationed in order to be paroled. The soldiers were furious. The statistics show[2] that strong Confederate armies were surrendered in this section of the country, when, as a matter of fact, the governor of Alabama had for two years been unable to secure sufficient military support to enforce the laws over more than half of the state.[3]

It is difficult to estimate the number of disaffected persons within the limits of the state. Probably in southeast Alabama there were in all, of tories and deserters, 1000 who at times were actively hostile to the Confederate authorities, and who committed depredations on the loyal people, and 1000 or 1500 more would include the "mossbacks" and obstructionists, who were without the courage to do more than keep out of the army and talk sedition. In addition to the 2576 enlistments in the Federal army credited to Alabama, it is probable that several hundred more were enlisted in northern regiments. Some of these were the Confederate prisoners captured late in the war and enlisted as "Galvanized Yankees" in the United States regiments sent West to fight the Indians.

Of deserters, tories, and "mossbacks" there could not have been less than 8000 or 10,000 in north Alabama. Of these, at least half were in active depredation all over the section. There were several thousand deserters from the Alabama troops, most of them from north Alabama and from commands stationed near their homes. At the beginning of the war there were probably no more than 2000

---

[1] Report of the Secretary of War, 1865, Vol. I, p. 45; "Confederate Military History," Vol. XII, p. 501.

[2] Report of the Secretary of War, Vol. I, p. 45; "Confederate Military History," Vol. XII, p. 501.

[3] I am indebted to old soldiers for descriptions of conditions in north and west Alabama before and following Taylor's surrender. All agree in their accounts of the conditions in Alabama and Mississippi at that time.

men who were wholly disaffected,[1] and these only to the extent of desiring neutrality for themselves.

On November 30, 1864, the Confederate "Deserter Book" showed that since April, 1864, 7994 Alabama soldiers had deserted or been absent without leave from the armies of the West and of Northern Virginia. Of these 4323 were again in the ranks, leaving still to be accounted for 3671 men. There were many deserters in the hills of Alabama from the commands from other states. After the fall of Atlanta, the number of stragglers and deserters greatly increased, and late in 1864 it was estimated that 6000 of them were in the state, some in every county; there being no longer a force to drive them back to the army. For a year or more the force for this purpose had been very weak.[2]

Much of the toryism and of the trouble resulting from it was due to' the weak policy of the Confederate authorities in dealing with discontent and in protecting the loyal people in exposed districts. Many a man had to desert in order to protect his family from outlaws, and was then easily driven into toryism.

There was a mild annoyance of the more peaceable tories by the Confederate officials in the spasmodic attempts to enforce the conscription laws, but it amounted to very little. The loyal southern people suffered more from the depredations of the disaffected "union" people of north and southeast Alabama than the latter suffered from all causes combined. The state and Confederate authorities were very lenient — too much so — in their treatment of these people. There was no great need of a strong Confederate force in north Alabama, since only raids, not invasions in force, were to be feared; yet the governments — both state and Confederate — were guilty of neglect in leaving so many of the people at the mercy of the outlaws when, as shown in several instances, two or three thousand good soldiers could march through the country and scatter the bands that infested it. Assuming that the state had a right to demand obedience and support from its citizens, it was weak and

---

[1] These estimates are based on half a hundred other estimates made during the war by state, Confederate, and Federal officials, and by other observers, and from estimates made by persons familiar with conditions at that time. They are rather too small than too large. O. R., Ser. IV, Vols. I to IV *passim*.

[2] O. R., Ser. IV, pp. 880, 881.

K

reprehensible conduct on the part of the authorities to allow three or four thousand malcontents and outlaws to demoralize a third of the state. Often the families of tories and "mossbacks" were supplied from the state and county stores for the destitute families of soldiers, while the men of such families were in the Federal service or were hiding in the woods, caves, and ravines, or were plundering the families of loyal soldiers. Not enough arrests were made, and too many were released. The majority of the troublesome class was of the kind who preferred to take no stand that incurred the fulfilment of obligations. In an emergency they would incline toward the stronger side. Prompt and rigorous measures, similar to the policy of the United States in the Middle West, stringently maintained, would have converted this source of weakness into a source of strength, or at least would have rendered it harmless. The military resources of that section of the state could then have been better developed, the helpless people protected, outlaws crushed, and there would have been peace after the war was ended.[1] As it was, the animosities then aroused smouldered on until they flamed again in one phase of the Ku Klux movement.[2]

SEC. 5.   PARTY POLITICS AND THE PEACE MOVEMENT

Political Conditions, 1861–1865

When, by the passage of the ordinance of January 11, 1861, the advocates of immediate secession had gained their end, the strong men of the victorious party, for the sake of harmony, stood aside, and intrusted much of the important work of organizing the new government to the defeated coöperationist party, who, to say the least, disapproved of the whole policy of the victors. The delegates chosen to the Provisional Congress were: R. H. Walker of Huntsville, a Union Whig, who had supported Bell and Everett and opposed secession; Robert H. Smith, a pronounced Whig, who had supported Bell and Everett and opposed secession; Colin J. McRae of Mobile, a commission merchant, a Whig; John Gill Shorter of Eufaula, who had held judicial office for nine years; William P. Chilton of Montgomery, for several years chief justice and before that an active Whig; Stephen F. Hale of Eutaw, a Whig who supported Bell and

---

[1] See also Pollard, " Lost Cause," p. 563 ; Schwab, p. 190.   [2] See below, Ch. XXI.

GOVERNOR THOMAS H. WATTS.   GOVERNOR JOHN GILL SHORTER.

GOVERNOR ANDREW B. MOORE.   BISHOP R. H. WILMER.

CIVIL WAR LEADERS.

Everett; David P. Lewis of Lawrence, an "unconditional Unionist" who had opposed secession in the convention of 1861, and who, in 1862, deserted to the Federals; Dr. Thomas Fearn of Huntsville, an old man, a Union Whig; and J. L. M. Curry of Talladega, the only consistent Democrat of the delegation, the only one who had voted for Breckenridge, and the only one with practical experience in public affairs. The delegation was strong in character, but weak in political ability and not energetic.[1] The delegation elected to the first regular Congress was more representative and more able.

In August, 1861, John Gill Shorter, a State Rights Democrat, was elected governor by a vote of 57,849 to 28,127 over Thomas Hill Watts, also a State Rights Democrat, who had voted for secession, but who had formerly been a Whig. Watts was not a regular candidate since he had forbidden the use of his name in the canvass.[2] For a time the people enthusiastically supported the administration. Governor Shorter's message of October 28, 1861, to the legislature closed with the words: "We may well congratulate ourselves and return thanks that a timely action on our part has saved our liberties, preserved our independence, and given us, it is hoped, a perpetual separation from such a government. May we in all coming time stand separate from it, as if a wall of fire intervened."[3] The legislature in 1861 declared that it was the imperative duty as well as the patriotic privilege of every citizen, forgetting past differences, to support the policy adopted and to maintain the independence assumed. To this cause the members of the general assembly pledged their lives, fortunes, and sacred honor.[4] A year later the same body declared that Mobile, then threatened by the enemy, must never be desecrated by the polluting tread of the abolitionist foe. It must never be surrendered, but must be defended from street to street, from house to house, and at last burned to the ground rather than surrendered.[5] The same legislature, elected in 1861 when the war feeling was strong, stated in August, 1863, that the war was unprovoked and unjust on the part of the United States government, which

---

[1] See DuBose, "Yancey," pp. 566, 567, and Brewer and Garrett under the names of the above.

[2] Brewer, p. 126; Garrett, p. 723.   [3] O. R., Ser. IV, Vol. I, p. 709.

[4] Joint Resolution, Acts of 1st Called Sess., 1861, p. 142.

[5] Joint Resolution, Acts of Called Sess. and 2d Regular Sess., 1862, p. 202.

was conducting it in utter disregard of the principles which should control and regulate civilized warfare. They renewed the pledge never to submit to abolitionist rule. The people were urged not to be discouraged by the late reverses, nor to attribute their defeats to any want of courage or heroic self-sacrifice on the part of the armies. All the resources of the state were pledged to the cause of independence and perpetual separation from the United States. It was the paramount duty, the assembly declared, of every citizen to sustain and make effective the armies by encouraging enlistments, by furnishing supplies at low prices to the families of soldiers, and by upholding the credit of the Confederate government. To enfeeble the springs of action by disheartening the people and the soldiers was to strike the most fatal blow at the very life of the Confederacy.[1]

This resolution was called forth partly by the constant criticism that the "cross-roads" politicians and a few individuals of more importance were directing against the civil and military policy of the administration. The doughty warriors of the office and counter were sure that the "Yankees" should have been whipped in ninety days. That the war was still going on was proof to them that those at the head of affairs were incompetent. These people had never before had so good an opportunity to talk and to be listened to. Those to whom the people had been accustomed to look for guidance were no longer present to advise. They had marched away with the armies, and there were left at home as voters the old men, the exempts, the lame, the halt, and the blind, teachers, preachers, officials, "bomb-proofs," "feather beds"[2] — all, in short, who were most unlikely to favor a vigorous war policy and who, if subject to service, wanted to keep out of the army. Consequently, among the voting population at home, the war spirit was not as high in 1863 as it had been before so many of the best men enlisted in the army.[3] The occupation of north Alabama by the enemy, short crops in 1862, and reverses in the field such as Vicksburg and Gettysburg, had a chilling

---

[1] Acts of Called Sess. and 3d Regular Sess., 1863, p. 52.

[2] A "bomb-proof" was a person who secured a safe position in order to keep out of service in the field. A "feather bed" was one who stayed at home with good excuse, — a teacher, agriculturist, preacher, etc., who had only recently been called to such profession.

[3] By act of the legislature soldiers in the field were to vote, but no instance is found of their having done so.

effect on the spirit of those who had suffered or were likely to suffer. The conscription law was unpopular among those forced into the service; it was much more disliked by those who succeeded for a time in escaping conscription. These lived in constant fear that the time would come when they would be forced to their duty.[1]

Further, the official class and the lawmakers were not up to the old standard of force and ability. The men who had the success of the cause most at heart usually felt it to be their duty to fight for it, if possible, leaving lawmaking and administration to others of more peaceable disposition. Some of the latter were able men, but few were filled with the spirit that animated the soldier class. Many of these unwarlike statesmen in the legislature and in Congress thought it to be their especial duty to guard the liberties of the people against the encroachments of the military power. They would talk by the hour about state rights, but would allow a few thousand of the sovereign state's disloyal citizens to demoralize a dozen counties rather than consent to infringe the liberties of the people by making the militia system more effective to repress disorder. They succeeded in weakening the efforts of both state and Confederate governments, and their well-meant arguments drawn from the works of Jefferson were never remembered to their credit. One of the best of these men — Judge Dargan, a member of Congress from Mobile — seems to have had a very unhappy disposition, and he spent much of his time writing to the governor and to the President in regard to the critical state of the country and suggesting numberless plans for its salvation. Among many things that were visionary he advanced some original schemes. In 1863 he proposed a plan for the gradual emancipation of slaves, later a plan for arming them, and suggested that blockade running be prohibited, as it was ruining the country.[2]

Even while the tide of war feeling was at the flood there occurred instances of friction between the state and the Confederate governments. In December, 1862, the legislature complained of the continued use of the railroads by the Confederate government, to the exclusion of private transportation. The railroads were built, it

[1] See Hannis Taylor, "Political History of Alabama," in "Memorial Record of Alabama," Vol. I, p. 82.

[2] Jones, "A Rebel War Clerk's Diary," Vol. I, pp. 250, 335, 391; Schwab, "Confederate States," p. 210; Garrett, p. 385; Brewer, p. 411.

was stated, for free intercourse between the states, and, since the blockade had become effective, were more important than ever in the transportation of the necessaries of life.[1] The legislature complained about the conduct of the Confederate officers in the state, about impressment, taxation, and redemption of state bonds, the state's quota of troops for the Confederate service, about arms and supplies purchased by the state, and about trade through the lines. Suits were brought again and again in the state courts by the strict constructionists to test the constitutionality of the conscript laws and the law forbidding the hiring of substitutes. But the courts declared both laws constitutional.[2] The lawmakers of the state were much more afraid of militarism than of the Federal invasion or domestic disorder, and refused to organize the militia effectively.[3]

The military reverses in the summer of 1863 darkened the hopes of the people and chilled their waning enthusiasm, and the effect was shown in the elections of August. Thomas H. Watts, who had been defeated in 1861, was elected governor by a vote of 22,223 to 6342 over John G. Shorter, who had been governor for two years. Watts had a strong personal following, which partly accounted for the large majority; but several thousand, at least, were dissatisfied in some way with the state or the Confederate administration. Jemison, a former coöperationist, took Yancey's place in the Confederate Senate. J. L. M. Curry was defeated for Congress because he had strongly supported the administration. The delegation elected to the second Congress was of a decidedly different temper from the delegation to the first Congress. A large number of hitherto unknown men were elected to the legislature.[4]

At the close of the term of Governor Shorter, the new legislature passed resolutions indorsing his policy in regard to the conduct of the war and commending his wise and energetic administration.[5] Other resolutions were passed which would seem to indicate that the

---

[1] Acts of 2d Regular Sess., 1862, p. 200.

[2] Annual Cyclopædia (1862), p. 9; Schwab, "Confederate States," pp. 195, 196; Brewer, 127; Garrett, pp. 722, 724. See *infra*, p. 97.

[3] Shorter's Proclamation, Dec. 22, 1862, in Moore, "Rebellion Record," Vol. IV, and above, p. 88.

[4] Annual Cyclopædia (1863), p. 6; O. R., Ser. IV, Vol. II, p. 126; Brewer, pp. 66, 126, 460; Garrett, p. 722; Hannis Taylor, in "Memorial Record of Alabama," p. 82.

[5] Acts, 3d Regular Sess., 1864, p. 217.

war feeling ran as high and strong as ever. In fact, it was only the voice of the majority, not of all, as before. There was a strong minority of malcontents who pursued a policy of obstruction and opposition to the measures of the administration and thereby weakened the power of the government. It was believed by many that Watts, who had been a Whig and a Bell and Everett elector, would be more conservative in regard to the prosecution of the war than was his predecessor. There were numbers of people in the state who believed or professed to believe that it was possible to end the war whenever President Davis might choose to make peace with the enemy. Others, who saw that peace with independence was impossible, were in favor of reconstruction, that is, of ending the war at once and returning to the old Union, with no questions asked. They believed that the North would be ready to make peace and welcome the southern states back into the Union on the old terms. These constituted only a small part of the population, but they had some influence in an obstructive way and were great talkers. Any one who voted for Watts from the belief that he would try to bring about peace was much mistaken in the man. It was reported that he was in favor of reconstruction. This he emphatically denied in a message to the legislature: "He who is now . . . in favor of reconstruction with the states under Lincoln's dominion, is a traitor in his heart to the state . . . and deserves a traitor's doom. . . . Rather than unite with such a people I would see the Confederate states desolated with fire and sword. . . . Let us prefer death to a life of cowardly shame." [1] Though Watts was elected somewhat as a protest against the war party, he was in favor of a vigorous prosecution of the war. However, at times, he had trouble with the Confederate government, and we find him writing about "the tyranny of Confederate officials," that "the state had some rights left," that "there will be a conflict between the Confederate and state authorities unless the conscript officials cease to interfere with state volunteers and state officials." [2]

[1] Annual Cyclopædia (1863), p. 7. Francis Wayland, Jr., in a "Letter to a Peace Democrat" in the *Atlantic Monthly*, Dec., 1863, quotes Governor Watts as saying immediately after he had been elected: "If I had the power I would build up a wall of fire between Yankeedom and the Confederate States, there to burn for ages." See also O. R., Ser. IV, Vol. I, p. 120; McMorries, "History of the First Alabama Regiment of Infantry."

[2] O. R., Ser. IV, Vol. III, pp. 37, 463, 466, 817, 820. See also above, pp. 97, 103, 104.

The governor was in favor of supporting the war, and recommended the repeal of some of the state laws obstructing Confederate enlistments; he was willing for any state troops that were available to go to the aid of another state, and he desired to aid in returning deserters to the army; but he opposed the manner of execution of laws by the Confederate government. He demanded for the state the right to engage in the blockade trade in order to secure necessaries. He also protested against the proposed policy of arming the slaves.[1]

During the year 1864 the legislature protested against the action of Confederate conscript officers who insisted on enrolling certain state officials. It was ordered that the reserves, when called out for service, should not be put under the command of a Confederate officer. The first-class reserves were not to leave their own counties. An act was passed to protect the people from "oppression by the illegal execution of the Confederate impressment laws."[2] Confederate enrolling officers who forced exempt men into the army were made liable to punishment by heavy fine.[3]

An Alabama newspaper, in the fall of 1864, advocated a convention of the states in order to settle the questions at issue, to bring about peace, and to restore the Union. Such a proposition found supporters in the legislature. A resolution was introduced favoring reconstruction on the basis of the recent platform of the Democratic party and McClellan's letter of acceptance.[4] The resolution was to this effect: if the Democratic party is successful in 1864, we are willing to open negotiations for peace on the basis indicated in the platform adopted by the convention; provided that our sister states of the Confederacy are willing. A lengthy and heated discussion followed. The governor sent in a message asking "who would desire a political union with those who have murdered our sons, outraged our women, with demoniac malice wantonly destroyed our property, and now seek to make slaves of us!" It would cause civil war, he said, if the people at home attempted such a course. After the reading of the message and some further debate, both houses united in a declaration that extermination was preferable to reconstruction according to the *Lincoln* plan. The proposed resolution, the extended

---

[1] O. R., Ser. IV, Vol. III, pp. 683, 685, 735, 736.   [2] Act, Oct. 7, 1864.
[3] Act, Dec. 12, 1864.   [4] See McPherson, " Rebellion," pp. 419–421.

debate, the governor's message, all clearly indicate a strong desire on the part of some to end the war and return to the Union.[1]

With the opening of 1865 conditions in Alabama were not favorable to the war party: the old coöperationists, with other malcontents, were charging the Davis administration with every political crime; the state administration was disorganized in half the counties; deserters and stragglers were scattered throughout the state; and many of the state and county officials were disaffected. Those who were in favor of war were in the armies. Had the war continued until the August election, there is no doubt that an administration would have been elected which would have refused further support to the Confederacy. Had it not been for fear of the soldier element, the malcontents at home could have controlled affairs in the fall of 1864. For a year there had been indications that the discontented were thinking of a *coup d'état* and an immediate close of the war. The formation of secret societies pledged to bring about peace was a sign of formidable discontent.

The Peace Society

It was after the reverses of 1863 that the enthusiasm of the people for the war very perceptibly declined. For the first time, many felt that perhaps after all their cause would not win, and that the horrors of war might be brought home to them by hostile invasion of their country. Public opinion was more or less despondent. There was a searching for scapegoats and a more pronounced hostility to the administration. The "cross-roads" statesmen were sure that a different policy under another leader would have been crowned with success, though what this policy should have been, perhaps no two would have agreed. This feeling was largely confined to the less well informed, but it was also found in a number of the old-time conservatives who would never believe that extreme measures were justifiable in any event, and who could never get over a feeling

---

[1] The "Confederate Military History" states that in 1864 the people hoped for terms of peace, believing that Democratic successes in the northern elections would result in an armistice, and later reconstruction ; that the people were always ready to go back to the principles of 1787, and it was believed that Davis was willing, but that the unfavorable elections of 1864 and the military interference by the Federal administration in the border states killed this constitutional peace party. See Vol. I, pp. 505, 537.

of horror at all that the Democrats might do. If left alone, they thought, time would have brought all things right in the end. It was as painful to them to think that Lincoln was marching armies over the fragments of the United States Constitution, as that the Davis administration was strangling state sovereignty in the Confederate States. Their minds never rose above the narrow legalism of their books. But they were few in numbers as compared with the more ignorant people (who were conscious only of dissatisfaction and suffering) who had willingly plunged into the war "to whip the Yankees in ninety days," and who now thought that all that had to be done to bring peace was to signify to the North a willingness to stop fighting. This course, many thought, need not result in a loss of their independence. Later they were minded to come back into the Union on the old terms, and later still they were ready to make peace without conditions and return to the Union. It seems never to have occurred to them that northern opinion had changed since 1861, and that severe terms of readmission would be exacted. The hardest condition likely to be imposed, they thought, would be the gradual emancipation of the slaves. As a rule, they owned few slaves, but such a condition would probably have been considered harder by them than by the larger slaveholders who felt that slavery had come to an end, no matter how the struggle might result.

This dissatisfaction culminated in the formation of numerous secret or semi-secret political organizations which sprang up over the state, and which together became generally known as the "Peace Society," though there were other designations. Often these organizations were formed for purposes bordering on treason; often not so, but only for constitutional opposition to the administration. The extremes grew farther apart as the war progressed, until the constitutional wing withdrew or ceased to exist, and the other became, from the point of view of the government, wholly treasonable in its purposes. These organizations had several thousand members, at least half the active males left in the state.

The work of the peace party was first felt in the August elections of 1863. The governor, though a true and loyal man, was elected with the help of a disaffected party, and a disaffected element was elected to the legislature and to Congress. Six members of Congress from Alabama were said to be "unionists," that is, in favor of ending the war at once and returning to the Union.[1] A Confederate official who had wide opportunities for observation reported that the district (Talladega) in which he was stationed had been carried by the peace party under circumstances that indicated treasonable influence. Unknown men were elected to the legislature and to other offices by a secret order which, he stated, had for its object the encouragement of desertion, the protection of deserters, and resistance to the conscription laws. Some men of influence and position belonged to it, and the leaders were believed to be in communication with the enemy. The entire organization was not disloyal, but he feared that the controlling element was faithless. The election had been determined largely by the votes of stragglers and deserters and of paroled Vicksburg soldiers who, it was found later, had been "contaminated" by contact with the western soldiers of Grant's army.[2] By this he evidently meant that the soldiers had been initiated into the "Peace Society."

A few months later the "Peace Society" appeared among the soldiers of General Clanton's brigade stationed at Pollard, in Conecuh County. Some of the soldiers had served in the army of Tennessee, and had there been initiated into this secret society. Clanton, who was strongly disliked by General Bragg and not loved by General Polk, had much trouble with them because he asserted that the order appeared first in Bragg's army and spread from thence. Later

---

[1] Williamson R. W. Cobb of Jackson County, a very popular politician, a member of the 36th Congress, met his first defeat in 1861, when a candidate for the Confederate Congress. In 1863 he was successful over the man who had beaten him in 1861. After the election, if not before, he was in constant communication with the enemy and went into their lines several times. The Congress expelled him by a unanimous vote. It was rumored that President Lincoln intended to appoint him military governor, but he killed himself accidentally in 1864. Cobb was a "down east Yankee" who had come into the state as a clock pedler. He had no education and little real ability, but was a smooth talker and was master of the arts of the demagogue. In political life he was famed for shaking hands with the men, kissing the women, and playing with the babies. At a Hardshell foot-washing he won favor by carrying around the towels, in striking contrast with his Episcopalian rival, who sat on the back bench. Cobb was for the Confederacy as long as he thought it would win ; when luck changed, he proceeded to make himself safe. After his desertion he lost influence among the people of his district. See Brewer, pp. 286, 287 ; McPherson, pp. 49, 400, 402, 411.

[2] O. R., Vol. II, p. 726 (W. T. Walthall, commandant of conscripts for Alabama, Talladega, Aug. 6, 1863). In the fall of 1864 a secret peace society was discovered in southwest Virginia, North Carolina, and Tennessee. O. R., Ser. IV, Vol. III, pp. 802-820.

developments showed that he was correct.[1] It was in December, 1863, that the operations of the order among the soldiers were exposed. A number of soldiers at Pollard determined to lay down their arms on Christmas Day, as the only means of ending the war. These troops, for the most part, were lately recruited from the poorer classes of southwest Alabama by a popular leader and had never seen active service. They were stationed near their homes and were exposed to home influences. Upon them and their families the pressure of the war had been heavy.[2] Many of them were exempt from service but had joined because of Clanton's personal popularity, because they feared that later they might become liable to service, and because they were promised special privileges in the way of furloughs and stations near their homes. To this unpromising material had been added conscripts and substitutes in whom the fires of patriotism burned low, and who entered the service very reluctantly. With them were a few veteran soldiers, and in command were veteran officers. A secret society was formed among the discontented, with all the usual accompaniment of signs, passwords, grips, oaths, and obligations. Some bound themselves by solemn oaths never to fight the enemy, to desert, and to encourage desertion — all this in order to break down the Confederacy. General Maury, in command at Mobile, concluded after investigation that the society had originated with the enemy and had entered the southern army at Cumberland Gap.[3]

In regard to the discontent among the soldiers, Colonel Swanson of the Fifty-ninth and Sixty-first Alabama[4] regiments (consolidated) stated that there was a general disposition on the part of the poorer classes, substitutes, and foreigners to accept terms and stop the war. They had nothing anyway, so there was nothing to fight for, they said. There was no general matured plan, and no leader, Colonel Swanson thought.[5] Major Cunningham of the Fifty-seventh Alabama Regiment[6] reported that there had been considerable manifestation

[1] O. R., Ser. I, Vol. XXVI, Pt. II, pp. 555–557.

[2] O. R., Ser. I, Vol. XXVI, Pt. II, p. 548.

[3] O. R., Ser. I, Vol. XXVI, Pt. II, pp. 551, 552.

[4] The 61st Alabama Regiment was composed largely of conscripts under veteran officers. It was evidently at first called the 59th. Brewer, p. 673.

[5] O. R., Ser. I, Vol. XXVI, Pt. II, p. 550.

[6] The 57th Alabama Regiment was recruited in the counties of Pike, Coffee, Dale, Henry, and Barbour. See Brewer, p. 669.

of revolutionary spirit on account of the tax-in-kind law and the impressment system, and that there was much reckless talk, even among good men, of protecting their families from the injustice of the government, even if they had to lay down their arms and go home.[1] General Clanton said that the society had existed in Hilliard's Legion and Gracie's brigade, and that few men, he was sure, joined it for treasonable purposes.[2] Before the appointed time—Christmas Day — sixty or seventy members of the order mutinied and the whole design was exposed. Seventy members were arrested and sent to Mobile for trial by court-martial.[3] There is no record of the action of the court. The purged regiments were then ordered to the front and obeyed without a single desertion. Bolling Hall's battalion, which was sent to the Western army for having in it such a society, made a splendid record at Chickamauga and in other battles, and came out of the Chickamauga fight with eighty-two bullet-holes in its colors.[4]

During the summer and fall of 1863 and in 1864 the Confederate officials in north Alabama often reported that they had found certain traces of secret organizations which were hostile to the Confederate government. The Provost-Marshal's Department in 1863 obtained information of the existence of a secret society between the lines in Alabama and Tennessee, the object of which was to encourage desertion.

Confederate soldiers at home on furlough joined the organization and made known its object to the Confederate authorities. The members were pledged not to assist the Confederacy in any way, to encourage desertion of the north Alabama soldiers, and to work for a revolution in the state government. Stringent oaths were taken by the members, a code of signals and passwords was used, and a well-organized society was formed. The bulk of the membership con-

[1] O. R., Ser. I, Vol. XXVI, Pt. II, p. 550.

[2] O. R., Ser. I, Vol. XXVI, Pt. II, p. 556. The 59th Alabama Regiment was formed from a part of Hilliard's Legion. Brewer, p. 671.

[3] O. R., Ser. I, Vol. XXVI, Pt. II, pp. 552, 556.

[4] O. R., Ser. I, Vol. XXVI, Pt. II, p. 556; Brewer, "Alabama," p. 671. It may be that the 59th Regiment here spoken of as consolidated was not the 59th under the command of Bolling Hall, but was merely the first number given to the regiment, which later became the 61st. See Brewer, pp. 671, 673. However, the society existed in Bolling Hall's regiment.

sisted of tories and deserters, with a few discontented Confederates. Their society gave information to the Federals in north Alabama and Tennessee and had agents far within the Confederate lines, organizing discontent. General Clanton early in 1864 endeavored to break up the organization in north Alabama and made a number of arrests, but failed to crush the order.

In middle Alabama, about the same time (the spring of 1864), the workings of a treasonable secret society were brought to light. Colonel Jefferson Falkner of the Eighth Confederate Infantry overheard a conversation between two malcontents and began to investigate. He found that in the central counties a secret society was working to break down the Confederate government and bring about peace. The plans were not perfected, but some were in favor of returning to the Union on the Arkansas or Sebastian platform,[1] others wanted to send to Washington and make terms, and still others were in favor of unconditional submission. As to methods, the malcontents meant to secure control of the state administration, either by revolution or by elections in the summer of 1865, then they would negotiate with the United States and end the war. The society had agents in both the Western army and the Army of Northern Virginia, tampering with the soldiers and endeavoring to carry the organization into the Federal army. The leaders in the movement hoped to organize into one party all who were discontented with the administration. If successful in this, they would be strong enough either to overthrow the state government, which was supported only by home guards, or by obstruction to force the state government to make peace. The oaths, passwords, and signals of this society were similar to those of the north Alabama organization, with which it was in communication. Conscript officers, county officials, medical boards, and members of the legislature were members of the order. If a deserter were arrested, some member released him; the members claimed that the society caused the loss of the battle of Missionary Ridge and the surrender at Vicksburg.

The strength of the so-called Peace Society lay in Alabama, Georgia, Tennessee, and North Carolina. The organizers were called Eminents. They gave the "degree" to (that is, initiated)

---

[1] See Nicolay and Hay, "Lincoln," Vol. VIII, pp. 410–415; McPherson, "Rebellion," pp. 320–322.

those whom they considered proper persons. No records were kept; the members did not know one another except by recognition through signals. They received directions from the Eminents, who accommodated their instructions to the person initiated. An ignorant but loyal person was told that the object of the order was to secure a change of administration; the disloyal were told that the purpose was to encourage desertion and mutiny in the army, to injure loyal citizens, and to overthrow the state and Confederate governments. Owing to the non-intercourse between members there were many in the order who never knew the real objects of the leaders or Eminents, who intended to use the organization to further their designs in 1865. The swift collapse of the Confederacy in the spring of 1865 anticipated the work of the secret societies. The anti-Confederate element was, however, left somewhat organized through the work of the order.[1]

Reconstruction Sentiment

Besides the open obstruction of politicians, officials, and legislature, and the secret opposition of the peace societies, there was a third movement for reconstruction. This movement took place in that part of Alabama held by the Federal armies, and the reconstruction meetings were encouraged by the Union army officers. The leaders were D. C. Humphreys and Jeremiah Clemens, whose defection has been noted before. A more substantial element than the tories and deserters supported this movement — the dissatisfied property

[1] O. R., Ser. I, Vol. XXXIII, Pt. III, pp. 682, 683, and Vol. XXII, Pt. I, p. 671; Ser. IV, Vol. III, pp. 393-397. A fuller account of the Peace Society will be found in the *South Atlantic Quarterly*, July, 1903. Some of the prominent leaders in the Peace Society were said to be: Lewis E. Parsons, later provisional governor, said to be the head of it; Col. J. J. Seibels of Montgomery; R. S. Heflin, state senator from Randolph County; W. W. Dodson, William Kent, David A. Perryman, Lieut.-Col. E. B. Smith, W. Armstrong, and A. A. West, of Randolph County; Capt. W. S. Smith, Demopolis; L. McKee and Lieut. N. B. DeArmon.

General James H. Clanton testified in 1871 that while in the Alabama legislature during the war L. E. Parsons, afterwards governor, introduced resolutions invoking the blessings of heaven on the head of Jefferson Davis and praying that God would spare him to consummate his holy purposes. Jabez M. Curry charged Parsons with being a "reconstructionist" during the war, that is, with being disloyal to the government. Parsons had two young sons in the Confederate army, and one of them was so indignant at the charge against his father that he shot and wounded Curry. Dr. Ware of Montgomery afterwards made the same charge. Ku Klux Rept., Ala. Test., p. 234.

holders who were afraid of confiscation. Several Confederate officers were drawn into the movement later.[1]

Early in 1864, Humphreys[2] issued an elaborate address renouncing his errors. There was no hope, he told his fellow-citizens, that foreign powers would intervene. Slavery as a permanent institution must be given up. Law and order must be enforced and constitutional authority reëstablished. Slavery was the cause of revolution, and as an institution was at an end. With slavery abolished, there was, therefore, no reason why the war should not end. The right to regulate the labor question would be secured to the state by the United States government. At present labor was destroyed, and in order to regulate labor, there must be peace. The address was printed and distributed throughout the state with the assistance of the Federal officials. A number of the packages of these addresses was seized by some women and thrown into the Tennessee River.[3] Jeremiah Clemens, who had deserted in 1862, issued an address to the people of the South advocating the election of Lincoln as President.[4] March 5, 1864, a reconstruction meeting, thinly attended, was held in Huntsville under the protection of the Union troops. Clemens presided. Resolutions were passed denying the legality of secession because the ordinance had not been submitted to the people for their ratification or rejection. Professions of devotion and loyalty to the United States were made by Clemens, the late major-general of Alabama militia and secessionist of 1861.[5] A week later the same party met again. No young men were present, for they were in the army. All were men over forty-five, concerned for their property. Clemens spoke, denouncing the "twenty-negro" law. The Gilchrist story was here originated by Clemens and told for the first time. The story was that J. G. Gilchrist of Montgomery County went to the Secretary of War, Mr. Walker, and urged him to begin hostilities by firing on Fort Sumter, saying, "You must sprinkle blood in the face of the people of Alabama or the state will

[1] See O. R., Ser. I, Vol. XLIX, Pt. I, p. 718. "Confederate Military History," Vol. I, pp. 505, 509, 511, 512, 537.

[2] A Douglas Democrat, a Douglas elector, and a strong secessionist, who had deserted to the enemy. Brewer, p. 364.

[3] N. Y. Times, Feb. 14, 1864; Annual Cyclopædia (1864), pp. 10, 11; N. Y. Daily News, April 16, 1864, from Columbus (Ga.) Sun.

[4] N. Y. Tribune, May 23, 1865.   [5] N. Y. World, March 28, 1864.

be back into the Union within ten days." In closing, Clemens said, "Thank God, there is now no prospect of the Confederacy succeeding."

D. C. Humphreys then proposed his plan: slavery was dead, but by submitting to Federal authority gradual emancipation could be secured, and also such guarantees as to the future status of the negro as would relieve the people from social, economic, and political dangers. He expressed entire confidence in the conservatism of the northern people, and asserted that if only the ordinance of secession were revoked, the southern people would have as long a time as they pleased to get rid of the institution of slavery. In case of return to the Union the people would have political coöperation to enable them to secure control of negro labor. "There is really no difference, in my opinion," he said, "whether we hold them as slaves or obtain their labor by some other method. Of course, we prefer the old method. But that is not the question." He announced the defection from the Confederacy of Vice-President Stephens, and bitterly denounced Ben Butler, Davis, and Slidell, to whose intrigues he attributed the present troubles. Resolutions were proposed by him and adopted, acknowledging the hopelessness of secession and advising a return to the Union. Longer war, it was declared, would be dangerous to the liberties of the people, and the restoration of civil government was necessary. The governor was asked to call a convention for the purpose of reuniting Alabama to the Union. It was not expected, it was stated, that the governor would do this; but his refusal would be an excuse for the independent action of north Alabama and a movement toward setting up a new state government. Busteed could then come down and hold a "bloody assize, trying traitors and bushwhackers." [1]

In the early winter of 1864–1865, the northern newspaper correspondents in the South [2] began to write of the organization of a strong peace party called the "State Rights party," in Georgia, Alabama, and Mississippi. The leaders were in communication with the Washington authorities. They claimed that each state

[1] *N. Y. Times*, March 24, 1864; *N. Y. World*, March 28, 1864. Busteed was a newly appointed Federal judge who afterward became notorious in "carpet-bag" days. He succeeded George W. Lane in the judgeship.

[2] There were several regular, reliable correspondents in north Alabama, for the New York, Boston, and Chicago papers. Their accounts are corroborated by the reports made later by Confederate and Federal officials.

L

had the right to negotiate for itself terms of reconstruction. The plan was to secure control of the state administration and then apply for readmission to the Union. The destruction of Hood's army removed the fear of the soldier element. Several thousand of Hood's suffering and dispirited soldiers took the oath of allegiance to the United States, or dispersed to their homes. Early in 1865 peace meetings were held in Georgia, Alabama, and Mississippi, within the Confederate lines; commissioners were sent to Washington; and the tories and deserters organized. A delegation waited on Governor Watts to ask him to negotiate for the return of the state to the Union, but did not get, nor did they expect, a favorable answer from him. The peace party expected to gain the August elections and elect as governor J. C. Bradley of Huntsville, or M. J. Bulger of Tallapoosa.[1] The plan, then, was not to wait for the inauguration in November, but to have the newly elected administration take charge at once. It was continually reported that General P. D. Roddy was to head the movement.[2]

There is no doubt that during the winter of 1864–1865 some kind of negotiation was going on with the Federal authorities. J. J. Giers, who was a brother-in-law of State Senator Patton,[3] was in constant communication with General Grant. In one of his reports to Grant he stated that Roddy and another Confederate general had sent Major McGaughey, Roddy's brother-in-law, to meet Giers near Moulton, in Lawrence County, to learn what terms could be obtained for the readmission of Alabama. Major McGaughey said that the people considered that affairs were hopeless and wanted peace. If the terms were favorable, steps would be taken to induce Governor Watts to accept them. If Watts should refuse, a civil and military movement would be begun to organize a state government for Alabama which would include three-fourths of the state. The plan, it was stated, was indorsed by the leading public men.

---

[1] At this time Bulger was in active service. See Brewer, "Alabama," pp. 548, 660; "Confederate Military History" — Alabama, see Index. Bradley was a north Alabama man who had gone over to the enemy to save his property. This was his chief claim to notoriety. He became a prominent "scalawag" later.

[2] *N. Y. Herald*, Nov. 29, 1864; *N. Y. Times*, Feb. 10, 1865; *Boston Journal*, Nov. 15, 1864; *The World*, March 28, 1864, Feb. 11, 1865; O. R., Ser. I, Vol. XLIX, Pt. I, pp. 590, 659.

[3] Later governor, succeeding Parsons.

The peace leaders wanted Grant, or the Washington administration, to announce at once a policy of gradual emancipation in order to reassure those afraid of outright abolition, and to "disintegrate the rebel soldiery" of north Alabama, which they said was never strongly devoted to the Confederacy. It was asserted that all the counties north of the cotton belt and those in the southeast were ready for a movement toward reconstruction. Giers stated that approaches were then being made to Governor Watts. Andrew Johnson, the newly elected Vice-President, vouched for the good character of Giers.[1] Ten days later Giers wrote Grant that on account of the rumors of the submission of various Confederate generals he had caused to be published a contradiction of the report of the agreement with the Confederate leaders. He further stated that one of Roddy's officers, Lieutenant W. Alexander, had released a number of Federal prisoners without parole or exchange, according to agreement.[2] In several instances, in the spring of 1865, subordinate Confederate commanders proposed a truce, and after Lee's surrender and Wilson's raid this was a general practice. During the months of April and May, there was a combined movement of citizens and soldiers in a number of counties in north Alabama to reorganize civil government according to a plan furnished by General Thomas, Giers being the intermediary.[3] On May 1 General Steele of the second army of invasion was informed at Montgomery by J. J. Scibels, L. E. Parsons, and J. C. Bradley — all well-known obstructionists — that two-thirds of the people of Alabama would take up arms to put down the "rebels."[4] Colonel Seibels alone of that gallant company had ever taken up arms for any cause. The other two and their kind may have been, and doubtless often were, warlike in their conversation, but they never drew steel to support their convictions.

It is quite likely that the strength of the disaffection, especially in north and east Alabama, was exaggerated by the reports of both Union and Confederate authorities. There never had been during the war much loyalty, in the proper sense of the word, to the United

[1] Letter from Giers at Decatur, Jan. 26, 1865; O. R., Ser. I, Vol. XLIX, Pt. I, pp. 590, 718. See also Report of Joint Committee on Reconstruction, Pt. III, pp. 13-15, 60, 64.

[2] Giers, from Nashville, to Grant; O. R., Ser. I, Vol. XLIX, Pt. I, p. 659.

[3] Judging from the correspondence of Giers, the plan had the approval of General Grant. [4] O. R., Ser. I, Vol. XLIX, Pt. II, p. 560.

States. There was much pure indifference on the part of some people who desired the strongest side to win as soon as possible and leave them in safety. There was much discontent on the part of others who had supported the Confederacy for a while, but who, for various reasons, had fallen away from the cause and now .wanted peace and reunion. There was a very large element of outright lawlessness in the opposition to the Confederate government. The lowest class of men on both sides or of no side united to plunder that defenceless land between the two armies. This class wanted no peace, for on disorder they thrived. For years after the war ended they gave trouble to Federal and state authorities. The discontent was actively manifested by civilians, deserters, "mossbacks," "bomb-proofs," and "feather beds." These had never strongly supported the Confederacy. It was largely a timid, stay-at-home crowd, with a few able but erratic leaders. The soldiers may have been dissatisfied, — many of them were, — and many of them left the army in the spring of 1865 to go home and plant crops for the relief of their suffering families. Many of them in the dark days after Nashville and Franklin took the oath of allegiance and went home, sure that the war was ended and the cause was lost. Yet these were not the ones found in such organizations as the Peace Society. That was largely made up of people whom the true soldier despised as worthless. There were few soldiers in the peace movement and these only at the last.

The peace party, however, was strong in one way. All were voters and, being at home, could vote. The soldiers in the army had no voice in the elections. The malcontents, had they possessed courage and good leaders, could have controlled the state after the summer of 1864. The able men in the movement were not those who inspired confidence in their followers. There were no troops in the state to keep them down, and the only check seems to have been their fear of the soldiers, who were fighting at the front, in the armies of Lee and Johnston, of Wheeler and Hood and Taylor. They were certainly afraid of the vengeance of these soldiers.[1] It was much better that the war resulted in the complete destruction of the southern cause, leaving no questions for future controversy, such as would have arisen had the peace party succeeded in its plans.

[1] This fear is expressed in all their correspondence.

CHAPTER IV

ECONOMIC AND SOCIAL CONDITIONS

SEC. I. INDUSTRIAL DEVELOPMENT DURING THE WAR

EARLY in the war the blockade of the southern ports became so effective that the southern states were shut off from their usual sources of supply by sea. Trade through the lines between the United States and the Confederate States was forbidden, and Alabama, owing to its central location, suffered more from the blockade than any other state. For three years the Federal lines touched the northern part of the state only, and, as no railroads connected north and south Alabama, contraband trade was difficult in that direction. Mobile, the only port of the state, was closely blockaded by a strong Federal fleet. The railroad communications with other states were poor, and the Confederate government usually kept the railroads busy in the public service. Consequently, the people of Alabama were forced to develop certain industries in order to secure the necessaries of life. But outside these the industrial development was naturally in the direction of the production of materials of war.

Military Industries

During the first two years of the war volunteers were much more plentiful than equipment. The arms seized at Mount Vernon and other arsenals in Alabama were old flint-locks altered for the use of percussion caps and were almost worthless, being valued at $2 apiece. These were afterwards transferred to the Confederate States, which returned but few of them to arm the Alabama troops.[1] Late in 1860 a few thousand old muskets were purchased by the state from the arsenal at Baton Rouge, Louisiana, for $2.50 each. A few Mississippi rifles were also secured, and with these the Second Alabama

[1] Davis, " Rise and Fall of the Confederate Government," Vol. I, p. 471; O. R., Ser. I, Vol. III, p. 440.

Infantry was armed. These rifles, however, required a special kind of ammunition, and this made them almost worthless. Other arms were found to be useless for the same reason. Both cavalry and

infantry regiments went to the front armed with single and double barrelled shot-guns, squirrel rifles, muskets, flint-locks, and old pistols. No ammunition could be supplied for such a miscellaneous collection. Many regiments had to wait for months before arms could be obtained. Before October, 1861, several thousand men had left Alabama unarmed, and several thousand more, also unarmed, were left waiting in the state camps.[1] In 1861 the state legislature bought a thousand pikes and a hundred bowie-knives to arm the Forty-eighth Militia Regiment, which was defending Mobile.

The sum of $250,000 was appropriated to lend to those who would manufacture firearms for the government.[2] In 1863 the Confederate Congress authorized the enlistment of companies armed with pikes who should take the places of men armed with firearms when the latter were dead or absent.[3] Private arms — muskets, rifles, pistols, shot-guns, carbines — were called for and purchased from the owners

---

[1] Miller, "History of Alabama," p. 158; Davis, "Confederate Government," Vol. I, p. 476; O. R., Ser. I, Vol. III, p. 440.

[2] Acts of 2d Called and 1st Regular Sess. (1861), pp. 75, 211.

[3] April 10, 1862, Pub. Laws, C.S.A., 1st Cong., 1st Sess.

when not donated.[1] An offer was made to advance fifty per cent of the amount necessary to set up machinery for the manufacture of small arms.[2] Old Spanish flint-lock muskets were brought in from Cuba through the blockade, altered, and placed in the hands of the troops.[3]

In 1862 a small-arms factory was established at Tallassee which employed 150 men and turned out about 150 carbines a week. At the end of 1864 it had produced only 6000.[4] At Montgomery the Alabama Arms Manufacturing Company had the best machinery in the Confederacy for making Enfield rifles. At Selma were the state and Confederate arsenals, a navy-yard, and naval foundry with machinery of English make, of the newest and most complete pattern. It had been brought through the blockade from Europe and set up at Selma because that seemed to be a place safe from invasion and from the raids of the enemy. Here the vessels for the defence of Mobile were built, heavy ordnance was cast, with shot and shell, and plating for men-of-war. The armored ram *Tennessee*, famous in the fight in Mobile Bay, the gunboats *Morgan, Selma*, and *Gaines* were all built at the Selma navy-yard — guns, armor, and everything being manufactured on the spot. When the *Tennessee* surrendered, after a terrible battle, its armor had not been penetrated by a single shot or shell. The best cannon in America were cast at the works in Selma. The naval foundry employed 3000 men, the other works as many more. Half the cannon and two-thirds of the fixed ammunition used during the last two years of the war were made at these foundries and factories. The foundry destroyed by Wilson was pronounced by experts to be the best in existence. It could turn out at short notice a fifteen-inch Brooks or a mountain howitzer. Swords, rifles, muskets, pistols, caps, were manufactured in great quantities. There were more than a hundred buildings, which covered fifty acres; and after Wilson's destructive work, Truman, the war correspondent, said that they presented the greatest mass of ruins he had ever seen.[5]

[1] April 16, 1862, Pub. Laws, C.S.A., 1st Cong., 1st Sess.; Governor's Proclamation, March 1, 1862.

[2] April 17, 1862, Pub. Laws, C.S.A., 1st Cong., 1st Sess.

[3] O. R., Ser. I, Vol. III, pp. 870, 875.

[4] O. R., Ser. IV, Vol. III, pp. 986, 987; Davis, Vol. I, p. 480; "Southern Hist. Soc. Papers," Vol. II, p. 61.

[5] Miller, "History of Alabama," pp. 180, 181; Davis, Vol. I, pp. 480, 481; Hardy, "History of Selma," pp. 46, 47; *N. Y. Times*, Nov. 2, 1865 (Truman); O. R.,

There was a navy-yard on the Tombigbee, in Clarke County, near the Sunflower Bend. Several small vessels had been completed and several war vessels, probably gunboats, were in process of construction here when the war ended; both vessels and machinery were destroyed by order of the Confederate authorities.[1]

Gunpowder was scarce throughout the war, and nitre or saltpetre, its principal ingredient, was not to be purchased from abroad. A powder mill was established at Cahaba,[2] but the ingredients were lacking. Charcoal for gunpowder was made from willow, dogwood, and similar woods. The nitre on hand was soon exhausted, and it was sought for in the caves of the limestone region of Alabama and Tennessee. In north Alabama there were many of these large caves. The earth in them was dug up and put in hoppers and water poured over it to leach out the nitre. The lye was caught (just as for making soft soap from lye ashes), boiled down, and then dried in the sunshine.[3] The earth in cellars and under old houses was scraped up and leached for the nitre in it. In 1862 a corps of officers under the title of the Nitre and Mining Bureau [4] was organized by the War Department to work the nitre caves of north Alabama which lay in the doubtful region between the Union and the Confederate lines, and which were often raided by the enemy. The men were subjected to military discipline and were under the absolute command of the superintendent, who often called them out to repulse Federal raiders. As much as possible in this department, as in the others, exempts and negroes were used for laborers. For clerical work those disabled for active service were appointed, and instructions were

Ser. IV, Vol. III, pp. 986, 987. The arsenal was commanded by Col. J. L. White; the naval foundries and the rolling mills were under the direction of Capt. Catesby ap Roger Jones, the designer of the *Virginia;* Commodore Ebenezer Farrand superintended the construction of war vessels at the Selma navy-yard. Captain Jones cast the heavy ordnance for the forts at Mobile, Charleston, and Wilmington. Five gunboats were built at Selma in 1863 and two or three others in 1864–1865. The ram *Tennessee,* built in 1863–1864, was constructed like the *Virginia,* but was an improvement except for the weak engines. When the keel of the *Tennessee* was laid, in the fall of 1863, some of the timbers to be used in her were still standing in the forest, and the iron for her plates was ore in the mines. Scharf, "Confederate Navy," pp. 50, 534, 550, 555; "Northern Alabama Illustrated," p. 654; Maclay, "History of United States Navy," Vol. II, pp. 446, 447; Wilson, "Ironclads in Action," Vol. I, p. 116.

[1] Ball, "Clarke County," p. 765.   [2] O. R., Ser. IV, Vol. II, pp. 29, 102.
[3] Miller, pp. 201, 230; Davis, Vol. I, p. 473; Porcher, p. 378.
[4] April 11, 1862, Pub. Laws, C. S. A., 1st Cong., 1st Sess.

issued that employment should be given to needy refugee women.[1] These important nitre works were repeatedly destroyed by the Federals, who killed or captured many of the employees.[2] In the district of upper Alabama, under the command of Captain William Gabbitt, whose headquarters were at Blue Mountain (now Anniston), most of the work was done in the limestone caves of the mountain region.[3] Several hundred men — whites and negroes — were employed in extracting the nitre from the cave earth. To the end of September, 1864, this district had produced 222,665 pounds of nitre at a cost of $237,977.17, war prices.[4]

The supply from the caves proved insufficient, and artificial nitre beds or nitraries were prepared in the cities of south and central Alabama. It was necessary to have them near large towns, in order to obtain a plentiful supply of animal matter and potash, and the necessary labor. Efforts were also made to induce planters in marl or limestone counties to work plantation earth.[5] Under the supervision of Professor W. H. C. Price, nitraries were established at Selma, Mobile, Talladega, Tuscaloosa, and Montgomery. Negro labor was used almost entirely, each negro having charge of one small nitre bed. To October, 1864, the nitraries of south Alabama produced 34,716 pounds at a cost of $26,171.14, which was somewhat cheaper than the nitre from the caves. From these nitraries better results were obtained than from the French, Swedish, and Russian nitraries which served as models. The Confederate nitre beds were from sixteen to twenty-seven months old in October, 1864, and hence not at their best producing stage. Yet, allowing for the difference in age, they gave better results, as they produced from 2.57 to 3.3 ounces of nitre per cubic foot, while the average European nitraries at four years of age gave 4 ounces per cubic foot. Earth from under old houses and from cellars produced from 2 to 4 ounces to the cubic foot. Nitre caves produced from 6 to 12 ounces per cubic foot. Most of the nitre thus obtained was made into powder at the mills in Selma. There were some private manufacturers of nitre, and to encourage

[1] O. R., Ser. IV, Vol. III, pp. 195, 697.
[2] O. R., Ser. IV, Vol. III, p. 695.
[3] One of the most valuable of these caves was the "Santa Cave." See O. R., Ser. IV, Vol. II, pp. 29, 102.
[4] O. R., Ser. IV, Vol. III, pp. 695, 698.
[5] O. R., Ser. IV, Vol. II, pp. 29, 102.

these the Confederate Congress authorized the advance to makers of fifty per cent of the cost of the necessary machinery.[1]

The state legislature appropriated $30,000 to encourage the manufacture and preparation of powder, saltpetre (nitre), sulphur, and lead. Little of the last article was found in Alabama.[2] Some of the powder works were in operation as early as 1861, and in that year the War Department gave Dr. Ullman of Tallapoosa a contract to supply 1000 to 1500 pounds of sulphur a day.[3]

The Confederate Nitre and Mining Bureau had charge of the production of iron in Alabama for the use of the Confederacy. The mines were principally in the hilly region south of the Tennessee River, where several furnaces and iron works were already established before the war. Two or three new companies, with capital of $1,000,000 each, had bought mineral lands and had commenced operations when the war broke out. The Confederate government bought the property or gave the companies financial assistance. The iron district was often raided by the Federals, who blew up the furnaces and wrecked the iron works.[4] The Irondale works, near Elyton, were begun in 1862, and made much iron, but they also were destroyed in 1864 by the Federals.[5] Other large iron furnaces, with their forges, foundries, and rolling-mills, were destroyed by Rousseau's raid in 1864. The government employed several hundred conscripts and several thousand negroes in the mines and rolling-mills. It also offered fifty per cent of the cost of equipment to encourage the opening of new mines by private owners.[6] There is record of only about 15,000 tons of Alabama iron being mined by the Confederacy, but probably there was much more.[7] The iron was sent to Selma, Montgomery, and other places for manufacture. The ordnance cast in

---

[1] In 1861 the War Department gave Leonard and Riddle of Montgomery an order for 60,000 pounds of nitre, and a company near Larkinsville in north Alabama was making 700 pounds a day, which it sold to the government at 22 to 35 cents a pound. O. R., Ser. IV, Vol. I, p. 556.

[2] April 17, 1862. Pub. Laws, C.S.A., 1st Cong., 1st Sess.; Acts of Ala., Dec. 7, 1861, and Dec. 2, 1862; O. R., Ser. IV, Vol. III, pp. 195, 698, 702, 987; Davis, Vol. I, pp. 316, 473, 477; Miller, pp. 201, 230; Schwab, "Confederate States," p. 270; Annual Cyclopædia (1862) Le Conte's "Autobiography," p. 184.

[3] O. R., Ser. IV, Vol. I, p. 556.

[4] Somers, "Southern States," p. 162.   [5] Somers, p. 175.

[6] April 9, 1862, Pub. Laws, C.S.A., 1st Cong., 1st Sess.

[7] O. R., Ser. IV, Vol. III, pp. 695, 700, 702, 990.

Selma was of Alabama iron; and after the war, when the United States sold the ruins of the arsenal, the big guns were cut up and sent to Philadelphia. Here the fine quality of the iron attracted the attention of experts and led to the development by northern capital of the iron industry in north Alabama.

The Confederate government encouraged the building and extension of railroads, and paid large sums to them for the transportation of troops, munitions of war, and military supplies.[1] Several lines of road within the state were made military roads, and the government extended their lines, built bridges and cars, and kept the lines in repair.[2] In 1862 $150,000 was advanced to the Alabama and Mississippi Railway Company, to complete the line between Selma and Meridian,[3] and the duty on iron needed for the road was remitted.[4] On June 25 of this year this road was seized by the military authorities in order to finish it,[5] and because of the lack of iron D. H. Kenny was directed (July 21, 1863) to impress the iron and rolling stock belonging to the Alabama and Florida Railway, the Gainesville Branch of

[1] Freight rates in Alabama were as follows in December, 1862: —

1. Ammunition	. . . .	$0.60 per 100 lbs., per 100 miles.
2. (Second class)	. . . .	0.30 per 100 lbs., per 100 miles.
3. Live stock	. . . .	30.00 per car, per 100 miles.
4. Hay, fodder, wagons, ambulances, etc.	. .	20.00 per car, per 100 miles.

Troops were to be carried for 2½ to 3½ cents a mile per man. O. R., Ser. IV, Vol. II, p. 276.

[2] Charles T. Pollard, president of the Montgomery and West Point R.R., who ran his road under direction of the government, reported, April 4, 1862, that he had placed the whole line between Montgomery and Selma under contract, and that it would be completed within the year if iron could be obtained. He thought the road between Selma and Meridian ought to be completed at once. O. R., Ser. IV, Vol. I, pp. 10, 48. On Sept. 14, 1864, it was reported that the grading was finished on the road between Montgomery and Union Springs, but that no iron could be obtained. O. R., Ser. IV, Vol. III, p. 576.

[3] O. R., Ser. IV, Vol. I, p. 941 ; Pub. Laws, C.S.A., Feb. 15, 1862.

[4] On April 4, 1862, the Secretary of War wrote to A. S. Gaines that the road from Selma to Demopolis had been completed ; from Demopolis to Reagan, a distance of 24 miles, a part of the grading had been done ; while the road from Reagan to Meridian, a distance of 27 miles, had been graded, bridged, and some iron had been laid. O. R., Ser. IV, Vol. I, pp. 1048–1049, 1061. Gaines stated, April 24, 1852, that on the Mississippi end of the road the road was completed to within 8 miles of Demopolis, Ala., and was being built at the rate of 3 miles a week. Connection was made by boat to Gainesville, within 2 miles of which a spur of the Mobile and Ohio, 21 miles long, had been completed. O. R., Ser. IV, Vol. I, p. 1089.

[5] O. R., Ser. IV, Vol. I, p. 1171.

the Mobile and Ohio, the Cahaba, Marion, and Greensborough Railroad, and the Uniontown and Newberne Railroad. The Alabama and Mississippi road was a very important line, since it tapped the supply districts of Mississippi and the Black Belt of Alabama. There were many difficulties in the way of the builders. In 1862 the locomotives were wearing out and no iron was to be obtained. In the fall of the same year the planters withdrew their negroes who were working on the road, and left the bridges half finished. But finally, in December, 1862, the road was completed.[1] In the fall of 1862 a road between Blue Mountain, Alabama, and Rome, Georgia, was planned, and $1,122,480.92 was appropriated by the Confederate Congress, a mortgage being taken as security.[2] This road was graded and some bridges built and iron laid, but was not in running order before the end of the war.

Telegraph lines, which had been few before the war, were now placed along each railroad, and several cross-country lines were put up. The first important new line was along the Mobile and Ohio Railroad, from Mobile to Meridian.[3]

Private Manufacturing Enterprises

Both the state and the Confederate government encouraged manufactures by favorable legislation. The Confederate government was always ready to advance half of the cost of the machinery and to take goods in payment. A law of Alabama in 1861 secured the rights of inventors and authors. All patents under the United States laws prior to January 11, 1861, were to hold good under the state laws, and the United States patent and copyright laws were adopted for Alabama.[4] Later, jurisdiction over patents, inventions, and copyrights was transferred to the Confederate government. A bonus of five and ten cents apiece on all cotton and wool cards made in Alabama was offered by the legislature in December, 1861.[5] All employees in iron mills, in foundries, and in factories supplying the state

[1] O. R., Ser. IV, Vol. I, pp. 1089, 1145; Vol. II, pp. 106, 148, 149, 655.

[2] O. R., Ser. IV, Vol. II, pp. 144–145; Vol. III, p. 312; Stats.-at-Large, Prov. Cong., C.S.A., Feb. 15, 1862; Pub. Laws, C.S.A., 1st Cong., 1st Sess., April 7 and Oct. 2, 1862.

[3] O. R., Ser. IV, Vol. I, p. 783.

[4] Acts, Feb. 8, 1861.   [5] Acts, 2d Called and 1st Regular Sess., p. 70.

or Confederate governments with arms, clothing, cloth, and the like were declared by the state exempt from military duty.

Factories were soon in operation all over the state, especially in central Alabama.   In all places where there were government factories there also were found factories conducted by private individuals. In 1861 there were factories at Tallassee, Autaugaville, and Prattville, with 23,000 spindles and 800 employees, which could make 5000 yards of good tent cloth a day.[1] And other cotton mills were established in north Alabama as early as 1861.[2] The Federals burned these buildings and destroyed the machinery in 1862 and 1863.   There was the most "unsparing hostility displayed by the northern armies to this branch of industry.   They destroyed instantly every cotton factory within their reach."[3]

At Tuscaloosa were cotton and shoe factories, tanneries, and an iron foundry.   A large cotton factory was established in Bibb County, and at Gainesville there were workshops and machine-shops.   In addition to the government works, Selma had machine-shops, car shops, iron mills, and foundries, cotton, wool, and harness factories, conducted by private individuals.   There were cotton and woollen factories at Prattville and Autaugaville, and at Montgomery were car shops, harness shops, iron mills, foundries, and machine-shops. The best tent cloth and uniform cloth was made at the factories of Tallassee.   The state itself began the manufacture of shoes, salt, clothing, whiskey, alcohol, army supplies, and supplies for the destitute.[4] Extensive manufacturing establishments of various kinds in Madison, Lauderdale, Tuscumbia, Bibb, Autauga, Coosa, and Tallapoosa counties were destroyed during the war by the Federals. There were iron works in Bibb, Shelby, Calhoun, and Jefferson counties, and in 1864 there were a dozen large furnaces with rolling-mills and foundries in the state.[5] However, in that year the governor complained that though Alabama had immense quantities of iron ore, even the planters in the iron country were unable to get sufficient

[1] Governor Moore to Sec. L. P. Walker, July 2, 1861, O. R., Ser. IV, Vol. I, p. 493; Somers, p. 136.

[2] Schwab, "Confederate States," p. 271.   [3] Somers, p. 136.

[4] Acts, Dec. 13, 1864, Acts of Ala., 2d Called and 1st Regular Sess. *passim*.

[5] Le Conte states that in 1863 he found the only Bessemer furnace in the Confederacy at Shelbyville; it was the first that he had ever seen. "Autobiography," pp. 184–185. It was probably the first in America.

iron to make and mend agricultural implements, since all iron that
was mined was used for purposes of the Confederacy.[1] The best and
strongest cast iron used by the Confederacy was made at Selma and
at Briarfield. The cotton factories and tanneries in the Tennessee
valley were destroyed in 1862 by the Federal troops.[2]

Salt Making

Salt was one of the first necessaries of life which became scarce
on account of the blockade. The Adjutant and Inspector-General
of Alabama stated, March 20, 1862, that the Confederacy needed
6,000,000 bushels of salt, and that only an enormous price would
force the people to make it.   In Montgomery salt was then very scarce,
bringing $20 per sack, and speculators were using every trick and
fraud in order to control the supply.[3] The poor people especially soon
felt the want of it, and in November, 1861, the legislature passed an
act to encourage the manufacture of salt at the state reservation in
Clarke County.[4] The state government even began to make salt at
these salt springs. At the Upper Works, near Old St. Stephens,
600 men and 120 teams were employed at 30 furnaces, which were
kept going all the time, the production amounting to 600 bushels a
day. These works were in operation from 1862 to 1865. The
Lower Works, near Sunflower Bend on the Tombigbee River, for
four years employed 400 men with 80 teams at 20 furnaces. The
production here was about 400 bushels a day. The Central Works,
near Salt Mountain, were under private management, and, it is said,
were much more successful than the works under state management.[5]
The price of salt at the works ranged from $2.50 to $7 a bushel
in gold, or from $3 to $40 in currency. From 1861 to 1865, 500,000
bushels of good salt were produced each year.

.   [1] O. R., Ser. IV, Vol. III, p. 3.

[2] Miller, pp. 179, 180, 181, 193; Davis, Vol. I, p. 481; *Montgomery Advertiser*,
July 14, 1867; *N. Y. Herald*, May 15, 1865.

[3] O. R., Ser. IV, Vol. I, p. 1010.

[4] This act authorized the governor to lease the salt springs belonging to the state
and to require the lessee to sell salt at 75 cents a bushel at the salt works. The state
paid 10 cents a bushel bounty and advanced $10,000 to the salt maker. Acts, Nov. 11
and Nov. 19, 1861.

[5] One private maker with one furnace and from 15 to 20 hands made 60 bushels a
day. Another, with 15 hands, burning 5 cords of wood, made 36 bushels a day. There
were also many other private salt makers.

To obtain the salt water, wells were bored to depths ranging from 60 to 100 feet, — one well, however, was 600 feet deep, — while in the bottom or swamp lands brine was sometimes found at a depth of 8 feet. The water at first rose to the surface and overflowed about 30 gallons a minute in some wells, but as more wells were sunk the brine ceased to flow out and had to be pumped about 16 feet by steam or horse power. It was boiled in large iron kettles like those then used in syrup making and which are still seen in remote districts in the South. Seven or eight kettles of water would make one kettle of salt. This was about the same percentage that was obtained at the Onondaga (New York) salt springs. About the same boiling was required as in making syrup from sugar-cane juice. The wells were scattered for miles over the country and thousands of men were employed. For three years more than 6000 men, white and black, were employed at the salt works of Clarke County, from 2000 to 3000 working at the Upper Works alone. All were not at work at the furnaces, but hundreds were engaged in cutting and hauling wood for fuel, and in sacking and barrelling salt. It is said that in the woods the blows of no single axe nor the sound of any single falling tree could be distinguished; the sound was simply continuous. Nine or ten square miles of pine timber were cleared for fuel.

The salt was sent down the Tombigbee to Mobile or conveyed in wagons into the interior of Alabama, Mississippi, and Georgia. These wagons were so numerous that for miles from the various works it was difficult to cross the road. The whole place had the appearance of a manufacturing city. These works had been in operation to some extent since 1809. The wells were exhausted from 1865 to 1870, when they began flowing again.

Besides the smaller works and large private works there were hundreds of smaller establishments. When salt was needed on a plantation in the Black Belt, the overseer would take hands, with pots and kettles, and go to the salt wells, camp out for several weeks, and make enough salt for the year's supply. All private makers had to give a certain amount to the state.[1] People from the interior of the state and from southeast Alabama went to the Florida coast and made salt by boiling the sea water. The state had salt works at Saltville, Virginia, but found it difficult to get transportation for

[1] Ball, "Clarke County," pp. 645–649, 765; "Our Women in War," p. 275 et seq.

the product. Salt was given to the poor people by the state, or sold to them at a moderate price. The legislature authorized the governor to take possession of all salt when necessary for public use, paying the owners a just compensation; $150,000 was appropriated for this purpose in 1861, and in 1862 it was made a penal offence to send salt out of the state.[1] A Salt Commission was appointed to look after the salt works owned by the state in Louisiana. A private salt maker in Clarke County made a contract to deliver two-fifths of his product to the state at the cost of manufacture, and the state purchased some salt from the Louisiana saltbeds.[2] As salt became scarcer the people took the brine in old pork and beef barrels and boiled it down. The soil under old smoke-houses was dug up, put in hoppers, and bleached like ashes, and the brine boiled down and dried in the sunshine.[3]

At Bon Secour Bay, near Mobile, there were salt works consisting of fifteen houses, capable of making seventy-five bushels per day from the sea-water. In 1864 these were burned by the Federals, who often destroyed the salt works along the Florida coast.[4] At Saltmarsh, ten miles west of Selma, there were works which furnished much of the salt used in Mississippi, central Alabama, and east Georgia during the years 1862, 1863, and 1864. Wells were dug to the depth of twelve or fifteen feet, when salt water was struck. The wells were then curbed, furnaces of lime rock were built, and upon them large kettles were placed. The water was pumped from the wells and run into the kettles through troughs, then boiled down, and the moisture evaporated by the sun. The fires were kept up day and night. A large number of blacks and whites were employed at these wells, and, as salt makers were exempt from military duty, the work was quite popular.[5]

Besides the industries above mentioned there were many minor enterprises. Household manufactures were universal. The more

[1] Acts, Nov. 9, 1861, and Dec. 9, 1862.

[2] Acts, Dec. 9, 1862, Oct. 11, 1864, and Dec. 13, 1864.

[3] Miller, "Alabama," pp. 156, 167, 230; Hague, "Blockaded Family"; "Our Women in War," pp. 267, 268.

[4] N. Y. Herald, Sept. 20, 1864 ; Miller, p. 167.

[5] American Cyclopædia (1864), p. 10 ; N. Y. Times, April 15, 1864. To show the character of the white laborers employed in the salt works: in reconstruction days, a prominent negro politician told how, when a slave, he had to keep accounts, and read and write letters for the whites at the salt works, who were very ignorant people.

important companies were chartered by the legislature. The acts of the war period show that in 1861 there were incorporated six insurance companies and the charters of others were amended to suit the changed conditions; three railroad companies were incorporated, and aid was granted to others for building purposes. Roads carrying troops and munitions free were exempted from taxation. Two mining and manufacturing companies were incorporated, four iron and coal companies, one ore foundry, an express company,[1] a salt manufacturing company, a chemical manufacturing company, a coal and leather company, and a wine and fruit company. In 1862 the legislature incorporated four iron and foundry companies, a railroad company, the Southern Express Company, a gas-light company, six coal and iron companies, a rolling-mill, and an oil company, and amended the charters of four railroad companies and two insurance companies. In 1864 two railroad companies were given permission to manufacture alcohol and lubricating oil, and the Citronelle Wine, Fruit, and Nursery Company was incorporated. Various other manufacturing companies — of drugs, barrels, and pottery — were established.

Besides salt the state made alcohol and whiskey for the poor. Every man who had a more than usual regard for his comfort and wanted to keep out of the army had a tannery in his back yard, and made a few shoes or some harness for the Confederacy, thus securing exemption.

Governor Moore, in his message to the legislature on October 28, 1861, said: "Mechanical arts and industrial pursuits, hitherto practically unknown to our people, are already in operation. The clink of the hammer and the busy hum of the workshop are beginning to be heard throughout our land. Our manufactories are rapidly increasing and the inconvenience which would result from the continuance of the war and the closing of our ports for years would be more than compensated by forcing us to the development of our abundant resources, and the tone and the temper it would give to our national character. Under such circumstances the return of peace would find us a self-reliant and truly independent people."[2]

[1] Later the Southern Express Company, which is still in existence. It was the southern division of the Adams Express Company.

[2] O. R., Ser. IV, Vol. I, p. 711.

M

And had the war ended early in 1864, the state would have been well provided with manufactures.

The raids through the state in 1864 and 1865 destroyed most of the manufacturing establishments. The rest, whether owned by the government or private persons, were seized by the Federal troops at the surrender and were dismantled.[1]

Sec. 2. Confederate Finance in Alabama

Banks and Banking

In a circular letter dated December 4, 1860, and addressed to the banks, Governor Moore announced that should the state secede from the Union, as seemed probable, $1,000,000 in specie, or its equivalent, would be needed by the administration. The state bonds could not be sold in the North nor in Europe, except at a ruinous discount, and a tax on the people at this time would be inexpedient. Therefore he recommended that the banks hold their specie. Otherwise there would be a run on the banks, and should an extra session of the legislature be called to authorize the banks to suspend specie payments, such action would produce a run and thus defeat the object. He requested the banks to suspend specie payments, trusting to the convention to legalize this action.[2] The governor then issued an address to the people stating his reasons for such a step. It was done, he said, at the request and by the advice of many citizens whose opinions were entitled to respect and consideration. Such a course, they thought, would relieve the banks from a run during the cotton season, would enable them to aid the state, would do away with the expense of a special session of the legislature, would prevent the sale of state bonds at a great sacrifice, and would prevent extra taxation of the people in time of financial crisis.[3]

Three banks — the Central, Eastern, and Commercial — suspended at the governor's request and made a loan to the state of $200,000 in coin. Their suspension was legalized later by an ordi-

---

[1] Miller, pp. 179, 180, 181, 193; Davis, Vol. II, p. 481; *Montgomery Advertiser*, July 14, 1867; *N. Y. Herald*, May 15, 1865; Acts of the General Assembly of Alabama, 1861-1864, *passim*. The Freedman's Bureau was largely supported by sales of the remnants of iron works, etc.

[2] Smith, " Debates," pp. 38, 39.   [3] Smith, " Debates," pp. 37, 39.

nance of the convention. The Bank of Mobile, the Northern Bank, and the Southern Bank refused to suspend, though they announced that the state should have their full support. The legislature passed an act in February, 1861, authorizing the suspension on condition that the banks subscribe for ten year state bonds at their par value. The bonds were to stand as capital, and the bills issued by the banks upon these bonds were to be receivable in payment of taxes. The amount which each bank was to pay into the treasury for the bonds was fixed, and no interest was to be paid by the state on these bonds until specie payments were resumed. All the banks suspended under these acts, and thus the government secured most of the coin in the state.[1] In October, 1861, before all the banks had suspended, state bonds at par to the amount of $975,066.68 had been sold — all but $28,500 to the banks. By early acts specie payments were to be resumed in May, 1862, but in December, 1861, the suspension was continued until one year after the conclusion of peace with the United States. By this law the banks were to receive at par the Confederate treasury notes in payment of debts, their notes being good for public dues. The banks were further required to make a loan to the state of $200,000 to pay its quota of the Confederate war tax of August 16, 1861. So the privilege of suspension was worth paying for.[2]

The banking law was revised by the convention so that a bank might deposit with the state comptroller stocks of the Confederate States or of Alabama, receiving in return notes countersigned by the comptroller amounting to twice the market value of the bonds deposited. If a bank had in deposit with the comptroller under the old law any stocks of the United States, they could be withdrawn upon the deposit of an equal amount of Confederate stocks or bonds of the state. The same ordinance provided that none except citizens of Alabama and members of state corporations might engage in the banking business under this law. But no rights under the old law

[1] In his message of Oct. 25, 1861, Governor Shorter made a report showing that the finances of the state for 1861 were in good condition, and advised against levying a tax on the people to pay the state's quota of the Confederate tax. He stated that the banks had done good service to the state; that, though in time of peace they were a necessary evil, now they were a public necessity; that all the money used to date by the state in carrying on the war had come from the banks. O. R., Ser. IV, Vol. I, pp. 697-700.

[2] O. R., Ser. IV, Vol. I, pp. 697-699; Acts of Gen. Assembly, Feb. 2, Nov. 27 and 30, and Dec. 7 and 9, 1861; Patton's Message, Jan. 16, 1866.

were to be affected. It was further provided that subsequent legislation might require any "free" bank to reduce its circulation to an amount not exceeding the market value of the bonds deposited with the comptroller. The notes thus retired were to be cancelled by the comptroller.[1] The suspension of specie payments was followed by an increase of banking business; note issues were enlarged; eleven new banks were chartered,[2] and none wound up affairs. They paid dividends regularly of from 6 to 10 per cent in coin, in Confederate notes, or in both. Speculation in government funds was quite profitable to the banks.

Issues of Bonds and Notes

The convention authorized the general assembly of the state to issue bonds to such amounts and in such sums as seemed best, thus giving the assembly practically unlimited discretion. But it was provided that money must not be borrowed except for purposes of military defence, unless by a two-thirds vote of the members elected to each house; and the faith and credit of the state was pledged for the punctual payment of the principal and interest.[3]

The legislature hastened to avail itself of this permission. In 1861 a bond issue of $2,000,000 for defence, and not liable to taxation, was authorized at one time; at another, $385,000 for defence, besides an issue of $1,000,000 in treasury notes receivable for taxes. Of the first issue authorized, only $1,759,500 were ever issued. Opposition to taxation caused the state to take up the war tax of $2,000,000 (August 19, 1861), and for this purpose $1,700,000 in bonds was issued, the banks supplying the remainder. There was a relaxation in taxation during the war; paper money was easily printed, and the people were opposed to heavy taxes.[4]

In 1862 bonds to the amount of $2,000,000 were issued for the benefit of the indigent. The governor was given unlimited authority to issue bonds and notes, receivable for taxes, to "repair the treasury," and $2,085,000 in bonds were issued under this permit. These bonds

---

[1] Ordinance No. 33, amending sections 1373, 1375, 1393, of the Code, March 16, 1861.

[2] In 1861 two banks were chartered, two in 1862, five in 1863, and two in 1864. Several of these were savings-banks.

[3] Ordinance No. 18, Jan. 19, 1861 ; Nos. 35 and 36, March 18, 1861.

[4] Schwab, p. 302 ; Davis, Vol. I, p. 495 ; Journal of the Convention of 1865, p. 61 ; Acts of Ala , Jan. 29, Feb. 6 and 8, Dec. 10, 1861 ; Stats.-at-Large, Prov. Cong., C. S. A., Feb. 8, 1861 ; Miller, " Alabama," pp. 152, 157.

drew interest at 6 per cent, ran for twenty years, and sold at a premium of from 50 per cent to 100 per cent.   Bonds were used both for
civil and for military purposes, but chiefly for the support of the
destitute.   Treasury notes to the amount of $3,500,000 were issued,
drawing interest at 5 per cent, and receivable for taxes.   The Confederate Congress came to the aid of Alabama with a grant of $1,200,000
for the defence of Mobile.[1]   In 1863 notes and bonds for $4,000,000
were issued for the benefit of indigent families of soldiers, and $1,500,-
000 for defence; $90,000 in bonds was paid for the steamer *Florida*,
which was later turned over to the Confederate government.[2]   In
1864 $7,000,000 was appropriated for the support of indigent fami-
lies of soldiers, and an unlimited issue of bonds and notes was authorized.[3]   In 1862 the Alabama legislature proposed that each state
should guarantee the debt of the Confederate States in proportion
to its representation in Congress.   This measure was opposed by
the other states and failed.[4]   A year later a resolution of the legislature declared that the people of Alabama would cheerfully submit to
any tax, not too oppressive in amount or unequal in operation, laid
by the Confederate government for the purpose of reducing the volume
of currency and appreciating its value.   The assembly also signified
its disapproval of the scheme put forth at the bankers' meeting at
Augusta, Georgia — to issue Confederate bonds with interest payable
in coin and to levy a heavy tax of $60,000,000 to be paid in coin or
in coupons of the proposed new issue.[5]

The Alabama treasury had many Confederate notes received for
taxes.   Before April 1, 1864 (when such notes were to be taxed one-
third of their face value), these could be exchanged at par for twenty-
year, 6 per cent Confederate bonds.   After that date the Confederate
notes were fundable at 33⅓ per cent of their face value only.[6]   After
June 14, 1864, the state treasury could exchange Confederate notes
for 4 per cent non-taxable Confederate bonds, or one-half for 6 per
cent bonds and one-half for new notes.   The Alabama legislature

[1] Journal of the Convention, 1865, p. 61 ; Acts of Ala., Nov. 8, Dec. 4, 8, and 9,
1862 ; Miller, p. 168.
[2] Jour. of the Convention of 1865, p. 61 ; Acts of Ala., Aug. 29, Dec. 8, 1863 ;
Miller, pp. 186, 189.
[3] Miller, p. 215 ; Acts of Ala., Oct. 7 and Dec. 13, 1864.
[4] Resolutions of Gen. Assembly, Dec. 1, 1862 ; Schwab, p. 50.
[5] Resolutions, Dec. 8, 1863.   [6] Confederate Funding Act, Feb. 17, 1864.

of 1864 arranged for funding the notes according to the latter method.[1] The Alabama legislature of 1861 had made it lawful for debts contracted after that year to be payable in Confederate notes.[2] Later a meeting of the citizens of Mobile proposed to ostracize those who refused to accept Confederate notes. Cheap money caused a clamor for more, and the heads of the people were filled with *fiat* money notions. The rise in prices stimulated more issues of notes. On February 9, 1861, $1,000,000 in state treasury notes was issued, and in 1862 there was a similar issue of $2,000,000 more. These state notes were at a premium in Confederate notes, which were discredited by the Confederate Funding Act of February 17, 1864. Confederate notes were eagerly offered for state notes, but the state stopped the exchange.[3] December 13, 1864, a law was passed providing for an unlimited issue of state notes redeemable in Confederate notes and receivable for taxes.

Private individuals often issued notes on their own account, and an enormous number was put into circulation. The legislature, by a law of December 9, 1862, prohibited the issue of "shinplaster" or other private money under penalty of $20 to $500 fine, and any person circulating such money was to be deemed the maker. It was not successful, however, in reducing the flood of private tokens; the credit of individuals was better than the credit of the government.

Executors, administrators, guardians, and trustees were authorized to make loans to the Confederacy and to purchase and receive for debts due them bonds and treasury notes of the Confederacy and of Alabama and the interest coupons of the same. One-tenth of the Confederate $15,000,000 loan of February 28, 1861, was subscribed in Alabama.[4] In December, 1863, the legislature laid a tax of 37½ per cent on bonds of the state and of the Confederacy unless the bonds had been bought directly from the Confederate government or from the state.[5] This was to punish speculators. After October 7, 1864, the state treasury was directed to refuse Con-

---

[1] Acts of Ala., Oct. 7, 1864; Schwab, pp. 73, 74.   [2] Acts of Ala., Dec. 10, 1861.

[3] Acts of Ala., *passim*. Notes of the state and of state banks were hoarded, while Confederate notes were distrusted. Pollard, "Lost Cause," p. 421.

[4] Acts of Ala., Nov. 9, 1861; Schwab, p. 8. It was considered a matter of patriotism to invest funds in Confederate securities. Not many other investments offered; there was little trade in negroes. Pollard, "Lost Cause," p. 424.

[5] Acts of Ala., Dec. 8, 1863.

federate notes issued before February 17, 1864 (the date of the Funding Act) in payment of taxes except at a discount of 33⅓ per cent. Later, Confederate notes were taken for taxes at their full market value.[1]

Gold was shipped through the blockade at Mobile to pay the interest on the state bonded debt held in London. It has been charged that this money was borrowed from the Central, Commercial, and Eastern banks and was never repaid, recovery being denied on the ground that the state could not be sued.[2] But the banks received state and Confederate bonds under the new banking law in return for their coin. The exchange was willingly made, for otherwise the banks would have had to continue specie payments or forfeit their charters. And to continue specie payments meant immediate bankruptcy.[3] After the war, the state was forbidden to pay any debt incurred in aid of the war, nor could the bonds issued in aid of the war be redeemed. The banks suffered just as all others suffered, and it is difficult to see why the state should make good the losses of the banks in Confederate bonds and not make good the losses of private individuals. To do either would be contrary to the Fourteenth Amendment.

The last statement of the condition of the Alabama treasury was as follows: —

Balance in treasury, September 30, 1864	$3,713,959
Receipts, September 30, 1864, to May 24, 1865 . . .	3,776,188
Total	$7,490,147
Disbursements, September 30, 1864, to May 24, 1865 . .	6,698,853
Balance in treasury, September 30, 1864, to May 24, 1865	$791,294

The balance was in funds as follows: —

Checks on Bank of Mobile, payable in Confederate notes .	$11,440
Certificate of deposit, Bank of Mobile, payable in Confederate notes	1,330
Confederate and state notes in treasury	517,889
State notes, change bills (legal shinplasters) . . .	250,004
Notes of state banks and branches	358
Bank-notes	424
Silver	337
Gold on hand	497
Gold on deposit in northern banks	35
Balance	$791,294

[1] Acts of Ala., Dec. 13, 1864.

[2] Clark, "Finance and Banking," in the "Memorial Record of Alabama," Vol. I, p. 341. Statement of J. H. Fitts. [3] Patton's Message, Jan. 16, 1866.

To dispose of nearly $7,000,000 in small notes must have kept the treasury very busy during the last seven months of its existence. It is interesting to note that the treasury kept at work until May 24, 1865, six weeks after the surrender of General Lee.

Special Appropriations and Salaries

Besides the regular appropriations for the usual expenses of the government, there were many extraordinary appropriations. These, of course, were for the war expenses which were far greater than the ordinary expenses. The chief item of these extraordinary appropriations was for the support of the indigent families of soldiers, and for this purpose about $11,000,000 was provided. For the military defence of the state several million dollars were appropriated, much of this being spent for arms and clothing for the Alabama troops, both in the Confederate and the state service. Money was granted to the University of Alabama and other military schools on condition that they furnish drill-masters for the state troops without charge. Hospitals were furnished in Virginia and in Alabama for the Alabama soldiers. The gunboat *Florida* was bought for the defence of Mobile, and $150,000 was appropriated for an iron-clad ram for the same purpose. Loans were made to commanders of regiments to buy clothing for their soldiers, and the state began to furnish clothing, $50,000 being appropriated at one time for clothing for the Alabama soldiers in northern prisons. By March 12, 1862, Alabama had contributed $317,600 to the support of the Army of Northern Virginia.[1] Much was expended in the manufacture of salt in Alabama and in Virginia, which was sold at cost or given away to the poor; in the purchase of salt from Louisiana to be sold at a low price, and in bounties paid to salt makers in the state who sold salt at reasonable prices. The state also paid for medical attendance for the indigent families of soldiers. When the records and rolls of the Alabama troops in the Confederate service were lost, money was appropriated to have new ones made. Frequent grants were made to the various benevolent societies of the state whose object was to care for the maimed and sick soldiers, the widows and the orphans. Cotton and wool cards and agricultural implements were purchased and distributed

---

[1] Jones, "Diary," Vol. I, p. 114. North Carolina alone had contributed more — $325,000.

among the poor. Slaves and supplies were taken for the public
service and the owners compensated.

The appropriations for the usual expenses of the government were
light, seldom more than twice the appropriations in times of peace,
notwithstanding the depreciated currency. The salaries of public
officers who received stated amounts ranged from $1500 to $4000 a
year in state money. In 1862 the salaries of the professors in the
State University were doubled on account of the depreciated currency,
the president receiving $5000 and each professor $4000.[1] The
members of the general assembly were more fortunate. In 1864
they received $15 a day for the time in session, and the clerks of the
legislature, who were disabled soldiers or exempt from service, or
were women, were paid the same amount. The salt commissioners
drew salaries of $3000 a year in 1864 and 1865, though this amount
was not sufficient to pay their board for more than six months. Salaries were never increased in proportion to expenses. The compensation, in December, 1864, for capturing a runaway slave was $25,
worth probably 50 cents in coin. For the inaugural expenses of
Governor Watts, $500 in paper was appropriated.[2] Many laws were
passed, regulating and changing the fees and salaries of public officials. In October, 1884, for example, the salaries of the state officials, tax assessors and collectors, and judges were increased 50 per
cent. Besides the general depreciation of the currency, the variations of values in the different sections of the state rendered such
changes necessary. In the central part, which was safe for a long
time from Federal raids, the currency was to the last worth more,
and the prices of the necessaries of life were lower than in the more
exposed regions. This fact was taken into consideration by the
legislature when fixing the fees of the state and county officers in the
various sections of the state.

Taxation

As a result of the policy adopted at the outset of meeting the
extraordinary expenses by bond issues,[3] the people continued to pay

---

[1] Clark, "Education in Alabama," p. 90.   [2] Acts of Ala., Dec. 7, 1863.

[3] The state authorities considered it inexpedient to levy heavier state taxes. The
people had always been opposed to heavy state taxes, but paid county taxes more will-

the light taxes levied before the war, and paid them in paper money. Though falling heavily on the salaried and wage-earning classes, it was never a burden upon the agricultural classes except in the poorest white counties. The poll tax brought in little revenue. Soldiers were exempt from its payment and from taxation on property to the amount of $500. The widows and orphans of soldiers had similar privileges. A special tax of 25 per cent on the former rate was imposed on all taxable property in November, 1861, and a year later, by acts of December 9, 1862, a far-reaching scheme of taxation was introduced. Under this poll taxes were levied as follows: —

White men, 21 to 60 years	$0.75
Free negro men, 21 to 50 years	5.00
Free negro women, 21 to 45 years	3.00
Slaves (children to laborers in prime)	0.50 to 2.00
More valuable slaves	2.00 and up

And other taxes as follows: —

Crop liens	33⅓ %
Hoarded money	1 %
Jewellery, plate, furniture	½ %
Goods sold at auction	10 %
Imports	2 %
Insurance premiums (companies not chartered by state)	2 %
Playing cards, per pack	$1.00
Gold watches, each	1.00
Gold chains, silver watches, clocks	0.50
Articles raffled off	10 %
Legacies, profits and sales, incomes	5 %
Profits of Confederate contractors	10 %
Wages of Confederate officials	10 %
Race tracks	10 %
Billiard tables, each	$150.00
Bagatelle	20.00
Tenpin alleys, each	40.00
Readings and lectures, each	4.00
Pedler	100.00
Spirit rapper, per day	500.00
Saloon-keeper	$40.00 to 150.00
Daguerreotypist	10.00 to 100.00
Slave trader, for each slave offered for sale	20.00

ingly. So the gift of $500,000 to the Confederate government in 1861 and the $2,000,000 war tax of the same year were assumed by the state, and bonds were issued. Stats.-at-Large, Prov. Cong., C.S.A., Feb. 8, 1861; Acts of Ala., Nov. 27, 1861.

In 1863 a tax of 37½ per cent was laid on Confederate and state bonds not in the hands of the original purchaser;[1] 7½ per cent was levied on profits of banking, railroad companies, and on evidence of debt; 5 per cent on other profits not included in the act of the year before. The tax on gold and silver was to be paid in gold and silver; on bank-notes, in notes; on bonds, in coupons.[2] In December, 1864, the taxes levied by the laws of 1862 and 1863 were increased by 33½ per cent. Taxes on gold and silver were to be paid in kind or in currency at its market value.[3] This was the last tax levied by the state under Confederate rule. From these taxes the state government was largely supplied.

A number of special laws were passed to enable the county authorities to levy taxes-in-kind or to levy a certain amount in addition to the state tax, for the use of the county. The taxes levied by the state did not bear heavily upon the majority of the people, as nearly all, except the well-to-do and especially the slave owners, were exempt. The constant depreciation of the currency acted, of course, as a tax on the wage-earners and salaried classes and on those whose income was derived from government securities.

While the state taxes were felt chiefly by the wealthier agricultural classes and the slave owners, this was not the case with the Confederate taxes. The loans and gifts from the state, the war tax of August 19, 1861, the $15,000,000 loan, the Produce Loan, and the proceeds of sequestration — all had not availed to secure sufficient supplies. The Produce Loan of 1862 was subscribed to largely in Alabama, the Secretary of the Treasury issuing stocks and bonds in return for supplies,[4] and $1,500,000 of the $15,000,000 loan was raised in the state. Still the Confederate government was in desperate need. The farmers would not willingly sell their produce for currency which was constantly decreasing in value, and, when selling at all, they were forced to charge exorbitant prices because of the high prices charged them for everything by the speculators.[5] The speculator also ran up the prices of supplies beyond the reach of the government purchasing agents who had to buy according to the list of prices issued by impressment commissioners. So in the spring

---

[1] Another measure aimed at the speculator. [2] Acts of Ala., Dec. 8, 1863.
[3] Acts of Ala., Dec. 13, 1864. [4] Pub. Laws, 1st Cong., 1st Sess., April 21, 1862.
[5] Pollard, "Lost Cause," p. 427.

of 1863 all other expedients were cast aside and the Confederate government levied a genuine "Morton's Fork" tax. No more loans of paper money from the state, no more assumption of war taxes by the state governments because the people were opposed to any form of direct taxation, no more holding back of supplies by producers and speculators who refused to sell to the Confederate government except for coin; the new law stopped all that.[1]

First there was a tax of 8 per cent on all agricultural products in hand on July 1, 1863, on salt, wine, and liquors, and 1 per cent on all moneys and credits. Second, an occupation tax ranging from $50 to $200 and from 2½ per cent to 20 per cent of their gross sales was levied on bankers, auctioneers, brokers, druggists, butchers, fakirs, liquor dealers, merchants, pawnbrokers, lawyers, physicians, photographers, brewers, and distillers; hotels paid from $30 to $500, and theatres, $500. Third, there was an income tax of 1 per cent on salaries from $1000 to $1500 and 2 per cent on all over $1500. Fourth, 10 per cent on all trade in flour, bacon, corn, oats, and dry goods during 1863. Fifth, a tax-in-kind, by which each farmer, after reserving 50 bushels of sweet and 50 bushels of Irish potatoes, 20 bushels of peas or beans, 100 bushels of corn or 50 bushels of wheat out of his crop of 1863, had to deliver (at a depot within 8 miles) out of the remainder of his produce for that year, 10 per cent of all wheat, corn, oats, rye, buckwheat, rice, sweet and Irish potatoes, hay, fodder, sugar, molasses, cotton, wool, tobacco, peas, beans, and peanuts; 10 per cent of all meat killed between April 24, 1863, and March 1, 1863.[2]

By this act $9,500,000 in currency was raised in Alabama. Alabama, with Georgia and North Carolina, furnished two-thirds of the tax-in-kind. Though at first there was some objection to the tax-in-kind because it bore entirely on the agricultural classes, yet it was a just tax so far as the large planters were concerned, since the depreciated money had acted as a tax on the wage-earners and salaried classes, who had also some state tax to pay. The tax-in-kind fell heavily upon the families of small farmers in the white counties, who had no negro labor and who produced no more than the barest necessaries of life. To collect the tax-in-kind required an army of

[1] Pub. Laws, C.S.A., 1st Cong., 3d Sess., April 24, 1863.
[2] See also Curry, "Confederate States," p. 110.

tithe gatherers and afforded fine opportunities of escape from military service. The state was divided into districts for the collection of all Confederate taxes, with a state collector at the head. The collection districts were usually counties, following the state division into taxing districts. In 1864 the tobacco tithe was collected by treasury agents and not by the quartermaster's department, which had formerly collected it.[1] The tax of April 24, 1863, was renewed on February 17, 1864, and some additional taxes laid as follows: —

Real estate and personal property	5 %
Gold and silver ware, jewellery	10 %
Coin	5 %
Credits	5 %
Profits on liquors, produce, groceries, and dry goods	10 %

On June 10, 1864, an additional tax of 20 per cent of the tax for 1864 was laid, payable only in Confederate treasury notes of the new issue. Four days later an additional tax[2] was levied as follows: —

Real estate and personal property and coin	5 %
Gold and silver ware	10 %
Profits on liquors, produce, groceries, and dry goods	30 %
Treasury notes of old issue (after January, 1865)	100 %

The taxes during the war, state and Confederate, were in all five to ten times those levied before the war. Never were taxes paid more willingly by most of the people,[3] though at first there was opposition to them. It is probable that the authorities did not, in 1861 and 1862, give sufficient consideration to the fact that conditions were much changed, and that in view of the war the people would willingly have paid taxes that they would have rebelled against in times of peace.

Of the tax-in-kind for 1863, $100,000 was collected in Pickens county alone, one of the poorest counties in the state. The produce was sent in too freely to be taken care of by the government quartermasters, and, as there was enough on hand for a year or two, much of it was ruined for lack of storage room.[4] An English traveller in east Alabama, in 1864, reported that there was abundance. The tax-in-kind was working well, and enough provisions had already been collected for the western armies of the Confederacy to last until

---

[1] Pub. Laws, C.S.A., 1st Cong., 4th Sess., Jan. 30, 1864.
[2] Pub. Laws, C.S.A., 2d Cong., 1st Sess., June 10 and 14, 1864.
[3] Miller, " Alabama," p. 190.   [4] *N. Y. Times*, Feb. 2, 1864.

the harvest of 1865.[1] There were few railroads in the state and the rolling stock on these was scarce and soon worn out. So the supplies gathered by the tax-in-kind law could not be moved. Hundreds of thousands of pounds of beef and bacon and bushels of corn were piled up in the government warehouses and at the depots, while starvation threatened the armies and the people also in districts remote from the railroads or rivers. At the supply centres of Alabama and along the railroads in the Black Belt there were immense stores of provisions. When the war ended, notwithstanding the destruction by raids, great quantities of corn and bacon were seized or destroyed by the Federal troops.[2]

Impressment

The state quite early began to secure supplies by impressment. Salt was probably the first article to which the state laid claim. Later the officials were authorized to impress and pay for supplies necessary for the public service. In 1862 the governor was authorized to impress shoes, leather, and other shoemakers' materials for the use of the army. The legislature appropriated $250,000 to pay for impressments under this law.[3] In case of a refusal to comply with an order of impressment the sheriff was authorized to summon a *posse comitatus* of not less than 20 men and seize double the quantity first impressed. In such cases no compensation was given.[4] The people resisted the impressment of their property. By a law of October 31, 1862, the governor was empowered to impress slaves, and tools and teams for them to work with, in the public service against the enemy, and $1,000,000 was appropriated to pay the owners.[5] Slaves were regularly impressed by the Confederate officials acting in coöperation with the state authorities, for work on fortifications and for other public service. Several thousand were at work at Mobile at various times. They were secured usually by requisition on the state government, which then impressed them. In December, 1864, Alabama was asked for 2500 negroes for the Confederate service.[6] The people

---

[1] Fitzgerald Ross, " Cities and Camps of the Confederate States," pp. 237, 238.

[2] Miller, p. 230.   [3] Acts of Ala., Nov. 19, 1862.

[4] Acts of Ala , Nov. 17, 1862.   [5] Acts of Ala., Oct. 31, 1862.

[6] O. R., Ser. II, Vol. III, p. 933; G. O., 86, A. and I. G. Office, Richmond, Dec. 12, 1864; Miller, pp. 198, 199 ; Beverly, " History of Alabama,"; A. C. Gordon, in *Century Magazine*, Sept., 1888 ; David Dodge, in *Atlantic Monthly*, Aug., 1886.

were morbidly sensitive about their slave property, and there was much discontent at the impressment of slaves, even though they were paid for. As the war drew to a close, the people were less and less willing to have their servants impressed.

In the spring of 1863, the Confederate Congress authorized the impressment of private property for public use.[1] The President and the governor each appointed an agent, and these together fixed the prices to be paid for the property taken.[2] Every two months they published schedules of prices, which were always below the market prices.[3] Evidently impressment had been going on for some time, for, in November, 1862, Judge Dargan, member of Congress from Alabama, wrote to the President that the people from the country were afraid to bring produce to Mobile for fear of seizure by the government. In November, 1863, the Secretary of War issued an order that no supplies should be impressed when held by a person for his own consumption or that of his employees or slaves, or while being carried to market for sale, except in urgent cases and by order of a commanding general. Consequently the land was filled with agents buying a year's supply for railroad companies, individuals, manufactories, and corporations, relief associations, towns, and counties — all these to be protected from impressment. Most speculators always had their goods on the way to market for sale. The great demand caused prices to rise suddenly, and the government, which had to buy by scheduled prices, could not compete with private purchasers; yet it could not legally impress. There was much abuse of the impressment law, especially by unauthorized persons. It was the source of much lawless conduct on the part of many who claimed to be Confederate officials, with authority to impress.[4] The legislature frequently protested against the manner of execution of the law. In 1863 a state law was passed which indicates that the people had been suffering from the depredations of thieves who pre-

[1] Pub. Laws, C.S.A., 1st Cong., 3d Sess., March 26, 1863.
[2] A conference of impressment commissioners met in Augusta, Ga., Oct. 26, 1863. Among those present were Wylie W. Mason, of Tuskegee, Ala., and Robert C. Farris, of Montgomery, Ala. See O. R., Ser. IV, Vol. II, pp. 898–906.
[3] Schwab, p. 202 ; Saunders, " Early Settlers." Schedules were printed in all the newspapers, and many have been reprinted in the Official Records.
[4] Jones, " Diary," Vol. I, p. 194 ; Miller, " Alabama," pp. 198, 199 ; Pollard, " Lost Cause," pp. 487–488.

tended to be Confederate officials in order to get supplies. It was made a penal offence in 1862 and again in 1863, with from one to five years' imprisonment and $500 to $5000 fine, to falsely represent one's self as a Confederate agent, contractor, or official.[1] The merchants of Mobile protested against the impressment of sugar and molasses, as it would cause prices to double, they said.[2] There was much complaint from sufferers who were never paid by the Confederate authorities for the supplies impressed. Quartermasters of an army would sometimes seize the necessary supplies and would leave with the army before settling accounts with the citizens of the community, the latter often being left without any proof of their claim. In north Alabama, especially, where the armies never tarried long at a place, the complaint was greatest. To do away with this abuse resulting from carelessness, the Secretary of War appointed agents in each congressional district to receive proof of claims for forage and supplies impressed.[3] The state wanted a Confederate law passed to authorize receipts for supplies to be given as part of the tax-in-kind.[4] The unequal operation of the impressment system may be seen in the case of Clarke and Monroe counties. In the former, from 16 persons, property amounting to $1700 was impressed. In Monroe, from 37 persons $60,000 worth was taken. The delay in payment was so long that the money was practically worthless when received.[5]

Debts, Stay Laws, Sequestration

In the secession convention the question of indebtedness to northern creditors came up, and Watts of Montgomery proposed confiscation, in case of war, of the property of alien enemies and of debts due northern creditors. The proposal was supported by several members, who declared that the threat of confiscation would do much to promote peace. But the majority of the convention were opposed to any measure looking toward confiscation, and the matter was carried over for the Confederate government to settle.[6]

Stay laws were enacted in Alabama on February 8, 1861, and on

---

[1] Acts of Ala., Nov. 25, 1863.   [2] Jones, "Diary," Vol. I, p. 301.
[3] Pub. Laws, C.S.A., 2d Cong., 1st Sess., June 14, 1864 ; Saunders, "Early Settlers."
[4] Resolutions of Gen. Assembly, Nov. 26, 1864.
[5] Ball, "Clarke County," p. 501.   [6] Smith, "Debates," pp. 174–183.

December 10, 1861. The Confederate Provisional Congress enacted a law (May 21, 1861) that debtors to persons in the North (except in Delaware, Maryland, Missouri, and the District of Columbia) be prohibited from paying their debts during the war.[1] They should pay the amount of the debt into the Confederate treasury and receive a certificate relieving them from their debts, transferring it to the Confederate treasury. A Confederate law of November 17, 1862, provided that when payment of the interest on a debt was proffered in Confederate treasury notes and refused, it should be unlawful for the plaintiff to secure more than $\frac{1}{4}$ of 1 per cent interest. On August 30, 1861, Congress, in retaliation for the confiscation and destruction of the property of Confederate citizens, passed the Sequestration Act, which held all property of alien enemies (except citizens of the border states) as indemnity for such destruction and devastation.[2] Under the Sequestration Act receivers were appointed in each county to take possession of all property belonging to alien enemies. They were empowered to interrogate all lawyers, bank officials, officials of corporations engaged in foreign trade, and all persons and agents engaged for persons engaged in foreign trade, for the purpose of discovering such property. The proceeds were to be held for the indemnity of loyal citizens suffering under the confiscation laws of the United States.[3] Later the property thus seized was sold and the money paid into the Confederate treasury.[4] In the last days of the war (February 15, 1865), the Sequestration Act was extended to include the property of disloyal citizens who had gone within the Federal lines to escape military service, or who had entered the Union service to fight against the Confederacy.[5]

In December, 1861, a law was passed by the legislature which

---

[1] Stats.-at-Large, Prov. Cong., C.S.A.

[2] Stat.-at-Large, Prov. Cong., 2d Sess.; McPherson, "Rebellion," pp. 203, 204. European merchants and capitalists also had a large trade with the South when the war broke out, and thus sustained great losses. They had made large advances to southern planters and merchants, and were also interested in property in the South. Proceeds were remitted to foreign creditors or owners in Confederate or state currency or bonds for there was no other form of remittance. Robertson, "The Confederate Debt and Private Southern Debts" (English pamphlet).

[3] McPherson, "Rebellion," pp. 203, 204; Acts of Prov. Cong., Aug. 30, 1861; Benjamin's "Instructions to Receivers," Sept. 12, 1861.

[4] Stats.-at-Large, Prov. Cong., 3d Sess., Feb. 15, 1862.

[5] McPherson, "Rebellion," p. 613.

N

provided that no suit by or for an alien enemy for debt or money should be prosecuted in any court in Alabama. No execution was to be issued to an alien enemy, and suits already brought could be dismissed on the motion of the defendant.[1] In Alabama much of the time of the Confederate district courts was taken up by sequestration cases. In fact, they did little else. However, but little money was ever turned into the Confederate treasury from this source.[2]

Just as the state sent nearly all its coin through the blockade to pay the interest of its London debt, so the Mobile, Montgomery, or Selma merchant cancelled his indebtedness and sent money, as he was able, during the early years of the war, to his northern and European creditors. Most debts due to northerners were concealed from the government. The stringent laws passed against it were of no avail. As a source of revenue the sequestration of the property of alien enemies hardly paid expenses. After all, however, the northern creditor probably lost nearly all his accounts in the South in the general wreck of property in 1865.

Trade, Barter, Prices

After the outbreak of war, business was soon almost at a standstill. The government monopolized all means of transportation for military purposes. There were few good railroads in the state and few good wagon roads. In one section there would be plenty, while seventy-five or a hundred miles away there would be great suffering from want. Depreciated currency and the impressment laws made the producer wary of going to market at all. He preferred to keep what he had and live upon it, effecting changes in the old way of barter. Cows, hogs, chickens, mules, farm implements, cotton, corn, peas — all were exchanged and reëxchanged for one another. The farmer tended more and more to become independent of the merchant and of money. Consequently the townspeople suffered. Confederate money, at first received at par, soon began to depreciate, though the most patriotic people considered it their duty to accept it at its par value.[3]

[1] Acts of Ala., Dec. 10, 1861.

[2] Two years after the passage of the Sequestration Law its entire proceeds in the Confederacy amounted to less than $2,000,000. Pollard, " Lost Cause," p. 220.

[3] Suspension of specie payments had been made in order to prevent a drain on the banks. The Confederate government took possession of some of the coin, while much

ALABAMA MONEY.

CONFEDERATE POSTAGE
STAMPS.

PRIVATE MONEY. Printed in large sheets on one side only and never used. The other side is a state bill similar to the one above. Paper was scarce, and the state money was printed so that when cut apart the private money was destroyed.

At the end of 1861, Confederate money was worth as much [1] as Federal, but it had depreciated. Often private credit was better than public, and individuals in need of a more stable circulating medium issued notes or promises to pay which in the immediate neighborhood passed current at their face value. Great quantities of this "card money" or shinplasters were issued, and in some communities it almost supplanted the legal money as a more reliable medium of exchange. The Alabama legislature passed severe laws against the practice of issuing "card money," but with little effect.

The effect of depreciation of paper money was the same as a tax so far as the people were concerned. Forced into circulation, it supported the government, but it gradually depreciated and each holder lost a little. Finally, when almost worthless, it was practically repudiated by the state and by the Confederacy, and funding laws were passed, providing for the redemption of old notes at a low rate in new issues. Depreciation of the currency caused extravagance and other more evil results. A person who handled much money felt that he must at once get rid of all that came into his possession in order to avoid loss by depreciation. Consequently there was speculation, reckless spending, and extravagance. Money would be spent for anything offered for sale. If useful things were not to be had, then luxuries would be bought, such as silks, fancy articles, liquors, etc., from blockade-runners. This was especially the case in Selma, Mobile, and Montgomery, and in northern Alabama. Persons formerly of good character frequently drifted into extravagant and dissipated habits, because they tried to spend their money and there were not enough legitimate ways in which to do so.

was used in the contraband and blockade trade. All this contributed to discredit Confederate paper currency. Pollard, "Lost Cause," p. 421. In May, 1862, General Beauregard seized $500,000 in coin from a bank in Jackson, Ala. The coin belonged to a New Orleans bank and had been sent out to prevent confiscation by Butler. Confederate money was almost worthless at Mobile in 1864, while in the interior of the state it still had a fair value.

[1] Confederate paper held up well in 1861 and 1862, though prices were very high. The people were opposed to fixing a depreciated value to Confederate money, but they were forced to do so by speculators. The money was worth more the farther away from Richmond, though comparison with gold should not be made, as gold was scarce, and prices in gold fell. Board, which formerly cost $2 a day, could now be had for fifty cents in gold. Gold was not a standard of value, but an article of commerce with a fictitious value. Pollard, "Lost Cause," p. 425.

Depreciation, speculation, and scarcity caused prices to rise, especially the prices of the necessaries of life. These varied in the different sections of the state. In Mobile, in 1862, prices were as follows: —

Shoes, per pair .	$25.00
Boots, per pair .	40.00
Overcoats, each .	25.00
Hats, each	15.00
Flour, per barrel	$40.00 to 60.00
Corn, per bushel	3.25
Butter, per pound	1.75
Bacon, per pound	10.00
Soap, per pound (cheap)	1.00
Candles, per pound	2.50
Sugar, per pound	$ 0.50 to .75
Coffee, per pound	1.75 to 3.25
Tea, per pound .	10.00 to 20.00
Cotton and wool cards, per pair	2.00
Board per week at the Battle House, in 1862	$3.50 ; in 1863, 8.00 [1]

In May, 1862, at Huntsville, then in the hands of the Federals, some prices were, in Federal currency: —

Green tea (poor quality), per pound	$4.00
Common rough trousers, per pair	13.00
Boots, per pair .	25.00
Shoes, per pair .	$5.00 to 12.00 [2]

In 1863, in south Alabama, in Confederate currency: —

Meat, per pound	$4.00
Lard, per pound	6.00
Salt, per sack at the works	$80.00 to 95.00
Wheat, per bushel	10.00
Corn, per bushel	3.00
A cow (worth $15 in 1860)	127.00 [3]

In March, 1864, prices in Selma were as follows: —

Salt, per bushel .	$30.00
Calico, per yard	10.00
Women's common shoes, per pair	60.00
Men's rough boots, per pair	125.00
Cotton cards (worth $1.75 in Connecticut)	85.00 [4]

[1] Clark, " Finance and Banking Memorial Record," Vol. I, p. 341 ; " Two Months in the Confederate States by an English Merchant," pp. 111, 115; DeBow's Review for 1866.

[2] O. R., Ser. IV, Vol. X, Pt. II, p. 639.

[3] Ball, " Clarke County," pp. 294, 295 ; Miller, p. 230 ; oral accounts.

[4] N. Y. Times, April 5, 1864 (from Mobile papers).

In August, 1864, the prices in Mobile were: —

Flour, per barrel	$250.00 to $300.00
Bacon, per pound	3.00 to 5.00
Cotton thread, per spool	6.00 to 12.00
Calico, per yard	12.50 to 15.00
Common shoes, per pair	150.00 to 175.00
Boots, per pair	250.00 to 300.00
Nails, per pound	4.00
Cotton shirts (each worth 50 to 60 c. in Massachusetts)	50.00 to 60.00 [1]

In November, 1864, Colonel Dabney paid the following prices in Montgomery: —

Bacon, per pound	$3.50
Beef, per pound	$2.00 to 2.50
Potatoes, per bushel	6.00
Wood, per cord	50.00
Board, per day	30.00 [2]

In Russell County and east Alabama the following prices were paid in 1863-1864: —

A calico dress (9 yards)	$108.00
A plain straw hat	100.00
Half a quire of note paper	40.00
Morocco shoes	375.00
Coffee, per pound	$30.00 to 70.00
Corn, per bushel	12.00 to 13.00
Wax candles, each	.10
Wages, per day	30.00
Soldier's pay, per month (which he seldom received)	11.00 [3]

In southwest Alabama, in December, 1864, prices were: —

A mule (worth before the war $75.00 to $120.00)	$800.00 to $1200.00
A horse (worth before the war $120.00 to $250.00)	1200.00 to 2500.00
A wagon and team cost	2940.00
Beef cattle, each	930.00 [4]

At the close of 1864, in Mobile, Alabama, $1 in gold was worth $25 in state currency, and prices were as follows: —

Wheat, per bushel	$30.00 to $40.00
Corn, per bushel	10.00
Coffee, per pound	20.00
Fresh beef, per pound	150.00

[1] *N. Y. Times*, Sept. 6, 1864.   [2] Smedes, "A Southern Planter," p. 226.
[3] Hague, "Blockaded Family," *passim*; "Our Women in the War," *passim*; Jacobs, "Drug Conditions."
[4] Ball, "Clarke County," p. 501.

Bacon, per pound	$4.00
Domestics, per yard	5.00
Calico, per yard	15.00
A horse	$1500.00 to 2000.00
Salt, per sack	150.00 to 200.00
Quinine, per ounce	150.00 [1]

The War Department published, on September 26, 1864, the following prices [2] as agreed upon by the commissioners of February 17, 1864, for the states east of the Mississippi: —

Bacon, per pound	$2.50
Fresh beef, per pound	.70
Flour, per barrel	40.00
Meal, per bushel	4.00
Rice, per pound	.30
Peas, per bushel	6.50
Sugar, per pound	3.00
Coffee, per pound	6.00
Candles, per pound	3.75
Soap, per pound	1.00
Vinegar, per gallon	2.50
Molasses, per gallon	10.00
Salt, per pound	.30

The commissioners' prices were always lower than the prevailing market price.

A little property or labor would pay a large debt. Merchants did not want to be paid in money, and were sorry to see a debtor come in with great rolls of almost worthless currency. Barter was increasingly resorted to. There were so many different series and issues of money and so many regulations concerning it that no one could know them all, and this operated to discredit the currency. Besides, it was known that much of it was counterfeited at the North and quantities sent South. Prices advanced rapidly in 1865; state money was worth more than Confederate money, though it was much depreciated. Board was worth $600 a month; meals, $10 to $25 each; a boiled egg, $2; a cup of imitation coffee, $5. After the news of Lee's surrender, few would accept the paper money, though for

---

[1] Miller, p. 232. A negro went to a conscript camp in 1864 with a fifty-cent jug of whiskey. He gave his master a bottleful from the jug, replacing what he had taken out by water. The resulting mixture he sold for $5 a drink, a drink being a cap-box full. Each drink poured out of the jug was replaced by the same measure of water. In this way he made $300 before the mixture was so diluted that the thirsty soldiers would not buy. Related by the negro's master.

[2] O. R., Ser. IV, Vol. III, p. 686.

two or three months longer, in remote districts, state money remained in circulation.

When Wilson's army was marching into Montgomery, a young man asked an old negro woman who stood gazing at the soldiers if she could give him a piece of paper to light his pipe. She fumbled in her pocket and handed him a one-dollar state bill. "Why, auntie, that is money!" remarked the young man. "Haw, haw!" the old crone chuckled, "light it, massa; don't you see de state done gone up?"[1]

SEC. 3. BLOCKADE-RUNNING AND TRADE THROUGH THE LINES

Blockade-running

For several months after the secession of the state, its one important seaport — Mobile — was open, and export and import trade went on as usual. The proclamation of Lincoln, April 19, 1861, practically declared a blockade of the ports of the southern states. A vessel attempting to enter or to leave was to be warned, and if a second attempt was made, the vessel was to be seized as a prize.[2] By proclamations of April 27 and August 16, 1861, the blockade was extended and made more stringent. All vessels and cargoes belonging to citizens of the southern states found at sea or in a port of the United States were to be confiscated.[3] As the summer advanced, the blockade was made more and more effective, until finally, at the end of 1861, the port of Mobile was closed to all but the professional blockade-runners.[4] The fact that the legislature in the fall of 1861 was fostering various new industries and purchasing certain articles of common use shows that the effects of the blockade were beginning to be felt.[5]

[1] *Montgomery Daily Advertiser*, April 18, 1865. But for another month state money circulated in Montgomery.

[2] See Messages and Papers of the Presidents, Vol. VI, p. 14.

[3] Messages and Papers of the Presidents, Vol. VI, pp. 15, 37.

[4] In 1860 the South exported $150,000,000 worth of cotton, and Mobile was the second cotton port of America. Scharf, "History of the Confederate Navy," pp. 439, 533. Besides the regular ship channel there were two shallow entrances to Mobile Bay, through which blockade-runners passed. Soley, "The Blockade and the Cruisers," p. 134. Regular water communication with New Orleans was kept up until 1862 through Mississippi Sound. Scharf, p. 535; Maclay, "A History of the United States Navy," Vol. II, p. 445.

[5] Miller, "Alabama," p. 167; Acts of the Called Sess. (1861), p. 123; Acts of 2d Called and 1st Regular Sess. (1861), pp. 151, 168, 214, 278.

At first the general confidence in the power of King Cotton made most southern people desire to let the blockade assist the work of war, and, by creating a scarcity of cotton abroad, cause foreign governments to recognize the Confederate government and raise the blockade.[1] The pinch of want soon made many forget their faith in the power of cotton; there was a general desire to get supplies through the blockade and to send cotton in exchange. The state administration was distinctly in favor of blockade-running and foreign trade.[2] In 1861 the legislature incorporated two "Direct Trading Companies," giving them permission to own and sail ships between the ports of the state and the ports of foreign countries for the purpose of carrying on trade.[3] The general regulation of foreign commerce, however, fell to the Confederate government, which was distinctly opposed to all blockade-running not under its immediate control and supervision. The state authorities complained that the course of the Confederate administration was harsh and unnecessary. The state was willing to prohibit blockade-running on private account, but insisted that its public vessels be allowed to import supplies needed by the state. The complaint about restrictions on trade was general throughout the southern states and, in October, 1864, the southern governors, in a meeting in Augusta, Georgia, Governor Watts of Alabama taking a leading part, declared that each state had the right to export its productions and import such supplies as might be necessary for state use or for the use of

---

[1] The blockading force before Mobile in 1861 often consisted of only one vessel (Soley, p. 134), and the people of Mobile believed that foreign nations would not recognize the blockade as effective. There was an English squadron under Admiral Milne in the Gulf, and on Aug. 4, 1861, the *Mobile Register and Advertiser* said that a conflict between the English and United States forces was expected; the English were then to raise the blockade. Scharf, p. 442.

[2] This, however, was not the plan favored by Ex-Gov. A. B. Moore, who, on Feb. 3, 1862, wrote to President Davis stating his belief that the permission given by the Federal fleet to export cotton was a "Yankee trick" to get cotton to leave port in order to seize it. He thought that the Confederate government should forbid all exportation of cotton until the close of the war. "This leaky blockade system should be deprecated as one [in which the parties] are either dupes or knaves and [is] not in the least calculated to demonstrate the fact that our cotton crops are a necessity to the commerce of the world." If cotton was not a necessity to Europe, then the sooner the South knew it the better; if it was a necessity, the sooner Europe knew it the better. O. R., Ser. IV, Vol. I, p. 905.

[3] Acts of Feb. 6 and Dec. 10, 1861.

the state troops in the army, state vessels being used for this purpose. The governors united in a request to Congress to remove the restrictions on such trade.[1] But the Confederate administration to the last retained control of foreign trade. Agents were sent abroad by the Treasury and War Departments[2] who were instructed to send on vessels attempting to run the blockade, first, arms and ammunition; second, clothing, boots, shoes, and hats; third, drugs and chemicals that were most needed, such as quinine, chloroform, ether, opium, morphine, and rhubarb. These agents were instructed to see that all vessels leaving for southern ports were laden with the articles named. Such part of the cargoes as was not taken by the government was sold at auction to the highest bidder. These blockade auction sales were attended by merchants from the inland towns, whose shelves were almost bare of goods during three years of the war.[3] For two years military and naval supplies were the most important articles brought into the southern ports. The Alabama troops were in great need of all kinds of war equipment, and the state administration made every effort to obtain military supplies from abroad. Shipments of arms from Europe were made to the West Indies, generally to Cuba, and thence smuggled into Mobile and other Gulf ports. The shipments were always long delayed while waiting for a favorable opportunity to attempt a run. A large proportion of the blockade-runners making for Mobile were captured by the United States vessels.[4] Dark nights, and rainy, stormy weather furnished the opportunity to the runners to slip into or out of a port. Once at sea, nothing could catch them, since they were built for fast sailing rather than for capacity to carry freight.[5]

[1] O. R., Ser. IV, Vol. III, p. 735; Ser. I, Vol. XXXIII, Pt. III, p. 805.

[2] The Confederate War and Treasury Departments required that each steamship coming and going should reserve one-half its tonnage for government use. The owners of an outgoing vessel had to make bond to return with one-half the cargo for the government and the other half in articles the importation of which was not prohibited by the Confederate government. The Confederate government paid five pence sterling a pound on outgoing freight, payable in a British port. On return freight £25 a ton was paid in cotton at a Confederate port. The expenses of one blockade-runner for one trip amounted to $80,265; while the gross profits were $172,000, leaving a net gain of $91,735 on the trip. Scharf, pp. 481, 485.

[3] Joseph Jacobs, "Drug Conditions."   [4] Soley, pp. 44, 156.

[5] See Taylor, "Running the Blockade." A typical blockade-runner of 1862–1864 was a long, low, slender, rakish sidewheel steamer, of 400 to 600 tons, about nine times as long as broad, with powerful engines, twin screws, and feathering paddles. The

Most of the arms secured by Alabama came by way of Cuba, as did nearly all the supplies that entered the port of Mobile or were smuggled in on boats along the coast.   Havanna was 590 miles from Mobile, and between these ports most of the blockade trade of the Gulf Coast was carried on.   One shipment, welcomed by the state authorities, was a lot of condemned Spanish flint-lock muskets, which were remodelled and repaired and placed in the hands of the state troops.   Machinery for the naval foundry and arsenal at Selma and for the navy-yard on the Tombigbee was brought through the blockade from England *via* the West Indies.   The Confederate government, besides taking its own half of each cargo, had the first choice of all other goods brought through the blockade and usually chose shoes, clothing, and medicine.   The state could only make contracts for the importation of supplies; it could not import them on its own vessels.   The Confederate government paid high prices for goods, but, on the whole, paid much less than did the private individual for the remainder of the cargo when sold at auction.   The merchants made large profits on the few articles of merchandise secured by them.   Speculators bought up lots of merchandise at Mobile and carried them far inland, to the small towns and villages of the Black Belt and farther north, and secured fabulous prices in Confederate money for ordinary calico, shoes, women's apparel, etc.   The central part of the state was more completely shut from the outside world than any other section of the South.   The Federal lines touched the northern part of the state, but the traffic carried on through the lines seldom reached the central counties.   Consequently, the arrival of a merchant in the Black Belt village with a small lot of blockade calicoes, shoes, hats, scented soap, etc., was a great event, and people came from far and near to gaze upon the fine things exhibited in the usually empty show windows.   Few had sufficient Confederate money to buy the commonest articles, but some one could always be found to purchase the latest useless trifle that came from abroad.[1]

funnels were short and could be lowered to the deck. It was painted a dull gray or lead color, and the masts being very short, it could not be seen more than two hundred yards away. When possible to obtain it, anthracite coal was burned, and when running into port all lights were turned out and the steam blown off under water. Scharf, p. 480; Soley, p. 156 ; Spears, Vol. IV, p. 55.

[1] "Two Months in the Confederate States by English Merchant," p. 111 ; Taylor, " Running the Blockade "; Hague, " A Blockaded Family " ; " Our Women in War," *passim ;* Jacobs, " Drug Conditions."

In exchange for goods thus imported, the blockade-runners carried out cargoes of cotton. As has been stated, the Confederate administration was in charge of cotton exportation. The Confederate Treasury Department purchased in Alabama 134,252 bales of cotton for $13,633,621.90 — that is, $101.55 a bale. This cotton was to be sold abroad for the benefit of the Confederate government. Nearly all the cotton purchased by the government was in the great producing states of Alabama, Mississippi, and Louisiana. Alabama furnished more than any other state. In 1864 3226 bales of cotton were shipped from Mobile by the Treasury Department, and the proceeds applied to the support of the Erlanger Loan. To avoid competition between the departments of the government, it was agreed, June 1, 1864, that all stores for shipment should be turned over to the Treasury, transported to the vessels by the War Department, and consigned to Treasury agents in the West Indies or in Europe. It was to be sold finally by the Treasury agent at Liverpool and the proceeds placed to the credit of the Treasury. The export business was under the direction of the Produce Loan Office, which had charge of all government cotton and tobacco. Contracts were usually made with companies, to whom the government turned over the cotton for shipment. In November, 1864, there were 115,450 bales of government cotton in Alabama, 18,802 bales having been sold. It is hardly possible that it was all exported; some of it was sold through the lines.[1] It was found very difficult to secure bagging and ties sufficient to bale the cotton for shipping.

The state lost much as well as gained by trade through the blockade. The risks were great and the exporters had to have a large share of the profit; but arms, medicine, and blankets were valuable and very necessary. In spite of regulations, the blockade-runners brought in more luxuries than necessaries, causing much extravagance, and there were people who objected to the practice altogether. In March, 1863, the Mobile Committee of Safety reported that there were several vessels then in the harbor fitting out to carry cotton to Cuba. They were of the opinion that the government ought not to allow them to depart, since the country could not afford to lose

[1] Report of A. Roane, Chief of the Produce Loan Office; Richmond, to Secretary of Treasury Trenholm, Oct. 30, 1864, in H. Mis. Doc., No. 190, 44th Cong., 1st Sess.; "Two Months in the Confederate States," p. 111.

the vessels with their machinery, which could not be replaced. Governor Shorter agreed with them, and a protest was made to the Richmond authorities; but the vessels went out.[1] Judge Dargan, whom many things troubled, wrote to the Richmond authorities that the blockade-runners were ruining the country by supplying the enemy with cotton and bringing in return useless gewgaws.[2]

From March 1, 1864, to the end of the war, the Confederate government succeeded better in regulating the imports by blockade-runners. But after August, when Farragut captured the forts defending the harbor entrance, the port of Mobile received little from the outside world. Before the stringent regulations of the Confederacy went into force, blockade-running was demoralizing. The importers refused to accept paper money for their goods, and thus discredited currency while draining specie from the country. High prices and extortion followed. Cotton, instead of being exchanged for British gold, brought in trinkets, silks, satins, laces, broadcloths, brandy, rum, whiskey, fancy slippers, and ladies' goods generally. Curiously enough, there was great demand for these, in spite of the wants of the necessaries of life, medicine, and munitions of war. Delicate women, old persons, and children suffered most from the effects of the blockade. As Spears says, there were many tiny graves made in the South because the blockade kept out necessary medicines.[3]

The blockade reduced the Confederacy; the Union navy rather than the Union army was the prime factor in crushing the South; it made possible the victories of the army. As it was, the blockade-runners probably postponed the end for a year or more.[4] Though the number of blockade-runners increased in the latter part of 1864 and in 1865, Alabama profited but little; her one good seaport was closed in August, 1864, by Farragut's fleet, and with the fleet came the last regular blockade-runner. As the warships were moving up to engage the forts, a blockade-runner passed in with them unnoticed.[5] Small boats still brought in supplies.

---

[1] O. R., Ser. IV, Vol. II, p. 462.
[2] Jones, "A Rebel War Clerk's Diary," Vol. I, p. 350.
[3] Scharf, pp. 484, 486; Spears, Vol. IV, p. 56.
[4] Bancroft, "Seward," Vol. II, p. 209; Wilson, "Ironclads in Action," Vol. I, pp. 196–197.
[5] Scharf, p. 487; Wilson, pp. 187, 192.

Trade through the Lines

The early policy of the Confederate administration was to bring the North to terms by shutting off the cotton supply and by ceasing to purchase supplies which had heretofore been a source of great profit to northern merchants, and was, on the whole, consistently adhered to during the war. The state administration held the same theory until one-fourth of its people were destitute; then it was ready to relax restrictions on trade.[1] Individuals who had plenty of cotton and little to eat and wear soon came to the conclusion that traffic with the North would do no harm, but much good. The United States wanted the products of the South, and made stronger efforts to get them than the blockaded South made to get supplies by the exchange. Until the very last, the North was more active in commercial intercourse than the South, notwithstanding the fearful want all over the southern country. The policy of the North was to have all trade in southern products pass through the hands of its own Treasury agents, who were to strip such products of all extraordinary profits for the benefit of the United States Treasury, and to see that the Confederacy profited as little as possible.[2] The Confederate States government, when forced to allow some kind of trade through the lines, sought to sell only government cotton or to force traders to traffic under its license. The state administration, at times, worked in its agents under Confederate license in order to get supplies for the destitute in the counties near the lines of the enemy. Few regulations of com-

---

[1] Scharf, p. 446, says that the press and public sentiment were against allowing shipment of cotton to districts or through ports held by the United States. When in danger of capture the cotton was burned. Pollard states that the Richmond authorities were opposed to allowing any extensive cotton trade through the lines or through blockaded ports, because it was believed that the Union finances were in bad condition and would not stand the loss of cotton manufacturing. Moreover, the Confederate authorities were afraid of the demoralization caused by contraband trade, and also feared that Europe might consider that licensed trade through ports in possession of the enemy, like New Orleans, was a confession of the weakness of King Cotton, and would refuse to recognize the Confederacy. "Lost Cause," pp. 484–485.

[2] The North was determined to show that cotton was not king, and to do this it must get all the cotton possible from the South by allowing a contraband trade in which nearly or quite all the profits on the cotton should be stripped off, leaving only the bare cost to the Confederate government or cotton planter. The North was willing that the South should sell all its cotton, but the North was to be middleman. Scharf, p. 443; "Personal Memoirs of U. S. Grant," Vol. I, p. 331.

mercial intercourse were made by the Confederate States, but many were made by the United States. The Confederate States had the problem almost under control; the United States did not, and had to try to regulate what it could not prohibit.

Trade along the Tennessee and Mississippi frontier was subject to the following regulations on the side of the United States: Trade was carried on under the control of the Treasury Department; all trade had to be licensed; there were numerous officials to regulate the trade and the army was directed to assist traders; no coin, no foreign money, and no supplies were to be allowed to get to the Confederates; the trader must not go within Confederate territory; until 1864 the southern seller, whither Confederate or Union, when he went beyond the lines could get only 25 per cent of the New York value of his produce; from 1864 to 1865 he could get 75 per cent of the value if the cotton were not produced by slave labor; in all cases the seller had to take the oath of allegiance to the United States. These regulations were gradually repealed during the latter part of 1865 and early in 1866.[1]

The legislation of the Confederate States was not so full, but the policy was about the same and more consistently enforced. In 1862 the Confederate Congress made it unlawful to sell in any part of the Confederate States in the possession of the enemy any cotton, tobacco, rice, sugar, molasses, or naval stores.[2] Licenses, however, for the sale of certain merchandise could be obtained from the Secretary of War. Trade through the lines was not under the supervision of Treasury officials but was looked after by the generals commanding the frontier. In 1864 a law of Congress prohibited the export of

---

[1] The various proclamations, orders, regulations, and laws affecting commercial intercourse between the United States and the Confederate States will be found in a compilation of the United States Treasury Department entitled " Acts of Congress and Rules and Regulations prescribed by the Secretary of the Treasury, in pursuance thereto, with the approval of the President, concerning Commercial Intercourse with and in States and parts of States declared in insurrection, Captured, Abandoned, and Confiscable Property, the care of freedmen, and the purchase of products of insurrectionary districts on government account." The proclamations of the President will be found in the Messages and Papers of the Presidents. See also Sen. Ex. Doc., No. 56, 40th Cong., 2d Sess., and No. 23, 43d Cong., 3d Sess., p. 58; Ho. Ex. Doc., No.   , 45th Cong., 2d Sess., p. 36; Ho. Mis. Doc., No. 190, 44th Cong., 1st Sess., p. 39. A fuller account of the trade regulations is in the *South Atlantic Quarterly*, July, 1905.

[2] Act, April 19, 1862, Pub. Laws, C.S.A., 1st Cong., 1st Sess.

military and naval stores, and agricultural production, such as cotton and tobacco, except under regulations prescribed by the President.[1]

But the restrictions were not strictly enforced. It was not possible to do so; commerce would find a way in spite of the war. The people of Alabama were, on the whole, disposed to approve the policy of the Confederate authorities, but, when want and destitution came, the owners of cotton proceeded to find a way to sell a few bales. Early in 1863 north Alabama was occupied by the Federals, and trade began along the line of the Tennessee River. Later, there were trade lines to the northwest through Mississippi, and to the northeast through Georgia and Tennessee.[2] After the capture of New Orleans, cotton was sent through Mississippi to New Orleans, or to the banks of the Mississippi River, and always found purchasers. There was a thriving trade between Mobile and New Orleans during the Butler régime in the latter city.

By the trade through the lines, the people of Alabama secured more of the scarcer commodities than by the blockade-running. Much of the trade was carried on by firms in Mobile that had agents or branch houses in New Orleans. Three pounds of cotton were exchanged for one of bacon; army supplies, clothing, blankets, and medical stores were secured in exchange for cotton; salt was also a commodity much in demand. For three years, from 1862 to 1864, trade was quite brisk between the two cities, some of it under license by the Confederate Secretary of War, and some of it purely contraband. As long as Butler controlled New Orleans there was no trouble.[3] When General Canby went to New Orleans, he reported that English houses in Mobile were making contracts to export 200,000 bales of

---

[1] Act, Feb. 6, 1864, Pub. Laws, C.S.A., 1st Cong., 4th Sess.

[2] The state officials in 1862–1863 planned to exchange cotton from Mississippi and Alabama with the cotton speculators in Tennessee for bacon. Davis opposed (Pollard, p. 481), but, nevertheless, the change was made. Along the Tennessee River there was much trading with the enemy. In order to conform with the United States regulations forbidding the payment of coin for Confederate staples, the northern speculator bought Confederate and state money, often at a high price ($100 gold for $225 in Confederate currency or $120 to $125 in Alabama, Georgia, or South Carolina banknotes), with which to carry on the cotton trade. O. R., Ser. IV, Vol. II, p. 10.

[3] Shorter, who was opposed to contraband trade, complained in July, 1862, that the cotton speculators in Mobile had an understanding with Butler and Farragut by which salt was allowed to come in and cotton, in unlimited quantities, allowed to go out. O. R., Ser. IV, Vol. II, p. 21.

cotton *via* New Orleans, and expected to realize $10,000,000 net profits. Canby was of the opinion that the cotton trade aided the Confederates. The character of the Treasury agents in charge of the cotton trade was bad; they were likely to do anything for gain. He stated on the authority of a New Orleans banker, who was the agent of a cotton speculator, that Confederate agents would come to New Orleans with United States legal tender notes and invest in sterling with him, drawing against cotton which was ostensibly purchased from "loyal" or foreign citizens.[1] The speculators would give information to the Confederates with regard to the movements of the Federals, in order that the Confederates might preserve cotton that would in an emergency be destroyed. The speculators would buy the cotton later.

In 1864 a New York manufacturer testified that he had made contracts with firms in Selma, Montgomery, and Mobile to take pay for debts due him in cotton delivered through the lines at New Orleans. The price was $1.24 to $1.30 a pound in New York. Treasury agents made similar contracts for Alabama cotton to be delivered through New Orleans, Pensacola, or through the lines in Mississippi, Tennessee, and Georgia. One agent, H. A. Risley, made contracts with half a dozen persons for more than 350,000 bales of cotton, the bulk of which was to come from Alabama. Most of this, it is needless to say, was not delivered.[2]

The Confederate officials tried to manage that only government cotton went out under the licenses from the War Department and that only necessary supplies were imported in exchange. But there was much abuse of the privilege and much private smuggling of cotton in 1864, through the Mississippi to New Orleans and the river; and on September 22, 1864, General Dick Taylor (at Selma) annulled all cotton export contracts in the Department of Alabama, Mississippi, and East Louisiana. However, he said, the Confederate authorities would purchase necessaries imported and would pay for them in cotton at 50 cents a pound. This cotton could then be carried beyond the lines. No luxuries were to be imported, under penalty of confiscation.[3]

[1] Ho. Ex. Doc., No. 16, 38th Cong., 2d Sess.
[2] Ho. Rept., No. 24, 38th Cong., 2d Sess.
[3] Ho. Ex. Doc., No. 16, 38th Cong., 2d Sess.

Surgeon Potts, of the Confederate army, stationed at Montgomery, secured medical supplies from the Federal lines in Louisiana and Mississippi, both by water and by land, sending cotton in exchange. One of the last reports made to President Davis was by Lieutenant-Colonel Brand, of Miles's Louisiana Legion, who stated (April 9, 1865, at Danville, Virginia) that on March 21, 1865, a Mr. McKnight of the Alabama Reserves had presented a permit to General Hodges in Louisiana for indorsement and orders for a grant to escort 1,666,666⅔ pounds of cotton (about 4000 bales) through southwestern Mississippi and eastern Louisiana to exchange for medical supplies for Surgeon Potts. Brand was of the opinion that this was merely a scheme to sell cotton and not to get medicines, as he had known of only one wagon-load of medical supplies that had gone through his territory to Dr. Potts. McKnight had no government cotton to carry, for there was none in that section of the country, but he expected to buy it as a speculation. This practice, Brand stated, was common. Even government cotton would be sold for coffee, soap, flour, etc., under the name of medical supplies, and these would be sold by the speculators.[1]

In north Alabama a brisk trade was carried on for three years with the connivance of the Federal officers, many of whom were interested in the fleecy staple in spite of orders forbidding such conduct.[2] Negroes were given "free papers" in order that they might go in and out of the lines of the armies on contraband trade. The Confederate officials on the border were also often implicated in the traffic or connived at it through a desire to see poor people get supplies.[3]

One of the mildest charges against the Federal General O. M. Mitchel was that he had profited by speculation in the contraband

---

[1] O. R., Ser. IV, Vol. III, pp. 1180, 1181. Davis probably made his last official indorsement on this report, Apr. 10, 1865. He forwarded it to the Adjutant and Inspector-General with instructions to look into the matter.

[2] Somers, "The Southern States since the War," p. 134. General Grant, July 21, 1863, stated that this trade through west Tennessee was injurious to the United States forces. "Restriction, if lived up to," he said, "makes trade unprofitable and hence none but dishonest men go into it. I will venture to say, that no honest man has made money in west Tennessee in the last year, while many fortunes have been made there during the time." So vexed was General Grant with the speculators that, early in 1865, he suspended all permits, but within a month he had to remove the suspensions. Scharf, pp. 443, 446, 447.

[3] Taylor, "Destruction and Reconstruction," pp. 227, 235.

O

trade in cotton while he was in command in north Alabama.   It was alleged that he used United States transportation to haul cotton when the transportation was needed for other purposes.   Mitchel claimed that personally he had received no profit from his trade; it appeared, however, that he had used his official position to advance the interests of his brother-in-law and his son-in-law.   The discussion over his case brought out the fact that the northern cotton speculator or agent would go into the Confederate lines and buy cotton at ten and eleven cents a pound, Confederate currency, and take the cotton North and realize immense profits.[1]   Mitchel and other Federal officers, it was shown, approved and assisted the trade beyond the lines.[2]

Individual permits were sometimes given by President Lincoln, authorizing the bearers to go within the Confederacy, without restriction, and get cotton and other southern produce.   Sometimes, after bringing it out, these people lost their cotton to United States Treasury agents, because the permission given by the President was not in accordance with the Treasury regulations.   In north Alabama several agents got into trouble in this way.   Lincoln, it seems, understood that the laws gave him authority to issue permits to trade within the Confederate lines.[3]

In 1864, when cotton was selling at forty to fifty cents a pound in coin, numbers of Federal officers resigned in order to speculate in cotton.   A former beef contractor who had grown rich in the cotton trade was said to have controlled almost the whole of Huntsville. Both hotels, the waterworks, and the gas works belonged to him, and there was complaint of his extortions.[4]

Small packages, especially of quinine, were sent South through the Adams Express Company, which would guarantee to deliver them within the Confederacy.[5]   This caused speculation, and it was finally stopped.   Women passed through the lines and brought back quinine and other medicines concealed in their clothing.   A druggist in middle Alabama determined to carry on a contraband trade in

---

[1] Confederate currency was plentiful in the North, where it was made even more cheaply than in the South, and the southerners did not notice the difference.

[2] O. R., Ser. I, Vol. X, Pt. II, pp. 291–293, 638–640.

[3] Ho. Rept., No. 83, 45th Cong., 3d Sess. ; No. 618, 46th Cong., 2d Sess.

[4] N. Y. Herald, April 7, 1864.

[5] Jacobs, " Drug Conditions," p. 7.   The Southern Express Company worked in connection with the Adams, of which it had been a part before 1861.

cotton and drugs. The South had prohibited private trade in cotton; the North forbade the sale of medical supplies to the Confederates. But following the example of many others, he went into north Mississippi, loaded a wagon with cotton, and carried it to Memphis, then held by the Federals, and sold it for a high price in United States money. He then exchanged his wagon for an ambulance with a white canvas cover, on which was painted the word "SMALLPOX" in large letters, and over which fluttered a yellow flag. He loaded the ambulance with quinine, ether, morphine, and other valuable drugs, and other articles of merchandise scarce in Alabama. The yellow flag and the magic word "SMALLPOX" kept people away, and, after many adventures, he finally reached home.[1] Only by such methods could the beleaguered people obtain the precious medicines.

One of the last contracts on record in respect to trade through the lines was a deal made on January 6, 1865, by Samuel Noble and George W. Quintard, his agent, both of Alabama, to deliver several thousand bales of cotton to an agent of the United States Treasury.[2] There is evidence that some of the cotton was delivered.

The illicit trade in cotton by private parties became so flagrant that in the winter of 1864–1865, a fresh Confederate regiment, which had not yet been touched by the fever of speculation, was sent from the interior of Georgia to guard part of the frontier in Alabama and Mississippi. One of the first persons captured smuggling a cotton train through the lines was the wife of the Confederate commanding general, who, of course, released her.[3] Much of the trade was carried on by poor people who had a few bales of cotton and who were obliged to sell it or suffer from want. This fact caused the Confederate officers to be lax in the enforcement of the regulations.[4]

---

[1] Jacobs, "Drug Conditions," pp. 7–10.

[2] Ho. Repts., 38th Cong., 2d Sess., p. 174. Before this, Samuel Noble of Rome, Georgia, representing himself as a "loyal" man (he was introduced and vouched for by George W. Quintard), made a contract with a United States Treasury agent to deliver 250,000 bales of cotton from Alabama, Georgia, Louisiana, and South Carolina. In Alabama at that time he owned 800 bales at Selma, 1256 at Mobile, and had much more contracted for. The cotton was to be delivered at Huntsville, Mobile, and places in the adjoining states. Noble was to get three-fourths of the proceeds, according to the regulations. Ho. Rept., No. 24, 38th Cong., 2d Sess.

[3] Statement of Professor O. D. Smith of Auburn, Ala., who was then a Confederate bonded agent operating in north Alabama.

[4] Taylor, "Destruction and Reconstruction," p. 232.

The extraordinary prices of cotton in the outside world brought little gain to the blockaded Confederacy. Before the cotton could be brought into the Union lines or beyond the blockade, all the profits had been absorbed by the Confederate speculator, or, most often, by the Union speculators and Treasury agents. Theoretically, the regulations of the United States should have brought much profit to the Federal government. In fact, as Secretary Chase reported, the United States did not realize a great deal from Confederate staples brought into the Union lines. These frauds and the demoralizing effects of the system were evidenced by many reports from officers from the army and navy.[1]

But in spite of the demoralizing effects of the contraband trade within the Confederacy and in spite of the extremely low prices obtained for Confederate staples, much-needed supplies were sent in in such quantities as to enable the contest to be maintained much longer than otherwise it would have lasted. Owing to its interior location, it is probable that Alabama profited less by this trade than the other states.

SEC. 4. SCARCITY AND DESTITUTION

When the men went away to the army, many poor families began to suffer for the necessaries of life. The suffering was greater in the white counties, where slaves were relatively few, many families feeling the touch of want as soon as the breadwinners left. The Black Belt had plenty, such as it was, until the end of the war.

The first legislature, after the secession of the state, levied a special tax of 25 per cent of the regular tax for the next year to provide for the destitute families of absent volunteers.[2] A month later a law was passed permitting counties to assume the tax and to pay the amount into the state treasury, and thus secure exemption from the state tax.[3] The county commissioners were directed to appropriate money from the county treasury for the support of the

---

[1] Letter of Secretary Chase to Hon. E. B. Washburne, in Ho. Mis. Doc., No. 78, 38th Cong., 1st Sess.

[2] Acts of Gen. Assembly, Nov. 11, 1861. As early as Jan. 14, 1861, Governor Moore reported that the poorest classes were in want and that much suffering, perhaps starvation, would result unless aid were given. O. R., Ser. IV, Vol. I, p. 51. The soldiers' families were reported to be almost destitute in April, 1861. *Idem*, p. 220.

[3] Acts of Gen. Assembly, Dec. 31, 1861.

indigent families of soldiers.[1] This was to secure immediate relief, which was imperatively necessary, since the special tax for their benefit would not be collected until the next year.

Early in 1862 portions of north Alabama were so devastated by the Federals that many people, to escape starvation, had to "refugee" to other parts of the country, usually to middle Alabama, there to be supported by the state. At this time all crops were short, owing to a drought, and the poorer people suffered greatly.[2] Speculators had advanced the prices on food, and wage-earners were unable to buy. Impressment by the government made farmers afraid to bring produce to town.[3]

The county commissioners were authorized in 1862 to levy for the next year a tax equal to the regular state tax and to use it for the benefit of the destitute.[4] The state also made an appropriation of $2,000,000 for the same purpose. This appropriation was to be distributed by the county commissioners in the form of supplies or money. The families of substitutes were not made beneficiaries of this fund.[5] The sum of $60,000 was appropriated for cotton and wool spinning cards, which were to be purchased abroad and distributed among the counties in proportion to the white population. They were sold at cost to those able to buy,[6] and several distributions were made to the needy families of soldiers.[7] Salt was the scarcest of all the necessaries of life. The state took entire charge of the whole supply that was for sale and sold it at a moderate price, sometimes at cost, and to those in great need it was furnished free.[8] The county commissioners were authorized to hire and rehire slaves and take in return provisions, which were distributed among the poor families of soldiers.[9] The commissioners of Sumter and Walker counties were permitted to borrow $10,000 in each county for the poor, and to levy a tax of 50 per cent of the state tax with which to repay the borrowed money.[10]

Judge Dargan, member of Congress, wrote to President Davis

[1] Act of Gen. Assembly, Dec. 29, 1861.
[2] Annual Cyclopædia (1862), p. 9.
[3] Jones, "Diary," Vol. I, pp. 194, 198.
[4] Act of Gen. Assembly, Nov. 8, 1862.
[5] Act of Gen. Assembly, Nov. 11, 1862.
[6] Act of Gen. Assembly, Nov. 8, 1862.
[7] Act of Gen. Assembly, Oct. 16, 1864.
[8] Acts of Gen. Assembly, Oct. 9 and Dec. 9, 1862, and Aug. 29, 1863. Miller, "Alabama," p. 167.
[9] Acts of Gen. Assembly, Nov. 26, 1862.   [10] Act of Gen. Assembly, Nov. 28, 1862.

in the winter of 1862 that many people of Mobile were destitute.[1] Mobile was farther away from country supplies, and the people suffered greatly. In the spring of 1863 there was suffering in the southern white counties. A party of women, the wives and daughters of soldiers, raided a provision shop in Mobile, when there were instances of dire distress in the families of soldiers.[2] The richer citizens of the city gave $130,000 to support a free market, where for a while 4000 needy persons were furnished daily. Another contribution of $70,000 was raised to clothe a thousand destitute families.[3]

In 1863 the non-combatants of north Alabama suffered more than in the previous year. Houses had been burned, grain and provisions destroyed, and many were homeless and destitute. Numbers were driven from the country by the persecutions of the Federals and tories. The Confederate war tax and the state tax were suspended in districts invaded by the enemy,[4] and in August, 1863, the legislature appropriated $1,000,000 for the support of the destitute families of soldiers during the next three months. Twenty-five pounds of salt were also given to each member of a soldier's family as a year's supply.[5] Probate judges impressed provisions and paid for them out of this million-dollar fund. In November, 1863, an appropriation of $3,000,000 was made for the support of soldiers' families during the coming year. In counties held by the enemy where there were no commissioners' courts, the probate judges paid to soldiers' families their share of the appropriation. The county commissioners were authorized to impress provisions for the poor if they were unable to buy them.[6] Washington County was permitted to borrow $10,000 for the relief of soldiers' families.[7] The policy of giving a county permission to raise money for its own poor was much opposed on the ground that the counties which had furnished most soldiers and where the destitution was greatest were the least able to pay. The legislature declared then that the poor soldiers' families should be the charge of the state.[8] The sum of

---

[1] Jones, " Diary," Vol. I, p. 194.   [2] Annual Cyclopædia (1863), p. 6.
[3] *N. Y. Herald*, Dec. 26, 1863.
[4] Act, April 19, 1862, Pub. Laws, C.S.A., 1st Cong., 18th Sess; Act of Gen. Assembly, Dec. 5, 1863.
[5] Act of Gen. Assembly, Aug. 29, 1863.   [6] Act of Gen. Assembly, Aug. 27, 1863.
[7] Act of Gen. Assembly, Aug. 27, 1863.
[8] Resolutions of Gen. Assembly, Aug. 27, 1863.

$500,000 was appropriated for the destitute of north Alabama, who had lost everything from the seizure and destruction by the enemy. Disloyal persons and their families were not entitled to aid.[1] Macon County was authorized to levy a tax-in-kind for the poor, and Pike County a tax-in-kind and a property and income tax, practically a duplicate of the Confederate tax.[2]

The legislature of 1864 appropriated $5,000,000 for soldiers' families,[3] and made a special appropriation of $180,000 for the poor in the counties of Cherokee, De Kalb, Morgan, St. Clair, Marshall, and Blount, which were overrun by the enemy.[4] The probate judge of Cherokee County was authorized to act for De Kalb because the probate judge of that county had been carried off by the Federals.[5] In Lawrence County the Federals raided the probate judge's office, and took $3000 belonging to the destitute, and the agent was robbed of $3887.50 while trying to carry it to Moulton. Both losses were made good by the state.[6]

Statutes were repeatedly passed, prohibiting the distilling of grain for the purpose of making alcoholic liquors. The state placed this industry under the supervision of the governor, and alcohol and whiskey were distributed among the counties where most needed, to be sold at a moderate price for medicinal purposes, and the profit given to the poor, or to be given away upon physicians' prescriptions. Later the prohibition was extended to include potatoes, peas, and even molasses and sugar. This prohibition was not a temperance measure, but was designed to preserve as foodstuffs the grain, molasses, peas, and potatoes.[7]

The county commissioners usually had charge of the destitute, and looked after the collection of the special taxes which were levied for the benefit of the poor. They also distributed the supplies, purchased or collected by the tax-in-kind, among the needy people after investigating the merits of each case. In those portions of the state overrun by the enemy or liable to repeated invasion, the probate judge of the county was authorized to take charge of

---

[1] Act of Gen. Assembly, Dec. 8, 1863.
[2] Acts of Gen. Assembly, Dec. 4 and Dec. 7, 1863.
[3] Acts of Gen. Assembly, Oct. 7, 1864, and Dec. 13, 1864.
[4] Act of Gen. Assembly, Dec. 9, 1864.   [5] Act of Gen. Assembly, Dec. 13, 1864.
[6] Act of Gen. Assembly, Dec. 4, 1864.
[7] Acts of Gen. Assembly, Dec. 8, 1862, Aug. 27 and 29, 1863, and Dec. 13, 1864.

all matters relating to the relief of the destitute. Many thousand dollars' worth of supplies were furnished the northern counties when they were within the Federal lines or between the hostile lines. Many of the supplies sent there fell into the hands of tories or Federals, and many undeserving persons obtained assistance. Confederate sympathizers within the Federal lines had a struggle to live, and numbers, completely ruined by the ravages of the Federals and tories, had to flee to the central and southern counties.

The quartermaster-general of the state had charge of the state distribution among the counties, and among the Confederate soldiers. There was an agent of the state whose business it was to look after claims for pay and bounty due the families of deceased soldiers. It is safe to say that little was ever collected on this account.[1] The Confederate soldiers, as plentiful as paper money was, were rarely paid. Much of their supplies came from home. The Confederate government could not supply them even with blankets and shoes. This the state undertook to do and with some degree of success. And at one time, however (1862), after impressing all the leather and shoes in the state, only one thousand pairs could be secured.[2] Agents were sent with the armies going north into Kentucky and Maryland to buy supplies of blankets, shoes, woollen clothing, and salt, for the state. Blankets could not be obtained except by capture, running the blockade, or purchase through the lines, as there was not a blanket factory in the Confederacy in 1862. In the following year the carpets in the state capitol were torn up and sent to the Alabama soldiers to be used as blankets.[3] In 1863 the legislature asked Congress to exempt from payment of the tax-in-kind the people of that part

[1] Acts of Gen. Assembly, Dec. 8, 1863. There were Confederate soldiers who were paid only twice in two years' service, and then not enough to buy a new uniform. The following incident is related of the 9th Alabama Infantry: at Chancellorsville some Federals had been captured by the regiment, and as they were being sent back over the field covered with dead Federals, one of the prisoners remarked: "You rebs are sharper than you used to be. You used to shoot us anywhere; now you shoot us in the head so as not to bloody our clothes." The 9th was a regiment of sharpshooters from north Alabama. The narrator says that the prisoner was alluding to "the practice of stripping the dead of their clothing to cover our nakedness." — "The Land We Love," Vol. II, pp. 216.

[2] The legislature had offered $200,000 for 50,000 pairs of shoes, but received none.

[3] Miller, p. 167; Acts of Gen. Assembly, Dec. 8, 1863; O. R., Ser. IV, Vol. II, pp. 32, 196.

of north Alabama which was subject to the invasions of the enemy. This was done. Congress was also asked to exempt from the payment of this tax those families of soldiers whose support was derived from white labor.[1] As a result of economic conditions the taxation fell upon the slave owners of central and south Alabama. But the suffering was much greater among the people whose supplies came from white labor. These were the people assisted by the state and county appropriations. Yet when they were able to pay the tax-in-kind, they, at times, almost rebelled against it.

It has been estimated that from the latter part of 1862 to the close of the war at least one-fourth of the white population of the state was supported by the state and counties. This estimate does not include the soldiers.[2] A letter written in April, 1864, to the governor, from Talladega County discloses the following facts in regard to that county: With a white population of 14,634, it had furnished up to April, 1864, 27 companies of volunteers, not counting those who volunteered in other regiments or who furnished substitutes or were enrolled in the reserves or militia. The citizens of the county pledged the soldiers that they would raise $20,000 annually, if necessary, for the support of the soldiers' families. In May, 1861, 30 persons received aid from the county; in April, 1864, 3799. In 1863, the county received about $80,000 from the state for the poor, and 25 pounds of salt for each member of needy families of soldiers. In addition to this the people of the county raised in that year, for the poor, $7276 in cash, 2570 bushels of corn, 102 bushels of wheat, and 16 sacks of salt. The county bought 21,755 bushels of corn at $3 a bushel, and sold it at 50 cents a bushel to the poor; 920 bushels of wheat at $10 a bushel and sold it at $2 a bushel; 233 sacks of salt at $80 per sack, and sold it at $20 per sack. The destitute families were those of laborers who had joined the army. They lived mostly in the hill country, where they suffered much from the tories. Many were refugees from north Alabama.[3] In May, 1864, 1600 soldiers' families in Randolph County were supported by the state and county. Many thousand bushels of corn brought from middle Alabama had to be hauled 40 miles from the railway. Eight thousand people, or one-third of the population, were destitute. The same condition

---

[1] Resolutions of Gen. Assembly, Nov. 28, 1863.
[2] Miller, " Alabama," p. 229.   [3] Miller, p. 198.

existed in other white counties.[1]   Colonel Gibson, probate judge of Lawrence County, relates an experience of his in caring for the destitute.   He went in person to Gadsden for 100 sacks of salt.   He found the sacks in a very bad condition, and repaired the whole lot with his own hands so as to preserve the precious contents.   This judge, with his own money, bought cotton cards for the poor people of his county as well as salt, which at that time cost $100 a barrel.[2] The people who had supplies gave to those who had none, and thus supplemented the work of the state.   They felt it a duty to divide to the last with the deserving families of the poorer soldiers.[3]

Early in the war, in order to provide against famine, the authorities, state and Confederate, began to urge the people to plant food crops only.   They were asked to plant no cotton, except for home needs.   Corn, wheat, beans, peas, potatoes, and other farm produce and live stock were essential.[4]   During the winter of 1862–1863 there was much distress among the poor people in the cities and towns, and the next spring the senators and representatives of Alabama united in an address to the people, asking them to stop raising cotton and raise more foodstuffs and live stock.   Governor Shorter begged the people to raise food crops to keep the soldiers from starving. The planters were asked as a patriotic duty to raise the largest possible quantities of supplies.   The Confederate Congress also urged the people to raise provision crops instead of cotton.[5]   Though hard to convince that cotton was not king, the people in 1863 and 1864 turned their attention more to food crops, and had transportation facilities been good in 1864 and 1865, there need not have been any suffering in the state, and the armies could have been fed better.[6]

Because of the few railways, and the bad roads, often people in one section of the state would be starving when there was an

[1] Miller, "Alabama," pp. 198, 199, 229.   [2] Saunders, "Early Settlers," p. 68.

[3] Saunders, "Early Settlers," p. 206; Hague, "Blockaded Family"; Clayton, "White and Black under the Old Régime"; "Our Women in the War."

[4] Governor Shorter's Proclamation, March 1, 1862; Annual Cyclopædia (1862), p. 9.

[5] Annual Cyclopædia (1863), p. 6; Resolution, April 4, 1863, Pub. Laws, 15th Cong., 3d Sess.

[6] A report to Davis in October, 1864, stated that Alabama, Georgia, and Mississippi had been supplying the Confederate armies.   Georgia was exhausted, and Alabama, having sent 125,000 pounds of bacon, could do no more.   Pollard, "Lost Cause," pp. 648-649.   But in remote counties were large stores of supplies that could not be moved for want of transportation facilities.

abundance a hundred miles away. In the upper counties, when the soldiers' families failed to make a crop, and when supplies were hard to get, the probate judges would give the women certificates, and send them down into the lower country for corn. Women whose husbands were at home hiding to escape the conscript officer or the squad searching for deserters, young girls, and old women came in droves into the central counties both by railway and by boat, for free passage was given them, getting off at every landing and station. With large sacks, these "corn women," as they were called, scoured the country for corn and other provisions. Something was always given them, and these supplies were sent to the station or landing for them. Money was sometimes given to them, and a crowd of "corn women" on their way home would have several hundred dollars and quantities of provisions. These women were usually opposed to the war, and hated the army and every one in it; the negro they especially disliked. The "corn women" became a nuisance to the overseers and planters' wives on the plantations.[1]

When there was plenty in the country, the towns and the armies were often in want. Speculators controlled the prices on whatever found its way to the market. In 1861 Governor Moore issued a proclamation condemning the extortion of tradesmen, who were buying up the necessaries of life for the purposes of speculation. Such, he declared, was unpatriotic and wicked.[2] The legislature made such an action a penal offence, and to buy up provisions and clothing on the false pretence of being a Confederate agent was "felony."[3] In 1862 some officers of the Quartermaster's Department were found guilty of speculation in food supplies.[4] To prevent extortion the legislature afterwards enacted that on all goods for sale or speculation, except medicine and drugs, a profit of 15 per cent only could be made. All over that amount was to be paid into the state treasury.[5] Millers were not to take more than one-eighth for toll.[6]

At times it was unlawful to buy corn or other grain for shipment

---

[1] "Our Women in the War," p. 275 et seq.
[2] Moore, "Rebellion Records," p. 3; O. R., Ser. IV, Vol. I, p. 701.
[3] Acts of Gen. Assembly, Nov. 11, 1862.
[4] Jones, "Diary," Vol. I, p. 198; Schwab, p. 180.
[5] Acts of Gen. Assembly, Nov. 8, 1862.   [6] Act of Gen. Assembly, Dec. 13, 1864.

and sale in another part of the state or in other states. The military authorities in charge of the railroads sometimes prohibited the shipment of grain or supplies away from the regions where the armies were likely to camp or to march. In December, 1862, it was enacted that no one except the producer or miller should sell corn without a license from the judge of probate, which license limited the sale to one county for one year at a profit of not more than 20 per cent.[1] However, in 1863 the legislature authorized T. B. Bethea of Montgomery to sell corn bought in Marengo County in any market in the state.[2]

Distress was produced in south Alabama by General Pemberton's order prohibiting shipment by private individuals from Mississippi to Alabama on the railways.[3]

In each state and later in each congressional district there were price commissioners appointed, whose duty it was to fix schedules of prices at which the articles of common use and necessity were to be sold by the owners or paid for by the government when impressed. These prices were fixed for the whole state, were usually for a term of three months, and were often below the real market value. Consequently this had no effect except to make the people hide their supplies from the government.[4] Prices necessarily varied greatly in the different sections of the state, and what was a reasonable value in central Alabama was unreasonably low in north Alabama or at Mobile. In 1863 a Confederate quartermaster in north Alabama insisted that the price commissioners must raise their prices or he would be unable to buy for the army. He wrote that wool and woollen and leather goods sold at Mobile in December, 1863, for from three to five times as much as the scheduled prices of November 1, 1863. Prices in north Alabama, he added, must be made higher than in south Alabama because there was barely enough in that section for the people themselves ito live on.[5]

For months after the end of the war the inhabitants of the hill and mountain districts of north Alabama and of the pine barrens

---

[1] Act of Gen. Assembly, Dec. 8, 1862.

[2] Act of Gen. Assembly, Dec. 8, 1863.   [3] O. R., Ser. I, Vol. X, p. 971.

[4] In September, 1864, Surgeon Richard Potts was instructed to buy all the apple brandy to be had, at not more than $35 a gallon, but to purchase as a private individual in order not to have to pay too much. O. R., Ser. IV, Vol. III, p. 682.

[5] Saunders, "Early Settlers of Alabama," p. 29; O. R., Ser. IV, Vol. I, p. 608.

of south Alabama were on the verge of starvation, and a number
of deaths actually occurred.   The Black Belt fared better, and recovered more quickly from the devastation of the armies.

SEC. 5.   THE NEGRO DURING THE WAR

Military Uses of Negroes

The large non-combatant negro population was not wholly a
source of military and economic weakness to the state.   In many
respects it was a source of strength to the military authorities, who
employed negroes in various capacities, thus relieving whites for
military service.   They were employed as teamsters, cooks, nurses,
and attendants in the hospitals, laborers on the fortifications at
Mobile, Montgomery, and Selma, around the ordnance factories at
Selma, in the salt works of Clarke County, and at the nitre works of
central and southern Alabama.   Half as many whites could be released for war as there were negroes employed in military industries.
The negroes employed by the authorities were usually chosen because
trustworthy, and they were as devoted Confederates as the whites,
all in all, perhaps, more so.   They were efficient and faithful, and
rarely deserted to the enemy or allowed themselves to be captured,
though many opportunities were offered in north Alabama.[1]

After the secession of the state and before the formation of the
Confederacy numerous offers of the services of negro men were made
by their masters.   The legislature passed an act to regulate the
use of men so proffered.[2]   Where the negroes were employed in
great numbers by the government they worked under the supervision,
not of a government overseer, but of one appointed by the master
who supported the negroes, and who was paid or promised pay for
their work.   In the early part of the war the white soldiers wanted
to fight, but not to dig trenches, cook, drive teams, or play in the
band.   Congress authorized, in 1862, the employment of negroes
as musicians in the army, and the enlistment of four cooks, who
might be colored, for each company.[3]   In the same year the state

---

[1] See also article by C. C. Jones, Jr., in *Magazine of American History*, Vol. XVI,
pp. 168–175 ; J. W. Beverly (colored), " History of Alabama," p. 22.

[2] Act, Jan. 31, 1861 ; Beverly, " Alabama," p. 200.

[3] April 15 and 21, 1862, Pub. Laws, C.S.A., 1st Cong., 2d Sess.

legislature authorized the governor to impress negroes to work on the fortifications.[1] The state government impressed numbers of negroes as laborers in the various state industries, such as nitre and salt working, building railroads, and hauling the tax-in-kind. The legislature, in August, 1863, declared that negroes ought to be placed in all possible positions in the workshops and as laborers, and the white men thus released should be sent to the army.[2]

Most of the impressment of blacks was done by the Confederate government. The Confederate Impressment Act of March 26, 1863, provided that no farm slave should be impressed before December 1. On February 17, 1864, free negroes were made liable to service in the army as laborers and teamsters. Before the passage of this act free negroes had often been hired as substitutes, and sent to the army as soldiers in place of those who preferred the comforts of home.[3] Bishop-General Polk made a general impressment of negroes in north Alabama to work on the defences in his department, and many protests were made by the owners. A public meeting was held in April, 1864, in Talladega County to protest against further impressment of negroes. This county, in December, 1862, sent 90 negroes to the fortifications; in January, 1863, 120 more were sent; in February, 1863, 160; in March, 1863, 160; and so on. Talladega was one of the counties that had to furnish supplies to the destitute mountain counties, and the loss of labor was severely felt. Randolph and other north Alabama counties made similar protests. From north Alabama 2500 negroes were taken at one time to work on the fortifications in the Tennessee valley; this frequently occurred. Central and south Alabama and southeast Mississippi furnished many negroes to work on the fortifications at Selma, Montgomery, and Mobile. After Farragut passed the forts at Mobile, 4500 negroes were at once set to throwing up earthworks and soon had the city in safety.[4] The lines of earthworks then made by the negroes still stretch for miles around the city, through the pine woods, almost as well defined as when thrown up.

When the crack regiments of young men from the black counties

---

[1] Acts, Oct. 31 and Nov. 20, 1862.   [2] Resolutions, Aug. 29, 1863.

[3] I have known two men who hired negro substitutes to go to the army, and the negroes having been killed in battle, the whites were forced to go.

[4] Beverly, "Alabama," p. 200; Miller, "Alabama," pp. 198, 199, 207; Curry, "Civil History," p. 110; O. R., Ser. IV, Vol. III, p. 933.

went to Virginia, early in 1861, nearly every soldier had with him a negro servant who faithfully took care of his "young master" and performed the rough tasks that fell to the soldier — splitting wood, digging ditches about the camp, hauling, and building. The Third Alabama regiment of infantry, one of the best, left Alabama a thousand strong in rank and file and several hundred strong in negro servants. Two years later there were no negro servants; they had been sent home when their masters were killed, or because they were needed at home, or they had been sold and "eaten up" by the youngsters, who now had to do their own work.[1] Only the officers kept body-servants after the first year or two. These servants were always faithful, even unto death. The old Confederate soldiers have pleasant recollections of the devotion of the faithful black who "fought, bled, and died" with him for four years in dreary camp and on bloody battle-field. The old soldier-servants who survive tell with pride of the times when with "young master" and "Mass Bob Lee" they "fowt the Yankees in Virginny" or at "Ilun 10." Many a bullet was sent into the northern lines by the slaves secretly using the white soldiers' guns. When capture was imminent, the negro servant would take watches, papers, and other valuables of the master, and, making his way through the enemy's lines, return to the old home with messages and directions from his master, then in prison. In battle the slave was close at hand to aid his master when wounded or exhausted. With a pine torch at night he searched among the wounded and dead for his master. Finding him wounded, he cared for him faithfully, bore him to hospital or friendly house, or carried him a long journey home. Finding him dead, the devoted slave performed the last duties and alone often buried his master, and then went sadly home to break the news. Sometimes he managed to carry home his master's body, that it might lie among kindred in the family burying-ground. If he could not do that, he carried to his mistress his master's sword, horse, trinkets, and often his last message.[2]

The negroes were more willing to serve as soldiers than the whites were for them to serve. The slave owner did not like the idea of

[1] John S. Wise, "End of an Era," pp. 161, 212, speaks of the impression made by the 3d Alabama before and after the two years' service. The privates in one company in this regiment paid tax on $3,000,000.

[2] See also Beverly, " Alabama," p. 200. Several of these old body-servants have related their experiences to me.

having the negro fight, because it was felt that fundamentally the black was the cause of strife. Others were sensitive about using slave property to fight the quarrels of free men. As the years went on opinion was more and more favorable to negro enlistment, but it was too late before the Confederate government took up the matter.[1]

The average white person and the private soldiers generally were opposed to the enlistment of the negroes. The white soldier thought it was a white man's duty and privilege to serve as a soldier and that the fight was a white man's fight. To make a negro a soldier was to grant him military equality at least. To enlist negroes meant to abolish slavery, sooner or later: negro soldiers would be emancipated at once; the rest would be freed gradually. The non-slaveholders were more opposed to such a scheme than the slaveholders. The negro would have made a good soldier under his master, but he was worth almost as much to the Confederacy to raise supplies and perform labor.[2]

The free negro population, though less than 3000 in number, were devoted supporters of the Confederacy, and nearly all free black men were engaged in some way in the Confederate service. Some entered the service as substitutes, others as cooks, teamsters, and musicians. In Mobile they asked to be enlisted as soldiers under white officers. The skilful artisans usually stayed at home at the urgent request of the whites, who needed their work, but, nevertheless, they contributed. All accounts agree that they never avoided payment of the tax-in-kind, and other contributions. One of the best-known of the free negroes was Horace Godwin (or King)[3] of Russell County. He was a constant and liberal contributor to the support of the Confederacy. He also furnished clothes and money to the sons of his former master who were in the army, and erected a monument over the grave of their father.

---

[1] *Sewanee Review*, Vol. II, pp. 94–95 ; Acts of Ala., Nov. 20, 1863, and Resolution of Aug. 29, 1863 ; Annual Cyclopædia (1865), p. 10.

[2] See also C. C. Jones, Jr., in the *Magazine of American History*, Vol. XVI, pp. 168–175. When the war ended General (now Senator) Morgan was recruiting near Selma for a Confederate negro brigade.

[3] His master was named Godwin. Horace learned to make bridges, and became so skilful and was so much in demand that he was set free. By special act of the Alabama legislature he was given civil rights and at once he became a slave owner. After the war he was in Republican politics for a while, but soon went back to bridge-building.

Negroes on the Farms

During the war the greater part of the farm labor in the white counties was done by old men, women, and children, and in the Black Belt by the negroes. Usually the owner, who was perhaps entitled to exemption under the "twenty-negro" law, went to war and left his family and plantation to the care of the blacks. In no known instance was the trust misplaced. There was no insubordination among the negroes, no threat of violence. The negroes worked contentedly, though they were soon aware that if the war went against their masters their freedom would result.[1] Under the direction of the mistress, advised once in a while by letter from the master in the army, the black overseer controlled his fellow-slaves, planted, gathered, and sold the crops, paid the tax-in-kind (under protest), and cared for the white family.[2] In a day's ride in the Black Belt no able-bodied white man was to be found.[3] When raiders came, the negroes saved the family valuables and concealed the farm cattle in the swamps, and though often mistreated by the plundering soldiers because they had hidden the property, they were faithful. Women and children felt safer then, when nearly all the white men were away, than they have ever felt since among free negroes.[4] The Black Belt could never again send out one-half as many whites to war, in proportion, as in 1861–1865.

[1] Some masters, like General John B. Gordon, informed their slaves that the victory of the North meant the freedom of the negroes. See Ku Klux Rept., Ga. Test., and *Sewanee Review*, Vol. II, p. 95. I have been told by ex-slaves that the negroes in the quarters believed from the first that their freedom would follow the defeat of the masters, but that few slaves believed that their masters could be defeated.

[2] The following are some of the various occupations in which slaves relieved whites: spinners, weavers, dyers, cutters and dressmakers, body-servants, butlers, coachmen, gardeners, carpenters, planters, brick masons, painters, tanners, shoemakers, harness makers, barrel makers, wheelwrights, blacksmiths, machinists, engineers, millers, seine and sail makers, and ship carpenters, besides farm occupations. Nearly all of the skilled laborers were negroes. Their industrial capacity was even greater during the war than in time of peace. President Winston in Proceedings of Fourth Conference for Education in the South, pp. 40, 41. See also the books of Miss Hague, Mrs. Clayton, and Booker T. Washington.

[3] Harrison, "Gospel Among the Slaves," p. 299.

[4] See Mallard, pp. 209, 210 ; Hague, "Blockaded Family" ; Clayton, "White and Black" ; "Our Women in War" ; *Sewanee Review*, Vol. II, p. 95.

P

Fidelity to Masters

The negroes had every opportunity to desert to the Federals, except in the interior of the state, but desertions were infrequent until near the close of the war. In the Tennessee valley many were captured and carried off to work in the Federal camps. Numbers of these captives escaped and gladly returned home. As the Federal armies invaded the neighboring states, negroes from Georgia, Tennessee, Florida, and Mississippi were sent into the state to escape capture. In many instances the refugee slaves were in charge of one of their own number — the overseer or driver. The invading armies in 1865 found numbers of negro refugees doing their best to keep out of the way of the Federals. As a rule only the negroes of bad character or young boys deserted to the enemy or gave information to their armies. The young negroes who followed the Federal raiders did not meet with the treatment expected, and were glad enough to get back home. Most of the negroes disliked and feared the invaders until they came as intensely as the whites did.[1]

The devotion and faithfulness of the house-servants and of many of the field hands where they came in contact with the white people at "the big house" cannot be questioned.[2] On the part of these there was a desire to acquit themselves faithfully of the trust imposed in them.[3] It is one of the beautiful aspects of slavery. Yet this will not account for the good behavior of the blacks on the large plantations where a white person was seldom seen. They were as faithful almost as the house-servants. It was the faithfulness of trained obedience rather than of love or gratitude, for these were fleeting emotions in the soul of the average African.[4] On the other hand, the negro did not harbor malice or hatred. Constitutionally good-

---

[1] See Mallard, p. 210; *Sewanee Review*, Vol. II, pp. 94–95; *Southern Magazine*, Jan., 1874.

[2] It has been estimated that one-fourth of the total number of negroes was not engaged in field labor, but in some kind of service which brought them into close relations with the whites. Tillinghast, "Negro in Africa and America," p. 126. And on the farms and smaller plantations also the blacks knew their "white folks."

[3] See W. H. Thomas, "American Negro," p. 41.

[4] The experiences of Reconstruction showed that the negro had only to feel the touch of a stronger hand, and, with most of them, the attachments of a lifetime were of no force. The negro was as wax in the hands of a stronger race. Hence the influence of the carpet-baggers, who were for a time the stronger power.

natured, the negroes were as faithful to a harsh and strict master as to one who treated them as men and brothers. Where one would expect a desire and an effort for revenge, there was nothing of the sort. Not so much love and fidelity, but training and discipline, made insurrection impossible among the blacks. Moreover, the negro lacked the capacity for organization under his own leaders. Had there been strong leaders and agitators, especially white ones, it is likely that there would have been insurrection, and a negro rising in Marengo County would have disbanded the Alabama troops. But the system of discipline prevented that.

The good church people maintain that one of the strongest influences to hold the negro to his duty was his religion. He had often been carefully instructed by preachers, black and white, and by his white master, and his religion was a real and living thing to him. Invariably the influence of the sturdy old black plantation preacher was exerted for good. This influence was strongly felt on the large plantations, where the negroes seldom held converse with white men.[1]

The negroes were frightened, during the last months of the war, at possible capture by the Federals and forced enlistment or deportation to freedom and work in camps. They had somewhat the small white child's idea of a "Yankee" as some kind of a thing with horns. When the end was at hand and the bonds of the social order were loosening, the negro heard more of the freedom beyond the blue armies, and some of them hoped for and welcomed the invaders. When the armies came at last, most of the negroes helped, as before, to save all that could be saved from the plunderers. At the worst, the negro celebrated freedom by quitting work and following the armies. Much stealing was done by them with the encouragement of their deliverers, but the behavior of the blacks was always better than that of the invaders. Many rode off the plantation stock in order to be

---

[1] Harrison, "Gospel among the Slaves," pp. 299, 300; McTyeire, "A History of Methodism"; Riley, "Baptists in Alabama"; Mallard, "Plantation Life," p. 74 *et seq.* W. H. Thomas (colored), "American Negro," pp. 41, 149, gives as reasons why the slaves did not revolt during the war : (1) genuine affection for the whites ; (2) the desire on the part of the negro to do the duty intrusted to him ; (3) and most important — the supreme and all-pervading influence of religion. The mission work among the negroes was kept up all during the war. Harrison, pp. 292-300; Tichenor, "Work of Southern Baptists among the Negroes " (pamphlet).

able to follow the army to freedom and no work. Some burned buildings, etc., because the army did. Most of the former house-servants remained faithful to the whites until it was no longer safe for a black man to be the friend of a native white.

On the whole the behavior of the slaves during the war, whatever may be the causes, was most excellent. To the last day of bondage the great majority were true against all temptations. With their white people they wept for the Confederate slain, were sad at defeat, and rejoiced in victory.[1]

SEC. 6.   SCHOOLS AND COLLEGES; NEWSPAPERS AND PUBLISHING
HOUSES

Schools and Colleges

During the first year of the war the higher institutions of learning kept their doors open and the common schools went on as usual. The strongest educational institution was the University of Alabama, which was supported by state appropriations. In 1860 a military department was established at the university under Captain Caleb Huse, U.S.A., who afterwards became a Confederate purchasing agent in Europe. This step was not taken in anticipation of future trouble with the United States, but had been contemplated for years. The student body had been rather turbulent and hard to control, and for the sake of order they were put under a strict military discipline similar to the West Point system. Many students resigned early in 1861 and went into the Confederate service. Others, proficient in drill, were ordered by the governor to the state camps of instruction to drill the new regiments. There were no commencement exercises in 1861; but the trustees met and conferred degrees upon a graduating class of fifty-two, the most of whom were in the army.

The fall session of 1861 opened with a slight increase of students,

---

[1] Harrison, pp. 299, 300. For general information in regard to the negroes during the war, consult Beverly (colored), "Alabama," pp. 201, 202; Miller, "Alabama," pp. 142–157; Mallard, "Plantation Life"; Washington, "Up from Slavery"; Washington, "Future of the American Negro"; Thomas, "The American Negro"; Tillinghast, "Negro in Africa and America"; Hague, "A Blockaded Family"; Clayton, "White and Black under the Old Régime"; Smedes, "Southern Planter"; "Our Women in War."

but they were younger than usual, — from fourteen to seventeen years, and not as well prepared as before the war. Parents sent young boys to school to keep them out of the army; many went to get the military training in order that they might become officers later; the state needed officers and encouraged military education. The university was required to furnish drill-masters to the instruction camps without expense to the state. As soon as the boys were well drilled they usually deserted school and entered the Confederate service. This custom threatened to break up the school, and in 1862 all students were required to enlist as cadets for twelve months, and were not permitted to resign. Yet they still deserted in squads of two, three, and four, and went to the army. Recruiting officers would offer them positions as officers, and they would accept and leave the university. The students refused to study seriously anything except military science and tactics. Numbers refused to take the examinations in order that they might be suspended or expelled, and thus be free to enlist.

In 1862–1863, 256 students were enrolled, — more than ever before, — but mostly boys of fourteen and fifteen. The majority of them were badly prepared in their studies, and it was necessary to establish a preparatory department for them. In 1863–1864 there were 341 boys enrolled — younger than ever. At the end of this session the first commencement since 1860 was held, and degrees were conferred on a few who had enlisted and on one or two who had not. The enrolment during the session of 1864–1865 was between 300 and 400 — all young boys of twelve to fifteen. The cadets were called out several times during this session to ·check Federal raids. Little studying was done; all were spoiling for a fight. When Croxton came, one night in 1865, the long roll was beaten, and every cadet responded. Under the command of the president and the commandant they marched against Croxton, whose force outnumbered theirs six to one. There was a sharp fight, in which a number of cadets were wounded, and then the president withdrew the corps to Marion in Perry County, where it was disbanded a few days later. It was now the end of the war. Croxton had imperative orders to burn the university buildings, and they were destroyed. There was a fine library, and the librarian, a Frenchman, begged in vain that it might be spared. The officers who fired the library saved one volume — the Koran — as a souvenir of the occasion.[1]

The Hospital for the Deaf and Dumb at Talladega and the Insane Asylum were continued throughout the war by means of state aid, and after the collapse of the Confederacy were not destroyed by the Federals.[2] La Grange College, a Methodist institution at Florence, in north Alabama, lost its endowment during the war, and after the occupation of that section by the Federals was closed. After the war it was given to the state, and is now one of the State Normal Colleges. In 1861, Howard College, the Baptist institution at Marion, sent three professors and more than forty students to the army. Soon there was only one professor left to look after the buildings; the rest of the faculty and all of the students had joined the army. The endowments and equipment of the college were totally destroyed. Nothing was left except the buildings.

The Southern University at Greensboro kept its doors open for three years, but had to close in 1864 for want of students and faculty. Most of its endowment was lost in Confederate securities. After two years of war the East Alabama College at Auburn suspended exercises. The buildings were then used as a Confederate hospital. The endowment was totally lost in Confederate bonds, and after the war the property was given to the state for the Agricultural and Mechanical College, now the Alabama Polytechnic Institute. The Catholic College at Spring Hill near Mobile, the Judson Institute at Marion, a well-known Baptist College for women, and the Methodist Woman's College at Tuskegee managed to keep going during the war.[3] The student body at both male and female colleges was composed of younger and younger students each successive year. In 1865 only children were found in any of them.

In 1860 there were many private schools throughout the state. Every town and village had its high school or academy. For several

---

[1] W. G. Clark, "Education in Alabama," pp. 87–92; W. G. Clark, "The Progress of Education," in "Memorial Record," Vol. I, p. 160; Acts, 1st Called Sess. (1861), p. 56; N. Y. Daily News, May 29, 1865; Century Magazine, Nov., 1889. In recent years Congress has made a grant of lands in north Alabama to replace the burned buildings. Rept. Comr. of Ed., 1899–1900, Vol. I, p. 484.

[2] Clark, "Education in Alabama," pp. 149, 152, 153, 156; "Northern Alabama Illustrated," p. 453.

[3] Clark, "Education in Alabama," pp. 164, 174, 179, 180.

years before the war military schools had been springing up over the state. State aid was often given these in the form of supplies of arms. Several were incorporated in 1860 and 1861. Private academies were incorporated in 1861 in Coffee, Randolph, and Russell counties, with the usual provision that intoxicating liquors should not be sold within a mile of the school. Charters of several schools were amended to suit the changed conditions. These schools were all destroyed, with the exception of Professor Tutwiler's Green Springs School, which survived the war, though all its property was lost,[1] and two schools in Tuscaloosa. One of these, known as "The Home School," was conducted by Mrs. Tuomey, wife of the well-known geologist, and the other by Professor Saunders in the building later known as the "Athenæum."[2]

The only independent city public school system was that of Mobile, organized in 1852, after northern models. The Boys' High School in this city was kept open during the war, though seriously thinned in numbers. The lower departments and the girls' schools were always full.[3] The state system of schools was organized in 1855 on the basis of the Mobile system. It was not in full operation before the war came, though much had been done.

During the first part of the war public and private schools went on as usual, though there was a constantly lessening number of boys who attended. Some went to war, while others, especially in the white counties, had to stop school to look after farm affairs as soon as the older men enlisted. Teachers of schools having over twenty pupils were exempt,[4] but as a matter of fact the teachers who were physically able enlisted in the army along with their older pupils. The teaching was left to old men and women, to the preachers and disabled soldiers; most of the pupils were small girls and smaller boys. The older girls, as the war went on, remained at home to weave and spin or to work in the fields. In sparsely settled com-

[1] Clark, " Education in Alabama," pp. 204, 208, 259; Acts, 1st Called Sess. (1861), pp. 67, 70, 82, 113; Acts, 2d Called Sess. and 1st Regular Sess., pp. 92, 93, 94; Brewer, " Alabama," p. 347.

[2] " Northern Alabama Illustrated," p. 513.

[3] Clark, " Education in Alabama," pp. 6, 7, 224, 226, 229, 239, 259; Ingle, " Southern Side-Lights," p. 172.

[4] Pub. Laws, C.S.A., 1st Cong., 1st Sess., April 21, 1862; 1st Cong., 2d Sess., Oct. 11, 1862.

munities it became dangerous, on account of deserters and outlaws, for the children to make long journeys through the woods, and the schools were suspended. The schools in Baldwin County were sus-pended as early as 1861.[1]

Legislation for the schools went on much as usual. After the first year few new schools were established, public or private. Ap-propriations were made by the legislature and distributed by the county superintendents. When the Federals occupied north Alabama, the legislature ordered that school money should be paid to the county superintendents in that section on the basis of the estimates for 1861.[2] The sixteenth section lands were sold when it was possible and the proceeds devoted to school purposes.[3] A Confederate military academy was established in Mobile and conducted by army officers. The purpose of this institute was to give practical training to future officers and to young and inexperienced officers.

Few, if any, of the schools were entirely supported by public money. The small state appropriation was eked out by contributions from the patrons in the form of tuition fees. These fees were paid sometimes in Confederate money, but oftener in meat, meal, corn, cloth, yarn, salt, and other necessaries of life. The school terms were shortened to two or three months in the summer and as many in the winter. The stronger pupils did not attend school when there was work for them on the farm; consequently the summer session was the more fully attended. The school system as thus conducted did not break down, except in north Alabama, until the surrender, though many schools were discontinued in particular localities for want of teachers or pupils.

The quality of the instruction given was not of the best; only those taught who could do little else. The girls are said to have been much better scholars than the boys, whose minds ran rather upon military matters. Often their play was military drill, and listening to war stories their chief intellectual exercise.[4]

Some rare and marvellous text-books again saw the light during the war. Old books that had been stored away for two generations

[1] Acts, 1st Called Sess. (1861), p. 82.   [2] Acts (1862), p. 97.
[3] Acts, 2d Called and 1st Regular Sess. (1861), pp. 65, 182, 183, 223, 253, 255; Acts of 1863 and 1864, *passim*.
[4] My chief source of information in regard to the common schools during the war has been the accounts of persons who were teachers and pupils in the schools.

were brought out for use. Webster's "blue back" Speller was the chief reliance, and when the old copies wore out, a revised southern edition of the book was issued. Smith's Grammar was expurgated of its New Englandism and made a patriotic impression by its exercises. Davies's old Arithmetics were used, and several new mathematical works appeared. Very large editions of Confederate text-books were published in Mobile, and especially in Richmond; South Carolina, North Carolina, and Georgia also furnished Confederate text-books to Alabama. Mobile furnished Mississippi.[1] I have seen a small geography which had crude maps of all the countries, including the Confederate States, but omitting the United States. A few lines of text recognized the existence of the latter country. Another geography was evidently intended to teach patriotism and pugnacity, to judge from its contents. Here are some extracts from W. B. Moore's Primary Geography: "In a few years the northern states, finding their climate too cold for the negroes to be profitable, sold them to the people living farther south. Then the northern states passed laws to forbid any person owning slaves in their borders. Then the northern people began to preach, to lecture, and to write about the sin of slavery. The money for which they had sold their slaves was now partly spent in trying to persuade the southern states to send their slaves back to Africa. . . . The people [of the North] are ingenious and enterprising, and are noted for their tact in 'driving a bargain.' They are refined and intelligent on all subjects but that of negro slavery; on this they are mad. . . .

[1] From 1863 to 1865 W. G. Clark and Co. of Mobile, the chief educational publishers of the state, brought out a series of five readers, "The Chaudron Series," — by Adelaide de V. Chaudron, a well-known writer of Mobile. Large numbers were sold. S. H. Goetzel of Mobile published Madame Chaudron's spelling-book, of which 40,000 copies were sold in 1864 and 1865. W. G. Clark and Co. printed a revision of Colburn's Mental Arithmetic in 1864. A Mental Arithmetic by G. Y. Browne of Tuscaloosa is dated Atlanta, 1865, but was probably published in North Carolina. In 1864 W. G. Clark and Co. announced "A Book of Geographical Questions." Before the close of the war Confederate text-books were quite common in the state. The series were usually named "Confederate," "Dixie," "Texas," "Virginia," etc. Stephen B. Weeks, in "A Preliminary Bibliography of Confederate Text-books" (Rept. of Comr. of Ed., 1898–1899, Vol. I, p. 1139), lists 16 primers, 14 spellers, 29 readers, 4 geographies, 1 dictionary, 12 arithmetics, 12 grammars, 8 books in foreign languages, 20 Sunday-school and religious works, and 10 miscellaneous educational publications. Those published in Georgia, North and South Carolina, and Virginia sold largely in Alabama. Few came from the West. See also Yates Snowden, "Confederate Books."

This [the Confederacy] is a great country! The Yankees thought to starve us out when they sent their ships to guard our seaport towns. But we have learned to make many things; to do without others.

"Q. Has the Confederacy any commerce?

"A. A fine inland commerce, and bids fair, sometime, to have a grand commerce on the high seas.

"Q. What is the present drawback to our trade?

"A. An unlawful blockade by the miserable and hellish Yankee nation." [1]

In some families the children were taught at home by a governess or by some member of the family. This was the case especially in the Black Belt, where there were not enough white children to make up a school. Many mistresses of plantations were, however, too busy to look after the education of their children, and the latter, when old enough, would be sent to a friend or relative who lived in town, in order to attend school.[2] Sometimes a planter had a school on his plantation for the benefit of his own children. To this school would be admitted the children of all the whites on the plantation, and of the neighbors who were near enough to come.[3]

Newspapers

In 1860 there were ninety-six periodicals of various kinds published in Alabama. About twenty-five of these suspended publication during the war and were not revived afterwards. Numbers of others suspended for a short time when paper could not be secured or when being moved from the enemy. The monthly publications — usually agricultural — all suspended. The so-called "unionist" newspapers of 1860 went to the wall early in the war or were sold to editors of different political principles.[4] In spite of the existence of war, the circulation decreased. Most of the reading men were in the army; the people at home became less and less able to pay for a newspaper as the war progressed, and many persons read a

---

[1] See Weeks, " Bibliography of Confederate Text-books."

[2] See Mrs. Clayton, " White and Black," p. 115, and Hague, " Blockaded Family."

[3] See Hague, " A Blockaded Family." Miss Hague was a teacher in a plantation school during the war.

[4] W. W. Screws, " Alabama Journalism," in " Memorial Record," Vol. II, pp. 195, 234.

single copy, which was handed around the community. People who could not read would subscribe for newspapers and get some one to read for them. An eager crowd surrounded the reader. Papers left for a short time in the post-office were read by the post-office loiterers as a right. Few war papers are now in existence, there were so many uses for them after they were read.

It is said that the newspaper men did more service in the field in proportion to numbers than any other class. At the first sound of war many of them left the office and did not return until the struggle was ended. Often every man connected with a paper would volunteer, and the paper would then cease to be issued. There were instances when both father and son left the newspaper office, and one or both were killed in the war. Colonel E. C. Bullock of the Alabama troops was a fine type of the Alabama editor. The law exempted from service one editor and the necessary printers for each paper. But little advantage was taken of this; few able-bodied newspaper men failed to do service in the field.[1]

Sometimes in north Alabama publication had to cease because of the occupation of the country by the Federal forces, which confiscated or destroyed the printing outfits. It was difficult to get supplies of paper, ink, and other newspaper necessaries. No new lots of type were to be had at all during the whole war. Some papers were printed for weeks at a time on blue, brown, or yellow wrapping-paper. The regular printing-paper was often of bad quality and the ink was also bad, so that to-day it is almost impossible to read some of the papers. Others are as white and clean as if printed a year ago. A bound volume presents a variegated appearance — some issues clear and white and strong, others stained and greasy from the bad ink. The type was often so worn as to be almost illegible. In some instances, when the sense could be made out, letters were omitted from words, and even words were omitted, in order to save the type for use elsewhere.

The reading matter in the papers was not as a rule very exciting. Brief summaries were given of military operations, in which the Confederates were usually victorious, and of political events, North and South. One of the latest war papers that I have seen chronicles

---

[1] Screws, pp. 194, 195, 205, 212, 218, 233, 234 ; Pub. Laws, C.S.A., 1st Cong., 1st Sess., April 21, 1862; 2d Sess., Oct. 11, 1862; Yates Snowden, "Confederate Books."

the defeat of Grant by Lee about April 10, 1865. Letters were printed from the editor in the field; former employees also wrote letters for the paper, and items of interest from the soldiers' letters were published. New legislation, state and Confederate, was summarized. The governor's proclamations were made public through the medium of the county newspapers. It was about the only way in which the governor could reach his people. The orders and advertisements of the army commissaries and quartermasters and conscript officers were printed each week; there were advertisements for substitutes, a few for runaway negroes, and a very few trade advertisements. If a merchant had a stock of goods, he was sure to be found without giving notice. Notices of land sales were frequent, but very few negroes were offered for sale. The price of slaves was high to the last, a sentimental price. Many papers devoted columns and pages to the printing of directions for making at home various articles of food and clothing that formerly had been purchased from the North — how to make soap, salt, stockings, boxes without nails, coarse and fine cloth, substitutes for tea, coffee, drugs, etc.

Mobile, Montgomery, Selma, and Tuscaloosa were the headquarters of the strongest newspapers. The *Mobile Tribune* and the *Register and Advertiser* were suppressed when the city fell ; the material of the latter was confiscated. Both had been strong war papers. In April, 1865, the *Montgomery Advertiser* sent its material to Columbus, Georgia, to escape destruction by the raiders, but Wilson's men burned it there. In Montgomery the newspaper files were piled in the street by Wilson and burned; and when Steele came, with the second army of invasion, the *Advertiser*, which was coming out on a makeshift press, was suppressed, and not until July was it permitted to appear again. The *Montgomery Mail*, edited by Colonel J. J. Seibels, who had leanings toward peace, began early in 1865 to prepare the people for the inevitable. Its attitude was bitterly condemned by the *Advertiser* and by many people, but it was saved from destruction by this course.[1]

[1] Screws, pp. 161, 166, 188, 192, 231.

Publishing Houses

Most of the people of Alabama had but little time for reading, and those who had the time and inclination were usually obliged to content themselves with old books. The family Bible was in a great number of homes almost the only book read. Most of the new books read were published in Atlanta, Richmond, or Charleston, though during the last two years of the war Mobile publishers sent out many thousand volumes. W. G. Clark and Co., of Mobile, confined their attention principally to text-books, but S. H. Goetzel was more ambitious. His list includes text-books, works on military science and tactics, fiction, translations, music, etc. The best-selling southern novel published during the war was "Macaria," by Augusta J. Evans of Mobile. It was printed by Goetzel, who also published Mrs. Ford's "Exploits of Morgan and his Men," which was pirated or reprinted by Richardson of New York. Evans and Cogswell of Charleston published Miss Evans's "Beulah." Both "Macaria" and "Beulah" were reprinted in the North. Goetzel bound his books in rotten pasteboard and in wall-paper. Goetzel was also an enterprising publisher of translations. In 1864 he published (on wrapping-paper) a four-volume translation, by Adelaide de V. Chaudron, of Muhlbach's "Joseph II and His Court." He published other translations of Miss Muhlbach's historical novels,—her first American publisher. Owen Meredith's poem, "Tanhauser," was first printed in America in Mobile. An opera of the same name was also published. Hardee's "Rifle and Infantry Tactics," in two volumes, and Wheeler's "Cavalry Tactics" were printed in large editions by Goetzel for the use of Alabama troops.

Lieutenant-Colonel Freemantle's book, "Three Months in the Southern States," was published in Mobile in 1864, and in the same year the works of Dickens and George Eliot were reprinted by Goetzel. An interesting book published by Clark of Mobile was entitled "The Confederate States Almanac and Repository of Useful Knowledge." It appeared annually to 1864 in Mobile and Augusta, and resembled the annual cyclopædias and year-books of to-day. Small devotional books and tracts were printed in nearly every town that had a printing-press. It is said that the church societies published no doctrinal or controversial tracts. Hundred of different tracts, such as Cromwell's "Soldier's Pocket Bible," were printed for distribution among the soldiers. But not enough Bibles and Testaments could be made. The northern Bible societies "with one exception" refused to supply the Confederate sinners. The American Bible Society of New York gave hundreds of thousands of Bibles, Testaments, etc., principally for the Confederate troops. At one time 150,000 were given, at another 50,000, and the work was continued after the war. In 1862 the British and Foreign Bible Society gave 310,000 Bibles, etc., for the soldiers, and gave unlimited credit to the Confederate Bible Society.[1]

After the surrender the material of the newspapers and publishing houses was confiscated or destroyed.

Sec. 7. The Churches during the War

Attitude of the Churches toward Public Questions

The religious organizations represented in the state strongly supported the Confederacy, and even before the beginning of hostilities several of them had placed themselves on record in regard to political questions. As a rule, there was no political preaching, but at conferences and conventions the sentiment of the clergy would be publicly declared.

The Alabama Baptist Convention, in 1860, declared, in a series of resolutions on the state of the country, that though standing aloof for the most part from political parties and contests, yet their retired position did not exclude the profound conviction, based on unquestioned facts, that the Union had failed in important particulars to answer the purpose for which it was created. From the Federal government the southern people could no longer hope for justice, protection, or safety, especially with reference to their peculiar property, recognized by the Constitution. They thought themselves entitled to equality of rights as citizens of the republic, and they meant to maintain their rights, even at the risk of life and all things held dear. They felt constrained "to declare to our brethren and fellow-citizens, before mankind and before our God, that we hold ourselves subject to the call of proper authority in defence of the sovereignty and

---

[1] See also Yates Snowden, "Confederate Books." I have examined copies of most of the books mentioned.

independence of the state of Alabama and of her sacred right as a sovereignty to withdraw from this Union, and to make any arrangement which her people in constituent assemblies may deem best for securing their rights. And in this declaration we are heartily, deliberately, unanimously, and solemnly united." [1] Bravely did they stand by this declaration in the stormy years that followed. A year later (1861) the Southern Baptist Convention adopted resolutions sustaining the principles for which the South was fighting, condemning the course of the North, and pledging hearty support to the Confederate government. [2] Like action was taken by the Southern Methodist Church, but little can now be found on the subject. One authority states that in 1860 the politicians were anxious that the Alabama Conference should declare its sentiment in regard to the state of the country. This was strongly opposed and frustrated by Bishops Soule and Andrew, who wanted to keep the church out of politics. [3] From another account we learn that in December, 1860, a meeting of Methodist ministers in Montgomery declared in favor of secession from the Union. [4]

In 1862 a committee report to the East Liberty Baptist Association urged "one consideration upon the minds of our membership: the present civil war which has been inaugurated by our enemies must be regarded as a providential visitation upon us on account of our sins." This called forth warm discussion and was at once modified by the insertion of the words, "though entirely just on our part." [5]

In 1863 the Alabama ministers — Baptist, Methodist Episcopal South, Methodist Protestant, United Synod South, Episcopal, and Presbyterian — united with the clergy of the other southern states in "The Address of the Confederate Clergy to Christians throughout the World." The address declared that the war was being waged to achieve that which it was impossible to accomplish by violence, viz. to restore the Union. It protested against the action of the North in forcing the war upon the South and condemned the abolitionist policy of Lincoln as indicated in the Emancipation Proc-

---

[1] Riley, "History of the Baptists of Alabama," p. 279.
[2] McPherson, "Rebellion," p. 514.
[3] Smith, "Life and Letters of James Osgood Andrew," p. 473.
[4] N. Y. World, Dec. 26, 1860.   [5] Riley, "Baptists of Alabama," p. 291.

lamation. It made a lengthy defence of the principles for which the South was fighting.[1]

By law ministers were exempt from military service.[2] But nearly all of the able-bodied ministers went to the war as chaplains, or as officers, leading the men of their congregations. It was considered rather disgraceful for a man in good physical condition to take up the profession of preaching or teaching after the war began. Young men "called to preach" after 1861 received scant respect from their neighbors, and the government refused to recognize the validity of these "calls to preach." The preachers at home were nearly all old or physically disabled men. Gray-haired old men made up the conferences, associations, conventions, councils, synods, and presbyteries. But to the last their spirit was high, and all the churches faithfully supported the Confederate cause. They cheered and kept up the spirits of the people, held society together against the demoralizing influences of civil strife, and were a strong support to the state when it had exhausted itself in the struggle. They gave thanks for victory, consolation for defeat; they cared for the needy families of the soldiers and the widows and orphans made by war. The church societies incorporated during the last year of the war show that the state relief administration had broken down. Some of them were, "The Methodist Orphans' Home of East Alabama," "The Orphans' Home of the Synod of Alabama," "The Samaritan Society of the Methodist Protestant Church," "The Preachers' Aid Society of the Montgomery Conference of the Methodist Episcopal Church South." The Episcopal Church was incorporated in order that it might make provision for the widows and orphans of soldiers.[3]

In 1861 the Presbyterian, Cumberland Presbyterian, Episcopal, and Methodist churches in Huntsville sent their bells to Holly Springs, Mississippi, and had them cast into cannon for a battery to be called the "Bell Battery of Huntsville." Before they were used the cannon were captured by the Federals when they invaded north Alabama in 1862.[4]

Each command of volunteers attended church in a body before

---

[1] McPherson, "Rebellion," p. 591.

[2] Pub. Laws, C.S.A., 1st Cong., 1st Sess., April 21, 1862, and 2d Sess., Oct. 11, 1862.

[3] Acts of Ala., Dec. 9, 12, and 13, 1864.   [4] *N. Y. Times*, Aug. 30, 1865.

departing for the front.   On such occasions there were special services in which divine favor was invoked upon the Confederate
cause and its defenders.   Religion exercised a strong influence over
the southern people.   The strongest demominations were the Methodists and the Baptists.   Nearly all the soldiers belonged to some
church, the great majority to the two just named.   The good influence
of the chaplains over the undisciplined men of the southern armies
was incalculable.   To the religious training of the men is largely
due the fact that the great majority of the soldiers returned but little
demoralized by the four years of war.[1]

Not only was the southern soldier not demoralized by his army
life, but many passed through the baptism of fire and came out better
men in all respects.   The "poor whites," so-called, arrived at true
manhood, they fought their way into the front of affairs, and learned
their true worth.   The reckless, slashing temper of the young bloods
disappeared.   All were steadied and sobered and imbued with greater
self-respect and respect for others.   And the work of the church
at home and in the army aided this tendency;   its democratic
influences were strong.

The white congregations at home were composed of women, old
men, cripples, and children.   Among the women the religious spirit
was strongest;   it accounts in some degree for their marvellous courage and constancy during the war.   They were often called to church
to sanctify a fast.   The favorite readings in the Bible were the first
and second chapters of Joel.   They worked and fasted and prayed
for protection and for victory.[2]   The Bible was the most commonly
read book in the entire land.   The people, naturally religious before
the war, became intensely so during the struggle.[3]

The Churches and the Negroes

After the separation of the southern churches from the northern
organizations the religious instruction of the negroes was conducted

---

[1] Rev. J. William Jones, "The Great Revival in the Southern Armies"; Rev. J.
William Jones, "Confederate Military History," Vol. XII, p. 119 *et seq.*; Bennett, "The
Great Revival in the Southern Armies"; Alexander, "History of the Methodist Church
South," p. 74.

[2] Hague, "Blockaded Family," pp. 111, 112, 142; Ball, "Clarke County," p. 283.

[3] For one instance, see Hague, "Blockaded Family," p. 141; and for others, Jones
on the "Morale of the Confederate Armies," in Vol. XII, "Confederate Military History."

Q

under less difficulties, and greater progress was made.   There was
no longer danger of interference by hostile mission boards controlled
by antislavery officials.[1]   The mission work among the negroes
was prospering in 1861, and while the white congregations were often
without pastors during the war, the negro missions were always supplied.[2]   Many negro congregations were united to white ones and
were thus served by the same preacher; others were served by regular circuit riders.   Some of the best ministers were preachers to
the blacks, and were most devoted pastors.   One winter a preacher
in the Tennessee valley, when the Federals had burned the bridges,
swam the river in order to reach his negro charge.   The faithful

[1] By the Alabama Conference of the Methodist Episcopal Church South, there was
appropriated for slave missions in the state

From 1829 to 1844	$17,366.36
From 1845 to 1864	340,166.67

Before the separation the planters were not favorably inclined toward Methodist
missionaries on account of the attitude of the northern section of the church.   They
preferred the Baptists and Presbyterians, who did most of their work with the blacks in
connection with the white congregations.   After the separation, in 1845, there was a
greater demand for Methodist missionaries.   Many planters of the Episcopal Church
paid the salaries of Baptist and Methodist missionaries to their slaves, and erected
chapels for their use.   Harrison, "Gospel among the Slaves," pp. 302, 312, 313, 326.
In 1860 there were 20,577 negro southern Methodists in Alabama, about half of whom
were attached to the white churches and the rest to plantation missions.   The number
was rapidly increasing.   The number of negro Baptists was much greater, but there are
no exact statistics of membership.   There were smaller numbers in all the other churches.

[2] The following statistics relate to colored mission work by the Methodists : —

YEAR	NUMBER OF MISSIONS	MEMBERS	MISSIONARIES	APPROPRIATIONS
1859	38	8381	39	$25,849.10
1860	40	9208	40	27,091.66
1861	40	——	40	27,091.66
1862	36	8962	35	10,800.00
1863	37	9020	37	31,311.59
1864	22 (Montgomery Conference)	5153	22	24,508.00
1864	23 (Mobile Conference)	5684	33	26,938.16
1865				Some money was raised in 1864 for 1865.

The General Conference raised, in 1862, $93,509.87 for negro missions; in 1864,
$158,421.96; and, for 1865, $80,000.

blacks were waiting for him and built him a fire of pine knots. He preached and dried his clothes at the same time.[1]

The fidelity of the slave during these trying times called forth expressions of gratitude from the churches, and all of them did what they could to better his social and religious condition.[2] Often when there was no white preacher, the old negro plantation preacher took his place in the pulpit and preached to the white and black congregation.[3] The good conduct of the slaves during the war was due in large degree to the religious training given them by white and black preachers and by the families of the slaveholders. The old black plantation preacher was a tower of strength to the whites of the Black Belt.[4] The missions were destroyed by the victorious Unionists, and the negro members of the southern churches were encouraged to separate themselves from the "rebel" churches; and never since have the southern religious organizations been able to enter successfully upon work among the blacks.

The Federal Armies and the Southern Churches

With the advance of the Federal armies came the northern churches. Territory gained by northern arms was considered territory gained for the northern churches. Ministers came, or were sent down, to take the place of southern ministers, who were prohibited from preaching. The military authorities were especially hostile to the Methodist Episcopal Church South,[5] and to the Protestant Episcopal Church, annoying the ministers and congregations of these bodies in every way. They were told that upon them lay the blame for the war; they had done so much to bring it on. There were very few "loyal" ministers and no "loyal" bishops, but the Secretary of War at Washington, in an order dated November 30, 1863, placed at the disposal of Bishop Ames of the northern Methodist Church, all houses of worship belonging to the southern Methodist Church in which a "loyal" minister, appointed by a "loyal" bishop, was

---

[1] Harrison, p. 314.   [2] Riley, "Baptists of Alabama."   [3] Hague, pp. 10, 11.

[4] Riley, "Baptists of Alabama," pp. 286, 300; McTyeire, "A History of Methodism," p. 671; Tichenor, "The Work of the Baptists among the Negroes." The war records of the churches show that sometimes the slaves gave more money for church purposes than the whites ; for example, in the Methodist church of Auburn, Ala.

[5] Smith, "Methodists in Georgia and Florida."

not officiating. It was a matter of the greatest importance to the government, the order stated, that Christian ministers should by example and precept support and foster the "loyal" sentiment of the people. Bishop Ames, the order recited, enjoyed the entire confidence of the War Department, and no doubt was entertained by the government but that the ministers appointed by him would be "loyal." The military authorities were directed to support Bishop Ames in the execution of his important mission.[1] A second order, dated January 14, 1864, directed the military authorities to turn over to the American Baptist Home Mission Society all churches belonging to the southern Baptists. Confidence was expressed in the "loyalty" of this society and its ministers.[2] Other orders placed the Board of Home Missions of the United Presbyterian Church in charge of the churches of the Associate Reformed Church, and authorized the northern branches of the (O. S. and N. S.) Presbyterians to appoint "loyal" ministers for the churches of these denominations in the South.

Lincoln seems to have been displeased with the action taken by the War Department, but nothing more was done than to modify the orders so as to concern only the "churches in the rebellious states."[3]

Under these orders churches in north Alabama were seized and turned over to the northern branches of the same denomination. In some of the mountain districts this was not opposed by the so-called "union" element of the population. But in most places bitter feelings were aroused, and controversies began which lasted for several years after the war ended. The northern churches in some cases attempted to hold permanently the property turned over to them during the war. In central and south Alabama, where the Federal forces did not appear until 1865, these orders were not enforced.

In the section of the country occupied by the enemy, the military authorities attempted to regulate the services in the various churches. Prayer had to be offered for the President of the United States and for the Federal government. It was a criminal offence to pray for the Confederate leaders. Preachers who refused to pray "loyal"

---

[1] McPherson, p. 521.   [2] McPherson, p. 521.
[3] McPherson, pp. 521, 522; Nicolay and Hay, Vol. V, p. 337.

prayers and preach "loyal" sermons were forbidden to hold services. In Huntsville, in 1862, the Rev. Frederick A. Ross, a celebrated Presbyterian clergyman, was arrested by General Rousseau, and sent North for praying a "disloyal" prayer in which he said, "We pray Thee, O Lord, to bless our enemies and to remove them from our midst as soon as seemeth good in Thy sight." He seems to have been released, for in February, 1865, General R. S. Stanley wrote to General Thomas's adjutant-general protesting against the policy of the provost-marshal in Huntsville, who had selected a number of prominent men to answer certain test questions as to "loyalty." If not answered to his satisfaction, the person catechized was to be sent beyond the lines. Among other prominent citizens two ministers — Ross and Bannister — were selected for expulsion. These, General Stanley said, had never taken part in politics, and he thought it was a bad policy. However, he stated that General Granger wanted the preachers expelled.[1]

Throughout the war there was a disposition on the part of some army officers to compel ministers of southern sympathies to conduct "loyal" services — that is, to preach and pray for the success of the Federal government. It was especially easy to annoy the Episcopal clergy, on account of the formal prayer used, but other denominations also suffered. In one instance, a Methodist minister was told that he must take the oath (this was soon after the surrender) and pray for the President of the United States, or he must stop preaching. For a time he refused, but finally he took the oath, and, as he said, "I prayed for the President; that the Lord would take out of him and his allies the hearts of beasts and put into them the hearts of men, or remove the cusses from office. The little captain never asked me any more to pray for the President and the United States."[2]

In the churches the situation at the close of the war was not promising for peace. Some congregations were divided; church property was held by aliens supported by the army; "loyal" services were still demanded; the northern churches were sending agents

[1] See *Gulf States Hist. Mag.*, Sept., 1902, on "The Churches in Alabama during Civil War and Reconstruction"; O. R., Ser. I, Vol. XLIX, Pt. I, p. 718; *Southern Review*, April, 1872, p. 414; *Boston Journal*, Nov. 15, 1864; McTyeire, "A History of Methodism," p. 673.

[2] Richardson, " Lights and Shadows of Itinerant Life," p. 183.

to occupy the southern field; the negroes were being forcibly separated from southern supervision; the policy of "disintegration and absorption" was beginning. Consequently the church question during Reconstruction was one of the most irritating.[1]

SEC. 8. DOMESTIC LIFE

Society in 1861

During the early months of 1861 society was at its brightest and best. For several years social life had been characterized by a vague feeling of unrest. Political questions became social questions, society and politics went hand in hand, and the social leaders were the political leaders. The women were well informed on all questions of the day and especially on the burning sectional issues that affected them so closely. After the John Brown episode at Harper's Ferry, the women felt that for them there could be no safety until the question was settled. They were strongly in favor of secession after that event if not before; they were even more unanimous than the men, feeling that they were more directly concerned in questions of interference with social institutions in the South. There was to them a great danger in social changes made, as all expected, by John Brown methods.[2]

Brilliant social events celebrated the great political actions of the day. The secession of Alabama, the sessions of the convention, the

[1] See Whitaker's paper in Transactions Ala. Hist. Soc., Vol. IV, p. 211 *et seq.*

[2] Col. Higginson seems to understand the influence of the women, but not the reason for their interest in public questions. He says: "But for the women of the seceding states, the War of the Rebellion would have been waged more feebly, been sooner ended, and far more easily forgotten. . . . Had the voters of the South been all women, it would have plunged earlier into the gulf of secession, dived deeper, and come up even more reluctantly." Higginson, "Common Sense about Women," pp. 54, 209. Professor Burgess, with a better understanding, explains the reason for the interest of the women in sectional questions. He says that, after the attempt of John Brown to incite the slaves to insurrection, " especially did terror and bitterness take possession of the hearts of the women of the South, who saw in slave insurrection not only destruction and death, but that which to feminine virtue is a thousand times worse than the most terrible death. For those who would excite such a movement or sympathize with anybody who would excite such a movement, the women of the South felt a hatred as undying as virtue itself. Men might still hesitate . . . but the women were united and resolute, and their unanimous exhortation was: 'Men of the South, defend the honor of your mothers, your wives, your sisters, and your daughters. It is your highest and most sacred duty.'" Burgess, "Civil War and the Constitution," Vol. I, p. 42.

meeting of the legislature, the meeting of the Provisional Congress, the inauguration of President Davis — all were occasions for splendid gatherings of beauty and talent and strength. There were balls, receptions, and other social events in country and in town. There was no city life, and country and town were socially one. Enthusiasm for the new government of the southern nation was at fever heat for months. At heart many feared and dreaded that war might follow, but had war been certain, the knowledge would have turned no one from his course. When war was seen to be imminent, enthusiasm rose higher. Fear and dread were in the hearts of the women, but no one hesitated. From social gayety they turned to the task of making ready for war their fathers, brothers, husbands, and sweethearts. They hurriedly made the first gray uniforms and prepared supplies for the campaign. When the companies were fitted out and ready to depart, there were farewell balls and sermons, and presentations of colors by young women. These ceremonies took place in the churches, town halls, and court-houses. Speeches of presentation were made by young women, and of acceptance by the officers. The men always spoke well. The women showed a thorough acquaintance with the questions at issue, but most of their addresses were charges to the soldiers, encouragement to duty. "Go, my sons, and return victorious or fall in the cause of the South," or a similar paraphrase, was often heard. One lady said, "We confide [to you] this emblem of our zeal for liberty, trusting that it will nerve your hearts and strengthen your hands in the hour of trial, and that its presence will forbid the thought of seeking any other retreat than in death." Another maiden told her soldiers that "we who present this banner expect it to be returned brightened by your chivalry or to become the shroud of the slain." "The terrors of war are far less to be feared than the degradation of ignoble submission," the soldiers were assured by another bright-eyed girl. The legends embroidered or woven into the colors were such as these: "To the Brave," "Victory or Death," "Never Surrender." [1]

There were dress parades, exhibition drills, picnics, barbecues; and then the soldiers marched away. After a short season of feverish social gayety, the seriousness of war was brought home to the peo-

[1] "Our Women in War," *passim;* Ball, "Clarke County," pp. 261–274; oral accounts, scrap-books, letters.

ple, and those left behind settled down to watch and wait and work and pray for the loved ones and for the cause. It was soon a very quiet life, industrious, strained with waiting and listening for news. For a long time the interior country was not disturbed by fear of invasion. Life was monotonous; sorrow came afresh daily; and it was a blessing to the women that they had to work so hard during the war, as constant employment was their greatest comfort.

Life on the Farm

The great majority of the people of Alabama lived in the country on farms and plantations. They had been dependent upon the North for all the finer and many of the commoner manufactured articles. The staple crop was cotton, which was sold in exchange for many of the ordinary necessaries of life. Now all was changed. The blockade shut off supplies from abroad, and the plantations had to raise all that was needed for feeding and clothing the people at home and the soldiers in the field. This necessitated a change in plantation economy. After the first year of war less and less cotton was planted, and food crops became the staple agricultural productions. The state and Confederate authorities encouraged this tendency by advice and by law. The farms produced many things which were seldom planted before the war, when cotton was the staple crop. Cereals were cultivated in the northern counties and to some extent in central Alabama, though wheat was never successful in central and south Alabama. Rice, oats, corn, peas, pumpkins, ground-peas, and chufas were grown more and more as the war went on. Ground-peas (called also peanuts, goobers, or pindars, according to locality) and chufas were raised to feed hogs and poultry. The common field pea, or "speckled Jack," was one of the mainstays of the Confederacy. It is said that General Lee called it "the Confederacy's best friend." At "laying by" the farmers planted peas between the hills of corn, and the vines grew and the crop matured with little further trouble. Sweet potatoes were everywhere raised, and became a staple article of food.

Rice was stripped of its husk by being beaten with a wooden pestle in a mortar cut out of a section of a tree. The threshing of the wheat was a cause of much trouble. Rude home-made flails were used, for there were no regular threshers. No one raised much of it, for it was a great task to clean it. One poor woman who had a small patch of wheat threshed it by beating the sheaves over a barrel, while bed quilts and sheets were spread around to catch the scattering grains. Another placed the sheaves in a large wooden trough, then she and her small children beat the sheaves with wooden clubs. After being threshed in some such manner, the chaff was fanned out by pouring the grain from a measure in a breeze and catching it on a sheet.

Field labor was performed in the Black Belt by the negroes, but in the white counties the burden fell heavily upon the women, children, and old men. In the Black Belt the mistress of the plantation managed affairs with the assistance of the trusty negroes. She superintended the planting of the proper crops, the cultivation and gathering of the same, and sent to the government stores the large share called for by the tax-in-kind. The old men of the community, if near enough, assisted the women managers by advice and direction. Often one old gentleman would have half a dozen feminine planters as his wards. Life was very busy in the Black Belt, but there was never the suffering in this rich section that prevailed in the less fertile white counties from which the white laborers had gone to war. In the latter section the mistress of slaves managed much as did her Black Belt sister, but there were fewer slaves and life was harder for all, and hardest of all for the poor white people who owned no slaves. When few slaves were owned by a family, the young white boys worked in the field with them, while the girls of the family did the light tasks about the house, though at times they too went to the field. Where there were no slaves, the old men, cripples, women, and children worked on the little farms. All over the country the young boys worked like heroes. All had been taught that labor was honorable, and all knew how work should be done. So when war made it necessary, all went to work only the harder; there was no holding of hands in idleness. The mistress of the plantation was already accustomed to the management of large affairs, and war brought additional duties rather than new and strange problems; but the wife of the poor farmer or renter, left alone with small children, had a hard time making both ends meet.

Home Industries; Makeshifts and Substitutes

Many articles in common use had now to be made at home, and the plantation developed many small industries. There was much joy when a substitute was found, because it made the people independent of the outside world. Farm implements were made and repaired. Ropes were made at home of various materials, such as bear-grass, sunflower stalks, and cotton; baskets, of willow branches and of oak splints; rough earthenware, of clay and then glazed; cooking soda from seaweed and from corn-cob ashes; ink from nut-galls or ink balls, from the skin of blue fig, from green persimmons, pokeberries, rusty nails, pomegranate rind, and indigo. Cement was made from wild potatoes and flour; starch from nearly ripe corn, sweet potatoes, and flour. Bottles or gourds, with small rolls of cotton for wicks, served as lamps, and in place of oil, cotton-seed oil, ground-pea or peanut oil, and lard were used. Candles made of wax or tallow were used, while in the "piney woods" pine knots furnished all the necessary illumination. Mattresses were stuffed with moss, leaves, and "cat-tails." No paper could be wasted for envelopes. The sheet was written on except just enough for the address when folded. In other instances wall-paper and sheets of paper with pictures on one side and the other side blank were folded and used for envelopes. Mucilage for the envelopes was made from peach-tree gum. Corn-cob pipes with a joint of reed or fig twig for a stem were fashionable. The leaves of the China tree kept insects away from dried fruit; the China berries were made into whiskey and were used as a basis for "Poor Man's" soap. Wax myrtle and rosin were also used in making soap. Beer was made from corn, persimmons, potatoes, and sassafras; "lemonade" from may-pops and pomegranates. Dogwood and willow bark were mixed with smoking tobacco "to make it go a long way." Shoes had to be made for white and black, and back-yard tanneries were established. The hides were first soaked in a barrel filled with a solution of lye until the hair would come off, when they were placed in a pit between alternate layers of red oak bark and water poured in. In this "ooze" they soaked for several months and were then ready for use. The hides of horses, dogs, mules, hogs, cows, and goats were utilized, and shoes, harness, and saddles were made on the farm.

All the domestic animals were now raised in larger numbers, especially beef cattle, sheep, goats, and hogs. Sheep were raised principally for their wool. The work of all was directed toward supplying the army, and the best of everything was sent to the soldiers.

Home life was very quiet, busy, and monotonous, with its daily routine of duty in which all had a part. There were few even of the wealthiest who did not work with their hands if physically able. Life was hard, but people soon became accustomed to makeshifts and privation, and most of them had plenty to eat, though the food was usually coarse. Corn bread was nearly always to be had; in some places often nothing else. After the first year few people ever had flour to cook; especially was this the case in the southern counties. When a family was so fortunate as to obtain a sack or barrel of flour, all the neighbors were invited in to get biscuits, though sometimes all of it was kept to make starch. Bolted meal was used as a substitute for flour in cakes and bread. Most of the meat produced was sent to the army, and the average family could afford it only once a day, many only once a week. When an epidemic of cholera killed the hogs, the people became vegetarians and lived on corn bread, milk, and syrup; many had only the first.[1] Tea and coffee were very scarce in the interior of Alabama, and small supplies of the genuine were saved for emergencies. For tea there were various substitutes, among them holly leaves, rose leaves, blackberry and raspberry leaves; while for coffee, rye, okra seed, corn, bran, meal, hominy, peanuts, and bits of parched or roasted sweet potatoes were used. Syrup was made from the juice of the watermelon, and preserves from its rind. The juice of corn-stalks was also made into syrup. In south Alabama sugar-cane and in north Alabama sorghum furnished "long sweetening." The sorghum was boiled in old iron kettles, and often made the teeth black. In south Alabama syrup was used instead of sugar in cooking. In grinding sugar-cane and sorghum, wooden rollers often had to be made, as iron ones were scarce. However, when they could be obtained, they were passed from family to family around the community.

---

[1] One of my acquaintances says that quite often she had only bread, milk, and syrup twice a day. Sometimes she was unable to eat any breakfast, but after spinning an hour or two she was hungry enough to eat. To many the diet was very healthful, but the sick and the delicate often died for want of proper food.

Clothes and Fashions

Before the war most articles of clothing were purchased in the North or imported from abroad. Now that the blockade shut Alabama off from all sources of supply, the people had to make their cloth and clothing at home. The factories in the South could not even supply the needs of the army, and there was a universal return to primitive and frontier conditions. Old wheels and looms were brought out, and others were made like them. The state government bought large quantities of cotton and wool cards for the use of poor people. The women worked incessantly. Every household was a small factory, and in an incredibly short time the women mastered the intricacies of looms, spinning-wheels, warping frames, swifts, etc. Negro women sometimes learned to spin and weave. The whites, however, did most of it; weaving was too difficult for the average negro to learn. The area devoted to the cultivation of cotton was restricted by law, but more than enough was raised to supply the few factories then operating, principally for the government, and to supply the spinning-wheels and hand looms of the people.

As a rule, each member of the family had a regularly allotted task for each day in spinning or weaving. The young girls could not weave, but could spin;[1] while the women became expert at weaving and spinning and made beautiful cloth. All kinds of cotton goods were woven, coarse osnaburgs, sheetings, coverlets, counterpanes, a kind of muslin, and various kinds of light cloth for women's dresses. Wool was grown on a large scale as the war went on, and the women wove flannels, plaids, balmorals, blankets, and carpets.[2] Gray jeans was woven to make clothing for the soldiers, who had almost no clothes except those sent them by their home people. A soldier's pay would not buy a shirt, even when he was paid, which was seldom the case. Nearly every one wove homespun, dyed with home-made dyes, and it was often very pretty. The women took more pride in their neat homespun dresses than they did before the war in the possession of silks and satins. And there was friendly rivalry between them in

[1] At the close of the war my mother was twelve years old; for more than two years she had been doing a woman's task at spinning. Her sister had been spinning for a year, though she was only six years old.

[2] Many of the heavier articles woven during the war, such as coverlets, counterpanes, rugs, etc., are still, after forty years, almost as good as new.

spinning and weaving the prettiest homespun as there was in making the whitest sugar, the cleanest rice, and the best wheat and corn. But they could not make enough cloth to supply both army and people, and old clothes stored away were brought out and used to the last scrap. When worn out the rags were unravelled and the short threads spun together and woven again into coarse goods. Pillow-cases and sheets were cut up for clothes and were replaced by homespun substitutes, and window curtains were made into women's clothes. Carpets were made into blankets. There were no blanket factories, and the legislature appropriated the carpets in the capitol for blankets for the soldiers.[1] Some people went to the tanyards and got hair from horse and cow hides and mixed it with cotton to make heavy cloth for winter use, which is said to have made a good-looking garment. Once in a long while the father or brother in the army would send home a bolt of calico, or even just enough to make one dress. Then there would be a very proud woman in the land. Scraps of these rare dresses and also of the homespun dresses are found in the old scrap-books of the time. The homespun is the better-looking. No one saw a fashion plate, and each one set the style. Hoop-skirts were made from the remains of old ones found in the garrets and plunder rooms. It is said that the southern women affected dresses that were slightly longer in front than behind, and held them aside in their hands. Sometimes fortunate persons succeeded in buying for a few hundred dollars some dress material that had been brought through the blockade. A calico dress cost in central Alabama from $100 to $600, other material in proportion. Sewing thread was made by the home spinners with infinite trouble, but it was never satisfactory. Buttons were made of pasteboard, pine bark, cloth, thread, persimmon seed, gourds, and wood covered with cloth. Pasteboard, for buttons and other uses, was made by pasting several layers of old papers together with flour paste.[2]

Sewing societies were formed for pleasure and to aid soldiers and the poor. At stated intervals great quantities of clothing and supplies were sent to the soldiers in the field and to the hospitals. All

[1] Acts, Dec., 1861, 2d Called and 1st Regular Sess., p. 70.

[2] Hague, "Blockaded Family," *passim ;* Miller, pp. 223–232; "Our Women in the War," p. 275 *et seq. ;* Clayton, "White and Black under the Old Régime," pp. 112–149; Porcher, "Resources of the Southern Fields and Forests," pp. 70, 107, 284–295, 351, 372, 657.

women became expert in crocheting and knitting — the occupations for leisure moments. Even when resting, one was expected to be doing something. Many formed the habit of knitting in those days and keep it up until to-day, as it became second nature to have something in the hands to work with. Many women who learned then can now knit a pair of socks from beginning to end without looking at them. After dark, when one could not see to sew, spin, or weave, was usually the time devoted to knitting and crocheting, which sometimes lasted until midnight. Capes, sacks, vandykes, gloves, socks and stockings, shawls, underclothes, and men's suspenders were knitted. The makers ornamented them in various ways, and the ornamentation served a useful purpose, as the thread was usually coarse and uneven, and the ornamentation concealed the irregularities that would have shown in plain work. The smoothest thread that could be made was used for knitting. To make this thread the finest bolls of cotton were picked before rain had fallen on them and stained the fibre.

The homespun cloth had to be dyed to make it look well, and, as the ordinary dye materials could not be obtained, substitutes were made at home from barks, leaves, roots, and berries. Much experimentation proved the following results: Maple and sweet gum bark with copperas produced purple; maple and red oak bark with copperas, a dove color; maple and red walnut bark with copperas, brown; sweet gum with copperas, a nearly black color; peach leaves with alum, yellow; sassafras root with copperas, drab; smooth sumac root, bark, and berries, black; black oak bark with alum, yellow; artichoke and black oak, yellow; black oak bark with oxide of tin, pale yellow to bright orange; black oak bark with oxide of iron, drab; black oak balls in a solution of vitriol, purple to black; alder with alum, yellow; hickory bark with copperas, olive; hickory bark with alum, green; white oak bark with alum, brown; walnut roots, leaves, and hulls, black. Copperas was used to "set" the dye, but when copperas was not to be had blacksmith's dust was used instead. Pine tree roots and tops, and dogwood, willow bark, and indigo were also used in dyes.[1]

[1] Clayton, "White and Black under the Old Régime"; Hague, "Blockaded Family," passim; Miller, p. 229; Jacobs, "Drug Conditions," p. 16; oral accounts; Porcher, passim.

Shoes for women and children were made of cloth or knitted uppers or of the skins of squirrels or other small animals, fastened to leather or wooden soles. A girl considered herself very fortunate if she could get a pair of "Sunday" shoes of calf or goat skin. There were shoemakers in each community, all old men or cripples, who helped the people with their makeshifts. Shoes for men were made of horse and cow hides, and often the soles were of wood. A wooden shoe was one of the first things patented at Richmond. Carriage curtains, buggy tops, and saddle skirts furnished leather for uppers, and metal protections were placed on leather soles. Little children went barefooted and stayed indoors in winter; many grown people went barefooted except in winter. Shoe blacking was made from soot mixed with lard or oil of ground-peas or of cotton-seed. This was applied to the shoe and over it a paste of flour or starch gave a good polish.

Old bonnets and hats were turned, trimmed, and worn again. Pretty hats were made of cloth or woven from dyed straw, bulrushes, corn-shucks, palmetto, oat and wheat straw, bean-grass, jeans, and bonnet squash, and sometimes of feathers. The rushes, shucks, palmetto, and bean-grass were bleached by boiling and sunning. Bits of old finery served to trim hats as well as feathers from turkeys, ducks, and peafowls, with occasional wheat heads for plumes. Fans were made of the palmetto and of the wing feathers and wing tips of turkeys and geese. Old parasols and umbrellas were re-covered, but the majority of the people could not afford cloth for such a purpose. Hair-oil was made from roses and lard. Thin-haired unfortunates made braids and switches from prepared bark.

The ingenious makeshifts and substitutes of the women were innumerable. They were more original than the men in making use of what material lay ready to hand or in discovering new uses for various things. The few men at home, however, were not always of the class that make discoveries or do original things. In an account of life on the farms and plantations in the South during the war, the white men may almost be left out of the story.

Drugs and Medicines

After the blockade became effective, drugs became very scarce and home-made preparations were substituted. All doctors became botanical practitioners. The druggist made his preparations from herbs, roots, and barks gathered in the woods and fields. Manufacturing laboratories were early established at Mobile and Montgomery to make medical preparations which were formerly procured abroad. Much attention was given to the manufacture of native preparations, which were administered by practitioners in the place of foreign drugs with favorable results. Surgeon Richard Potts, of Montgomery, Alabama, had exclusive charge of the exchange of cotton for medical supplies, and when allowed by the government to make the exchange, it was very easy for him to get drugs through the lines into Alabama and Mississippi. But this permission was too seldom given.[1]

Quinine was probably the scarcest drug. Instead of this were used dogwood berries, cotton-seed tea, chestnut and chinquapin roots and bark, willow bark, Spanish oak bark, and poplar bark. Red oak bark in cold water was used as a disinfectant and astringent for wounds. Boneset tea, butterfly or pleurisy root tea, mandrake tea, white ash or prickly ash root, and Sampson's snakeroot were used in fever cases. Local applications of mustard seed or leaves, hickory leaves, and pepper were used in cases of pneumonia and pleurisy, while sumac, poke root and berry, sassafras, alder, and prickly ash were remedies for rheumatism, neuralgia, and scrofula. Black haw root and partridge berry were used for hemorrhage; peach leaves and Sampson's snakeroot for dyspepsia and sassafras tea in the spring and fall served as a blood medicine. The balsam cucumber was used for a tonic, as also was dogwood, poplar, and rolled cherry bark in whiskey. Turpentine was useful as an adjunct in many cases. Hops were used for laudanum; may-apple root or peach tree leaf tea for senna; dandelion, pleurisy root, and butterfly weed for calomel. Corks were made from black gum roots, corn-cobs, and old life preservers. Barks were gathered when the sap was running, the roots after the leaves were dead, and medicinal plants when they were in bloom.[2] Opium was made from the poppy, cordials from the blackberry, huckleberry, and persimmon, brandy from watermelons and fruits, and wine from the elderberry.[3] Whiskey made in the hills of north Alabama, in gum log stills, formed the basis of nearly all medicinal preparations. The state had agents who looked after the proper distribution of the whiskey among the counties. The

---

[1] O. R., Ser. IV, Vol. III, pp. 1073-1075; Jacobs, "Drug Conditions."

[2] Jacobs, pp. 4-6, 12-14, 16-21; Porcher, p. 65.   [3] Hague, "Blockaded Family."

castor beans raised in the garden were crushed and boiled and the oil skimmed off.[1]

Social Life during the War

Life in the towns was not so monotonous as in the country. In the larger ones, especially in Mobile, there was a forced gayety throughout the war. Many marriages took place, and each wedding was usually the occasion of social festivities. In the country "homespun" weddings were the fashion — all parties at the wedding being clad in homespun. Colonel Thomas Dabney dined in Montgomery in November, 1864, with Mr. Woodleaf, a refugee from New Orleans. "They gave me," he said, "a fine dinner, good for any time, and some extra fine music afterwards, according to the Italian, Spanish, and French books, for we had some of each sort done up in true opera fashion, I suppose. It was a *leetle* too foreign for my ear, but that was my fault, and not the fault of the music."[2] The people were too busy for much amusement, yet on the surface life was not gloomy. Work was made as pleasant as possible, though it could never be made play. The women were never idle, and they often met together to work. There were sewing societies which met once a week for work and exchange of news. "Quiltings" were held at irregular intervals, to which every woman came armed with needle and thimble. At other times there would be spinning "bees," to which the women would come from long distances and stay all day, bringing with them in wagons their wheels, cards, and cotton. When a soldier came home on furlough or sick leave, every woman in the community went to see him, carrying her work with her, and knitted, sewed, or spun while listening to news from the army. The holiday soldier, the "bomb-proof," and the "feather bed" received little mercy from the women; a thorough contempt was the portion of such people. "Furlough" wounds came to receive slight sympathy.[3] The soldiers

---

[1] Jacobs, "Drug Conditions," pp. 4-6, 12-14, 16-21 ; Hague, "Blockaded Family," *passim ;* "Our Women in the War " ; Ball, "Clarke County " ; Miller, "Alabama " ; Porcher ; Pub. So. Hist. Ass'n, March, 1903.

[2] Smedes, "A Southern Planter," p. 226.

[3] In the early part of the war when a soldier received a slight wound he was given a furlough for a few weeks until he was well again. Slight wounds came to be called "furloughs," and some soldiers when particularly homesick are said to have exposed themselves unnecessarily in order to get a "furlough."

R

always brought messages from their comrades to their relatives in the community, which was often the only way of hearing from those in the army. Letters were uncertain, the postal system never being good in the country districts. Postage was ten to twenty cents on a letter, and one to five cents on small newspapers. Letters from the army gave news of the men of the settlement who were in the writer's company or regiment, and when received were read to the neighbors or sent around the community. Often when a young man came home on furlough or passed through the country, there would be many social gatherings or "parties" in his honor, and here the young people gathered. There were parties for the older men, too, and dinners and suppers. Here the soldier met again his neighbors, or rather the feminine half of them, anxious to hear his experiences and to inquire about friends and relatives in the army. The young people also met at night at "corn shuckings" and "candy pullings," from which they managed to extract a good deal of pleasure. At the social gatherings, especially of the older people, some kind of work was always going on. Parching pindars to eat and making peanut candy were amusements for children after supper.

The intense devotion of the women to the Confederate cause was most irritating to a certain class of Federal officers in the army that invaded north Alabama. They seemed to think that they had conquered entrance into society, but the women were determined to show their colors on all occasions and often had trouble when boorish officers were in command. A society woman would lose her social position if seen in the company of Federal officers. When passing them, the women averted their faces and swept aside their skirts to prevent any contact with the hated Yankee. They played and sang Confederate airs on all occasions, and when ordered by the military authorities to discontinue, it usually took a guard of soldiers to enforce the order. The Federal officers who acted in a gentlemanly manner toward the non-combatants were accused by their rude fellows and by ruder newspaper correspondents of being "wound round the fingers of the rebel women," who had some object to gain. When the people of a community were especially contemptuous of the Federals, they were sometimes punished by having a negro regiment stationed as a garrison. Athens, in Limestone county, one of the most intensely southern towns, was garrisoned by a regiment of negroes recruited in the immediate vicinity.[1]

For the negroes in the Black Belt life went on much as before the war. More responsibility was placed upon the trusty ones, and they proved themselves worthy of the trust. They were acquainted with the questions at issue and knew that their freedom would probably follow victory by the North. Yet the black overseer and the black preacher, with their fellow-slaves, went on with their work. The master's family lived on the large plantation with no other whites within miles and never felt fear of harm from their black guardians. The negroes had their dances and, 'possum hunts on Saturday nights after the week's work was done. There was preaching and singing on Sunday, the whites often attending the negro services and *vice versa*. Negro weddings took place in the "big house." The young mistresses would adorn the bride, and the ceremony would be performed by the old white clergyman, after which the wedding supper would be served in the family dining room or out under the trees. These were great occasions for the negroes and for the young people of the master's family. The sound of fiddle and banjo, songs, and laughter were always heard in the "quarters" after work was done, though Saturday night was the great time for merrymaking. In July and August, after the crops were "laid by," the negroes had barbecues and picnics. To these the whites were invited and they always attended. The materials for these feasts were furnished by the mistress and by the negroes themselves, who had garden patches, pigs, and poultry. The slaves were, on the whole, happy and content.

The clothes for the slaves were made under the superintendence of the mistress, who, after the war began, often cut out the clothes for every negro on the place, and sometimes assisted in making them. Some of the negro women had spinning-wheels and looms, and clothed their own families, while others spun, wove, and made their clothes under the direction of the mistress. But most of them could not be trusted with the materials, because they were so unskilful. It took a month or two twice a year to get the negroes into their new outfits. The rule was that each negro should have two suits of heavy material for winter wear and two of light goods for summer. To

[1] See *Boston Journal*, Sept. 29 and Nov. 15, 1864.

clothe the negroes during the war time was a heavy burden upon the mistress.

To those negroes who did their own cooking rations were issued on Saturday afternoon. Bacon and corn meal formed the basis of the ration, besides which there would be some kind of "sweetening" and a substitute for coffee.[1] Special goodies were issued for Sunday. The negroes in the Black Belt fared better during the war than either the whites or the negroes in the white counties. When there were few slaves or in the time of great scarcity, the cooking for whites and blacks was often done in the house kitchen by the same cooks. This was done in order to leave more time for the negroes to work and to prevent waste. Where there were many slaves, there was often some arrangement made by which cooking was done in common, though there were numbers of families that did their own cooking at home all the time. When meat was scarce, it was given to the negro laborers who needed the strength, while the white family and the negro women and children denied themselves.

As the Confederate government did not provide well for the soldiers, their wives and mothers had to supply them. The sewing societies undertook to clothe the soldiers who went from their respective neighborhoods. Once a week or once a month, a box was sent from each society. One box sent to the Grove Hill Guards contained sixty pairs of socks, twenty-five blankets, thirteen pairs of gloves, fourteen flannel shirts, sixteen towels, two handkerchiefs, five pairs of trousers, and one bushel of dried apples. Other boxes contained about the same. Hams and any other edibles that would keep were frequently sent and also simple medicine chests. When blankets could not be had, quilts were sent, or heavy curtains and pieces of carpet. With the progress of the war, there was much suffering among the soldiers and their destitute families that the state could do but little to relieve, and the women took up the task. Besides the various church aid societies, we hear of the "Grove Hill Military Aid Society" and the "Suggsville Soldiers' Aid Society," both of Clarke County; the "Aid Society of Mobile"; the "Montgomery Home Society" and the "Soldiers' Wayside Home," in Montgomery; the "Wayside Hospital" and the "Ladies' Military Aid Society" of Selma; the "Talladega Hospital"; the "Ladies' Humane Society"

---

[1] See Mrs. Clayton's "White and Black" in regard to rations for negroes.

of Huntsville,[1] and many others. The legislature gave financial aid
to some of them. Societies were formed in every town, village, and
country settlement to send clothing, medicines, and provisions to the
soldiers in the army and to the hospitals. The members went to
hospitals and parole camps for sick and wounded soldiers, took them
to their homes, and nursed them back to health. "Wayside Homes"
were established in the towns for the accommodation of soldiers travelling to and from the army. Soldiers on sick leave and furlough
who were cut off from their homes beyond the Mississippi came to
the homes of their comrades, sure of a warm welcome and kind attentions. Poor soldiers sick at home were looked after and supplies sent
to their needy families.

The last year of the war a bushel of corn cost $13, while a soldier's
pay was $11 a month, paid once in a while. So the poor people be-
came destitute. But the state furnished meal and salt to all[2] and the
more fortunate people gave liberally of their supplies. Many of the
poorer white women did work for others — weaving, sewing, and
spinning — for which they were well paid, frequently in provisions,
which they were in great need of. Some made hats, bonnets, and
baskets for sale. The cotton counties supported many refugees from
the northern counties, and numerous poor people from that section
imposed upon the generosity of the planting section. The overseers,
white or black, had a dislike for those to whom supplies were given;
they also objected to the regular payment of the tax-in-kind, and to
impressment which took their corn, meat, horses, cows, mules, and
negroes, and crippled their operations. The mistresses had to
interfere and see that the poor and the government had their
share.

In the cities the women engaged in various patriotic occupations,
— sewing for the soldiers, nursing, raising money for hospitals, etc.
The women of Tuskegee raised money to be spent on a gunboat for
the defence of Mobile Bay. They wanted it called *The Women's
Gunboat.*[3] "A niece of James Madison" wrote to a Mobile paper,

---

[1] See Acts of Ala., Nov. 28 and 30, 1861, Dec. 9, 1862, and Dec. 8, 1863;
Transactions Ala. Hist. Soc., Vol. IV, pp. 219 *et seq.*

[2] It was estimated that one-fourth of the people of the state were furnished for
three years with meal and salt.

[3] Moore, " Rebellion Record," Vol. IV (1862).

proposing that 200,000 women in the South sell their hair in Europe to raise funds for the Confederacy. The movement failed because of the blockade.[1] There were other similar propositions, but they could not be carried out, and year after year the legislatures of the state thanked the women for their patriotic devotion, their labors, sacrifices, constancy, and courage.

The music and songs that were popular during the war show the changing temper of the people. At first were heard joyous airs, later contemptuous and defiant as war came on; then jolly war songs and strong hymns of encouragement. But as sorrow followed sorrow until all were stricken; as wounds, sickness, imprisonment, and death of friends and relatives cast shadow over the spirits of the people; as hopes were dashed by defeat, and the consciousness came that perhaps after all the cause was losing, — the iron entered into the souls of the people. The songs were sadder now. The church hymns heard were the soul-comforting ones and the militant songs of the older churchmen. The first year were heard "Farewell to Brother Jonathan," "We Conquer or We Die;" then "Riding a Raid," "Stonewall Jackson's Way," "All Quiet Along the Potomac," "Lorena," "Beechen Brook," "Somebody's Darling," "When the Cruel War is O'er," "Guide Me, O Thou Great Jehovah." "Dixie" was sung and played during the entire time, whites and blacks singing it with equal pleasure. The older hymns were sung and the doctrines of faith and good works earnestly preached. The promises were, perhaps, more emphasized. A deeply religious feeling prevailed among the home workers for the cause.

The women had the harder task. The men were in the field in active service, their families were safe at home, there was no fear for themselves. The women lived in constant dread of news from the front; they had to sit still and wait, and their greatest comfort was the hard work they had to do. It gave them some relief from the burden of sorrow that weighed down the souls of all. To the very last the women hoped and prayed for success, and failure, to many of them, was more bitter than death. The loss of their cause

---

[1] *N. Y. News*, March 29, 1864, from the *Richmond Whig*, from the *Mobile Evening News;* oral accounts. There were numbers of women who actually cut off their hair, thinking that it could be sold through the blockade. For a while they were hopeful and enthusiastic in regard to the plan of selling their hair.

hurt them more deeply than it did the men who had the satisfaction of fighting out the quarrel, even though the other side was victorious.[1]

[1] P. A. Hague's " Blockaded Family" is the best account of life in Alabama during the war. Mrs. Clayton's " White and Black under the Old Régime" is very good, but brief. "Our Women in the War" is a valuable collection of articles by a number of women. Nearly all the incidents mentioned I have heard related by relatives and friends. " John Holden, Unionist," by T. C. De Leon, gives a good account of life in the hill country. Mary A. H. Gay's " Life in Dixie during the War" and Miller's " History of Alabama" give information based on personal experiences. Porcher's " Resources of the Southern Fields and Forests," published in 1863, is a mine of information in regard to economic conditions in the South. Porcher quotes much from the newspapers and from correspondence. The second edition, published in 1867, omits much of the more interesting material.

PART III

THE AFTERMATH OF WAR

CHAPTER V

SOCIAL AND ECONOMIC DISORDER

Sec. 1. Loss of Life and Property

The Loss of Life

The surviving soldiers came straggling home, worn out, broken in health, crippled, in rags, half starved, little better off, they thought, than the comrades they had left under the sod of the battle-fields on the border. In the election of 1860 about 90,000 votes were cast, nearly the entire voting population, and about this number of Alabama men enlisted in the Confederate and Union armies. Various estimates were made of Alabama's losses during the war, most of which are doubtless too large. Among these Governor Parsons, in his inaugural address, gives the number as 35,000 killed or died of wounds and disease, and as many more disabled.[1] Colonel W. H. Fowler, for two years the state agent for settling the claims of deceased soldiers and also superintendent of army records, states that he had the names of nearly 20,000 dead on his lists and believed this to be only about half of the entire number; that the Alabama troops lost more heavily than any other troops. He asserted that of the 30,000 Alabama troops in the Army of Northern Virginia over 9000 had died in

---

[1] In his inaugural proclamation of July 20 (or 21), 1865, Governor Parsons gives the following figures : —

Alabama male population (1860), 15 to 60 years	126,587
Connecticut male population (1860), 15 to 60 years	120,249
Alabama soldiers enlisted	122,000
Connecticut soldiers enlisted	40,000
Alabama soldiers died in service	35,000
Alabama soldiers disabled	35,000

N. Y. Times, Aug. 2, 1865 ; *N. Y. Herald*, Aug. 11, 1865 ; Parsons's Message, Nov. 22, 1865 ; Parsons's Speech at Cooper Institute, Nov. 13, 1865.

service, and of those who were retired, discharged, or who resigned, about one-half were either dead or permanently disabled.[1] These estimates are evidently too large, and they probably form the basis of the statements of Governors Parsons and Patton. Governor Patton estimated that 40,000 had died in service, while 20,000 were disabled for life, and that there were 20,000 widows and 60,000 orphans.[2] A *Times* correspondent places the loss in war at 34,000.[3] The strongest regiments were worn out by 1865. At Appomattox, when three times as many men surrendered as were in a condition to bear arms, the Alabama commands paroled hardly enough men in each regiment to form a good company. Though the average enlistment had been 1350 to the regiment, one of the best regiments — the Third Alabama Infantry — paroled: from Company B, 8 men; from Company D, 7 men; Company G, 4; Company E, 7; while the Fifth Alabama paroled: from Company A, 2; B, 7; C, 2; E, 2; F, 1; K, 3. The Twelfth Alabama: Company A, 4; C, 6; D, 6; E, 4; G, 3; I, 5; M, 4. Sixth Alabama (over 2000 enlistments): D, 2; F, 2; I, 5; M, 4. Sixty-first Alabama: B, 2; C, 4; E, 1; G, 5; I, 4; K, 3. Fifteenth Alabama: C, 8. Forty-eighth Alabama: C, 6; K, 7. Ninth Alabama: 70 men in all — an average of 7 to a company. Thirteenth Alabama: 85 men in all. Forty-first Alabama: 74 men in all. Forty-first, Forty-third, Fifty-ninth, Sixtieth, and Twenty-third: 220 men in all. Some companies were entirely annihilated, having neither officer nor private at the surrender. A company from Demopolis is said to have lost all except 7 men, that is, 125 by death in the service.[4] The census of 1866 contains the names of 8957 soldiers killed in battle, 13,534 who died of disease or wounds, and 2629 disabled for life.[5] These are the only facts obtainable on which to base calculations, yet the census was very imperfect, as hundreds of families were broken up, thousands of men forgotten, and there was no one to give information regarding them to the census taker.

---

[1] Fowler's Report, Transactions Ala. Hist. Soc., Vol. II, p. 188.

[2] Ho. Mis. Doc., No. 114, 39th Cong., 1st Sess.

[3] *N. Y. Times*, Oct. 31, 1865.

[4] Southern Hist. Soc. Papers, Vol. XV (Paroles at Appomattox); Miller, "History of Alabama," p. 233; Brewer, "Regimental Histories."

[5] Census of 1866, *Selma Times and Messenger*, March 24, 1868.

The white population decreased 3632 from 1860 to 1866, according to the census of the latter year. But for the war, according to rate of increase from 1850 to 1860, there should have been an increase of 50,000. In 1870 the census showed a further decrease of 1415, due, perhaps, to the great mortality just after the war. In other words, the white population was about 100,000 less in 1870 than it would have been under normal conditions, without immigration. Contemporary accounts state that the negro suffered much more than the whites in the two years immediately following the war, from starvation, exposure, and pestilence, and the census of 1866 showed a decrease of 14,325 in the colored population, when there should have been an increase of nearly 70,000 according to the rate of 1850 to 1860, besides the 20,000 that it has been estimated were sent into the interior of the state from other states to escape capture by the raiding Federals. The census of 1866 was not accurate, for the negroes at that time were in a very unsettled condition, wandering from place to place. However, in 1870, the number of negroes had increased 37,740 over the numbers for 1860, while the number of whites had decreased several thousand, which would seem to indicate that the census of 1866 was defective. But there is no doubt that the negroes suffered terribly during this time.[1]

Destruction of Property

Governor Patton, in a communication to Congress dated May 11, 1866, gives the property losses in Alabama as $500,000,000,[2] which sum doubtless includes the value of the slaves, estimated in 1860 at $200,000,000, or about $500 each.[3] The value of other property in 1860 has been estimated at $640,000,000, the assessed value, $256,428,893, being 40 per cent of the real value.[4]

[1] WHITES					BLACKS				
1860	.	.	.	. . 526,271	1860	.	.	. .	. 437,770
1866	.	.	.	. . 522,799	1866	.	.	. .	. 423,445
1870	.	.	.	. . 521,384	1870	.	.	. .	. 475,510

Censuses of 1860, 1866, 1870.

[2] Ho. Mis. Doc., No. 114, 39th Cong., 1st Sess.
[3] Miller, "History of Alabama," p. 141.
[4] Miller, "Alabama," p. 141 (Auditor's Report).

A comparison of the census statistics of 1860 and of 1870 after five years of Reconstruction will be suggestive: —

	1860	1870
Value of farms	$175,824,032	$54,191,229
Value of live stock	43,411,711	21,325,076
Value of farm implements	7,433,178	5,946,543
Number of horses	127,000	80,000
Number of mules	111,000	76,000
Number of oxen	88,000	59,000
Number of cows	230,000	170,000
Number of other cattle	454,000	257,000
Number of sheep	370,000	241,000
Number of swine	1,748,000	719,000
Improved land in farms, acres	6,385,724	5,062,204
Corn crop, bushels	33,226,000	16,977,000
	(35,053,047 in 1899)	
Cotton crop, bales	989,955	429,482
	(1,106,840 in 1899)	

Not until 1880 was the acreage of improved lands as great as in 1860.[1] Live stock, valued at $43,000,000 in 1860, is still to-day $7,000,000 behind. Farm implements and machinery in 1900 were worth $1,000,000 more than in 1860, having doubled in value in the last ten years.[2] Land improvements and buildings, worth $175,000,-000 in 1860, were in 1900 still more than $30,000,000 below that mark. The total value of farm property in 1860 was $226,669,511; in 1870, $97,716,055;[3] and in 1900, $179,339,882. Though the population has increased twofold since 1860[4] and the white counties have developed and the industries have become more varied, agriculture has not yet reached the standard of 1860, the Black Belt farmer is much less prosperous, and the agricultural system of the old cotton belt has never recovered from the effects of the war. From the theoretical point of view the abolition of slavery should have resulted in loss only during the readjustment of industrial conditions. Yet $200,000,000 capital had been lost; and, as a matter of fact, the statistics of agriculture show that, while in the white counties in 1900 there was a greater yield of the staple crops, — cotton and corn,

[1] 1860, 6,385,724 acres; 1880, 6,375,706 acres.
[2] 1860, $7,433,178; 1890, $4,511,645; 1900, $8,675,900.
[3] Which must be reduced by one-fifth for depreciated currency.
[4] See Census Bulletin, No. 155, 12th Census.

—in the black counties the free negroes of double the number do not yet produce as much as the slaves of 1860.[1]

The manufacturing establishments that had existed before the war or were developed during that time were destroyed by Federal raids, or were seized, sold, and dismantled after the surrender because they had furnished supplies to the Confederacy. The public buildings used by the Confederate authorities in all the towns and all over the country were burned or were turned over to the Freedmen's Bureau. The state and county public buildings in the track of the raiders were destroyed. The stocks of goods in the stores were exhausted long before the close of the war. All banking capital, and all securities, railroad bonds and stocks, state and Confederate bonds, and currency were worth nothing. All the accumulated capital of the state was swept away; only the soil and some buildings remained. People owning hundreds of acres of land often were as destitute as the poorest negro. The majority of people who had money to invest had bought Confederate securities as a patriotic duty, and all the coin had been drawn from the country. The most of the bonded debt was held in Mobile, and that city lost all its capital when the debt was declared null and void.[2] This city suffered severely, also, from a terrible explosion soon after the surrender. Twenty squares in the business part were destroyed.[3]

Thousands of private residences were destroyed, especially in north Alabama, where the country was even more thoroughly devastated than in the path of Sherman through Georgia. The third year of the war had seen the destruction of everything destructible in north Alabama outside of the large towns, where the devastation was usually not so great. In Decatur, however, nearly all the buildings were burned; only three of the principal ones were left standing.[4] Tuscumbia was practically destroyed, and many houses were condemned for army use.[5] The beautiful buildings of the Black Belt

[1] Census, 1860 and 1900; Miller, " Alabama," p. 235.

[2] *N. Y. Times*, Nov. 2, 1865 (Truman).

[3] The explosion was caused by fire reaching the ordnance stores left by the Confederate troops. One of the cotton agents claimed that 9000 bales of cotton were destroyed for him in the explosion. But the government held otherwise. It was charged, without satisfactory proof, that the cotton agents caused the explosion to cover their shortage.

[4] " Northern Alabama Illustrated," p. 321.

[5] " Northern Alabama Illustrated," p. 427.

were out of repair and fast going to ruin. Many of the fine houses in the cities — especially in Mobile — had fallen into the hands of the Jews. One place, which was bought for $45,000 before the war, was sold with difficulty in 1876 for $10,000. Before the war there were sixteen French business houses in Mobile; none survived the war. The port of Mobile never again reached its former importance. In 1860, 900,000 bales of cotton had been shipped from the port; in 1865-1866, 400,000 bales; in 1866-1867, 250,000 bales; in 1876, 400,000 bales. There was no disposition on the part of the Washington administration to remove the obstructions in Mobile harbor. They were left for years and furnished an excuse to the reconstructionists for the expenditure of state money.[1] Nearly all the grist-mills and cotton-gins had been destroyed, mill-dams cut, and ponds drained. The raiders never spared a cotton-gin. The cotton, in which the government was interested, was either burned or seized and sold, and private cotton, when found, fared in the same way. Cotton had been the cause of much trouble to the commanders on both sides during the war; it was considered the mainstay of the South before the war and the root of all evil. So of all property it received

DEVASTATION
BY INVADING ARMIES
1861-1865.

- - - 1861
- . - 1862
- . - 1863
- - - 1864
——— 1865

---

[1] M. G. Molinari, "Lettres sur les États-Unis et le Canada," p. 233; Somers, "Southern States," pp. 181, 183.

the least consideration from the Federal troops, and was very easily turned into cash. All farm animals near the track of the armies had been carried away or killed by the soldiers (as at Selma), or seized after the occupation by the troops. Horses, mules, cows, and other domestic animals had almost disappeared except in the secluded districts. Many a farmer had to plough with oxen. Farm and plantation buildings had been dismantled or burned, houses ruined, fences destroyed, corn, meat, and syrup taken. The plantations in the Tennessee valley were in a ruined condition. The gin-houses were burned, the bridges ruined, mills and factories gone, and the roads impassable.[1] In the homes that were left, carpets and curtains were gone, for they had been used as blankets and clothes, window glass was out, furniture injured or destroyed, and crockery broken. In the larger towns, where something had been saved from the wreck of war, the looting by the Federal soldiers was shameful. Pianos, furniture, pictures, curtains, sofas, and other household goods were shipped North by the Federal officers during the early days of the occupation. Gold and silver plate and jewellery were confiscated by the bummers who were with every command. Abuses of this kind became so flagrant that the northern papers condemned the conduct of the soldiers, and several ministers, among them Henry Ward Beecher, rebuked the practice from the pulpit.[2]

Land was almost worthless, because the owners had no capital, no farm animals, no farm implements, in many cases not even seed. Labor was disorganized, and the product of labor was most likely to be stolen by roving negroes and other marauders. Seldom was more than one-third of a plantation under cultivation, the remainder growing up in broom sedge because laborers could not be gotten. When the Federal armies passed, many negroes followed them and never returned. Numbers of them died in the camps. When the war ended, many others left their old homes, some of whom several

---

[1] Somers, "Southern States," p. 114; Ho. Ex. Doc., No. 114, 39th Cong., 1st Sess.

[2] John Hardy, " History of Selma," pp. 51, 52; Reid, "After the War," pp. 211, 214, 222, 371; Miller, "Alabama," pp. 233-235; Ho. Mis. Doc., No. 114, 39th Cong., 1st Sess. (Patton to Congress) ; N. Y. Times, Nov. 2, Oct. 31, and Aug. 17, 1865; Riley, "History of Conecuh County"; Riley, " Baptists of Alabama," pp. 304, 305; Brewer, "Alabama," pp. 65, 69; Brown, "Alabama," pp. 254, 256; DuBose, " Alabama," pp. 114, 115; "Our Women in the War," p. 277 et seq.

s

years later came straggling back.[1]   Land that would produce a bale
of cotton to the acre, worth $125, and selling in 1860 for $50 per
acre at the lowest, was now selling for from $3 to $5 per acre.   Among
the negroes, especially after the occupation, there was a general belief,
which was carefully fostered by a certain class of Federal officials
and by some leaders in Congress, that the lands would be confiscated
and divided among the "unionists" and the negroes.   When the state
seceded, it took charge of the public lands within its boundaries
and opened them to settlement.   After the fall of the Confederacy
those who had purchased lands were required to rebuy them from
the United States or to give up their claims.   Some lands were
abandoned, as the owners were able neither to cultivate nor to sell
them, for there was no capital.   In Cumberland, a village, at one
time there were ninety advertisements of sales posted in the hotel.
The planters often found themselves amid a wilderness of land, without laborers, and often rented land free to some white man or to a
negro who would pay the taxes.[2]   Many hundreds of the people
could see no hope whatever for the future of the state, and certainly
the North was not acting so as to encourage them.   Hence there
was heavy emigration to Brazil, Cuba, Mexico, the northern and
western states, and much property was offered at a tenth of its value
and even less.

The heaviest losses fell upon the old wealthy families, who, by
the loss of wealth and by political proscription, were ruined.   In
middle life and in old age they were unable to begin again, and for
a generation their names disappear from sight.   Losses, debts,
taxes, and proscriptions bore down many, and few rose to take their
places.[3]   The poorer people, though they had but little to lose, lost
all, and suffered extreme poverty during the latter years of the war
and the early years of Reconstruction.   No wonder they were in despair and seemed for a while a menace to public order.   To the power
and influence of the leaders succeeded in part a second-rate class —
the rank and file of 1861 — upon whom the losses of the war fell
with less weight, and who were thrown to the front by the war which
ruined those above and those below them.   They were the sound,
hard-working men — the lawyers, farmers, merchants, who had for-

---

[1] Somers, "Southern States," p. 115.   [2] Somers, "Southern States," p. 115.
[3] Somers, "Southern States," p. 114.

merly been content to allow brilliant statesmen to direct the public affairs. Now those leaders were dead or proscribed, for poverty, war, reconstruction, and political persecution rapidly destroyed the old ruling element, and deaths among them after the war were very common. The men who rescued the state in 1874 were the men of lesser ability of 1860, farmer subordinates in the political ranks.[1]

The Wreck of the Railways

The steamboats on the rivers were destroyed. At that time the steamers probably carried as much freight and as many passengers as did the railroads, and served to connect the railway systems. The railroads also were in a ruined condition; depots had been burned, bridges and trestles destroyed, tracks torn up, cross-ties burned or were rotten, rails worn out or ruined by burning, cars and locomotives worn out or destroyed or captured. The boards of directors and the presidents of the roads, because of the aid they had given the Confederacy, were not considered safe persons to trust with the reorganization of the system, and, in August, 1865, Stanton, the Secretary of War, directed that each southern railway be reorganized with a "loyal" board of directors.

In 1860 there were about 800 miles of railways in Alabama. Nearly all of the roads were unfinished in 1861, and, except on the most important military roads, little progress was made in their construction during the war — only about 20 or 30 miles being completed. During this time all roads were practically under the control of the Confederate government, which operated them through their own boards of directors and other officials. The various roads suffered in different degrees. At the close of the war, the Tennessee and Alabama Railroad had only two or three cars that could be used, the rails also were worn out, the locomotives out of order and useless, nearly all the depots, bridges, and trestles destroyed, as well as all of its shops, water tanks, machinery, books, and papers. The Memphis and Charleston, extending across the entire northern part of the state, fell into the hands of the Federals in 1862, who captured at Huntsville nearly all of the rolling stock and destroyed the shops

[1] Reid, "After the War," pp. 222, 371; Ball, "Clarke County," p. 294; Riley, "Baptists of Alabama," pp. 304–305; *N. Y. Times*, Oct. 31, 1865; *N. Y. Herald*, July 23, 1865.

and the papers. The rolling stock had been collected at Huntsville, ready to be shipped to a place of less danger; but because of the treachery of a telegraph operator who kept the knowledge of the approaching raid from the officials, all was lost, for to prevent its falling into the hands of the enemy much more was destroyed than was captured. When the Federals were driven from a section of the road, they destroyed it in order to prevent the Confederates from using it. The length of this road in the state was 155 miles, and 140 miles of the track were torn up, the rails heated in the middle over fires of burning cross-ties, and the iron then twisted around trees and stumps so as to make it absolutely useless. In 1865 very little machinery of any kind was left. Besides this the company lost heavily in Confederate securities, and the other losses (funds, etc.) amounted to $1,195,166.79.

The Mobile and Ohio lost in Confederate currency $5,228,562.23. Thirty-seven miles of rails were worn out, 21 miles were burned and twisted, 184 miles of road cleared of bridges, trestles, and stations, the cross-ties burned, and the shops near Mobile destroyed. There were 18 of 59 locomotives in working order, 11 of 26 passenger cars, 3 of 11 baggage cars, 231 of 721 freight cars. The Selma and Meridian lost its shops and depots in Selma and Meridian, and its bridges over the Cahaba and Valley creeks. It sustained a heavy loss in Confederate bonds and currency. The Alabama and Tennessee Rivers Railroad lost a million dollars in Confederate funds, its shops, tools, and machinery at Selma, 6 bridges, its trestles, some track and many depots, its locomotives and cars. The Wills Valley Road suffered but little from destruction or from loss in Confederate securities. The Mobile and Great Northern escaped with a loss of only $401,190.37 in Confederate money, and $164,800 by destruction, besides the wear and tear on its track and rolling stock in the four years without repairs. The Alabama and Florida Road lost in Confederate currency $755,343,21. It had at the end of the war only 4 locomotives and 40 cars of all descriptions. The people were so poor that in the summer of 1865 this road, on a trip from Mobile to Montgomery and return, a distance of 360 miles, collected in fares only $13. The Montgomery and West Point, 161 miles in length, and one of the best roads in the state, probably suffered the heaviest loss from raids. It lost in currency $1,618,243, besides all of its rolling stock that was in running order; much of the track was torn up and rails twisted, all bridges and tanks and depots were destroyed. Both Rousseau and Wilson tore up the track and destroyed the shops and rolling stock at Montgomery and along the road to West Point and also the rolling stock that had been sent to Columbus, Georgia. After the surrender an old locomotive that had been thrown aside at Opelika and 14 condemned cars were patched up, and for a while this old engine and a couple of flat cars were run up and down the road as a passenger train. The worn strap rails used in repairing gave much trouble. The fare was 10 cents a mile in coin or 20 cents in greenbacks.[1] Every road in the South lost rolling stock on the border. The few cars and locomotives left to any road were often scattered over several states, and some of them were never returned.

As the Federal armies occupied the country, they took charge of the railways, which were then run either under the direction of the War Department or the railroad division of the army. After the war they were returned to the stockholders as soon as "loyal" boards of directors were appointed or the "disloyal" ones made "loyal" by the pardon of the President. Contractors who undertook to re-open the roads in the summer of 1865 were unable to do so because the negroes refused to work. The companies were bankrupt, for all money due them was Confederate currency, and all they had in their possession was Confederate currency. Many debts that had been paid by the roads during the war to the states and counties now had to be paid again. All of the nine roads in the state attempted reorganization, but only three were able to accomplish it, and these then absorbed the others. None, it appears, were abandoned.[2]

---

[1] An indignant northern newspaper correspondent appealed to the military authorities to check this "rebellious discrimination," but nothing was done. The railroad officials, as well as all other southern people, were now suspicious of paper money.

[2] Ho. Repts., Vol. IV, 39th Cong., 2d Sess., on "Affairs of Southern Railroads"; Trowbridge, "The South," p. 451; Reid, "After the War," p. 212; Brewer, "Alabama," pp. 78, 79; Miller, "Alabama," pp. 141, 234; *N. Y. World*, July 18, 1865; *Selma Times*, Jan. 25 and Feb. 2, 1866; *N. Y. Times*, Oct. 31, 1865; April 25 and July 2, 1866; Berney, "Handbook of Alabama"; Hodgson, "Alabama Manual and Statistical Register."

Sec. 2. The Interregnum; Lawlessness and Disorder

Immediately after the surrender of the armies a general demand arose from the people throughout the lower South that the governors convene the state legislatures for the purpose of calling conventions which, by repealing the ordinance of secession and abolishing slavery, could prepare the way for reunion. This, it was thought, was all that the North wanted, and it seemed to be in harmony with Lincoln's plan of restoration. General Richard Taylor, when he surrendered at Meridian, Mississippi, advised the governors of Tennessee, Alabama, and Mississippi to take steps to carry out such measures; and General Canby, to whom Taylor surrendered the department, indorsed the plan, as did also the various general officers of the armies of occupation. But these generals were not in touch with politics at Washington. The Federal government outlawed the existing southern state governments, leaving them with no government at all. Governor Watts and ex-Governors Shorter and Moore were arrested and sent to northern prisons. A number of prominent leaders, among them John Gayle of Selma and ex-Senators Clay and Fitzpatrick, were also arrested. The state government went to pieces. General Canby was instructed by President Johnson to arrest any member of the Alabama legislature who might attempt to hold a meeting of the general assembly. Consequently, from the first of May until the last of the summer the state of Alabama was without any state government;[1] and it was only after several months of service as provisional governor that Parsons was able to reorganize the state administration.

For six months after the surrender there was practically no government of any kind in Alabama except in the immediate vicinity of the military posts, where the commander exercised a certain authority over the people of the community. A good commander could do little more than let affairs take their course, for the great mass of the people only wanted to be left alone for a while. They were tired of war and strife and wanted rest and an opportunity to work their crops and make bread for their suffering families. The strong-

---

[1] *N. Y. Herald*, June 17 and Aug. 30, 1865; Taylor, "Destruction and Reconstruction," pp. 227, 228; Miller, "History of Alabama," p. 237; McCulloch, "Men and Measures," p. 235.

est influence of the respectable people was exerted in favor of peace and order.   While much lawlessness appeared in the state, it was not as much as might have been expected under the existing circumstances at the close of the great Civil War.   Much of the disorder was caused by the presence of the troops, some of whom were even more troublesome than the robbers and outlaws from whom they were supposed to protect the people.   The best soldiers of the Federal army had demanded their discharge as soon as fighting was over, and had gone home.   Those who remained in the service in the state were, with few exceptions, very disorderly, and kept the people in terror by their robberies and outrages.   Especially troublesome among the negro population, and a constant cause of irritation to the whites, were the negro troops, who were sent into the state, the people believed, in order to humiliate the whites.   They were commanded by officers who had been insulted and threatened all during the war because of their connection with these troops, and this treatment had embittered them against the southern people.   The negro troops were stationed in towns where Confederate spirit had been very strong, as a discipline to the people.   For months and even years after the surrender the Federal troops in small detachments were accustomed to march through the country, searching for cotton and other public property and arresting citizens on charges preferred by the tories or by the negroes, many of whom spent their time confessing the sins of their white neighbors.   The garrison towns suffered from the unruly behavior of the soldiers.   The officers, who were only waiting to be mustered out of service, devoted themselves to drinking, women, and gambling.   The men followed their example.   The traffic in whiskey was enormous, and most of the sales were to the soldiers, to the lowest class of whites, and to the negroes.   The streets of the towns and cities such as Montgomery, Mobile, Selma, Huntsville, Athens, and Tuscaloosa, were crowded with drunken and violent soldiers.   Lewd women had followed the army and had established disreputable houses near every military post, which were the centre and cause of many lawless outbreaks.   Quarrels were frequent, and at a disorderly ball in Montgomery, in the fall of 1865, a Federal officer was killed.   The peaceable citizens were plundered by the camp followers, discharged soldiers, and the deserters who now crawled out of their retreats.   Sometimes these marauders dressed in the Federal uniforms when on their expeditions, in order to cast suspicion on the soldiers, who were often wrongfully charged with these crimes.[1]

As one instance of the many outrages committed at this time the following may be cited: in the summer of 1865, when all was in disorder and no government existed in the state, a certain "Major" Perry, as his followers called him, went on a private raid through the country to get a part of anything that might be left. He was one of the many who thought that they deserved some share of the spoils and who were afraid that the time of their harvest would be short. So it was necessary to make the best of the disordered condition of affairs. Perry was followed by a few white soldiers, or men who dressed as soldiers, and by a crowd of negroes. At his saddle-bow was tied a bag containing his most valuable plunder. From house to house in Dallas and adjoining counties he and his men went, demanding valuables, pulling open trunks and bureau and wardrobe drawers, scattering their contents, and choosing what they wanted, tearing pictures in pieces, and scattering the contents of boxes of papers and books in a spirit of pure destructiveness. At one house they found some old shirts which the mistress had carefully mended for her husband, who had not yet returned from the army. One of the marauders suggested that they be added to their collection. "Major" Perry looked at them carefully, but, as he was rather choice in his tastes, rejected them as "damned patched things," spat tobacco on them, and trampled them with his muddy boots. Incidents similar to this were not infrequent, nor were they calculated to soften the feelings of the women toward the victorious enemy. Their cordial hatred of Federal officers was strongly resented by the latter, who were often able to retaliate in unpleasant ways.[2]

In southeast Alabama deserters from both armies and members of the so-called First Florida Union Cavalry continued for a year after the close of the war their practice of plundering all classes of people and sometimes committing other acts of violence. Some

---

[1] *N. Y. Herald,* July 17 and 20, 1865; *N. Y. World,* July 20, 1865; *N. Y. Times,* Aug. 17 and Dec. 27, 1865; Miller, "History of Alabama," pp. 235, 237; Herbert, "The Solid South," pp. 18, 19; Ku Klux Rept., Ala. Test., p. 451; oral accounts.

[2] "Our Women in the War," p. 279; Riley, "Baptists of Alabama," pp. 304, 305. See also Elizabeth McCracken, "The Southern Woman and Reconstruction," in the *Outlook,* Nov., 1903.

persons were robbed of nearly all that they possessed.[1] Joseph Saunders, a millwright of Dale County, served as a Confederate lieutenant in the first part of the war. Later he resigned, and being worried by the conscript officers, allied himself with a band of deserters near the Florida line, who drew their supplies from the Federal troops on the coast. Saunders was made leader of the band and made frequent forays into Dale County, where on one occasion a company of militia on parade was captured. The band raided the town of Newton, but was defeated. After the war, Saunders with his gang returned and continued horse-stealing. Finally he killed a man and went to Georgia, where, in 1866, he himself was killed.[2] He was a type of the native white outlaw.

The burning of cotton was common. Some was probably burned because the United States cotton agents had seized it, but the heaviest loss fell on private owners. A large quantity of private cotton worth about $2,000,000, that had escaped confiscation and had been collected near Montgomery, was destroyed by the cotton burners.[3] Horse and cattle thieves infested the whole state, especially the western part. Washington and Choctaw counties especially suffered from their depredations.[4] The rivers were infested with cotton thieves, who floated down the streams in flats, landed near cotton fields, established videttes, went into the fields, stole the cotton, and carried it down the river to market.[5] A band of outlaws took passage on a steamboat on the Alabama River, overcame the crew and the honest passengers, and took possession of the boat.[6]

A secret incendiary organization composed of negroes and some discharged Federal soldiers plotted to burn Selma. The members of the band wore red ribbon badges. One of the negroes informed the authorities of the plot and of the place of meeting, and forty of the band were arrested. The others were informed and escaped. The military authorities released the prisoners, who denied the charge, though some of their society testified against them.[7] There were

---

[1] Miller, "History of Alabama," p. 238 ; Patton's Message, Jan. 16, 1866.

[2] Brewer, "Alabama," pp. 205, 206.

[3] *N. Y. Times*, Nov. 2, 1865 (Truman).

[4] *N. Y. Herald*, Oct. 5, 1895 ; Report of Carl Schurz.

[5] *Chicago Tribune*, (fall of) 1865, Montgomery correspondence.

[6] Governor Patton's Message, Jan. 16, 1866.

[7] Oral accounts ; *Daily News*, Sept. 3, 1865 (Selma correspondence).

incendiary fires in every town in the state, it is said, and several were almost destroyed.

The bitter feeling between the tories and the Confederates of north Alabama resulted in some places in guerilla warfare. The Confederate soldiers, whose families had suffered from the depredations of the tories during the war, wanted to punish the outlaws for their misdeeds, and in many cases attempted to do so. The tories wanted revenge for having been driven from the country or into hiding by the Confederate authorities, so they raided the Confederate soldiers as they had raided their families during the war. Some of the tories were caught and hanged. In revenge, the Confederates were shot down in their houses, and in the fields while at work, or while travelling along the roads. The convention called by Governor Parsons declared that lawlessness existed in many counties of the state and authorized Parsons to call out the militia in each county to repress the disorder. They also asked the President to withdraw the Federal troops, which were only a source of disorder,[1] and gave to the mayors of Florence, Athens, and Huntsville special police powers within their respective counties in order to check the lawless element, which was especially strong in Lauderdale, Limestone, and Madison counties.[2] These counties lay north of the Tennessee River, along the Tennessee border. There was a disposition on the part of the civil and military authorities in Alabama to attribute the lawlessness in north and northwest Alabama to bands of desperadoes from Tennessee and Mississippi, but north Alabama had numbers of marauders of her own, and it is probable that Tennessee and Mississippi had little to do with it. Half a dozen men, where there was no authority to check them, could make a whole county uncomfortable for the peaceable citizens.[3]

The Federal infantry commands scattered throughout the country were of little service in capturing the marauders. General Swayne repeatedly asked for cavalry, for, as he said, the infantry was the source of as much disorder as it suppressed. The worst outrages, he added, were committed by small bands of lawless men organized

---

[1] Ordinances, No. 4, Sept. 20, 1865, and No. 54, Sept. 30, 1865.

[2] Reid, "After the War," pp. 351, 352; Ordinance, No. 43, Sept. 30, 1865.

[3] *Daily Times*, Aug. 17, Nov. 2, and Dec. 27, 1865; Report of Carl Schurz; oral accounts.

under various names, and whose chief object was robbery and plunder.[1] After the establishment of the provisional government an attempt was made to bring to trial some of the outlaws who had infested the country during and after the war, and who richly deserved hanging. They were of no party, being deserters from both armies, or tories who had managed to keep out of either army. However, when arrested they raised a strong cry of being "unionists" and appealed to the military authorities for protection from "rebel" persecution, though the officials of the Johnson government in Alabama were never charged by any one else with an excess of zeal in the Confederate cause. The Federal officials released all prisoners who claimed to be "unionists." Sheriff Snodgrass of Jackson County arrested fifteen bushwhackers charged with murder. They claimed to be "loyalists," and General Kryzyanowski, commanding the district of north Alabama, ordered the court to stop proceedings and to discharge the prisoners. This was not done, and Kryzyanowski sent a body of negro soldiers who closed the court, released the prisoners, and sent the sheriff to jail at Nashville.[2] The military authorities allowed no one who asserted that he was a "unionist" to be tried for offences committed during the war, and any effort to bring the outlaws to trial resulted in an outcry against the "persecution of loyalists."

In August, 1865, Sheriff John M. Daniel of Cherokee County arrested and imprisoned a band of marauders dressed in the Federal uniform, though they had no connection with the army. A short time afterwards the citizens asked him to raise a *posse* and arrest a similar band which was engaged in robbing the people, plundering houses, assaulting respectable citizens, and threatening to kill them. And as such occurrences were frequent, Sheriff Daniel, after consulting with the citizens, summoned a *posse comitatus* and went in pursuit of the marauders. One squad was encountered which surrendered without resistance. A second, belonging to the same band, approached, and, refusing to surrender, opened fire on the sheriff's party. In the fight the sheriff killed one man. Upon learning that his prisoners were soldiers and were on detail duty, he desisted

---

[1] Report of the Freedmen's Bureau, Oct. 24, 1865; Patton's Message, Jan. 16, 1866; Report of the Joint Committee on Reconstruction, Pt. III, p. 140.

[2] *N. Y. Times*, Oct. 10, 1865. See also Resolutions of Legislature, 1865-1866.

from further pursuit, released the citizens who were held as prisoners by the soldiers, and turned his prisoners over to the military authorities. This was on August 24. Daniel was at once arrested by the military authorities and confined in prison at Talladega in irons. Six months later he had had no trial, and the general assembly petitioned the President for his release, claiming that he had acted in the faithful discharge of his duty.[1] The memorial asserts that such outrages were of frequent occurrence. Another petition to the President asked for the withdrawal of the troops, whose presence caused disorder, and who at various times provoked unpleasant collisions. Many of the troops, remote from the line of transportation, subsisted their stock upon the country. This was a hardship to the people, who had barely enough to support life.[2]

For several years the arbitrary conduct of some of the soldiers was a cause of bad feeling on the part of the citizens.[3]   But the soldiers were very often blamed for deeds done by outlaws disguised as Federal troops.   In northern Alabama a party of northern men bought property, and complained to Governor Parsons of the depredations of the Federal troops stationed near and asked for protection.   Parsons could only refer their request to General Davis at Montgomery, and in the meantime the troops complained of drove out of the community the signers of the request for protection.   One of them, an ex-captain in the United States army, was ordered to leave within three hours or he would be shot.[4]   The soldiers, except at the important posts, were under slack discipline, and their officers had little control over them.   At Bladen Springs some negro troops shot a Mr. Bass while he was in bed and beat his wife and children with ramrods.   They drove the wife and daughters of a Mr. Rhodes from home and set fire to the house.   The citizens fled from their homes, which were pillaged by the negro soldiers in order to get the clothing, furniture, books, etc.   The trouble originated in the refusal of the white people to associate with the white officers of the colored troops.[5]   These negroes had little respect for their officers and

---

[1] Joint Memorial and Resolutions of the General Assembly, in Acts of Ala. (1865–1866), pp. 598–600.

[2] Memorial and Joint Resolutions, Acts of Ala. (1865–1866), pp. 601–603.

[3] Miller, "Alabama," p. 242.

[4] *N. Y. Herald*, Dec. 15, 1865.

[5] The wife of one of these officers was a notorious prostitute.

threatened to shoot their commanding officers.[1] At Decatur the
negro troops plundered and shot into the houses of the whites. In
Greensboro a white youth struck a negro who had insulted him, and
was in turn slapped in the face by a Federal officer, whom he at once
shot and then made his escape. The negro population, led by negro
soldiers, went into every house in the town, seized all the arms, and
secured as a hostage the brother of the man who had escaped. A
gallows was erected and the boy was about to be hanged when his
relatives received an intimation that money would secure his release.
With difficulty about $10,000 was secured from the people of the town
and sent to the officer in command of the district. No one knows
what he did with the money, but the young man was released.[2]

Before the close of 1865, the commanding officers were reducing
the troops to much better discipline and many were withdrawn.
The provisional government also grew stronger, and there was considerably less disorder among the whites, though the blacks were
still demoralized.

SEC. 3. THE NEGRO TESTING HIS FREEDOM

The conduct of the negro during the war and after gaining his
freedom seemed to convince those who had feared that insurrection
would follow emancipation that no danger was to be feared from this
source. Most of the former slaveholders, who were better acquainted
with the negro character and who knew that the old masters could
easily control them, at no time feared a revolt of the blacks unless
under exceptional circumstances. It was only when the wretched
characters who followed the northern armies gained control of the
negro by playing upon his fears and exciting his worst passions that
the fear of the negro was felt by many who had never felt it before,
and who have never since been entirely free from this fear.

When the Federal armies passed through the state, the negroes
along the line of march followed them in numbers, though many
returned to the old home after a day or two. Yet all were restless
and expectant, as was natural. During the war they had understood

---

[1] *Selma Times*, Feb. 22, 1866.

[2] From Ms. account by a citizen of Greensboro. The young man who came so
near hanging was some years later a hotel proprietor in Birmingham and created much
newspaper discussion by ordering General Sherman to leave his hotel.

the questions at issue so far as they themselves were concerned, and now that the struggle was decided against their masters they looked for stranger and more wonderful things, not so much at first, however, as later when the negro soldiers and the white emissaries had filled their minds with false impressions of the new and glorious condition that was before them.   For several weeks before the master came home from the army the negroes knew that, as a result of the war, they were free.   They, however, worked on, somewhat restless, of course, until he arrived and called them up and informed them that they were free.   This was the usual way in which the negro was informed of his freedom.   The great majority of the blacks, except in the track of the armies, waited to hear from their masters the confirmation of the reports of freedom.   And the first thing the returning slaveholder did was to assemble his negroes and make known to them their condition with its privileges and responsibilities.   It did not enter the minds of the masters that any laws or constitutional amendments were necessary to abolish slavery.   They were quite sure that the war had decided the question.   Some of the legal-minded men, those who were not in the army and who read their law books, were disposed to cling to their claims until the law settled the question. But they were few in number.[1]

How to prove Freedom

The negro believed, when he became free, that he had entered Paradise, that he never again would be cold or hungry, that he never would have to work unless he chose to, and that he never would have to obey a master, but would live the remainder of his life under the tender care of the government that had freed him.   It was necessary, he thought, to test this wonderful freedom.   As Booker Washington says, there were two things which all the negroes in the South agreed must be done before they were really free: they must change their names and leave the old plantation for a few days or weeks.   Many of them returned to the old homes and made contracts with their masters for work, but at the same time they felt that it was not proper to retain their old master's name, and accordingly took new ones.[2]

[1] See Mrs. Clayton, " White and Black Under the Old Régime," pp. 152–153.
[2] Washington, " Up From Slavery," pp. 23, 24.

Upon leaving their homes the blacks collected in gangs at the cross-roads, in the villages and towns, and especially near the military posts. To the negro these ordinary men in blue were beings from another sphere who had brought him freedom, which was something that he did not exactly understand, but which he was assured was a delightful state. The towns were filled with crowds of blacks who left their homes with absolutely nothing, thinking that the government would care for them, or, more probably, not thinking at all. Later, after some experience, they were disposed to bring with them their household goods and the teams and wagons of their former masters. This was the effect that freedom had upon thousands; yet, after all, most of the negroes either stayed at their old homes, or, that they might feel really free, moved to some place near by. But among the quietest of them there was much restlessness and neglect of work. Hunting and fishing and frolics were the duties of the day. Every man acquired in some way a dog and a gun as badges of freedom. It was quite natural that the negroes should want a prolonged holiday to enjoy their new-found freedom; and it is rather strange that any of them worked, for there was a universal impression, vague of course in the remote districts — the result of the teachings of the negro soldiers and of the Freedmen's Bureau officials — that the government would support them. Still some communities were almost undisturbed. The advice of the old plantation preachers held many to their work, and these did not suffer as did their brothers who flocked to the cities. Many negro men seized the opportunity to desert their wives and children and get new wives. It was considered a relic of slavery to remain tied to an ugly old wife, married in slavery. Much suffering resulted from the desertion, though, as a rule, the negro mother alone supported the children much better than did the father who stayed.[1]

In many districts the negro steadily refused to work, but persisted in supporting himself at the expense of the would-be employer. Thousands of hogs and cattle that had escaped the raiding armies or the Confederate tithe gatherer went to feed the hungry African

---

[1] *Columbus* (Ga.) *Sun*, Nov. 22, 1865; *The World*, July 20, 1865; *N. Y. Herald*, July 23, 1865; Parsons's Speech, Cooper Institute, Nov. 13, 1865; Riley, " Baptists of Alabama," pp. 305, 307; Ball, "Clarke County," p. 294; Herbert, "Solid South," pp. 19, 20; Miller, " History of Alabama," Ch. CXLI; oral accounts.

whom the Bureau did not supply. The Bureau issued rations only three times a week, and as the homeless negro had nowhere to keep provisions for two or three days, there would be a season of plenty and then a season of fasting. The Bureau reached only a small proportion of the negroes; and, of those it could reach, many, in spite of the regulations, neglected to apply for relief. By causing the negroes to crowd into the towns and cities the Bureau brought on much of the want that it did not relieve. The complaint was made that in the worst period of distress the soldiers in charge of the issue of supplies made no effort to see that the negroes were cared for. It was easier also for the average negro to pick up pigs and chickens than to make trips to the Bureau. During the summer the roving negro lived upon green corn from the nearest fields and blackberries from the fence corners and pine orchards. With the approach of winter suffering was sure to come to those who were now doing well in a vagrant way, but winter was to them too far in the future to trouble them.

The negroes soon found that freedom was not all they had been led to expect. A meeting of 900 blacks held near Mobile decided by a vote of 700 to 200 to return to their former masters and go to work to make a living, since their northern deliverers had failed to provide for them in any way.[1]

The negro preacher, especially those lately called to preach, and the northern missionaries had, during the summer and fall, a flourishing time and a rich harvest. A favorite dissipation among the negroes was going to church services as often as possible, especially to camp-meetings where he or she could shout. It was another mark of freedom to change one's church, or to secede from the white churches. All through the summer of 1865 the revival meetings went on, conducted by new self-"called" colored preachers and the missionaries. The old plantation preachers, to their credit be it remembered, frowned upon this religious frenzy. The people living near the places of meetings complained of the disappearance of poultry and pigs, fruit and vegetables after the late sessions of the African congregations. The various missionaries filled the late slave's head with false notions of many things besides religion, and gathered thousands into their folds from the southern religious organizations.

[1] *N. Y. Herald*, Aug. 27, 1865; *Mobile Register*, Aug. 16, 1865.

Baptizings were as popular as the opera among the whites to-day. That ceremony took place at the river or creek side. Thousands were sometimes assembled, and the air was electric with emotion. The negro was then as near Paradise as he ever came in his life. The Baptist ceremony of immersion was preferred, because, as one of them remarked, "It looks more like business." Shouting they went into the water and shouting they came out. One old negro woman was immersed in the river and came out screaming: "Freed from slavery! freed from sin! Bless God and General Grant!" [1]

Suffering among the Negroes

The negroes massed in the towns lived in deserted and ruined houses, in huts built by themselves of refuse lumber, under sheds and under bridges over creeks, ravines, and gutters, and in caves in the banks of rivers and ravines. Many a one had only the sky for a roof and the ground in a fence corner for a bed. They were very scantily clothed. Food was obtained by begging, stealing, or from the Bureau. Taking from the whites was not considered stealing, but was "spilin de Gypshuns." The food supply was insufficient, and was badly cooked when cooked at all. It was not possible for the army and the Freedmen's Bureau, which came later, to do half enough by issuing rations to relieve the suffering they caused by attracting the negroes to the cities. While in slavery the negro had been forced to keep regular hours, and to take care of himself; he had plenty to eat and to wear, and, for reasons of dollars and cents, if for no other, his health was looked after by his master. Now all was changed. The negroes were like young children left to care for themselves, and even those who remained at home suffered from personal neglect, since they no longer could be governed in such matters by the directions of the whites. Among the negroes in the cities and in the "contraband" camps the sanitary conditions were very bad. To make matters infinitely worse disease in its most loathsome forms broke out in these crowded quarters. Smallpox, peculiarly fatal to negroes, raged among them for two years and carried off great numbers. The Freedmen's Bureau had established hospitals

[1] *Huntsville Advocate*, July 26 and Nov. 9, 1865 ; McTyeire, "History of Methodism"; Riley, "Baptists of Alabama"; conversations with various negroes and whites.

T

for the negroes, but it could not or would not care for the smallpox patients as carefully as for other sickness. In Selma, for instance, the city authorities had been sending the negroes who were ill to one of the city hospitals. But the military authorities interfered, took the negroes away, and informed the city authorities that the negroes were the especial wards of the government, which would care for them at all times. When smallpox broke out, the military authorities in charge of the Bureau refused to have anything to do with the sick negroes, and left them to the care of the town.[1] Consumption and venereal diseases now made their appearance. The relations of the soldiers of the invading army and the negro women were the cause of social demoralization and physical deterioration. An eminent authority states that from various causes the efficient negro population was reduced by one-fourth.[2] Though this estimate must be too large, still the negro population decreased between 1860 and 1866, as the census of the latter year shows,[3] in spite of the fact that thousands of negroes[4] were sent into Alabama during the war from Georgia, Mississippi, Tennessee, and Florida to escape capture by the Federal armies. The greatest mortality was among the negroes in the outskirts of the cities and towns. Some of the loss of population must be ascribed to the enrolment of negroes as soldiers and to the capture of slaves by the Federal armies.[5] For several years after the war young negro children were scarce in certain districts. They had died by hundreds and thousands through neglect.[6]

---

[1] Hardy, "History of Selma," p. 85.   [2] *DeBow's Review*, March, 1866.

[3] Negro population in 1860	.	.	.	.	.	.	.	437,770
Negro population in 1866	.	.	.	.	.	.	.	423,325
Decrease	.	.	.	.	.	.	.	14,445

[4] Estimated 20,000 — Census of 1866.

[5] *Southern Mag.*, Jan., 1874. Authorities as already noted and *DeBow's Review*, March, 1866; *Montgomery Advertiser*, March 21, 1866; Hardy, "History of Selma," p. 85; *N. Y. Times*, Oct. 31, 1865; *Huntsville Advocate*, Nov. 9, 1865; *N. Y. Herald*, July 17, 1865; *N. Y. News*, Sept. 7 and Dec. 4, 1865; Census of 1866 in *Selma Times and Messenger*, March 24, 1868; Mrs. Clayton, "White and Black," pp. 152, 153; "Our Women in the War"; Thomas, "The American Negro," p. 190; Report of the Joint Committee, Pt. III, p. 140; B. C. Truman, Report to the President, April 9, 1866; Carl Schurz, Report to the President, see Sen. Ex. Doc., No. 2, 39th Cong., 1st Sess.; General Grant, Report to the President, Sen. Ex. Doc., No. 2, 39th Cong., 1st Sess.

[6] *Southern Mag.*, Jan., 1874.

Relations between Whites and Blacks

For a year or two the relations between the blacks and whites were, on the whole, friendly, in spite of the constant effort of individual northerners and negro soldiers to foment trouble between the races. As a result of the work of outsiders, there was a growing tendency to insolent conduct on the part of the younger negro men, who were convinced that civil behavior and freedom were incompatible. On the part of some there was a disposition not to submit to the direction of the white men in their work, and the negro's advisers warned him against the efforts of the white man to enslave him. Consequently he refused to make contracts that called for any responsibility on his part, and if he made a contract the Bureau must ratify it, and, as he had no knowledge of the obligation of contracts, he was likely to break it. In an address of the white ministers of Selma to the negroes, they said that papers had been circulated among the negroes telling them that they were hated and detested by the whites, and that such papers caused bad feeling, which was unfortunate, as the races must live together, and the better the feeling, the better it would be for both. At first, the address added, there was some bad feeling when certain negroes, in order to test their freedom, became impudent and insulting, but on the part of the white man this feeling was soon changed. Later the negroes were poisoned against their former masters by listening to lying whites, and then they refused to work. The ministers warned the negroes against their continual idleness and their immoral lives, and told them that those of them who pretended to work were not making one bushel of corn where they might make ten, and that the whites wanted workers. The self-respecting negroes were asked to use their influence for the bettering of the worthless members of their race.[1]

When the negroes became convinced that the government would not support them entirely, they then took up the notion that the lands of the whites were to be divided among them. In the fall of 1865 there was a general belief that at Christmas or New Year's Day a division of property would be made, and that each negro would get his share — "forty acres of land and an old gray mule" or the equivalent in other property. The soldiers and the officials of the Freed-

---

[1] Protestant Episcopal Freedmen's Commission, Occasional Papers, Jan., 1866.

men's Bureau were responsible for putting these notions into the heads of the negroes, though General Swayne endeavored to correct such impressions. The effect of the belief in the division of property was to prevent steady work or the making of contracts. Many ceased work altogether, waiting for the division. In many cases northern speculators and sharpers deceived the negroes about the division of land, and, in this way, secured what little money the latter had.

The trust that the negro placed in every man who came from the North was absolute. They manifested a great desire to work for those who bought or leased plantations in the South, and nearly all observers coming from the North in 1865 spoke of the alacrity with which the blacks entered into agreements to work for northern men. At the same time there was no ill feeling toward the southern whites; only, for the moment, they were eclipsed by these brighter beings who had brought freedom with them. Two years' experience at the most resulted in a thorough mutual distrust. The northern man could make no allowances for the difference between white and negro labor, he expected too much; the negro would not work for so hard a taskmaster.

The northern newspaper correspondents who travelled through the South in 1865 agreed that the old masters were treating the negroes well, and that the relations between the races were much more friendly than they had expected to find. When cotton was worth fifty cents a pound, it was to the interest of the planter to treat the negro well, especially as the negro would leave and go to another employer on the slightest provocation or offer of better wages. The demand for labor was much greater than the supply. The lower class of whites, the "mean" or "poor whites," as the northern man called them, were hostile to the negro and disposed to hold him responsible for the state of affairs, and, in some cases, mistreated him. The negro, in turn, made many complaints against the vicious whites, and against the policemen in the towns, who were not of the highest type, and who made it hard for Sambo when he desired to hang around town and sleep on the sidewalks. One correspondent said that the Irish were especially cruel to the negroes.

The negro freedman undoubtedly suffered much more from mistreatment by low characters than the negro slave had suffered. In slavery times his master saw that he was protected. Now he had no one to look to for protection. The strongest influence of the great majority of the whites was used against any mistreatment of the negro, and the meaner element of the whites was suppressed as much as it was possible to do when there was no authority except public opinion. All in all the negro had less ill treatment than was to be expected, and suffered much more from his own ignorance and the mistaken kindness of his friends.[1]

Sec. 4. Destitution and Want in 1865 and 1866

When the war ended, there was little good money in the state, and industry was paralyzed. The gold and silver that remained was carefully hoarded, and for months there was none in circulation except in the towns. A Confederate officer relates that on his way home, in 1865, he gave $500 in Confederate currency to a Federal soldier for a silver dime, and that this was the only money he saw for several weeks. The people had no faith in paper money of any kind, and thought that greenbacks would become worthless in the same way as Confederate currency. All sense of values had been lost, which may account for the fabulous and fictitious prices in the South for several years after the war, and the liberality of appropriations of the first legislature after the surrender, which in small matters was severely economical. The legislators had been accustomed to making appropriations of thousands and even millions of dollars, with no question as to where the money was to come from, for the state had three public printers to print money. Now it was hard to realize that business must be brought to a cash basis.

Here and there could be found a person who had a bale or two of cotton which he had succeeded in hiding from the raiders and the Treasury agents. This was sold for a good price and relieved the wants of the owner; but those who had cotton to sell often spent the money foolishly for gewgaws and fancy articles to eat and wear, such as they had not seen for several years. There was an almost maddening desire for the things which they had once been accustomed

[1] *N. Y. Times*, Aug. 17, 1865, Jan. 25, Feb. 12, and July 2, 1866; *N. Y. Herald*, June 24, 1866; *The Nation*, Feb. 15 and April 19, 1866; Reid, "After the War," pp. 369–371; Reports of Grant, Truman, and Schurz; Report of the Joint Committee on Reconstruction (Fisk); Herbert, "Solid South," p. 20; Paper by Petrie in Transactions Ala. Hist. Soc., Vol. IV, p. 465.

to, and which the traders and speculators now placed in tempting array in the long-empty store windows. But the majority of the people had no cotton to sell, and in many cases a pig or a cow was driven ten or fifteen miles to sell for a little money to buy necessaries, or frequently trinkets.

In certain parts of the state the crops planted by the negroes were in good condition in April, 1865, but after the invasions they were neglected, and in thousands of cases the negroes went away and left them. In the white counties conditions were as bad as it was possible to be. Half of the people in them had been supported by state and county aid which now failed. Nearly all the men were injured or killed, and there were no negroes to work the farms. The women and the children did everything they could to plant their little crops in the spring of 1865, but often not even seed corn was to be had. All over the state, where it was possible, the returning soldiers planted late crops of corn, and in the Black Belt they were able to save some of the crops planted by the negroes. But in the white counties, especially in the northern part of the state, nothing could be done. Often the breadwinner had been killed in the war, and the widow and orphans were left to provide for themselves. The late crops were almost total failures because of the drought, not one-tenth of the crop of 1860 being made. In this section everything that would support life had been stripped from the country by the contending armies and the raiding bands of desperadoes. A double warfare had devastated the country, "tories" raiding their neighbors and *vice versa;* and the bitter state of feeling prevented neighbor from relieving neighbor. But the "Unionists," who were sure that their turn had come, wanted the destitute cared for, even if some were fed "who curse us as traitors." This part of the country had been supported by the central Black Belt counties, but in 1865 the supply was exhausted. In the cotton counties there was enough to support life, and had the negroes remained at home and worked, they would not have suffered. As it was, those who left the plantation were decimated by disease and want. Soon after the occupation, the army officers distributed the supplies captured from the Confederates among the needy whites and blacks who applied for aid. But many out of reach of aid starved, and especially did this happen among the aged and helpless who made no appeal for aid, but who died in silence from want of shelter and food.

After several months the Freedmen's Bureau, under the charge of General Swayne, who was a man of discretion and common sense, and who understood the real state of affairs, extended its assistance to the destitute whites. Among the negroes the Bureau created much of the misery it relieved, for in the cotton belt there was enough to support life; and had the negroes not flocked to the Bureau, they would have lived in plenty. Besides, the aged and infirm negroes were not assisted by the Bureau, but remained with their master's people, who took care of them. But the generous assistance extended by that much-abused institution saved many a poor white from starvation. In the fall of 1865 139,000 destitute whites were reported to the provisional government. They were mostly in the mountain counties of north and northeast Alabama, though in southeast Alabama there was also much want. And in Governor Parsons's last message to the legislature (December, 1865), he stated that those in need of food numbered 250,000.[1] A state commissioner for the destitute was appointed to coöperate with General Swayne and the Freedmen's Bureau. The legislature appropriated $500,000 in bonds to buy supplies for the poor, but the attitude of Congress toward the Johnson state governments prevented the sale of state securities. However, the governor went to the West and succeeded in getting some supplies. In December, 1865, it was believed that there were 200,000 people who needed assistance in some degree.

The failure of the crops in 1865 left affairs in even a worse condition than before. Small farmers could not subsist while making a new crop, and many widows and children were in great need. Some of the latter walked thirty or forty miles for food for themselves and for those at home.[2]

In January, 1866, the state commissioner, M. H. Cruikshank, reported to Governor Patton that 52,921 whites were entirely destitute.

[1] Brown, "Alabama," p. 259.

[2] *Montgomery Advertiser*, Dec., 1865, and Jan. 31, 1866; *N. Y. Times*, Oct. 31 and Dec. 27, 1865; *N. Y. News*, Dec. 4, 1865; *N. Y. Herald*, Dec., 1865, and Jan. 31, 1866; Ho. Ex. Doc., No. 70, 39th Cong., 1st Sess.; Ho. Mis. Doc., No. 42, 39th Cong., 1st Sess. (W. H. Smith); Sen. Ex. Doc., No. 6, 39th Cong., 2d Sess. (Swayne's Report); Riley, "Baptists of Alabama," p. 305; Trowbridge, "The South," p. 445; Miller, "Alabama," pp. 228, 229; Somers, "South since the War," p. 134; *Huntsville Advocate*, Nov. 23, 1865.

These were mostly in the counties of Bibb, Shelby, Jefferson, Talladega, St. Clair, Cherokee, Blount, Jackson, Marshall, all white counties; nine other counties had not been heard from.[1] During the same month, a Freedmen's Bureau official who travelled through the counties of Talladega, Bibb, Shelby, Jefferson, and Calhoun reported that the suffering among the whites was appalling, especially in Talladega County. The Freedmen's Bureau had neglected the poor whites, though there was little suffering in the richer sections where the negroes lived. He stated that near Talladega many white families were living in the woods with no shelter except the pine boughs, and this in the middle of winter.[2]

In Randolph County, in January, 1866, the probate judge said that 5000 persons were in need of aid. Most of these had been opposed to the Confederacy. The "unionists" complained that the Confederate foragers had discriminated against them, which, while very likely true, was more than offset by the depredations of the tories and Federals on the Confederate sympathizers. All accounts agree that the Confederate sympathizers were in the worse condition; many of them had not tasted meat for months. But charges were brought that the probate judges of the provisional government, who certainly were not strong Confederates, did not fairly distribute provisions among the "damned tories," as the latter complained that they were called.[3] The state commissioner could relieve only about one-tenth of the destitute whites. In January, 1866, he gave assistance in the form of meal, corn (and sometimes a little meat) to 5245 whites and 2426 blacks; in February, to 13,083 whites and to 4107 blacks; and in March, to 17,204 whites and to 5877 blacks, most of whom were women and children, the men receiving assistance being old, infirm, or crippled. General Swayne of the Freedmen's Bureau helped Cruikshank in every way he could, and took charge of some of the negroes. But owing to the failure of the crops in 1865, the situation was growing worse,

[1] *Montgomery Advertiser*, Jan. 31, 1866.

[2] Ho. Ex. Doc., No. 70, 39th Cong., 1st Sess.; Buckley's Report, Jan. 16, 1865; Report of John H. Hurst and A. B. Strickland, Oct. 4, 1865.

[3] Swayne's Report, Oct. 31, 1866; R. T. Smith to Swayne, Jan. 6, 1866 (in Ho. Ex. Doc., No. 70, 39th Cong., 1st Sess.); W. H. Smith, D. C. Humphreys, and J. J. Giers, Memorial to Congress, Ho. Mis. Doc., No. 42, 39th Cong., 1st Sess.; Patton's Message, Jan. 16, 1866.

and there was no hope for any relief until the summer of 1866 when vegetables and corn would ripen.[1]

In May, 1866, Governor Patton said that of 20,000 widows and 60,000 orphans, three-fourths were in need of the necessaries of life, that they had been able to do very little for themselves, even those who had land being unable to work it to any advantage, and that their corn crop of the previous year had failed.[2]   There is little doubt that many died from lack of food and shelter during 1865 and 1866, but in the disordered times incomplete records were kept.   Many cases of starvation were reported, especially in north Alabama, but few names can now be obtained.   Near Guntersville there were three cases of starvation, while hundreds were in an almost perishing condition.   From Marshall County, where, it was said, there were 2180 helpless and destitute persons and 2000 who were able to work, but could get nothing to do, it was reported that not more than twenty people had more than enough to supply their own needs. The people of Cherokee County, when on the verge of starvation, appealed to south Alabama for aid.   They asked for corn, and said that if they could not get it they must leave the country.   Hundreds, they said, had not tasted meat for months, and farm stock was in a wretched condition.   Nashville sent $15,000 and Montgomery $10,000 to buy provisions for them.[3]   From Coosa County much distress was reported among the old people, widows, children, refugees, and the families whose heads had returned from the army too late to make a crop.   However, the negroes in this section who had remained on their farms had made good crops and were doing well.[4] In the valley of the Coosa, in northeast Alabama, several cases of starvation were reported.   One woman went seventeen miles for a peck of meal, but died before she could reach home with it.   Another, after fasting three days, walked sixteen miles to obtain supplies, and failing, died.   One family lived on boiled greens, with no salt nor pepper, no meat nor bread.   An old woman, living eighteen miles from Guntersville, walked to that village to get meal for her grandchildren.   It has been estimated that there were 20,000 people

---

[1] Report of M. H. Cruikshank, March, 1866.

[2] Ho. Mis. Doc., No. 114, 39th Cong., 1st Sess; *National Intelligencer*, Oct. 2, 1866.

[3] *Huntsville Independent*, April 3 and 19, 1866; *Selma Times*, June 9, 1866; oral accounts.

[4] W. Garrett to Swayne, Jan. 15, 1866, in Ho. Ex. Doc., No. 70, 38th Cong., 1st Sess.

in the five counties south of the Tennessee river — Franklin, Lawrence, Morgan, Marshall, De Kalb — in a state of want bordering on starvation.[1]

The majority of the destitute whites never appealed for aid, but managed, though half starved, to live until better times. Numbers left the land of famine and went where there was plenty, and where they could get work. Others who could not emigrate and those broken in spirit received assistance. From January to September, 1866, 15,000 to 20,000 whites, and 4000 to 14,000 negroes were aided each month by the Freedmen's Bureau and by the state. Most of these were women and children, the rule being not to assist able-bodied whites except in extreme cases.

In 1866 the state succeeded in selling some of its bonds, and raised money in other ways. Much was spent for supplies for the poor, for in 1866 the crops almost failed again. From November, 1865, to September, 1866, the Freedmen's Bureau and the state commissioner issued, to black and white, 3,789,788 rations. There were also large donations from the West and from Tennessee and Kentucky. After this the Freedmen's Bureau gave less, though during the year from September, 1866, to September, 1867, it issued 214,305 rations to whites and 274,399 to blacks. To the whites, and partly to the blacks, the issue of provisions was made under the general supervision of General Swayne, and through state agents in each county who were acceptable to Swayne.[2]

In November, 1867, the Freedmen's Bureau reported that there were 10,000 whites and 50,000 blacks without means of support, and 450,000 rations per month were asked for. It would have been much better to have put an end to relief work, since by this time the officials of the Freedmen's Bureau were very active in politics and showed a disposition to report their political henchmen as destitute and in need of support. And in another way there was much abuse of the

[1] *Chicago Tribune*, June 2, 1866 (Correspondent at Bellefonte, Jackson County); *Huntsville Independent*, April 3 and 19, 1866; Reports of General Swayne, 1865–1866.

[2] March 8, 1867, General Howard of the Freedmen's Bureau reported that in Alabama there were 10,000 whites and 5000 blacks in a destitute condition, and that during the next five months, owing to the failure of the crops in 1866, there would be needed 2,250,000 rations valued at $562,500, or 25 cents per ration. Sen. Ex. Docs., No. 1, 40th Cong., 1st Sess. Report of Swayne, Oct. 31, 1866; Report of Com. Bureau, Nov. 1, 1867; G. O., No. 4, Hq. Dist. of Ala., Montgomery, Oct. 10, 1866.

charity of the government, for some broken-down, spiritless people would never work for themselves as long as they could draw rations for nothing. The negroes, especially, were demoralized by the issue of rations. Fear of the contempt of their neighbors would drive all but the meaner class of whites back to work, but the negro came to believe that he would be supported the rest of his life by the government.

As late as October, 1868, it was reported that there was great want in middle and south Alabama, and soup houses were established by the state and the Bureau in Mobile, Huntsville, Selma, Montgomery, and other central Alabama towns.[1] The location of the soup kitchens, and the date, lead one to suspect that politics, perhaps, had something to do with the matter. These towns were the very places where there was less want than anywhere else in the state, but Grant was to be elected, and there were many negro votes.

For more than two years after the war in all the small towns were seen emaciated persons who had come long distances to get food. General Swayne thought the condition of the poor white much worse than that of the negro. The latter, he said, was hindered by no wounds nor by a helpless family, for his aged and helpless kin were cared for at the old master's. The "refugees," as the poor whites were called who had but little and lost all by the war, lived in a different part of the country, — in the mountains and in the pine woods, — beyond the reach of work or help, clinging to the old home places in utter hopeless desolation. For the negro, Swayne thought, there was hope, but for the "refugee" there was none; he existed only.[2]

It was years before a large number of the people again attained a comfortable standard of living. Some gave up altogether. Many died in the struggle. Numbers left the country; others, in reach of assistance, became trifling and worthless from too much aid. In later years the opening of mines and the building of railroads in north Alabama, the lumber industry and the rapid development of south Alabama, saved the "refugee" from the fate that General Swayne thought was in store for him.

[1] Freedmen's Bureau Report, Oct. 24, 1868.
[2] Swayne's Report, Nov., 1866; Sen. Ex. Doc., No. 6, 39th Cong., 2d Sess.; Reid, "After the War," p. 221 ; Freedmen's Bureau Report, Nov. 1, 1866, Nov. 1, 1867, Oct. 2, 1868 ; and other authorities noted above.

CHAPTER VI

CONFISCATION AND THE COTTON TAX

SEC. I. CONFISCATION FRAUDS

Restrictions on Trade in 1865

AT the time of the collapse of the Confederacy trade within the state of Alabama was subject to the following regulations: gold and silver was in no case to be paid for southern produce; all trade was to be done through officers appointed by the United States Treasury Department;[1] the state was divided into districts and sub-districts called agencies, under the superintendence of these Treasury agents, whose business it was to regulate trade, and collect captured, abandoned, and confiscable property; in making purchases of cotton, and other produce the agents were to pay only three-fourths of the value, or to purchase the produce at three-fourths its value, and then at once resell it to the former owner at full value, with permission to export or ship to the North; in order to get permission to sell, the owner must take the Lincoln amnesty oath of December 8, 1863; there was, besides, an internal revenue tax of two cents a pound, and a shipping fee of four cents a pound.[2] So for a month after the surrender the person who owned cotton near any port or place of sale had to sell to United States Treasury agents, or pretended agents, and have twenty-five per cent to fifty per cent of the value of his cotton deducted before it could be sent North. On May 9, 1865, a regulation provided that "all cotton not produced by persons *with their own labor* or with the labor of *freedmen* or others employed and *paid* by them, must, before shipment to any port or

---

[1] These were general agents, supervising special agents, assistant special agents, local special agents, agency aids, aids to the revenue, customs officers, and superintendents of freedmen. Rules and Regulations, July 29, 1864. Ho. Mis. Doc., No. 190, 44th Cong., 1st Sess.

[2] Amended regulations, Sec. IV, March 30, 1865.

place in a loyal state, be sold to and resold by an officer of the government . . . and before allowing any cotton or other product to be
shipped . . . the proper officer must require a certificate from the
purchasing agent or the internal revenue officer that the cotton proposed to be shipped had been resold by him or that 25 per cent of
the value thereof has been paid to such purchasing agent in money." [1]

This was in accord with the general policy of Johnson, at first,
viz. to punish the slaveholding class and to favor the non-slaveholders.
Cotton was then worth $250 or more a bale, and cotton raised by
slave labor had to pay the 25 per cent tax — $60 to $75. However,
the regulations ordered that no other fees were to be exacted after
the fourth was taken. Nearly all the cotton not yet destroyed was
in the Black Belt, and was raised by slave labor. The few people
who had cotton raised by their own labor might sell it after paying
the tax of three cents a pound, or $12 to $15 a bale.

May 22, 1865, the proclamation of the President removed restrictions on commercial intercourse except as to the right of the United
States to property purchased by agents in southern states, and except
as to the 25 per cent tax on purchases of cotton. No exceptions
were made to the 25 per cent tax. The ports were to be opened to
foreign commerce after July 1, 1865.[2] After June 30, 1865, restrictions as to trade were removed except as to arms, gray cloth, etc.[3]
And after August 29, 1865, even contraband goods might be admitted
on license.[4]

Federal Claims to Confederate Property

The confiscation laws relating to private property under which
the army and Treasury agents were acting in Alabama in 1865 were:
(1) the act of July 17, 1862, which authorized the confiscation and
sale of property as a punishment for "rebels"; (2) the act of March
12, 1863, which authorized Treasury agents to collect and sell "captured and abandoned" property, — but a "loyal" owner might
within two years after the close of the war prove his claim, and "that

[1] Rules and Regulations, Sec. IX, Treasury Department, May 9, 1865. Renewed
by Circular Instructions, May 16, 1865, and in force to June 30, 1865. In Alabama the
regulation was enforced during the entire summer. Ho. Rept., No. 83, 45th Cong.,
3d Sess.

[2] McPherson, " Reconstruction," p. 9.

[3] Proclamations, June 13 and 23, 1865.   [4] Proclamation, Aug. 29, 1865.

he has never given any aid or comfort" to the Confederacy, and then receive the proceeds of the sales, less expenses; (3) the act of July 2, 1864, authorizing Treasury agents to lease or work abandoned property by employing refugee negroes. "Abandoned" property was defined by the Treasury Department as property the owner of which was engaged in war or otherwise against the United States, or was voluntarily absent. According to this ruling all the property of Confederate soldiers was "abandoned" and might be seized by Treasury agents. North Alabama suffered from the operation of these laws from their passage until late in 1865, the rest of Alabama only in 1865.

The blockade prevented the people from disposing of most of the cotton raised during the war; there were heavy crops in 1860, 1861, 1862, and small ones in 1863 and 1864. The number of bales produced in 1859 was 989,955; in 1860, about the same; and less in 1861 and 1862.

Comparatively little cotton was sent out on blockade-runners, and not very much was sent through the lines from the cotton belt proper, so that at the close of the war there were many thousands of bales of cotton in the central counties of the state. Cotton was selling for high prices — 30 cents to $1.20 a pound, or $200 to $500 a bale. It was almost the sole dependence of the people to prevent the severest suffering. The state and Confederate governments had some kind of a claim on much of the cotton early in 1865. No one knew how much nor exactly where all of the Confederate cotton was stored, and it bore no marks that would distinguish it from private cotton. But the records surrendered by General Taylor and others showed who had subscribed to the Cotton or Produce Loan. Many thousand bales had been destroyed by the raiders in 1864 and 1865, and many thousand more had been burned by Confederate authorities to prevent its falling into the hands of the Federals.[1]

---

[1] Wilson burned at Selma 32,000 bales, and at Columbus, Ga., 150,000 bales, much of which came from Alabama. During the raid he destroyed 275,000 bales, 125,000 of which were burned in Alabama. The Confederates destroyed at Montgomery 80,000 bales (other accounts say 97,000 and 125,000; see Greeley, Vol. II, p. 19). Government cotton was, of course, the first destroyed, and there is no doubt but that nearly all of it was burned either by the raiders or by the Confederates to prevent its falling into the hands of the enemy. Cotton was also destroyed at Mobile and by the Federal armies that came up from the South.

On October 30, 1864, a report was made to Secretary of the Treasury[1] Trenholm which showed the amount of Confederate cotton in the southern states. By far the greater part that was still on hand was in Alabama. In this state the Confederacy had received as subscriptions to the Produce Loan, 134,252 bales, at an average cost of $101.55, in all, $13,633,621.90. Other sales or subscriptions on other products to this Produce or Cotton Loan raised the amount in Alabama to $16,691,500. Alabama, as one of the producing states, and the one least affected by the ravages of war, furnished to all of these loans more produce than any other state.[2] The people, unable to sell their cotton abroad, exchanged some of it for Confederate bonds. Several thousand bales (6000 in 1864) were gathered by the cotton tithe. After shipping several thousand bales through the blockade, and smuggling some through the lines, and after some destruction by the enemy, or to prevent seizure by the enemy, there remained in the state, in the fall of 1864, 115,450 bales of Confederate cotton. Nearly all of this was destroyed in 1865, before the surrender, by Federals and Confederates, and very little remained which the Federal government could rightfully claim as Confederate property. This claim was based on the theory that cotton subscribed to the Produce Loan was devoted to the aid of the Confederacy, in intention at least, and therefore was forfeited to the United States, even though the owner had never delivered the cotton or other produce, and though the United States held that the Confederacy could not legally acquire property.[3] There were three classes of property claimed by the United States: (1) "captured" property or anything seized by the army and navy; (2) "abandoned" property, the owner being in the Confederate service, no matter whether his family were present or not; (3) "confiscable" property, or that liable to seizure and sale under the Confiscation Act of July

---

[1] Report of A. Roane, Chief of the Produce Loan, C.S.A. Office, in Ho. Mis. Doc., No. 190, 44th Cong., 1st Sess.

[2] Roane then estimated that by April 1, 1865, the Confederacy owned in all no more than 150,000 bales. Dr. Curry, a member of the Confederate Congress, stated that only 250,000 bales were ever owned by the Confederate government. "Civil History," pp. 115, 128. F. S. Lyon, when a member of the Confederate Congress in 1864, found that the Confederacy had a claim on about 150,000 bales scattered over ten states. Ku Klux Rept., Ala. Test., 1426.

[3] J. Barr Robertson, "The Confederate Debt and Private Southern Debts," p. 25.

17, 1862. Until 1865, all sorts of property were seized and used by the Federal forces, or, if portable, sent North for sale. Live stock, planting implements and machinery, wagons, etc., were in some cases sent North and sold;[1] but most was used on the spot.

After the surrender the Secretary of Treasury ordered household furniture, family relics, books, etc., to be restored to all "loyal" owners or to those who had taken the amnesty oath.[2] In no case had a person who could not prove his or her "loyalty" any remedy against seizure of property. Until the surrender the people of north Alabama were despoiled of all property that could be moved, and after the surrender the same policy was pursued all over the state, especially in regard to cotton. No right of property in cotton was there recognized, but by a previous law a "loyal" owner had until two years after the war to prove his claim and his "loyalty."[3]

The Attorney-General delivered an opinon, July 5, 1865, that cotton and other property seized by the agents or the army was *de facto* and *de jure, captured* property, and that neither the President nor the Secretary of the Treasury had the power to restore such property to the former owners. They must go through the courts, and under the laws only "loyal" claimants had any basis for claims, and "loyalty" must first be determined by the courts.[4] After the opinion of the Attorney-General, Secretary McCulloch followed it so far as

---

[1] Ho. Ex. Doc., No. 78, 38th Cong., 1st Sess. (Chase).
[2] Circular, Sept. 9, 1865.   [3] Act, March 12, 1863.
[4] Ho. Ex. Doc., No. 114, 39th Cong., 2d Sess.; Treasury Department Doc., No. 2261. According to a decision of the Supreme Court in case of Klein *vs.* United States (13 Wallace, 128), " disloyal" owners might become "loyal" by pardon and thus have all rights of property restored. This was the effect of proclamations of the President. "The restoration of the proceeds [then] became the absolute right of persons pardoned." See. Ho. Repts., No. 784, 51st Cong., 1st Sess., and No. 1377 ; 52d Cong., 1st Sess. The Attorney-General stated that " Congress took notice of the fact that captures of private property on land had been made and would continue to be made by the armies as a necessary and proper means of diminishing the wealth and thus reducing the powers of the insurgent rulers," and that after a seizure had been made there could be no question of whether the usages of war were observed or violated, except through the courts ; the President and the Secretary of the Treasury had no discretion in the matter. Ho. Ex. Doc., No. 114, 39th Cong., 1st Sess. According to the opinion of the United States law officers, " No one who submitted to the Confederate States, obeyed their laws, and contributed to support their government ought to recover under the statute " of March 12, 1863. See Sen. Ex. Doc., No. 22, 40th Cong., 2d Sess.

captures by the army were concerned, but still continued to "revise the mistakes" of the cotton agents who "frequently seized the property of private individuals." Proof of "loyalty" was, however, required in all cases before restoration, and the fourteen classes excepted by the amnesty proclamation of May 29, 1865, could get no restoration. In all cases the expenses charged against the property had to be paid before the owner could get it. After April 4, 1867, by request of the Joint Sub-Committee on Retrenchment, no further releases of any kind were made.[1] On March 30, 1868, a joint resolution of Congress covered into the Treasury all money received from sales of property in the South. After this only an act of Congress could restore the proceeds to the owner.[2]

The result was in the long run that the "disloyal" owners never received restoration of their property seized by the army, and by the Treasury agents during and after the war, but claim agents and perjurers have pursued a thriving business in proving "loyal" claims against the Treasury. "Disloyal" persons, whose property was liable to confiscation, and who could not recover in the Court of Claims, were, as decided by that body: those who served in the military, naval, or civil service of the state or the Confederacy; those who voted for secession or for secession candidates; those who furnished supplies to the Confederacy, engaged in business that aided the Confederacy, subscribed to its loans, resided or removed voluntarily within the Confederate lines, or sold produce to the Confederacy. Women who had sons or husbands in the Confederate army, or who belonged to "sewing societies," or made flags and clothing for, or furnished delicacies to, Confederate soldiers were "disloyal" and could not recover property. "Loyalty" had to be proven, not only for the original owner, but also for the heirs and claimants. The claims of deserters were allowed. In order to test the "loyalty" of claimants, they were asked to answer in writing lists of questions (numbering at various times 49, 62, 79, and 80 questions) regarding their conduct during the war. The questions covered several hundred points, and embraced every possible activity from 1861 to 1865. No man and few women who lived within the state until 1865 could,

---

[1] Secretary McCulloch to President of the Senate, Jan. 16, 1869. Sen. Ex. Doc., No. 22, 40th Cong., 2d Sess., No. 37, 39th Cong., 25th Sess.

[2] Department Circular, No. 4, Jan. 9, 1900; 15 Stats.-at-Large, p. 251.

U

without perjury, pass the examination and prove a claim. Yet numbers have proved claims.[1]

Cotton Frauds and Stealing

The minority report of the Ku Klux Committee in 1872 asserted that, of the 5,000,000 bales of cotton in the South at the close of the war, 3,000,000 had been seized by United States Treasury agents or pretended agents.[2] The Gulf states, and especially Alabama, were for a year or more filled with agents and "cotton spies," seeking Confederate cotton and other property. They were paid a percentage of what they seized — 25 to 50 per cent. Native scoundrels united with these, and all reaped a rich harvest.[3]

On much of the cotton subscribed to the Confederate Produce Loan the government had advanced a small amount to the owner and allowed him to keep it. In many cases no payment had been made. The farmer considered that the cotton still belonged to him, but that the Confederacy had a claim on a part of it. The records kept were imperfect, and few persons knew just what was Confederate cotton and what was not. Much of the cotton subscribed had been destroyed or sent to government warehouses in Selma, Mobile, Montgomery, and Columbus, where it was burned in April and May, 1865. Of course each man considered that the cotton destroyed was Confederate cotton, and that all left was private cotton. In most cases the claim of the government was very shadowy. Where cotton was still in the hands of the planter, private and government cotton could not be distinguished. The records did not show whether a man had kept or delivered the cotton he had subscribed to the Produce Loan. The agents proceeded upon the assumption that he had kept it, and that all he had kept was government cotton.[4] No proof to the contrary would convince the average agent. Secretary

---

[1] See Ho. Mis. Doc., No. 16, 42d Cong., 2d Sess.; No. 12, 42d Cong., 3d Sess.; No. 23, 43d Cong., 1st Sess.; No. 18, 43d Cong., 2d Sess.; No. 30, 44th Cong., 1st Sess.; No. 4, 45th Cong., 2d Sess.; Nos. 10 and 30, 46th Cong., 2d Sess.; also Treasury Department Doc., No. 2261 (1901); Department Circular, No. 4. Jan. 9, 1900.

[2] Sen. Rept., No. 41, Pt. I, pp. 442, 445, 42d Cong., 2d Sess.

[3] Ku Klux Rept., Ala. Test., p. 1941.

[4] Curry, "Civil History Confederate States," pp. 115, 126, 128. See testimony of Lieut.-Col. Hunter Brooke in Rept. Joint Committee on Reconstruction, Pt. III, p. 115.

McCulloch said, "I am sure I sent some honest cotton agents South; but it sometimes seems very doubtful whether any of them remained honest very long."[1] It was said that Secretary Chase had foreseen the trouble that would result if the cotton were confiscated, and had proposed to leave all cotton in the hands of the former owners who then held it. When the records were certain, the cotton might be confiscated; but in most cases there were no correct records. Such a policy would have been generous and magnanimous, and would have had a good effect.[2] The plan of Chase was not accepted, and a carnival of corruption followed. In August, 1865, President Johnson wrote to General Thomas, "I have been advised that innumerable frauds are being practised by persons assuming to be Treasury agents, in various portions of Alabama, in the collection of cotton pretended to belong to the Confederate States government."[3] The thefts of the Treasury agents and the worst characters of the army did much to arouse bitter feelings among the people who lost their only possession that could be turned into ready money. It was assumed, as a general rule, that all cotton belonged to the government until the real owner could prove his claim and his "loyalty," and of course he could seldom do this to the satisfaction of the agent or of the army officer who was bent on supplementing his pay. Cotton had been all along an object of the special hostility of Federals. The old southern belief that cotton was king and the hopes that Confederates had founded on this belief were well known. "Cotton is the root of all evil" was a common declaration of the invading army and of the cotton agents. When no other private property was taken or destroyed, cotton was sure to be. Every cotton-gin and press in reach of the armies was burned from 1863 to 1865. There seemed to be an intense desire to destroy the royal power of King Cotton. As opportunity offered, officers in the army, contrary to orders, began to interest themselves in speculations in cotton — captured, purchased, or stolen. The small garrisons were not officered by the best men of the army, and many who would never have touched money from any other kind of plunder thought it perfectly legitimate to fill their pockets by the seizure and sale of cotton. They

[1] Whitelaw Reid, " After the War," p. 204.
[2] Reid, " After the War," pp. 208, 209.
[3] Miller, " Alabama," p. 236.

did not consider it defrauding the government, for the latter, they knew, had no more title to it than they had.[1]

The disposition of the cotton collectors to regard the people as without rights resulted in the growth of a feeling on the part of the latter that it was perfectly legitimate to keep the government and its rascally agents from profiting by the use of Confederate property. In every way people began to hinder the agents and the army in its work of collecting cotton. Colonel Hunter Brooke stated, in 1866, that most of the people who had subscribed cotton to the Confederate government or on whose cotton the Confederates had some claim utterly refused to recognize the title of the United States to that property and refused to give any assistance to the authorities in tracing the cotton. At times the citizens rose in rebellion against the invasion of Treasury agents and the military escorts sent with them. A cotton spy was sent into Choctaw County to collect information about cotton stealing. He had an escort of twenty soldiers, but the people drove them out. A battalion of cavalry was then sent. Steamers sent up the rivers to get the cotton seized by the agents were sometimes fired upon.[2]

Not only cotton but stores collected on private plantations for the army, no matter whether private property or not, were seized. Horses and mules used in the Confederate service were taken, notwithstanding the terms of surrender and the fact that the Confederate soldiers owned the cavalry horses.[3] The counties of Cherokee,

---

[1] One who suffered writes from Selma: "Our cotton, the only thing left us with which to buy the necessaries of life, was seized at the point of the bayonet under the plea that it was Confederate cotton and that it was being seized by the government for its own use, whereas it was taken by the officers and sold, and the money put into their own pockets. It was then worth $255 a bale. Gen. —— commanded at this place, and he and his staff coined money faster than a mint could turn it out." Judge B. H. Craig. In July, 1865, a train of wagons at Talladega was sent to the ginnery of Ross Green, at Alexandria, and 59 bales of cotton, Green's own property, worth $100 a bale in gold, were carried off. Miller, p. 236.

[2] Testimony in Rept. of Joint Committee on Reconstruction, Pt. III, p. 115; Ku Klux Rept., Ala. Test., p. 1426. F. S. Lyon said that the people would have been better reconciled to the confiscation had the cotton been sold for the benefit of the United States, but it was plainly stolen by the agents and the army, and they began to resist in every way. Some of them concealed Confederate cotton; some stole from the government, some from the agents what the latter had stolen from them; some went into partnership with the agents. No one believed that any one except the original owner had a right to the cotton, and they did anything to get even.

[3] Miller, p. 236; N. Y. Times, March 2 and Aug. 30, 1865. In the Black

Franklin, Jackson, Jefferson, Lauderdale, Limestone, Madison, Morgan, St. Clair, Walker, and Winston — all white counties — lost principally corn, fodder, provisions, harness, mules, horses, and wagons.[1]

As to cotton, much pure stealing was done by the followers of the army and thieving soldiers and some natives, but sooner or later the officials became implicated in it, since only by their permission could the commodity be shipped. A thieving southerner would find where a lot of cotton was stored and inform a soldier, usually an officer, who would make arrangements to ship the cotton, and the two would divide the profits. Planters who were afraid that their cotton would be seized by Treasury agents went into partnership with Federal officers and shipped their cotton to New Orleans or to New York. No one outside the ring could ship cotton until five or ten dollars a bale was paid the military officers who controlled affairs. Along the line of the Mobile and Ohio Railway 10,000 bales of cotton were said to have been stolen from the owners and sold in Mobile and New Orleans. The thieves often paid $75 a bale to have the cotton passed through to New Orleans.[2]

But all petty thievery went unnoticed when the Treasury agents began operations. They harried the land worse than an army of bummers. There was no protection against one; he claimed all cotton, and, unless bribed, seized it. Thousands of bales were taken to which the government had not a shadow of claim. In November, 1865, the *Times* correspondent (Truman) stated that nearly all the Treasury agents in Alabama had been filling their pockets with cotton money, and that $2,000,000 were unaccounted for. One agent took 2000 bales on a vessel and went to France. Their method of proceeding was to find a lot of cotton, Confederate or otherwise, and give some man $50 a bale to swear the cotton belonged to him, and that it had never been turned over to the Confederate States. Then the agent shipped the cotton and cleared $100 a bale.[3]

Belt the United States military authorities collected the tax-in-kind which had been levied by the Confederate authorities but not collected. One planter had to pay one thousand bushels of corn, two barrels of syrup, and smaller quantities of other produce. From those who refused to pay the tax was taken forcibly. See Ku Klux Rept., p. 446 (F. S. Lyon).

[1] Ho. Mis. Doc., No. 30, 46th Cong., 2d Sess.

[2] Trowbridge, "The South," p. 447; Reid, "After the War," pp. 208, 209, 375; *N. Y. Times*, Aug. 30, 1865; *N. Y. Herald*, June 23, 1865.

[3] *N. Y. Times*, Aug. 30 and Nov. 2, 1865; *De Bow's Review*, 1866; oral accounts.

Secretary McCulloch said that the most troublesome and disagreeable duty that he was called upon to perform was the execution of the law in regard to Confederate property. The cotton agents, being paid by a commission on the property collected, were disposed so seize private property also. There was no authority at hand to check them. And people were disposed, he thought, to lay claim to Confederate cotton and "spirited away" much of it, while on the other hand much private property was taken by the agents.[1]

Five years later the testimony taken in Alabama at the instance of the minority members of the Ku Klux Committee exposed the methods of the cotton agents.[2] The country swarmed with agents or pretended agents and their spies or informers; the commission given was from one-fourth to one-half of all cotton collected; everybody's cotton was seized, but for fear of future trouble a proposition from the owner to divide was usually listened to and a peaceable settlement made; when private or public cotton was shipped it was consigned by bales and not by pounds; the various agents through whose hands it passed were in the habit of "tolling" or "plucking" it, often two or three times, about one-fifth at a time; in this way a bale weighing 500 pounds would be reduced to 200 or 300 pounds; even after the private cotton arrived at Mobile or New Orleans, paying "toll" all the way, it was liable to seizure by order of some Treasury agent; as a rule, terms could be arranged by which a planter might keep one-fourth to three-fourths of his cotton, whether Confederate or not; it was safer for the agent to take a part of the cotton with the consent and silence of the owner than to steal both from the owner and from the government for which he pretended to work, and in this way the owners saved some for themselves; much private cotton was seized on the plantations near the rivers before the owners came home from the war; cotton seized in the Black Belt was shipped to Simeon Draper, United States cotton agent, New York, while that from north Alabama was sent to William P. Mellen, Cincinnati;[3] complaint was made by those few owners who succeeded in tracing

---

[1] McCulloch, "Men and Measures," pp. 234, 235.

[2] Sen. Rept., No. 41, Pt. 1, 42d Cong., 2d Sess., pp. 442–445.

[3] The minority Ku Klux Report asserted that it was a well-known fact that Draper when appointed cotton agent was a bankrupt, and that when he died he was a millionnaire.

their cotton that, after being reduced by "tolling" or "plucking," [1] it was sold by the agent in the North, by samples which were much inferior to the cotton in the bales, and in this way the purchaser, who was in partnership with the agents, would pay ten or fifteen cents a pound for a lot of cotton certainly not worth more than that if the samples were honest, but which was really good cotton, worth 35 cents to $1.20 a pound in New York.

So in case the Secretary of the Treasury could be brought to "revise the mistakes" of his agents, the owner would get only the small sum paid in for inferior cotton, and even this was reduced by excessive charges and fees.[2] There was also complaint that when a lot of private cotton was seized and traced to Draper, the latter would inform the owners that only a small proportion of what had been seized was received,[3] and that had been sold at a low price. It was afterwards shown that Draper never gave receipts for cotton received. There was nothing businesslike about the cotton administration. Cotton was consigned to Draper or Mellen by the bale and not by the pound. A bale might weigh 200 or 500 pounds. As soon as cotton was seized the bagging was stripped off, and it was then repacked in order to prevent identification.[4] Many persons who knew nothing of the law and who saw that their property was unsafe were induced by the Treasury agents to surrender their cotton to the United States government, even though there might be no claim against it, the agents promising that the United States would pay to the owners the proceeds upon application to the Treasury Department. When the Secretary of the Treasury discovered this, and when the agent would certify that such was the case, his "mistake was revised" and the money received from the sale of cotton was refunded.[5] The owner had no remedy if the agent declined to cer-

[1] The cotton secured in this way was, it was claimed, sold as "waste," "trash," or "dog tail" to some friend of the agent, who would divide with the latter.

[2] All freight, agency, auctioneer, insurance, storage, etc., charges, and fees for legal advice, were charged against the cotton, and had to be paid before it was restored.

[3] Probably Draper was correct here. The agents would consign to him all cotton that they felt sure the government had record of, and the rest they sold for their own benefit.

[4] Ho. Mis. Doc., No. 190, 44th Cong, 1st Sess.

[5] Secretary McCulloch to President of the Senate, March 2, 1867, in Sen. Ex. Doc. No. 37, 39th Cong., 2d Sess. In this way, during the summer of 1865, $616,844.34 was restored to owners, and to the end of 1866 $1,018,459.83 was restored. Most of the owners lived in Alabama and Louisiana.

tify, and he usually declined, since the cotton had probably never been turned over to the United States by him.

The experience of Hon. F. S. Lyon [1] is typical of many in the Black Belt. He stated [2] that after the surrender of Taylor, General Canby issued an order that all who had sold cotton to the Confederate government must now surrender it to United States authorities under penalty of confiscation of other property to make good the failure to deliver Confederate cotton. Under this order some cotton was seized to replace Confederate cotton that had disappeared. United States army wagons, guarded by soldiers, went over the country day and night, gathering cotton for persons who pretended to be Treasury agents. Lyon had 384 bales of Confederate cotton which were claimed by General Dustin, a cotton agent (later a carpet-bag politician), and Lyon agreed to haul it to the railroad, under an "agreement" with Dustin. But one night a train of army wagons, guarded by soldiers, came and carried off 26 bales, and the next day, 70 bales. (They had asked the manager "if he would accept $2000 and sleep soundly all night.") The wagons were traced to Uniontown, and the commanding officer there was induced to hold the cotton until the question was settled. General Hubbard, commanding the district, arrested one Ruter, who, with the soldiers, had taken the cotton. Ruter claimed to be acting under the authority of a cotton agent in Mississippi, but could show no evidence of his authority, and his name was not on the list of authorized agents. However, General Hubbard was ordered by superior authority to regard Ruter as a cotton agent and to discharge him. The 70 bales were lost.

The Mobile agent, Dustin, [3] would not make a decision in disputed cases because he was afraid of appeal to Washington. A proposition to divide the profits, however, would always secure from him a declaration that the cotton had no claims against it. Lyon reported that not one-tenth of the cotton seized was consigned to govern-

---

[1] See Brewer, p. 375, and Garrett, p. 587. Lyon was one of the most useful, reliable, and respected public men of Alabama and his account is entitled to confidence. He had been a lawyer, clerk of the senate, senator, member of Congress, state bank commissioner, presidential elector, member Confederate Congress, etc.

[2] Letter to F. P. Blair, in Sen. Rept., No. 41, Pt. I, p. 445, 42d Cong., 2d Sess.

[3] Under the reconstruction government Dustin held the office of major-general of militia.

ment agents, but that the agents usually sold it on the spot to cotton buyers. The planter was held responsible for cotton sold or subscribed to Confederate government. Cotton stolen from the agent had to be made good by the person from whom the agent had seized it. Seed cotton was often hauled away at night by pretended agents. In every part of the cotton belt the looting of cotton went on.

There were frequent changes of agents. As soon as a man became rich his place would be taken by another. The chief cotton agents sold for high prices appointments as collecting agents. The new agents often seized the cotton that through bribery had escaped former agents; and in this way the same lot would be seized two or three times. One cotton agent, a mere youth, at Demopolis received as his commission for one month 400 bales of cotton which netted him $80,000. The Treasury Department made a regulation allowing one-fourth to a person who had kept the Confederate cotton and delivered it safely to the United States authorities, but the agents did not make known the regulation, and the one-fourth went to them.[1]

There were complaints of the seizure of cotton grown after the war. The Planters' Factory of Mobile lost 240 bales of cotton grown in 1865. This company was made up of "Union" and northern men who were able to obtain an order for the release of the cotton. There was of course no way to tell what cotton was seized, and 240 bales of "dog tail," worth six cents a pound, were turned over to the factory instead of the good cotton, worth sixty cents a pound.[2]

Dishonest Agents Prosecuted

The Federal grand jury reported that at the end of the war there were 150,000 bales of cotton in Alabama to which the government

---

[1] See Ku Klux Rept., pp. 444–446. Letter of F. S. Lyon to General Blair. Also Ku Klux Rept., Ala. Test., pp. 1410–1426, 1661.

Lyon had been agent for the Confederate Produce Loan, and consequently knew what was government cotton and what was not. After the war he acted as attorney for those whose cotton was unlawfully seized. The general officers commanding in his district approved his conduct, but he was hated by the cotton agents, who frequently complained of his "rebellious conduct." Lyon tried to save even the cotton pledged to the Confederacy, on the ground that the promise or sale had not been completed and that the transaction was void from the beginning, and that the right of capture did not exist after the close of the war.

[2] Ho. Mis. Doc., No. 190, 44th Cong., 1st Sess., p. 146.

had clear title;[1] the records showed the history and location of each bale, and these records were placed in the hands of the cotton agents; the papers of two agents, in south Alabama, Dexter and Tomeny, showed that while a large part of this cotton had been shipped but little of it had been consigned to the government, the bulk of it having become a source of private profit to the agents; the 20,000 bales turned over to the government by these agents had been much reduced in weight, in some cases as much as one-third, and exorbitant expenses had been charged against them; large quantities of cotton had been fraudulently released to parties who presented fictitious claims; cotton belonging to private individuals had often been seized, and release refused unless the owner sold at a ruinous sacrifice to S. E. Ogden and Company, who seemed to be on the inside at New York; cotton thus seized was not released except through the influence of Ogden and Company, and it was said that Tomeny openly advised some parties to make arrangements with Ogden and Company, who paid less than half-price for cotton under such circumstances.[2] The grand jury declared that in Alabama 125,000 bales had been stolen by agents. Tomeny, who seems to have secured a much smaller share of the spoils than Dexter, stated that when he began business in November, 1865, nearly all cotton had been collected or stolen, and that not a hundred bales had been received by himself except from other agents who had collected it. He consigned all his cotton to Simeon Draper, in New York City. None was released to Ogden and Company, and they bought only one lot of cotton that had been seized — 505 bales seized from Ellis and Alley, themselves cotton agents under the First Agency. This lot, Tomeny claimed, was bought by Ogden and Company without his knowledge or consent.[3]

Two cotton agents, T. C. A. Dexter and T. J. Carver, were finally arraigned, in the fall and winter of 1865, in the Federal courts, and Judge Busteed proceeded to try them; but they denied the jurisdiction of the court, and the army interfered and stopped the proceedings, whereupon Busteed closed the court. Then a military

[1] Calculation based on subscriptions to Produce Loan. Most of it had been destroyed.

[2] *N. Y. Times*, June 2, 1865; *Huntsville Advocate*, May 26, 1866. Report of Grand Jury.

[3] *N. Y. Times*, June 2, 1866.

commission was convened, and before it the cases were tried. Lieutenant-Colonel Hunter Brooke presided over the commission. The culprits denied the legality of this trial by a military commission in time of peace and ultimately were pardoned on this account. Carver was convicted of fraud in the collection of cotton, and was fined $90,000 and sentenced to imprisonment for one year and until the fine should be paid. Carver had paid Dexter $25,000 for his commission as cotton agent. So it seems the office must have carried with it certain opportunities. Dexter was convicted of fraud in the cotton business and for selling the appointment to Carver. Only 3321 bales of government cotton could be traced directly to his stealing.[1] He was fined $250,000 and imprisoned for one year and until the fine should be paid.[2]

Statistics of the Frauds

The minority report of the Ku Klux Committee asserted, as has been said, that in 1865 there were 5,000,000 bales of cotton in the South, and that the agents seized 3,000,000 bales for themselves and for the government;[3] Dr. Curry said that there were about 250,000 bales of Confederate cotton;[4] another expert estimate placed the total number of bales of Confederate cotton at 150,000 on April 1, 1865; after April 1, many thousand bales were destroyed in Alabama, where most of the Confederate cotton was gathered; the report of A. Roane, in 1864, showed 115,000 bales in Alabama. It is not probable, after all the burnings which later took place in Alabama,

---

[1] Worth $500,000, at the lowest price.

[2] G. O., No. 55, Department of Ala., Oct. 30, 1865; G. O., No. 8, Department of Ala., Feb. 14, 1866; Ms. records in War Department archives. For years these men were in prison while their friends were working to secure their release. The principal arguments for Dexter's release were the virtue of his wife's relations in New England and the illegality of the trial before the military commission in time of peace. Judging from the tone of the indorsements he was probably released, though there is no record of the fact in the archives. The manuscript proceedings of the trial show that thousands of bales of cotton had been "spirited away," but everything was in such a state of confusion that little could be plainly proven against the agents. Only one thing was certain, "that much more cotton was seized for the government than was received by the government." The investigation was hushed up as soon as possible; too many were implicated.

[3] Sen. Rept., No. 41, Pt. I, pp. 442, 445, 42d Cong., 2d Sess. This estimate is probably too large for both numbers.

[4] "Civil History, Confederate States," pp. 115, 128.

that there was much government cotton left in Alabama, 20,000 bales at the most.

Secretary McCulloch, on March 2, 1867, reported that the total receipts from captured and abandoned property amounted to $34,052,809.54, netting $24,742,322.55.[1] The cotton sold for $29,518,041.17.[2] The records show that only 115,000 bales were turned over to the United States, and of these Draper received 95,840½ bales which he sold for about $15,000,000 when cotton was worth 33 cents to $1.22 a pound, and a bale weighed 400 to 450 pounds. This cotton was worth in New York $500,000,000.[3] The records of the agencies were badly kept or not kept at all, and many agents made no reports. The government never knew how many bales had been collected in its name.

The First Special Agency reported that in Alabama it had seized cotton (after June 1, 1865) in the counties of Greene, Marengo, Perry, Dallas, Pickens, Montgomery, Sumter, and Tuscaloosa, during October, November, and December, 1865, and January, 1866. This agency had, before June 1, 1866,[4] shipped 5697 bales to the government agent in New York, who sold them for $750,702.68, and had made charges of $209,338.58 for freight, fees, etc., $35 a bale. The Ninth Agency, under the notorious T. C. A. Dexter and J. M. Tomeny, gathered cotton from the counties of Dallas, Marengo, Sumter, Montgomery, Wilcox, Lowndes, Barbour, Butler, Tuscaloosa, Macon, and Mobile. This agency had thirty-six collecting agents, and turned over to the government only 9,712 bales, which sold for $1,412,335.68, with fees and charges amounting to $540,962.38.[5]

[1] Sen. Ex. Doc., No. 37, 39th Cong., 2d Sess.

[2] Sen. Ex. Doc., No. 56, 40th Cong., 2d Sess.

[3] Sen. Rept., No. 41, Pt. I, p. 444, 42d Cong., 2d Sess.

[4] After which date confiscation was forbidden by Treasury regulation.

[5] An example of the way charges were piled up: A lot of 448 bales of cotton was seized in Eufaula, Alabama, and shipped to New York, via Appalachicola. The expenses were : —

Expenses to and at Appalachicola	$24,264.85
Freight	4,164.69
Expenses at New York	2,500.05
Information and collecting	30,893.31
Total expenses	61,822.90
Gross proceeds of sale	78,352.56
Net proceeds of sale	16,529.66

Sen. Ex. Doc., No. 23, 43d Cong., 2d Sess.

Most of the government cotton was consigned to New York agents and sold there.[1]

The army quartermasters at Mobile received 19,396 bales of cotton, of which 6149 were delivered to Dexter and 9741 were, it was claimed, destroyed by the great explosion. Dexter turned over to the government only 7469 bales and Tomeny 7732, other agents accounted for enough to bring the total up to about 30,000 bales. Dexter sold $823,947 worth of other property.[2]

The Freedmen's Bureau in Alabama was supported for two years by the sale of confiscated property, of which no accounts were kept. The army also sold cotton and other confiscated property and used the proceeds. "Abandoned" cotton netted to the Treasury $2,682,271.69. After June 30, according to Treasury records, 33,638 bales (worth $7,650,675.93, but netting only $4,886,671) were illegally seized. It is this money which is still held because the former owners once subscribed to the Confederate Produce Loan. "Loyal" claimants, 22,298 in number in 1871, were asking damages to the amount of $60,258,150.44. When Congress, on March 30, 1868, called into the Treasury all proceeds of captured and abandoned property, it was found that Jay Cooke and Company had $20,000,000, which they had been using in their business for years. The cotton agents and others interested lobbied persistently in Washington

The following cotton statistics show how the Mobile agents ran up expenses: —

J. R. Dillon, 1st Agency:	Cotton sales	$57,033.66
	Total proceeds of all sales . .	129,076.33
	Expenses, total	64,350.01
S. B. Eaton, 1st Agency:	Cotton sold	15,963.01
	Total receipts	27,799.48
	Total expenses	27,799.48
T. C. A. Dexter, 9th Agency:	Cotton sold	39,945.39
	Total receipts	783,152.62
	Expenses	485,137.77
J. M. Tomeny, 9th Agency:	Cotton sold	14,159.51
	Total receipts	208,185.63
	Expenses	208,185.63
Total expenses of every kind amounted to		6,546,000.95
On receipts of		34,396,189.95
Of which cotton sold for		29,518,041.17

[1] Sen. Ex. Doc., No. 56, 40th Cong., 2d Sess.
[2] Ho. Ex. Doc., No. 97, 39th Cong., 2d Sess.

against legislation in behalf of claimants, fearing investigation and exposure.

The statistics given in the public documents are often those for the whole South, but usually only for Alabama, Mississippi, and Louisiana. Seldom can the figures for Alabama be separated from the others. Alabama lost more from the invasion of Treasury agents than any other state, since in 1865 she had more cotton and other property, and many more agents visited her soil. The United States Treasury received only a small fraction of the confiscated property, and most of the proceeds of that have been released to people who were willing to commit perjury in order to get it.[1]

Under the act of March 12, 1863, "loyal" owners had until two years after the war to file claims, and by February, 1888, $9,864,300.75 had been paid out to satisfy these people. Since 1888, $520,700.18 has been paid out. Under the act of May 18, 1872, providing for return of proceeds of cotton seized illegally after June 30, 1865, 1337 claims were filed, 339 of which were from Alabama. These Alabama claims called for 23,529 bales. Only a very small amount ($195,896.21) was returned to the claimants, because the records showed that most of them had once sold cotton to the Confederate government. Therefore, they now say, all cotton seized after June 30, 1865, was Confederate cotton, and the proceeds will be held. Only about four and a half millions now (1904) remain in the Treasury, as the proceeds of all the cotton seized. This is the amount for which the cotton seized after June 30, 1865, was sold. All other proceeds have either been returned to "loyal" claimants or have been absorbed by expenses. Very few, if any, claimants not able to prove "loyalty" have been able to secure restoration, since "loyalty" was in most cases a prerequisite to consideration.[2]

---

[1] See Ku Klux Rept., pp. 443–446; Sen. Ex. Doc., No. 37, 39th Cong., 2d Sess.; Ho. Ex. Doc., No. 97, 39th Cong., 2d Sess.; Ho. Ex. Doc., No. 113, 41st Cong., 2d Sess.; Sen. Ex. Doc., No. 23, 43d Cong., 2d Sess.; Department Circular, No. 4, Jan. 9, 1900.

[2] Department Circular, No. 4, Jan. 9, 1900; Sen. Ex. Doc., No. 23, 43d Cong., 2d Sess. There are imperfect records of only two Alabama agencies, which reported a certain number of bales seized. The other agencies did not report their operations in Alabama. The agents not reporting were: J. R. Dillon, H. M. Buckley, S. B. Eaton, E. P. Hotchkiss, L. Ellis, A. D. Banks, James and Ellis Carver, and perhaps others. None of the numerous collecting agents made reports or kept records. In 1876, thirty-three cotton agents were defaulters to the United States, one man owing the United

The confiscation policy, it may be concluded, profited the government nothing; the Treasury agents and pretended agents were enriched by their stealings and but few were punished; nearly all private cotton was lost; the people were reduced to more desperate want and exasperated against the government which, it seemed, had acted upon the assumption that the ex-Confederates had no rights whatever.

SEC. 2. THE COTTON TAX

Another heavy burden imposed on the prostrate South was the tax levied by the United States government on each pound of cotton raised. An act of July, 1862, imposed a tax of one-half cent a pound on cotton, but this tax could be collected only on that part of the crop that was brought through the lines by speculators. January 30, 1864, the tax was increased to two cents a pound, collectible on all cotton coming from the Confederate States. This was raised to two and a half cents a pound on March 3, 1865, and to three cents a pound, or $15 a bale, on July 13, 1866.[1] After the war the tax bore with crushing weight on the impoverished farmers.[2] On March 2, 1867, in anticipation of Reconstruction, the tax was reduced to two and a half cents a pound, or $12.50 a bale, to take effect after September 1, 1867. A year later, partly because of the decided objections of those carpet-baggers, scalawags, and negroes who had small farms and whose remonstrances had more influence than those of the planters, the tax was discontinued on all cotton raised after the crop of 1867. The tax was a lien on the cotton from the time it was baled until the tax was paid, and was often collected in the states to which the cotton was shipped.

States $337,460.44. Of these, sixteen were not to be found anywhere. Four of the defaulters had operated in Alabama. These men were by their own records defaulters — having failed to turn over to the government the proceeds of sales they had reported. Ho. Mis. Doc., No. 190, 44th Cong., 1st Sess.

[1] In addition to the tax of twenty-five per cent on purchases of cotton levied by a Treasury regulation during the war and in force during 1865. Treasury regulations, May 9, 1865. See also President's proclamation, in McPherson, "Reconstruction," p. 9.

[2] Governor Patton, in his message of Nov. 12, 1866, stated that the cotton tax of three cents a pound was oppressive and unjust, a burden on the farmers and on the laborers also; that the tax went into the United States Treasury and then passed into the hands of the manufacturers as a gratuity of three cents per pound; that there was no way of getting the ruinous tax raised or lightened unless by an appeal in the form of a petition; that the people of Alabama had no voice in the government; that this "law paralyzes our energies and represses the development of our resources and is injurious to the whole country." Governor's Message, House Journal, 1866–1867, p. 21.

The collections in the South amounted to the following sums: —

For the year ending June 30, 1863	$351,311.48
For the year ending June 30, 1864	1,268,412.56
For the year ending June 30, 1865	1,772,983.48
For the year ending June 30, 1866	18,409,654.90
For the year ending June 30, 1867	23,769,078.80
For the year ending June 30, 1868	22,500,947.77
Total, ...	$68,072,388.99 [1]

Of this tax Alabama paid within her borders $10,388,072.10,[2] and since she was one of the three great cotton states, her share of the tax paid in northern ports must have been several million dollars more. Of the other cotton states, — Georgia, Louisiana, Mississippi, Texas, Tennessee, and Arkansas, — all except Georgia, which paid about a million dollars more than Alabama, suffered in less degree.

From April 1, 1865, to February 1, 1866, Alabama paid in other taxes, into the United States Treasury, $1,747,563.51, of which $1,655,-218.31 was internal revenue, and from September 1, 1862, to January 30, 1872, $14,200,982 internal revenue.[3] The former sum was much more than the Federal government spent in Alabama during that year for the relief of the destitute, both black and white. The cotton spirited away by thieves and confiscated by the government would have paid several times over all the expenses of the army and the Freedmen's Bureau during the entire time of the occupation. Many times as much money was taken from the negro tenant in the form of this cotton tax as was spent in aiding him. The most crushing weight of the tax came in 1866 and 1867, and it was much heavier than the taxation imposed by the Confederate and state governments even in the darkest days of the war. Had the price of cotton remained high, the tax would not have borne so heavily on the people; but with the decline of the price the tax finally amounted to a third of the net value of the cotton, while the amount raised in these years was about one-fifth of the value of the farming lands.[4] The tax absorbed all the profits of cotton planting and left the farmer nothing.

[1] Twenty states and territories are not included in these sums, as no reports were received from them. Ho. Ex. Doc., No. 181, 42d Cong., 3d Sess., and Sen. Ex. Doc., No. 2, 39th Cong., 2d Sess.

[2] Ho. Ex. Doc., No. 181, 42d Cong., 3d Sess.

[3] Ho. Ex. Doc., No. 47, 39th Cong., 1st Sess.; Ho. Ex. Doc., No. 181, 42d Cong., 3d Sess.

[4] $54,191,229 in 1870.

A letter from the Secretary of the Treasury in reference to the propriety of refunding the money received from the cotton tax stated some of the arguments of the opponents of the tax. It was claimed (1) that the tax was unconstitutional because it was not uniform and because it was virtually a tax upon exports; (2) that the tax was unequal and oppressive in its operations because it fell entirely upon cotton producers; (3) that it was levied without the consent of the people and when they were not represented in Congress; and (4) that in addition to the cotton tax the producers of the cotton were subject to all taxes paid by citizens of other states.[1] These objections were answered by the Secretary, who said that the tax was added to the price of cotton and was borne by the consumer, not the producer, and that it was the fault of the cotton states that they were not represented. He asserted that the tax on cotton was an excise like that on tobacco and whiskey.[2]

In 1866 an effort was made in Congress to raise the tax to five cents a pound. Such a tax, they said, would raise $66,000,000, or, at the least, $50,000,000 a year, of which Alabama's share would be about $12,000,000 to $15,000,000. The Committee on the Revenue reported that such a tax "will not prove detrimental to any national interest." The testimony of experts was quoted to prove that the tax would fall upon the consumer, though most of the experts, who were manufacturers from New England, said that on account of the great demand and excessive prices of cotton goods the tax would fall upon the manufacturer for the present time. Nevertheless, they were all in favor of the proposed tax, except one manufacturer and one planter from Georgia, who objected on the ground that the producer would have the burden to bear.[3]

The business men of New York and other northern cities opposed

---

[1] Ho. Ex. Doc., No. 181, 42d Cong., 3d Sess.

[2] The cotton tax was justified on the ground that while Alabama had paid $14,200,982 from 1862 to 1872, New Jersey had paid a total tax of $48,528,298, the two states having very nearly the same population. But no account was taken of the fact that for four years no tax was collected from Alabama by the United States, while nearly all of the movable wealth was destroyed during the war, and that in 1865 property was almost non-existent in Alabama. New Jersey, however, was a rich state. Alabama had besides paid an enormous war tax and had been looted of millions of dollars' worth of cotton. And in Alabama there were 500,000 negroes who paid no tax, while most of the population of New Jersey were taxpayers. Ho. Ex. Doc., No. 181, 42d Cong., 3d Sess.

[3] Ho. Ex. Doc., No. 34, 39th Cong., 1st Sess.

x

the tax and defeated the extra levy. The New York Chamber of Commerce, when the measure to raise the cotton tax to five cents a pound was proposed, memorialized Congress against the injustice of the tax. The memorial stated that the North and the West must not take advantage of the South in the days of her weakness; that the cultivation of cotton should not be thus discouraged. It was shown that the manufacturer would be protected by the drawback of five cents a pound allowed on cotton goods exported, while the cotton farmer would pay a five-cent tax. By the operation of such a tax, they stated, the rich would be made richer, and the poor made poorer. That in the proposed law "there is a want of impartiality which is calculated to provoke hostility at the South, and to excite in all honest minds at the North the hope that such a purpose will not prevail."[1]

By the people who had to pay the tax it was considered an unjust and purely vindictive measure, which was the more exasperating because they had no voice in the matter and because no attention was paid to their remonstrances. They complained that it was levied as a penalty, that it was confiscation under color of law. They felt that it was a blow of revenge aimed at them when there was no fear of resistance or hope of protection, as no other part of the country had its exports taxed.[2] The fact that the tax was removed because of the objections of the carpet-baggers, scalawags, and negroes, instead of pleasing the whites, was a source of irritation to them. The respectable people had asked for justice and it was refused them, but was granted to those who were of opposing politics. Those who paid the tax never believed that the mass of the people at the North were in favor of such a measure, and they hoped that favorable elections would reverse the policy of Congress, which, then recognizing the unconstitutionality of the tax, would refund it, if not to individuals, at least to the states in proportion to the amount raised in each, or, that Congress would give it to the states as a long-time loan.[3]

---

[1] Sen. Mis. Doc., No. 100, 39th Cong., 1st Sess. (A. A. Low, Chairman of Committee of the N. Y. Chamber of Commerce).

[2] Ku Klux Rept., Ala. Test., pp. 383, 403 (General Pettus); Journal of the Convention of 1867.

[3] See Saunders, "Early Settlers," p. 31 (Reverdy Johnson to Saunders). Jan. 18, 1872, the Alabama legislature (Republican Senate and Democratic House) memorialized Congress, asking to have the cotton tax refunded to the impoverished people, and

For years there was a belief among the farmers that the unjust tax
would be refunded, and the cotton tax receipts were carefully preserved against a day of reimbursement, but, like the negroes' "forty
acres and a mule," the money never came.[1]

stating that the tax was "most unjust and oppressive, a direct tax upon industry"; that
to refund the tax would be "evenhanded but tardy justice." Acts of Ala., 1871-1872,
pp. 445-446. A similar petition was made on Feb. 23, 1875. Acts of Ala., 1874-1875,
p. 674.

[1] In December, 1903, Representative J. S. Williams of Mississippi introduced a
measure in Congress to refund the amount of the cotton tax to the southern states.

CHAPTER VII

THE TEMPER OF THE PEOPLE, 1865-1866

After the Surrender

THE paroled Confederate soldier returned to his ruined farm and went to work to keep his family from extreme want. For him the war had decided two questions, the abolition of slavery, and the destruction of state sovereignty. Further than that he did not expect the effects of the war to extend, while punishment, as such, for the part he had taken in the war[1] was not thought of. He knew that there would be a temporary delay in restoring former relations with the central government, but political proscription and humiliation were not expected. That after a fair fight, which had resulted in their defeat, they should be struck when down, was something that did not occur to the soldiers at all. No one thought of further opposition to the United States; the results of the war were accepted in good faith, and the people meant to abide by the decision of arms. Naturally, there were no profuse expressions of love for the United States, — which was the North, — but there was an earnest desire to leave the past behind them and to take their place and do their duty as citizens of the new Union.[2]

---

[1] It is difficult to understand now how thoroughly the Confederate soldier realized that the questions at issue were decided against him. But that it was a crime to have been a Confederate soldier, he did not understand. See also testimony of John B. Gordon and of Edmund W. Pettus in the Ku Klux Testimony.

[2] A neglected point of view is the attitude of the Confederate soldier. He had surrendered with arms in hand, and certain terms had been made with him, as he thought, a contract, embodied in the parole. This he believed secured his rights in return for laying down arms, and that as long as he was law-abiding his rights were to be inviolate. He was well pleased with the "spirit of Appomattox," but nearly all that happened after Appomattox was in violation, he felt, of the terms of surrender. The whole radical programme was contrary to the contract made with men who had arms in their hands. Lee had decided that there should be no guerilla warfare, and in return certain moral obligations rested on the North. See the statements of General (now Senator) Edmund W. Pettus, in Ku Klux Rept, Ala. Test., pp. 377, 383, and of General John B. Gordon, in Ga. Test., pp. 314, 332, 333, 343.

The women and the children, who heard with a shock of the surrender, felt a terrible fear of the incoming armies. The raids of the latter part of the war had made them fear the northern soldiers, from whom they expected harsh treatment. The women had been enthusiastic for the Confederate cause; their sacrifices for it had been incalculable, and to many the disappointment and sorrow were more bitter than death. The soldier had the satisfaction of having fought in the field for his opinions, and it was easier for him to accept the results of war. A certain class of people who had served during the war at duties which kept them at home professed to be afraid of hanging, of confiscation, of negro suffrage and negro equality, and many other horrible things; they were loud in their denunciation of the surrender; they would have "fought and died in the last ditch," they declared. It is hard to see how they could so flatter themselves as to think the conqueror would hold them responsible for anything, unless for their violent talk on political questions before and during the war.

Such was the state of feeling in the first stage, before there was any general understanding of the nature of the questions to be solved or of the conflicting policies. News from the outside world came in slowly; each country community was completely cut off from the world; the whole state lay prostrate, breathless, exhausted, resting. Little interest was shown in public questions; the long strain had been removed, and the people were dazed about the future. There was no information from abroad except through the army officials, who reported the news to suit themselves. The railroads and steamboats were not running; for months there was no post-office system, and for years the service was poor. The people settled down into a lethargy, seemingly indifferent to what was going on, and exhibiting little interest in the government and in politics. Some persons dumbly awaited the worst, but the soldiers feared nothing; at present they took no interest in politics; they were working, when they were able, to provide for their families.

With many people there was a disposition to see in the defeat the work of God. There was a belief that fate, destiny, or Providence had been against the South, and this state of mind made them the more ready to accept as final the results of war. The fear expressed by northern politicians that in case of foreign war the South would

side with the enemy was without cause. The South had had enough
and too much of war. It disliked England and France more than it
hated the North, because they had withheld their aid after seeming to
promise it.

From the general gloom and seeming despair the young people
soon recovered to some degree, and among them there was much
social gayety of a quiet sort. For four years the young men and
young women had seen little of each other, and there had been comparatively few marriages. Now they were glad to be together again,
and all the surviving young men proceeded to get married at once.
This revival of spirits did not extend to the older people. Nearly
all were grieving over the loss of sons, brothers, husbands, or relatives. Much that made life worth living was lost to them forever,
and unable to adapt themselves to changed conditions or to recover
from the shock of grief and the strain of war, they died one after the
other, until soon but few were left.[1]

One of the first things to awaken the people of Alabama from
the blank lethargy into which they had fallen was the question of
what was to be done by the United States government with the Confederate leaders who had been arrested. President Davis and Vice-
President Stephens, Senator Clay, the war governors, — Moore,
Shorter, and Watts, — Admiral Semmes, several judicial officers of
the state, and many minor officials were arrested and imprisoned in
the North. Davis, Moore, and Clay were known to be in feeble
health, and from them came accounts of harsh treatment. The
arrests of lesser personages were purely arbitrary, and in most cases
were probably done by the military without any higher authority.
It was announced unofficially that all who had held office before the
war and who had supported the Confederacy, even those who had
never taken an oath to support the Constitution and laws of the
United States, would be arrested and tried for treason.[2] During the
spring and summer of 1865 rumor was busy. Thus, fear of arrest
and imprisonment, the sympathy of the people for their leaders who

---

[1] See "Our Women in the War," p. 280 ; Ball, "Clarke County," p. 463; Le Conte,
"Autobiography," p. 236.

[2] *N. Y. Herald*, June 17 and Aug. 30, 1865 ; *N. Y. Times*, Aug. 17 and Oct. 31,
1865 ; Mrs. Clay, "A Belle of the Fifties"; *Nation*, Feb. 15, 1865 ; oral accounts;
Clayton, "White and Black under the Old Régime."

were being made to suffer as scapegoats, the irritating methods of the Freedmen's Bureau, the work of various political and religious emissaries among the negroes, and the confiscation of property served progressively to awaken the people from the stupor into which they had fallen, and they began to take an interest in affairs of such vital importance to them. The newspapers began to discuss the problems of Reconstruction and to condemn the treatment of the political prisoners from the South. This renewed interest was characterized by a section of the northern press and by prominent politicians as "disloyalty," — a proof of a "rebellious" spirit which ought to be chastised.

"The Condition of Affairs in the South"

The President, who began with a vindictive policy, gradually modified it until it was as fair as the South could expect from him. To support his policy, he sent agents to the South to ascertain the state of feeling here and the exact condition of affairs. These agents were General Grant, the head of the army, Carl Schurz, a sentimental foreign revolutionist and politician with an implicit belief in the Rights of Man, and Benjamin C. Truman, a well-known and able journalist.

General Grant reported: "I am satisfied that the thinking men of the South accept the present condition of affairs in good faith. The questions that have heretofore divided the sentiment of the people of the two sections, slavery and state rights, or the right of a state to secede from the Union, they regard as having been settled by the highest tribunal — arms — that man can resort to." He believed that acquiescence in the authority of the general government was universal, but that the demoralization following four years of civil war made it necessary to post small garrisons throughout the South until civil authority was fully established.[1]

The report of Carl Schurz was distinctly unfavorable to the south-

[1] Letter concerning affairs at the South, Dec. 18, 1865, Sen. Ex. Doc., No. 2, 39th Cong., 2d Sess.; McPherson, "Reconstruction," p. 67. General Grant's conclusions were undoubtedly correct, but they evidently could not be based on the information gathered in a week's journeying through the South. This gave the Radicals an opportunity to attack his report as being based on insufficient information. But General Grant knew the men against whom he had fought, he had talked with many of the representative men of the South, and through military channels was well informed as to actual conditions at the South.

erners. He made a classification of the people into four divisions: (1) The business and professional men and men of wealth who were forced into secession. These, though prejudiced, were open to conviction, and accepted the results of the war. However, as a class, they were neither bold nor energetic. (2) The professional politicians who supported the policy of the President and wanted the state readmitted at once, as they hoped then to be able to arrange things to suit themselves. (3) A strong lawless element, idlers and loiterers, who persecuted negroes and "union" men, and in politics would support the second class. They appealed to the passions and prejudices of the masses and commanded the admiration of the women. (4) The mass of the people, who were of weak intellect, with no definite ideas about anything; who were ruled by those who appealed to their impulses and prejudices. He stated, however, that all were agreed that further resistance to the government was useless and that all submitted to its authority. The people, he said, were hostile toward the soldiers, northern men, unionists, and negroes; their loyalty was only submission to necessity; and they still honored their old political leaders.[1]

B. C. Truman, the journalist, after a long stay in the South, of which about two months were spent in Alabama, reported to the President that the southerners were loyal to the government and were cheerfully submissive and obedient to the law. The fates were against them, the people thought, and it was the will of God that they should lose; the dream of independence was over, and secession would never be thought of again; the war had decided this question, and the decision was accepted. The Confederate soldier, the backbone and sinew of the South, who must be the real basis of reconstruction and worthy citizenship, was exerting his influence for peace and reconciliation;

---

[1] Report of Carl Schurz, Sen. Ex. Doc., No. 2, 39th Cong., 1st Sess. Schurz made a journey of more than two months through the southern states. Judging from the testimony which he submits, his confidence must have been confined to the officers of the Freedmen's Bureau. As a foreigner (a German), he would not be able, even if so inclined, to ascertain anything of the sentiments of the representative people. However, his report was evidently not based entirely on the evidence submitted with it; if it had been, it would have been even more unfavorable. In *McClure's Magazine*, January, 1904, Schurz has an article which is practically a rewriting of this report made nearly forty years before. He repeats some of the same stories told him then, and endeavors to reconcile his attitude in 1865–1866 with his course as a Liberal Republican in 1871–1872.

there were few more potent influences at work in promoting real and lasting reconciliation and reconstruction than that of the Confederate soldier. The fear that in case of foreign war the South would fight against the United States he knew to be unfounded; the soldiers hated England, and would fight for the United States; this, Hardee, McLaws, and Forrest had told him; but, he added, the soldiers preferred to have no war at all, they had had all that they wanted. At the collapse of the Confederacy, there had been a general feeling of despair. The people at home, especially, had expected the worst; and the reaction was wrongly called "disloyal." The people were gradually returning to old attachments, but that they would repudiate their old leaders was not to be expected; neither would they acknowledge any wrong in their former belief in slavery and the right of secession, though ready to grant that those no longer existed. They were better friends to the negro than the northern men who came South; and the courts, magistrates, and lawyers would see that justice was done the negro.[1]

In order to produce a report which would justify the action of Congress in opposing the President's plan,[2] a committee of Congress for several months held an inquest at Washington and examined selected witnesses who gave the desired testimony relative to the condition of affairs in the South. The committee consisted of six senators and nine representatives. Only three Democrats were on this committee, and not one of them was on the sub-committee that took testimony relating to affairs in Alabama.[3] All sessions of the sub-committees were held in Washington, far removed from the state under inquisition. Care was exercised in calling as witnesses only Republicans, and these usually were not citizens of the state. No citizens of Alabama testified except two deserters,[4] one tory,[5] and one

---

[1] Report of Benjamin C. Truman to the President, April 9, 1866, Sen. Ex. Doc., No. 43, 39th Cong., 1st Sess.; *N. Y. Times*, March 2, 1865. Truman spent two months in Alabama, and saw many prominent men whom Schurz did not see, and came in contact with thousands of other citizens. His aim was to picture conditions as they were. The newspaper correspondents, regardless of politics, gave better accounts than the volunteer officers, who had little training or education and much prejudice.

[2] See Blaine, Vol. II, p. 127.

[3] The sub-committee: Senator Harris (New York) and Senator Boutwell (Massachusetts) and Morrill (Vermont) from the House.

[4] Smith and Humphreys.

[5] J. J. Giers.

man who, during the war, had been an agent of the Confederate government "to examine political prisoners," [1] but who told the committee that during the war he had been a "union" man. A witness from Ohio claimed to be a citizen of Alabama.[2] Another witness was a cotton speculator from Massachusetts, and still another, a land office man from the North. Three hailed from Illinois, three from Iowa, one each from California and Minnesota, and the remainder were from the North, with the exception of General George H. Thomas, who had been a Virginian and who had not been allowed to remain in ignorance of what the Virginians called his "treasonable" conduct toward his native state. Three were connected with the Freedmen's Bureau, already fiercely criticised in all sections of the country, and twelve were, or had been, connected with the army, and for short periods had served in some part of Alabama.[3]

Of the five men who resided in the state, each was bitter in denunciation of existing conditions and tendencies in Alabama. The course they had taken during the war made it impossible for them to attain to any position of honor or profit so long as the Confederate sympa-

[1] M. J. Saffold. He was pardoned by President Johnson for that offence.

[2] George E. Spencer, Colonel 1st Alabama Union Cavalry.

[3] The witnesses who furnished testimony to the Congressional committee were : —

NAME	NATIVITY	REMARKS
1. Warren Kelsey	Massachusetts	Cotton speculator
2. General Edward Hatch	Iowa	Volunteer army
3. General George E. Spencer	Iowa	Volunteer army
4. William H. Smith	Alabama	Deserter
5. J. J. Giers	Alabama	Tory
6. Mordecai Mobley	Iowa	
7. General George H. Thomas	Virginia	U. S. Army
8. General Clinton B. Fisk	North	Freedmen's Bureau
9. M. J. Saffold	Alabama	"Union" man
10. D. C. Humphreys	Alabama	Deserter
11. Colonel Milton M. Bane	Illinois	Volunteer army
12. General Joseph R. West	California	Volunteer army
13. Colonel Hunter Brooke	North	Volunteer army
14. General Grierson	Illinois	Volunteer army
15. General Swayne	North	Freedmen's Bureau
16. General C. C. Andrews	Minnesota	Volunteer army
17. General Chetlain	Illinois	Volunteer army
18. General Tarbell	North	Volunteer army

thizers were not proscribed. Existing institutions must be over-thrown before they could hope for political preferment.[1]

The conflicting stories of most of the witnesses neutralized one another, and the remainder corroborated the testimony of General Wager Swayne, the head in Alabama of that much-hated institution, the Freedmen's Bureau. General Swayne stated that he had been agreeably disappointed in the temper of the people. In most of his conclusions he agreed with Truman. He said that he had observed a gradual cessation of disorder, the opening of courts to the negro, and favorable legislation for him; but a marked increase of political animosity. He thought the northerner was well treated except so-cially. He thought the people were determined to make it honorable to have been engaged in "rebellion" and dishonorable to have been a "unionist" among them during the war.[2] The statements of General Swayne were probably as near to the truth as the average human being could attain to.[3] His account was from the northern stand-point, but was as impartial as any one could make at that time.[4] A few weeks later he said that the bluster of a few irreconcilables should not be exaggerated into the threatening voice of a whole people.[5] This he repeatedly asserted.

[1] One of these men (W. H. Smith) became the first scalawag governor of Alabama, another (George E. Spencer) became a United States senator by negro votes, the third (Giers) was provided for in the departments at Washington, the fourth (Saffold) became a circuit judge in Alabama, and the fifth (Humphreys) a judge of the Supreme Court of the District of Columbia. See Herbert, "The Solid South," pp. 19, 20.

[2] Testimony of General Swayne, Report of the Joint Committee on Reconstruction, 1866, Pt. III, pp. 138–141.

[3] Other witnesses gave, in some respects, more favorable testimony, though most of them were very much more bitter. General Swayne showed no bias except the natural bias of one who did not understand the people, and who had no sympathy with any of the southern social or political principles. Of the northern men he was the best quali-fied by experience and observation to testify as to conditions in the South. He was an intelligent, educated man, trained in the law, and had a good military record. Most of the others were distinctly below his standard, — ignorant, prejudiced officers of volunteers from the West.

[4] General Swayne was in Alabama nearly three years as the head of the unpopular Freedmen's Bureau, and his accounts, from first to last, of conditions in Alabama were marked by a fairness which can be found in but little of the official correspondence from the South. He believed in the Freedmen's Bureau, in negro suffrage, and in the politi-cal proscription of white leaders; but his feelings influenced his judgment but little, and, unlike other Bureau officials, he never made misrepresentations.

[5] *The Nation*, Feb. 15, 1866.

Ex-Governor Andrew B. Moore spoke for the people when he said: "Slavery and the right of secession are settled forever. The people will stand by it." Rev. Thomas O. Summers, who lived in the heart of the Black Belt, said, "I have not found a planter who does not think the abolition of slavery a great misfortune to both races; but all recognize abolition to be an accomplished fact."[1]

The people had little faith in the free negro as a laborer, but were disposed to make the best of a bad situation and to give the negro a fair chance. The old soldiers took a hopeful view, and the great wrong of Reconstruction was not so much in the enfranchising of the ignorant slave as in the proscription and humiliation of the better whites with the alienated negro as an instrument.

There was no indication at this time that the people could ever be united into one political party. Before the war party lines had sharply divided the people, and the divisions were deep and political prejudices strong, though not based to any great extent on differences of principles. The war had served to unite the people only temporarily, and the last years of the struggle showed that this temporary union would fall to pieces when the pressure from without was removed. When normal conditions should be restored, local political strife was sure to be warm and probably bitter, and parties would separate along the old Whig and Democratic lines. At this time there was a disposition on the part of Whig and Democrat, secessionist and coöperationist, each to charge the responsibility for present evils upon the other, and by the "bomb-proof" people there was much talk of the "twenty-nigger law," of "the rich man's war and the poor man's fight," etc., in order to discredit the former leaders.[2]

The "Loyalists"

An unpleasant and violent part of the population was the Union "loyal" or tory party, consisting of a few thousand persons who had now returned from the North or had crept out of their hiding-places and were demanding the punishment of the "traitors" who had carried the state into war. Hanging, imprisonment, disfranchisement, confiscation, banishment, was the programme demanded by

[1] *Huntsville Advocate*, July 26, 1865.
[2] Herbert, "Solid South," pp. 29, 30; *Atlantic Monthly*, Feb., 1901.

them. From the Johnson régime in the state they could hope only for toleration, never for official preferment, nor even for respect. They demanded the assistance of the Federal government to place them in power and maintain them there.[1]

About this time it became difficult to distinguish the various species of "loyal" men or "loyalists." There were: (1) Those who had taken the side of the United States in the war. These numbered two or three thousand and they were "truly loyal," as they were called. (2) Those who had escaped service in the Confederate army by hiding out or by desertion, or who engaged in secret movements intended to overthrow the Confederate government. These claimed and were accorded the title of "loyalists" or "union" men. (3) All who during the war became in any way disaffected toward the Confederate or state government and gave but weak support to the cause asked to be called "loyalists" or "unionists." (4) All negroes were, in the minds of the northern radical politician, "loyalists" by virtue of their color, and had all the time been "devoted to the Union"; the fact, of course, was that the negroes had been about as faithful as their masters to the Confederate cause. (5) All who took the oath in 1865 or were pardoned by the President and who promised to support the government thereby acquired the designation of "loyal" men. These included practically all the population except negroes and the first class. (6) A small number included in the fifth class who were conservative people, and who now used their influence to bring about peace and reconstruction. This was the best class of the citizens, and the majority of them were old soldiers, — men like Clanton, Longstreet, Gordon, and Hardee. (7) Later, only those who approved the policy of Congress were "loyal," while those who disapproved were "disloyal." The first and second classes coalesced at once, and finally they admitted the right of the third class to bear the designation "loyal." They, for a long time, would not admit the claims of the negro to "loyalty," but at last political necessity drove them to it; they denied always that the sixth class had any right to share the rewards of "loyalty." These various definitions of loy-

---

[1] See Memorial of William H. Smith, J. J. Giers, and D. C. Humphreys to Congress, Feb., 1866, in Ho. Mis. Doc., No. 42, 39th Cong., 1st Sess. Testimony of the same and of M. J. Saffold in Report of Joint Committee on Reconstruction, 1866; letter of D. H. Bingham from West Point, New York; Reid, "After the War," *passim*.

alty were made by the men themselves, by the various political parties, and by the party newspapers. Every man in the South was some kind of a "loyalist," and most of them were also "disloyal," according to the various points of view.

Treatment of Northern Men

There was no question more irritating to both sides than that of social relations between the southern people and the northerners. After the first weeks of occupation the relations between the enlisted men of the Union army and the native whites became somewhat friendly and in most cases remained so, while, with few exceptions, the regular officers and the people maintained friendly relations, in public matters, at least. The volunteers, however, were much more disagreeable, especially the volunteer officers, who lacked the social training of the regulars. Too often the northerners seemed to feel that they had conquered in war the right to enter the most exclusive southern society, and individuals made themselves disliked more than ever by striving to obtain social recognition where they were not known and were not desired. They had a newspaper knowledge of social conditions before the war, and, while professing to scorn the pretensions of the "southern chivalry and beauty," yet were very desirous of closer acquaintance with both, and especially the latter. Soon after the armies of occupation came, matters were pretty bad for the southern people. The less refined subordinate volunteer officers almost demanded entrance, and even welcome, into southern social circles. They found that while the southern men would meet them courteously in business relations and in public places, they were never invited to the homes. On all occasions the women avoided meeting the northern men; this was their own wish, as well as that of their male relatives. They felt the losses of war more keenly than did the men because they had lost more. All of them had lost some loved one in the war, and quite naturally had no desire to meet in social relations the men who had overcome their country and possibly killed their fathers, brothers, husbands, lovers. They must have time to bury their dead, and it was long before the sight of a Federal soldier caused other than bitter feelings of sorrow and loss. Yet most of the northerners overlooked this fact. The southern women reigned supreme over society; the death in the war of so large a number of young men had only strengthened the influence of the women; as a rule, they were better educated than the men, especially the young men, whose education had been interrupted by the war.[1]

When the families of the northern people came South, the doors of the southern homes were not opened to them. The northerners resented this ostracism by the southerners, and the coldness of society toward them caused many a sarcastic and sneering letter to be written home or to the newspapers.[2] There was constant interference in semi-social relations: the mistress of the house was told how she must treat her colored cook; the employer was warned that his conduct must be more respectful toward the negroes in his employ; ex-Confederates were forbidden to wear their uniforms, or even to use their buttons; nor could southern airs be sung or played.[3] The soldiers would crowd a woman off the sidewalk in order to make her look at them. Women would go far out of the way to avoid meeting

[1] See Le Conte, "Autobiography," p. 236 ; Montgomery correspondent in *N. Y. Daily News*, May 7, 1866.

[2] A newspaper correspondent, the guest of ex-Governor C. C. Clay, wrote : " While the Yankee boldly marched in at the front door into his [Clay's] parlors and best chambers to dream loyal dreams and rest now that the warfare's o'er, the quondam aristocrat [a son of ex-Governor Clay, editor of a paper in Huntsville, had been outlawed for his sentiments during the occupation of north Alabama by the Federal troops and was in hiding] must plod around to the rear and there eat the (corn) bread of mad passion weighed down with mad remorse." Letter from a travelling correspondent of the *N. Y. Times*, Aug. 17, 1865. The *Times* usually had very little of such correspondence. The *Times*, the *Herald*, and the *World* had good correspondents in the South, especially during Reconstruction.

[3] An old Alabama river steamboat captain had had his boat burned by Wilson, but had secured another. The Federal army regarded him as a most unmitigated " rebel." He would play " Dixie " in spite of all prohibitions. He was finally arrested on a more serious charge.

" What do you answer to the charge against you?"

" Faith, an' which one? "

" That you refuse to take the bodies of dead Federal soldiers on your boat to Montgomery."

"No, no, that's not true. God knows it would be the pleasure of my life to take the whole Yankee nation up the river *in that same fix*." " Our Women in the War," p. 281.

Colonel Robert McFarland returned to Florence in the only suit he possessed — a gray uniform. He was peremptorily ordered by the Federal officers not to wear it. He was in a quandary until a friend secured a long linen duster for him to wear. "Northern Alabama," p. 291.

a Federal officer, and when forced to pass one, would sweep their skirts aside as if to avoid contagion. Forthwith the man insulted indited an epistle in which such incidents were related and the size of the ladies' feet and ankles and the poverty-stricken appearance of their dress commented upon. This naturally found its way into the newspapers, as home letters from soldiers usually do. Soldiers, white and black, would sit on the back fence and jeer at the former mistress of slaves as she worked at the family washing. United States flags were hung over the sidewalks to force the women to walk under them, and in some instances, when they refused to do so and went out into the street, efforts were made to force them to pass under the flag. For refusal and for exceedingly "disloyal" remarks made under the excitement of such treatment, several were arrested and lectured by coarse officials. Drunken soldiers terrorized women in the garrison towns. A lot of drunken officers in a launch in Mobile Bay habitually terrified pleasure parties of women who were on the bay in small boats. The officers invited the women to balls and entertainments, but the latter paid no attention to what they considered impertinence. This angered the officers. The northern newspapers of 1865, 1866, and 1867 have many letters from correspondents in the South complaining of social neglect or ostracism. Letters were written about the coarseness, unlovely tempers, and character of the southern men and women who, it was insisted, were of the best families.[1]

These letters the violent southern press afterward made a practice of copying for political reasons.[2] The more incorrigible officers were accustomed to express their most offensive sentiments in regard to

[1] Gen. T. Kilby Smith, on Sept. 14, 1865, in Mobile, made a statement for Carl Schurz in which he asserted that one of the most intelligent, well-bred, pious ladies of Mobile wanted the military authorities to whip or torture into a confession of theft two negroes whom she suspected of stealing. She considered it a hardship, he said, that a negro might not be whipped or tortured in order to force a confession, when there was no evidence against him. "I offer this," he wrote, "as an instance of the feeling that exists in all classes against the negro." See Doc. No. 9, accompanying the report of Schurz.

[2] I have seen a coarse article reflecting on the character of southern women originally published in the *Tribune* and copied in a small Alabama paper each issue for several weeks. It asserted in thinly veiled terms that many of the young southern women were too intimate with negro men; the solution of the race question by amalgamation was asserted as sure to come; details of such a solution were suggested, and examples of what was taking place were cited.

negro inequality, the position of the negro, the slavery question, and the treatment of the negro by the whites.   The Bureau officials were cordially disliked for their tendency to such conduct.   Though only a small portion of the northerners and Federal officials were guilty of offensive actions, the relations in many places being kindly and the conduct of most of the officers considerate and courteous, yet the insolent behavior of some caused all to be blamed.[1]

The question of the social standing of the tory element may be summed up in a few words.   They were mercilessly ostracized and thoroughly despised by the Confederate element of the population at that time, and the same feeling of social contempt had descended to their children's children.   It is rather a feeling of indifference now, but the result is even more deadly.   The true Unionist was disliked but respected.

All the witnesses called before the sub-committee at Washington complained of the dislike exhibited toward "unionists" and northerners.   It was a burning question and had much influence on the later course of reconstruction.[2]

Immigration to Alabama

As soon as the war was ended, there was an influx of northern men and northern capital into Alabama.   Cotton was selling at a

---

[1] General Terry attempted to explain the condition of affairs by saying that the results of the war were but the legitimate consequence of a conflict between an inferior and a superior race. "Land We Love," Vol. IV, p. 243. Gen. T. Kilby Smith, in September, 1865, complained that Federal officers were not received in society in Mobile. General Wood, he said, had been six weeks in Mobile, "ignored socially and damned politically"; and this, he said, in a community which before the war was considered one of the most refined and hospitable of all the southern maritime cities, the favorite home of army and naval officers. Doc. No. 9, accompanying the report of Schurz.

[2] In addition to references cited above, see also *Huntsville Advocate*, March 9 and 23, July 26, 1865 ; Ho. Mis. Doc., No. 42, 39th Cong., 1st Sess.; Sen. Mis. Doc., No. 43, 39th Cong, 1st Sess. (Truman); Reid, "After the War," pp. 211, 212, 218, 219; "The Land We Love," *passim ;* "Our Women in the War," p. 279 *et passim ;* Abbott, "The Rights of Man," pp. 224-226 ; Clayton, "White and Black," pp. 150-152 ; Clay, "A Belle of the Fifties" ; Straker, "The New South Investigated," pp. 24, 57 ; Report of the Joint Committee, 1866, Pt. III ; *N. Y. Daily News*, April 16, 1864, and Dec. 4, 1865; Reports of Schurz, Truman, and Grant; Reports of the Freedmen's Bureau; *Southern Magazine*, 1874 (DeLeon); *N. Y. Times*, Oct. 31, 1865 ; *N. Y. Herald*, July 23, 1865 ; Miller, "Alabama," pp. 233-251 ; Columbus (Ga.) *Sun*, March 22 and April 19, 1865 ; *The Nation*, Feb. 15, 1866 ; Ku Klux Rept., Ala. Test., *passim ;* Reconstruction articles in *Atlantic Monthly*, 1901.

fabulous price, — 40 to 50 cents a pound, $200 to $250 a bale, — and the newcomers expected to make fortunes in a few years. They were welcomed by the planters who wanted to sell or to lease their plantations, which, for want of funds, they were unable to cultivate. General Swayne said that in 1866 there were 5000 northern men[1] in Alabama engaged in trading and planting. They were sought for as partners or as overseers by those who hoped that northern men could control free negro labor. Lands were sold or leased at low prices, and many soldiers, especially officers, decided to buy land and raise cotton. Numbers of large plantations in the Black Belt were bought or leased by officers of the army, all of whom had lofty ideas as to what they were going to do. The soil was fertile, cotton was selling for high prices, and the free blacks, they were sure, would work for them out of gratitude and trust. They wanted to help reconstruct southern industry, and to show what could be done toward developing the great natural resources of the state. They embarked in large enterprises, and as long as their money lasted bought everything that was offered for sale. Their success or failure was dependent largely upon the negro laborer, who was to make the cotton, and the new planters made extraordinarily liberal terms with him. They dealt with the negro as if he were a New Englander with a black skin, and they purchased expensive machinery for him to use. They would not listen to southern advice, but went as far as possible to the opposite extreme from southern methods of farming. All suggestions were met with the assurance that the southern man was used only to slaves, and could not know how free men would work.

Reports, generally false and made mainly for political purposes, were continually published by the northern press in regard to the ill treatment of northern men who wished to make their homes in the South.[2] But not a single authenticated case of violence to such persons can be found to have taken place in Alabama.

In some localities, on account of bands of outlaws, for several

---

[1] Trowbridge, "The South," p. 448.

[2] Thomas W. Conway, of the Freedmen's Bureau, who passed through the state in 1866, stated that there were men in Alabama who, rather than sell their lands to northern men or borrow money in the North, would see their plantations lie waste, and before they would hire their former slaves as free laborers they would starve. The spirit of hatred toward northern men was universal, he said. Report to Chamber of Commerce, New York, June 7, 1866.

months after the war it was not safe for any stranger to settle. The ignorant whites had no liking for the northern men (and may not have to this day). The better class of people was in favor of much immigration from the North, and Governor Parsons made a tour through the North to induce northern men and capital to come to Alabama.[1] The people had no capital, and wanted to induce those who possessed it to come and live in the state. The testimony of travellers was that the accounts of cruelty and intolerance toward northerners were almost entirely false; that they were welcomed if they did not attempt to stir up trouble between the races.[2] The refusal of Congress to recognize the state government and the rejection of the members elected to Congress caused a fresh outburst of bitter feeling against the North; but General Swayne, who had the best opportunities for observation, said that rudeness and insult and the occasional attentions of a horse-thief were the worst things that had happened to the northern settlers.[3]

These northern men meant well but, as a rule, were incompetent as farmers and business men. Consequently they failed, and most of them never quite understood the reasons for their failure. They knew next to nothing of plantation economy, and the negroes were their only teachers. Most of them were from the West, and had never seen cotton growing before. It was almost pathetic to see these 5000 northerners risking all they possessed upon their faith in the negro, and losing. The northern merchant gave the negro unlimited credit and lost; the planter gave his tenant all he asked for, whenever it pleased him to ask. The farm stock was driven to camp-meetings

[1] Jan. 17, 1867, the state legislature declared that the reports published in the northern papers that it was unsafe for northern men to reside in Alabama were false. The lower house declared that "we, in the name of the people of Alabama, most cordially invite skilled labor and capital from the world, and particularly from all parts of the United States, and pledge the hearty coöperation and support of the state." Annual Cyclopædia (1867), p. 15. For several years every inducement was offered by the planters to encourage immigration to the Black Belt. As late as 1869 immigration conventions were held. Annual Cyclopædia (1869), p. 10. During 1865 the north Alabama "unionists" hoped to see northern white men come in and take the place of the negroes. The Nation, Aug. 17, 1865.

[2] Report of Truman, Sen. Ex. Doc., No. 43, 39th Cong., 1st Sess.; Reid "After the War," passim; Trowbridge, "The South," p. 448; N. Y. Times, Nov. 10, 1865, July 2 and Oct. 31, 1866; General Swayne's testimony, Report Joint Committee, Pt. III, p. 141; General Tarbell's testimony, Report Joint Committee, Pt. III, pp. 155, 156.

[3] Report Joint Committee, 1866, Pt. III, pp. 139–141.

and frolics while the grass was killing the cotton. Mills and factories were built and negro laborers employed, but the negroes, because of a lack of quickness and sensitiveness of touch, proved to be unfit for factory work. Besides, the noise of the machinery made them sleepy, and it was beyond their power to report for work at a regular hour each morning. At first, the negroes showed great confidence in the northern man and were glad to work for him, but too much was required of them, and after a year or two the disgust was mutual. The revulsion of feeling following failure and disappointment and ostracism injured the South by creating hostile opinion in the North. Nearly all the northern men went home, but the less desirable ones remained to assist in the political reconstruction of the state, when many of them became state officials.[1]

Troubles in the Church

At the close of the war, the churches were in a disturbed condition, owing to the attitude of the Washington government. Most of the southern churches held by the northern organizations were restored to their former owners. The northern Methodist Church caused irritation by retaining southern church property that had been placed under its control by the military authorities. But the most aggravated ill feeling was aroused in the Protestant Episcopal Church.

After the collapse of the Confederate government, Bishop Wilmer of Alabama directed the Episcopal clergy to omit that portion of the prayer mentioning the President of the Confederate States. Further, he ordered that when civil authority should be restored, the prayer for the President of the United States should be used.[2] Bishop Wilmer, consecrated in 1862, had never made a declaration of conformity to the constitution and canons of the church in the United States, and, consequently, even by the northern Episcopal Church, was not considered amenable to its constitution.[3]

---

[1] In addition to the above references, see *The World*, Nov. 13, 1865 ; *N. Y. Times*, July 2 and Sept. 9, 1866 ; *N. Y. Herald*, July 23 and Aug. 28, 1865 (Swayne); Truman's Report, April 9, 1866; Swayne's Report, Jan., 1866; *Harper's Monthly Magazine*, Jan., 1874.

[2] Pastoral Letters, May 30 and June 20, 1865.

[3] Perry, "History of the American Episcopal Church," Vol. II, p. 328 *et seq.*; Whitaker, "The Church in Alabama," pp. 172-175; *N. Y. Herald*, Sept. 4, 1865; Wil-

For several months his directions were not noticed by the Federal authorities, and services were held in conformity to the bishop's orders. In September, "Parson" William G. Brownlow of Tennessee, it is said, brought the matter of the Wilmer pastoral letters to the attention of General George H. Thomas, who commanded the Military Division of the Tennessee, to which belonged the Department of Alabama. Thomas, like Wilmer, was a Virginian, and was regarded by the latter and other southerners as a traitor to his native state. Thomas was peculiarly sensitive to such a charge, and disliked Wilmer, who had expressed his opinion in regard to the matter. So it was easy to secure his interference. General Woods, at Mobile, was directed to investigate the matter. An officer was sent to ask Wilmer when he intended to order the clergy to pray for the President of the United States. The bishop refused to direct its use at the dictation of the military authority, or while the state was under military domination, since no one desired "length of life," nor the least prosperity to such a government.[1] The result was the argumentative order which follows:[2] —

HEADQUARTERS DEPARTMENT OF ALABAMA,
MOBILE, ALA., Sept. 20, 1865.

General Order No. 38:

The Protestant Episcopal Church of the United States has established a form of prayer to be used for "the President of the United States and all in civil authority." During the continuance of the late wicked and groundless rebellion the prayer was changed to one for the President of the Confederate States, and so altered, was used in the Protestant Episcopal churches of the Diocese of Alabama.

Since the "lapse" of the Confederate government, and the restoration of the authority of the United States over the late rebellious states, the prayer for the President has been altogether omitted in the Episcopal churches of Alabama.

This omission was recommended by the Rt. Rev. Richard Wilmer, Bishop of Alabama, in a letter to the clergy and laity, dated June 20, 1865. The only reason given by Bishop Wilmer for the omission of a prayer, which, to use his own language, "was established by the highest ecclesiastical authorities, and has

mer, "The Recent Past from a Southern Standpoint," p. 143. Gen. T. Kilby Smith said that Wilmer had great influence among the better class of people, especially the women. Doc. No. 9, accompanying the report of Carl Schurz.

[1] Perry, "History of the American Episcopal Church," Vol. II, p. 328 *et seq.;* Whitaker, pp. 175, 176; Wilmer, pp. 143–145.

[2] Whitaker, p. 177; Wilmer, "Recent Past," p. 145. A copy of the order was also found in the War Department archives.

for many years constituted a part of the liturgy of the church," is stated by him in the following words : —

" Now the church in this country has established a form of prayer for the President and all in civil authority. The language of the prayer was selected with careful reference to the subject of the prayer — all in civil authority — and she desires for that authority prosperity and long continuance. No one can reasonably be expected to desire a long continuance of military rule. Therefore, the prayer is altogether inappropriate and inapplicable to the present condition of things, when no civil authority exists in the exercise of its functions. Hence, as I remarked in the circular, we may yield a true allegiance to, and sincerely pray for grace, wisdom, and understanding in behalf of a government founded on force, while at the same time we could not in good conscience ask for its continuance, prosperity, etc."

It will be observed from this extract, first, that the bishop, because he cannot pray for the continuance of " military rule," therefore declines to pray for those in authority ; second, he declares the prayer inappropriate and inapplicable, because no civil authority exists in the exercise of its functions. On the 20th of June, the date of his letter, there was a President of the United States, a Cabinet, Judges of the Supreme Court, and thousands of other civil officers of the United States, all in the exercise of their functions. It was for them specially that this form of prayer was established; yet the bishop cannot, among all these, find any subject worthy of his prayers.

Since the publication of this letter a civil governor has been appointed for the state of Alabama, and in every county judges and sheriffs have been appointed, and all these are, and for weeks have been, in the exercise of their functions ; yet the prayer has not been restored.

The prayer which the bishop advised to be omitted is not a prayer for the continuance of military rule, or the continuance of any particular form of government or any particular person in power. It is simply a prayer for the temporal and spiritual weal of the persons in whose behalf it is offered — it is a prayer to the High and Mighty Ruler of the Universe that He would with His power behold and bless His servant, the President of the United States, and all others in authority; that He would replenish them with grace of His holy spirit that they might always incline to His will and walk in His ways ; that He would endow them plenteously with heavenly gifts, grant them in health and prosperity long to live, and finally, after this life, to attain everlasting joy and felicity. It is a prayer at once applicable and appropriate, and which any heart not filled with hatred, malice, and all uncharitableness, could conscientiously offer.

The advice of the bishop to omit this prayer, and its omission by the clergy, is not only a violation of the canons of the church, but shows a factious and disloyal spirit, and is a marked insult to every loyal citizen within the department. Such men are unsafe public teachers, and not to be trusted in places of power and influence over public opinion.

It is therefore ordered, pursuant to the directions of Major-General Thomas, commanding the military division of Tennessee, that said Richard Wilmer, Bishop of the Protestant Episcopal Church of the Diocese of Alabama, and the Protestant Episcopal clergy of said diocese be, and they are hereby suspended from their functions, and forbidden to preach, or perform divine service; and that their places of worship be closed until such time as said bishop and clergy show a sincere return to their allegiance to the government of the United States, and give evidence of a loyal and patriotic spirit by offering to resume the use of the prayer for the President of the United States and all in civil authority, and by taking the amnesty oath prescribed by the President.

This prohibition shall continue in each individual case until special application is made through the military channels to these headquarters for permission to preach and perform divine service, and until such application is approved at these or superior headquarters.

District commanders are required to see that this order is carried into effect.
By order of
Major-General CHARLES R. WOODS,
FREDERICK H. WILSON, A. A.-G.

Wilmer denied the right of civil or military officials to interfere in such matters. Prayer, he said, was religious, not political, and was not to be prescribed by secular authority.[1] Woods threatened to use force, and had the churches closed by soldiers. St. John's Church in Montgomery having been closed by the military authorities, the congregation attempted to meet in Hamner Hall, a school building, but was dispersed by soldiers at the point of the bayonet. Much to the indignation of Generals Woods and Thomas, services were held in private houses.[2] The House of Bishops of the northern church protested against this edict to the President. Wilmer appealed to Governor Parsons and found that the "civil governor" of G. O. No. 38 was only a subordinate military official with no power. President Johnson at first refused to interfere, but was finally induced to direct Thomas to revoke the suspension of the clergy. This was done in the following remarkable order:[3] —

HEADQUARTERS
MILITARY DIVISION OF THE TENNESSEE,
NASHVILLE, TENN., Dec. 22, 1865.

General Orders No. 40:

Armed resistance to the authority of the United States having been put down, the President, on the 29th of May last, issued his Proclamation of Amnesty, declaring that armed resistance having ceased in all quarters, he invited those lately in rebellion to reconstruct and restore civil authority, thus proclaiming the magnanimity of our government towards all, no matter how criminal or how deserving of punishment.

[1] Pastoral Letter, Sept. 28, 1865.
[2] Whitaker, pp. 180, 181; Wilmer, pp. 145, 146; *Montgomery Mail*, Oct. 2, 1865.
[3] Whitaker, p. 182; Wilmer, p. 146; Copy of order in War Department archives. Republished on G. O. 2, Jan. 10, 1866, Hq. Dept. Ala., Mobile.

Alarmed at this imminent and impending peril to the cause in which he had embarked with all his heart and mind, and desiring to check, if possible, the spread of popular approbation and grateful appreciation of the magnanimous policy of the President in his efforts to bring the people of the United States back to their former friendly and national relations one with another, an individual, styling himself Bishop of Alabama, forgetting his mission to preach peace on earth and good will towards man, and being animated with the same spirit which through temptation beguiled the mother of men to the commission of the first sin — thereby entailing eternal toil and trouble on earth — issued, from behind the shield of his office, his manifesto of the 20th of June last to the clergy of the Episcopal Church of Alabama, directing them to omit the usual and customary prayer for the President of the United States and all others in authority, until the troops of the United States had been removed from the limits of Alabama; cunningly justifying this treasonable course, by plausibly presenting to the minds of the people that, civil authority not yet having been restored in Alabama, there was no occasion for the use of said prayer, as such prayer was intended for the civil authority alone, and as the military was the only authority in Alabama it was manifestly improper to pray for the continuance of military rule.

This man in his position of a teacher of religion, charity, and good fellowship with his brothers, whose paramount duty as such should have been characterized by frankness and freedom from all cunning, thus took advantage of the sanctity of his position to mislead the minds of those who naturally regarded him as a teacher in whom they could trust, and attempted to lead them back into the labyrinths of treason.

For this covert and cunning act he was deprived of the privileges of citizenship, in so far as the right to officiate as a minister of the Gospel, because it was evident he could not be trusted to officiate and confine his teachings to matters of religion alone — in fact, that religious matters were but a secondary consideration in his mind, he having taken an early opportunity to subvert the church to the justification and dissemination of his treasonable sentiments.

As it is, however, manifest that so far from entertaining the same political views as Bishop Wilmer, the people of Alabama are honestly endeavoring to restore the civil authority in that state in conformity with the requirements of the Constitution of the United States, and to repudiate their acts of hostility during the past four years, and have accepted with a loyal and becoming spirit the magnanimous terms offered them by the President; therefore, the restrictions heretofore imposed upon the Episcopal clergy of Alabama are removed, and Bishop Wilmer is left to that remorse of conscience consequent to the exposure and failure of the diabolical schemes of designing and corrupt minds.

By command of
Major-General THOMAS.
WILLIAM D. WHIPPLE,
Assistant Adjutant-General.

Wilmer had won, and three days after the order was promulgated in Alabama he directed the use of the prayer for the President of the United States. Two months earlier, the General Council of the Confederate States had provided for such a prayer, but this provision was not to have the force of law in any diocese until approved by the bishop. This was to enable Wilmer to win the fight and then to resume the use of the prayer.[1]

The General Council of the Confederate Church, in November, 1865, decided that each diocese should decide for itself whether to remain in union with the General Council (of the Confederate States) or to withdraw and unite with the General Convention (of the United States). A small party in the northern church wanted "to keep the southern churchman out for a while in the cold," and "to put the rebels upon stools of repentance," but better feeling and better policy prevailed. The southern church was met halfway by the northern church, and the only important reunion of churches separated by sectional strife was accomplished. The diocese of Alabama was the last to join, Bishop Wilmer making the declaration of conformity January 31, 1866.[2]

[1] Whitaker, p. 186; *Mobile Register*, Jan. 9, 1866; *Montgomery Mail*, Jan. 19, 1866.

[2] Annual Cyclopædia (1865), p. 25; Wilmer, pp. 147–152; Whitaker, pp. 189–194; Perry, Vol. II, p. 328 *et seq.* The northern conferences of the Methodist Protestant Church returned in 1877 to the southern organization. See "Statistics of Churches," p. 566.

PART IV

PRESIDENTIAL RESTORATION

CHAPTER VIII

FIRST PROVISIONAL ADMINISTRATION

Sec. i. Theories of Reconstruction

Owing to the important bearing upon the problem of Reconstruction of the disputes between the President and Congress in regard to the status of the seceded states, it will be of interest to examine the various plans and theories for restoring the Union. From the beginning of the war the question of the status of the seceded states was discussed both in Congress and out, and with the close of the war it became of the gravest importance. There was nothing in the Constitution to guide the President or Congress, though each sought to base a policy on that ancient instrument. Many questions confronted them. Were the states in the Union or out? If in the Union, what rights had they? If out of the Union, were they conquered territories subject to no law but the will of the United States government, or were they United States territory with rights under the Constitution? Must they be reconstructed or restored, and who was to begin the movement — the people of the states, Congress, or the President? Were the states in their corporate capacity, or the people as individuals, responsible for secession? What punishment was to be inflicted, and on whom or what must it fall — the people or the states? Who or what decides who are the political people of the state? Exactly what was a state? Was the Union the old Union of Washington, or a new one? Congress and the President could never agree in their answers to these questions.[1]

Conservative Theories

As to the status of the seceded states and the proper method of Reconstruction, all interested persons had theories, but the only one which was logical and consistent with regard to the "Constitution

[1] See Messages and Papers of the Presidents, Vol. X, p. 562.

as it was" was the so-called Southern theory. This theory was that secession having failed, state sovereignty was at an end; the doctrine was worthless; secession was a nullity, and therefore the states were not out of the Union; the state was indestructible. The war was prosecuted against individuals and not against states, and the consequences must fall upon individuals; the states had all the rights they ever possessed, but, being out of their proper relation to the Union, its officers must take the oath of allegiance to the United States government, representatives must be sent to Congress, and the people must submit to the authority of the government. Then the Union would be restored as it was.[1] At the fall of the Confederacy the general belief was that restoration would proceed along these lines. Many of the higher officials of the United States army were of the same opinion, and on this theory the celebrated Johnston-Sherman convention was drawn up by General Sherman, which promised amnesty to the people and recognition of the state governments as soon as the officials should have taken the oath of allegiance.[2] Likewise, in the Southwest, General Dick Taylor, with the approval of General Canby, advised the governors of the states in his department to take steps toward restoring their states to their former relations to the Union. General Thomas, and perhaps General Grant, had likewise advised the people of north Alabama, and the subordinate Federal commanders in the Southwest favored such reconstruction and were inclined to help along the movement. But orders from Washington put an end to any such course by directing the arrest of all state officials who endeavored to act. Among those who had taken steps to restore the former relations with the Union were the governors of Alabama, Mississippi, and Florida.[3]

The Presidential and Democratic theories, like the Southern theory, were based on the doctrine of the indestructibility of the state. In the beginning the Democratic theory would have recognized the state governments of the seceded states and thus practically coincided with the later Southern theory. The Presidential theory, as formulated later, would not have recognized the state governments,

---

[1] See Dunning, " Essays on the Civil War and Reconstruction," pp. 100–103.

[2] McPherson, " Reconstruction," pp. 121, 122, 504, 505.

[3] Taylor, " Destruction and Reconstruction " ; Report of Joint Committee on Reconstruction, Pt. III, pp. 15, 60.

and to this view the Democrats came after the war. The Union was indestructible and was composed of indestructible states. To assert that the states as states were not in the Union was to admit the success of secession and the dissolution of the Union. But the people as insurgents were incapable of political recognition by the United States government. So the state after the war was in a condition of suspended animation: the so-called state governments were not governments in a constitutional sense; the President could have the citizens tried for treason and punished, or he could pardon them and thus restore to them all their former rights, which, of course, included the right to reëstablish their governments and to resume their former relations with the Union. Congress had no power to interfere or to disfranchise any man, nor to regulate the suffrage in any way. Its only part in Reconstruction was to admit to Congress the representatives of the states as soon as constitutional government was restored by the people with the assistance of the President.[1]

The earliest legislative declaration touching this subject was in the Crittenden Resolutions passed by the House of Representatives on July 22, 1861.[2] Two days later practically the same resolutions were introduced in the Senate by Andrew Johnson of Tennessee and passed with only five dissenting voices.[3] They declared that "war is not waged upon our part in any spirit of oppression, nor for any purpose of conquest or subjugation, nor for the purpose of overthrowing or interfering with the rights or established institutions of these states, but to defend and maintain the supremacy of the Constitution with all the dignity, equality, and rights of the several states unimpaired; and that as soon as these objects are accomplished the war ought to cease."[4] To this declaration of principles the Democratic party adhered throughout the war and after. The Union as it was must be restored and maintained, one and indivisible.[5]

President Lincoln had no such regard for the "sacred rights of a state" as had the Democrats and his successor, Andrew Johnson. In his inaugural address he asserted that the Union existed before the states and was perpetual; that no state could withdraw from the Union; that secession was null and void; and that the Union was

---

[1] See Dunning, "Essays," pp. 103–104.   [2] With only two dissenting votes.
[3] Some of these were southerners who were about to withdraw.
[4] *Cong. Globe*, July 22, 24, 25, 1861.   [5] *Cong. Globe*, Dec. 5, 1862.

unbroken.[1] In the formation of the provisional governments by the aid of the military authorities in Tennessee, Arkansas, and Louisiana, Lincoln showed that he expected the political institutions of 1861 to be restored. In December, 1863, be brought forth this plan for restoration: When one-tenth of the voting population of a state in 1861 should take an oath to support the Constitution and should establish a government on the basis of the state constitution and laws in 1861, such a government would be recognized as the government of the state.[2] In July, 1864, he announced by proclamation that he was unwilling to commit himself formally to any fixed plan of restoration. This was in answer to the Wade-Davis bill passed by Congress, which, if approved, would set aside the governments he had erected in Louisiana, Tennessee, and Arkansas, and it showed that he considered it the prerogative of the executive to bring about and recognize the restored government.[3] These restored states he expected to take their places in the Union on the old terms,[4] for as soon as the people submitted and civil governments were established, constitutional relations would be resumed, and Congress would be obliged to admit their representatives.[5] Early in the war, he said nothing about abolition, but rather to the contrary. Later he advocated gradual and compensated emancipation by state action. At the close of the war, after the practical, if not the theoretical, abolition of slavery, he suggested that the newly established governments might, as a measure of expediency, confer the privilege of voting upon the best negroes.[6] He considered the matter of the suffrage beyond the control of the central government. The enfranchisement of the negro as a measure of revenge, and as a means of keeping the southern whites down and the Republican party in power, never entered his thoughts.

President Johnson succeeded to the policy of Lincoln, or, at least, to Lincoln's belief that restoration was a matter for the executive attention, not for the legislative. He asserted that secession

[1] Messages and Papers of the Presidents, Vol. VI, pp. 5-12.

[2] Proclamation, Dec. 8, 1863, in Messages and Papers of the Presidents, Vol. VI, p. 213.

[3] Proclamation, July 8, 1864, Messages and Papers of the Presidents, Vol. VI, p. 223.

[4] Lincoln to Reverdy Johnson, Nicolay and Hay, p. 349.

[5] Nicolay and Hay, Vol. IX, p. 457; Vol. X, p. 123.

[6] Nicolay and Hay, Vol. VIII, p. 434.

ANDREW JOHNSON.

CHARLES SUMNER.

THADDEUS STEVENS.

RECONSTRUCTION LEADERS.

was null and void from the beginning; that a state could not commit treason; that by the attempted revolution the vitality of the state was impaired and its functions suspended but not destroyed; that it was the duty of the executive to breathe into the inanimate state the life-giving breath of the Constitution. He recognized no power in Congress to pass laws preliminary to or restricting the admission of duly qualified representatives of the states.[1]

The plan of Lincoln was, in theory and at first in practice, objectionable. It would recognize as the political people of a state the loyal minority, which would be an oligarchy, and the principle of the rule of majorities would thus be repudiated. Those who claimed to be loyal were not promising material for a new political people, and the "10 per cent" governments were treated with just contempt. But the plan was based, not on any narrow principle of legality, but on the broader grounds of justice and expediency, and was capable of expansion into a very different plan from what it was in the beginning. As applied to Louisiana and Arkansas, it was severely, and in theory justly, criticised on the ground that the President was assuming absolute authority in dealing with the seceded states, and that by this plan the entire political power would be given to a small class not capable of using it. As later modified, his plan would have admitted to participation in Reconstruction nearly or quite all the citizens of the southern states.

President Johnson, a war Democrat, gave promise of being more harsh than Lincoln in the work of restoration. Lincoln's policy was based on expediency; Johnson's, on the narrow legal principles of a State Rights Democrat. He had a strong regard for the "sacred rights of a state." He proposed to reëstablish the state governments by means of a political people of the lower classes, and the old political leaders were to be disfranchised. Lincoln imposed certain conditions on individuals as a prerequisite to participation in reconstruction. Having created by the pardoning power a political people, he expected the initiative to come from them. The executive then retired into the background and waited the impulse of the people. He shrank from interfering with the states, not from any great respect for their rights, but from motives of policy. As Johnson applied his theory, there was little initiative left to the people. The execu-

---

[1] Message, Dec. 4, 1865, in Messages and Papers of the Presidents, Vol. VI, p. 379.

z

tive authority as the source of power set the machinery of restoration in motion, and the people were obliged to do as he ordered, many of them being at first excluded from participation. The whole programme was prescribed by him, and he watched every step of the progress made. For a firm believer in the rights of states he took strange liberties with them while restoring their suspended animation. Lincoln advised a limited suffrage for the blacks; but negroes could have no part in the Johnson scheme. Like Lincoln, however, Johnson so modified his plan that practically all the white people were to take part in the reëstablishment of the government. The conservative theories contemplated restoration, not reconstruction.

Radical Theories

The Republican majority in Congress soon advanced from the position taken in the Crittenden-Johnson resolutions. Most of the Republican party had no fixed opinions in regard to Reconstruction, but formed a kind of a centre or swamp between the Democrats and the President on the one extreme, and the Radicals on the other. The plan of Lincoln, as first announced and applied, was offensive to all parties, and some leaders never seem to have recognized that the President had, to any appreciable degree, modified his policy. The extreme Radicals were not sorry to have the matter of reconstruction fall from the hands of the wise and kind Lincoln into those of the narrow and vindictive Johnson. But the seeming defection of the latter soon disappointed those who were in favor of harsh measures in dealing with the defeated southerners. The best-known of the Radical theories advanced in opposition to the presidential policy were (1) the State Suicide theory of Charles Sumner, (2) the Conquered Province theory of Thaddeus Stevens, and (3) the Forfeited Rights theory, practically the same as the Conquered Province theory, but expressed in less definite language for the benefit of the more timid members of the Republican party.

Charles Sumner, the Radical leader of the Senate, set forth the Suicide theory in a series of resolutions to the effect that the ordinances of secession were void, and, when sustained by force, amounted to abdication by the state of all constitutional rights; that the treason involved worked instant destruction of the body politic, and the state became territory under the exclusive control of Congress. Consequently, there were no state governments in the South, and all peculiar institutions had ceased to exist — among them slavery. Sumner constantly asserted that Congress now had exclusive jurisdiction over the southern territory.[1] He made strong objection to the despotic power of the President as applied in dealing with the seceded states, and declared that the executive was encroaching upon the sphere of Congress, which was the proper authority to organize the new governments. The seceded states, he affirmed, by breaking the constitutional compact had committed suicide, and no longer had corporate existence, and that the "loyalists," who were few in number, should not have the power formerly possessed by all. The whole South was a "tabular rasa," "a clean slate," upon which Congress might write the laws.[2] The existence of slavery was declared to be incompatible with a republican form of government, which it was the duty of Congress to establish. For it is necessary to such a form of government that there be absolute equality before the law, suffrage for all, education for all, the choice of "loyal" citizens for office, and the exclusion of "rebels." The negro must take part in Reconstruction, for his vote would be needed to support the cause of human rights and "the party of the Union" — meaning, of course, the Republican party.[3]

Sumner cared little for the Constitution except for the clause about guaranteeing a republican form of government to the states, and on this he based the power of Congress to act. The Declaration of Independence was to him the supreme law and above the Constitution, and to make the government conform to that document was his aim. He wearied his colleagues with his continual harping on the Declaration of Independence as the fundamental law, upon which footing the seceded states must return. That, he declared, would destroy slavery and all inequality of rights, political and civil.[4]

The Conquered Province theory was originated by Thaddeus Stevens, the Radical leader of the House of Representatives, who, however, refused to call it a theory. He made no attempt to harmonize his plan with the Constitution, and frankly expressed his

[1] *Cong. Globe*, Feb. 11, 1862. [2] *Atlantic Monthly*, Oct., 1863.
[3] *Globe*, Feb. 25, 1865, and Dec. 4, 1865. See Henry Adams, " Historical Essays."
[4] Speeches in the *Globe*, 1865–1867.

opinion that there was nothing in the Constitution providing for such an emergency; that the laws of war alone should govern the action of Congress, allowing no constitutions to interfere.[1] It was impossible to execute the Constitution in the seceded states, he said, which the victors must treat "as conquered provinces and settle them with new men and exterminate or drive out the present rebels as exiles from this country."[2] Every inch of the soil of the southern states should be held for the costs of the war, to pay damages to the "loyal" citizens and pensions to soldiers and their families, and slavery should be abolished.[3] Secession, according to Stevens, was so far successful that the southern states were out of the Union and the people had no constitutional rights.[4] All ties were broken by the war. The states in their corporate capacities made war, and were out of the Union so far as the conqueror might choose to consider them, and must come back into the Union as new states or remain as conquered provinces with no rights except such as the conqueror might choose to grant. Perpetual ascendency of the North must be secured by giving the ballot to the negro, by confiscation, and by banishment. The Constitution, in his opinion, had been torn to atoms; it was now a "bit of worthless parchment," and there could be no reconstruction on the basis of that instrument. Congress had absolute jurisdiction over the whole question.[5] Stripped of its violence, Stevens's theory was probably the correct one from the point of view of public law. It was more in accord with historical facts. It recognized the great changes wrought by war in the structure of the government. It was frank, explicit, and practical. Unfortunately, the statesmanship necessary to carry to success such a plan was entirely lacking in its supporters.

Sumner would limit the authority of Congress only by the provisions of the Declaration of Independence; Stevens would have Congress unchecked by any law. By martial law and the law of nations, he meant no law at all, as his utterances show; nothing must stand in the way of the absolute powers of Congress. Both theories agreed in reducing the states to a territorial status. Sumner would

---

[1] *Globe*, Aug. 2, 1861.   [2] *Globe*, Jan. 8, 1863.
[3] *Globe*, Jan. 22, 1864.   [4] *Globe*, Jan. 8, 1863.
[5] *Globe*, Dec. 4, 1865, March 10, 1866; Taylor, "Destruction and Reconstruction," p. 244.

leave the people of these states the rights of people in the United States territories. Stevens would deny that they had any such rights whatever under any law, but that they were to be considered conquered foes, with their lives, liberty, and property at the mercy of the conqueror.[1]

The Forfeited Rights theory, patched up to suit the more timid Radicals who would not concede that the states had succeeded in getting outside of the Union or that they could be destroyed, was, in effect, the Stevens theory, though recognizing some kind of a survival of the states. The names and boundaries of the states alone survived; the political institutions were entirely destroyed, and must be reconstructed by Congress.

It is a waste of time to try to find a basis in the old Constitution for any of the theories advanced. If a legal basis must be had, it will have to be found in the Constitution as revolutionized by seventy-five years of development and four years of war. The main purposes of the congressional plans were to reduce the late dictatorial powers of the President, to remove forever from political power the political leaders of the South, to give the ballot to the negro as a measure of revenge and to assure the continuation in power of the Republican party.[2]

Owing to the fact that Congress was not in session for several months after the downfall of the Confederacy, the President had a good opportunity to put into operation the executive plan for restoring the southern states to their proper standing in the Union.

Sec. 2. Presidential Plan in Operation

Early Attempts at Restoration

In the early spring of 1865, Governor Watts, in a speech calling upon the people to make renewed exertions against the invader, said: "We hold more territory than a year ago, more of Texas, Louisiana, and Arkansas, Georgia is overrun but is ready to rise. Our financial condition is better than four years ago. Arms, com-

---

[1] See also Dunning, " Essays," pp. 106–108.

[2] See Dunning, " Essays," pp. 99–112 ; Texas versus White (1869), 7 Wallace 700; Scott, " Reconstruction during the Civil War"; McCarthy, " Lincoln's Plan of Reconstruction "; Burgess, " Reconstruction and the Constitution," pp. 1–143.

missary and quartermaster's stores are more abundant now."[1]   But there were no more men.   A month later Lee had started on the march to Appomattox; two months later Dick Taylor was surrendering the last Confederate armies east of the Mississippi; three months later the war governors of Alabama were in northern prisons, and not a vestige of the Confederate or state governments remained.   There was no government.

Even before the collapse of the Confederacy there were indications of an approaching revolution in the state government, to be carried out by the union of all discontented factions.   The object was to gain control of the state government or to organize a new one and return to the Union.   This movement was strongest in north Alabama and was supported and encouraged by the Federal military authorities.   One of the disaffected clique testified before the Subcommittee on Reconstruction that in the last years of the war a "Reconstruction" or "Union" party was organized in Alabama, which, at the time of the surrender, had a majority in the lower house of the legislature.[2]   But the Senate, elected in 1861, held over and prevented any action by the House.   During the year 1865 the "Union" party hoped to secure both the governorship and the Senate in the first elections which were to occur under the new constitution, and thus secure control of the state.   But the invasion and surrender stopped the movement.[3]

There were indications during the winter and spring of 1865 that Reconstruction movements were going on in the northern half of the state.   After the invasion of the state in April many people more influential than the ordinary peace party men began to think of Reconstruction.   General Thomas authorized the citizens of Morgan, Marshall, Lawrence, and the neighboring counties to organize a civil government based on the Alabama laws of 1861.   J. J. Giers, a brother-in-law of State Senator Patton (later governor), was sent by the military leaders to "reorganize civil law."   Thomas invited

---

[1] *N. Y. Times*, April 4, 1865.   [2] Elected in 1863.

[3] Testimony of M. J. Saffold, Report Joint Committee, 1866, Pt. III, p. 60.   The "union" men greatly exaggerated the strength of the "union" sentiment in the state during the war and their individual part in the peace movement.   This was necessary in order to secure recognition as representatives of a strong "union" element. When the plan of the President was so modified as to leave them in their natural position of no influence, they became very bitter against it and played the martyr act to perfection.

the people of the other northern counties to do likewise and thus show that they were "forced into rebellion." Colonel Patterson of the Fifth Alabama Cavalry accepted the terms for his forces, and Giers stated that Roddy's men were so pleased with Thomas's letter that they released their prisoners and stopped fighting. A Reconstruction meeting was held at Somerville, Morgan County, and was largely attended by soldiers. This was early in April.[1] In the central and southern portions of the state the movement did not begin until the Federal forces traversed the country. General Steele with the second army of invasion reported from Montgomery, May 1, 1865, that J. J. Seibels, L. E. Parsons, and J. C. Bradley[2] had approached him and had told him that two-thirds of the people of the state would take up arms to "put down the rebels."[3] A meeting was held at Selma, in Dallas County, on May 10, and called upon the governor to convene the legislature and take the state back into the Union. Judge Byrd,[4] one of the speakers, said that the war had decided two things — slavery and the right of secession — and both against the South. He counselled a spirit of conciliation and moderation, and in this he expressed the general sentiment of the people.[5]

A more important meeting was held the next day in Montgomery. A number of the more prominent politicians met to take steps to place the state in the way of readmission to the Union.[6] George Reese[7] of Chambers County presided over the meeting and Albert Roberts was secretary. Seibels introduced resolutions, which were adopted, pledging to the United States government earnest and zealous coöperation in the work of restoring the state of Alabama to its proper relation with the Union at the earliest possible moment. The murder

[1] Testimony of J. J. Giers, Report Joint Committee, Pt. III, p. 15; O. R., Ser. I, Vol. XLIX, Pt. II, pp. 473, 485, 505, 506.

[2] See pp. 143–148. [3] O. R., Ser. I, Vol. XLIX, Pt. II, p. 560.

[4] Judge Byrd was elected to the Supreme Court in 1865. He was a distant relative of Colonel William Byrd, of Westover, Va., Esq. Brewer, p. 224.

[5] General C. C. Andrews, in O. R., Ser. I, Vol. XLIX, Pt. II, p. 727; N. Y. Commercial Advertiser, May 27, 1865; N. Y. Tribune, June 2, 1865.

[6] There were present : Ex-Gov. John G. Shorter, M. A. Baldwin (Attorney-General, Brewer, p. 445), W. B. Bell, A. B. Clitherall (Brewer, p. 479), all of whom had been ardent secessionists, and L. E. Parsons (see p. 143), Col. J. C. Bradley, Col. J. J. Seibels (Brewer, p. 459; see p. 143), W. J. Bibb, J. G. Strother, M. J. Saffold (Brewer, p. 215), George Goldthwaite (Brewer, p. 451, A. and I. General). It was a fairly representative body of government officials and "stay-at-homes."

[7] Garrett, p. 166. Reese was a "Union" man.

of Lincoln and the attempt on the life of Seward were condemned as "acts of infamous diabolism revolting to every upright heart." The bad effect the crime would have on political matters was deplored. The desire was expressed that all guilty of participation in the attempt might be brought to speedy and condign punishment, and "we shall hold as enemies all who sympathize with the perpetrators of the foul deed." The majority reported a memorial to the President asking him to permit the governor of Alabama to convene the legislature, which would call a convention in order to restore the state to her political relations to the United States. This they believed was the most speedy method. But if this were not permitted, then the President was requested to appoint a military governor from among the most prominent and influential "loyal" men of the state and invest him with the power to call a convention. They were encouraged to ask this, the memorial stated, by the recent statement of the President of the principle that the states which attempted to secede were still states, and not being able to secede would not be lost in territorial or other division. "To forever put an end to the doctrine of secession; to restore our state to her former relations to the Union under the Constitution and the laws thereof; to enable her to resume the respiration of her life's breath in the Union, — is a work in which we in good faith pledge you our earnest and zealous coöperation, and we hazard nothing in the assurance that the people of Alabama will concur with us with a majority approaching almost unanimity."

Colonel J. C. Bradley presented a memorial from the minority of the committee. It was the same as the other memorial, except that the part relating to the appointment of a military governor was omitted. Such an official was not desired nor needed, he stated. After some discussion both memorials were adopted and each person present signed the one he preferred. The chairman appointed a committee to bear the memorials to the President. The general sentiment of the meeting and of the people seemed to be that, since they had failed to maintain their independence, there was nothing left to do but to accept as a working basis the theory that a state could not secede, and to get straight into the Union by having the President restore the suspended animation of the Constitution. The best and shortest way, they thought, was for Governor Watts to convene the legislature, which should begin the work, and a convention of the people would complete it. Governor Watts and the Supreme Court (Stone and Phelan) approved the action of the meeting, though they took no part in it.[1]

Another meeting on the same day (May 11), at Guntersville, in Marshall County, in the heart of the devastated section of the state, proposed to submit cheerfully to the decision of war and return to the Union. Two soldiers, Major A. C. Baird and Colonel J. L. Sheffield,[2] were the leaders in the meeting.[3] Two mass-meetings were held in Covington County (one at Andalusia on May 17) and passed resolutions favoring a restoration of the Union. The Union General Asboth said that these people had returned to their allegiance early in April and had organized and armed to resist the "rebels." The resolutions were signed by 280 and 376 persons respectively. Asboth reported great excitement on account of the action taken by the meeting.[4] On May 23 there was a meeting of citizens in Franklin County. James W. Ligon was president, H. C. Tompkins, vice-president, and R. B. Lindsey (governor in 1870–1872) addressed the meeting. This meeting seems to have been behind the times, for it accepted the overtures of Thomas made April 13, and promised to assist cheerfully in restoring law and order. They were anxious to resume former friendly relations to the United States and wanted a state convention called to settle matters.[5]

About this time the President, General Grant, and Stanton, by repeated orders, managed to reach the generals who were encouraging the movement toward Reconstruction, and put an end to their plans by ordering them not to recognize the state government in Alabama and to prevent the assembly of the legislature.[6] Thereupon, on

---

[1] *N. Y. Commercial Advertiser*, May 27, 1865; *N. Y. Tribune*, June 2, 1865; *Montgomery Mail*, May 12, 1865. The members of the committee which went to Washington were: Joseph C. Bradley, L. E. Parsons, M. J. Saffold, Lewis Owen, George S. Houston, James Birney, W. J. Bibb, John M. Sutherlin, Albert Roberts, Luke Pryor. None of the committee had been secessionists. Reese had been a "Union" man, Saffold a "political agent." W. J. Bibb had made a visit to Washington during the war and had a consultation with Lincoln. Parsons was a "Union" man. Houston and Pryor (see Brewer, pp. 324, 326) were neither "Union" nor "secessionist," but "constitutional." The others were unknown to public life.

[2] Formerly colonel of the 48th Alabama Infantry.

[3] *N. Y. Daily News*, May 29, 1865.   [4] O. R., Ser. I, Vol. XLIX, Pt. II, p. 826.

[5] O. R., Ser. I, Vol. XLIX, Pt. II, p. 971.

[6] O. R., Ser. I, Vol. XLIX, Pt. II, pp. 810, 854, 877.

May 23, a memorial was signed by 106 prominent citizens of Mobile, asking the President to take steps to enable Alabama to be restored to the Union. Robert H. Smith[1] and Percy Walker[2] were sent as a committee to General Granger, who commanded in the city, to ask him to transmit the memorial to the President. General Granger did so with the indorsement that no impediment existed to immediate restoration, that the signers were influential men and represented the sentiment of the people of the state.[3] At Athens, in Limestone County, the citizens met and adopted resolutions declaring that all must be restored to the Union; that the state officials should be recognized, but that a new election should be held under the laws of Alabama as they were before secession; that a convention was not necessary and in the present unsettled condition of the county it would be dangerous to hold one; that the constitution of 1819, changed by amendment, should be used. The murder of Lincoln was deplored.[4] Similar meetings were held all over the state, especially in north Alabama.[5]

The "loyal" element held a meeting in north Alabama about the first of June.[6] Resolutions were introduced by K. B. Seawell to the effect that the government of Alabama had been illegally set aside in 1861 by a combination of persons regardless of the best interests of the state, that secession was not the act of the people, and that the Confederacy was a usurpation. It was decided that Alabama must go back to the Union, and the authority of the United States was invoked to enable "loyal" citizens to form a state government.[7] The sentiments of the more violent "unionists" or tories may be understood from a letter of D. H. Bingham,[8] then at West Point, New York. He said that reconstruction must not be com-

---

[1] Member of Congress, Confederate colonel of the 36th Alabama, former Whig. Brewer, p. 425.

[2] Former Whig, Adjutant and Inspector-General during the war. Brewer, p. 397.

[3] *N. Y. Herald*, June 15, 1865.

[4] *N. Y. World*, June 13, 1865. The absence of the old names in all these movements is noticeable. The old leaders had been strongly in favor of the Confederacy and now took back seats while smaller men came forward. They never came into power again.

[5] *Huntsville Advocate*, July 19, 1865.

[6] In one of the mountain counties, but the exact location was never named in any of the accounts of the convention.

[7] *N. Y. Herald*, June 17, 1865.

[8] He represented Talladega in the convention of 1867.

mitted to the hands of the "rebels"; that Parsons, who was spoken of for provisional governor, was not one of the "union" men of Alabama and would use his influence to secure control to the old slave dynasty; that his appointment would be unfair to the "union" men; that the masses were coerced and deluded into fighting the battles of slavery; "I, George W. Lane,[1] and J. H. Larcombe," he said, "never gave way to secession." The non-slaveholding whites in slaveholding districts were trained to obey, he wrote, and the official class used its influence to keep the non-slaveholders in ignorance. Hence the small number of slaveholders (of whom most were owners of few slaves and hence were union men) controlled the "union" population of over 5,000,000. He said that the Alabama delegates, then in Washington,[2] were not inactive in producing these results, though they claimed to be "unionists." They were once "union" men, but went over. Now they alleged that they were carried into rebellion by a great wave of public feeling. Such men should not be trusted until they had passed through a probationary state.[3]

The southerners who wanted immediate restoration of constitutional rights and privileges on the basis of the Crittenden Resolution of 1861,[4] soon found that this plan would not work; so, to make the best of a bad situation, all accepted the Johnson plan and declared that the state, since it had not had the right to secede, must still be in the Union. The press and the prominent men, even those who would be disfranchised by the President's plan, gave it a hearty support in order to give peace to the land and restore civil government.[5] At this time the Johnson plan promised to be one of merciless proscription of the prominent men. As Johnson himself expressed it: "The American people must be made to understand the nature of the crime, the length, the breadth, the depth, and height of treason. For the thousands who were driven into the infernal rebellion there

---

[1] See above, p. 125.

[2] Parsons, Bradley, Houston, Nicholas Davis, Pryor, Saffold, Bibb, Roberts, etc.

[3] Letter in *N. Y. Herald,* June 17, 1865.

[4] See McPherson, "Rebellion," p. 286.

[5] The *Mobile Register* and *Advertiser* (John Forsyth, editor) supported the President's policy: "The states were never out of the Union"—July 18, 1865. The *Huntsville Advocate,* July 19, said, "The presidential policy is simple, direct, and emphatic." Henry W. Hilliard, General Cullen A. Battle, Ex-Governors Shorter, Moore, Watts, and Fitzpatrick declared that there would be no opposition but a hearty effort "to get straight."

should be amnesty, conciliation, clemency, and mercy. For the leaders, justice — the penalty and the forfeit should be paid. The people must understand that treason is the blackest of crimes and must be punished." [1] The leaders were not afraid of such threats and meant not to stand in the way. The people intended to make the best they could out of a bad state of affairs. They believed then and always that their cause was right, secession justifiable and necessary; that the provocation was great, and that they were the aggrieved party; that the abolitionists and fanatics forced secession and civil war. But since they were beaten in war, after they had done all that men could do, they meant to accept the result and abide by the decision of the sword. There was a general purpose to stand by the government — certainly no dream of opposition to it. The people meant (which was neither treasonable nor unreasonable) to ally themselves to the more conservative political party in the North in order to secure as many advantages as possible to the South. Their aim was to preserve as much of their old constitution as they could, all the while recognizing that state sovereignty and slavery ended with the war. Their course in ceasing at once all useless opposition and proceeding to secure reinstatement on the old terms was, *The Nation* declared, "a display of consummate political ability." Southerners like to think that had Lincoln lived his plan would have succeeded, and that the most shameful chapter of American history would not have to be written. [2] Johnson helped to ruin his own cause and his supporters along with it. The people never seem to have taken seriously the proposed merciless plans of Johnson, and the opposition of moderate advisers and the pleasure of pardoning southern "aristocrats" (and later Radical criticism) caused a distinct modification of his policy in the direction of mildness until the proscriptive part was almost lost sight of. [3]

The southern leaders [4] saw clearly that there was no hope for their party unless the President could win the fight against the Radicals

---

[1] Lilian Foster, "Andrew Johnson: Services and Speeches," pp. 199, 210, "Address to Loyal Southerners," April, 1865.

[2] There is little reason to believe that Lincoln could have succeeded in the struggle with Congress.

[3] See Foster, "Andrew Johnson," for change of feeling in Johnson as expressed in his speeches in 1865 and 1866.

[4] "President Tamers" the Radicals called them.

in Congress, and they attempted to disarm northern hostility outside Congress until the Radical party, aided by the rash conduct of the President, educated the people of the North to the proper point for approving drastic measures.[1]

The President begins Restoration

On May 29 the President began his attempt at restoration by proclaiming amnesty to all, except certain specified classes of persons. They were pardoned and therefore restored to all rights of property, except in slaves, on condition that the following oath be taken: —

" I   do solemnly swear (or affirm) in the presence of Almighty God, that I will henceforth faithfully support, protect, and defend the Constitution of the United States, and the Union of the states thereunder; and that I will, in like manner, abide by and faithfully support all laws and proclamations which have been made during the existing rebellion, with reference to the emancipation of slaves: So help me God."[2]

Fourteen classes of people were excluded from the benefits of this proclamation; of these twelve were affected in Alabama: —

(1) The civil or diplomatic officers, or domestic or foreign agents of the Confederacy; (2) those who left judicial positions under the United States to aid the Confederacy; (3) all above the rank of colonel in the army and lieutenant in the navy; (4) those who left seats in the United States Congress and aided the Confederacy; (5) those who resigned commissions in the United States army and navy to escape service against the Confederacy; (6) persons who went abroad to aid the Confederacy in a private capacity; (7) graduates of the naval and military academies who were in the Confederate service; (8) the war governors of Confederate states; (9) those who left the United States to aid the Confederacy; (10) Confederate sailors (considered as pirates); (11) all in confinement as prisoners of war or for other offences; (12) those who supported the Confederacy and whose taxable property was over $20,000.

The classes excluded embraced practically all Confederate and state officials, for the latter had acted as Confederate agents, all the old political leaders of the state, many of the ablest citizens who had not been in politics but had attained high position under the Confederate government or in the army, the whole of the navy, — officers and men, — several thousand prisoners of war, a number of political

---

[1] McCulloch, p. 517 and Preface; *Nation*, Oct. 26, 1865; Mayes, "L. Q. C. Lamar"; Reid, "After the War," pp. 404, 405, 578; *Mobile Register and Advertiser*, July 18, 1865; *Huntsville Advocate*, July 18, 1865.

[2] McPherson, p. 10; Messages and Papers of the Presidents, Vol. VI, p. 310.

prisoners, and every person in the state whose property in 1861 was assessed at $20,000 or more. According to the proclamation the assessment was to be in 1865, but it was made on the basis of 1861, at which time slaves were included and a slaveholder of very moderate estate would be assessed at $20,000. In 1865 there were very few people worth $20,000.

It was provided that persons belonging to these excepted classes might make special application to the President for pardon, and the proclamation promised that pardon should be freely granted.[1] The oath could be taken before any United States officer, civil, military, or naval, or any state or territorial civil or military officer, qualified to administer oaths.[2] In Alabama 120 army officers were sent into all the counties to administer the amnesty oath. These officers were strict in barring out "all improper persons" and subscription went on slowly until the military commander issued orders that all who were eligible must take the oath. Less than 50,000 persons took the oath; 90,000 had voted in 1860.

There was a fight for appointment to the provisional governorship. William H. Smith of Randolph and D. C. Humphreys of Madison, both of whom had opposed secession, then entered the Confederate service, and later deserted; D. H. Bingham of Limestone, who had been a tory during the war; and L. E. Parsons of Talladega, who had aided the Confederacy materially and damned it spiritually — all wanted to oversee the restoration of the state.[3]

June 21, 1865, the President, acting as commander-in-chief of the army and under the clause in the Constitution requiring the United States to guarantee to each state a republican form of government and protect each state against invasion and domestic violence,[4] proceeded to breathe the breath of life into the prostrate state by appointing Lewis E. Parsons provisional governor.[5]

---

[1] McPherson, p. 10.

[2] G. O., Nos. 5, 13, and 14, Department of Alabama, 1865.

[3] N. Y. Herald, June 21, 1865; Brewer and Garret, sub. nom.

[4] Article II, section 2 : Article IV, section 4.

[5] Lewis Eliphalet Parsons, born 1817, Boone County, New York, was the son of a farmer and the grandson of the celebrated Jonathan Edwards. He came to Alabama in 1840 and practised law in Talladega, was a Whig, later a Douglas Democrat. and on both sides during the war. See above, p. 143.

It was made the duty of Parsons to call a convention of delegates chosen by the "loyal"[1] people of the state. This convention was to amend or alter the state constitution to suit the changed state of affairs, to exercise all the powers necessary to enable the people to restore the state to its constitutional relations with the central authority, and to set up a republican form of government. All voters and delegates must have taken the oath of amnesty, and must have the qualifications for voters prescribed by the Alabama constitution and laws prior to the secession of the state. This excluded the fourteen proscribed classes and said nothing of the negroes. The convention, when assembled, was to prescribe qualifications for voters and for office holders. The military and naval officers of the United States were directed to assist the provisional officials and to refrain from hindering and discouraging them in any way. The Secretary of State was directed to put in force in the state of Alabama all laws of the United States, the administration of which belonged to the State Department. The Secretary of the Treasury was directed to nominate assessors, collectors, and other treasury officials, and to put into execution in Alabama the revenue laws of the United States. The Postmaster-General was ordered to establish post-offices and post routes and to enforce the postal laws. The Attorney-General and the Federal judges were directed to open the United States courts in the state. The Secretary of the Navy and the Secretary of the Interior were ordered to put in execution the regulations of their respective departments, so far as related to Alabama.[2]

In making appointments to office in the southern states, the departments were to give preference to "loyal"[3] persons of the district or state where they were to serve. If no "loyal" persons could be found in the state or district, such persons might be imported from other states or districts.

In this measure the difference appears between the Lincoln and the Johnson plan of restoration. Lincoln believed that the executive should only make things easy for the people to erect a government for themselves. He kept as much as possible in the background

---

[1] Here "loyal" seems to mean those who had taken the amnesty oath.
[2] Messages and Papers of the Presidents, Vol. VI, p. 323.
[3] Those who could take the iron-clad test oath of 1862.

and let it appear that the movement originated with the people. Several times he merely suggested that negroes with certain qualifications should be granted the suffrage. Johnson, on the other hand, made it clear that he was the source of all authority in the movement. He himself made stringent regulations of the suffrage, thus creating a body of citizens, and set up a government of his own for the purpose of creating a new state government. The people were to do as he bade them. He did not suggest negro suffrage in any form and was, like most southern Unionists, opposed to it. The Johnson provisional government was a military government with the President as the source of authority. Parsons was a military governor appointed by the commander-in-chief and paid by the War Department.[1] Lincoln's provisional government would have been popular government based on election by the people.

The appointment of Parsons gave general satisfaction to all parties except the more violent tory element in the northern part of the state, who wanted men like D. H. Bingham or William H. Smith. A correspondent of *The Nation* who travelled among them in August, 1865, when this element of the people seemed likely to form a strong portion of the new ruling class of the South, before the President modified his plans, said of them: they are ignorant and vindictive, live in poor huts, drink much, and all use tobacco and snuff; they want to organize and receive recognition by the United States government in order to get revenge — really want to be bushwhackers, supported by the Federal government; they "wish to have the power to hang, shoot, and destroy in retaliation for the wrongs they have endured"; they hate the "big nigger holders," whom they accuse of bringing on the war and who, they are afraid, would get into power again; they are the "refugee," poor white element of low character, shiftless, with no ambition.[2] To proscribe the mass of leading citizens, the experienced men in public affairs, as Johnson's plan at first promised to do, would have had serious results, but his later, more liberal, policy restored the rights of all except the more prominent. But the old leaders were never again leaders, thinking it more politic to put forward less well-known men. At first Johnson had the mountaineer's dislike of the "slave aris-

[1] Sen. Ex. Doc., No. 26, p. 97, 39th Cong., 1st Sess.
[2] James Redpath in *The Nation*, Aug. 17, 1865, condensed.

tocracy," as he called it, and his plan was devised to humiliate and ruin this class.[1]

A month after his appointment Governor Parsons issued (July 20) a proclamation to the people, drawn largely from the census of 1860, showing how prosperous the state was at that time and inviting attention to the present condition of affairs. The question of slavery and secession, he said, had been decided against the South, but every political and property right, except slavery, still remained. He thus repudiated any former belief he may have had in the right of secession. A funny comparison was made in exuberant language and with many mixed metaphors, likening the Union to a steamship and the state of Alabama to a man swimming around in the water, trying to get on board. The following officers of the Confederate state government who were in office on the 22d of May,[2] 1865, were reappointed to serve during the continuance of the provisional government: justices of the peace, constables, members of common councils, judges of courts, except probate, county treasurers, tax collectors and assessors, coroners, and municipal officers. Judges of probate and sheriffs who were in office on May 22 were directed to take the amnesty oath and serve until others were appointed. All officers reappointed were to take the amnesty oath and give new bond. The right was reserved to remove any officer for disloyalty or for misconduct in office. Thus there was a continuity between .the Confederate administration and the "restoration" administration.

The civil and criminal laws of the state as they stood on January 11, 1861, except as to slavery, were declared in full force, and an election of delegates to a constitutional convention was ordered for August 31, and the convention was to meet on September 10.[3] No one could vote in the election or be a candidate for election to the convention who was not a legal voter according to the law on January 11, 1861, and all voters and candidates must first take the amnesty oath or must have been pardoned by the President. Instructions were given as to how a person who was excluded from the benefits of the amnesty proclamation might proceed in order to secure a

[1] See Foster, "Andrew Johnson," pp. 199, 210, 214, 220, 250.

[2] The 22d of May was the date when the Confederate state government ceased to exist.

[3] Garrett, p. 735, says Aug. 30 and Sept. 12. The convention met on Sept. 12.

2 A

pardon. A list of questions was appended by which "an improper person" might test his case and see how bad it was. They ran like this : —

(1) Are you under arrest ? Why ? (2) Did you order, advise, or aid in the taking of Fort Morgan and Mount Vernon ? (3) Have you served on any "vigilance" committee for the purpose of trying cases of disloyalty to the Confederate States ? (4) Did you order any persons to be shot or hung for disloyalty to the Confederate States ? (5) Did you shoot or hang such a person ? (6) Did you hunt such a person with dogs ? (7) Were you in favor of the so-called ordinance of secession ? (8) You are not bound to answer any except the first of these questions. (9) Will you be peaceable and loyal in the future ? (10) Have proceedings been instituted against you under the Confiscation Act ? (11) Have you in your possession any property of the United States ?[1]

Parsons appointed to assist him a full staff of secretaries as follows : Wm. Garrett, Secretary of State; M. A. Chisholm, Comptroller of Accounts; L. P. Saxton, Treasurer; —— Collins, Adjutant-General; M. H. Cruikshank, Commissioner for the Destitute; John B. Taylor, Superintendent of Education.

A report on the condition of the treasury on September 1, 1865, shows that of $791,294 in the treasury on May 24, 1865, only $337 was in silver and $532 in gold. The rest was in state and Confederate money, now worthless. The financial status of the provisional treasury was uncertain. Receipts from July 20 to September 21, 1865, were $1766 and disbursements had been $1572. The bonded debt of the state, held in London, was $1,336,000, in New York, $2,109,000, a total of $3,445,000.[2]

Parsons could hardly do otherwise than reappoint the old state officials as temporary officers, but it created some dissatisfaction in the state and much in the North; and in truth the Confederate state officers in 1865 were not, in general, very efficient, being old men, cripples, incapables, "bomb-proofs," "feather beds," and deadheads. They were not much liked by any party unless perhaps by the few who put them in office. The *Huntsville Advocate* may have been voicing the objections of either "tory" or "rebel" when it condemned Governor Parsons's reappointment of the *de facto* state officers —

[1] Parsons's Proclamation, July 20 (or 22), 1865; in *N. Y. Herald*, July 26 and Aug. 11, 1865; Garrett, p. 735; McPherson, p. 21.

[2] Parsons's Message to Convention, Sept. 21, 1865 ; Proclamation, July 20, 1865 ; in *N. Y. Herald*, Aug. 11, 1865.

"they are not the proper persons to rekindle the fires of patriotism in the hearts of the people."[1]

The provisional governor was obliged to rely upon inferior material in restoring the state government. Though the President's plan soon was shorn of its worst proscriptive features, the work of restoration had begun by excluding the natural leaders from a share in the upbuilding of the state, and they were thus rendered somewhat indifferent to the process. The class to whom the task fell was good, but it was not the best. The best men went into the southern army or otherwise committed themselves strongly to the cause of the Confederacy. The strong men of the state who sulked in their tents during the war were few in numbers, and they were usually disgruntled and cranky, and now, without influence, were much disliked by the people. The so-called "union" men who stayed at home in "bomb-proof" offices, or as teachers, overseers, ministers, etc., were not the kind of men to reconstruct the shattered government. The few who had openly espoused the Union cause had not the character, experience, and training necessary to fit them to rule a state. Though the administration began on a basis of very inferior material, yet the modification of the plan of the President gradually admitted the second-rate leaders to political privileges, and, had the experiment continued, they would have gradually resumed control of the politics of the state. It was in some degree the hope of this that made them willing to submit to proscription and exclusion for a while and support the reconstruction measures of the President. They hoped for better times.[2]

Parsons revised the official lists thoroughly, and many of the old officers were discharged and new ones appointed. However, they had little to do; the army and the Freedmen's Bureau usurped their functions. A proclamation of August 19, 1865, directed the probate judge, sheriff, and clerk in each county to destroy, after August 31, old jury lists and make new ones from the list of names of "loyal" citizens who had taken the amnesty oath and registered. Circuit court judges were directed to hold special sessions of court for the trial of state cases and to have their grand juries inquire particularly into the cases of cotton and horse stealing, now common crimes.[3]

---

[1] *Huntsville Advocate*, Aug. 17, 1865.

[2] See McCulloch, p. 517 and *passim; N. Y. Tribune*, May 4, 1866; *Mobile Times*, April 25, 1866.

[3] *N. Y. Herald*, Sept. 3, 1865.

" Proscribing Proscription "

One of the principal occupations of the provisional government was securing pardons for those who were excluded from the general amnesty of May 29, 1865. Governor Parsons was for reconciliation, and those who hoped to profit by the disfranchisement of the leaders complained of the lenient treatment of the latter. Parsons's policy of "proscribing proscription" was greatly disliked by those who would profit by disfranchisement. If it were continued, they saw there would be no spoils for them. One of the aggrieved parties related a case which might well have been his own: A prominent "union" man went to the President to get his pardon, stating that he had been as much a Union man as possible for the last four years. "I am delighted to hear that," the President said. Directly the "union" man said that he had been forced to become somewhat implicated in the rebellion, that he had been obliged to raise money by selling cotton to the Confederates, and, as he was worth over $20,000, it was necessary to get a pardon. "Well, sir," the President answered, "it seems that you were a Union man who was willing to let the Union slide. Now I will let you slide." On the other hand, Judge Cochran of Alabama told the President that he had been a rabid, bitter, uncompromising rebel; that he had done all he could to cause secession, and had fought in the ranks as a private; that he regretted very much that the war had resulted as it had; that he was sorry they had not been able to hold out longer. But he now accepted the results. The President asked: "Upon what ground do you base your application for pardon? I do not see anything in your statement to justify you in making such an application." Judge Cochran replied, "Mr. President, I read that where sin abounds, mercy and grace doth much more abound, and it is upon that principle that I ask for pardon." The pardon was granted.[1]

The President in the end granted pardons to nearly all persons who applied for them, but not a great number applied. The total number pardoned in Alabama from April 15, 1865, to December 4, 1868, was less than 2000, and of these most were those who had been worth over $20,000 in 1861 and had aided the Confederacy with their

---

[1] Testimony of M. J. Saffold, Report of Joint Committee, 1866, Pt. III, pp. 59–63.

substance. For this offence (for offence it was in Johnson's eyes) 1456 people (of whom 72 were women) were pardoned before the general amnesty in 1868.[1] How many of this class of excepted persons did not ask for pardon is not known. It is certain that all who possessed that amount of wealth assisted the Confederacy. Half at least of the $20,000 must have been slave property.[2]

Few of the state and Confederate officials applied for pardon. Many worth over $20,000 in 1861 did not apply. Most of those who were wealthy in 1861 lost all they had in the war. To December 31, 1867, the President had pardoned in Alabama only 12 generals, viz. Battle, Baker, F. M. Cockerill, Clayton, Deas, Duff C. Green, Holtzclaw, Morgan, Moody, Pettus, Roddy, and Wood; 11 members of the Confederate Congress had been pardoned, 1 former United States judge, 1 former member United States Congress, 1 West

[1] Ho. Ex. Doc., No. 16, 40th Cong., 2d Sess.

[2] Others were pardoned for having aided the Confederacy in the following occupations : agents of the Nitre and Mining Bureau ; tax collector and state assessor ; tax receiver (Confederate) ; general officer of the Confederate army ; postmasters who had held office before the war ; members of the state legislature ; cotton agents ; foreign agents and commissioners ; graduates of West Point and Annapolis ; resigning United States service to join Confederacy ; mail contractors ; clerks of the Confederate government ; state and Confederate judges ; members of Congress ; receivers of subscriptions for the Confederacy ; marshals and deputy marshals ; clerks of state and Confederate courts ; agents for the purchase of supplies ; members of advisory board ; cotton bond agent ; Confederate government official ; commissioner of appraisement ; depositary ; route agent ; commissioner of Indian affairs ; member of convention of 1861 ; prize commissioner ; commissioner to take testimony ; Indian agent ; Confederate financial agent ; commissioner to examine prisoners held by military authorities ; agent of the Produce Loan ; receiver of the tax-in-kind ; leaving loyal state ; commissioner of "fifteen million loan" ; agent to receive subscriptions for cotton and produce loans ; depot agent to receive the tax-in-kind ; agent under sequestration laws ; enrolling officer ; impressment agent ; Treasury agent ; Confederate contractor ; sequestration commissioner ; agent to collect provisions for the army ; district attorney ; state printer ; border agriculturist ; custom officer ; agent to receive titles ; commissioner to examine political prisoners. Ho. Ex. Doc., No. 16, 40th Cong., 2d Sess., gives a list of those pardoned. Some of the more well-known men pardoned were : R. M. Patton, "agent for the sale of rebel bonds, and worth over $20,000" ; Nicholas Davis, "member of rebel provisional Congress" ; Charles Hays, worth over $20,000 ; Benjamin Fitzpatrick, "resigned United States Senate" ; J. G. Gilchrist, "member of Secession Convention" ; S. F. Rice, worth over $20,000 ; S. S. Scott, Indian agent ; H. C. Semple, worth over $20,000 ; Thomas H. Watts, "member of rebel convention, voted for ordinance of secession, colonel in rebel army, attorney-general of the would-be Southern Confederacy, rebel governor of Alabama, and worth $20,000" ; M. J. Saffold, "commissioner to examine political prisoners, and state printer."

Point graduate; 2 naval officers, and 2 governors. These were the only prominent political leaders who applied for pardon.[1]

SEC. 3. THE "RESTORATION" CONVENTION

Personnel and Parties

The election for delegates was held August 31, and the convention met in Montgomery September 12 and adjourned on September 30. The total vote cast for delegates was about 56,000,[2] a very large vote when all things are considered. This being a representative body of the men who were to carry out the Johnson plan of restoration, it will be of interest to examine closely the personnel of the convention. There were 99 delegates, of whom only 18 were under forty years of age, the majority being over fifty; it was a body of old rather than middle-aged men; 26 were natives of Alabama; 24 were born in Georgia; Virginia, North Carolina, and South Carolina furnished 28; Maryland, Kentucky, and Tennessee, 14; 6 were from northern states, and 1 from Ireland. There were 23 Methodists; 19 Baptists; 16 Presbyterians (the most able members), and 5 Episcopalians; 34 belonged to no church (not a mark of respectability at that time). There were 33 lawyers and 42 farmers and planters; 6 physicians, 9 merchants, 2 teachers, and 7 ministers. The proportion of ministers and non-church-members is remarkable. As to politics, 45 were old Whigs and had voted for Bell and Everett electors in 1861, 24 voted for Breckenridge, and 30 for Douglas; 18 had been in favor of immediate secession and a few of these were now called "precipitators"; 11 had been in the convention of 1861, and 10 had then voted for secession. Only one member of the convention of 1861 from the southern and central parts of the state was returned to the convention of 1865. All the others had by their course in the war made themselves ineligible. Fifty-two had had no previous experiences in public life. There were two ex-governors, two former members of Congress, and one who had been minister to Belgium.[3]

There were several extreme "union" men, a few "precipitators,"

---

[1] The names and offences of those pardoned are given in Ho. Ex. Doc., No. 99, 39th Cong., 1st Sess.; No. 16, 40th Cong., 2d Sess.; and No. 31, 39th Cong., 2d Sess.

[2] *N. Y. Herald*, Oct. 15, 1865.   [3] *Montgomery Daily Advertiser*, Oct. 1, 1865.

who, however, made no factious opposition, and a large majority of conservative men. The votes on test questions showed a wide difference between the extremists from north Alabama and the other members. The proportion was about 63 conservatives to 36 north Alabama anti-Confederates. It was the old sectional division. The minority was made up about equally of rampant "union" men and old con-

servative Whigs; the majority, of the more liberal Whigs and conservative Democrats. Neither party was as united as the parties had been in 1861. There were almost as many minor divisions as there were members, but the most of them acted together in order to transact business, and none were allowed to obstruct. As a body the convention was much inferior in ability to that of 1861 and lacked experience. Nearly all were men of ordinary ability, while those

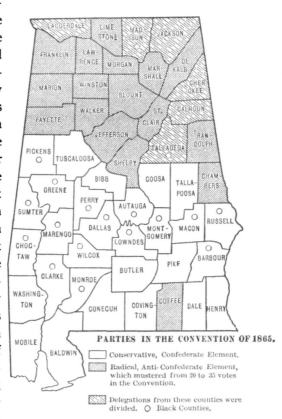

PARTIES IN THE CONVENTION OF 1865.

☐ Conservative, Confederate Element.

▨ Radical, Anti-Confederate Element, which mustered from 20 to 35 votes in the Convention.

▨ Delegations from these counties were divided. ○ Black Counties.

of 1861 were the best from both sections of the state. Yet this was quite a respectable conservative body.[1] The secessionists and former Democrats were the ablest members, and were more inclined to accept the results of war in a philosophical spirit, and, making the best of things, to go to work to bring order out of political chaos. The *Herald* correspondent said that John A. Elmore was the strongest

[1] *N. Y. Herald,* Sept. 26 and Oct. 15, 1865.

man in the convention. He had been an ardent secessionist of the Yancey school, yet in the convention he did more than any other man to bring the weaker men around to correct views and harmony of action.[1]

Ex-Senator and Ex-Governor Fitzpatrick was chosen to preside, and Governor Parsons administered the amnesty oath. The convention at once notified President Johnson of the desire and intention of the people to be and to remain loyal citizens of the United States. It indorsed his administration and policy and asked him to pardon all who were not included in the amnesty proclamation of May 9, 1865.[2]

Debates on Secession and Slavery

The debate on the action to be taken as to the ordinance of secession was warm and extended over the entire session. The dispute was concerning the form of words to be used in repealing or otherwise getting rid of the ordinance of secession. One delegate proposed that it be declared "unconstitutional and therefore illegal and void"; another wanted it declared "null and void"; another, "the so-called ordinance of secession, null and void"; others, "unconstitutional, null and void"; "unauthorized, null and void"; or "unauthorized and void from the beginning." The minority proposition to declare it "unauthorized, null and void," was laid on the table by a vote of 69 to 21, the minority being from north Alabama. A proposition to declare it "unconstitutional, null and void" was lost by the same vote. And all similar propositions fared about the same.[3] However, a proposition to say that "it is and was unconstitutional" secured 34 votes against 59. Clark of Lawrence, who had been in the convention of 1861, wanted this convention to declare the ordinance of secession "unauthorized, null and void," because, he said, in 1861, the majority of the people voted for "union and coöperation," and that, as the convention refused to submit its work to the people, the people were misrepresented and the ordinance of secession was unauthorized. Yet he would not say that it was unconstitutional and void from the beginning. Other members said that the convention of 1861 had full authority. From the act of the

---

[1] *N. Y. Herald*, Sept. 26, 1865.   [2] Journal of the Convention, 1865, p. 28.

[3] Journal of the Convention, 1865, pp. 16, 57, 58 ; *N. Y. Herald*, Sept. 26 and Oct. 15, 1865.

legislature of 1860 which provided for the calling of the convention, the people understood that it had full authority and they also knew that it would use its authority to secede. "Unauthorized" would mean that there was no cause for calling the convention of 1861, and would even deny the right to secede as a revolutionary right. It would mean consent to the doctrine of passive obedience, and also that the convention of 1861 and those who supported it had usurped authority, and "we thereby impliedly should leave the memory of our dead who died for their country to be branded as traitors and rebels and turn over the survivors, so far as we are concerned, to the gibbet." [1] The ordinance favored by the majority of the convention declared that the ordinance of secession "is null and void," and was adopted by a unanimous vote. [2] All other ordinances, resolutions, and proceedings of the convention of 1861, and such provisions of the constitution of 1861 as were in conflict with the Constitution of the United States, were declared null and void. [3]

The state bonded debt in aid of the war was $3,844,500, which was held principally in Mobile. There were other indirect war debts, but no one knew the amount. On a test vote early in the session the convention was divided, 58 to 34, against repudiating the war debt. [4] Later, by a vote of 60 to 19, all debts created by the state of Alabama, directly or indirectly in aid of the war, were declared void, and the legislature was forbidden to pay any part of it, or of any debts contracted directly or indirectly by the Confederacy or its agents or by its authority. [5]

---

[1] Annual Cyclopædia (1865), pp. 16, 17 ; Journal of the Convention, 1865, pp. 57, 58.

[2] The vote cast was 92, probably all who were present. Journal of the Convention, p. 59; *N. Y. Herald*, Sept. 26, 1865 ; Shepherd, " Constitution and Ordinances," 1865, p. 48 ; Code of 1867, Ordinance No. 13, Sept. 25, 1865. Early in the session Mardis of Shelby, a "loyal" member, proposed a resolution to the effect that the ordinance of secession was "unconstitutional and therefore illegal and void, [and that] the leaders of the rebellion having been forced to lay down their arms and turn over to the conservative people of the state the reigns of the civil government by which the state has become more peaceful and loyal to the United States government. She is now entitled to all the rights as before ordinance of secession." Journal of the Convention, 1865, p. 16. The resolutions of the " loyalists " were curiosities, and the secretary did not always expurgate bad spelling, etc.

[3] Shepherd, " Constitution and Ordinances," 1865, p. 49 ; Ordinance No. 14.

[4] *N. Y. Herald*, Sept. 22, 1865.

[5] Annual Cyclopædia (1865), p. 17 ; *N. Y. Times*, Sept. 29, 1865 ; *N. Y. Herald*, Oct. 15, 1865 ; Shepherd, " Constitution and Ordinances," 1865, pp. 53, 54 ; Ordinances

In the debate in regard to the abolition of slavery, Mr. Coleman of Choctaw [1] desired to know by what authority the people of Alabama had been deprived of their constitutional right to property in slaves.[2] He urged the convention not to pass an ordinance to abolish slavery, but to leave the President's proclamations and the acts of Congress to be tested by the Supreme Court; that there was no such thing as secession; a state could not be guilty of treason, and Alabama had committed no crime; individuals had done so; others were loyal and were entitled to their rights. Not only those who had always been loyal but also those who had taken the amnesty oath were entitled to their property;[3] those pardoned by the President were entitled to the same rights, and Congress had no authority to seize property except during the lifetime of the criminal. The Federal government had no right to nullify the Constitution. The abolition of slavery should be accepted as an act of war, not as the free and voluntary act of the people of Alabama which latter course would prevent the "loyalists" of Alabama, from receiving compensation for slaves. He denied that slavery was non-existent; Lincoln's proclamation did not destroy slavery; it was a question for the Supreme Court to decide, and to admit that Lincoln's proclamation destroyed slavery was to admit the power of the President and Congress to nullify every law of the state. For all these reasons it was inexpedient for the convention to declare the abolition of slavery.

Judge Foster of Calhoun answered that the war had settled the question of slavery and secession; that the question of slavery was beyond the power of the courts to decide, and, besides, a decision of the Supreme Court would not be respected. The question had to be decided by war, and having been so decided, there was no appeal from the decision. The institution of slavery had been destroyed

Nos. 25–28, September, 1865. In spite of this ordinance certain war debts were paid. Fowler, Superintendent of Army Records, was paid $3000 for his work during the war, the legislature buying the records from him. Coleman, a Confederate judge, was paid for services during the war. See Acts 65–66 and the Journal of the Convention of 1867. The newspaper reports give summaries of the debates on the more important ordinances ; the Journal of the Convention gives only the votes and resolutions.

[1] Chairman of the committee on suffrage, Convention of 1901.

[2] It seems to have been taken for granted by the convention that slavery was already abolished.

[3] The amnesty proclamation expressly excepted property in slaves.

by secession. The question was not open for discussion. Slavery, he said, does not exist, is utterly and forever destroyed, — by whom, when, where, is no matter. The power of arms is greater than all courts. Citizens should begin to make contracts with their former slaves. Should the Supreme Court declare the proclamations of the Presidents and the acts of Congress unconstitutional, slavery would not be restored. Whether destroyed legally or illegally, it was destroyed, and the people had better accept the situation and restore Federal relations.[1]

Mr. White of Talladega[2] proposed to abide by the proclamations of the President and the acts of Congress until the Supreme Court should decide the question of slavery. White said that he had opposed secession as long as he could; that the states were not out of the Union, but had all their rights as formerly.[3] Mr. Lane of Butler wanted an ordinance to the effect that since the institution of slavery had been destroyed in the state of Alabama by act of the Federal government, therefore slavery no longer exists. This was lost by a vote of 66 to 17.[4] On September 22, 1865, an ordinance was adopted by a vote of 89 to 3 which declared that the institution of slavery having been destroyed, neither slavery nor involuntary servitude should thereafter exist in the state, except as a punishment for crime. All provisions in the constitution regarding slavery were struck out, and it was made the duty of the next legislature to pass laws to protect the freedmen in the full employment of all their rights of person and property and to guard them and the state against any evils that might arise from their sudden emancipation.[5] Mr. Taliafero Towles of Chambers, a "loyalist," proposed an ordinance to make all "free negroes"[6] who were not inhabitants of the state

---

[1] Annual Cyclopædia (1865), p. 14; *N. Y. Times*, Sept. 30, 1865.

[2] "Loyalist," and later a "scalawag."   [3] *N. Y. Herald*, Oct. 15, 1865.

[4] Journal of the Convention, 1865, p. 49.

[5] Journal of the Convention, 1865, pp. 49, 50; *N. Y. Herald*, Oct. 15, 1865; Shepherd, "Constitution and Ordinances," 1865, p. 45, Ordinance No. 6. The three members who voted against the abolition ordinance were Crawford of Coosa, Cumming of Monroe, and White of Talladega. They wanted to let the Supreme Court decide. The Supreme Court of Alabama, a year later, held that, as a matter of history which the court would recognize, slavery was dead as a result of war before the passage of the ordinance of Sept. 22, 1865.

[6] That class of men called all negroes "free negroes" and "freedmen" for years after the war as a term of contempt.

before 1861 leave the state. Mr. Langdon of Mobile regretted
this proposition, and thought it would do harm. Mr. Towles explained that he lived near the Georgia line and that he was much
annoyed by the negroes who came into Alabama from Georgia. Mr.
Patton[1] of Lauderdale opposed such a policy. It was unwise, he
said; let people go where they pleased; he would invite people
from all parts of the Union to Alabama. Mr. Mudd of Jefferson
thought that such a measure would be extremely unwise. Mr.
Hunter of Dallas said that it was very unwise, that it would do no
good, and at such a time would be harmful. Passions must be
allayed. Towles withdrew the resolution.[2]

Mr. Saunders of Macon introduced a memorial to the President
to release President Davis. It was referred to a committee and
was not heard from.[3] General Swayne of the Freedmen's Bureau
sent to the convention a memorial from a negro mass-meeting in
Mobile praying for the extension of suffrage to them. It was unanimously laid on the table.[4]

"A White Man's Government"

General Swayne had made an arrangement with the governor
by which the state officials were required to act as agents of the
Freedmen's Bureau. The convention now passed an ordinance
requiring these officers to continue to discharge the duties of agents
of the Bureau "until the adjournment of the next general assembly."
Seventeen north Alabama men opposed the passage of this ordinance.[5]

Mr. Patton of Lauderdale proposed an ordinance in regard to
the basis of representation in the general assembly. It was not
correctly understood in north Alabama, which section, thinking it
called for representation based on population, rose in wrath. The
Huntsville Advocate said: "This is a white man's government
and a white man's state. We are opposed to any changes in the
convention except such as are necessary to get the state into the
Union again."[6] Mr. Patton explained that the purpose of his meas-

---

[1] Afterwards second provisional governor.   [2] N. Y. Times, Sept. 30, 1865.

[3] N. Y. Herald, Oct. 15, 1865.   [4] N. Y. Times, Sept. 30, 1865.

[5] Journal of the Convention, 1865, p. 80; Shepherd, "Constitution and Ordinances," 1865, p. 61, Ordinance No. 34.

[6] Huntsville Advocate, Sept. 28, 1865. A "Johnson reconstruction paper."

ure was to base representation on the white population. He cheerfully indorsed north Alabama doctrine, "This is a white man's government and we must keep it a white man's government."[1] The ordinance as passed provided for a census in 1866, and the apportionment of senators and representatives according to white population as ascertained by the census. The delegates from the white counties of north Alabama and southeast Alabama voted for the ordinance, and thirty delegates from the Black Belt voted against it.[2]

This measure destroyed at a blow the political power of the Black Belt, and had the Johnson government survived, the state would have been ruled by the white counties instead of by the black counties. This was partly the result of antagonism between the white and black counties.

Early in the session Mr. Sheets of Winston, "loyalist," demanded that all amendments to the Constitution adopted by the convention should be referred to the people for ratification or rejection, except such as related to slavery.[3] Mr. Webb of Greene, chairman of the Committee on the Constitution, reported that, on account of the state of the times, it was not expedient to refer the amendments to the people. Mr. Clark of Lawrence[4] wanted the people to have an opportunity to show whether they favored the work of the convention. He said that, in 1861, had the ordinance of secession been referred to the people, it would have been defeated.

The members who were in favor of not sending the amendments to the people said that there was not time, and that there were too many other elections; that the people had confidence in the convention or they would not have elected the delegates who were there. But the north Alabama delegates insisted that their constituents not only expected to have the amendments submitted to them, but that they (the delegates) had pledged that they would have the amendments sent before the people.[5] The north Alabama party could not consistently do anything but object to the adoption of the constitution by proclamation. Some had never recognized the supreme

[1] *Huntsville Advocate*, Oct. 12, 1865.

[2] Shepherd, p. 57, Ordinance No. 30 ; Journal of the Convention, 1865, pp. 67, 68. See Constitution of 1865, Article IV, Section 4.

[3] Journal of the Convention, 1865, p. 34.

[4] A member of the convention of 1861.

[5] *N. Y. Herald*, Oct. 15, 1865.

authority of a constitutional convention; others were opposed to the expediency of adoption by proclamation. By a vote of 61 to 25 the constitution was proclaimed in force without reference to the people.[1]

Legislation

The convention did some important legislative work necessary to put the business of administration in running order again. All the laws enacted during the war not in conflict with the United States Constitution, and not relating to the issue of money and bonds nor to appropriations, were ratified and declared in full force since their dates.[2] All officials acts of the state and county officials, all judgments, orders, and decrees of the courts, all acts and sales of trustees, executors, administrators, and guardians, not in conflict with United States Constitution were ratified and confirmed. Deeds, bonds, mortgages, and contracts made during the war were declared valid and binding. But in cases where payments were to be made in Confederate money the courts were to decide what the true value of the consideration was at the time.[3] Divorces granted during the war by the chancery court were declared valid.[4] Marriages between negroes, whether during slavery or since emancipation, were declared valid; and in cases where no ceremony had been performed, but the parties recognized each other as man and wife, such relationship was declared valid marriage. The children of all such marriages were declared legitimate. Fathers of bastard negro children were required to provide for them. The freedmen were placed under the same laws of marriage as the whites, except that they were not required to give bond.[5] The legislature was commanded to pass laws prohibiting the intermarriage of whites with negroes or with persons of mixed blood.[6]

In view of the lawlessness prevailing in some of the counties, the provisional governor was authorized to call out the militia in each county, and the mayors of Huntsville, Athens, and Florence were given police jurisdiction over their respective counties until the

---

[1] Journal of the Convention, 1865, p. 74.

[2] Shepherd, p. 44, Ordinance No. 5. [3] Shepherd, p. 54, Ordinance No. 26.

[4] Shepherd, p. 46, Ordinance No. 7. [5] Shepherd, p. 63, Ordinance No. 39.

[6] Shepherd, p. 74, Ordinance No. 42. See Constitution, 1865, Article IV, Section 31.

legislature should act. The ante-bellum militia code was declared in force, and all other laws in regard to the militia were repealed.[1]

The governor was ordered to pay the interest on the bonded debt of the state that was made before 1861, and the convention pledged the faith of the people that the old debt should be paid in full with interest.[2] The state was divided into six congressional districts. The negro was no longer counted in the "Federal number," and the representation of the state in Congress was thus reduced. Elections were ordered for various offices in November and December, 1865, and March and May, 1866. The provisional governor was authorized to act as governor until another was elected and inaugurated. It was ordered that in the future no convention be held unless first the question of convention or no convention be submitted to the people and approved by a majority of those voting.[3]

Finally, the convention asked that the President withdraw the troops from the state, the people and the convention having complied with all the conditions and requirements necessary to restore the state to its constitutional relations to the Federal government.[4] The convention adjourned on September 30, having been in session ten days in all. The constitution went into effect gradually, Parsons enforcing some of it; Patton and the newly elected legislature organized the government under it from December, 1865, to May, 1866. But it never became more than a provisional constitution, which was set aside by the President at pleasure.

Sec. 4. "Restoration" Completed

By convention ordinance and by constitutional amendment the civil rights of the freedmen were made secure, family relations legalized, property rights secured; the courts of law were open to them, and in all cases affecting themselves, their evidence was admissible. The admission of negro testimony was generally approved by the bar and the magistracy, but disliked by the ignorant classes of whites. All magistrates and judicial officers who refused to admit negro testimony or to act as Bureau agents were removed from office by the governor. One mayor (of Mobile) and one judge were removed.

[1] Shepherd, pp. 44, 53, 65, Ordinances Nos. 4, 23, 43.
[2] Shepherd, pp. 49, 62, 68, Ordinances Nos. 15, 37, 49.
[3] Ordinances Nos. 8, 16, 22, 33.   [4] Shepherd, p. 70.

Affairs were going on well, though the civil government was weakened and lost prestige by being subordinated to the military authorities.[1] The convention having authorized Parsons to organize the militia to aid in restoring order, several companies were organized and instructed to act solely in aid of the civil authorities and in subordination to them. They were to act alone only when there was no civil officer present.[2]

Among the whites there was a vague but widespread fear of negro insurrections, and toward Christmas this fear increased. The negroes were disappointed because of the delayed division of lands, and their temper was not improved by the reports of adventurers, black and white, who came among them as missionaries and sharpers. There was a general and natural desire among the freedmen to get possession of firearms, and all through the summer and fall they were acquiring shotguns, muskets, and pistols in great quantities. Most of the guns were worthless army muskets, but new arms of the latest pattern were supplied by their ardent sympathizers in the belief that the negroes were only seeking means of protection. A sharper who claimed to be connected with the government travelled through some of the black counties, telling the negroes that they were mistreated and must arm themselves for protection. He sold them certificates for $2.50 each which he said would entitle the bearers to muskets if presented at the arsenals at Selma, Vicksburg, etc.[3] Hence arose the fears of the whites who were poorly armed.

In several instances where there was fear of negro insurrection the civil authorities, backed by the militia, searched negro houses for concealed weapons, and sometimes found supplies of arms, which were confiscated. There was a general desire to disarm the freedmen until after Christmas, when the expected insurrection failed to materialize; but no order for disarming was issued by the governor, and a bill for that purpose was defeated in the legislature. Some of the militia companies undertook to patrol the country to scare the negroes with a show of force,[4] and in some places disguised patrols rode through the negro settlements to keep them in order.

---

[1] *N. Y. Herald*, Oct. 15, 1865; Sen. Ex. Doc., No. 26, 39th Cong., 1st Sess. (Parsons); Report Joint Committee, 1866, Pt. III, pp. 138–141.

[2] Parsons's Proclamation, Sept. 28, 1865.   [3] *Montgomery Advertiser*, May 12, 1866.

[4] In Macon, Russell, and Lowndes counties.

There were several instances of unauthorized disarming and lawless plunder under the pretence of disarming the blacks, by marauders who took advantage of the state of public feeling and followed the example of the disguised patrol bands. General Swayne himself was afraid of negro insurrection, and before Christmas did not interfere with the attempts of the whites to control the blacks. After Christmas the negroes quieted down, and most of them made some pretence of working. The next case of disarming that occurred brought the interference of General Swayne, who ordered that neither the civil nor the military authorities should again interfere with the negroes under any pretext, unless by permission from himself. He threatened to send a negro garrison into any community where the blacks might be interfered with. After that, he says, the people were "more busy in making a living," and the militia organizations disbanded. Two classes of the population were now beyond the reach of the civil government, the "loyalists" and the negroes, and the civil authorities maintained that these were the source of most disorder.[1]

An act of Congress, July 2, 1862, prescribed that every person elected or appointed to any office under the United States government should, before entering upon the duties of the office, subscribe to the "iron-clad" test oath,[2] which obliged one to swear that he had never aided in any way the Confederate cause. Outside of the few genuine Union men of North Alabama, there were not half a dozen respectable white men in the state who could take

---

[1] *N. Y. Daily News*, Sept. 7, 1865; *N. Y. Tribune*, Feb. 6, 1866; Swayne's Report, Jan., 1866, in Ho. Ex. Doc., No. 70, 39th Cong., 1st Sess.; Report Joint Committee of Reconstruction, 1866, Pt. III, p. 140 (Swayne).

[2] "I, *A. B.*, do solemnly swear (or affirm) that I have never voluntarily borne arms against the United States since I have been a citizen thereof; that I have voluntarily given no aid, countenance, counsel or encouragement to persons engaged in armed hostility thereto; that I have never sought nor accepted nor attempted to exercise the functions of any office whatever, under any authority or pretended authority, in hostility to the United States; that I have not yielded a voluntary support to any pretended government, authority, power or constitution within the United States, hostile or inimical thereto; and I do further swear (or affirm) that, to the best of my knowledge and ability, I will support and defend the Constitution of the United States against all enemies, foreign and domestic; that I will bear true faith and allegiance to the same; that I take this obligation freely, without any mental reservation or purpose of evasion, and that I will well and faithfully discharge the duties of the office on which I am about to enter. So help me God." McPherson, "Reconstruction," p. 193.

2 B

such an oath. Those who had been opposed to secession had nearly all aided in the prosecution of the war or had held office under the Confederate government. The thousands who had fallen away from the Confederates in the last year of the war could not take the oath. The women could not take it, and few even of the negroes could. Those who could take the oath were detested by all, and the unfitness of such persons for holding office was clearly recognized by the administration. By law, certain Federal offices had to be filled by men who lived in the county or state. The Federal service did not exist in Alabama at the end of the war, and the President and Cabinet, agreeing that the requirement of the oath could not be enforced, made temporary appointments in the Treasury and postal service of men who could not take the oath. In Alabama the men appointed were the old conservatives, those who had opposed secession. The officers appointed were marshals and deputy marshals, collectors and assessors of internal revenue, customs officers, and postmasters. Objection was made in Congress to the payment of these officers, and Secretary McCulloch of the Treasury made a report on the subject. He stated that it was difficult to find competent persons who could take the oath, and that it was better for the public service and for the people that their own citizens should perform the unpleasant duty of collecting taxes from an exhausted people. There was no civil government whatever, and it was necessary that the Federal service be established. In regard to future appointments, he said, it would be difficult, if not impossible, to find competent men in the South who could take the oath, that very few persons of character and intelligence had failed to connect themselves in some way with the insurgent cause. The persons who could present clean records for loyalty would have been able to present equally fair records to the Confederate government had it succeeded, or else they lacked the proper qualifications. Northern men of requisite qualifications would not go South for the compensation offered. For the government to collect taxes in the southern states by the hands of strangers was not advisable. Better for the country politically and financially to suspend the collection of internal revenue taxes in the South for months or years than to collect them by men not identified with the taxpayers in sympathy or interest. It would be a calamity to the nation and to the cause of civil liberty everywhere if, instead of a policy of conciliation, the action of the government should tend to intensify sectional feeling. To make tax-gatherers at the South of men who were strangers to the people would be a most unfortunate course for the government to pursue, and fatal consequences, he thought, would follow such a policy. He asked that the oath be modified so that the men in office could take it.[1] The Postmaster-General made similar recommendations.[2]

For years after the war the test oath obstructed administration and justice in the South. The Alabama lawyers could not take the oath, and United States courts could not be held because there were no lawyers to practise before them. There were many cases of property libelled which should have come before the United States courts, but it was not possible.[3] As men of character could not be found to fill the offices, the Post-office Department tried to get women to take the post-offices, but they could not take the test oath. Many post-offices remained closed, and mail matter was sent by express. Letters were thrown out at a station or given to a negro to carry to the proper person. Juries in the Federal courts had to take practically the same oath as the "iron-clad," and the jury oath was in existence long after the others were modified. So for years a fair jury trial was in many localities impossible.[4]

The effect of the proscription by the test oaths of the only men who were fit for office was distinctly bad. It drove the old Whig-coöperationist-Unionist men into affiliation with the secessionists and Democrats. The division of the whites into different parties

---

[1] Ho. Ex. Doc., No. 81, 39th Cong., 1st Sess., McCulloch, Report, March 19, 1866; McCulloch, "Men and Measures," pp. 227, 233. The Finance Committee reported in favor of paying these officials, accepting as correct the secretary's statement. They were paid, in spite of the opposition of Sumner, who voted not to pay "those rebels." McCulloch, p. 232.

[2] On March 17, 1866, the Postmaster-General, in a letter to the President, stated that the test oaths of July 2, 1862, and March 3, 1863, hindered the reconstruction of the postal service in the South. Of 2258 mail routes in 1861, only 757 had been restored. Before the war there were 8902 postmasters, and in 1866 there were but 2042, of whom 420 were women and 865 others could not take the oath. Ho. Ex. Doc., No. 81, 39th Cong., 1st Sess.

[3] *N. Y. News*, Dec. 8 and Oct. 23, 1865; *N. Y. Times*, July 2, 1866.

[4] Cox, "Three Decades," p. 603; Reid, "After the War," pp. 401, 402; *N. Y. Daily News*, Oct. 23 and Dec. 8, 1865; *N. Y. Times*, July 2, 1866.

was made less likely. The Senate regularly rejected nominations made by the President of men who could not take the oath,[1] and the military authorities were inclined to enforce the taking of the test oath by the state and local officials of the provisional government.[2]

The convention ordered an election, on November 30, for governor, state and county officials, and legislature. There were three candidates for governor, all respectable, conservative men, old-line Whigs, from north Alabama, the stronghold of those who had opposed secession. They were R. M. Patton of Lauderdale, M. J. Bulger of Tallapoosa, and W. R. Smith of Tuscaloosa.[3] The section of Alabama where the spirit of secession had been strongest refrained from putting forward any candidate. The radical "loyalists" had no candidate. The few prominent men of that faction saw that it would be political suicide for them to commit themselves to the Johnson plan after he had begun the pardoning process, and were now working to overthrow the present political institutions. Only in case the plan of the Radicals in Congress should succeed would the "loyalists" get any share in the spoils. The Conservative candidates were in sympathy with the north Alabama desire for "a white man's government." Mr. Patton in the late convention had secured the revision of the constitution so as to base representation on the white population. During the war General M. J. Bulger, the second candidate, made a speech at Selma in which he said he had opposed secession and had refused to sign the ordinance, but had deemed it his duty to fight when the time came and had served throughout the war. There could be, he said, no negro suffrage, no negro

---

[1] *Selma Times*, April 10, 1866. The rejection of such men as Dr. F. W. Sykes of Lawrence as tax commissioner was especially discouraging to the anti-Democratic party in the state. Sykes had been an obstructionist in the legislature during the war. Brewer, p. 309.

[2] One official who had suffered from objections made against his past record inserted the following advertisement in the *Selma Times*, April 11, 1866: —

"Having been elected twice, given three approved bonds, and sworn in five times, I propose opening the business of the city courts of Selma.

"E. M. GARRETT,
"*Clerk City Court of Selma.*"

[3] There were no nominating conventions; the candidates were announced by caucuses of friends. Several other men were spoken of, but the contest narrowed down to three.

equality.[1] W. R. Smith had been the leader of the coöperationists in the convention of 1861. The election resulted in the choice of R. M. Patton of Lauderdale over Bulger and Smith by a good majority.[2]

The new legislature met on November 20, but Patton was not inaugurated until a month later, owing to the refusal of the Washington administration to allow Parsons to resign the government into the hands of what the administration intended should be the permanent, "restored" state government. The object in the delay was the desire of the President to have the Thirteenth Amendment ratified before he relinquished the state government. It was a queer mixture of a government—an elected constitutional legislature and a governor and state administration appointed by the commander-in-chief of the army.[3] The legislature was recognized, but the governor elected at the same time was not. Several acts of legislation were done by this military-constitutional government during the thirty days of its existence, the most important being the ratification of the Thirteenth Amendment by the legislature. This was done with the understanding, the resolution stated, that it did not confer upon Congress the power to legislate upon the political status of the freedmen in Alabama.[4] The amendment was ratified December 2, 1865, and

[1] *N. Y. Times*, Nov. 10, 1865.

[2] R. M. Patton, 21,442; M. J. Bulger, 15,234; W. R. Smith, 8194. The total vote was 44,870; the registration to Sept. 22, 1865, had been 65,825; the vote for delegates to the convention had been about 56,000; the vote for presidential electors in 1860 had been 89,579. The falling off in the vote may be explained by the death and disfranchisement of voters and by the indifference of south Alabama people to the north Alabama candidates.

[3] The convention in September had proceeded to correct the theory of the situation by conferring the powers of a civil governor upon Parsons, and authorizing him to act as governor until the elected governor should be qualified.

[4] McPherson, "Reconstruction," p. 21. Alabama was the twenty-seventh state to ratify, and with seven other seceding states made up the necessary three-fourths of the thirty-six states. So far the Johnson state governments were recognized. *Tribune Almanac*, 1866. Later, when all that the "restoration" administration had done was found to be useless or worse than useless, an Alabama writer, in "The Land We Love," complained: —

"The constitutional amendment abolishing slavery could only be passed constitutionally when the southern states were in the Union. We were then in the Union for the few weeks during which time this was being done. For this brief privilege we lost 4,000,000 of slaves valued at $1,200,000,000. We have every reason to be thankful for being wakened out of our brief dream of being in the Union. A few

on the 10th, Secretary Seward telegraphed to Parsons that the time had arrived when in the judgment of the President the care and conduct of the proper affairs of the state of Alabama might be remitted to the constitutional authorities chosen by the people. Parsons was relieved, the instructions stated, from the trust imposed in him as provisional governor. When the governor-elect should be qualified, Parsons was to transfer papers and property to him and retire.[1] On the strength of these instructions Governor Patton was inaugurated December 13, 1865. In his inaugural address the new governor said that the extinction of slavery was one of the inevitable results of the war. "We shall not only extend to the freedmen all their legitimate rights," he stated, "but shall throw around them such effectual safeguards as will secure them in their full and complete enjoyment. At the same time it must be understood that politically and socially ours is a white man's government. In the future, as has been the case in the past, the state affairs of Alabama must be guided and controlled by the superior intelligence of the white man. The negro must be made to realize that freedom does not mean idleness and vagrancy. Emancipation has not left him where he can live without work."[2]

Though Patton was inaugurated on December 13, the Washington authorities did not authorize the formal transfer of the government until December 18, and the charge was made on December 20, 1865.

The legislature at once elected ex-Governor Parsons and George S. Houston to the United States Senate. The people had already elected six congressmen of moderate politics.[3] So far as concerned

more weeks of such costly sleep would have stripped us entirely of houses and lands."

[1] *N. Y. Herald*, Dec. 19, 1865.

[2] Inaugural Addresses, Dec. 13, 1865; Annual Cyclopædia (1865), p. 19.

[3] Both Parsons and Houston had been "Unionists," but neither could have subscribed to the oath exacted from members of Congress. The representatives chosen were: (1) C. C. Langdon, Whig, Bell and Everett man, of northern birth, opposed secession, a member of the legislature of 1861; (2) George C. Freeman, Whig, Bell and Everett man, opposed secession, captain and major 47th Alabama; (3) Cullen A. Battle, Democrat, major-general C.S.A.; (4) Joseph W. Taylor, Whig, Bell and Everett man, opposed secession; (5) Burwell T. Pope, Whig, opposed secession; (6) Thomas J. Foster, Whig, Bell and Everett man, opposed secession. None of the congressmen-elect could subscribe to the test oath. The people would have voted for no man who could take the test oath.

the state of Alabama, the presidential plan of restoration was complete, if Congress would recognize the work.

A proclamation of the President on December 1, revoking and annulling the suspension of the writ of *habeas corpus*, expressly excepted all the southern states and the southern border states. It was not until April 2, 1866, that the President declared the rebellion at an end.[1] He had little faith in his restored governments, or else he liked to interfere, and he still retained the power to do so.

[1] McPherson, p. 15.

CHAPTER IX

THE SECOND PROVISIONAL ADMINISTRATION

Status of the Provisional Government

It was generally understood in the state that while Congress was opposed to the presidential plan of restoration and repudiated it as soon as it convened, yet if the state conventions should abolish slavery, and the state legislatures should ratify the Thirteenth Amendment, their representatives would be admitted to Congress. This was the meaning, it seemed, of a resolution offered in the Senate December 4, 1865, by Charles Sumner, one of the most radical of the Radical leaders.[1] On the same day, in the House of Representatives, Thaddeus Stevens, the Radical leader of the lower house, introduced a resolution, which was adopted, to appoint a joint committee of the Senate and House to inquire into conditions in the southern states. Until the committee should make a report, no representatives from the southern states should be admitted to Congress.[2] Under this resolution, the Committee of Fifteen on Reconstruction was appointed. In order to support a report in favor of the congressional plan of reconstruction and to justify the overturning of the southern state governments, the committee took testimony at Washington which was carefully calculated to serve as a campaign document. Such Radicals as Stevens professed to believe that the arbitrary rule of the President was hateful to the southern people. Stevens said: "That they would disregard and scorn their present constitutions forced upon them in the midst of martial law, would be most natural and just. No one who has any regard for freedom of elections can look upon these governments, forced upon them in duress, with any favor."[3] Just exactly how much of this he meant may be inferred from his later

---

[1] *Cong. Globe*, Dec. 4, 1865.

[2] *Globe*, Dec. 4, 1865. This was a distinct refusal to recognize, for the present at least, the restoration as done by the President.

[3] *Cong. Globe*, Dec. 18, 1865.

course as leader of the Radicals of the House, in the movement which forced the negro-carpet-bag government upon the southern states. Now Stevens proposed to "take no account of the aggregation of whitewashed rebels who, without any legal authority, have assembled in the capitals of the late rebel states and simulated legislative bodies."[1]

The Republican caucus instructed Edward McPherson, clerk of the House, to omit from the roll the names of the members-elect from the South as certified by the Secretary of State. This was done, and the southern congressmen were not even allowed the usual privileges of contestants.[2]

As soon as the leaders in Congress felt that they were strong enough to carry through their plan to destroy the governments erected under the President's plan, they agreed that no senator or representative from any southern state should be admitted to either branch of Congress until both houses should have declared such state entitled to representation.[3] The state governments were recognized as provisional only, and for a year or more Congress was occupied in the fight with the President over Reconstruction. The consequence was that Patton became provisional governor of a territory and not the constitutional governor of a state. The state suffered from much government at this time. First, came the military authorities with military commissions; then, the Freedmen's Bureau with its courts supported by the military; the Bureau also acted independently of the army and with civilian officers; it was also a part of the Parsons provisional government, and later of the Patton government, and so controlled the minor officials of the state administration. To complicate matters further, the President constantly interfered by order or direction with all the various administrations, for all were subject to his supervision. The many governments were bound up with one

[1] Herbert, "Solid South," p. 12.

[2] McPherson made a collection of extracts from various newspapers relating to his action in omitting the names of the southern members. Few of the editorials seem to indicate any belief that a grave constitutional question was to be settled. Most of the editors believed that he had exceeded his authority, but approved his action because the southern members were Democrats. The general opinion seemed to be that their politics alone was a cause of offence. See McPherson's scrap-book, "The Roll of the 39th Congress," in the Library of Congress.

[3] *Globe*, March 2, 1866.

another, and by interfering with the action of one another increased the general confusion.   The people lost respect for authority, and only public opinion served to regulate the conduct of individuals.

Legislation about Freedmen

For several months the industrial system was entirely disorganized, especially in the neighborhood of the cities, and many people realized the absolute necessity of laws to regulate negro labor.   The negro insisted on taking a living from the country without working for it.   There were also fears of insurrection by the idle negroes who were waiting for the division of spoils, and General Swayne of the Bureau felt a touch of the apprehension.[1]

When the legislature met, a few of the demagogues who had told their constituents that they would soon regulate all troubles introduced many bills to regulate labor, and thousands of copies were printed for distribution.   On December 15 it was agreed to print ten thousand copies of all bills relating to freedmen.[2]   This was done, and though the governor had not approved them, the country members went home with pockets full of bills introduced by themselves, to show to their constituents and to scare the negroes into work.   The regulations proposed made special provision for the freedmen, and under different circumstances it would have been well for the negro if they had been passed into law and enforced; but it was not good policy at this time to propose such regulations, in view of the fact that the Radicals were watching for such action and hoping for it.   However, it is probable that nothing that the southern whites could have done would have met with the approval of the Radicals.

Governor Patton asked General Swayne for advice in regard to the pending bills relating to freedmen, and Swayne informed him of the probable bad effect on public opinion in the North.   After Christmas the Senate passed some obnoxious bills, and these the governor vetoed.   The other bills that came up from the lower house failed to pass in the Senate.   Similar bills, modified in many details, but which would have been of much use could they have been enforced as law, were passed by both houses only to be vetoed by the governor.   The

[1] Swayne's Report, Oct. 31, 1866, Sen. Ex. Doc., No. 6, 39th Cong., 1st Sess.
[2] Acts of Ala. (1865-1866), p. 601.

negroes were now showing a disposition to work, and the legislature did not attempt to pass the bills over the governor's veto. Next, a law relating to contracts between whites and blacks was attempted. General Swayne was known to favor such a law, but Governor Patton vetoed it. He declared that such a law would cause much trouble; he had information that everywhere freedmen were going to work on terms satisfactory to both parties and that they were disposed to discharge their obligations, and there should not be, he said, one law for whites and another for blacks; special laws for regulating contracts between whites and freedmen would do no good and might cause harm; the common law gave sufficient remedy for violations of contracts, viz. damages. General Swayne had been strongly of the opinion that contracts regularly made and carefully inspected on behalf of the negro were necessary. Later he came to the conclusion that the negro needed no protection by contract or by special law; that he had a much better protection in the demand for his labor, and would only be injured by artificial safeguards; contracts would cause litigation, and it was best for both parties to be able to break an engagement at pleasure. He was of the opinion that the whites preferred contracts, while the negro disliked to bind himself to anything. Hunger and cold, he declared, were the best incentives to labor. Swayne further reported that all objectionable bills relating to freedom had been vetoed.[1]

A bill passed both houses to extend to freedmen the old criminal laws of the state formerly applicable to free persons of color. Governor Patton vetoed the bill on the ground that a system of laws enacted during slavery was not applicable to present conditions. He showed how the proposed laws would act, and the legislature not only accepted the veto, but repealed all such laws then in the code and on the statute books.[2] At the close of the session there were two laws on the statute books which made a distinction before the law between negroes and whites. The first made it a misdemeanor, with a pen-

---

[1] Swayne's Reports, Dec. 26, 1865, Jan. 31, 1866, and Oct. 31, 1866, in Ho. Ex. Doc., No. 70, 39th Cong., 1st Sess., and Sen. Ex. Doc., No. 6, 39th Cong., 1st Sess.; Patton's Message, Jan. 16, 1866; *N. Y. Times*, Jan. 18, 1866; *N. Y. Evening Post*, Jan. 29, 1865; McPherson, "Reconstruction," p. 21; McPherson's scrap-book, "Freedmen's Bureau Bill," 1866.

[2] McPherson, "Reconstruction," pp. 21, 22; Act, approved Feb. 23, 1866, Penal Code of Ala., pp. 6–8; Acts of Ala. (1865–1866), pp. 121, 124.

alty of $100 fine and ten days' imprisonment, to purchase or receive from a "free person of color" any stolen goods, knowing the same to have been stolen.[1]

The second act gave the freedmen the right to sue and be sued, to plead and be imprisoned, in the state courts to the same extent as whites. They were competent to testify only in open court, and in cases in which freedmen were concerned directly or indirectly. Neither interest in the suit nor marriage should disqualify any black witness.[2] This law, if restrictive at all, was never in force in the lower courts where minor magistrates and judicial officers presided; for, by the order of the convention and later of the legislature, the state officials were *ex officio* agents of the Freedmen's Bureau, and sworn to make no distinction between white and black.[3]

Two laws were passed for the purpose of regulating labor, in theory applicable equally to white and black. They had the approval of General Swayne, who was always present when labor legislation was discussed.[4] The first law made it a misdemeanor to interfere with, to hire, entice away, or induce to leave the service of another any laborer or servant who had made a contract in writing, as long as the contract was in force, unless by consent of the employer given in writing or verbally "in the presence of some reputable white person." The penalty for inducing a laborer to break a contract was a fine of $50 to $500, — in no case less than double the amount of the injury sustained by the employer; and half the fine was to go to the injured

[1] Acts of Ala. (1865–1866), Act of Dec. 15, 1865; Penal Code of Ala., p. 12. The compilers of the Penal Code placed this act in the Code separate from the rest, as irreconcilable with the provisions of the Code and with other legislation. That is, they refused to codify it and left it for the courts to decide. The law was meant to suppress a common practice of encouraging negroes to steal cotton, etc., for sale.

[2] Acts of Ala. (1865–1866), p. 98; Penal Code, pp. 164, 165. In one respect the negro had a better standing in court than the white: he was a competent witness in his own behalf, and his wife might also be a witness.

[3] Acts, Dec. 11 and 26, 1865. See below, Ch. XII.

[4] In an interview with General Swayne, in 1901, he informed me that he was present when the bills were drawn up. The governor and the president of the Senate in consultation decided that all measures already brought forward should be vetoed or dropped; the apprentice and contract laws as they stood on the statute book were then drawn up, and no objection was made to them by General Swayne, who was present by request. He made suggestions as to what would be acceptable to the Bureau and to northern public opinion.

party.[1] The compilers of the Penal Code refused to incorporate this statute into the code on the ground that it was inconsistent with other provisions of the code as adopted by the legislature. The Penal Code had an old ante-bellum provision which made it a penal offence to entice, decoy, or persuade a servant or apprentice to leave the service of his master. The penalty was a fine of $20 to $100, and imprisonment for not more than three months might also be allowed.[2]

The second labor law defined the relations of master and apprentice. The war had made orphans of many thousand children, white and black, and there were few people who could look after them. Under slavery no regulation of such things had been necessary for negro children. Now the children were running wild, in want, neglected, becoming criminals and vagabonds. Negro fathers ran off when freedom came, left their wives and children, and took unto themselves other and younger wives. The negro mother, left alone, often incapable and without judgment, could not support her children; and many negro children were found both of whose parents had died, or who had deserted them. As a result of the war, there were many white orphan children and many widowed mothers who were unable to care for their children. For years (1862–1875) there was much suffering among the children of the poorer whites and the negroes. The apprentice law was an extension of an old statute, and was designed to make it possible to care for these dependent children. It was made the duty of county officials to report to the probate courts all minors under the age of eighteen who were destitute orphans, or whose parents refused or were unable to support them; and the court was to apprentice them to suitable persons. In case the minor were the child of a freedman, the former owner should have the preference when he or she should be proven a suitable person. In such cases the probate judge was to keep a record of all the proceedings. The master to whom the minor was apprenticed was obliged to give bond that he would furnish the apprentice sufficient food and clothing, treat him humanely, furnish medical attention in case of sickness, and teach or have him taught to read and write, whether white or black, if under the age of fifteen.

---

[1] Acts of Ala. (1865–1866), pp. 111, 112 (Act of Feb. 16, 1866); Penal Code, p. 13.

[2] Penal Code, pp. 50, 51.

Power was given to inflict such punishment as a father or guardian might inflict on a child or ward, but in no case should the punishment be cruel. In case the apprentice should leave the employment of the master without the consent of the latter, he might be arrested by the master and carried before a justice of the peace, whose duty it was to remand the apprentice to the service of his master. If the apprentice refused to return, he was to be committed to jail until the next session of the probate court, which would investigate the case, and, if convinced that the apprentice had not good cause for leaving his master, would punish the apprentice under the vagrancy laws. If the court should decide that the apprentice had good cause to leave his master, he was to be released from the indenture and the master fined not more than $100, which was to be given to the apprentice. Apprenticeship was to end at the age of twenty-one for men and eighteen for women. Parents could bind out minor children under the regulations of this act.[1] It was a penal offence to sell or give intoxicating liquors to apprentices or to gamble with them.[2]

The definition of vagrancy was extended to include stubborn and refractory servants, laborers, and servants who loitered away their time or refused, without cause, to comply with a contract for service. A vagrant might be fined $50 and costs, and hired out until the fine was paid, but could not be hired for a longer time than six months. The proceeds of fines and hiring in all cases were to go to the county treasury for the benefit of the poor.[3]

[1] Acts of Ala. (1865-1866), pp. 128-131 (Act Feb. 23, 1866).

[2] Penal Code, pp. 34, 35.

[3] Penal Code of Ala., pp. 10-12; Acts of Ala. (1865-1866), pp. 119-121. This was another act which the compilers refused to incorporate into the Penal Code. It was an amendment to the law already on the statute books, and the constitution of the state provided that the law revised or amended must be set forth in full (Article IV, Section 2.) The next legislature repealed this and similar laws as being in conflict with the Code. Acts of Ala. (1866-1867), pp. 107, 115, 504. It was never in force, being practically repealed by the later adoption of the Penal Code, which had the old ante-bellum law of vagrancy, which provided a fine of $10 to $50 for the first offence, and for a second conviction, $50 to $100 and hard labor for not more than six months. (See Penal Code, p. 37). The laws regulating labor and vagrancy were so carelessly drawn that it would have been practically impossible to enforce them. Not only were they technically unconstitutional, but they were also in conflict with the provisions of the Code. The consequence was confusion and the suspension of both Code and statutes. Colonel Herbert, in "The Solid South" (pp. 31-36), gives a summary of similar laws of the northern states which were more stringent than the Alabama laws. As a matter

These statutes form the so-called "Slave Code" or "Black Code" of the state which was so harshly criticised by the Radicals as being designed to reënslave the negroes.[1] There is no doubt that if enforced they would have affected the blacks more than the whites, though they were meant to apply to both.[2] Something of the kind was felt to be a necessity. There were hundreds of negroes wandering about the country, living by petty theft, and some rascally whites made it a business to purchase stolen property, especially cotton, from them. White vagrants were numerous. The refuse of both armies and numbers of the most worthless whites, who had lost all they had in the war, travelled about the country as tramps, their sole occupation being to victimize the ignorant by some scheme. Stringent laws, strictly enforced, would have done much to restore order.[3]

The Negro under the Provisional Government

The lawlessness prevalent in the state consequent upon civil war and emancipation had resulted in filling the jails with all sorts and conditions of criminals — mostly negroes — who were charged with minor offences, such as stealing, fighting, burning, which were committed during the jubilee after the coming of the Federal troops. They were clearly guilty of the crimes alleged, since they were imprisoned by consent of the Freedmen's Bureau, which allowed no negro to be arrested without its permission. There were some whites confined for similar small offences, and there were many "union" men, or "rebels," according to locality, who were under arrest for crimes committed during the war. Most of the crimes were not seri-

of fact, all the states had similar laws, but in the South they had always been a dead letter on the statute book.

[1] See Blaine, "Twenty Years," Vol. II, p. 93.

[2] It was not possible then, nor is it now, to pass any law in regard to labor contracts, vagrancy, or minor crimes, that would not affect the negroes to a much greater degree than the whites. All laws regulating society, if strictly enforced, would bear with much greater force upon blacks than upon whites.

[3] Neither Swayne nor Howard made any objection to the apprentice and vagrancy laws, and so far as I can gather from the reports of General Swayne, they were not enforced. If so, there were no results unfavorable to the freedmen. In 1901, in an interview, Swayne stated that all measures that he considered objectionable had either failed to pass the Senate or had been vetoed by the governor. He intimated that he had a great deal to do with the suppression of such measures and the framing of new ones.

ous or were committed under the abnormal conditions of war. The governor, after consultation with General Swayne, "with entire single-ness of purpose" (Swayne), issued a proclamation of amnesty and pardon[1] for all offences, except murder and rape, committed between April 13, 1861, and July 20, 1865.[2] Many hundred prisoners were thus liberated, among them eight hundred freedmen[3] confined for penitentiary offences. No bad results followed.[4]

By state law and military order the negro was now freed from slavery and given all the civil rights possessed by the whites, unless in certain cases of law between whites in the higher courts where the negro was not permitted to testify. In all cases concerning his own race, directly or indirectly, his standing before the court was the same as that of a white or better. The races were forbidden to intermarry. The apprentice and vagrancy laws, which were meant to regulate the economic relations between the races, could not be enforced because of technical and practical difficulties, and because the officials who were to enforce them were *ex officio* agents of the Bureau and therefore forbidden to enforce such laws. The Bureau upheld the negro in all his rights and much beyond. There was the most urgent demand for his labor, and to secure his wages there was a lien on the employer's crop. The negro was free to come and go when he pleased, and his pleasure led him to do this so often that written contracts fell into immediate disfavor on account of the useless liti-gation and disputes that ensued. Many of the more thrifty blacks began to acquire small bits of property.

The travellers who visited the South in the fall of 1865 and in 1866 agreed (except Schurz) that there was no thought of reënslave-ment of the negro by the white; that the white was more afraid of the negro than the negro of the white; that there was no need of protection, for the demand for his labor would protect him. There were more colored artisans than white, and all were sure of employ-ment. At first the strong conviction that they were not free unless they were careering around the country in idleness resulted in a gen-

---

[1] Feb. 13, 1866.

[2] The date of the beginning of the provisional government.

[3] General Swayne's account.

[4] *Montgomery Advertiser*, Feb. 14, 1865; Swayne's Report, Oct. 31, 1866; Swayne's Testimony, Report Joint Committee, Pt. III, pp. 138–141.

eral wandering. In the fall and winter a large majority returned to their old homes. "Once being assured of their liberty to go and come at will, they generally returned to the service of the southerner." [1] The courts gave substantial justice, it was reported; the judge and jury would prefer the case of a black to that of a mean white man; negro testimony in lawsuits was more and more favored, and the standing of the negro in the courts became more and more secure. Conditions as to the treatment of the negroes were steadily improving.[2] An unfriendly critic who travelled through the Gulf states said that the negro was fairly well paid and fairly well treated.[3] A charge to the grand jury of Pike County by Judge Henry D. Clayton, on September 9, 1866, will serve to show the sentiments of the judicial officers and members of the bar as well as juries. It was reprinted at the North as a campaign document. The following is a summary:—

A certain class of our population is clothed with civil rights and privileges that it did not possess until recently, and in dealing with them some embarrassment will be felt. One of the results of the war was the freedom of the black race. We deplore the result as injurious to the country and fatal to the negroes, but we are in honor bound to observe the laws which acknowledge their freedom. "When I took off my sword in surrender, I determined to observe the terms of that surrender with the same earnestness and fidelity with which I first shouldered my musket." We may cherish the glorious memories of that past, in the history of which there is nothing of which we need be ashamed, but now we have to reëstablish society and rebuild our ruined homes. Those unwilling to submit to this condition of things may seek homes abroad.[4] We are bound to this soil for better or for worse. What is our duty? Let us deal with the facts as they are. The negro has been made free, though he did not seek freedom. Nominally free, he is beyond expression helpless by his want of self-reliance, of experience, of ability to understand and appreciate his condition. For promoting his welfare and adapting him to this new

---

[1] Truman's Report, April 19, 1866; Mrs. Clayton, "White and Black," p. 152 *et passim;* "Our Women in the War," *passim; The Nation,* Oct. 5, 1865; Reid and Trowbridge.

[2] Truman's Report, April 19, 1865.   [3] *The Nation,* Feb. 15, 1866.

[4] Referring to the emigration movement to Mexico, Brazil, Europe, etc.

2 C

relation to society, all agencies from abroad will prove inadequate. The task is for us who understand him. To remedy the evil growing out of abolition two things are necessary: (1) we must recognize the freedom of the race as a fact, enact just and humane laws, and willingly enforce them; (2) we must in all our relations with the negro treat him with perfect fairness. We shall thus convince the world of our good faith, get rid of the system of espionage [the Freedmen's Bureau] by removing the pretext for its necessity, and secure the services of the negroes, teach them their place, and convince them that we are their friends. We need the labor of the negro and it is worth the effort to secure it. We owe the negro no grudge; he has done nothing to provoke our hostility; freedom was forced upon him. "He may have been the companion of your boyhood; he may be older than you, and perhaps carried you in his arms when an infant. You may be bound to him by a thousand ties which only a southern man knows, and which he alone can feel in all their force. It may be that when, only a few years ago, you girded on your cartridge box and shouldered your trusty rifle to go to meet the invaders of your country, you committed to his care your home and your loved ones; and when you were far away upon the weary march, upon the dreadful battle-field, in the trenches, and on the picket line, many and many a time you thought of that faithful old negro, and your heart warmed toward him." [1]

Movement toward Negro Suffrage

The Freedmen's Bureau and the provisional government had set aside, repealed, or suspended laws which treated the negro as a separate class. It was soon seen that the civil government had little real authority, being frequently overruled by the officials of the army

[1] This charge was published in the general presentments of the Pike County grand jury and was immediately taken up by the northern Democratic and the conservative Republican papers and given a wide publication. Mrs. Clayton republished it in her book (pp. 156–165). Judge Clayton was disfranchised by the Reconstruction Acts, and not until 1874 was he again able to hold judicial office. The bench and bar were generally in favor of admitting the negro to the fullest standing in the courts. Under slavery, when a case turned on negro testimony, extra-legal trials were often held and the decision given by "lynch-law" jury, the court officials presiding. In 1865 the lawyers and judges were ready to admit negro testimony, according to General Swayne, but made more or less objection in order not to alienate those of the people who objected.

and Bureau and by the President. The civil officials became accustomed to considering Swayne or Woods, the commander of the troops in Alabama, rather than the state government, as the source of authority. It was known that the Radicals were bent on giving the ballot to the negro and on disfranchising southern political and military leaders. Some politicians began to consider the question of giving the ballot to the negro under certain restrictions. This was not done from any faith in the political intelligence of the negro, or belief that he was fitted for or needed the exercise of the franchise; for it was and is an article of the political faith of the southern people that the exercise of suffrage is a high privilege, an historical and inherited right, not the natural and absolute right of all men. The reasons were very different, and were based entirely on expediency and necessity: (1) Such action would forestall the Radical programme and disarm, to some extent, the hostile party at the North. (2) It would enable the native leaders, by conferring the privilege on the negro, to gain his confidence, control his vote, and thereby make it harmless. It was certain, it seemed, that two widely separated white political parties would arise as soon as outside pressure should be removed, and each hoped to get control of most of the negro vote. (3) Such a measure would increase the representation of the state in the Congress, thus giving them needed strength at a critical period. (4) The Black Belt hoped in this way to regain its former political influence. The new constitution, by making the white population the basis of representation, had transferred political supremacy to the white counties.

As early as October, 1865, Truman remarked that some leaders were thinking of giving the ballot to the negroes. He thought that suffrage for the negroes would harm them and would inflame the lower classes of whites against them. But if left to the leaders and politicians, they, for the sake of increased representation in Congress, would bring the people around, and by 1870 the negro would be voting.[1] About the same time a correspondent of *The Nation* observed that there was no great objection to giving the negro the ballot because the white leaders thought that they could control it. It would not be opposed by the planters of the South, but by the middle and poorer classes, — the merchants, mechanics, and laborers.[2] Early in 1866

[1] Sen. Ex. Doc., No. 43, 39th Cong., 1st Sess.
[2] *The Nation*, Oct. 5, 1865.

Representative Brooks [1] of Lowndes, a black county, introduced a bill in the lower house providing for a qualified negro suffrage based on education and property.   It was laid on the table, but not before a calm and dispassionate discussion.   The bill proposed by Brooks was opposed more because it disfranchised a large number of whites than because it gave suffrage to the negro.   The debates showed that later the legislature would do something along that line if assured that such a course would result in readmission into the Union.   In the discussion the idea was urged that something must be done to prevent the Radicals from taking the question of suffrage to the central government.   This, it was held, would be dangerous to the South, with its peculiar population, to which general Federal legislation would not well apply, and hence it would be dangerous for the suffrage question to become one of national instead of state concern.   Then, too, the people were intensely weary of provisional rule, and wanted to resume their proper position in the Union. [2]

The people of the north Alabama white counties, the hilly section of the state, were opposed to any form of negro suffrage, though some of their leaders who understood the state of affairs were willing to think of it as a last resort to defeat the intentions of the Radicals. The Black Belt people, who had less prejudice against the negro and who were sure that they could control him and gain in political power, were more favorably inclined.   Left alone, the various interests would have united to carry through the project in time.   Suffrage so conferred upon the blacks would have been strictly limited, — a premium offered, not a right acknowledged, — under the control of the native white leaders and supporting their interests, just exactly the situation of the lower-class voters everywhere else, and the reverse of the southern situation since 1867.

One of the north Alabama leaders, L. Pope Walker, [3] after consulting with other prominent men, went to Montgomery and conferred with General Swayne in regard to the state of affairs.   Swayne gave assurance that a qualified negro suffrage would be favorably received

[1] Brooks was a cousin of Preston Brooks of South Carolina, and had been president of the convention of 1861. The measure was indorsed by Governor Patton, Judge Goldthwaite, and a respectable minority. Ku Klux Rept., Ala. Test., p. 226.

[2] McPherson's scrap-book, " Fourteenth Amendment," p. 55.

[3] First Confederate Secretary of War, brigadier-general, C.S.A.

at the North, would create a good impression, and assist, perhaps, in an early restoration of the state to the Union. He knew that suffrage for the negro brought about in this way would result in gaining the black vote for the southern and probably for the Democratic party. Though a believer in the rights of all men to vote and a strong Republican, Swayne was not then committed to the Radical programme and was ready to encourage the movement. An opportunity for the entering wedge was now at hand. Many of the minor magistrates and the sheriffs were also administering the affairs of the Freedmen's Bureau, and consequently were more or less under the direction of Swayne, who was the assistant commissioner in Alabama. His instructions to agents, before the convention, directed that all laws be administered without regard to color. Governor Parsons approved these directions and required all provisional officers to take oath accordingly. The convention sanctioned this arrangement, and ordered it to continue until the close of the next general assembly. This general assembly had practically continued the arrangements already made. In consequence, the state officials, whether willingly or not, were still, at the time when the movement for negro suffrage began, obliged to obey the directions of Swayne. The bulk of the people being opposed to the movement, it was proposed to make an experiment on the responsibility of the Freedmen's Bureau and to use that much-disliked institution as an instrument, for the people would not be much surprised at anything it would do. So the sheriff of Madison County, in the winter of 1866–1867, when some local election was at hand, wrote to General Swayne, asking if the election laws also were to be carried out regardless of color. He announced his willingness to carry out instructions. Here was an opportunity to begin the experiment, but public feeling became so irritated by the Radical measures in Congress that nothing was done, the election was not held, and the Reconstruction Acts, coming soon after, prejudiced the people more strongly than ever against anything of the kind.[1]

[1] For this incident my authority is a statement of General Swayne made to me in 1901. He was much interested in the movement, and was positive that in time the native whites would have given the suffrage to the negro had not the Reconstruction Acts and other legislation so alienated the races. General Swayne gave me full explanations of his policy in Alabama. His death, a year after the interview, prevented him from verifying some details. His account, though given thirty-five years after the occur-

About December 1, 1866, a bill was introduced into the state legislature "to amend the constitution of the state according to impartial suffrage, and then ask representation, leaving the amnesty question in the hand of Congress." Reporting this action to Chief Justice Chase, Swayne added: "This I am told is popular, and the member is sustained by his constituents." [1] The legislature, at the same time, intended to reject the Fourteenth Amendment.

It has been stated that in February, 1867, an effort was made, with the indorsement of the President, to induce the southern legislatures which had rejected the Fourteenth Amendment to adopt a qualified negro suffrage. This was tried in Alabama and North Carolina, and probably hastened congressional Reconstruction. [2]

With the passage of the Reconstruction Acts and other congressional action in regard to the negroes, affairs changed complexion rapidly. The alienation of the races began. It was seen that the negro vote would now be controlled by worthless outsiders and native whites. The expected division of the whites into two well-defined parties did not occur; there was an almost united white party. A few whites, indeed, there were who were ready to try negro suffrage, not those, however, who had been thinking of it during the past two years. The result of the war had intensified party spirit. The old "Union" men were intensely bitter against the secessionists or "precipitators," and in the present crisis some otherwise good citizens were so blinded by party passion as to put revenge above the welfare of their country, and were ready to accept the aid of their former slaves in their fight against the men whom they considered responsible for the present condition of affairs. Others who now took up negro suffrage were mere politicians, content to take office at any price to the country, and who could never hope for office until existing institutions were destroyed. [3]

rences, was correct so far as I could compare it with the printed matter available. It agreed almost exactly with his reports as printed in the public documents, though he had not those at hand, and had not seen them for thirty years. I have several times been told by old citizens that negroes voted in 1866, in minor elections, by consent of the whites.

[1] "Diary and Correspondence of S. P. Chase," in the Annual Report of the Amer. Hist. Assn. (1902), Vol. II, p. 517.

[2] Stephen B. Weeks, in *Polit. Sci. Quarterly* (1894), Vol. IX, pp. 683–684.

[3] See Herbert, "Solid South," pp. 29, 30, 37.

New Conditions of Congress and Increasing Irritation

The first general assembly under the provisional government ratified the Thirteenth Amendment, "with the understanding that it does
not confer upon Congress the power to legislate upon the political
status of freedmen in this state."[1] The same legislature requested
the President to order the withdrawal of the Federal troops on duty
in Alabama, for their presence was a source of much disorder and
there was no need of them.[2]

The President was asked to release Hon. C. C. Clay, Jr., who
was still in prison.[3] At the end of the session a resolution was adopted
approving the policy of President Johnson and pledging coöperation
with his "wise, firm, and just" work; asserting that the results of
the late contest were conclusive, and that there was no desire to renew
discussion on settled questions; denouncing the misrepresentations
and criminal assaults on the character and interest of the southern
people; declaring that it was a misfortune of the present political
conditions that there were persons among them whose interests were promoted by false representations; confidence was expressed in the power of the administration to protect the state from
malign influences; slavery was abolished and should not be reëstablished; the negro race should be treated with humanity, justice,
and good faith, and every means be used to make them useful and
intelligent members of society; but "Alabama will not voluntarily
consent to change the adjustment of political power as fixed by the
Constitution of the United States, and to constrain her to do so in
her present prostrate and helpless condition, with no voice in the
councils of the nation, would be an unjustifiable breach of faith."[4]

During the year 1866 there was a growing spirit of independence
in the Alabama politics. At no time had there been a subservient
spirit, but for a time the people, fully accepting the results of the
war, were disposed to do nothing more than conform to any reasonable
conditions which might be imposed, feeling sure that the North would

[1] Resolution, Dec. 2, 1865, Acts of Ala. (1865–1866), p. 598.
[2] Resolution, Jan. 16, 1866, Acts of Ala. (1865–1866), p. 603.
[3] Resolution, Dec. 15, 1865, Acts of Ala. (1865–1866), p. 604.
[4] Resolution, Feb. 22, 1866, Acts of Ala. (1865–1866), p. 607; McPherson, p. 22;
Selma Times, Feb. 27, 1867.

impose none that were dishonorable. To them at first the President represented the feeling of the people of the North, perhaps worse. The theory of state sovereignty having been destroyed by the war, the state rights theories of Lincoln and Johnson were easily accepted by the southerners, who were content, after Johnson had modified his policy, to leave affairs in his hands. When the serious differences between the executive and Congress appeared, and the latter showed a desire to impose degrading terms on the South, the people believed that their only hope was in Johnson. They believed the course of Congress to be inspired by a desire for revenge. Heretofore the people had taken little interest in public affairs. Enough voters went to the polls and voted to establish and keep in operation the provisional government. The general belief was that the political questions would settle themselves or be settled in a manner fairly satisfactory to the South. Now a different spirit arose. The southerners thought that they had complied with all the conditions ever asked that could be complied with without loss of self-respect. The new conditions of Congress exhausted their patience and irritated their pride. Self-respecting men could not tamely submit to such treatment.[1]

During the latter part of 1865 and in 1866, ex-Governor Parsons travelled over the North, speaking in the chief cities in support of the policy of the President. He asked the northern people to rebuke at the polls the political fanatics who were inflaming the minds of the people North and South. He demanded the withdrawal of the military. There had been, he said, no sign of hostility since the surrender; the people were opposed to any legislation which would give the negro the right to vote; and it was the duty of the President, not of Congress, to enforce the laws.[2]

Much angry discussion was caused by the passage of the Freedmen's Bureau Bill in 1866. The Bureau officials had caused themselves to be hated by the whites. They were a nuisance, when no worse, and useless,—a plague to the people. Though there were comparatively few in the state, they were the cause of disorder and ill-feeling between the races. Though there was now even less need of the institution than a year before, the new measure was much more

[1] See N. Y. Herald, April 17, 1866 (Alabama correspondence).
[2] McPherson's scrap-book, "The Campaign of 1866," Vol. I, pp. 84, 122.

offensive in its provisions.[1] There was great rejoicing when the President vetoed the bill, which the *Mobile Times* called "an infamous disorganization scheme of radicalism." The Bureau had become a political machine for work among white and black. The passage of the bill over the veto was felt to be a blow at the prostrate South.[2]

The Civil Rights Bill of 1866 was also a cause of irritation. There was a disposition among the officials of the Freedmen's Bureau to enforce all such measures before they became law. Orders were issued directing the application of the principles of measures then before Congress. The United States commissioner in Mobile decided that under the "Civil Rights Bill"[3] negroes could ride on the cars set apart for the whites. Horton, the Radical military mayor of Mobile, banished to New Orleans an idiotic negro boy who had been hired to follow him and torment him by offensive questions. Horton was indicted under the "Civil Rights Bill" and convicted. The people of Mobile were much pleased when a "Yankee official was the first to be caught in the trap set for southerners."[4]

Another citizen of Mobile, a magistrate, was haled before a Federal court, charged with having sentenced a negro to be whipped, contrary to the provisions of the "Civil Rights Bill." The magistrate explained that there was nothing at all offensive about the whipping. He had not acted in his magisterial capacity, but had himself whipped the negro boy for lying, stealing, and neglect of duty while in his employ.[5] The agent of the Bureau at Selma notified the mayor that the "chain gang system of working convicts on the streets had to be discontinued or he would be prosecuted for violation of the 'Civil Rights Bill.'"[6] Judge Hardy of Selma decided in a case brought before him that the "Civil Rights Bill" was unconstitutional. He declared it to be an attack on the independence of the judiciary.[7]

[1] See Burgess, "Reconstruction," pp. 64–67.

[2] McPherson's scrap-book, "Freedmen's Bureau Bill, 1866," pp. 47, 128.

[3] The reconstruction laws of Congress were almost invariably referred to as "Bills" even in official documents and military orders.

[4] McPherson's scrap-book, "Civil Rights Bill, 1866," pp. 136, 151.

[5] McPherson's scrap-book, "Civil Rights Bill, 1866," p. 135.

[6] McPherson's scrap-book, "Civil Rights Bill, 1866," p. 110.

[7] McPherson's scrap-book, "Civil Rights Bill, 1866," p. 120.

Rejection of the Fourteenth Amendment

In the fall of 1866 the proposed Fourteenth Amendment was submitted to the legislature. There was no longer any belief that further yielding would do any good; the more the people gave the more was asked. State Senator E. A. Powell wrote to John W. Forney that the people would do nothing about the Fourteenth Amendment because they were convinced that any action would be useless. Condition after condition had been imposed and had been absolved; slavery had been abolished, secession acknowledged a failure, and the war debt repudiated by the convention; the legislature had ratified the Thirteenth Amendment, had secured the negro in all the rights of property and person; and after all the state was no nearer to restoration.[1] This was the view of nearly all the newspapers of the state, and in this they represented popular opinion. They were intensely irritated by the fact that, although they had made so many concessions, still they were excluded from representation in Congress, and were heavily and unjustly taxed.[2] Moreover, they were opposed to the amendment because it branded their best men as traitors.[3] One newspaper, alone, advocated adoption of the amendment as the least of evils.[4]

John Forsyth, in the *Mobile Register*, said: "It is one thing to be oppressed, wronged, and outraged by overwhelming force. It is quite another to submit to voluntary abasement" by adopting the Fourteenth Amendment. It should be rejected, he said, because it would disfranchise the very best of the respectable whites, the beloved leaders of the people. Judge Busteed, in a charge to the Federal grand jury, delivered a political harangue advocating the adoption of the Amendment. Many ultra "union" men in north Alabama opposed the Amendment for three reasons: (1) though it would disfranchise the leaders, the great mass of the white people would still be allowed to vote, especially those who had not held civil office during the war; (2) some of these "union" men had been ardent secessionists at the beginning and had thus compromised themselves,

---

[1] McPherson's scrap-book, "Fourteenth Amendment," pp. 33, 34.

[2] The cotton tax, for instance.

[3] Ku Klux Rept., Ala. Test., p. 226.

[4] *N. Y. Tribune*, Nov. 30, 1866. I have not been able to discover what the name of the paper was, but very likely it was the *Mobile National*.

or had been elected to the legislature or to some "bomb-proof" office
during the war — as "obstructionists," they claimed — and the proposed amendment would disfranchise them along with the Confederate leaders; (3) this class as a rule disliked the negro and never wanted
negro suffrage if it were possible to secure the overthrow of existing
institutions without it.   Two planters of the Black Belt were ready
for negro suffrage to one "buckra." [1]   Those men who considered
themselves "unionists" wanted no negro suffrage, nor anything
so weak as the Fourteenth Amendment; but desired some kind of a
military régime in which the United States government should place
them in permanent possession of the state administration and exclude
all who were not like themselves.   The test should be a political
one, they said.   It seems to be a fact that a few hundred such men
with, at the most, five thousand followers expected to have the whole
state administration under their direction for years.   Yet it would
have required a special law of exemption for each of them in order
to protect them from the proscription which was to be visited upon
the ex-Confederates.   For these "unionists" had often betrayed
both sides during the war.   Their most patriotic duty had been
"obstruction."

By most persons the question of negro political rights was considered to belong to the state and was not a matter for the Federal
government to regulate.   "Loyalists" as well as "rebels" were afraid
to leave negro affairs to the regulation of Congress.   In his annual
message to the legislature, in November, 1866, Governor Patton
advised the legislature not to ratify the Fourteenth Amendment,
on the ground that it could do no good and might do harm.   It
involved a creation of a penalty after the act.   On this point, he said
that it was an *ex post facto* law, and contrary to the whole spirit of
modern civilization; that such a mode of dealing with citizens charged
with offences against government belonged only to despotic tyrants;
that it might accomplish revengeful purposes, but that was not the
proper mode of administering justice; that adoption would vacate
merely all offices in most of the unrepresented states — governors,
judges, legislators, sheriffs, justices of peace, constables — and the
state governments would be completely broken up and reduced to
utter and hopeless anarchy; that the disabilities imposed by the

[1] McPherson's scrap-book, "Fourteenth Amendment," pp. 39, 55, 56.

test oath were seriously detrimental to the interests of the government; that ratification of the Amendment could not accomplish any good to the country and might bring upon it irretrievable disaster.[1]

Under the circumstances, the legislature refused to consider the Amendment. But the governor during the next few weeks was induced by various considerations to recommend the ratification, and on December 7, 1866, he sent a special message stating that there was a purpose on the part of those who controlled the national legislation to enforce their own terms of restoration at all hazards; and that their measures would immeasurably augment the distress already existing and inaugurate endless confusion. The cardinal principle of restoration seemed to be, he said, favorable action on the Fourteenth Amendment. Upon principle he was opposed to it. Yet necessity must rule. So now he recommended reconsideration. If they should ratify and restoration should follow, they might trust to time and their representatives to mitigate its harshness. If they should ratify and admission should be delayed, it would serve as a warning to other states and thus prevent the necessary number for ratification.[2]

The message created excitement in the legislature and the chances were favorable for ratification; but ex-Governor Parsons, who was in the North, advised against it. He thought the northern people would support the President in the matter. The legislature refused to ratify by a vote of 27 to 2 in the Senate, and 69 to 8 in the House.[3] Potter of Cherokee gave notice that on January 15 he would move to reconsider the vote. Governor Patton, moreover, was convinced

[1] Governor's Message, Nov. 12, 1866, in House Journal (1866–1867), p. 35 ; *N. Y. Tribune*, Nov. 19, 1866 ; Annual Cyclopædia (1866), pp. 11, 12.

[2] House Journal (1866–1867), p. 198.

[3] McPherson, p. 194 ; McPherson's scrap-book, " Fourteenth Amendment," p. 55; *N. Y. Times*, Jan. 23, 1867. General Wager Swayne to S. P. Chase, Dec. 10, 1866, wrote, in substance, that — the evident intention of Congress to enforce its own plan makes it seem possible to secure from the Alabama legislature the ratification of the Amendment ; that the Senate was ready to ratify in spite of the governor's message against it, and of the certain disapproval of "the people, poor, ignorant, and without mail facilities," but a despatch had been sent to Parsons in the North for advice, and he advised rejection; inspired, it was asserted by the President, the cry was raised, "we can't desert *our* President," and the measure was lost ; but when they return (in January) they will be prepared for either course, and the governor will recommend ratification. "Diary and Correspondence of S. P. Chase," in the Annual Rept. of the Amer. Hist. Assn. (1902), Vol. II, pp. 516–517.

that Congress meant to carry out its plan of reconstruction, and that opposition might make matters worse. General Swayne kept a strong pressure upon him, assuring him that Congress would have its own way. During the Christmas holidays the governor made speeches in north Alabama in favor of ratifying the Amendment. Congress would require it, he said. On principle he opposed the measure, but it must come at last. "Look the situation squarely in the face," he said; only 2000 or 3000 men (himself included) would be deprived of office, and to oppose Congress was to ruin the state, to territorialize it. There were men in Washington, he said, who were already working in order to be made provisional governor under the new régime.[1] After the recess Patton sent a second message recommending that the Amendment be adopted, since it was the evident purpose of Congress to enforce their own terms.[2] For a day or two it was considered, General Swayne and the governor using their influence with the members, and it seemed almost sure to be ratified. But Parsons, then in Montgomery, telegraphed (January 17, 1867) to the President that the legislature was reconsidering the Amendment. Johnson replied saying that no possible good could come of such action; that he did not believe the people of the country would sustain "any set of individuals" in attempts to change the whole character of the government, but that they would uphold those who stood by the Constitution; and that there should be no faltering on the part of those who were determined to sustain the coördinate departments of the government in accordance with its original design. For the third time the Amendment failed to pass.[3] One of the last resolutions passed by the provisional legislature before it was abolished by the Reconstruction Acts was on February 1, 1867, in regard to memorializing Congress to establish a uniform system of bankruptcy. Relief was needed, they stated, "yet the promptings of self-respect forbid the propriety of further intruding our appeals upon a Congress which refuses to recognize the state of Alabama for any purpose other than that of taxation. It is a source of regret that Congress has assumed

---

[1] *N. Y. Times*, Jan. 9, 1867. Patton also went to Washington during the recess.

[2] Annual Cyclopædia (1866), pp. 11, 12.

[3] McPherson, pp. 352, 353; McPherson's scrap-book, "Fourteenth Amendment," pp. 60, 66. The telegrams are in the Impeachment Testimony, Vol. I, pp. 271-272. Interview with General Swayne, 1901.

an attitude toward the state of Alabama totally incompatible with the mutual obligations of allegiance and protection." [1]

Political Conditions, 1865-1867; Formation of Parties

In the convention of 1865 two well-defined parties had appeared, though generally, at that time, for the sake of harmony they acted together. These parties grew farther and farther apart. One of them, consisting of most of the people, especially of the central and southern section of the state, supported the policy of the President. The other party was a motley opposition. In it were the few original "Union" men, the tories, and many more self-styled "union" men, who saw an opportunity for advancement for themselves if the present government were overthrown. There were others who thought that the old ruling class should now retire absolutely from public life and allow their former followers to take their places. There was a fair sprinkling of respectable men who were bitterly opposed to any party or policy that suited the former Democrats, and believing that Congress would not be too severe, they were willing to see three or four thousand of the leaders disfranchised in order to get the state back into the Union. They were willing also to become leaders themselves in the place of those disfranchised.

During the year 1866 these parties were organized to some degree, held meetings, and made bids for northern support. The opposition worked into the hands of the Radical party at the North, though many of them did not favor the full Radical programme, especially as regarded negro suffrage. The other party took the name of the "Conservative" or "Democratic and Conservative." It was composed of former Democrats, Whigs, Know-nothings, Anti-Know-nothings, Bell and Everett men, — nearly all of the respectable voting people. These allied with the "Conservative" party in other southern states and with the Democrats in the North and formed the "National Union Party." Its platform was essentially the presidential plan of Reconstruction.[2] The campaign of 1866 was made on many issues, — the Civil Rights Bill, Freedmen's Bureau Bill, Fourteenth Amendment, the plans of Reconstruction. Ex-Governor Parsons and other prominent Alabamians spoke in the cities of the North in support of

---

[1] Annual Cyclopædia (1867), p. 15.   [2] See McPherson, pp. 118, 240, 241.

the policy of the President. Ex-Governor Shorter, in a public letter, said that he had been a "rebel" until the close of the war, and understood the feeling of the people of Alabama. There had not been since the surrender and there was not now, he said, any antagonism to the United States government, and Reconstruction based on the assumption of this would be harmful and hopeless. The people had given their allegiance to the government and had remodelled their state organizations in good faith.[1]

"Southern outrages" now began afresh. The Radical press and Radical politicians began to manufacture tales of outrage and cruelty on the part of the southern whites against negroes. There had been all along a disposition to look for "outrages" in the South, and the reports of Schurz and the Joint Committee on Reconstruction seemed to put the seal of truth on the tissue of falsehoods, and for campaign purposes "outrages" were increased. For several years, judging from some accounts, the entire white population — men, women, and children — must have given much of their time to persecuting, beating, and killing negroes and northern men. The Radical papers seized upon the silly things said or done by the idlers of bar-rooms and street corners or printed in the small newspapers and magnified them into the "threatening voice of a whole people." Against this mistake General Swayne repeatedly protested. He had no special liking for the southern people, but he scorned to misrepresent the true state of affairs for political capital. During his stay in the state (more than two years) the tenor of his reports was: There was no trouble from the southern whites; northern men were welcomed in a business way; disorder and lawlessness existed in sections of the state, but this was a natural result of long war and civil strife among the people. In his reports, Swayne repeatedly stated that as time went on the condition of affairs was gradually improving. Newspaper correspondents sent to write up conditions in the South went among the most worthless part of the population, in bar-rooms, hotel lobbies, on street corners, in country groceries, and wrote up the doings and sayings of these people as representative of all. Even E. L. Godkin was not above doing such a thing at times.[2]

[1] *N. Y. Herald*, July 19, 1866.
[2] According to his own report. See *Nation*, Feb. 15, 1866. Hart, "American History as told by Contemporaries," Vol. IV, p. 49.

These writers carefully recorded the idle talk about the negro and the North and dressed it up for Radical information. A favorite plan was to find some woman, coarse and vulgar and cruel-minded, and describe her and her speeches as representative of southern women. The southern newspapers republished such correspondence as specimens of Radical methods. The whites were more and more irritated. This aggravating correspondence and the more aggravating editorials continued in some papers long after the Reconstruction period.[1]

On the other hand, northern men received little or no social welcome in the South. Most of them would not have been sought after in any section; few representatives of northern culture came South. The indiscretions of some caused the ostracism of all. But that was not the sole reason. General Swayne seemed surprised at "social exclusion" and mentioned it before the Reconstruction sub-committee. But, said an Alabama correspondent, what else can he expect? Why is he surprised? Can the sister, the mother, and the father who have lost their loved ones care to meet those who did the deeds? They meet with respectful treatment; let them not ask too much.[2]

What the people needed and wanted was a settled and certain policy. The mixed administrations of the provisional authorities and the President, of the Freedmen's Bureau and the army, did not result in respect for the laws. The talk of confiscation and disfranchisement kept the people irritated. They thought that they had already complied with the conditions imposed precedent to admission to the Union and now believed that Congress was acting in bad faith. Many were willing to affiliate even with conservative Republicans in order to overthrow the Radicals. Much was hoped for in the way of good results from the "National Union" movement. Few or none of the northern business men in the state thought that the Radical plan was necessary. They did not expect or desire its success.[3]

---

[1] Report of B. C. Truman, April 9, 1866; Report of Joint Committee, 1866, Pt. III, *passim;* Report of Schurz with accompanying documents; *N. Y. Times,* Sept. 9 and Oct. 3, 1866; *Nation,* Feb. 15, *et passim; World* and *Tribune; Herald* and *Tribune* correspondent, 1865; *Montgomery Mail and Advertiser; Selma Times; Tuscaloosa Monitor and Blade,* 1865 to 1875. Of the New York papers the *Nation* and *Tribune* were especially violent at first, but changed later. The *Times* and the *Herald* had fair correspondents most of the time.

[2] *N. Y. Daily News,* May 7, 1866 (Montgomery correspondent).

[3] See *N. Y. Times,* Sept. 9, 1866 (Federal soldier), Oct. 3, 1866 (Ohio man); *N. Y. News,* May 7, 1866 (Montgomery correspondent).

There was a convention of the Conservative party at Selma in July, 1866. Delegates were elected to the National Union convention at Philadelphia.[1] The Selma convention indorsed the policy of Johnson and condemned the Radical party as the great obstacle to peace. The most prominent men of the state were present, representing both of the old parties — Whigs and Democrats.[2] The national platform adopted in Philadelphia stated the principles to which the southerners had now committed themselves, viz.: the war had decided the national character of the Constitution; but the restrictions imposed by it upon the general government were unchanged and the rights and authority of the states were unimpaired; representation in Congress and in the electoral college was a right guaranteed by the Constitution to every state, and Congress had no power to deny such right; Congress had no power to regulate the suffrage; there is no right of withdrawal from the Union; amendments to the Constitution must be made as provided for by the Constitution, and all states had the right to a vote on an amendment; negroes should receive protection in all rights of person and property; the national debt was declared inviolable, the Confederate debt utterly invalid; and Andrew Johnson's administration was indorsed.[3]

Ex-Governor Parsons and others from Alabama spoke in New York, New Jersey, Maine, and Pennsylvania, at National Union meetings. Parsons told the North that the conservative people of Alabama were in charge of the administration, and would not send extreme men to Congress; the representatives chosen had opposed secession. The "Union" party, — a large one in the state, — he said, had hoped that after the war each individual would have to answer for himself, but instead all were suffering in common.[4]

[1] Lewis E. Parsons (New York), Whig; George S. Houston; A. B. Cooper.(New Jersey), Whig; John Forsyth, State Rights Democrat; R. B. Lindsay (Scotch), Douglas Democrat; James W. Taylor, Whig; Benjamin Fitzpatrick, Douglas Democrat.

[2] Some of them were W. H. Crenshaw (Democrat), who presided, — Crenshaw was then president of the Senate; John G. Shorter (Democrat), war governor of Alabama; H. D. Clayton (Whig), Confederate general; C. C. Langdon (Whig); William S. Mudd (Whig); William Garrett (Whig); M. J. Bulger (Douglas Democrat), Confederate general; C. A. Battle (Democrat), Confederate general; A. Tyson (Whig). See Brewer and Garrett, and *N. Y. Times*, Aug. 3 and 9, 1866.

[3] McPherson, pp. 240, 241.

[4] *N. Y. Times*, Aug. 27, 1866. By "Union" party, Parsons evidently meant those who opposed secession.

2 D

The opposition party was weak in numbers and especially weak in leaders. The tory and deserter element, with a few from the obstructionists of the war time and malcontents of the present who wanted office, made up the native portion of the party. Northern adventurers, principally agents of the Freedmen's Bureau, teachers and missionaries, and men who had failed to succeed in some southern speculation, with a number of those who follow in the path of armies to secure the spoils, composed the alien wing of the opposition party.[1] The fundamental principle upon which the existence of the party was based required the destruction of present institutions and the creation of a new political people who should be kept in power by Federal authority. The northern soldiers of fortune saw at once that it would be necessary to give the ballot to the negro. The native Radicals disliked the idea of negro suffrage and seemed to think that the central government should proscribe all others, place them in power and hold them there by armed force until they could create a party.

Such a party could secure a northern alliance only with the extreme Radical wing of the Republican party. A convention of "Southern Unionists" was held in Washington, in July, 1866, which issued an address to the "loyalists" of the South, declaring that the reconstruction of the southern state governments must be based on constitutional principles, and the present despotism under an atrocious leadership must not be permitted to remain; the rights of the citizens must not be left to the protection of the states, but Congress must take charge of the matter and make protection coextensive with citizenship; under the present state governments, with "rebels" controlling, there would be no safety for loyalists, — they must rely on Congress for protection. A meeting of "southern loyalists" was called to be held in September, in Independence Hall in Philadelphia.[2] The Alabama delegates to this convention were George Reese, D. H. Bingham, M. J. Saffold, and J. H. Larcombe. This Philadelphia convention condemned the "rebellion as unparalleled for its causelessness, its cruelty, and its criminality." "The unhappy policy" of the President was "unjust, oppressive, and intolerable." The policy of Congress was indorsed, but regret was expressed that it did not pro-

[1] The northern business men were on the side of the whites.
[2] McPherson, p. 124.

vide by law for the greater security of the "loyal" people in the southern states. Demand was made for "the establishment of influences of patriotism and justice" in each of the southern states. Washington, Lincoln, the Declaration of Independence, Philadelphia, and Independence Hall — all were brought in. The question of negro suffrage was discussed, and most of the delegates favored it. Of the five delegates from Alabama, two announced themselves against it.[1] At a Radical convention in Philadelphia about the same time the delegates from Alabama were Albert Griffin, an adventurer from Ohio; D. H. Bingham, a bitter tory, almost demented with hate; and M. J. Saffold, who had been an obstructionist during the war. Here was the beginning of the alliance of carpet-bagger and scalawag that was destined to ruin the state in six years of peace worse than four years of war had done. The convention indulged in unstinted abuse of Johnson and demanded "no mercy" for Davis. Bingham was one of the committee that presented the hysterical report demanding the destruction of the provisional governments in the South. Saffold opposed the negro suffrage plank. He had no prejudice himself, he explained, but thought it was not expedient. He was hissed and evidently brought to the correct opinion.[2]

After the report of the Joint Committee on Reconstruction in 1866 it was believed by the Radicals that Congress would be victorious over the President, and the party in Alabama that expected to control the government under the new régime began to hold meetings and organize preparatory to dividing the offices. January 8-9, 1867, a thinly attended "Unconditional Union Mass-meeting" was held at Moulton, in Lawrence County. Eleven of the counties of north Alabama were represented, the hill and mountain people predominating. Nicholas Davis, who presided, said that none but "loyal" men must control the states, lately in rebellion.[3] The action of Congress was com-

---

[1] McPherson, p. 242.   [2] *N. Y. Times*, Sept. 8, 1866.

[3] Davis was of good middle-class Virginia stock. A Whig in politics, Mrs. Chesnut called him "a social curiosity." In convention of 1861 he voted against immediate secession, threatened resistance among the hills of north Alabama, and ended by signing the ordinance of secession; was chosen to succeed Dr. Fearn in the Confederate Provisional Congress; was appointed lieutenant-colonel of the 19th Alabama Infantry, but declined; commanded a battalion for a while; his "loyalty" consisted in his leaving the Confederate service and returning to Huntsville within the Federal lines. Brewer, p. 365, Garrett, pp. 341, 342; Smith's Debates, *passim*. He soon fell out with the carpet-baggers and "formed a party of one."

mended by the convention; the proposed Fourteenth Amendment was indorsed; and Congress was asked to distinguish between the "precipitators" and those "coerced or otherwise led by the usurpers." [1] They asked for $100 a year bounty for all Union soldiers from north Alabama, and for the compensation of Unionists for property lost during the war. The leaders here present were Freedmen's Bureau agents, Confederate deserters, and former obstructionists.[2]

A "Union" convention was held in Huntsville, March 4, 1867. Seventeen north Alabama counties were represented by much the same crowd that attended the Moulton convention.[3] General Swayne was there, carried along by the current, and, it was said, hoping for high office under the new régime.[4] The convention declared that a large portion of the people of the South had been opposed to secession, but rather than have civil war at home had acquiesced in the revolution; that the true position of these "unionists" now was with the party that would protect them against future rebellion; it was necessary that the Federal government be strengthened; the "union" men of each county were asked to hold meetings and send delegates to a state convention to be held during the summer.[5]

The spring of 1867 saw the white Radical party stronger than it ever was again. The few native whites who were to take part in the Reconstruction had chosen their side. After this time the party gradually lost all its respectable members. The carpet-baggers and

---

[1] The disposition of some of the north Alabama leaders (even among the Conservatives) to play the childish act was one of the disgusting features of Reconstruction.

[2] *N. Y. Times*, Jan. 23, 1867. Among those present were: D. C. Humphreys (Douglas Democrat), Confederate officer, who deserted to Federals (he was in the first carpet-bag legislature, and later judge of the Supreme Court of the District of Columbia; see Garrett, p. 364); John B. Callis, agent of the Freedmen's Bureau, Veteran Reserve Corps, member of Congress, 1868; C. C. Sheets, in convention of 1861, refused to sign ordinance of secession and deserted to Federals, a member of Congress, 1868; Thomas M. Peters, Whig, deserted to Federals, later judge of Supreme Court of Alabama (see Brewer, p. 309; Garrett, p. 440); F. W. Sykes, member of legislature during war, soon returned to Conservative party (Brewer, p. 309); J. J. Hinds, afterward a notorious scalawag.

[3] One new man was S. C. Posey of Lauderdale, who had been in the convention of 1861 and refused to sign the ordinance of secession and was in the legislature during the war. Returned soon to Conservative party. Brewer, p. 299, Garrett, p. 389.

[4] The Radical party might have done much worse than to send him to the Senate. Warren and Spencer, the senators elected, were far inferior in character and abilities to Swayne. He was too decent a man to suit the Radicals and was soon dropped.

[5] *N. Y. Herald*, March 6, 1867.

Bureau agents had not yet shown their strength. The scalawags did not foresee that to the carpet-baggers would fall the lion's share of the plunder, owing to their control over the negro vote.

The President's plan failed, not because of any inherent defect in itself, but because of the bungling manner in which it was administered. If President Jonhson had been content to place confidence in any one of the agencies to which were intrusted the government of the South, it would have been better. Had the governments set up by him been endowed with vigor, it is probable that Congress would not have fallen wholly under the control of the Radicals. The penalty for the indiscretions of the President was visited upon the South. To-day the southern people like to believe that, had Lincoln lived, his policy would have succeeded, and the horrors of Reconstruction would have been mitigated or prevented. Johnson's policy was that of Lincoln, except that he reserved to himself a much larger part in setting up and running the provisional governments. He established state governments, pronounced them constitutional, completed, perfected, and asked Congress to recognize them before he had proclaimed the rebellion at an end or restored the privilege of the writ of *habeas corpus*.[1]

He interfered himself, and allowed or ordered the army to interfere, in the smallest details of local administration. The military rule in Alabama was on the whole as well administered as it could be, which is seldom well. There were too few soldiers and the posts were too widely separated for the exercise of any firm or consistent authority. But the people were sorry to see even the worst of this give place to the reign of carpet-bagger, scalawag, and negro. The interference of the army and the President discredited the civil government in the minds of the people. The absolute rule of the President over the whole of ten states, though never used for bad purposes, was, nevertheless, not to be viewed with equanimity by those who were afraid of the almost absolute power that the executive had assumed during the war. That the power had not been used for bad purposes was no guarantee against future misuse. There was some excuse for the pretended fright of the Radical leaders, like Sumner and Stevens, and the real anxiety of more moderate men, at the dicta-

[1] The proclamation announcing that the rebellion had ended was issued April 2, 1866. McPherson, p. 15.

torial course of Johnson. But it must be said that a desire for a share in political appointments was a cause of much of this "real anxiety."

From 1865 to 1868, and even later, there was, for all practical purposes, over the greater part of the people of Alabama, no government at all. There was little disorder; the people were busy with their own affairs. Public opinion ruled the respectable people. Until the close of Reconstruction, the military and civil government touched the people mainly to annoy. From 1865 to 1874 government and respect for government were weakened to a degree from which it has not yet recovered. The people governed themselves extra-legally and have not recovered from the practice.

By taking cases from the civil authorities for trial before military commission, by dictating the course of the civil government, by nullifying the actions of the highest executive officers, the acts of the legislature, and the decisions of the highest courts, the army was mainly responsible for the lack of confidence in the civil administration.

CHAPTER X

MILITARY GOVERNMENT, 1865-1866

IN the account of the affairs thus far we have seen many evidences of the active participation of the military power of the United States in the conduct of government in Alabama. It will be useful at this point to examine with some care the form and scope of the authority concerned during the period of the provisional state government's existence.

The Military Division of the Tennessee (1863), under General Grant, included the Department of the Cumberland, under the command of General George H. Thomas. Several counties of north Alabama in the possession of the Federals formed a part of this department and for three years were governed entirely by the army, except for two short intervals, when the Federal forces were flanked and forced to retire. Anarchy then reigned, for the civil government had been almost entirely destroyed in ten of the northern counties. June 7, 1865, the Military Division of the Tennessee was reorganized under General Thomas, and included in it was the Department of Alabama, commanded by General C. R. Woods, with headquarters at Mobile. In October, 1865, Georgia and Alabama were united into a military province called the Department of the Gulf, under General Woods. This department was still in the Military Division of the Tennessee, commanded by General Thomas. June 1, 1866, Alabama and Georgia were formed into the Department of the South and were still in Thomas's Military Division of the Tennessee. General Woods commanded, with headquarters at Macon, Georgia. Alabama was ruled by General Swayne from Montgomery. August 6, 1866, the Military Division of the Tennessee was discontinued and was made a department, General Thomas retaining the command. In this department Georgia and Alabama formed the District of the Chattahoochee, with headquarters at Macon, commanded by General Woods. The Sub-district of Alabama was commanded by General Swayne, who was also in charge of the Freedmen's Bureau at Montgomery. This organization lasted until the Third Military District, under the Reconstruction Acts of March 2, 1867, was formed of Alabama, Florida, and Georgia, and General Thomas (immediately superseded by General Pope) was put in command.[1]

The Military Occupation

Within a month after the surrender of Lee, Alabama was occupied by Federal armies, and garrisons were being stationed at one or more points in all the more populous counties. Everywhere, the state and county government was broken up by the military authorities, who were forbidden to recognize any civil authority in the state. Into each of the 52 counties soldiers were sent to administer the oath of allegiance to the United States to any one who wished to take it. Most people were indifferent about it.[2]

For several months there was no civil government at all, and no government of any kind except in the immediate vicinity of the army posts and the towns where military officers and Freedmen's Bureau agents regulated the conduct of the negroes, and incidentally of the whites, well or badly, according to their abilities and prejudices. Some of the officers, especially those of higher rank, endeavored to pacify the land, gave good advice to the negroes, and were considerate in their relations with the whites; others incited the blacks to all sorts of deviltry and were a terror to the whites.[3] Each official in his little district ruled as supreme as the Czar of all the Russias. He was the first and last authority on most of the affairs of the community.

Early in the summer each city and its surrounding territory was formed into a military district under the command of a general

[1] Van Horne, Life of Thomas, pp. 153, 399, 400, 408 ; *Huntsville Advocate*, June 9, 1866 (for copy of order relating to Department of the South that I have not found elsewhere); G. O. No. 1, Mil. Div. Tenn., June 20, 1865 ; G. O. No. 118, W. Dept., June 27, 1865 ; G. O. No. 1, Dept. Ala., July 18, 1865 ; G. O. No. 1, Dist. Ala., June 4, 1866; G. O. No. 1, Dept. Tenn., Aug. 13, 1866 ; G. O. No. 42, Dept. Tenn., Nov. 1, 1866. The general and special orders cited in this chapter are on file in the War Department at Washington.

[2] O. R., Ser. I, Vol. XLIX, Pt. II, pp. 505, 560, 727, 826, 854, 971; Report of the Joint Committee on Reconstruction, Pt. III.

[3] Miller, "Alabama," p. 236 ; Acts of Ala. (1865-1866), pp. 598, 601.

officer, who was subject to the orders of General Woods at Mobile. There were the districts of Mobile, Montgomery, Talladega, and Huntsville — each with a dozen or more counties attached. Then there were isolated posts in each. The district was governed by the rules applying to a "separate brigade" in the army.[1] The different posts, districts, and departments were formed, discontinued, reorganized, with lightning rapidity. Hardly a single day passed without some change necessitated by the resignation or muster out of officers or troops. Commanding officers stayed a few days or a few weeks at a post, and were relieved or discharged. Some of the officers spent much of their time pulling wires to keep from being mustered out. Others resigned as soon as their resignations would be accepted. Few or none had any adequate knowledge of conditions in their own districts, nor was it possible for them to acquire a knowledge of affairs in the short time they remained at any one post.

After the establishment of the provisional government, the army was supposed to retire into the background, leaving ordinary matters of administration to the civil government. This it did not do, but constantly interfered in all affairs of government. The army officers cannot be blamed for their meddling with the civil administration, for the President did the same and seemed to have little confidence in the governments he had erected, though he gave good accounts of them to Congress. The struggle at Washington between the President and Congress over Reconstruction confused the military authorities as to the proper policy to pursue. The instructions from the President and from General Grant were sometimes in conflict.

In August, 1865, the military commander published the President's Amnesty Proclamation of May 29, 1865, and sent officers to each county to administer the oath.[2] Instructions were given that "no improper persons are to be permitted to take the oath." The oath was to be signed in triplicate, one copy for the Department of State, one for military headquarters, and one for the party taking the oath. Regulations were prescribed for making special applications for

---

[1] That is, the officers had the privileges and authority of officers of a division. G. O. Nos. 1, 9, 17, 29, 54, Dept. Ala., 1865; G. O. No. 1, Mil. Div. Tenn., 1865.

[2] The "Amnesty Oath." The oath of allegiance had already been administered to all who would take it. See McPherson, "Reconstruction," pp. 9, 10.

pardon by those excepted under the Amnesty Proclamation. There were 120 stations in the state where officials administered the oath of amnesty.[1] The military authorities gave the term "improper persons" a broad construction and excluded many who applied to take the oath. The various officers differed greatly in their enforcement of the regulations. Special applications for pardon had to go through military channels, and that meant delays of weeks or months; so, after civil officials were appointed in Alabama, "improper persons" took the oath before them, and then their papers were sent at once to Washington for the attention of the President. There was some scandal about the provisional secretary of state accepting reward for pushing certain applications for pardon. But there was no need to use influence, for the President pardoned all who applied.

Soon after Parsons was appointed provisional governor, an order stated that the United States forces would be used to assist in the restoration of order and civil law throughout the state and would act in support of the civil authorities as soon as the latter were appointed and qualified. The military authorities were instructed to avoid as far as possible any assumption or exercise of the functions of civil tribunals. No arrest or imprisonment for debt was to be made or allowed, and depredations by United States troops upon private property were to be repressed.[2]

The Army and the Colored Population

As acting agents of the Freedmen's Bureau, the army officers had to do with all that concerned the negroes; but sometimes, in a different capacity, they issued regulations concerning the colored race. It is difficult to distinguish between their actions as Bureau agents and as army officers. On the whole, it seems that each officer of the army considered himself *ex officio* an acting agent of the Bureau.

Soon after the occupation of Montgomery, an order was issued prohibiting negroes from occupying houses in the city without the consent of the owner. They had to vacate unless they could get permission. Negroes in rightful possession had to show certificates to that effect from the owner. All unemployed negroes were advised

---

[1] G. O. Nos. 13 and 14, Dept. Ala., 1865.

[2] G. O. No. 3, Dept. Ala., July 21, 1865. There was complaint about the stealing of cotton by troops.

to go to work, as the United States would not support them in idleness.[1] This order was intended to discourage the tendency of the negro population to flock to the garrison towns. The first troops to arrive were almost smothered by the welcoming blacks, who were disposed to depend upon the army for maintenance. The officers were at first alarmed at the great crowds of blacks who swarmed around them, and tried hard for a time to induce them to go back home to work. Their efforts were successful in some instances. In view of the fact that the posts and garrisons were the gathering places of great numbers of unemployed blacks, an order, issued in August, 1865, instructed the commanders of posts and garrisons to prohibit the loitering of negroes around the posts and to discourage the indolence of the blacks.[2]

In Mobile some kind of civil government must have been set up under the direction of the military authorities, for we hear of an order issued by General Andrews that in all courts and judicial proceedings in the District of Mobile the negro should have the same standing as the whites.[3] These may have been Bureau courts.

It was represented to the military commander that the negroes of Alabama had aided the Federals in April and May, 1865, by bringing into the lines, or by destroying, stock, provisions, and property that would aid the Confederacy, and that they were now being arrested by the officers of the provisional government for larceny and arson. So he ordered that the civil authorities be prohibited from arresting, trying, or imprisoning any negro for any offence committed before the surrender of Taylor (on May 4, 1865), except by permission of military headquarters or of the assistant commissioner of the Freedmen's Bureau.[4] When the Federal armies passed through the state in April and May, 1865, thousands of negroes had seized the farm stock and followed the army, for a few days at least. There was more of this seizure of property by negroes after garrisons were stationed in the towns. The order was so construed that practically no negro could be arrested for stealing when he was setting out for

[1] G. O. No. 6, Post of Montgomery, May 15, 1865. This order is printed on thin, blue Confederate writing paper, which seems to have been shaped with scissors to the proper size. Supplies had not followed the army.

[2] G. O. No. 24, Dept. of Ala., Aug. 25, 1865.

[3] G. O. No. 6, Post of Mobile, in *N. Y. Daily News*, June 27, 1865.

[4] G. O. No. 48, Dept. Ala., Oct. 18, 1865.

town and the Bureau. A few weeks before the order was issued, Woods stated, "I do not interfere with civil affairs at all unless called upon by the governor of the state to assist the civil authorities."[1]

Terrible stories of cruel treatment of the negroes were brought to Woods by the Bureau officials, and he sent detachments of soldiers to investigate the reports. Nothing was done except to march through the country and frighten the timid by a display of armed force, which was evidently all the agents wanted. One detachment scoured the counties of Clarke, Marengo, Washington, and Choctaw, investigating the reports of the agents.[2]

The commanding officers at some posts authorized militia officers of the provisional government to disarm the freedmen when outbreaks were threatened. But after Christmas General Swayne ordered that no authority be delegated by officers to civilians for dealing with freedmen, but that such cases be referred to himself as the assistant commissioner of the Freedmen's Bureau.[3] There had been great fear among some classes of people that the negroes would engage in plots to massacre the whites and secure possession of the property, which they were assured by negro soldiers and Bureau agents the governor meant them to have. About Christmas, 1865, the fear was greatest. For six months the blacks had been eagerly striving to get possession of firearms. The soldiers and speculators made it easy for them to obtain them. In Russell County $3000 worth of new Spencer rifles were found hidden in negro cabins.[4] There were few firearms among the whites, for all had been used in war and were therefore seized by the United States government. Some feared that the negroes were preparing for an uprising, but it is more probable that they merely wanted guns as a mark of freedom. The purchase of firearms by whites was discouraged by the army. The sale of arms and ammunition into the interior was forbidden, but speculators managed to sell both. General Smith, at Mobile, had one of them — Dieterich — arrested and confined in the military prison at Mobile.[5] The *Mobile Daily Register* was warned that it

[1] Statement of General Woods, Sept. 4, 1865, Document No. 11, accompanying the Report of Schurz.

[2] See statement of Woods, Sept. 4, 1865, Schurz's Report.

[3] G. O. No. 4, Dept. Ala., Jan. 26, 1866.

[4] *N. Y. Daily News*, Sept. 7, 1865.

[5] Statement of Gen. T. K. Smith, Sept. 14, 1865, in Schurz's Report.

must not print articles about impending negro insurrections,[1] a very good regulation; but the violent negro sheet in Mobile was not noticed, though it was a cause of excitement among the blacks.

In the fall of 1866 it was reported to the Secretary of State, Mr. Seward, that negroes were being induced to go to Peru on promise of higher wages. Seward induced Howard, the commissioner of the Freedmen's Bureau, to have the Bureau annul or disapprove all contracts of freedmen to go beyond the limits of the United States. General Swayne, who was now both assistant commissioner and military commander, was directed to enforce Howard's order in Alabama.[2]

Administration of Justice by the Army

From April to December, 1865, all trade and commerce had to go on under the regulations prescribed by the army. The restrictions placed on trade caused demoralization both in the army and among the Treasury agents, who worked under the protection of the military.[3] It was ordered that civilians guilty of stealing government cotton should be punished, after trial and conviction by military commission, according to the statutes of Alabama in force before the war. Later all cases of theft of government property were tried by military commission.[4]

When the cotton agents were tried by military commission[5] there arose a conflict of authority between the military authorities and the Federal Judge. One agent, T. C. A. Dexter, was arrested and sued out a writ of *habeas corpus* before Busteed, the Federal judge. The writ was served on General Woods and Colonel Hunter Brooke, who presided over the military commission. The officers declined to obey, saying that a military commission had been convened to try Dexter, and that no interference of the civil authorities would be permitted. Busteed ordered Dexter to be discharged, and Woods to appear before him and show why he should not be prosecuted for contempt of court. Woods paid no attention to this order, and Busteed sent the United States marshal to arrest him. The

---

[1] Statement of General Woods, Sept. 4, 1865.

[2] G. O. No. 5, Sub-dist. Ala., Oct. 13, 1866.   [3] See Ch. VI, sec. 1.

[4] G. O. No. 30, Dept. of Ala., Sept. 4, 1865; Statement of General Woods, Sept. 4, 1865, in Schurz's Report.

[5] See Ch. VI, sec. 1.

marshal reported that he was unable to get into the presence of Woods, because the military guard was instructed not to allow him to pass. Woods sent a message to Busteed that the writ had not been restored in Alabama. Busteed made a protest to the President and asserted that the trial could not lawfully proceed except in the civil courts. President Johnson sustained the course of General Woods, and thereby gave a blow to his provisional government, for Busteed at once adjourned his court — the only Federal court in the state. The sentiment of the people was with Busteed in spite of his own notorious character and that of the defendant. All wanted the civil government to take charge of affairs.[1]

Of the cases of civilians tried by summary courts in the summer of 1865, there is no official record; of the cases tried by military commission during 1865 and 1866, only incomplete records are to be found. A partial list of the cases, with charges and sentences, is here given: —

Wilson H. Gordon,[2] civilian, murder of negro, May 14, 1865. Convicted.

Samuel Smiley,[2] civilian, murder of negro, 1865. Acquitted.

T. J. Carver,[3] cotton agent, stealing cotton. Fined $90.000 and one year's imprisonment.

.T. C. A. Dexter,[4] cotton agent, stealing cotton (3321 bales) and selling appointment of cotton agent to Carver for $25,000. Fined $250,000 and imprisonment for one year.

William Ludlow,[5] civilian, stealing United States stock. Four years' imprisonment.

L. J. Britton,[6] civilian, guerilla warfare and robbery. Fined $5000 and imprisonment for ten years. (Fine remitted by reviewing officer.)

George M. Cunningham,[7] late Second Lieutenant 47th Ill. Vol. Inf., stealing government stores. Fined $500.

John C. Richardson,[8] civilian, guerilla warfare and robbery. Imprisonment for ten years.

Owen McLarney,[8] civilian assault on soldier. Acquitted.

William B. Rowls,[8] civilian, guerilla warfare and robbery. Imprisonment for ten years.

Samuel Beckham,[8] civilian, receiving stolen property. Imprisonment for three years.

---

[1] *N. Y. Herald*, Nov. 26 and Dec. 15, 1865.

[2] Document No. 19, accompanying Schurz's Report.

[3] G. O. No. 55, Dept. Ala., Oct. 30, 1865.   [4] G. O. No. 8, Dept. Ala., Feb. 17, 1866.

[5] G. O. No. 1, Dept. Ala., Jan. 5, 1866.   [6] G. O. No. 13, Dept. Ala., 1866.

[7] G. O. No. 17, Dept. Ala., 1866.   [8] G. O. No. 20, Dept. Ala., 1866.

John Johnson,[1] civilian, robbery and pretending to be United States officer. Fined $100, "to be appropriated to the use of the Freedmen's Bureau."

Abraham Harper,[1] civilian, robbery and pretending to be United States officer. Fined $100 "to be appropriated to the use of the Freedmen's Bureau."

Most of the civilians tried by the military commissions were camp followers and discharged soldiers of the United States army. Those charged with guerilla warfare were regularly enlisted Confederate soldiers and were accused by the tory element, who were guilty of most of the guerilla warfare.[2] It was impossible to punish outlaws for any depredations committed during the war, and for several months after the surrender, if they claimed to be "loyalists," which they usually did. The civil authorities were forbidden to arrest, try, and imprison discharged soldiers of the United States army for acts committed while in service.[3] A similar order withdrew all "loyal" persons from the jurisdiction of the civil courts so far as concerned actions during or growing out of the war.[4] The negroes had already been withdrawn from the authority of the civil courts so far as similar offences were concerned.[5]

Upon the complaint of United States officials collecting taxes and revenues of the refusal of individuals to pay, the military commanders over the state were ordered to arrest and try by military commission persons who refused or neglected "to pay these just dues." [6]

Numerous complaints of arbitrary arrests and of the unwarranted seizure of private property called forth an order from General Thomas, directing that the persons and property of all citizens must be respected. There was to be no interference with or arrests of

---

[1] G. O. No. 23, Dept. Ala., 1866.

There were other trials, but the records are missing and the names of the parties are unknown. A large number of cases were prosecuted before military commissions convened at the instance of the Freedmen's Bureau.

[2] For two years after the war the Confederate sympathizers in north Alabama suffered from persecution of this kind. During the war the Confederates in north Alabama had been classed as guerillas by the Federal commanders.

[3] G. O. No. 29, Mil. Div. Tenn., Sept. 21, 1865; G. O. No. 42, Dept. Ala., Sept. 26, 1865.

[4] G. O. No. 3, H. Q. A., Jan. 12, 1866; G. O. No. 7, Dept. Ala., Feb. 12, 1866.

[5] G. O. No. 48, Dept. Ala., Oct. 18, 1865.

[6] G. O. No. 6, Mil. Div. Tenn., Feb. 21, 1866.

citizens unless upon proper authority from the district commander, and then only after well-supported complaint.[1]

The local military authorities were directed to arrest persons who had been or might be charged with offences against officers, agents, citizens, and inhabitants of the United States, in cases where the civil authorities had failed, neglected, or been unable to bring the offending parties to trial. Persons so arrested were to be confined by the military until a proper tribunal might be ready and willing to try them.[2] This was another one of many blows at the civil government permitted by the President, who allowed the army to judge for itself as to when it should interfere.

These are the more important orders issued by the military authority relating to public affairs in Alabama during the existence of the two provisional or "Johnson" state governments. It will be seen from the scope of the orders that the local military officials had the power of constant interference with the civil government. A large part of the population was withdrawn from the jurisdiction of the civil administration. The officials of the latter had no real power, for they were subject to frequent reproof and their proceedings to frequent revision by the army officers. Both Governor Parsons and Governor Patton wanted the army removed, confident that the civil government could do better than both together. Parsons appealed to Johnson to remove the army or prohibit its interference.[3] He complained that the military officials had caused and were still causing much injustice by deciding grave questions of law and equity upon *ex parte* statements. Personal rights were subject to captious and uncertain regulations. The tenure of property was uncertain, and citizens felt insecure when the army decided complicated cases of title to land and questions of public morals. A military commission at Huntsville, acting under direction of General Thomas, had assumed to decide questions of title to property, and in one case, a widow was alleged to have been turned out of her home.[4] The citizens of Montgomery were indignant because the military authorities had issued licenses for the sale of liquor, and had permitted

---

[1] G. O. No. 25, Mil. Div. Tenn., Sept. 13, 1865.
[2] G. O. No. 44, H. Q. A., July 6, 1866; G. O. No. 13, Dept. of the South, July 21, 1866.
[3] Sen. Ex. Doc., No. 26, 39th Cong., 1st Sess.
[4] P. M. Dox to Governor Parsons, Sen. Ex. Doc., No. 26, 39th Cong., 1st Sess.

prostitution by licensing houses of ill repute. Circular No. 1, District of Montgomery, September 9, 1865, required that all public women must register at the office of the provost marshal; that each head of a disorderly house must pay a license tax of $25 a week in addition to $5 a week for each inmate, and that medical inspection should be provided for by military authority. In case of violation of these regulations a fine of $100 would be imposed for each offence, and ten to thirty days' imprisonment. The bishop and all the clergy of the Episcopal Church were suspended and the churches closed for several months because the bishop refused to order a prayer for the President.[1] The restaurant of Joiner and Company, at Stevenson, was closed by order of the post commander because two negro soldiers were refused the privilege of dining at the regular table.[2] Admiral Semmes, after being pardoned, was elected mayor of Mobile, but the President interfered and refused to allow him to serve. Many arrests and many more investigations were made at the instigation of the tory or "union" element, and on charges made by negroes.[3]

Relation between the Army and the People

The unsatisfactory character of the military rule was due in a large measure to the fact that the white volunteers were early mustered out, leaving only a few regulars and several regiments of negro troops to garrison the country.[4] These negro troops were a source of disorder among the blacks, and were under slack discipline. Outrages and robberies by them were of frequent occurrence. There was ill feeling between the white and the black troops. Even when the freedmen utterly refused to go to work, they behaved well, as a rule, except where negro troops were stationed. There is no reason to believe that it was not more the fault of the white officers than of the black soldiers, for black soldiers were amenable to discipline when they had respectable officers. Truman reported to the President that the negro troops

---

[1] See p. 327.   [2] *Selma Times*, Feb. 3, 1866.

[3] There were really three governments in Alabama based on the war powers of the President : (1) the army ruling through its commanders ; (2) the Freedmen's Bureau, with its agents ; (3) the provisional civil government.

[4] Circular No. 1, Aug. —, 1865; G. O. No. 21, Dept. Ala., April 9, 1866.

2 E

should be removed, because "to a great extent they incite the freed-men to deeds of violence and encourage them in idleness." [1]   The white troops, most of them regulars, behaved better, so far as their relations with the white citizens were concerned.   The general officers were as a rule gentlemen, generous and considerate.   So much so, that some rabid newspaper correspondents complained because the West Pointers treated the southerners with too much considera-tion.[2]   In the larger posts discipline was fairly good, but at small, detached posts in remote districts the soldiers, usually, but not always, the black ones, were a scourge to the state.   They ravaged the coun-try almost as completely as during the war.[3]   The numerous reports of General Swayne show that there was no necessity for garrisons in the state.   He wanted, he said, a small body of cavalry to catch fugitives from justice, not a force to overcome opposition.   The presence of the larger forces of infantry created a great deal of dis-order.   The soldiers were not amenable to civil law, the refining restraints of home were lacking, and discipline was relaxed.[4]

Of the subordinate officers some were good and some were not, and the latter, when away from the control of their superior officers and in command of lawless men, ravaged the back country and acted like brigands.   For ten years after the war the general orders of the various military districts, departments, and divisions are filled with orders publishing the results of court-martial proceedings, which show the demoralization of the class of soldiers who remained in the army after the war.   The best men clamored for their discharge when the war ended and went home.   The more disorderly men, for whom life in garrison in time of peace was too tame, remained, and all sorts of disorder resulted.   Finally "Benzine" boards, as they were called, had to take hold of the matter, and numbers of men

---

[1] *De Bow's Review*, 1866.   De Bow made a trip through the South.   *Nation*, Oct. 5 and 26, 1865 ; Truman, Report to President, April 9, 1866.   See also Grant, Letter to President, Dec. 18, 1865.

[2] Colonel Herbert says that the relations between the soldiers and the ex-Confed-erates were very kindly, but the latter hoped the army would soon be removed, when civil government was established.   "Solid South," p. 30.

[3] Miller, "Alabama," p. 242 ;   Resolutions of the Legislature, Jan. 16, 1866.

[4] Testimony of Swayne, Report Joint Committee, 1866, Pt. III, p. 139; various reports of Swayne as assistant commissioner of Freedmen's Bureau.   It was noticeable that when Swayne was placed in command of the army in the state there was less interference and better order than before, though he never obtained the cavalry.

who had done good service during the war were discharged because they were unable to submit to discipline in time of peace.

The rule of the army might have been better, especially in 1865, had there not been so many changes of local and district commanders and headquarters. Some counties remained in the same military jurisdiction a month or two, others a week or two, several for two or three days only. The people did not know how to proceed in order to get military justice. Orders were issued that business must proceed through military channels. This cut off the citizen from personal appeal to headquarters, unless he was a man of much influence. Often it was difficult to ascertain just what military channels were. Headquarters and commanders often changed before an application or a petition reached its destination.[1]

The President merited failure with his plan of restoration because he showed so little confidence in the governments he had established. He was constantly interfering on the slightest pretexts. He asked Congress to admit the states into the Union, and said that order was restored and the state governments in good running order, while at the same time he had not restored the writ of *habeas corpus*, had not proclaimed the "rebellion" at an end, and was in the habit of allowing and directing the interference of the army in the gravest questions that confronted the civil government. In this way he discredited his own work, even in the eyes of those who wished it to succeed. His intentions were good, but his judgment was certainly at fault.

---

[1] For instance: In the city of Mobile a petition of some kind might be made out in proper form and given to the commander of the Post of Mobile. The latter would indorse it with his approval or disapproval, and send it to the commander of the District of Mobile, who likewise forwarded it with his indorsement to the commander of the Department of Alabama at Mobile or Montgomery. In important cases the paper had to go on until it reached headquarters in Macon, Nashville, Louisville, Atlanta, or Washington, and it had to return the same way.

The following orders relate to the changes made so often : —

G. O. Nos. 1, 9, 10, 12, 17, 19, 20, 27, Dept. Ala., from July 18 to Sept. 1, 1865; G. O. No. 18, Dept. Ala., March 30, 1866; G. O. No. 1, Dist. Ala., June 1, 1866 ; G. O. No. 1, Sub-dist. Ala., Oct. —, 1866; G. O. No. 1, Mil. Div. Tenn., June 20, 1865 ; G. O. Nos. 1 and 42, Dept. of the Tenn., Aug. 13 and Nov. 1, 1866; G. O. No. 1, Dept. of the South, June 1, 1866; G. O. No. 1, Dept. of the Gulf, ——, 1865 ; G. O. No. 1, Dist. of the Chattahoochee, Aug. —, 1866.

There were numerous general orders from local headquarters of the same nature. See also Van Horne, " Life of Thomas," pp. 153, 399, 400, 418; and Sen. Ex. Doc., No. 13, 38th Cong., 2d Sess.

The army authorities went on in their accustomed way until Swayne was placed in command, June 1, 1866, when a more sensible policy was inaugurated, and there was less friction. Swayne aspired to control the governor and legislature by advice and demands rather than to rule through the army. There were few soldiers in the state after the summer of 1866. Order was good, except for the disturbing influence of negro troops and individual Bureau agents. There were in remote districts outbreaks of lawlessness which neither the army nor the state government could suppress. The infantry could not chase outlaws; the state government was too weak to enforce its orders or to command respect as long as the army should stay. At their best the army and the civil administration neutralized the efforts and paralyzed the energies of each other. There were two governments side by side, the authority of each overlapping that of the other, while the Freedmen's Bureau, a third government, supported by the army, was much inclined to use its powers. The result was that most of the people went without government.

On the 28th of March, 1867, the policy of Johnson came to its logical end in failure. General Grant then issued the order which overturned the civil government established by the President. In Alabama, which was to form a part of the Third Military District, all elections for state and county officials were disallowed until the arrival of the commander of the district. All persons elected to office during the month of March (after the passage of the Reconstruction Acts) were ordered to report to military headquarters for the action of the new military governor.[1] Military government then entered on a new phase.

---

[1] G. O. No. 1, Sub-dist. Ala., March 28, 1867.

CHAPTER XI

THE WARDS OF THE NATION

Sec. 1. The Freedmen's Bureau

Department of Negro Affairs

Any account of the causes of disturbed conditions in the South during the two years succeeding the war must include an examination of the workings of the Freedmen's Bureau, the administration of which was uniformly hostile to the President's policy and in favor of the Radical plans.

As soon as the Federal armies reached the Black Belt, it became a serious problem to care for the negroes who stopped work and flocked to the camps. Some of the generals sent them back to their masters, others put them to work as laborers in the camps and on the fortifications. Officers — usually chaplains — were temporarily detailed to look after the blacks who swarmed about the army, and thus the so-called "Department of Negro Affairs" was established extra-legally, and continued until the passage of the Freedmen's Bureau Act in 1865. The "Department" was supported by captured and confiscated property, and was under the direction of the War Department.[1]

For a year after north Alabama was overrun by the Federal troops, no attempt was made to segregate the blacks; but in 1863 a camp for refugees and captured negroes was established on the estate of ex-Governor Chapman, near Huntsville in Madison county, and Chaplain Stokes of the Eighteenth Wisconsin Infantry was placed in charge. It was not intended that the negroes should remain there permanently, but they were to be sent later to the larger concentration camps at Nashville. No records were kept, but the report of the inspector states that several hundred negroes were

[1] Freedmen's Bureau Report, Oct. 20, 1869; Ho. Ex. Doc., No. 143, 41st Cong., 2d Sess.

received before August, 1864, of whom only a small proportion was sent to Nashville. Those who remained were employed in cultivating the land, — planting corn, cotton, sorghum, and vegetables, — and in building log barracks and other similar houses. Schools were established for the children. The War Department issued three-fourths rations to the negroes, and the aid societies also helped them, although this colony was nearer self-sustaining than any other.[1]

In 1864 the Treasury Department assumed partial charge of negro refugees and captive slaves. Regulations provided that captured and abandoned property should be rented and the proceeds devoted to the purchase of supplies for the blacks, who, when possible, were to be employed as laborers. In each special agency there was to be a "Freedmen's Home Colony" under a "Superintendent of Freedmen," whose duty it was to care for the blacks in the colony, to obtain agricultural implements and supplies, and to keep a record of the negroes who passed through the colony. A classification of laborers was made and a minimum schedule of wages fixed as follows : —

No. 1 hands, males, 18 to 40 years of age, minimum wage, $25 per month; No. 2 hands, males, 14 to 18, 40 to 55 years of age, minimum wage, $20 per month; No. 3 hands, males, 12 to 14 years of age, minimum wage, $15 per month; corresponding classes of women, $18, $14, $10, respectively.

It was the duty of the superintendent to see that all who were physically able secured work at the specified rates. He acted as an employment agent, and the planters had to hire their labor through him. He exercised a general supervision over the affairs of all freedmen in the district. Beside paying the high wages fixed by the schedule, the planter was obliged to take care of the young children of the family hired by him; to furnish without charge a separate house for each family with an acre of ground for garden, medical attendance for the family, and schooling for the children; to sell food and clothing to the negroes at actual cost; and to pay for full time unless the laborer was sick or refused to work. Half the wages was paid at the end of the month, and the remainder at the end of the contract. Wages due constituted a first lien on the crop, which could not be moved until the superintendent certified that the wages

[1] Sen. Ex. Doc., No. 28, 38th Cong., 2d Sess.

had been paid or arranged for.   Not more than ten hours a day labor
was to be required.   Cases of dispute were to be settled by civil
courts (Union), where established, — otherwise the superintendent
was vested with the power to decide such cases.   Provision was
made for accepting the assistance of the aid societies, especially in
the matter of schools.[1]   Under such regulations it was hardly possible for the farmer to hire laborers, and we find that only 205 negroes
were disposed of by the colony near Huntsville.   If the wages could
have been paid in Confederate currency, they would have been
reasonable; but United States currency was required, and most
people had none of it.

In the fall of 1864 the army again took charge of negro affairs
and administered them along the lines indicated in the Treasury
regulations.   Wherever the army went its officers constituted themselves into freedmen's courts, aid societies, etc., and exercised absolute control over all relations between the two races and among the
blacks.

The Freedmen's Bureau Established

The law of March 3, 1865, created a Bureau in the War Department to which was given control of all matters relating to freedmen,
refugees, and abandoned lands.   All officials were required to take
the iron-clad test oath.[2]   No appropriation was made for the purpose
of carrying out this law, and for the first year the Bureau was maintained by taxes on salaries and on cotton, by fines, donations, rents
of buildings and lands, and by the sales of crops and confiscated
property.[3]   On July 16, 1866, a second Bureau Bill, amplifying the
law of March 3, 1865, and extending it to July 16, 1868, was passed
over the President's veto.   In 1868 the Bureau was continued for
one year, and on January 1, 1869, it was discontinued, except in
educational work.[4]   There is no indication that the provisions of
the laws had much effect on the administration of the Bureau.   From
the beginning it had entire control of all that concerned freedmen,

---

[1] Regulations, July 9, 1864.

[2] Stats.-at-Large, Vol. XIII, pp. 507–509.   See also O. O. Howard, "The Freedmen
during the War," in the *New Princeton Review*, May and Sept., 1886.

[3] Ho. Ex. Doc., No. 7, 39th Cong., 2d Sess.

[4] McPherson, "Reconstruction," pp. 69–74, 147–151, 349, 350, 378; Burgess, "Reconstruction," pp. 87–90.

who thus formed a special class not subject to the ordinary laws. In Alabama there were nearly 500,000 negroes thus set apart, of whom 100,000 were children and 40,000 were aged and infirm.[1]

It was several months before the organization of the Bureau was completed in Alabama. Meanwhile army officers acted as *ex officio* agents of the Bureau, and regulated negro affairs. They were disposed to persuade the negroes to go home and work, and not congregate around the military posts. They issued some rations to the negroes in the towns who were most in want, but discouraged the tendency to look to the United States for support. Only a small proportion of the race was affected by the operations of the Bureau during the months of April, May, and June, 1865. In north and south Alabama, above and below the Black Belt, the negroes were more under control of the Bureau than in the Black Belt itself. The assistant commissioner for Tennessee had jurisdiction over the negroes in north Alabama, who had been under nominal northern control since 1862. The Bureau was established at Mobile in April and May, under the control of the army, and was an offshoot of the Louisiana Bureau, T. W. Conway, assistant commissioner for Louisiana, being for a short while in charge of negro affairs in Alabama. At the same time there was at Mobile one T. W. Osborn, who was called the assistant commissioner for Alabama. Later he was transferred to Florida, and in July, 1865, General Wager Swayne succeeded Conway in Alabama.[2]

There were but few regular agents in Alabama before the arrival of General Swayne. A few stray missionaries and preachers, representing the aid societies, came in, and were placed in charge of the camps of freedmen near the towns. Conway appointed agents at Mobile, Demopolis, Selma, and Montgomery, who were officers in the negro regiments.[3] For several months the army officers were almost the only agents, and, as has been stated, the higher officials, and some of the subordinates pursued a sensible course, giving the negroes sensible advice, and laboring to convince them that they

---

[1] *N. Y. Times,* Oct. 31, 1865.

[2] Circular No. 16, Sept. 19, 1865 (Howard); Circular No. 6, June 13, 1865 (Howard); Ho. Ex. Doc., No. 70, 39th Cong., 1st Sess.; Circular No. 1, July 14, 1865 (Conway); Circular No. 2, July 14, 1865 (Conway).

[3] One of them — Chaplain C. W. Buckley — was guardian of the blacks at Montgomery. He afterwards played a prominent part in carpet-bag politics.

could not expect to live without work. Others encouraged them in idleness and violence and advised them to stop work and congregate in the towns and around the military posts. The black troops and their commanders were a source of disorder and cause of irritation between the races. The officers of these troops, and others also, were probably often sincere in their convictions that the southern white, especially the former slave owner, could not be trusted in anything where negroes were concerned, that he was the natural enemy of the black and must be guarded against.[1]

It was on June 20, 1865, that General Swayne was appointed assistant commissioner for Alabama, and on July 14, T. W. Conway directed all officials of the Bureau in the state (except those in north Alabama who were under the control of the assistant commissioner of Tennessee) to report to Swayne on his arrival.[2] On July 26 the latter assumed charge and appointed Charles A. Miller as his assistant adjutant-general, later another saviour of his country in Reconstruction days. General Swayne stated that on his arrival he was kindly received by most of the people, and that he was "agreeably disappointed" in the temper of the people and their attitude toward him. Howard's instructions made it the duty of the assistant commissioner or his agents to adjudicate all differences among negroes and between negroes and whites. Exclusive and final jurisdiction was vested in him.[3]

The Bureau in Alabama was organized in five departments: (1) the Department of Abandoned and Confiscated Lands; (2) the Department of Records (Labor, Schools, and Supplies); (3) the Department of Finance; (4) the Medical Department; (5) the Bounty Department. Before the end of August, 1865, the organization was completed, on paper, and the state had been divided into five districts, each controlled by a superintendent. These districts were:

---

[1] Ku Klux Rept., p. 441; *N. Y. World*, July 20, 1865; oral accounts and letters. It was on this theory that the Bureau was established, and at the head of the institution was placed General O. O. Howard, who was a soft-hearted, unpractical gentleman, with boundless confidence in the negro and none whatever in the old slave owner. A man of hard common sense like Sherman would have done less harm and probably much good with the Bureau.

[2] Ho. Ex. Doc., No. 70, 39th Cong., 1st Sess.

[3] Circular No. 5, June 2, 1865 (Howard); Circular No. 2, July 14, 1865 (Conway); Ho. Ex. Doc., No. 70, 39th Cong., 1st Sess.

(1) Mobile, with seven counties; (2) Selma, with ten counties; (3) Montgomery, with nine counties; (4) Troy, with six counties; (5) Demopolis, with eight counties; later, (6) north Alabama, consisting of twelve counties, was withdrawn from the jurisdiction of the assistant commissioner of Tennessee, General Fiske, and became the sixth division in Alabama.

The officials of the Freedmen's Bureau, except the state officials and subordinate employees, numbered, in 1865, twenty-seven army officers, and two civilians.[1] By November the Bureau was well organized, and as many offices as possible were established to examine into labor contracts. Each superintendent had charge of the issue of rations in the county where he was stationed, and in each of the other counties of his district he had an assistant superintendent. It was the duty of these seventy-five or more officers to investigate complaints against county or state officials, who had been made *ex officio* Freedmen's Bureau agents; and when a negro made a complaint, Swayne forced Parsons to appoint a new officer. Later, when complaint was made, Swayne would replace a civil agent by a regular Bureau agent. Thus the Bureau gradually passed out of the hands of the state officials. The superintendents and the assistant superintendents had the power to arrest outlaws and evil-doers. They could also delegate the charge of contracts to responsible persons. Depots were established from which supplies were issued to the counties, each county furnishing transportation and distributing the supplies under the observation of the superintendent.[2]

General Swayne was succeeded, January 14, 1868, by Brevet Brigadier-General Julius Hayden, who in turn was succeeded, March

---

[1] Freedmen's Bureau Report, Dec., 1865.

[2] In November, 1866, the following army officers, most of whom were members of the Veteran Reserve Corps, were made superintendents of these depots: Montgomery, Capt. J. L. Whiting, V.R.C.; Mobile, Brevet Major G. H. Tracy, 15th Infantry; Huntsville, Brevet Col. J. B. Callis, V.R.C.; Selma, Lieut. George Sharkley; Greenville, James F. McGogy, Late First Lieut. U.S.A.; Tuscaloosa, Capt. W. H. H. Peck, V.R.C.; Talladega, J. W. Burkholder, A.A.G., U.S.A.; Demopolis, Brevet Major C. W. Pierce, V.R.C. Other Bureau officials who afterward became well-known carpet-baggers were: Major C. A. Miller, 2d Maine Cavalry, A.A.G.; Major B. W. Norris, Additional Paymaster; Lieut.-Col. Edwin Beecher, Additional Paymaster; Rev. C. W. Buckley, Chaplain 47th U.S.C. Infantry. Other officers of the V.R.C. who arrived later were Capt. Roderick Theune, Lieuts. George F. Browing, G. W. Pierce, John Jones, P. E. O'Conner, and Joseph Logan. See Swayne's Report, Oct. 31, 1866; Sen. Ex. Doc., No. 21, 40th Cong., 2d Sess. With one exception these later assisted in Reconstruction.

31, 1868, by Brevet Brigadier-General O. L. Shepherd, Colonel of the Fifteenth Infantry, and he was relieved on August 18, 1868, by Brevet Lieutenant-Colonel Edwin Beecher, who wound up the affairs of the Bureau in the state, except the educational and bounty divisions.[1] The sub-districts were continued during the existence of the Bureau. These consisted of four to six counties each, and were sometimes under the charge of regular army officers, sometimes under civilians.[2] The *Tribune* correspondent had doubts of the benefits of the Freedmen's Bureau where army officers, especially West Pointers, were in charge. The West Pointers were strict with the negroes, there was no idleness; the negro had to work; and the officers always took the side of the white.[3]

Pressure from the northern Radicals was brought to bear on Swayne, as time went on, to force him to do away more and more with army officers and civil officials of the state, and to substitute civilians from the North, who had a different plan for helping the negro. The alien agents were opposed to Swayne's plan of appointing native whites as agents, and told him tales of outrage that had been committed, but he paid no attention to them. The Bureau officers told much more horrible tales than any of the army officers.[4]

The Nation's correspondent seemed disappointed because the Freedmen's Bureau and the people and the negro were getting along fairly well.[5]

The Freedmen's Bureau and the Civil Authorities

There was, according to the state laws of 1861, no provision for the negro in the courts, and Swayne asked Governor Parsons to issue a proclamation opening the courts to them and giving them full civil rights. He reminded Parsons that he (Parsons) was merely a military official, and that the law administered by him was martial law, which had its limits only in the discretion of the commander.

[1] Freedmen's Bureau Report, Oct. 24, 1869.
[2] Freedmen's Bureau Report, Oct. 24, 1868.
[3] McPherson's scrap-book, " Freedmen's Bureau Bill, 1866," p. 128.
[4] For examples, see Schurz's Report and accompanying documents, Nos. 20, 21, 22, 28; Taylor, " Destruction and Reconstruction "; article by Schurz in *McClure's Magazine*, Jan., 1904.
[5] *The Nation*, Feb. 15, 1866.

Parsons and his advisers thought that the people would oppose such action and so refused to issue the proclamation.[1]

Thereupon Swayne himself issued a proclamation, stating that exclusive control of all matters relating to the negroes belonged to him. He was unwilling, however, he said, to establish tribunals in Alabama conducted by persons foreign to her citizenship and strangers to her laws. Consequently, all judicial officers, magistrates, and sheriffs of the provisional government were made Bureau agents for the administration of justice to the negroes. The laws of the state were to be applied so far as no distinction was made on account of color. Processes were to run in the name of the provisional government and according to the forms provided by state law. The military authorities were to support the civil officials of the Bureau in the administration of justice. Each officer was to signify his acceptance of this appointment, and failure to accept or refusal to administer the laws without regard to color would result in the substitution of martial law in that community.[2]

This order was remarkable for several reasons. In the first place, it was rather an arrogant seizure of the provisional administration and subordination of it to the Bureau. All officials were forced to accept by the threat of martial law in case of refusal to serve. Again, Swayne was not in command of the military forces of the state, though the army was directed to support the Bureau. This law gave to Swayne unlimited discretion, so that by a short order he practically placed himself at the head of the whole administration, — civil and military, — and throughout his term of service in Alabama he never allowed anything to stand in his way.[3] Again, the act of March 3, 1865, provided that all officials of the Bureau must take the "iron-clad," and it is doubtful if a single state official could have taken it. Swayne did not require it.

As soon as Swayne's proclamation was made known, the majority of the judges and magistrates applied to Governor Parsons for instructions in the matter. Parsons, who disliked the Bureau, but who

[1] Report of the Joint Committee on Reconstruction, Pt. III, p. 138.

[2] G. O. No. 7, Montgomery, Aug. 4, 1865.

[3] No one ever knew exactly how far the military commander was bound to obey the assistant commissioner and *vice versa*. The problem was at last solved by making Swayne military commander also.

was a timid and prudent man, issued a proclamation requiring compliance, and even enforced compliance by removing those who refused and appointing in their places nominees of Swayne. The entire body of state and county officials finally signified their acceptance, and the negro was then given exactly the same civil rights as possessed by the whites.[1] Had all the state officials refused to serve, there would have ensued an interesting state of affairs; an official of the Freedmen's Bureau would have overturned the state government set up by the President. It was, however, done with a good purpose, and for a while worked well by not working at all. Swayne was a man of common sense, a soldier, and a gentleman, and honestly desired to do what was best for all — the negro first. He did not profess much regard for the native white, and he made it plain that his main purpose was to secure the rights which he thought the negro ought to have. Incidentally, he pursued a wise and conciliatory policy, as he understood it, toward the whites, for he saw that this was the best way to aid the negro. The work of the Bureau under his charge was probably the least harmful of all in the South, and for most of the harm done he was not responsible. General Swayne attributed what he termed his success with the Freedmen's Bureau to the fact that he used at first the native state and county officials as his agents, and thus dispensed to some extent with alien civilians and army officials, who were obnoxious to the mass of the people. The requisite number of army officials of proper character could not have been secured, and they would not have understood the conditions. The same was true of alien civilians. Even the best ones would have inclined toward the blacks in all things, and thus would have incensed the whites, or they would have been "seduced by social amenities" to become the instruments of the whites, or they would have become merchantable. In any case the negro would suffer. General Swayne said that he thoroughly understood that he was expected by the Radicals to pursue no such policy, and that he half expected to be forced from the service for so doing. Influence was brought to bear to cause him to change and with some success.

Later some few officials were removed, the most notable case

---

[1] Report of the Joint Committee on Reconstruction, Pt. III, p. 138 (testimony of General Wager Swayne).

being that of Major H. H. Slough and the police of Mobile.[1] It was reported to Swayne that Slough was not enforcing the laws without regard to color. A staff officer was sent at once to Mobile to demand instant acceptance or rejection of Swayne's proclamation. The mayor rejected it, and Swayne then informed Parsons that Mobile had to have either a new mayor, or martial law and a garrison of negro troops.[2] Parsons yielded, and made all the changes that Swayne demanded. Two commissions were made out, — one appointed John Forsyth as mayor, and the other, F. C. Bromberg, a "Union" man. Swayne was to deliver the commission he wished. He went to Mobile and decided to try Forsyth, who at that time was down the bay at a pleasure resort. Swayne went after him in a tug, and met a tug with Forsyth on board coming up the bay. He hailed it and asked it to stop, but the tug only went the faster. He chased it for several miles,[3] and at length the pursued boat was overtaken. Swayne called for Forsyth, and all thought that he was to be arrested. But to the great relief of the party the appointment as mayor was offered to him, and Forsyth soon decided to accept the office. As Swayne said, he was a "hot Confederate," a Democrat, and would fight, and no one would dare criticise him. He soon had the confidence of both white and black.[4]

The order admitting the testimony of and conferring civil rights upon the negro was favored by most of the lawyers of the state. The "testimony" was the fulcrum to move other things. The tendency of the law of evidence is to receive all testimony and let the jury decide. So there was no trouble from the lawyers, and their opinion greatly influenced the people. None of the respectable people of Alabama were opposed to allowing the negro to testify. They were not afraid of such testimony, for no jury would ever convict a reputable man on negro testimony alone. This was one objection to it — its unreliability and consequent possible injustice.

---

[1] Report of the Joint Committee on Reconstruction, Pt. III, p. 138.

[2] Swayne did not hesitate to intimidate such men as Parsons. He would treat old men — former senators, governors, and congressmen — as if they were bad boys; he himself was under thirty.

[3] The reason for this was that the day before several Federal drunken officers had been careering around the bay in a boat, and Forsyth, who was on this boat, did not want his party of ladies to meet them.

[4] Statement of Swayne, 1901; N. Y. News, Aug. 21, 1865.

Bureau supported by Confiscations

Landlords were prevented from evicting negroes who had taken possession of houses or lands until complete provision had been made for them elsewhere. Thus the negroes would do nothing and kept others from coming in their places.[1] "Loyal" refugees and freedmen were made secure in the possession of land which they were cultivating until the crops were gathered or until they were paid proper compensation.[2] Little captured, abandoned, or confiscated private property remained in the hands of the Bureau officials after the wholesale pardoning by the President. As soon as pardoned, the former owner regained rights of property except in slaves, though the personal property had been sold and the proceeds used for various purposes.[3] There was, however, a great deal of Confederate property and state and county property that had been devoted to the use of the Confederacy. In every small town of the state there was some such property — barns, storehouses, hospital buildings, foundries, iron works, cotton, supplies, steamboats, blockade-runners. An order from the President, dated November 11, 1865, directed the army, navy, and Treasury officials to turn over to the Freedmen's Bureau all real estate, buildings, and other property in Alabama that had been used by the Confederacy. The sale of this property furnished sufficient revenue for one year, and, until withdrawn several years later, the educational department was sustained by the proceeds of similar sales.[4] The failure of Congress to appropriate funds made it almost necessary to use state officials as agents, as there was no money to pay other agents. The Confederate iron works at Briarfield were sold for $45,000, three blockade-runners in the Tombigbee River for $50,000, and some hospital buildings for $8000. There was besides a large amount of Confederate property in Selma, Montgomery, Demopolis, and Mobile. Of private property, at the close of 1865, the Bureau was still holding 2116 acres of land and thirteen pieces of town property.[5] A year

[1] Circular No. 20 (Freedmen's Bureau), War Dept., Nov. 30, 1865.

[2] Circular No. 15, Sept. 12, 1865.   [3] McPherson, " Reconstruction," p. 13.

[4] Richardson, Messages and Papers of the Presidents, Vol. VI, p. 352; G. O. No. 64, Dept. Ala., Dec. 10, 1865; Swayne's Report, Jan. 31, 1865; Freedmen's Bureau Reports, Dec., 1865, and Nov., 1866.

[5] Freedmen's Bureau Report, Dec., 1895; Swayne's Reports, Jan. 31 and Oct. 31, 1866, in Ho. Ex. Doc., No. 70, and Sen. Ex. Doc., No. 6, 39th Cong., 1st Sess.

later all of this property, except seven pieces of town property, had been restored to the owners.[1]

In 1866 a blockade-runner was sold for $4000 and a war vessel in the Tombigbee for $27,351.93. The expenses of the Bureau in 1865, so far as accounts were kept, amounted to $126,865.77.[2] This sum was obtained from sales of Confederate property. There was, also, a tax on contracts of from 50 cents to $1.50, and a fee on licenses for Bureau marriages. But the money thus obtained seems to have been appropriated by the agents, who kept no record. Rations were issued by the army to the Bureau agents and there was no further accountability. No accounts were kept of the proceeds from the sales of abandoned and confiscated property, a neglect which led to grave abuses. All records were confused, loosely kept, and un-businesslike. There were, also, funds from private sources at the disposal of the authorities, besides the appropriations of 1866 and 1867, those in the former year being estimated at $851,500. There was little or no supervision over and no check on the operations of the agents. It has been stated that the salaries proper of the Bureau agents in Alabama amounted to about $50,000 annually.[3] State officials acting as agents received no salaries. It is impossible to ascertain the amount expended in Alabama, though the entire expenditure accounted for in the South was nearly twenty million dollars; much was not accounted for.

During the two decades preceding the war many individual planters had erected chapels and churches for the use of the negroes

---

[1] Freedmen's Bureau Report, Nov. 1, 1866.

[2] Ho. Rept., No. 121, 41st Cong., 2d Sess.; Sen. Ex. Doc., No. 6, 39th Cong., 1st Sess.

[3] Freedmen's Bureau Reports, Dec., 1865, and Nov., 1866; Ho. Ex. Doc., No. 142, 41st Cong., 2d Sess.; Miller, "History of Alabama," p. 240. Congress appropriated $20,000,000, and there was an immense amount of Confederate property confiscated and sold for the benefit of the Bureau. Of this no account was kept. One detailed estimate of Bureau expenses is as follows: —

Appropriations by Congress	$20,000,000
General Bounty Fund	8,000,000
Freedmen and Refugee Fund	7,000,000
Retained Bounty Fund (Butler)	2,000,000
School Fund (Confiscated Property)	2,500,000
Total	$39,500,000

Edwin De Leon, "Ruin and Reconstruction of the Southern States," in *Southern Magazine*, 1874. See also Ho. Ex. Doc., No. 142, 41st Cong., 2d Sess.

in the towns and on the plantations. Some few such buildings belonged to the negroes and were held in trust by the whites for them, but most of them were the property of the planters or of church organizations that had built them. General Swayne ordered that all such property should be secured to the negroes.[1] These buildings were used for schools and churches by the missionary teachers and religious carpet-baggers who were instructing the negro in the proper attitude of hostility toward all things southern.

The Bureau issued a retroactive order, requiring negroes to take out licenses for marriages, and all former marriages had to be again solemnized at the Bureau. Licenses cost fifty cents, which was considered an extortion and was supposed to be for Buckley's benefit.[2]

The Labor Problem

The Bureau inherited the policy of the "superintendents" in regard to the regulation of negro labor, and the first regulations by the Bureau were evidently modelled on the Treasury Regulations of July 29, 1864. The monthly wage was lowered, but there was the same absurd classification of labor with fixed wages. The first of these regulations, promulgated in Mobile in May, 1865, was to this effect : —

Laborers were to be encouraged to make contracts with their former masters or with any one else. The contracts were to be submitted to the "Superintendent of Freedmen" and, if fair and honest, would be approved and registered. A register of unemployed persons was to be kept at the Freedmen's Bureau, and any person by applying there could obtain laborers of both sexes at the following rates: first class, $10 per month; second class, $8 per month; third class, $6 per month; boys under 14 years of age, $3 per month; girls under 14 years of age, $2 per month. Colored persons skilled in trade were also divided into three classes at the following rates: men and women receiving the same, first class, $2.50 per day; second class, $2 per day; third class, $1.50 per day. Mechanics were also to receive not less than $5 per month in addition to first-class rates. Wages were to be paid quarterly, on July 1 and October 1, and the final

[1] G. O. No. 4, July 28, 1865.
[2] N. Y. News, Sept. 7, 1865 (Montgomery correspondent); Ku Klux Rept., p. 441; oral accounts.

2 F

payment on or before the expiration of the contract, which was to be made for not less than three months, and not longer than to the end of 1865. In addition to his wages, the contracts must secure to the laborer just treatment, wholesome food, comfortable clothing, quarters, fuel, and medical attendance. No contract was binding nor a person considered employed unless the contract was signed by both parties and registered at the Bureau office, in which case a certificate of employment was to be furnished. Laborers were warned that it was for their own interest to work faithfully, and that the government, while protecting them against ill treatment, would not countenance idleness and vagrancy, nor support those capable of earning an honest living by industry. The laborers must fulfil their contracts, and would not be allowed to leave their employer except when permitted by the Superintendent of Freedmen. For leaving without cause or permission, the laborers were to forfeit all wages and be otherwise punished. Wages would be deducted in cases of sickness, and wages and rations withheld when sickness was feigned for purposes of idleness, the proof being furnished by the medical officer in attendance. Upon feigning sickness or refusing to work, a laborer was to be put at forced labor on the public works without pay. A reasonable time having been given for voluntary contracts to be made, any negro found without employment would be furnished work by the superintendent, who was to supply the army with all that were required for labor, and gather the aged, infirm, and helpless into "home colonies," and put them on plantations. Employers and their agents were to be held responsible for their conduct toward laborers, and cruelty or neglect of duty would be summarily punished.[1] The ignorance of conditions shown by these seemingly fair regulations is equalled in other regulations issued by the Bureau agents during the summer and fall of 1865. It is no wonder that the negroes could not find work in Mobile when they wanted it.

Instructions from Howard directed that agreements to labor must be approved by Bureau officers. Overseers were not to be tolerated. All agents were to be classed as officers, whether they were enlisted men or civilians. Wages were to be secured by a lien on the crops or the land, the rate of pay being fixed at the wages paid

[1] *Montgomery Mail*, May 12, 1865.

for an able-bodied negro before the war, and a minimum rate was to be published. All contracts were to be written and approved by the agent of the Bureau, who was to keep a copy of the documents.[1]

At Huntsville, in north Alabama, orders were issued that freedmen must go to work or be arrested and forced to work by the military authorities. Contracts had to be witnessed by a friend of the freedmen, and were subject to examination by the military authorities. Breach of contract by either party might be tried by the provost marshal or by a military commission, and the property of the employer was liable to seizure for wages.[2]

At first the planters thought that they saw in the contract system a means of holding the negro to his work, and they vigorously demanded contracts.[3] This suited Swayne, and he issued the following regulations, which superseded former rules: —

1. All contracts with freedmen for labor for a month or more had to be in writing, and approved by an agent of the Freedmen's Bureau, who might require security.

2. For plantation labor: (a) contracts could be made with the heads of families to embrace the labor of all members who were able to work; (b) the employer must provide good and sufficient food, quarters, and medical attendance, and such further compensation as might be agreed upon; (c) such contracts would be a lien upon the crops, of which not more than half could be moved until full payment had been made, and the contract released by the Freedmen's Bureau agent or by a justice of the peace in case an agent was not at hand.

3. The remedies for violation of contracts were forfeiture of wages and damages secured by lien.

4. In case an employer should make an oath before a justice of the peace, acting as an agent of the Bureau, that one of his laborers had been absent more than three days in a month, the justice of the

---

[1] Howard's Circular, May 30, 1865; War Department Circular No. 11, July 12, 1865.

[2] *Huntsville Advocate*, July 26, 1865. This was when the army officials were conducting the Bureau. Later the civilian agents charged $2 for making every contract, and the negroes soon wanted the Bureau abolished so far as it related to contracts. *N. Y. Times*, March 12, 1866 (letter from Florence, Ala.). In Madison County some of the negroes tarred and feathered a Bureau agent who had been collecting $1.50 each for drawing contracts. *N. Y. Herald*, Dec. 22, 1867.

[3] Swayne's Report, Jan. 31, 1866.

peace could proceed against the negro as a vagrant and hand him over to the civil authorities.

5. Vagrants when convicted might be put to work on the roads or streets or at other labor by the county or municipal authorities, who must provide for their support; or they might be given into the charge of an agent of the Freedmen's Bureau. This was usually done and the agent released them. Besides this, he often interfered, and took charge of the negro vagrants convicted in the community.

6. All contracts must expire on or before January 1, 1866.[1]

The lien upon the crop was to be enforced by attachment, which must be issued by any magistrate when any part of the crop was about to be moved without the consent of the laborer. The plaintiff (negro) was not obliged to give bond.[2] These regulations had no effect in reorganizing labor, and were only a cause of confusion.

A committee of citizens of Talladega, appointed to make suggestions in regard to enforcing the regulations of the Freedmen's Bureau concerning contracts, reported that: (1) contracts for a month or more between whites and blacks should be reduced to writing and witnessed; (2) civil officers should enforce these contracts according to law and the regulations of the Freedmen's Bureau; (3) the law of apprenticeship should be applied to freedmen where minors were found without means of support; (4) civil officers should take duties heretofore devolving upon the Freedmen's Bureau in matters of contract between whites and blacks. This practically asked for the discontinuance of the Freedmen's Bureau as being superfluous.[3]

When enforced, the contract regulations caused trouble. The lien on the crop for the negro's wages prevented the farmer from moving a bale of cotton if the negro objected. No matter whether the negro had been paid or not, if he made complaint, the farmer's whole crop could be locked up until the case was settled by a magistrate or agent; and the negro was not backward in making claims

---

[1] These regulations bear the approval of the other two rulers of Alabama — General Woods and Governor Parsons. See G. O. No. 12, Aug. 30, 1865.

[2] G. O. No. 13, Sept., 1865. This order was in force until 1868. See *N. Y. World*, Nov. 20, 1867.

[3] These propositions were approved by A. Humphreys, assistant superintendent at Talladega, and by General Chetlain, commanding the District of Talladega. *Selma Times*, Dec. 4, 1865.

for wages unpaid or for violation of contract. The average southern farmer had to move a great part of his crop before he could get money to satisfy labor and other debts, and when the negro saw the first bale being moved, he often became uneasy and made trouble.[1] The contract system resulted in much litigation, of which the negro was very fond; he did not feel that he was really free until he had had a lawsuit with some one. It gave him no trouble and much entertainment, but was a source of annoyance to his employer. The Bureau agents were particular that no negro should work except under a written contract, as a fee of from fifty cents to a dollar and a half was charged for each contract. If a negro was found working under a verbal agreement, he and his employer were summoned before the agent, fined, and forced into a written contract. When the negroes refused to work, the planters could sometimes hire the Bureau officials to use their influence. The whites charged that it was a common practice for the agents to induce a strike, and then make the employers pay for an order to send the blacks back to work.[2] This was the case only under alien Bureau agents, for where the magistrates were agents, all went smoothly with no contracts. The end of 1865 and the spring of 1866 found the whites, who at first had insisted on written contracts, weary of the system and disposed to make only verbal agreements, and the negro had usually become afraid of a written contract because it might be enforced. The legislature passed laws to regulate contracts, which Governor Patton vetoed on the ground that no special legislation was necessary; the laws of supply and demand should be allowed to operate, he said. Swayne also said that contracts were not necessary, as hunger and cold on the part of one, and demand for labor on the part of the other, would protect both negro and white.[3]

Some planters, having no faith in free negro labor, refused to

---

[1] *Selma Messenger*, Nov. 15, 1865; *N. Y. World*, Nov. 20, 1867.

[2] Ku Klux Rept., p. 441 ; *N. Y. News*, Sept. 7, 1865 ; oral accounts.

[3] Swayne's Report, Jan., 1866. Rev. C. W. Buckley, in a report to Swayne (dated Jan. 5, 1866), of a tour in Lowndes County, stated that while the Bureau and the army and the "government of the Christian nation," each had done much good, all was as nothing to what God was doing. The hand of God was seen in the stubborn and persistent reluctance of the negro to make contracts and go to work; God had taught the 8,000,000 arrogant and haughty whites that they were dependent upon the freedmen ; God had ordained that "the self-interest of the former master should be the protection of the late slaves."

give the negro employment requiring any outlay of money. And "freedmen were not uncommon who believed that work was no part of freedom." There was a disposition, Swayne reported, to preserve as much as possible the old patriarchal system, and the general belief was that the negro would not work; and he did refuse to work regularly until after Christmas.[1] Some planters thought that the government would advance supplies to them,[2] and they asked Howard to bind out negroes to them. Howard visited Mobile and irritated the whites by his views on the race question.[3]

Freedmen's Bureau Courts

In Alabama, the state courts were made freedmen's courts, — to test, as Howard said, the disposition of the judges; Swayne says that it was done from reasons of policy, and because at first there were not enough aliens to hold Bureau courts. The reports were favorable except·from north Alabama, where the "unionists" were supposed to abound.[4] In all cases where the blacks were concerned the assistant commissioner was authorized to exercise jurisdiction, and the state laws relating to apprenticeship and vagrancy were extended by his order to include freedmen. The Bureau officials were made the guardians of negro orphans, but each city and county had to take care of its own paupers.[5] Freedmen's Bureau courts were created, each composed of three members appointed by the assistant commissioner, one of whom was an official of the Freedmen's Bureau, and two were citizens of the county. Their jurisdiction extended to cases relating to the compensation of freedmen to the amount of $300, and all other cases between whites and blacks, and criminal cases by or against negroes where the sentence might be a fine of $100 and one month's imprisonment.

In his report for 1866, Swayne states that "martial law administered concurrently" by provisional and military authorities was in force throughout the state; that the coöperation of the provisional government and the Freedmen's Bureau had secured to the freedmen the same rights and privileges enjoyed by the other non-voting inhabitants; in some cases, he said, on account of prejudice, the

---

[1] Swayne's Report, Oct. 31, 1865.   [2] Freedmen's Bureau Report, Oct. 24, 1868.
[3] De Bow's Review, 1866.   [4] Freedmen's Bureau Report, Dec., 1865.
[5] Howard's Circular Letter, Oct. 4, 1865.

laws were not executed, but this was not to be remedied by any number of troops, since no good result could be obtained by force.[1] During 1865 and 1866 General Swayne repeatedly spoke of the friendly relations between the Freedmen's Bureau and the state officials — Governors Parsons and Patton and Commissioner Cruikshank, who was in charge of relief of the poor.

By means of the Bureau courts the negro was completely removed from trial by the civil government or by any of its officers, except when the latter were acting as Bureau agents, which, as time went on, was less and less often the case, and the negro passed entirely under the control of the alien administration, and an army officer and two or three carpet-baggers administered what they called justice in cases where the negroes were concerned. The negroes frequently broke their contracts, telling the provost marshal that they had been lashed, and this caused the employer to be arrested and often to be convicted unjustly. The white planter was much annoyed by the disposition on the part of the blacks to transfer their failings to him in their tales to the "office," as the negro called the Bureau and its agents. "The phrase flashed like lightning through the region of the late Confederacy that at Freedmen's Bureau agencies 'the bottom rail was on top.' The conditions which this expression implied exasperated the whites in like ratio as the negroes were delighted."[2] In the Ku Klux testimony, the whites related their grievances against the Bureau courts conducted by the aliens: the Bureau men always took a negro's word as being worth more than a white's; the worst class of blacks were continually haling their employers into court; the simple assertion of a negro that he had not been properly paid for his work was enough to prevent the sale of a crop or to cause the arrest of the master, who was frequently brought ten or fifteen miles to answer a trivial charge involving perhaps fifty cents;[3] the negroes were taken from work and sent to places of refuge — "Home Colonies"[4] — where hundreds died of

[1] Report, Oct. 31, 1866.

[2] Herbert, "Solid South," p. 31; N. Y. News, Sept. 3, 1865 (Selma correspondent).

[3] In one case the agent in Montgomery sent to Troy, fifty-two miles distant, and arrested a landlord who refused to rent a house to a negro. The negro told the Bureau agent that he was being evicted.

[4] There were several plantations near Montgomery, Selma, Mobile, and Huntsville where negroes were thus collected.

disease caused by neglect, want, and unsanitary conditions; the Bureau courts encouraged complaints by the negroes; the trials of cases were made occasions for lectures on slavery, rebellion, political rights of negroes, social equality, etc., and the negro was by official advice taught to distrust the whites and to look to the Bureau for protection.[1] The Bureau perhaps did some good work in regulating matters among the negroes themselves, but when the question was between negro and white, the justice administered was rather one-sided.[2] Genuine cases of violence and mistreatment of negroes were usually not tried by the Bureau courts, but by military commission. The following humorous advertisement shows the result of a legitimate interference of the Bureau : —

" Do You Like
                The Freedmen's Court ? If so, come up to Burnsville and I will rent or sell you three nice, healthy plantations with *Freedmen*. Come soon and get a bargain. I am ahead of any farmer in this section, except on one place, which said court ' Busteed ' to-day because some of the Freedmen got flogged. — JOHN F. BURNS."[3]

The Bureau courts, after the aliens came into control, proceeded upon the general principle that the negro was as good as or better than the southern white, and that he had always been mistreated by the latter, who wished to still continue him in slavery or to cheat

---

[1] In Montgomery, the Rev. C. W. Buckley, a " hard-shell " preacher, looked after negro contracts. A negro was not allowed to make his own contract, but it must be drawn up before Buckley. When a negro broke his contract, Buckley always decided in his favor, and avowed that he would sooner believe a negro than a white man. His delight was to keep a white man waiting for a long time while he talked to the negro, turning his back to and paying no attention to the white caller. He preached to the negroes several times a week, not sermons, but political harangues. The audience was composed chiefly of negro women, who, if they had work, would leave it to attend the meetings. They would not disclose what Buckley said to them, and when questioned would reply, " It's a secret, and we can't tell it to white folks." Buckley advocated confiscation, but Swayne, who had more common sense, frowned upon such theological doctrines.

[2] Barker, a carriage-maker at Livingston, was arrested and confined in prison for some time, and finally was released without trial. He was told that a negro servant had preferred charges against him, and later denied having done so. Such occurrences were common. Ku Klux Rept. Ala. Test., pp. 357, 371, 390, 475, 487, 1132; Ho. Ex. Doc., No. 27, 39th Cong., 1st Sess.; Swayne's Reports, Dec., 1865, and Jan., 1866.

[3] *Selma Times*, April 11, 1866. Busteed was a much-disliked carpet-bag Federal judge. Mr. Burns survived the *Busting*, and was a member of the Constitutional Convention of 1901.

him out of the proceeds of his labor, and who, on the slightest provocation, would beat, mutilate, or murder the inoffensive black. The greatest problem was to protect the negroes from the hostile whites, the agents thought. The aliens did not understand the relations of slave and master, and assumed that there had always been hostility between them, and that for the protection of the negro this hostility ought to continue. A system of espionage was established that was intensely galling. Men who had held high offices in the state, who had led armies or had represented their country at foreign courts, — men like Hardee, Clanton, Fitzpatrick, etc., — were called before these tribunals at the instance of some ward of the nation, and before a gaping crowd of their former slaves were lectured by army sutlers and chaplains of negro regiments.[1]

Care of the Sick

The medical department of the Freedmen's Bureau gave free attendance to the refugees and freedmen. In 1865 there were in the state 4 hospitals, capable of caring for 646 patients, with a staff of 11 physicians and 26 male and 22 female attendants. In the hospitals in 1866 were 18 physicians and 16 male and 18 female attendants.[2] In 1866 there were 6 hospitals, which number was increased in 1867 to 8, with a staff of 13 physicians and 50 male and 40 female attendants. In 1868–1869 there were only three hospitals.

In 1865 no refugees were treated, but there were 2533 negro patients, of whom 602, or 24 per cent, died. To August 31, 1866, 271 refugees had been treated, of whom 8 died, and 4153 negroes, of whom 460 died. From September 1, 1866, to June 30, 1867, 220 refugees

---

[1] The Bureau courts continued to act even after the state was readmitted to the Union. In 1868, two constables arrested a negro charged with house-burning in Tuscumbia. Col. D. C. Rugg, the Bureau agent at Huntsville, raised a force of forty negroes and came to the rescue of the negro criminal. "If you attempt to put that negro on the train," he said, "blood will be spilled. I am acting under the orders of the military department." The officers were trying to take him to Tuscumbia for trial. Rugg thought the Bureau should try him, and said, "These men [the negroes] are not going to let you take the prisoner away, and blood will be shed if you attempt it." *N. Y. World*, Oct. 23, 1868; *Tuscaloosa Times.*

[2] Probably more. Freedmen's Bureau Report, Nov. 1, 1866.

were treated and 6 died; 2203 negroes, and 186 died; to October 31, 1866, 3801 freedmen, of whom 473 died, and 305 refugees, of whom 12 died. After July, 1868, 289 freedmen were treated.[1] These statistics show the relative insignificance of the relief work.

Smallpox was the most fatal disease among the negroes in the towns, and several smallpox hospitals were established. In Selma the complaint was raised that the assistant superintendent encouraged the negroes to stay in town, and insisted on caring for all their sick, but when an epidemic of smallpox broke out, he notified the city that he could not care for these cases. The Bureau sent supplies for distribution by the county authorities to the destitute poor and to the smallpox patients. But the relief work for the sick amounted to but little.[2]

The Issue of Rations

The Department of Records had charge of the issue of supplies to the destitute refugees and blacks. Among the whites of all classes in the northern counties there was much want and suffering. The term "refugee" was interpreted to include all needy whites,[3] though at first it meant only one who had been forced to leave home on account of his disloyalty to the Confederacy. The best work of the Bureau was done in relieving needy whites in the devastated districts; and for this the upholders of the institution have never claimed credit. The negro had not suffered from want before the end of the war, but now great crowds hastened to the towns and congregated around the Bureau offices and military posts. They thought that it was the duty of the government to support them, and that there was to be no more work.

Before June, 1865, rations were issued by the army officers. From June, 1865, to September, 1866, the Freedmen's Bureau issued 2,522,907 rations to refugees (whites) and 1,128,740 to freedmen.

---

[1] Bureau Reports, 1865–1869.

[2] Freedmen's Bureau Reports, 1865–1870; Hardy, "History of Selma"; *N. Y. World*, Nov. 13, 1865.

[3] The Southern Famine Relief Commission of New York, which worked in Alabama until 1867, reported that there was much greater suffering from want among the whites than among the blacks. This society sent corn alone to the state, — 65,958 bushels. See Final Proceedings and General Report, New York, 1867.

The following table shows the number of people fed each month in Alabama by the Freedmen's Bureau before October, 1866:—

	WHITE					BLACK				
Months	Men	Women	Boys	Girls	Total	Men	Women	Boys	Girls	Total
1865.										
Nov. .	72	483	821	875	2,521	327	656	346	615	1,944
Dec. .	271	909	1,059	1,090	3,329	464	860	345	574	2,243
1866.										
Jan. .	349	2,377	1,735	2,764	7,225	538	1,053	742	1,002	3,335
Feb. .	1,285	3,641	3,806	5,039	13,771	894	1,455	880	1,095	4,324
March .	1,181	4,971	5,796	6,758	18,616	995	2,007	1,389	1,662	6,053
April .	1,038	4,340	4,844	6,642	16,864	1,176	2,331	1,904	2,771	8,182
May .	1,743	5,821	6,939	9,064	23,567	1,479	3,433	2,898	3,576	14,526
June .	1,912	5,661	6,932	8,092	22,577	1,654	3,170	2,846	3,151	10,821
July .	1,585	5,036	7,108	8,076	21,805	1,294	2,472	2,379	2,648	8,793
Aug. .	1,376	4,528	5,932	6,836	18,672	1,178	2,025	2,112	2,247	7,562
Sept. .	1,368	4,454	5,547	6,543	17,912	1,242	2,225	1,939	2,126	7,532
Totals	12,180	42,201	50,429	61,779	166,589	11,241	21,687	17,780	21,407	72,115

Men, 23,421; women, 63,888; children, 151,295; aggregate, 238,704; rations issued, 3,789,788; value, $643,590.18.

During the month of September, 1865, 45,771 rations were issued to 1971 refugees, and 36,295 rations to 3537 freedmen; in October, 1865, 2875 refugees and 2151 freedmen drew 153,812 rations. From September 1, 1866 to September 1, 1867, 214,305 rations were issued to refugees and 274,329 to freedmen. From September 1, 1867, to September 1, 1868, refugees drew only 886 rations, and freedmen 86,021. Fewer and fewer whites and more and more freedmen were fed by the Bureau.[1]

In 1865 and 1866, the crops were poor, and in 1866 there were at least 10,000 destitute whites and 5000 destitute blacks in the state. The Bureau asked for 450,000 rations per month, but did not receive them. The agents were now (1866) beginning to use the issue of rations to control the negroes, and to organize them into political clubs or "Loyal Leagues." During this time (1866-1867), however, the state gave much assistance, and coöperated with the

[1] Freedmen's Bureau Reports, 1865-1868.

Freedmen's Bureau. Some of the agents of the Bureau sold the supplies that should have gone to the starving.[1]

The Bureau furnished transportation to 217 refugees and to 521 freedmen who wished to return to their homes, and to a number of northern school teachers. These transactions were not attended by abuses.[2]

Demoralization caused by the Freedmen's Bureau

After the Federal occupation, when the negroes had congregated in the towns, the higher and more responsible officers of the army used their influence to make the blacks go home and work. If left to these officers, the labor question would have been somewhat satisfactorily settled; they would have forced the negroes to work for some one, and to keep away from the towns. But the subordinate officers, especially the officers of the negro regiments, encouraged the freedmen to collect in the towns. Few supplies were issued to them by the army, and there was every prospect that in a few weeks the negroes would be forced by hunger to go back to work. The establishment of the Freedmen's Bureau, however, changed conditions. It assumed control of the negroes in all relations, and upset all that had been done toward settling the question by gathering many of the freedmen into great camps or colonies near the towns. One large colony was established in north Alabama, and many temporary ones throughout the state,[3] into which thousands who set out to test their new-found freedom were gathered. On one plantation, in Montgomery County, in July, 1865, 4000 negroes were placed. There was another large colony near Mobile.[4] A year later the Montgomery colony had 200 invalids. Perhaps more misery was caused by the Bureau in this way than was relieved by it. The want and sickness arising from the crowded conditions in the towns was only in slight degree relieved by the food distributed, and the hospitals opened. There were 40,000 old and infirm negroes in the state, and thousands died of disease. Not one-tenth did the Bureau reach. The helpless old negroes were supported by their former

---

[1] Ho. Rept., No. 121, 41st Cong., 2d Sess.

[2] Sen. Ex. Doc., No. 6, 39th Cong., 1st Sess.

[3] Freedmen's Bureau Report, Dec., 1865.

[4] Swayne's Report, Oct. 31, 1866; *N. Y. Daily News*, Sept. 7, 1865 (Montgomery correspondent).

masters, who now in poverty should have been relieved of their care. Those who were fed were the able-bodied who could come to town and stay around the office. The colonies in the negro districts became hospitals, orphan asylums, and temporary stopping places for the negroes; and the issue of rations was longest and surest at these places.[1] Several hundred white refugees also remained worthless hangers-on of the Bureau.

The regular issue of rations to the negroes broke up the labor system that had been partially established and prevented a settlement of the labor problem. The government would now support them, the blacks thought, and they would not have to work. Around the towns conditions became very bad. Want and disease were fast thinning their numbers. They refused to make contracts, though the highest wages were offered by those planters and farmers who could afford to hire them, and the agents encouraged them in their idleness by telling them not to work, as it was the duty of their former masters to support them, and that wages were due them, at least since January 1, 1863.[2] They told them, also, to come to the towns and live until the matter was settled.[3] Domestic animals near the negro camps were nearly all stolen by the blacks who were able but unwilling to work. These marauders were frequently shot at or were thrashed, which gave rise to the stories of outrage common at that time.

Doctor Nott of Mobile wrote that in or near Mobile no labor could be hired; that it was impossible to get a cook or a washerwoman, while hundreds were dying in idleness from disease and starvation, deceived by the false hopes aroused, and false promises of support by the government, made by wicked and designing men who wished to create prejudice against the whites, and to prevent the negroes from working by telling them that to go back to work was to go back to slavery. The negro women were told that women should not work, and they announced that they never intended to go to the field or do other work again, but "live like white ladies."[4] Wherever

---

[1] Trowbridge, "The South," p. 446.

[2] In the convention of 1867 this teaching bore fruit in the ordinance authorizing suits by former slaves to recover wages from Jan. 1, 1863.

[3] *N. Y. World*, Nov. 13, 1865 (Selma correspondent); oral accounts.

[4] *De Bow's Review*, March, 1866 (Dr. Nott); *N. Y. Times*, Oct. 3, 1865; *Montgomery Advertiser*, March 21, 1866.

it was active the Bureau demoralized labor by arousing false hopes and by unnecessary intermeddling. It has been claimed for the Bureau that it was a vast labor clearing-house, and that a part of its work was the establishment of a system of free labor.[1] In other states such may have been the case; in Alabama it certainly was not. The labor system partially established all over the Black Belt in 1865 was deranged wherever the Bureau had influence. The system proposed by the Bureau was simply that of old slave wages paid for work done under a written contract. The excessive wages and the interference of the agents in the making of contracts made it impossible for the system to work, and Swayne acquiesced in the nullification of the Bureau rules by black and white, saying that natural forces would bring about a proper state of affairs. Wherever the Bureau had the least influence, there industry was least demoralized. So far from acting as a labor agency, its influence was distinctly in the opposite direction wherever it undertook to regulate labor. The free labor system, such as it was, was already in existence when the Bureau reached the Black Belt, and, in spite of that institution, worked itself out.[2]

A general belief grew up among the freedmen that at Christmas, 1865, there would be a confiscation and division of all land in the South. The soldiers, — black and white, — the preachers, and especially the Bureau agents and the school-teachers, were responsible for this belief. Swayne reported that an impression, well-nigh universal, prevailed that the confiscation, of which they had heard for months, would take place at Christmas, and led them to refuse any engagement extending beyond the holidays, or to work steadily in the meantime.[3] Christmas or New Year's the negro thought would

---

[1] Du Bois in *Atlantic Monthly*, March, 1901.

[2] A Tallapoosa County farmer stated that for three years after the war the crops were very bad. Yet the whites who had negroes on their farms felt bound to support them. But if the whites tried to make the negroes work or spoke sharply to them, they would leave and go to the Bureau for rations. P. M. Dox, a Democratic member of Congress in 1870, said that in north Alabama, in 1866–1867, negro women would not milk a cow when it rained. Servants would not black boots. There was a general refusal to do menial service. Ala. Test., pp. 345, 1132. The Alabama cotton crop of 1860 was 842,729 bales; of 1865, 75,305 bales; of 1866, 429,102 bales; of 1867, 239,516 bales; of 1868, 366,193 bales. Of each crop since the war an increasingly large proportion has been raised by the whites.

[3] Swayne's Report, Oct. 31, 1866.

be the millennium. Each would have a farm, plenty to eat and drink, and nothing to do, — "forty acres of land and a mule." There is no doubt that the "forty acres and a mule" idea was partly caused by the distribution among the negroes of the lands on the south Atlantic coast by General Sherman and others, and by the provisions of the early Bureau acts. "Forty acres and a mule" was the expectation, and to this day some old negroes are awaiting the fulfilment of this promise.[1] Many went so far, in 1865, as to choose the land that would be theirs on New Year's Day; others merely took charge at once of small animals, such as pigs, turkeys, chickens, cows, etc., that came within their reach.[2]

On account of this belief in the coming confiscation of property and their implicit confidence in all who made promises, the negroes were deceived and cheated in many ways. Sharpers sold painted sticks to the ex-slaves, declaring that if set up on land belonging to the whites, they gave titles to the blacks who set them up. A document purporting to be a deed was given with one set of painted sticks. In part it read as follows : "Know all men by these presents, that a naught is a naught, and a figure is a figure; all for the white man, and none for the nigure. And whereas Moses lifted up the serpent in the wilderness, so also have I lifted this d—d old nigger out of four dollars and six bits. Amen. Selah!" In the campaign of 1868 this was circulated far and wide by the Democrats as a campaign document. There is record of the sale of painted sticks in Clarke, Marengo, Sumter, Barbour, Montgomery, Calhoun, Macon, Tallapoosa, and Greene counties, and in the Tennessee valley. The practice must have been general. In Sumter County, 1865–1866,

[1] Within the last five years I have seen several old negroes who said they had been paying assessments regularly to men who claimed to be working to get the "forty acres and the mule" for the negro. They naturally have little to say to white people on the subject. From what I have been told by former slaves, I am inclined to think that the negroes have been swindled out of many hard-earned dollars, even in recent times, by the scoundrels who claim to be paying the fees of lawyers at work on the negroes' cases.

[2] Swayne's Report, Oct. 31, 1866; Freedmen's Bureau Report, Dec., 1865; Grant's Report; Truman's Report, April 9, 1866; De Bow's Review, March, 1866; Montgomery Advertiser, March 1, 1866; N. Y. News, Nov. 25, 1865 (Selma correspondent); N. Y. World, Nov. 13, 1865; N. Y. Times, Oct. 31, 1865; N. Y. News, Sept., and Oct. 2, 7, 1865. B. W. Norris, a Bureau agent from Skowhegan, Maine, told the negroes the tale of "forty acres and a mule," and they sent him to Congress in 1868 to get the land for them. He told them that they had a better right to the land than the masters had. "Your work made this country what it is, and it is yours." Ala. Test., pp. 445, 1131.

the seller of sticks was an ex-cotton agent. He had secured the striped pegs in Washington, he said, and his charge was a dollar a peg. He instructed the buyer how to "step off" the forty acres, and told them not to encroach upon one another and to take half in cleared land and half in woodland.[1] In Clarke County, as late as 1873, the sticks were sold for three dollars each if the negro possessed so large a sum; but if he had only a dollar, the agent would let a stick go for that. Some of the negroes actually took possession of land, and went to work.[2] In Tallapoosa County the painted pegs were sold as late as 1870.[3] In 1902 a man was arrested in south Alabama for collecting money from negroes in this way. It was said that one cause of the survival of this practice was the course of Wendell Phillips, who, in the *Antislavery Standard*, advocated the distribution of land among the negroes, eighty acres to each, or forty acres and a furnished cottage. The speeches of Thaddeus Stevens on confiscation were widely distributed among the negroes. His Confiscation Bill of March, 1867, caused expectations among the negroes, who soon heard of such propositions.[4] General Wilson, on his raid, had taken all the stock from Montgomery and had left with the planters his broken-down mules and horses. The military authorities of the Sixteenth Army Corps had declared that these animals belonged to the planters, who had already used them a year. But the Rev. C. W. Buckley, a Bureau chaplain, promised them to the negroes, who began to take possession of them.[5]

The subordinate agents of the Bureau frequently were broken-down men who had made failures at everything they had undertaken;[6] some were preachers with strong prejudices, and others were the dregs of a mustered-out army, — all opposed to any settlement of the negro question which would leave them without an office. Such men sowed the seeds of discord between the races and taught the negro that he must fear and hate his former master, who desired above all things to reënslave him.[7] In this way they were ably abetted by the northern teachers and missionaries.

[1] Ala. Test., p. 314.   [2] Ball, "Clarke County," p. 627.   [3] Ala. Test., p. 1133.

[4] Ala. Test., p. 460; see Annual Cyclopædia (1867), article "Confiscation."

[5] *Montgomery Advertiser*, March, 1866. Buckley was known among the "malignants" as "the high priest of the nigger Bureau." *N. Y. World*, Dec. 22, 1867.

[6] *N. Y. Herald*, July 23, 1865; Herbert, "Solid South," p. 30.

[7] *DeBow's Review*, 1866; oral accounts.

There were some favorable reports from the Bureau in Alabama, principally from districts where the native whites were agents. But in the summer of 1866 Generals Steedman and Fullerton, accompanied by a correspondent, made a trip through the South inspecting the institution. They reported that in Alabama it was better conducted than elsewhere in the South; that all of the good of the system and not all of the bad was here most apparent. Over the greater part of the state, they said, it interfered but little with the negro, and consequently the affairs of both races were in better condition. General Patton thought that Swayne was the best man to be at the head of the Bureau, yet he was sure that the institution was unnecessary, its only use being to feed the needy, which could be done by the state with less demoralization. The negro, he said, should be left to the protection of the law, since there was no discrimination against him. As long as free rations were issued, the blacks would make no contracts and would not work. Swayne, Patton declared, was doing his best, but he could not prevent demoralization, and the very presence of the Bureau was an irritation to the whites, thus operating against the good of the negro. He stated that in Clarke and Marengo counties, where there were no agents, the relations between the races were more friendly than in any other black counties, and there the negro was better satisfied. The southern people knew the negro and his needs, Steedman and Fullerton reported, and he should be left to them; the Bureau served as a spy upon the planters; it was the general testimony that where there was no northern agent, there the negro worked better, and there was less disorder among the blacks and less friction between the races. The fact was clearly demonstrated in west Alabama, where there was little interference on the part of the Bureau, and where the negro did well.[1]

An account of conditions in one county where the agents were army officers and were somewhat under the influence of the native whites will be of interest. When the army and the Bureau came to Marengo County, the white people, who were few in number, determined to win their good will. There were "stag" dinners and feasts, and the eternal friendship of the officers, with few exceptions,

---

[1] *N. Y. Times*, Feb. 12, 1866 (letter of northern traveller); Steedman and Fullerton's Reports; *N. Y. Herald*, June 24, 1866; *Columbus* (Ga.) *Sun*, Nov. 22, 1865; *N. Y. Times*, Jan. 25, 1866.

2 G

was won. The exceptions were those who had political ambitions. The population, being composed largely of negroes, was under the control of the "office," which here did not heed the tales of "rebel outrages." The negro received few supplies and did well, though afterwards, in places doubtful politically, supplies were issued for political purposes. One planter in Marengo gave an order to the negroes on his plantation to do a certain piece of work. They refused and sent their head man to report at the "office." He brought back a sealed envelope containing a peremptory order to cease work. The negroes were ignorant of the contents, so the planter read the letter, called the negroes up, and ordered them back to the same work. They went cheerfully, evidently thinking it was the order of the Bureau. At any time the Bureau could interfere and say that certain work should or should not be done. Another planter lived twelve miles from Demopolis. One day ten or twelve of the negro laborers went to Demopolis to complain to the "office" about one of his orders. The planter went to Demopolis by another road, and was sitting in the Bureau office when the negroes arrived. They were confused and at first could say nothing. The planter was silent. Finally they told their tale, and the officer called for a sergeant and four mounted men. "Sergeant," he said, "take these people back to Mr. DuBose's on the *run!* You understand; on the *run!*" They ran the negroes the whole twelve miles, though they had already travelled the twelve miles. Upon their arrival at home the sergeant tied them to trees with their hands above their heads, and left them with their tongues hanging out. It was the most terrible punishment the negroes had ever received, and they never again had any complaints to pour into the ear of the "office." [1] The white soldiers usually cared little for the negroes, it is said.

From the first the Bureau was unnecessary in Alabama. The negro had felt no want before the beginning of the war, and the efforts of the general officers of the army, besides hunger and cold, would have soon forced him to work. He was not mistreated except in rare cases which did not become rarer under the Bureau. Cotton was worth fifty cents to a dollar a pound, and the extraordinary demand for labor thus created guaranteed good treatment. Much more suffering was caused by the congregation of the black population

[1] Account by Col. J. W. DuBose in manuscript.

in the towns than would have been the case had there been no relief. Not a one did it really help to get work, because no man who wanted work could escape a job unless it prevented, and with its red tape it was a hindrance to those who were industrious. Its interference in behalf of the negro was bad, as it led him to believe that the government would always back him and that it was his right to be supported. Thus industry was paralyzed. Yet as first organized by Swayne, the Bureau would have been endurable, though it would have been a disturbing element, and the negro would have been the greater sufferer from the disorder caused by it; but, as time went on, General Swayne was gradually forced by northern opinion to change his policy, and to put into office more and more northern men as subordinate agents. These men, of character already described, had to live by fleecing the negroes, by fees, and by stealing supplies.[1] Then, recognizing the trend of affairs and seeing their great opportunity, they began to organize the negro for political purposes; they themselves were to become statesmen. The Bureau was then manipulated as a political machine for the nomination and election of state and federal officers, and the public money and property were used for that purpose. The Howard Investigation refused to enter that field, but the testimony shows that the Bureau agents, teachers, the savings-bank, and missionaries industriously carried on political operations.[2]

In 1869 the Bureau was intrusted with the payment of bounties to the negro soldiers who had been discharged or mustered out. There were several thousand of these in Alabama. Gross frauds are said to have been perpetrated by the officials in charge of the distribution. The worst scandals were in north Alabama, where most of the negro soldiers lived.[3]

Sec. 2. The Freedmen's Savings-Bank

The Freedmen's Savings and Trust Company was an institution closely connected with the Freedmen's Bureau, and had the sanction

---

[1] Herbert, "Solid South," pp. 30, 31; *N. Y. Times*, Jan. 25, 1866.

[2] Ho. Rept., No. 121, 41st Cong., 2d Sess.; Ku Klux Rept., p. 441. See chapter in regard to Union League.

[3] See also DuBois, in *Atlantic Monthly*, March, 1901; Ho. Ex. Doc., No. 241, 41st Cong., 2d Sess.

and support of the government, especially of the Bureau officials. Many of the trustees of the bank were or had been connected with the Bureau,[1] and it was generally understood by the negroes that it was a part of the Bureau. It possessed the confidence of the blacks to a remarkable degree and gave promise of becoming a very valuable institution by teaching them habits of thrift and economy.[2]

The central office was in Washington, and several branch banks were established in every southern state. The Alabama branch banks were established at Huntsville, in December, 1865, and at Montgomery and Mobile early in 1866. The cashiers at the respective branches, when the bank failed, in 1874, were Lafayette Robinson, who seems to have been an honest man though he could not keep books, Edwin Beecher,[3] and C. R. Woodward, both of whom seem to have had some picturesque ideas as to their rights over the money deposited. A bank-book was issued to each negro depositor, and in the book were printed the regulations to be observed by him. On one cover there was a statement to the effect that the bank was wholly a benevolent institution, and that all profits were to be divided among the depositors or devoted to charitable enterprises for the benefit of freedmen. It was further stated that the "Martyr" President Lincoln had approved the purpose of the bank, and that one of his last acts was to sign the bill to establish it. On the cover of the book was the printed legend:[4] —

"I consider the Freedmen's Savings and Trust Company to be greatly needed by the colored people and have welcomed it as an auxiliary to the Freedmen's Bureau." — MAJOR-GENERAL O. O. HOWARD.

To the negro this was sufficient recommendation. There was also printed on the cover a very attractive table, showing how much a

[1] Ho. Rept., No. 121, p. 47, 41st Cong., 2d Sess.

[2] Some of the prominent incorporators were Peter Cooper, William C. Bryant, A. A. Low, Gerritt Smith, John Jay, A. S. Barnes, J. W. Alvord, S. G. Howe, George L. Stearns, Edward Atkinson, and A. A. Lawrence. The act of incorporation was approved by the President on March 3, 1865, at the same time the Freedmen's Bureau Bill was approved. Numbers of the incorporators and bank officials were connected with the Bureau. See Ho. Mis. Doc., No. 16, 43d Cong., 2d Sess.

[3] A Bureau paymaster.

[4] Ho. Mis. Doc., No. 16, 43d Cong., 2d Sess.

man might save by laying aside ten cents a day and placing it in the bank at 6 per cent interest. The first year the man would save, in this way, $36.99, the tenth year would find $489.31 to his credit. And all this by saving ten cents a day — something easily done when labor was in such demand. This unique bank-book had on the back cover some verses for the education of the freedmen. The author of these verses is not known, but the negroes thought that General Howard wrote them.

> " 'Tis little by little the bee fills her cell;
> And little by little a man sinks a well;
> 'Tis little by little a bird builds her nest;
> By littles a forest in verdure is drest;
> 'Tis little by little great volumes are made;
> By littles a mountain or levels are made;
> 'Tis little by little an ocean is filled;
> And little by little a city we build;
> 'Tis little by little an ant gets her store;
> Every little we add to a little makes more;
> Step by step we walk miles, and we sew stitch by stitch;
> Word by word we read books, cent by cent we grow rich."

The verses were popular, the whole book was educative, and it was not above the comprehension of the negro. If all the teaching of the negro had been as sensible as this little book, much trouble would have been avoided. It was a proud negro who owned one of these wonderful bank-books, and he had a right to be proud. Many at once began to make use of the savings-banks, and small sums poured in. Only the negroes in and near the three cities — Huntsville, Montgomery, and Mobile — where the banks were located seem to have made deposits, for those of the other towns and of the country knew little of the institution. During the month of January, 1866, deposits to the amount of $4809 were made in the Mobile branch. This was all in small sums and was deposited at a time of the year when money was scarcest among laborers.[1] In 1868 the interest paid on long-time deposits to depositors at Huntsville was $38.02; at Mobile, $1349.40. On May 1, 1869, the deposits at Huntsville amounted to $17,603.29; at Mobile, $50,511.66.

---

[1] Ho. Ex. Doc., No. 70, 39th Cong., 1st Sess.

The following statements of the two principal banks will show how the scheme worked among the negroes: —

	HUNTSVILLE BRANCH	MOBILE BRANCH
Total deposits to March 31, 1870 . . .	$89,445.10	$539,534.33
Total number of depositors	500	3,260
Average amount deposited by each . . .	$17.89	$165.60
Drawn out to March 31, 1870	70,586.60	474,583.60
Balance to March 31, 1870	18,858.50	64,750.83
Average balance due to each depositor . .	47.114	39.82
Spent for land (known)	1,900.00	50,000.00
Dwelling houses	800.00	——
Seeds, teams, agricultural implements . .	5,000.00	15,000.00
Education, books, etc.	1,200.00	——

STATEMENT OF THE BUSINESS DONE DURING AUGUST, 1872

	HUNTSVILLE	MOBILE	MONTGOMERY
Deposits for the month . . .	$7,343.50	$11,136.05	$8,522.90
Drafts for the month	10,127.61	18,645.62	8,679.60
Total deposits	416,617.72	1,039,097.05	238,106.08
Total drafts	364,382.51	933,424.30	213,861.71
Total due depositors . . .	52,235.21	105,672.75	24,244.37 [1]

These branch banks exercised a good influence over the negro population, even over those who did not become depositors. The negroes became more economical, spent less for whiskey, gewgaws, and finery, and when wages were good and work was plentiful, they saved money to carry them through the winter and other periods of lesser prosperity. Some of those who had no bank accounts would save in order to have one, or, at least, save enough money to help them through hard times. Much of the money drawn from the banks was invested in property of some kind. Excessive interest in politics prevented a proper increase in the number of depositors and in the amount of deposits.

In 1874, after the bank failed through dishonest and inefficient management, the liabilities to southern negro depositors amounted

[1] See Williams, "History of the Negro Race in America," Vol. II, p. 410. August was a month in which there was little money-making among the negroes. It was vacation time, between the "laying by" and the gathering of the crop.

to $3,299,201.[1] A total business of $55,000,000 had been done. The following table, compiled by Hoffman, will show the total business of the bank, 1866 to 1874.[2]

YEAR	TOTAL DEPOSITS	DEPOSITS EACH YEAR	DUE DEPOSITORS	GAIN EACH YEAR
1866	$305,167	$305,167	$199,283	$199,283
1867	1,624,853	1,319,686	366,338	167,054
1868	3,582,378	1,957,525	638,299	271,960
1869	7,257,798	3,675,420	1,073,465	435,166
1870	12,605,782	5,347,983	1,657,006	583,541
1871	19,952,947	7,347,165	2,455,836	798,829
1872	31,260,499	11,281,313	3,684,739	1,227,927
1873	————	————	4,200,000	————
1874	55,000,000	————	3,013,670	————

In Alabama the depositors lost, for the time at least, $35,963 at Huntsville; $29,743 at Montgomery; $95,144 at Mobile. After years of delay dividends were paid; but few of the depositors profited by the late payment.[3] The philanthropic incorporators took care to desert the failing enterprise in time, and Frederick Douglass, a well-known negro, was placed in charge to serve as a scapegoat. No one was punished for the crooked proceedings of the institution. Several of the incorporators were dead; the survivors pleaded good intentions, ignorance, etc., and finally placed the blame on their dead associates. Their sympathy for the negro did not go the length of assuming money responsibility for the operations of the bank, and thus saving the negro depositors. There were several of the incorporators who could have assumed all the liabilities and not felt the burden severely. Agents and lawyers got most of the later proceeds, and the good work was all undone, for the negro felt that the United States government and the Freedmen's Bureau had cheated him. It is said to have affected his faith in banks to this day.[4]

[1] Hoffman, "Race Traits and Tendencies," p. 290, says $3,013,699.

[2] Hoffman, p. 290; also Sen. Rept., No. 440, 46th Cong., 2d Sess. Williams, Vol. II, p. 411, states that the total deposits amounted to $57,000,000, an average of $284 for each depositor.

[3] Dividends were declared as follows : Nov. 1, 1875, 20%; March 20, 1875–1878, 10%; Sept. 1, 1880, 10%; June 1, 1882, 15%; May 12, 1883, 7%; making 62% in all. To 1886, $1,722,549 had been paid to depositors, and there was a balance in the hands of the government receivers of $30,476.

[4] Williams, "History of the Negro Race," Vol. II, pp. 403–410 ; Fred Douglass, "Life and Times," Ch. XIV; Ho. Mis. Doc., No. 16, 43d Cong., 2d Sess.; DuBois,

SEC. 3. THE FREEDMEN'S BUREAU AND NEGRO EDUCATION

As the Federal armies occupied southern territory and numbers of negroes were thrown upon the care of the government which gathered them into colonies on confiscated plantations, there arose a demand from the friends of the negro at the North that his education should begin at once. An educated negro, it was thought, was even more obnoxious to the slaveholding southerner than a free negro; hence educated negroes should be multiplied. No doubt was entertained by his northern friends but that the negro was the equal of the white man in capacity to profit by education. To educate the negro was to carry on war against the South just as much as to invade with armed troops, and various aid societies demanded that, as the negro came under the control of the United States troops, schools be established and the colored children be taught. The Treasury agents, who were in charge of the plantations and colonies where the negroes were gathered, were instructed by the Secretary to establish schools in each "home" and "labor" colony for the instruction of the children under twelve years of age. Teachers, supplied by the superintendent of the colony, who was usually the chaplain of a negro regiment, or by benevolent associations, were allowed to take charge of the education of the blacks in any colony they decided to enter.[1] Before the end of the war only three or four such schools were established in Alabama. One was on the plantation of ex-Governor Chapman, in Madison County, another at Huntsville, and one at Florence.

The law of March 3, 1865, creating the Freedmen's Bureau, gave to its officials general authority over all matters concerning freedmen. Nothing was said about education or schools, but it was understood that educational work was to be carried on and extended, and after the organization of the Bureau in the state of Alabama its "Department of Records" had control of the education of the negro. For the support of negro education the second Freedmen's Bureau Act, July 16, 1866, authorized the use of or the sale of all buildings and lands and other property formerly belonging to the Confederate States

"The Souls of Black Folk"; the various reports of the Freedmen's Bureau and of the commissioners appointed to settle the affairs of the Freedmen's Savings and Trust Company, to 1902; Hoffman, "Race Traits and Tendencies," pp. 289, 290; Fleming, "Documents relating to Reconstruction," Nos. 6 and 7.

[1] Regulations of the Treasury Dept., July 29, 1864.

or used for the support of the Confederacy. It directed the authorities of the Bureau to coöperate at all times with the aid societies, and to furnish buildings for schools where these societies sent teachers, and also to furnish protection to these teachers and schools.[1]

The southern churches had never ceased their work among the negroes during the war,[2] and immediately after the emancipation of the slaves all denominations declared that the freedmen must be educated so as to fit them for their changed condition of life.[3] The churches spoke for the controlling element of the people, who saw that some kind of training was an absolute necessity to the continuation of the friendly relations then existing between the two races. The church congregations, associations, and conferences, and mass meetings of citizens pledged themselves to aid in this movement. Dr. J. L. M. Curry first appeared as a friend of negro education when, in the summer of 1865, he presided over a mass meeting at Marion, which made provision for schools for the negroes. On the part of the whites whose opinion was worth anything, there was no objection worth mentioning to negro schools in 1865 and 1866.[4] In the latter year, before the objectionable features of the Bureau schools appeared, General Swayne commented upon the fact that the various churches had not only declared in favor of the education of the negro, but had aided the work of the Bureau schools and kept down opposition to them. He was, however, inclined to attribute this attitude somewhat to policy. He wrote with special approval of the assistance and encouragement given by the Methodist Episcopal Church South, through Rev. H. N. McTyeire (later bishop), who was always in favor of schools for negroes. He reported, also, that there was a growing feeling of kindliness on the part of the people toward the schools. Where there was prejudice the school often dispelled it, and the movement had the good will of Governors Parsons and Patton.[5]

---

[1] McPherson, "Rebellion," pp. 594, 595 ; McPherson, "Reconstruction," pp. 147–151.   [2] See Ch. IV, sec. 7.

[3] DuBois (*Atlantic Monthly*, March, 1901) declares that the opposition to the education of the negro was bitter, for the South believed that the educated negro was a dangerous negro. This statement is perhaps partially correct for fifteen or twenty years after 1870, but it is not correct for 1865–1869.

[4] *The Gulf States Hist. Mag.*, Sept., 1902; Report of General Swayne to Howard, Dec. 26, 1865. The evidence on this point that is worthy of consideration is conclusive. It is all one way. See also Chs. XIX and XX, below.

[5] Report of Swayne, Oct. 31, 1866.

Just after the military occupation of the state there was the greatest desire on the part of the negroes, young and old, for book learning. Washington speaks of the universal desire for education.[1] The whole race wanted to go to school; none were too old, few too young. Old people wanted to learn to read the Bible before they died, and wanted their children to be educated. This seeming thirst for education was not rightly understood in the North; it was, in fact, more a desire to imitate the white master and obtain formerly forbidden privileges than any real desire due to an understanding of the value of education; the negro had not the slightest idea of what "education" was, but the northern people gave them credit for an appreciation not yet true even of whites. There were day schools, night schools, and Sunday-schools, and the "Blue-back Speller" was the standard beginner's text. Yet, as Washington says, it was years before the parents wanted their children to make any use of education except to be preachers, teachers, Congressmen, and politicians. Rascals were ahead of the missionaries, and a number of pay schools were established in 1865 by unprincipled men who took advantage of this desire for learning and fleeced the negro of his few dollars. One school, established in Montgomery by a pedagogue who came in the wake of the armies, enrolled over two hundred pupils of all ages, at two dollars per month in advance. The school lasted one month, and the teacher left, but not without collecting the fees for the second month.[2]

When General Swayne arrived, he assumed control of negro education, and a "Superintendent of Schools for Freedmen" was appointed. The Rev. C. M. Buckley, chaplain of a colored regiment and official of the Freedmen's Bureau, was the first holder of this office. In 1868, after he went to Congress, the position was held by Rev. R. D. Harper, a northern Methodist preacher, who was superseded in 1869 by Colonel Edwin Beecher, formerly a paymaster of the Bureau and cashier of the Freedmen's Savings Bank in Montgomery. There also appeared a person named H. M. Bush as "Superintendent of Education," a title the Bureau officials were fond of assuming and which often caused them to be confused with the state officials of like title.[3]

[1] " Up from Slavery," pp. 29, 30.

[2] *Daily News*, Sept. 7, 1865 (Montgomery correspondence). Oral accounts.

[3] G. O. No. 11, July 12, 1865 (Montgomery); Freedmen's Bureau Reports, 1865-1869.

The sale of Confederate property at Selma, Briarfield, and other places, small tuition fees, and gifts furnished support to the teachers. General Swayne was deeply interested in the education of the blacks, and thought that northern teachers could do better work for the colored race than southern teachers. Most of the aid societies had spent their funds before reaching Alabama, but Swayne secured some assistance from the American Missionary Association. The teachers were paid partly by the Association, but mostly by the Bureau. The Pittsburg Freedmen's Aid Commission established schools in north Alabama, at Huntsville, Stevenson, Tuscumbia, and Athens, and also had a school at Selma. The Cleveland Freedmen's Union Commission worked in Montgomery and Talladega by means of Sunday-schools. 'A great many of the schools with large enrolments were Sunday-schools. The American Missionary Association, besides furnishing teachers to the Bureau, had schools of its own in Selma, Talladega, and Mobile. The American Freedmen's Union Commission (Presbyterian branch) also had schools in the state. The Freedmen's Aid Society of the Methodist Episcopal Church (North) did some work in the way of education, but was engaged chiefly in inducing the negroes to flee from the wrath to come by leaving the southern churches. At Stevenson and Athens schools were established by aid from England.[1] In 1866 the Northwestern Aid Society had a school at Mobile.[2] At the end of 1865, the Bureau had charge of eleven schools at Huntsville, Athens, and Stevenson, one in Montgomery with 11 teachers and 497 pupils, and one in Mobile with 4 teachers and 420 pupils.[3] Some ill feeling was aroused by the action of the Bureau in seizing the Medical College and Museum at Mobile and using it as a schoolhouse. Even the Confederate authorities had not demanded the use of it. Before the war it was said that the museum was one of the finest in America. Many of the most costly models were now taken away, and a negro shoemaker was installed in the chemical department.[4]

The attitude of the southern religious bodies enabled the Bureau to extend its school system in 1866, and to secure native white teachers.

[1] Swayne's Report, Oct. 31, 1866 ; Freedmen's Bureau Report, 1866.

[2] Swayne's Report., Oct. 31, 1866.

[3] Freedmen's Bureau Report, Dec., 1865 ; Ho. Ex. Doc., No. 70, 39th Cong., 1st Sess.

[4] *Daily News,* Oct. 21, 1865 (Mobile correspondent) ; *De Bow's Review,* 1866 (Dr. Nott).

Schools taught by native whites, most of whom were of good character, were established at Tuskegee, Auburn, Opelika, Salem, Greenville, Demopolis, Evergreen, Mount Meigs, Tuscaloosa, Gainesville, Marion, Arbahatchee, Prattville, Haynesville, and King's Station, — in all twenty schools. There were negro teachers in the schools at Troy, Wetumpka, Home Colony (near Montgomery), and Tuscaloosa. The native whites taught at places where no troops were stationed, and General Swayne stated that they were especially willing to do this work after the churches had declared their intention to favor the education of the negro. It was of such schools that he said their presence dispelled prejudice.[1] The history of one of these schools is typical: In Russell County a school was established by the Bureau, and Buckley, the Superintendent of Schools, who had no available northern teacher, allowed the white people to name a native white teacher. Several prominent men agreed that a Methodist minister of the community was a suitable person. The neighbors assured him that his family should not suffer socially on account of his connection with the school, and that they wanted no northern teacher in the community. The minister accepted the offer, was appointed by the Bureau, and the school was held in his dooryard, out buildings, and verandas, his family assisting him. The negroes were pleased, and big and little came to school. The relations between the whites and blacks were pleasant, and all went well for more than two years, until politics alienated the races, and the negroes demanded a northern teacher or one of their own color.[2] The schools at Huntsville, Mobile, Montgomery, Selma, Tuscumbia, Stevenson, and Athens, where troops were stationed, were reserved for the northern teachers who were sent by the various aid societies. The disturbing influence of the teachers was thus openly acknowledged. The Bureau coöperated by furnishing buildings, paying rent, and making repairs, and, in some instances, by giving money or supplies.[3]

The statistics of the Bureau schools are confused and incomplete. In 1866 one report states that there were 8 schools with 31 teachers and 1338 pupils under the control of the Bureau. General Swayne's

---

[1] Swayne's Report, Oct. 31, 1866.

[2] The account of this particular school was given me by Dr. O. D. Smith of Auburn, Ala., who was one of the men who chose the white teacher.

[3] Swayne's Report, Oct. 31, 1866.

list includes the schools at the various places named above, and reports 43 schools in 23 of the 52 counties, with 68 teachers and a maximum enrolment of 3220 pupils — the average being much less.[1] Buckley's report for March 15, 1867, gives the number of negro schools of all kinds as 68 day schools and 27 night schools. The total enrolment for the winter months had been 5352; the average attendance, 4217. At this time the Bureau was supporting 38 day schools, 19 night schools, and paying 49 teachers. Benevolent societies under supervision of the Bureau were conducting 21 day schools, 7 night schools, with 36 teachers and a total enrolment of 2157 pupils. Besides these there were 10 private schools with 443 pupils. In all the schools, there were 75 white and 20 negro teachers. There were more than 100,000 negro children of school age in the state who were not reached by these schools.

The following table, compiled from the semiannual reports on Bureau schools in Alabama, will show the slight extent of the educational work of the Bureau. The list includes all the schools in charge of the Bureau, or which received aid from the Bureau.

	July 1, 1867	July 1, 1868	Jan. 1, 1869	July 1, 1869	July 1, 1870
Day schools . . .	122	59	33	79	23
Night schools . . .	53	19	2	1	4
Private schools (negro teachers)	8	22	4	1	—
Semi-private . . .	25	48	25	55	2
Teachers transported by Bureau	122	22	29	3	—
School buildings owned by negroes	27	13	1	4	11
School buildings owned by Bureau	38	36	29	66	—
White teachers . . .	126	67	49	65?	—
Negro teachers . . .	24	28	12	23?	—
White pupils (refugees) .	23	—	—	—	—
Black pupils . . .	9,799	4,040	3,330	5,131	2,110
Tuition paid by negroes .	$1,542.00	$3,206.56	$1,431.50	$1,248.95	$1,446.30
Bureau paid for tuition .	6,693.00	2,097.73	1,219.75	2,938.50	22,559.88
Bureau paid for school expenses	18,685.07				
Total expenditures .	8,235.00	6,463.72	2,723.25	4,187.45	240,061.18

[1] Report, Oct. 31, 1866.

These statistics showing expenditures are not complete, but they are given as they are in the reports, which are carelessly made from carelessly kept and defective records. There was a disposition on the part of the Bureau to claim all the schools possible in order to show large numbers. Many of these so-called schools were in reality only Sunday-schools, — that is, they were in session only on Sundays, — (and the missionary Sunday-schools were counted), and were not as good as the Sunday-schools which for years before the war had been conducted among the negroes by the different churches. The Bureau did not consider of importance the private plantation and mission schools supported by the native whites, nor the state schools, which largely outnumbered the Bureau schools, but only those aided in some way by itself. The schools entirely under the control of the Bureau had small enrolment. Assistance was given to all the schools taught by northern missionaries, to some taught by native whites, and to some taught by negroes. It was given in the form of buildings, repairs, supplies, and small appropriations of money for salaries. Rent was paid by the Bureau for school buildings not owned by the schools or by the Bureau. Accounts were carelessly kept, and after General Swayne left, if not before, abuses crept in. At least one of the aid societies received money from the Bureau, and its representatives established a reputation for crookedness that was retained after the Bureau was a thing of the past. This society, — The American Missionary Association, — along with other work among the negroes, carried on a crusade against the Catholic Church which was endeavoring to work in the same field. Church work and educational work were not separated. A building in Mobile, valued at $20,000, was given by the Bureau to the association as a training school for negro teachers. The society charged the Bureau rent on this building, and there were other similar cases where the Bureau paid rent on its own buildings which were used by the aid societies.[1]

[1] Rent was usually paid at the rate of $20 a month for thirty pupils. Ho. Rept., No. 121, pp. 47, 369, 374, 377, 41st Cong., 2d Sess. The books of the American Missionary Association showed that it had received, in 1868 and 1869, from the Freedmen's Bureau for Alabama, the following amounts in cash, though how much it received before these dates is not known.

December, 1867	$4000.00
October, 1868	583.86
February, 1868	25.41 (?)

As already stated, for two years there was little or no opposition by the whites to the education of the negro, and to some extent they even favored and aided it. The story of southern opposition to the schools originated with the lower class of agents, missionaries, and teachers. Of course, to a person who had taken the abolitionist programme in good faith, it was incomprehensible that the southern whites could entertain any kindly or liberal feelings toward the blacks. But Buckley reported, as late as March 15, 1867, that the native whites favored the undertaking, and that no difficulty was experienced in getting southern whites to teach negro schools. Some of these teachers were graduates of the State University, some had been county superintendents of education. Crippled Confederate soldiers and the widows of soldiers sought for positions in the schools.[1] There were also some northern whites of common sense and good character engaged in teaching these Bureau schools. But too many of the latter considered themselves missionaries whose duty it was to show the southern people the error of their sinful ways, and who taught the negro the wildest of the social, political, and religious doctrines held at that time by the more sentimental friends of the ex-slaves.

The temper and manner and the beliefs in which the northern educator went about the business of educating the negro are shown in the reports and addresses in the proceedings of the National

January, 1869	$218.25
April, 1869	683.53
May, 1869	1397.49
June, 1869	95.87
July, 1869	527.00
September, 1869	3049.59
November, 1869	3469.50
December, 1869	2083.78
For building (?)	20,000.00

An item in the account of the Association was "Chicago to Mobile, $20,000." No one was able to explain what it meant unless it was the $20,000 building in Mobile used as a training school for negro teachers and on which the Bureau paid rent. In the southern states the Bureau paid to the American Missionary Association, as shown by the books of the latter, $213,753.22. Judging from the variable items not noted above, rent was evidently not included nor even all the cash. Ho. Rept., No. 121, p. 369 et seq., 41st Cong., 2d Sess. (Howard Investigation).

[1] Buckley's Report for March 15, 1867 ; Semiannual Report on Schools for Freedmen, July 4, 1867 ; General Clanton in Ku Klux Rept. Ala. Test.

Teachers' Association from 1865 to 1875. The crusade of the teachers in the South was directed by the people represented in this association, and its members went out as teachers. Some of the sentiments expressed were as follows: Education and Reconstruction were to go hand in hand, for the war had been one of "education and patriotism against ignorance and barbarism."[1] "The old slave states [were] to be a missionary ground for the national schoolmaster,"[2] and knowledge and intellectual culture were to be spread over this region that lay hid in darkness.[3] There was a demand for a national school system to force a proper state of affairs upon the South, for free schools were necessary, they declared, to a republican form of government, and the free school system should be a part of Reconstruction. The education of the whites as well as the blacks should be in the future a matter of national concern, because the "old rebels" had been sadly miseducated, and they had been able to rule only because others were ignorant and had been purposely kept in ignorance. Much commiseration was expressed for "the poor white trash" of the South. The "rebels" were still disloyal, and, as one speaker said, must be treated as a farmer does stumps, that is, they must be "worked around and left to rot out." The old "slave lords" must be driven out by the education of the people, and no distinction in regard to color should be allowed in the schools. ·The work of education must be directed by the North, for only the North had correct ideas in regard to education. Nothing good was found in the old southern life; it was bad and must give way to the correct northern civilization. The work of "The Christian Hero" was praised, and it was declared that it ought to inspire an epic even greater than the immortal epic of Homer.[4]

The missionary teachers who came South were supported by this sentiment in the North, and they could not look with friendly eyes upon anything done by the southern whites for the negroes. Altogether there were not many of these heralds of light, and it was a year before the character of their teaching became generally known

---

[1] Francis Wayland.　　　　[2] S. G. Greene, president of the association.

[3] President Hill of Harvard College.

[4] Reports, Proceedings, and Lectures of the National Teachers' Association, 1865 to 1880; Reports of the Freedmen's Aid Societies of the Methodist Episcopal Church. For results of the mistaken teachings of the radical instructors, see Page's article on "Lynching" in the *North American Review*, Jan., 1904.

to the whites or its results were plainly seen. Their dislike for all things southern was heartily reciprocated by the native whites, who soon acquired a dislike for the northern teacher which became second nature. The negro was taught by the missionary educators that he must distrust the whites and give up all habits and customs that would remind him of his former condition; he must not say master and mistress nor take off his hat when speaking to a white person. In teaching him not to be servile, they taught him to be insolent. The missionary teachers regarded themselves as the advance guard of a new army of invasion against the terrible South. In recent years a Hampton Institute teacher has expressed the situation as follows: "When the combat was over and the Yankee schoolma'ams followed in the train of the northern armies, the business of educating the negroes was a continuation of hostilities against the vanquished, and was so regarded to a considerable extent on both sides." The North in a few years became disappointed and indifferent, especially after the negro began to turn again to the southern whites.[1]

The negro schools felt the influence of the politics of the day, besides suffering from the results of the teachings of the northern pedagogues. Buckley made a report early in 1867, stating that conditions were favorable. On July 1, 1868, Rev. R. D. Harper, "Superintendent of Education," reported that there was a reaction against negro schools; that the whites were now hostile to the negro schools on account of their teachers, who, the whites claimed, upheld the doctrines of social and political equality; the negroes were too much interested in politics in 1867 and 1868, and spent their money in the campaigns; the teachers of the negro schools were intimidated, ostracized from society, and could not find board with the white people. Because of this, he said, some schools had been broken up. The civil authorities, he declared, winked at the intimidation of the teachers.[2] Beecher, the Assistant Commissioner and "Superintendent of Education," reported that the schools had been supported on confiscated Confederate property until 1869, and that this source of supply

---

[1] Miss Alice M. Bacon, in the Slater Fund Trustees, Occasional Papers, No. 7, p. 6. Armstrong, at Hampton, Va., was a shining exception to the kind of teachers described above.

[2] The Reconstruction government was now in power. There were, at this time, thirty-one Bureau schools at thirty-one points in the state.

2 H

being exhausted, the teachers were returning to the North. He reported that 100,000 children had never been inside a schoolhouse. The night schools were not successful because the negroes were unable to keep awake. A year later, Beecher reported that the schools were recovering from unfavorable conditions, and that some of the teachers who had proven to be immoral and incompetent had been discharged.

The last reports (1870) stated that there was less opposition by the whites to the Bureau schools.[1] This can be partly accounted for by the fact that the majority of the obnoxious northern teachers had returned to the North or had been discharged. The best ones, who had come with high hopes for the negroes, sure that the blacks needed only education to make them the equal of the whites, were bitterly disappointed, and in the majority of cases they gave up the work and left. Not all of them were of good character and a number were discharged for incompetency or immorality; others were coarse and rude. The respectable southern whites resigned as soon as the results of the teaching of the outsiders began to be realized, and those who remained were beyond the pale of society. The white people came to believe, and too often with good reason, that the alien teachers stood for and taught social and political equality, intermarriage of the races, hatred and distrust of the southern whites, and love and respect for the northern deliverer only. Social ostracism forced the white teachers to be content with negro society. Naturally they became more bitter and incendiary in their utterances and teachings. Some negroes were only too quick to learn such sentiments, and the generally insolent behavior of the negro educated under such conditions was one of the causes of reaction against negro education. The hostility against negro schools was especially strong among the more ignorant whites, and during the Ku Klux movement these people burned a number of schoolhouses and drove the teachers from the country where a few years before they had been welcomed by some and tolerated by all.

The results of the attempts by the Bureau and the missionary societies to educate the negro were almost wholly bad. DuBois makes the astonishing statement that the Bureau established the free

---

[1] Freedmen's Bureau Reports, 1867-1870.

public school system in the South.[1] It is true that some of the schools then established have survived, but there would have been many more schools to-day had these never existed. For the whites the public school system of Alabama existed before the war; the example of the Bureau in no way encouraged its extension for the blacks; reconstructive educational ideals caused a reaction against general public education. In 1865 to 1866 the thinking people of the state, such men as Dr. J. L. M. Curry and Bishop McTyeire, were heartily in favor of the education of the negro, and all the churches were also in favor of giving it a trial. As conditions were at that time, even the best plan for the education of the negro by alien agencies would have failed. General Swayne hoped to use both northern and southern teachers, but it was not possible that the temper of either party would permit coöperation in the work. Buckley seems to have had glimmerings of this fact, when he tried to get southern teachers for the schools. But the damage was already done. The logical and intentional result of the teachings of the missionaries was to alienate the races. If the negro accepted the doctrine of the equality of all men and the belief in the utter sinfulness of slavery and slaveholders, he at once found that the southern whites were his natural enemies.

Unwise efforts were made to teach the adult blacks, and they were encouraged to believe that all knowledge was in their reach; that without education they would be helpless, and with it they would be the white man's equal. Some of the negroes almost worshipped education, it was to do so much for them. The schools in the cities were crowded with grown negroes who could never learn their letters. All attempts to teach these older ones failed, and the failure caused grievous disappointment to many. The exercise of common sense by the teachers might have spared them this. But the average New England teacher began to work as if the negroes were Mayflower descendants. No attention was paid to the actual condition of the negroes and their station in life. False ideas about manual labor were put into their heads, and the training given them had no practical bearing on the needs of life.[2]

---

[1] *Atlantic Monthly*, March, 1901.

[2] Sir George Campbell, "White and Black," pp. 131, 383; Thomas, "The American Negro," p. 240; Washington, "The Future of the American Negro," pp. 25-27, 55; *De Bow's Review*, 1866; Slater Fund Trustees, Occasional Papers, No. 7. Wash-

From the table given above it will be seen that the Bureau schools reached only a very small proportion of the negro children. The missionary schools not connected with the Bureau were few. It is likely that for five years there were not more than two hundred northern teachers in the state, yet the effect of their work was, in connection with the operations of the political and religious missionaries, to make a majority perhaps of the white people hostile to the education of the negro. The crusading spirit of the invaders touched the most sensitive feelings of the southerners, and the insolence and rascality of the educated negroes were taken as natural results of education. The good was obscured by the bad. The innocent missionary suffered for the sins of the violent and incendiary. The educated black rascal was pointed out as a fair example of negro education. The damage was done, not so much by what was actually taught in the relatively few schools, as by the ideas caught by the entire negro population that came in contact with the missionaries. Naturally the blacks were more likely to accept the radical teachers. A most unfortunate result was the withdrawal of the southern church organizations and of all white southerners from the work of training the negro. The profession had been discredited. One of the hardest tasks of the negro educators of to-day — like Washington or Councill — is to undo the work of the aliens who wrought in passion and hate a generation before they began. The evil of the Bureau system did not die with that institution, but when the reconstructionists undertook to mould anew the institutions of the South, the educational methods of the Bureau and its teachers were transferred into the new state system which they helped to discredit.[1]

ington tells of the craze for the education in Greek, Latin, and theology. This education would make them the equal of the whites, they thought, and would free them from manual labor, and above all fit them for office-holding. Nearly all became teachers, preachers, and politicians. "Up from Slavery," pp. 30, 80, 81 ; "Future of the American Negro," p. 49.

[1] From the surrender of the Confederate armies, to his death in 1903, Dr. Curry was a stanch believer in the work for negro education. No other man knew the whole question so thoroughly as he. And he had the advantage of a close acquaintance with the negro from his early childhood. His observations as to the effects of alien efforts to educate the black will be found in the Slater Fund Occasional Papers, and in an address delivered before the Montgomery Conference in 1900. See also Ch. XIV.

Why the Bureau System Failed

There have been many apologies for the Freedmen's Bureau, many assertions of the necessity for such an institution to protect the blacks from the whites. It was necessary, the friends of the institution claimed, to prevent reënslavement of the negro, to secure equality before the law, to establish a system of free labor, to relieve want, to force a beginning of education for the negro, to make it safe for northern missionaries and teachers to work among the blacks. It was, of course, not to be expected that the victorious North would leave the negroes entirely alone after the war, and in theory there were only two objections to such an institution well conducted, — (1) it was not really needed, and (2) it was, as an institution, based on an idea insulting to southern white people. It meant that they were unfit to be trusted in the slightest matter that concerned the blacks. It was based on the theory that there was general hostility between the southern white and the southern black, and that the government must uphold the weaker by establishing a system of espionage over the stronger. The low characters of the officials made the worst of what would have been under the best agents a bad state of affairs. In 1865 it was necessary for the good of the negro that social and economic laws cease to operate for a while and allow the feelings of sentiment, duty, and gratitude of the Southern whites to work in behalf of the black and enable the latter to make a place for himself in the new order. After the surrender there was, on the part of the whites, a strong feeling of gratitude to the negroes, that was practically universal, for their faithful conduct during the war. The people were ready, because of this and many other reasons, to go to any reasonable lengths to reward the blacks. The Bureau made it impossible for this feeling to find expression in acts. The negro was taken from his master's care and in alien schools and churches taught that in all relations of life the southern white man was his enemy. The whites came to believe that negro education was worse than a failure. The southern churches lost all opportunity to work among the negroes. Friendly relations gave way to hostility between the races. The better elements in southern society that were working for the good of the black were paralyzed and the worst element remained active. The friendship of the native whites was of more value to the blacks than any amount of theoretical protection against inequalities in legislation and justice.   Finally, the claim that the Bureau was essential in establishing a system of free labor is ridiculous.   The reports of the Bureau officials themselves show clearly, though not consciously, that the new labor system was being worked out according to the fundamental economic laws of supply and demand, and largely in spite of the opposition of the Bureau with its red tape measures. The Bureau labor policy finally gave way everywhere before the unauthorized but natural system that was evolved.[1]

---

[1] I have talked with many who uniformly assert that they were unable to conform to the Bureau regulations.   It was better to let land remain uncultivated.   Wherever possible·no attention was paid to the rules.   The negro laborers themselves have no recollections of any real assistance in labor matters received from the Bureau.   They remember it rather as an obstruction to laboring freely.

PART V
CONGRESSIONAL RECONSTRUCTION

CHAPTER XII

MILITARY GOVERNMENT UNDER THE RECONSTRUCTION ACTS

SEC. I. THE ADMINISTRATION OF GENERAL POPE

The Military Reconstruction Bills

THE Radicals in Congress triumphed over the moderate Republicans, the Democrats, and the President, when, on March 2, 1867, they succeeded in passing over the veto the first of the Reconstruction Acts. This act reduced the southern states to the status of military provinces and established the rule of martial law. After asserting in the preamble that no legal governments or adequate protection for life and property existed in Alabama and other southern states, the act divided the South into five military districts, subject to the absolute control of the central government, that is, of Congress.[1] Alabama, with Georgia and Florida, constituted the Third Military District. The military commander, a general officer, appointed by the President, was to carry on the government in his province. No state interference was to be allowed, though the provisional civil administration might be made use of if the commander saw fit. Offenders might be tried by the local courts or by military commissions, and except in cases involving the death penalty, there was no appeal beyond the military governor. This rule of martial law was to continue until the people[2] should adopt a constitution providing for enfranchisement of the negro and for the disfranchisement of such whites as would be excluded by the proposed Fourteenth Amendment to the United States Constitution. As soon as this constitution should be ratified by the new electorate (a majority voting in the election) and the constitution approved by Congress, and the legislature elected under the new constitution should ratify the proposed Fourteenth

---

[1] The President and the Supreme Court now being powerless.

[2] That is, blacks and such whites as were not " disfranchised for participation in the rebellion or for felony."

Amendment, then representatives from the state were to be admitted to Congress upon taking the "iron-clad" test oath of July 2, 1862.[1] And until so reconstructed the present civil government of the state was provisional only and might be altered, controlled, or abolished, and in all elections under it the negro must vote and those who would be excluded by the proposed Fourteenth Amendment must be disfranchised.[2]

The President at once (March 11, 1867) appointed General George H. Thomas to the command of the Third Military District, with headquarters at Montgomery, but the work was not to General Thomas's liking, and at his request he was relieved, and on March 15 General Pope was appointed in his place.[3] Pope was in favor of extreme measures in dealing with the southern people and stated that he understood the design of the Reconstruction Acts to be "to free the southern people from the baleful influence of old political leaders."[4]

The act of March 2 did not provide for forcing Reconstruction upon the people. If they wanted it, they might initiate it through the provisional governments, or if they preferred, they might remain under martial law. While all people were anxious to have the state restored to the Union, most of the whites saw that to continue under martial law, even when administered by Pope, was preferable to Reconstruction under the proposed terms. Consequently the movement toward Reconstruction was made by a very small minority of the people and had no chance whatever of making any headway.

Therefore, in order to hasten the restoration of the states and to insure the proper political complexion of the new régime, Congress assumed control of the administration of the law of March 2, by the supplementary act of March 23, 1865. "To facilitate restoration" the commander of the district was to cause a registration of all men

---

[1] July 11, 1868, the oath was modified for those whose disabilities had been removed by Congress; Feb. 15, 1871, those not disfranchised by the Fourteenth Amendment were allowed to take the modified oath of July 11, 1868, instead of the iron-clad oath. See MacDonald, "Select Statutes." The Alabama representatives all took the "iron-clad" oath.

[2] Text of the Act, McPherson, "Reconstruction," pp. 191, 192; G. O. No. 2, 3d M. D., April 3, 1867. For criticism, Burgess, "Reconstruction," pp. 112-122; Dunning, "Civil War and Reconstruction," pp. 123, 126-135, 143.

[3] G. O. Nos. 10 and 18, H. Q. A., March 11 and 15, 1867; McPherson, p. 200.

[4] Report of Secretary of War, 1867, Vol. I, p. 321.

over twenty-one not disfranchised by the act of March 2, who could take the prescribed oath [1] before the registering officers. The commander was then to order an election for the choice of delegates to a convention. He was to apportion the delegates according to the registered voting population. If a majority voted against holding the convention, it should not be held. The boards of registration, appointed by the commanding general, were to consist of three loyal persons. They were to have entire control of the registration of voters, and the elections and returns which were to be made to the military governor. They were required to take the "iron-clad" test oath, and the penalties of perjury were to be visited upon official or voter who should take the oath falsely. After the convention should frame a constitution, the military commander should submit it to the people for ratification or rejection. The same board of registration was to hold the election. If the Constitution should be ratified by a majority of the votes cast in the election where a majority of the registered voters voted, and the other conditions of the act of March 2 having been complied with, the state should be admitted to representation in Congress.[2]

Pope assumes Command

On April 1, 1867, General Pope arrived in Montgomery and assumed command of the Third Military District. General

---

[1] The oath was: "I, —— ——, do solemnly swear (or affirm), in the presence of Almighty God, that I am a citizen of the State of Alabama; that I have resided in said State for —— months, next preceding this day, and now reside in the county of —— in said State; that I am twenty-one years old; that I have not been disfranchised for participation in any rebellion or civil war against the United States, nor for felony committed against the laws of any State or of the United States; that I have never been a member of any State legislature, nor held any executive or judicial office in any State and afterward engaged in insurrection or rebellion against the United States or given aid and comfort to the enemies thereof; that I have never taken an oath as a member of Congress of the United States, as an officer of the United States, or as a member of any State legislature, or as an executive or judicial officer of any State, to support the Constitution of the United States and afterwards engaged in insurrection or' rebellion against the United States or given aid and comfort to the enemies thereof; that I will faithfully support the Constitution and obey the laws of the United States, and will, to the best of my ability, encourage others to do so, so help me God!" McPherson, "Reconstruction," pp. 192, 205; G. O. No. 5, 3d M. D., April 8, 1867.

[2] McPherson, "Reconstruction," pp. 192–194; Burgess, "Reconstruction," pp. 129–135; Dunning, "Civil War and Reconstruction," pp. 124, 125.

Swayne was continued in command of Alabama as a sub-district. Pope announced that the officials of the provisional government would be allowed to serve out their terms of office, provided the laws were impartially administered by them. Failure to protect the people without distinction in their rights of person and property would result in the interference of the military authorities. Civil officials were forbidden to use their influence against congressional reconstruction. No elections were to be held unless negroes were allowed to vote and the whites disfranchised as provided for in the act of March 2. However, all vacancies then existing or which might occur before registration was completed would be filled by military appointment. The state militia was ordered to disband.[1] General Swayne proclaimed that he, having been intrusted with the "administration of the military reconstruction bill" in Alabama, would exact a literal compliance with the requirements of the Civil Rights Bill. All payments for services rendered the state during the war were peremptorily forbidden.[2] The *Herald* correspondent reported that Pope's early orders were favorably received by the conservative press of Alabama, and that there was no opposition of any kind manifested. The people did not seem to realize what was in store for them. The army thought necessary to crush the "rebellious" state was increased by a few small companies only, and now consisted of fourteen companies detached from the Fifteenth and the Thirty-third Infantry and the Fifth Cavalry, amounting in all to 931 men, of whom eight companies were in garrison in the arsenal at Mount Vernon and the forts at Mobile.[3] The rest were stationed at Montgomery, Selma, and Huntsville.

Writing to Grant on April 2, Pope stated that the civil officials were all active secessionists and would oppose Reconstruction. But the people were ready for Reconstruction, which he predicted would be speedy in Alabama. Five days later he wrote that there would be no trouble in Alabama; that Governor Patton and nearly all the civil officials and most of the prominent men of the state were in

---

[1] G. O. Nos. 1 and 2, 3d M. D., April 1 and 3, 1866; *N. Y. Herald*, April 6, 1867; Annual Cyclopædia (1867), p. 19; McPherson, pp. 201, 205; Report of Secretary of War, 1867, Vol. I, p. 322; Herbert, "Solid South," p. 38.

[2] G. O. No. 1, Dist. Ala., April 2, 1867; McPherson, p. 206.

[3] Report of Secretary of War, 1867, Vol. I, p. 466; *N. Y. Herald*, April 6, 1867.

favor of the congressional Reconstruction and were canvassing the state in favor of it.[1] He was evidently of changeable opinions. However, he was so impressed with the goodness of Alabama and the badness of Georgia, that, in order to be near the most difficult work, he asked Grant to have headquarters removed to Atlanta, which was done on April 11.[2]

The Georgia people were evidently so bad that they caused a change in his former favorable opinion of the people in general, or rather of the whites, for in a letter to Grant, July 24, 1867, we find a frank expression of his sentiments in regard to Reconstruction. He thought the disfranchising clauses were among the wisest provisions of the Reconstruction Acts; that the leading rebels should have been forced to leave the country and stay away; that all the old official class was opposed to Reconstruction and was sure to prevail unless kept disfranchised; that it was better to have incompetent loyal men in office than rebels of ability, — in fact, the greater the ability the greater the danger; that in order to retain the fruits of reconstruction the old leaders must be put beyond the power of returning to influence. He had by this time evidently become somewhat disgusted with the reconstructionists, for he intimated that none of the whites were fit for self-government, and was strongly of the opinion that, in a few years, intelligence and education would be transferred from the whites to the negroes. He predicted ten thousand majority for Reconstruction in Alabama, but thought that in case Reconstruction succeeded in the elections, some measures would have to be taken to free the country of the turbulent and disloyal leaders of the reactionary party, or there would be no peace.[3]

Control of the Civil Government

Pope instructed the post commanders in Alabama to report to headquarters any failures of civil tribunals to administer the laws in accordance with the Civil Rights Bill or the recent acts of Congress. They were, above all, to watch for discrimination on account of color, race, or political opinion. While not interfering with the

---

[1] Ho. Ex. Doc., No. 20, 40th Cong., 1st Sess.
[2] G. O. No. 52, H. Q. A., April 11, 1867.
[3] Report of Secretary of War, 1867, Vol. I, p. 353.

functions of civil officers, they were instructed to give particular attention to the manner in which such functions were discharged.[1] Civil officials were warned that the prohibition against their using influence against Reconstruction would be stringently enforced. They were not to give verbal or written advice to individuals, committees, or the public unless in favor of Reconstruction. Officials who violated this prohibition were to be removed from office and held accountable as the case demanded.[2] District and post commanders were ordered to report to Pope all state, county, or municipal officials who were "disloyal" to the government of the United States, or who used their influence to "hinder, delay, prevent, or obstruct the due and proper administration of the acts of Congress."[3] Later, Grant and Pope decided that the paroles of soldiers were still in force and that any attempt to "prevent the settlement of the southern question would be a violation of parole."[4]

In May, Pope issued orders informing the officials of Alabama of their proper status. There was no legal government in Alabama, they were told, and Congress had declared that no adequate protection for life and property existed. The military authorities were warned that upon them rested the final responsibility for peace and security. Consequently when necessary they were to supersede the civil officials. In towns, the mayor and chief of police were required to be present at every public meeting, with sufficient force to render disturbance impossible. It would be no excuse not to know of a meeting or not to apprehend trouble. Outside of towns, the sheriff or one of his deputies was to be present at such gatherings, and in case of trouble was to summon a posse from the crowd, but must not summon officers of the meeting or the speakers. It was declared the duty of civil officials to preserve peace, and assure rights and privileges to all persons who desired to hold public meetings. In case of disturbance, if it could not be shown that the civil officials did their full duty, they would be deposed and held responsible by the military authorities. When the civil authorities asked for it, the commanders of troops were to furnish detachments to be present at political meetings and prevent disturbance. The commanding officers

---

[1] G. O. No. 4, 3d M. D., April 4, 1867.　　[2] G. O. No. 10, 3d M. D., April 23, 1867.
[3] G. O. No. 48, 3d M. D., Aug. 6, 1867.　　[4] Annual Cyclopædia (1867), p. 17.

were to keep themselves informed in regard to political meetings and hold themselves ready for immediate action.[1]

From the beginning, Pope, supported and advised by General Swayne, pursued extreme measures. There were soon many complaints of his arbitrary conduct. In his correspondence with General Grant he complained of the attitude of the Washington administration toward his acts, and largely to support Pope (and Sheridan in the Fifth District), Congress passed the act of July 19, 1867, which was the last of the Reconstruction Acts, so far as Alabama was concerned. This law declared that the civil governments were not legal state governments and were, if continued, to be subject absolutely to the military commanders and to the paramount authority of Congress. The commander of the district was declared to have full power, subject only to the disapproval of General Grant, to remove or suspend officers of the civil government and appoint others in their places. General Grant was vested with full power of removal, suspension, and appointment. It was made the duty of the commander to remove from office all who opposed Reconstruction.[2] Pope had already been making use of the most extreme powers, and the only effect of the act was to approve his course. Pope gave the laws a very broad interpretation, believing that Reconstruction should be thoroughly done in order to leave no room for future trouble and embarrassment. Grant, on August 3, wrote to him[3] approving his sentiments, and went on to say: "It is certainly the duty of the district commander to study what the framers of the Reconstruction laws wanted to express, as much as what they do express, and to execute the law according to that interpretation."[4] This was certainly a unique method of interpretation and would justify any possible assumption of power.

There had been several instances of prosecution by state authori-

[1] G. O. No. 25, 3d M. D., May 29, 1867. (This was to favor Radical meetings. There were many stump speakers sent down from the North to tell the negro how to vote, and it was feared they might excite the whites to acts of violence.) *N. Y. Herald*, June 4, 1867 (explanatory order).

[2] McPherson, "Reconstruction," pp. 335, 336; Dunning, pp. 153, 154.

[3] As long as Pope was in command at Montgomery and Atlanta, he and Grant kept up a rapid and voluminous (on the part of Pope) correspondence. They were usually agreed on all that pertained to Reconstruction, both now being extreme in their views.

[4] Ho. Ex. Doc., No. 30, 40th Cong., 2d Sess.; No. 20, 40th Cong., 1st Sess.; McPherson, p. 312.

ties of soldiers and officials for acts which they claimed were done under military authority. Pope disposed of this question by ordering the civil courts to entertain no action against any person for acts performed in accordance with military orders or by sanction of the military authority. Suits then pending were dismissed. The military authorities were to enforce the order strictly and report all officials who might disobey.[1] A few weeks later a decree went forth that all jurors should be chosen from the lists of voters registered under the acts of Congress. They must be chosen without discrimination in regard to color, and each juror must take an oath that he was a registered voter. Those who could not take the oath were to be replaced by those who could.[2]

So much for the general regulation and supervision of the civil authorities by the army. There were but a few hundred troops intrusted with the execution of these regulations, which were, of course, enforced only spasmodically. The more prominent officials were closely watched, but the only effect in country districts was to destroy all government. Many judges, while willing to have their jurors drawn from the voting lists, refused to accept ignorant negroes on them, or to order the selection of mixed juries, and many courts were closed by military authority. Judge Wood, of the city court of Selma, had a jury drawn of whites. A military commission, sitting in Selma, refused to allow cases to be tried unless negroes were on the jury. Pope's order was construed as requiring negroes on each jury, and he so meant it.[3] Later, he published an order requiring jurors to take the "test oath," which would practically exclude all the whites.[4] Prisoners confined in jail under sentence by jurors drawn under the old laws were liberated by the army officers or by Freedmen's Bureau officials. Twice in the month of December, 1867, there were jail deliveries by military authorities in Greene County.[5]

Within the first month Pope began to remove civil officials and appoint others. Mayor Joseph H. Sloss of Tuscumbia was the

---

[1] G. O. No. 45, 3d M. D., Aug. 2, 1867; McPherson, p. 319.

[2] G. O. Nos. 53 and 55, 3d M. D., Aug. 19 and 23, 1867; Report of the Secretary of War, 1867, Vol. I, p. 331 ; McPherson, p. 319.

[3] See *Selma Messenger*, Jan. 17, 1868.   [4] See McPherson, p. 312.

[5] *Eutaw Whig and Observer*, Dec. 12 and 24, 1867.

first to go. Pope alleged that the election had not been conducted in accordance with the acts of Congress and forthwith appointed a new mayor. No complaint had been made, the removal being caused by outside influence.[1] At this election, negroes for the first time in Alabama had voted under the Reconstruction Acts. Sloss had received two-thirds of all votes cast. Evidently the blacks had been controlled by the whites, which was contrary to the spirit of the Reconstruction.

Immediately after a riot in Mobile [2] following an incendiary speech by "Pig Iron" Kelly of Pennsylvania, one of the visiting orators, Colonel Shepherd of the Fifteenth Infantry assumed command of the city. The police were suspended. Breach of the peace was punished by the military authorities. Out-of-door congregations after nightfall were prohibited. Notice of public meetings had to be given to the acting mayor in time to have a force on hand to preserve the peace. The publication of incendiary articles in the newspapers was forbidden. The provost guard was directed to seize all large firearms in the possession of improper persons and to search suspected persons for small arms. The special police, when appointed, were ordered to restrict their duties to enforcing the city ordinances. All offences against military ordinances would be attended to by the military authorities. A later order prohibited the carrying of large firearms without special permission. Deposits of such arms were seized.[3]

Pope declared all offices vacant in Mobile and filled them anew,[4] in the face of a report by Swayne that reasonable precautions had been taken to prevent disorder. The blame for this action of Pope's fell upon Swayne, who had to carry out the orders. The officers appointed by Pope refused to accept office, and then he seems to have offered to reappoint the old officials, and they declined. Thereupon he lost his temper and directed Swayne to fill the vacancies in the city government of Mobile "from that large class of citizens who have

[1] S. O. No. 2, 3d M. D., April 15, 1867; Annual Cyclopædia (1867), p. 20; *Montgomery Mail*, April 30, 1867.

[2] See p. 509.

[3] G. O. Nos. 35, 38, 40, Post of Mobile, 1867; Annual Cyclopædia (1867), pp. 20–23; *N. Y. Times*, May 21, 1867.

[4] *N. Y. World*, May 28, 1867; S. O. No. 34, 3d M. D., May 31, 1867; Herbert, "Solid South," p. 40; *N. Y. Times*, May 21, 1867.

2 I

heretofore been denied the right of suffrage and participation in municipal affairs and whose patriotism will prevent them from following this disloyal example." He was referring to the refusal of the former members of the city government to accept reappointment after suspension, and meant that negroes should now be appointed. Swayne offered positions to some of the most respected and influential negroes, who declined, saying that they preferred white officials. Negro policemen were appointed.[1] In October a case came up in Mobile which caused much irritation. The negro policemen were troublesome and insolent, and one day a little child ran out into the street in front of a team driven by a negro, who paid no attention to the mother's call to him to stop his horses. Some one snatched the baby from under the heels of the horses, and the scared and angry mother relieved her feelings by calling the driver a "black rascal." The negro policemen came to her house, arrested her, and with great brutality dragged her from the house and along the street. Another woman asked the negroes if they had a warrant for the arrest of the first woman. She was answered by the polite query, "What the hell is it your business?" Mayor Horton, Pope's appointee, fined the woman ten dollars[2] — for violation of the Civil Rights Bill, it is to be presumed, since that was considered to cover most things pertaining to negroes.

This Mayor Horton had a high opinion of his prerogatives as military mayor of Mobile. The *Mobile Tribune* had been publishing criticisms on his administration and also of Mr. Bromberg, one of his political brethren. Archie Johnson, a crippled, half-witted negro newsboy, was, it is said, hired to follow the mayor about, selling his *Tribune* papers, much to the annoyance of Mayor Horton. On one occasion Archie cried, "Here's yer *Mobile Tribune*, wid all about Mayor Horton and his Bromberg rats." This was too much for the military mayor, and, considering the offence as one against the Civil Rights Bill, he sentenced the negro to banishment to New Orleans. Archie soon returned and was again exiled by the mayor. Here was an opportunity for the people to get even

---

[1] S. O. No. 38, 3d M. D., June 6, 1867; S. O. No. 27, 3d M. D., May 22, 1867; *N. Y. Tribune*, June 12, 1867; *Selma Messenger*, June 18, 1867; *Evening Post*, May, 1867; Annual Cyclopædia (1867), pp. 20-25; *Mobile Register*, Oct. —, 1867.

[2] *Mobile Register*, Oct. —, 1867.

with Horton, and suit was brought in the Federal court before Busteed, who was now somewhat out with his party. Horton was fined for violation of the Civil Rights Bill.[1]

Many officials were removed and many appointments made by Pope. His removals and appointments included mayors, chiefs of police, tax assessors and collectors, school trustees, county commissioners, justices of the peace, sheriffs, judges, clerks of courts, bailiffs, constables, city clerks, solicitors, superintendents of schools, aldermen, common councils, and all the officials of Jones and Colbert counties.[2] Pope was roundly abused by the newspapers and by the people for making so many changes. I have been unable to find, however, the names of more than thirty-four officials of any consequence who were removed by Pope. He made 224 appointments to such offices, besides minor ones. A clean sweep of all officials from mayor to policemen was made in Mobile and again in Selma. Most vacancies were caused by expiration of term of office or by forced resignation.[3]

As there was need of money to pay the expense of the convention soon to assemble, and as the taxpayers were beginning to understand for what purposes their money was to be used and were in many instances refusing to pay, Pope issued an order to the post and detachment commanders directing them to furnish military aid to state tax-collectors.[4] The bitterest reconstructionists were heartily in favor of aid to the tax-collecting branch of the "rebel" administration. They needed money to carry out their plans. When the terms of the tax-collectors expired, they were ordered to continue in office until their successors were duly elected and qualified,[5] which, of course, meant to continue the present administration until the reconstructed government should take charge. Pope was very careful not to allow the civil government to spend any of the money coming in from taxes. He said that he thought it proper

[1] Herbert, "Solid South," pp. 40, 41; *N. Y. Times*, Dec. 27, 1867. See above, p. 393.

[2] S. O. Nos. 9, 10, 16, 18, 19, 20, 22, 24, 25, 26, 27, 31, 32, 35, 36, 37, 38, 39, 3d M. D., 1867; Report of the Secretary of War, 1867, Vol. I, p. 327. (Some of the persons appointed were B. T. Pope and David P. Lewis, judges; George P. Goldthwaite, solicitor; and B. F. Saffold, mayor of Selma.)

[3] Report of the Secretary of War, 1867, Vol. I, p. 364.

[4] G. O. No. 77, 3d M. D., Oct. 19, 1897; McPherson, p. 319.

[5] G. O. No. 103, 3d M. D., Dec. 21, 1867.

to prohibit the state treasurer from paying out money for the support of families of deceased Confederate soldiers, for wooden legs for Confederate soldiers, etc., since the convention soon to meet would probably not approve expenditure for such purposes.[1] Later the treasurer was ordered to pay the *per diem* of the delegates and the expenses of the convention, though Pope expressed doubt, for once, of his authority in the matter.[2]

General Swayne, at Montgomery, who had long been at the head of the Freedmen's Bureau in the state and also military commander of the District of Alabama since June 1, 1866, found himself relegated to a somewhat subordinate position after Pope assumed command in the Third District. The latter took charge of everything. If a negro policeman were to be appointed in Mobile, Pope made the appointment and issued the order. Nor did he always send his orders to Swayne to be republished. In consequence, Swayne dropped out of the records somewhat, but he had to bear much of the blame that should have fallen on Pope, though he was in full sympathy with the views of the latter. He was, however, a man of much more ability than Pope, of sounder judgment, and had had legal training. Consequently, Pope relied much upon him for advice in the many knotty questions that came up, often coming from Atlanta to Montgomery to see Swayne, and as a rule none of his well-known proclamations were ever issued when under the latter's influence. The orders written for him or outlined by Swayne were stringent, of course, but clear, short, and to the point. Pope's own masterpieces were long, rhetorical, and blustering. His favorite valedictory at the end of an order was a threat of martial law and military commissions.

General Swayne was still at the head of the Freedmen's Bureau, and in this capacity he made his authority felt. In April, 1867, he ordered probate judges to revise former actions in apprenticing minors to former owners and to revoke all indentures made since the war if the minors were able to support themselves. Though the vagrancy law had never been enforced and had been repealed by the legislature, he declared its suspension. The chain-gang

[1] Report of the Secretary of War, 1877, Vol. I, p. 333; McPherson, p. 316.

[2] S. O. 254, 3d M. D., Nov. 26, 1867; Pope to Swayne, Nov. 20, 1867; *N. Y. World*, Dec. 14, 1867.

system was abolished, except in connection with the penitentiary.[1] In the fall, in order to secure pay for negro laborers, he ordered a lien on the crops grown on the farm where they were employed. This lien was to attach from date of order and to have preference over former liens.[2]

Pope and the Newspapers

When Pope first assumed command, it was reported that the conservative papers were, at the worst, not hostile to him;[3] but within a few weeks he had aroused their hostility and the battle was joined. Pope believed that the papers had much to do with inciting hostility against the visiting orators from the North, resulting in such disturbances as the Kelly riot in Mobile. Consequently, instructions were issued prohibiting the publication of articles tending to incite to riot. This order was aimed at the conservative press. No one except the negroes paid much attention to the Radical press. However, after the Mobile trouble the military commander was somewhat nervous and wanted to prevent future troubles. The negroes, now much excited by the campaign, were supposed to be much influenced by the violent articles appearing in the Radical paper of Mobile, — the *National*. On May 30 an article was printed in that paper instructing the freedmen when, where, and how to use firearms. It went on to state: "Do not, on future occasions [like the Kelly riot], waste a single shot until you see your enemy, be sure he is your enemy, never waste ammunition, don't shoot until necessary, and then be sure to shoot your enemy. Don't fire into the air." Fearing the effect upon the negroes of such advice, the commanding officer at Mobile suppressed the edition of May 30, and prohibited future publication unless the proof should first be submitted to the commandant according to the regulations of May 19, ·issued by Pope. Instead of approving the action of the Mobile officer, Pope strongly disapproved of and revoked his orders. The Mobile commander was informed that it was the duty of the military authorities, not to restrict, but to secure, the utmost freedom of speech. No officers or soldiers should interfere with newspapers or speakers on any pretext whatever. "No satisfactory execution of the late

[1] G. O. No. 3, Sub-dist. Alabama, April 12, 1867 ; McPherson, p. 319.
[2] McPherson, p. 319. [3] *N. Y. Herald*, April 6, 1867.

acts of Congress is practicable unless this freedom is secured and its exercise protected," Pope said. However, "treasonable utterances" were not to be regarded as the legitimate exercise of the freedom of discussion.[1]

The conservative papers managed to keep within bounds, and Pope was unable to harm them. Finally he decided to strike at them through the official patronage. By the famous General Order No. 49,[2] he stated that he was convinced that the civil officials were obeying former instructions[3] only so far as their personal conversation was concerned, and were using their official patronage to encourage newspapers which opposed reconstruction and embarrassed civil officials appointed by military authority by denunciations and threats of future punishment. Such use of patronage was pronounced an evasion of former orders and an employment of the machinery of the state government to defeat the execution of the Reconstruction Acts. Therefore it was ordered that official advertising and official printing be given to those newspapers which had not opposed and did not then oppose Reconstruction or embarrass officials by threats of violence and of prosecution as soon as the troops were withdrawn.[4] This order affected nearly every newspaper in the state. There were sixty-two counties, and each had public printing and advertising. On an average, at least one paper for each county was touched in the exchequer, and as Pope reported, "a hideous outcry" arose from the press of the state.[5] There were only five or six Reconstruction papers in the state, and a modification of the order in practice was absolutely necessary. Pope was so roundly abused by the newspapers, North and South, and especially in Alabama and Georgia, that he seems to have been affected by it. He endeavored to explain away the order by saying that it related only to military officials and not to civil officials. He did not say that in the order, though he may have meant it, and was now using the remarkable method of interpretation suggested to him by Grant in regard to the Reconstruction Acts. Several accounts of newspapers for public advertisements were held up and payments disallowed.

---

[1] *N. Y. Tribune,* June 1, 1867; *N. Y. Herald,* June 4, 1867; G. O. No. 28, 3d M. D., June 3, 1867; Report of the Secretary of War, 1867, Vol. I, p. 326.

[2] Aug. 12, 1867.   [3] G. O. Nos. 1 and 10.

[4] G. O. No. 49, 3d M. D., Aug. 12, 1867.

[5] Report of the Secretary of War, 1867, Vol. I, p. 235.

The best-known of these papers were the *Selma Times* and the *Eutaw Whig and Observer*.[1] The order was strictly enforced until General Meade assumed command of the Third Military District.

Trials by Military Commissions

The newspapers state that many arrests of citizens were made by military authorities, and in the spring of 1868 they generally remarked that the jails were filled with prisoners thus arrested who were still awaiting trial. Most of these were probably arrested under the Pope régime, since Meade, his successor, was not so extreme. However, Pope, in spite of his threats, had but few persons tried by military commissions. D. C. Ballard was convicted of pretending to be a United States detective and of stealing ninety-five bales of cotton, and was sentenced to eight years' imprisonment.[2] One David J. Files was arrested for inciting the Kelly riot at Mobile. Pope said that he was the chief offender and had him imprisoned at Fort Morgan until he could be tried by a military commission. He was fined $100.[3] William A. Castleberry was convicted by a military commission, fined $200, and imprisoned for one year for purchasing stolen property and for assisting a deserter to escape. Jesse Hays, a justice of the peace in Monroe County, was sentenced to five months' imprisonment and fined $100 for prescribing a punishment for a negro that could not be prescribed for a white, that is, fifty lashes. Matthew Anderson and John Middleton, who were tried for carrying out the sentence imposed on the negro, were acquitted.[4] These are all the cases that I have been able to find of trial of civilians by military commission under Pope. In one case there was a direct interference by Pope with the administration of justice. Daniel and James Cash had been indicted in Macon County for murder and had made bond. They were later indicted and arrested in Bullock County. Pope ordered that they be released and that all civil officials let them alone.[5]

---

[1] *Selma Messenger*, Dec. 25, 1867.   [2] G. O. No. 25, 3d M. D., 1867.

[3] S. O. No. 53, 3d M. D., June 27, 1867; G. O. No. 44, 3d M. D., Aug. 1, 1867; Ho. Ex. Doc., No. 30, 40th Cong., 2d Sess.

[4] G. O. No. 94, 3d M. D., 1867.

[5] S. O. No. 96, 3d M. D., Aug 5. 1867; Ho. Ex. Doc., No. 30, 40th Cong., 2d Sess. There were other cases not referred to in general and special orders, but this was the only case in which Pope himself directly interfered.

Registration and Disfranchisement

But the prime object of Pope's administration was not merely to carry on the government in his military province, but to see that the Reconstruction was rushed through in the shortest possible time and in the most thorough manner, according to the intentions of the Congressional leaders as he understood them. As already stated, he had very clear ideas of what should be done, and from the first was hampered by no few doubts as to the limits of his power. The Reconstruction laws were given the broadest interpretation. In the liberal interpretation of his powers Pope was equalled only by Sheridan in the Fifth District.

A week after his arrival in Montgomery Pope directed Swayne to divide the state into registration districts. Army officers were to be used as registrars only when no civilians could be obtained. General supervisors were to look after the working of the registration, and there was to be a general inspector at headquarters. Violence or threats of violence against registration officials would be punished by military commission.[1] May 21, 1867, the state was divided into forty-two (later forty-four) registration districts, so arranged as to make the most effective use of the black vote.[2] A board of registration for each district was appointed, each board consisting of two whites and one negro. Since each had to take the "iron-clad" test oath, practically all native whites were excluded, those who were on the lists being men of doubtful character and no ability. There were numbers of northerners. For most of the districts the white registrars had to be imported. It is not saying much for the negro members to say that they were much the more respectable part of the boards of registration.[3] Again it was stated that in order to secure full registration, the compensation would be fixed at so much for each voter — fifteen to forty cents, the price varying according to density of population. Five to ten cents mileage was paid in order

[1] G. O. No. 5, 3d M. D., April 8, 1867.

[2] In this way, white majorities in ten counties were overcome by black majorities in the adjoining counties of the district.

[3] Of the registrars who later became somewhat prominent in politics, the whites were Horton, Dimon, Dereen, Sillsby, William M. Buckley, Stanwood, Ely, Pennington, Haughey — all being northern men. Of the negro members of the boards, Royal, Finley, Williams, Alston, Turner, Rapier, and King (or Godwin) rose to some prominence, and their records were much better that those of their white colleagues.

to enable the registrars to hunt up voters. They were directed to
inform the negroes what their political rights were and how necessary
it was for them to exercise those rights. Voters were to be registered
in each precinct, and later, in order to register those missed the first
time, the board was to sit, after due notice, for three days at each
county seat. Any kind of interference with registration, by threats
or by contracts depriving laborers of pay, was to be punished by military commission. The right of every voter under the acts of Congress
to register and to vote was guaranteed by the military. In case of
disturbance the registrars were to call upon the civil officials or upon
the nearest military authorities. If the former refused or failed to
protect the registration, they were to be punished by a military commission.[1] May 1, Colonel James F. Meline was appointed inspector
of registration for the Third Military District,[2] and William H. Smith
was appointed general supervisor for Alabama.[3] Boards of registration were authorized to report cases of civil officials using their
influence against reconstruction.[4] When a voter wished to remove
from his precinct after registration, he was to be given a certificate
which would enable him to vote anywhere in the state. If he should
lose this certificate, his own affidavit before any civil or military
official would suffice to obtain a new certificate.[5]

On June 1, Pope issued pamphlets containing instructions to
registrars which were especially definite as to those former state officials who should be excluded from registration. The list of those
who were to be disfranchised included every one who had ever been
a state, county, or town official and later aided the Confederacy;[6]
former members of the United States Congress, former United States
officials, civil and military, members of state legislatures and of the
convention of 1861; all officials of state, counties, and towns during
the war; and finally judicial or administrative officials not named
elsewhere.[7] The records fail to show that any officials were not ex-

---

[1] G. O. No. 20, 3d M. D., May 21, 1867.   [2] G. O. No. 12, 3d M. D., 1867.

[3] Smith was later the first Reconstruction governor of Alabama.

[4] G. O. No. 41, 3d M. D., 1867.   [5] G. O. No. 50, 3d M. D., Aug. 15, 1867.

[6] Governor, secretary of state, treasurer, comptroller, sheriff, judicial officers of every
kind, and all court clerks and other officials, commissioners, tax assessors and collectors,
county surveyors, treasurers, mayor, councilmen, justices of the peace, solicitors.

[7] Special Instructions to Registrars in Alabama, Report of the Secretary of War,
1867, Vol. I, p. 339.

cluded from registration except the keepers of poorhouses, coroners, and health officers. Instructions issued later practically repeated the first instructions and added former officials of the Confederate States to the list of disfranchised. The registrars were reminded to enforce the disfranchising clauses of the acts both as to voters and candidates.[1]

The stringent regulations of Pope caused much bitter comment, and the Washington administration was besought to revoke them. Complaints were coming in from other districts, and on June 18, 1867, at a Cabinet meeting, the questions in controversy were brought up point by point, and the Cabinet passed its opinion on them. A strict interpretation of the Reconstruction Acts was arrived at, which was much more favorable toward the southern people. Stanton alone voted against all interpretation favorable to the South. The interpretation of the acts thus obtained was issued as a circular, the opinion of the Attorney-General, through the War Department and sent to the district commanders on June 20.[2] As soon as Pope received a copy of the opinion of the Attorney-General he wrote to Grant protesting against the enforcement of the opinion as an order, so far as it related to registration. If enforced, his instructions to registrars would have to be revoked. According to all rules of military obedience, it was his duty to consider the instructions sent him through the adjutant-general's office as binding, though in this case the instructions were not in the technical form of an order, but he expressed doubt if they were to be considered as an order to him. Grant telegraphed to him to enforce his own construction of the acts until ordered to do otherwise.[3]

In order to remove all doubt in the matter, Congress, in the act of July 19, 1867, sustained Pope's interpretation of the acts and made it law. The construction placed upon the laws by the Cabinet was repudiated, and officers acting under the Reconstruction Acts were not to consider themselves bound by the opinion of any civil officer of the United States.[4] This was aimed at the Attorney-General and

[1] Registration Orders, June 17, 1867.
[2] Record of Cabinet Meeting, June 18, 1867, in Ho. Ex. Doc., No. 34, 40th Cong., 1st Sess.; Burgess, p. 136; Ho. Ex. Doc., No. 20, 40th Cong., 1st Sess.
[3] Ho. Ex. Doc., No. 20, 40th Cong., 1st Sess.; McPherson, p. 311. See above, p. 479.
[4] McPherson, pp. 335, 336; Burgess, pp. 138–142.

the Cabinet. The law also gave the registrars full judicial powers to investigate the records of those who applied for registration. Witnesses might be examined touching the qualifications of voters. The boards were empowered to revise the lists of voters and to add to or strike from it such names as they thought ought to be added or removed. No pardon or amnesty by the President was to avail to remove disability.[1]

The Elections and the Convention

After the passage of this law it was smooth sailing for Pope. Registration went on with such success that on August 31 he was induced to order an election to be held on October 1 to 4, for the choice of delegates to a convention, and an apportionment of delegates among the various districts was made at the same time. In the distribution the black counties were favored at the expense of the white counties.[2]

The work of the registrars was thoroughly done. The negro enrolment was enormous; the white enrolment was small. The registration of voters before the elections was: whites, 61,295; blacks, 104,518; total, 165,813.[3] For the convention and for delegates 90,283 votes were cast. Of these 18,553 were those of whites, and 71,730 were negro votes. Against holding a convention, 5583 white votes were cast, and 69,947 registered voters failed to vote — 37,159 whites and 32,788 blacks.[4] The names of the delegates chosen were published in general orders, and the convention was ordered to meet in Montgomery on November 5.[5] During the session of the convention Pope took a rest from his labors and spent some time in Montgomery. He was a great favorite with the reconstructionists and was accorded special honors by the convention. But he did not think as highly of reconstructionists as when he first assumed command, and the antics of the "Black Crook" convention

[1] McPherson, pp. 335, 336.
[2] G. O. No. 59, 3d M. D., Aug. 31, 1867; Journal of Convention of 1867, pp. 3–5; Report of the Secretary of War, 1867, Vol. I, pp. 356, 357; Tribune Almanac, 1868.
[3] Sen. Ex. Doc., No. 53, 40th Cong., 2d Sess. Tribune Almanac, 1867, 1868; Report of Col. J. F. Meline, Inspector of Registration, Jan. 27, 1868. These figures are based on the latest reports of 1867. According to the census of 1866, there would be in 1867, 108,622 whites over twenty-one years of age, and 89,663 blacks.
[4] Meline's Report, Jan. 27, 1868. See also Ch. XIII below.
[5] G. O. No. 76, Oct. 18, 1867 ; Journal of Convention of 1867, pp. 1–3.

made him nervous. After a month's session he was glad to see it disband.[1]

One of the last important acts of Pope's administration was to order an election for February 4 and 5, 1868, when the constitution should be submitted for ratification or rejection, and when by his advice candidates for all offices were to be voted for. Two weeks beforehand the registrars were to revise their lists, adding or striking off such names as they saw fit. Polls were to be opened at such places as the board saw fit. Any voter might vote in any place to which he had removed by making affidavit before the board that he was registered and had not voted before.[2]

Removal of Pope and Swayne

Both Pope and Swayne had been charged with being desirous of representing the states of the Third Military District in the United States Senate. Pope had made himself obnoxious to the President, and the white people of Alabama and Georgia were demanding his removal. So, on December 28, 1867, an order was issued by the President, relieving Pope and placing General Meade in command of the Third Military District. General Swayne was at the same time ordered to rejoin his regiment,[3] and a few days later his place was taken by General Julius Hayden.[4] The whites were greatly relieved and much pleased by the removal of both Pope and Swayne. The former had become obnoxious on account of the extreme measures he had taken in carrying out the Reconstruction Acts, on account of his irritating proclamations, his attitude toward the press, etc. General Swayne had long enjoyed the confidence of the best men. His influence over the negroes was supreme, and had been used to pro-

---

[1] McPherson, p. 319 ; Journal of Convention, 1867, pp. 110, 111, 276 ; *N. Y. World*, Dec. 14, 1867. When the convention passed a resolution indorsing the "firm and impartial, yet just and gentle," administration of Pope, three delegates voted against it because they said Pope had not done his full duty in removing disloyal persons from office but, after being informed of their politics, had left them in office. Journal of Convention, 1867, pp. 110, 111. For account of the convention, see below, Ch. XIV.

[2] G. O. No. 101, Dec. 20, 1867 ; McPherson, p. 319 ; Journal of Convention, p. 267.

[3] The 45th United States Infantry, a negro regiment.

[4] McPherson, p. 346 ; G. O. No. 104, H. Q. A. (A. G. O.), Dec. 28, 1867 ; G. O. No. 1, 3d M. D., Jan. 1, 1868.

mote friendly relations between the races. But as soon as the Reconstruction was taken charge of by Congress and party lines were drawn, all his influence, personal and official, was given to building up a Radical party in the state and to securing the negroes for that party. He was high in the councils of the Union League and controlled the conventions of the party. The change of rulers is said to have had a tranquillizing effect on disturbed conditions in Alabama.[1] But the people of Alabama would have been pleased with no human being as military governor invested with absolute power.

SEC. 2. THE ADMINISTRATION OF GENERAL MEADE

Registration and Elections

On January 6, 1868, General Meade arrived in Atlanta and assumed command of the Third Military District.[2] His first and most important duty was to complete the military registration of voters, and hold the election for ratification of the constitution and for the choice of officials under it. Registration had been going on regularly since the summer of 1867, and after the convention had adjourned there was a rush of whites to register in order to defeat the constitution by refraining from voting on it. As the time for the election drew near the friends of the Reconstruction, much alarmed at the tactics of the Conservative party, brought pressure to bear upon Grant, who suggested to Meade that an extension of time be made. Consequently, the time for the election was extended from two to five days in order to enable the remotest negro to be found and brought to the polls. At the same time the number of voting places was limited to three in each county,[3] in order to lessen the influence of the whites over the blacks.

General Meade was opposed to holding the election for state officials at the same time with that on ratification of the constitution. He thought it would be difficult to secure the adoption of the constitution on account of the proscriptive clauses in it, but in his opinion

---

[1] Herbert, "Solid South"; *N. Y. Times*, Jan. 24, 1868.

[2] G. O. No. 3, 3d M. D., Jan. 6, 1868.

[3] G. O. No. 16, 3d M. D., Jan. 27, 1868; Annual Cyclopædia (1868), p. 15; Report of Major-General Meade's Military Operations and Administration of the 3d M. D., etc. (pamphlet); *N. Y. Times*, Jan. 24, 1868.

the candidates[1] nominated by the convention were even more obnoxious to the people than the constitution, and many would refrain from voting on that account. Swayne, who seems to have still been in Montgomery, admitted the force of the objection, but Grant objected to any change until too late to make other arrangements.[2]

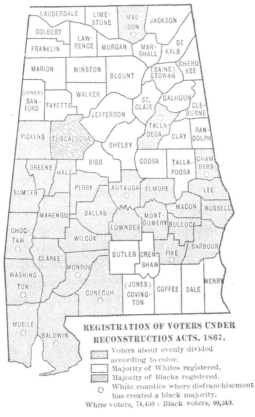

REGISTRATION OF VOTERS UNDER RECONSTRUCTION ACTS, 1867.

    Voters about evenly divided according to color.
    Majority of Whites registered.
    Majority of Blacks registered.
  O White counties where disfranchisement has created a black majority.
White voters, 74,450 : Black voters, 90,349.

After the lists were revised by Meade.

The election took place on February 1 to 5, and passed off without any disorder. Meade reported that the charges of fraud made by the Radicals were groundless, and that the constitution had been defeated on its merits, or rather demerits. Both the constitution and the candidates were obnoxious to a large number of the friends of Reconstruction. He reported that the constitution failed of ratification by 13,550 votes, and advised that the convention assemble again, revise the constitution of its proscriptive features, and again submit to it the people.[3]

[1] See Ch. XV for "convention" candidates.

[2] Report of Meade, etc., 1868; Telegrams of Meade to Grant, Jan. 11, 12, and 18, and of Grant to Meade, Jan. 13 and 18.

[3] Report of Meade, etc., 1868 ; Herbert, "Solid South," pp. 48, 49. In his first report Meade estimated that the constitution failed of ratification by 8114 votes (Herbert, "Solid South," p. 49). In his report at the end of the year, based on the official report of General Hayden, which was made a month after the election, he changed the number to 13,550. See also Ch. XVI, on the rejection of the constitution.

Administration of Civil Affairs

Pending the decision of the Alabama question by Congress, Meade carried on the military government as usual. He thoroughly understood that his power was unlimited. No more than Pope did he allow the civil government to stand in the way. There was, however, a vast difference in the administrations of the two men. Meade was less given to issuing proclamations, but was firmer and more strict, and less arbitrary. He was not under the influence of the Radical politicians in the slightest degree, and was abused by both sides, especially by the Radical adventurers. It was a thankless task, for which he had no liking, but his duty was done in a soldierly manner, and his administration was probably the best that was possible.

He made it clear to the civil authorities that he was the source of all power, and that they were responsible to him and must obey all orders coming from him. If they refused, he promised trial by a military commission, fine, and imprisonment. They must under no circumstances interfere, under color of state authority, with the military administration. He had no admiration for the "loyal" element; and when a bill was before Congress providing that the officials of the civil government be required to take the "iron-clad" test oath or vacate their offices, he made a strong protest and declared that he could not fill half the offices with men who could take the test oath.[1] After the February elections political influence was brought to bear to force Meade to vacate the offices of the civil government and to appoint certain individuals of the proper political beliefs. The persons voted for in the elections were clamorous for their places. Grant suggested that when appointments were made, the men recently voted for be put in. Meade resisted the pressure and made few changes, and these only after investigation. Removals were made for neglect of duty, malfeasance in office, refusing to obey orders, and "obstructing Reconstruction." Many appointments were made on account of the deaths or resignations of the civil officials.[2] Few of

---

[1] G. O. No. 42, 3d M. D., March 12, 1868; McPherson, p. 320; Meade's Report, 1868.

[2] In one case he reinstated Charles R. Hubbard, Clerk of the District Court, who had been removed by Swayne. This was contrary to instructions from the War Department, which forbade the reappointment of an officer who had been removed. Annual Cyclopædia (1868), p. 15.

the officials appointed by him could take the test oath, and he was much abused by the Radicals for saying that it would be impossible to fill half the offices with men who could take the oath. He was constantly besought to supersede the civil authority altogether and rule only through the army. In this connection, he reported that he was greatly embarrassed by the want of judgment and of knowledge on the part of his subordinates, and by the great desire of those who expected to profit from military intervention. So he issued an order informing the civil officials that as long as they performed their duties they would not be interfered with. The army officials were informed that they should in no case interfere with the civil administration before obtaining the consent of Meade; that the military was to act in subordination to and in aid of the civil authority;[1] and that no soldiers or other persons were to be tried in court for acts done by military authority or for having charge of abandoned land or other property.[2]

There was much disorder by thieves and roughs on the river boats during the spring of 1868. To facilitate trials of these lawbreakers, Meade directed that they be arrested and tried in any county in the state where found, before any tribunal having jurisdiction of such offences.[3]

The courts were not interfered with as under Pope's rule. The judges continued to have white jurors chosen, and the army officers, as a rule, approved. In one case, however, in Calhoun County, there was trouble. One Lieutenant Charles T. Johnson, Fifteenth Infantry, attended the court presided over by Judge B. T. Pope. He found that no negroes were on the jury, and demanded that the judge order a mixed jury to be chosen. The judge declined to comply, and Johnson at once arrested him. Johnson found that the clerk of the court did not agree with him, and he arrested the clerk also. Pope was placed in jail until released by Meade.[4] The conduct of Johnson was condemned in the strongest terms by Meade, who ordered him to be court-martialed. A general order was published

---

[1] Report of Meade, etc., 1868 ; G. O. No. 10, 3d M. D., Jan. 15, 1868.

[2] G. O. No. 7, Jan. 11, 1868, republishing G. O. No. 3, War Department, 1866.

[3] G. O. No. 47, 3d M. D., March 21, 1868.

[4] Pope was in feeble health, and this treatment hastened his death, which occurred shortly after being released from jail. Brewer, " Alabama," p. 524.

reciting the facts of the case and expressing the severest censure of the conduct of Johnson. Meade informed the public generally that even had Judge Pope violated previous orders, Johnson had nothing to do in the case except to report to headquarters. Moreover, Johnson was wrong in holding that all juries had to be composed partly of blacks. This order stopped interference with the courts in Alabama.[1]

Meade did not approve of Pope's policy toward newspapers, and on February 2, 1868, he issued an order modifying General Order No. 49 on the ground that it had in its operations proved embarrassing. In the future, public printing was to be denied to such papers only as might attempt to intimidate civil officials by threats of violence or prosecution, as soon as the troops were withdrawn, for acts performed in their official capacity. However, if there was but one paper in the county, then it was to have the county printing regardless of its editorial opinions. "Opposition to reconstruction, when conducted in a legitimate manner, is," the order stated, "not to be considered an offence." Violent and incendiary articles, however, were to be considered illegal,[2] and newspapers were warned to keep within the bounds of legitimate discussion. The Ku Klux movement, especially after it was seen that Congress was going to admit the state, notwithstanding the defeat of the constitution, gave Meade some trouble. Its notices were published in various papers, and Meade issued an order prohibiting this custom. The army officers were ordered to arrest and try offenders. Only one editor came to grief. Ryland Randolph, the editor of the *Independent Monitor*, of Tuscaloosa, was arrested by General Shepherd and his paper suppressed for a short time.[3]

General Meade was no negrophile, and hence under him there

---

[1] G. O. No. 53, 3d M. D., April 7, 1868; *N. Y. Herald*, April 1, 1868. Judge Pope was arrested for violating Pope's G. O. Nos. 53, 55, which certainly provided for mixed juries. Meade was simply putting his own interpretation on these orders.

[2] G. O. No. 22, 3d M. D., Feb. 2, 1868; Report of Meade, etc., 1868.

[3] Report of Meade, etc.. 1868; *Independent Monitor*, April and May, 1868. The *Independent Monitor* was a long-established and well-known weekly paper. F. A. P. Barnard, who was afterwards president of Columbia College, New York, was, when a professor at the University of Alabama, the editor of the *Monitor*, and under him it won a reputation for spiciness which it did not lose under Randolph. See also Ch. XXI, for Randolph and the Ku Klux Klan.

2 K

were no more long oration orders on the rights of "that large class of citizens heretofore excluded from the suffrage." He set himself resolutely against all attempts to stir up strife between the races, and quietly reported at the time, and again a year later, that the stories of violence and intimidation, which Congress accepted without question, were without foundation. He ordered that in the state institutions for the deaf, dumb, blind, and insane, the blacks should have the same privileges as the whites. The law of the state allowed to the sheriffs for subsistence of prisoners, fifty cents a day for white and forty cents a day for negro prisoners. Meade ordered that the fees be the same for both races, and that the same fare and accommodations be given to both. Swayne had abolished the chain-gang system the year before, because it chiefly affected negro offenders. Meade gave the civil authorities permission to restore it.[1]

The convention had passed ordinances which amounted to stay laws for the relief of debtors. In order to secure support for the constitution, it was provided that these ordinances were to go into effect with the constitution. Complaint was made that creditors were oppressing their debtors in order to secure payment before the stay laws should go into effect. Though opposed in principle to such laws, Meade considered that under the circumstances some relief was needed. The price of cotton was low, and the forced sales were ruinous to the debtors and of little benefit to the creditors. Therefore, in January, he declared the ordinances in force to continue, unless the constitution should be adopted. A later order, in May, declared that the ordinances would be considered in force until revoked by himself.[2]

Trials by Military Commissions

When the ghostly night riders of the Ku Klux Klan began to frighten the carpet-baggers and the negroes, Meade directed all officials, civil and military, to organize patrols to break up the secret organizations. Civil officials neglecting to do so were held to be guilty of disobedience of orders. Where army officers raised *posses*

[1] G. O. No. 31, Feb. 28, 1868; G. O. No. 44, March 18, 1868; G. O. No. 69, April 24, 1868; McPherson, p. 320; Report of Meade, etc., 1868.

[2] G. O. No. 6, Jan. 10, 1868 ; G. O. No. 79, May 20, 1868; McPherson, p. 320; Report of Meade, 1868.

to aid in maintaining the peace, the expenses were charged to the counties or towns where the disturbances occurred.[1]

Nearly all prisoners arrested by the military authorities were turned over to the civil courts for trial. Military commissions were frequently in session to try cases when it was believed the civil authorities would be influenced by local considerations. The following list of such trials is complete: H. K. Quillan of Lee County and Langdon Ellis, justice of the peace of Chambers County, were tried for "obstructing reconstruction" and were acquitted; Richard Hall of Hale County, tried for assault, was acquitted;[2] Joseph B. F. Hill, William Pettigrew, T. W. Roberts, and James Steele of Greene County were sentenced to hard labor for five years, for "whipping a hog thief, and threatening to ride him on a rail";[3] Samuel W. Dunlap, William Pierce, Charles Coleman, and John Kelley, implicated in the same case, were fined $500 each, and sentenced to one year's imprisonment; Frank H. Munday, Hugh L. White, John Cullen, and Samuel Strayhorn, charged with the same offence, were each fined $500, and sentenced to hard labor for two years;[4] Ryland Randolph, editor of the *Monitor*, was tried for "obstructing reconstruction" in his paper and for nearly killing a negro, and was acquitted. During the trial Busteed granted a writ of *habeas corpus*, and Meade and Grant both were prepared to submit to the decision of the court, but Randolph wanted the military trial to go on.[5]

Meade was much irritated by the careless conduct of officers in reporting cases for trial by military courts which were unable to stand the test of examination. After frequent failures to substantiate

[1] Report of Meade, 1868.

[2] G. O. No. 64, 3d M. D., April 19, 1868; *Selma Times and Messenger*, April 29, 1868.

[3] This was the offence according to conservative testimony. The Radical testimony did not differ greatly, but the "hog thief" happened to be a carpet-bag politician also.

[4] These were the "Eutaw cases," and were tried at Selma. Meade commuted some of the sentences at once. The prisoners were sent to Dry Tortugas, and were later pardoned by Meade. The officials spoiled the effect of his leniency by putting the pardoned prisoners ashore at Galveston, Texas, without money and almost without clothes, while some of the party were ill. Annual Cyclopædia (1868), p. 17; *Selma Times and Messenger*, May 5, 1868; *N. Y. World*, May 28, 1868; G. O. No. 80, 3d M. D., May 20, 1868.

[5] *Independent Monitor*, April and May, 1868; Report of Meade, 1868; G. O. No. 78, 3d M. D., May 13, 1868.

charges in cases sent up for trial, orders were issued that subordinate officials must exercise the greatest caution and care in preferring charges, and in all cases must state the reasons why the civil authorities could not act. Sworn statements of witnesses must accompany the charges, and the accused must be given an opportunity to forward evidence in his favor.[1]

The Soldiers and the Citizens

The troops in the state during 1867 and 1868, though sadly demoralized as to discipline, gave the people little trouble except in the vicinity of the military posts. The records of the courts-martial show that the negroes were the greatest sufferers from the outrages of the common soldiers. The whites were irritated chiefly by the arrogant conduct of a few of the post commanders and their subordinates. At Mount Vernon, Frederick B. Shepard, an old man, was arrested and carried before Captain Morris Schoff, who shot the unarmed prisoner as soon as he appeared. For this murder Schoff was court-martialed and imprisoned for ten years.[2] Johnson, the officer who arrested Judge Pope, was cordially hated in middle Alabama. He arrested a negro who refused to vote for the constitution; in a quarrel he took the crutch of a cripple and struck him over the head with it; hung two large United States flags over the sidewalk of the main street in Tuscaloosa, and when the schoolgirls avoided walking under them, it being well understood that Johnson had placed them there to annoy the women, he stationed soldiers with bayonets to force the girls to pass under the flags. For his various misdeeds he was court-martialed by Meade.[3]

Most of the soldiers had no love for the negroes, carpet-baggers, and scalawags, and at a Radical meeting in Montgomery, the soldiers on duty at the capitol gave three groans for Grant, and

---

[1] G. O. Nos. 64 and 65, 3d M. D., April 19 and 20, 1868.

During the eight months of Meade's administration in the Third District, there were thirty-two trials by military commission in Georgia, Florida, and Alabama. Only fifteen persons were convicted. The sentences in four cases were disapproved, in eight cases remitted, and two cases were referred to the President, leaving only one person confined in prison. Report of Meade, 1868.

[2] *Selma Messenger*, Oct. 25, 1867.

[3] *Montgomery Mail*, June 17, 1868; *Independent Monitor*, June 16, 1868.

three cheers for McClellan and Johnson.   For this conduct they were strongly censured by Major Hartz and General Shepherd, their commanders.[1]

The soldiers sent to Hale County knocked a carpet-bag Bureau agent on the head, ducked a white teacher of a negro school in the creek, and cuffed the negroes about generally.[2]

From Martial Law to Carpet-bag Rule

The act providing for the admission of Alabama in spite of the defeat of the constitution was passed June 25, 1868.[3]   Three days later Grant ordered Meade to appoint as provisional governor and lieutenant-governor those voted for[4] in the February elections, and to remove the present incumbents.[5]   So Smith and Applegate were appointed as governor and lieutenant-governor, their appointments to take effect on July 13, 1868, on which date the legislature said to have been elected in February was ordered to meet.[6]

Until the state should comply with the requirements of the Reconstruction Acts all government and all officials were to be considered as provisional only.   The governor was ordered to organize both houses of the legislature, and before proceeding to business beyond organization each house was required to purge itself of any members who were disqualified by the Fourteenth Amendment.[7]

A few days later, Congress having admitted the state to representation, Meade ordered all civil officials holding under the provisional civil government to yield to their duly elected successors.   The military commander in Alabama was directed to transfer all property and papers pertaining to the government of the state to the proper civil authorities and for the future to abstain from any interference or control over civil affairs.   Prisoners held for offences against the civil law were ordered to be delivered to state officials.[8]   This was, in theory, the end of military government in Alabama, though, in fact, the army retired into the background, to remain

---

[1] Annual Cyclopædia (1868), p. 17; *Montgomery Advertiser*, June 5, 1868.
[2] Ku Klux Rept., Ala. Test., pp. 1285-1286.
[3] McPherson, p. 337; see below, Ch. XV.
[4] Only the Radical candidates had been voted for.
[5] Report of Meade, 1868.   [6] G. O. No. 91, 3d M. D., June 28, 1868.
[7] G. O. No. 100, July 9, 1868.   [8] G. O. No. 101, July 14, 1868.

for six years longer the support and mainstay of the so-called civil government.[1]

The rule of the army had been intensely galling to the people, but it was infinitely preferable to the régime which followed, and there was general regret when the army gave way to the carpet-bag government.   In January, 1868, a day of fasting and prayer was observed for the deliverance of the state from the rule of the negro and the alien.

---

[1] The volume of orders numbered 598 in the Adjutant-General's office at Washington contains the General Orders of the Third Military District.   Volume 599 relates to civil affairs in the same district.

CHAPTER XIII

THE CAMPAIGN OF 1867

Attitude of the Whites

IN the preceding chapter the part of the army in executing the Reconstruction Acts has been set forth. In the three succeeding chapters I shall sketch the political conditions in the state during the same period. The people of Alabama had, for several months before March, 1867, foreseen the failure of the President's attempt at Reconstruction. The "Military Reconstruction Bill" was no worse than was expected; if liberally construed, it was even better than was expected. And there was a possibility that Reconstruction under these acts might be delayed and finally defeated. Though President Johnson was said to be hopeful of better times, the people of Alabama were decided that no good would come from longer resistance. A northern observer stated that they were so fearfully impoverished, so completely demoralized, by the break-up of society after the war, that they hardly comprehended what was left to them, what was required of them, or what would become of them. Still, they had a clear conviction that Johnson could do no more for them. Every one, except the negroes, was too much absorbed in the struggle for existence to pay much attention to politics. The whites seemed generally willing to do what was required of them, or rather to let affairs take their own course and trust that all would go well. They had given up hope of an early restoration of the Union, but the Radicals, they thought, could not rule forever.[1]

On March 19, 1867, Governor Patton published an address advising acquiescence in the plan of Congress. He had all along been opposed to Radical Reconstruction, but he now saw that it could not be avoided and wished to make the best of it. He said that a few thousand good men would be disfranchised, but that there were other

[1] *N. Y. Herald,* June 27, 1867.

good men and from these a wise and patriotic convention could be chosen. He advised that negro suffrage be accepted as a settled fact, with no ill feeling against the freedmen; that antagonism between the races should be discouraged, and that no effort be made to control the votes of the blacks.[1] More consideration, Patton thought, should have been given to Congress as the controlling power; antagonism to Congress had caused infinite mischief. It was folly, he added, to expect more favorable terms, and further opposition might cause harsher conditions to be imposed.[2]

Other prominent men advised the people to accept the plan of Congress and to participate in the Reconstruction. Nearly all the leading papers of the state, in order to make the best of a bad situation, now supported congressional Reconstruction. Consequently, when General Pope arrived in April, the people were ready to accept the situation in good faith, and desired that he should make a speedy registration of the voters and end the agitation.[3] Even at this late date the southern people seem not to have foreseen the inevitable results of this revolution in government.[4]

[1] Washington (in "The Future of the American Negro," pp. 11, 112, 136) thinks it unfortunate that the native whites did not make stronger efforts to control the politics of the negro, and prevent him from falling under the control of unscrupulous aliens. But any attempt to influence the negro voters was looked upon as "obstructing reconstruction," and, in fact, was contrary to the spirit of the reconstruction laws and rendered a person liable to arrest. This was recognized by Patton and others, who, however, never dreamed that the negroes would be so successfully exploited by political adventurers, or perhaps they would have pursued a different policy. General Clanton, the leader of the Conservatives, said that early in 1867 the whites had endeavored to keep the blacks away from Radical leaders by giving them barbecues, etc. On one occasion a Radical, who had once been kept from mistreating negroes by the military authorities at Clanton's request, told the negroes that the whites intended to poison them at the barbecue. Two long tables had been set, one for each race, and the preachers, speakers, and the whites were present, but the blacks did not come. Ku Klux Rept., Ala. Test., pp. 237, 246.

[2] N. Y. Herald, March 26, 1867.

[3] Herbert, "Solid South," p. 39; Herbert, "Political History" in "Memorial Record of Alabama," Vol. I, p. 88; Annual Cyclopædia (1867), p. 16.

[4] Northern observers who were friendly to the South saw the danger much more clearly than the southerners themselves, who seemed unable to take negro suffrage seriously or to consider it as great a danger as it is generally believed they did. Two years of the Freedmen's Bureau had not wholly succeeded in alienating the best of the whites and the negroes. The whites thought that the removal of outside interference would quiet the blacks. To give the negro the ballot was absurd, they thought, but they did not consider it necessarily as dangerous as it turned out to be. A remarkable prophecy

The Organization of the Radical Party

While a large number of the influential men of the state were ready to accept the situation, "not because we approve the policy of the reconstruction laws, but because it is the best we can do," and while a larger number were more or less indifferent, there were many who were opposed to Reconstruction on any such terms, preferring a continuance of the military government until passions were calmer and a more liberal policy proposed.   There was, however, no organized opposition to Reconstruction for two months or more, and even then it was rendered possible only by the arbitrary conduct of General Pope and the violent agitation carried on among the negroes by the Radical faction.   For several months, in the white counties of north Alabama the so-called "loyal" people, reënforced by numbers of the old "Peace Society" men, had been holding meetings looking toward organization in order to secure the fruits of Reconstruction. These meetings were continued, and by them it was declared that the people of Alabama were in favor of Reconstruction by the Sherman Bill, to which only the original secession leaders were opposed, and the Sherman plan, negro suffrage and all, was indorsed as a proper punishment for the planters.[1]   After the beginning of congressional Reconstruction, however, the centre of gravity in the Radical party shifted to the Black Belt, and no one any longer paid serious attention

of Reconstruction is found in Calhoun's Works, Vol. VI, pp. 309–310. The behavior of the negro during and after the war, in spite of malign influences, had been such as to reassure many whites, who began to believe that to accept negro suffrage and get rid of the Freedmen's Bureau and the army would be a good exchange. The northern friendly observers saw more clearly because, perhaps, they better understood the motives of the Radicals. The *N. Y. Herald* said: " Briefly, we may regard the entire ten unreconstructed southern states, with possibly one or two exceptions, as forced by a secret and overwhelming revolutionary influence to a common and inevitable fate. They are all bound to be governed by blacks, spurred on by worse than blacks — white wretches who dare not show their faces in respectable society anywhere. This is the most abominable phase barbarism has assumed since the dawn of civilization. It was all right and proper to put down the rebellion. It was all right, perhaps, to emancipate the slaves, although the right to hold them had been acknowledged before. But it is not right to make slaves of white men, even though they may have been former masters of blacks. This is but a change in a system of bondage that is rendered the more odious and intolerable because it has been inaugurated in an enlightened instead of a dark and uncivilized age." See Annual Register, 1867.

[1] See McPherson's scrapbook, "The Campaign of 1876," Vol. I, p. 105, for an account of a typical meeting.

to the few thousand "loyal" whites in north Alabama. The first negro meetings held were in the larger towns, Selma leading with a large convention of colored "Unionists," who, under the guidance of a few white officers of the Freedmen's Bureau, declared in favor of military Reconstruction.[1] The Montgomery reconstructionists held a meeting in the capitol "in which whites and blacks fraternized." The meeting was addressed by several "rebel" officers: A. C. Felder, ——— Doster, and H. C. Semple, and by General Swayne and John C. Keffer from the north. General Swayne and Governor Patton served as vice-presidents. The blacks were eulogized and declared capable of political equality; and it was urged that only those men in favor of military Reconstruction should be supported for office.[2] In Mobile, a meeting held on April 17 resolved that "everlasting thanks" were due to Congress for its wisdom in passing the Reconstruction Acts. Both whites and negroes spoke in favor of the rights of the negro to hold office, sit on juries, and ride in the same cars and eat at the same tables with whites. The prejudices of the whites, they declared, must give way. At a meeting of negroes only the next day one of the speakers made a distinction between political and social rights. He said that the latter would come in time but that the former must be had at once; they were defined as the right to ride in street cars with the whites, in first-class cars on the railroad, to have the best staterooms on the boats, to sit at public tables with whites, and to go to the hotel tables "when the first bell rang." What social rights were he did not explain. Negroes attended these meetings armed with clubs, pistols, muskets, and shotguns, most of which, of course, would not shoot; but several hundred shots were fired, much to the alarm of the near-by dwellers.[3]

To counteract the effect of these meetings, the "moderate" reconstructionists held a meeting in Mobile, April 19, presided over by General Withers, the mayor of the city. Several influential citizens and also a number of colored men were vice-presidents. Judge Busteed, a "moderate" Radical, spoke, urging all to take part in the Reconstruction and not leave it to the ignorant and vicious. Resolutions were passed to the effect that the blacks would be accorded every legal right and privilege. The "moderate" spirit of Pope was com-

---

[1] *Selma Times*, March 19, 1867.   [2] *N. Y. Herald*, March 27, 1869.
[3] *N. Y. Herald*, April 25, 1869; Annual Cyclopædia (1869), p. 19.

mended, and coöperation was promised him. All were urged to register and vote for delegates to the convention.[1]

A state convention of negroes was called by white Radical politicians to meet in Mobile on May 1, and in all of the large towns of the state meetings to elect delegates were held under the guidance of the Union League. The delegates came straggling in, and on May 2 and 3 the convention was held. It at once declared itself "Radical," and condemned the efforts of their oppressors who would use unfair and foul means to prevent their consolidation with the Radical party. Swayne and Pope were indorsed, a standing army was asked for to protect negroes in their political rights, and demand was made for schools, to be supported by a property tax. Violations of the Civil Rights Bill should be tried by military commission, and the Union League was established in every county. Finally, the convention resolved that it was the undeniable right of the negro to hold office, sit on juries, ride in any public conveyances, sit at public tables, and visit places of public amusement.[2]

The Alabama Grand Council of the Union League, the machine of the Radicals in Alabama,[3] met in April and formulated the principles upon which the campaign was to be conducted. Congress was thanked for putting the reorganization of the state into the hands of "Union" men; the return to the principle that "all men are created equal" and its application to a "faithful and patriotic class of our fellow-men" was hailed with joy; any settlement which denied the ballot to the negro could not stand, they asserted; and "while we believe that rebellion is the highest crime known to the law, and that those guilty of it hold their continued existence solely by the clemency of an outraged but merciful government, we are nevertheless willing to imitate that government in forgiveness of the past, and to reclaim to the Republican Union party all who, forsaking entirely the principles on which the rebellion was founded, will sincerely and earnestly unite with us in establishing and maintaining for the future a government of equal rights and unconditional loyalty;" "we consider

---

[1] Annual Cyclopædia (1869), p. 19; *N. Y. Herald*, April 25, 1869.

[2] *N. Y. Herald*, May 17, 1869; Annual Cyclopædia (1867), pp. 18, 21. It is noticeable all through Reconstruction that most of the demands for social rights or privileges came from Mobile mulattoes.

[3] For an estimate of the importance of the Union League, see Ch. XVI.

willingness to elevate to power the men who preserved unswerving adherence to the government during the war as the best test of sincerity in professions for the future;" and "if the pacification now proposed by Congress be not accepted in good faith by those who staked and forfeited their lives, their fortunes, and their sacred honor, in rebellion, then it will be the duty of Congress to enforce that forfeiture, by the confiscation of the lands at least of such a stiff-necked and rebellious people;" "the assertion that there are not enough intelligent and loyal men in Alabama to administer the government is false in fact, and mainly promulgated by those who aim to keep treason respectable by retaining power in the hands of its friends and votaries."[1] This was a declaration of principles to which self-respecting whites could hardly be expected to subscribe. That was the very reason for its proclamation. The Radical leaders in control of the machinery of the Union League began to discourage the accession of whites to the party. The negro vote was to be their support, and not too many whites were desired at the division of spoils.[2] Other causes conspired to drive the respectable people from the ranks of the reconstructionists. Prominent politicians were sent into the state to tell the negro that, having received his freedom from the Republican party, to it his vote was due. Senator Henry Wilson of Massachusetts made a bitter speech against the southern whites at the capitol in Montgomery. The negroes were informed that the Republican party was entitled to their votes, and the whites were asked to join them, as subordinates perhaps.[3] This speech was delivered on May 11, and from this date may be traced the organized opposition to Reconstruction. General James H. Clanton[4] replied to Wilson, maintaining that the southern

---

[1] McPherson, "Reconstruction," pp. 249, 250. The last assertion refers to such statements as those of Secretary McCulloch and the Postmaster-General in regard to the character of the "loyalists." See McCulloch, "Men and Measures," p. 228.

[2] See Herbert, "Solid South," p. 41.

[3] On March 15, 1867, Senator Wilson, in a speech in favor of negro suffrage, said that when the purpose of the act of March 2 was carried out, the "majority of these states will, within a twelvemonth, send here senators and representatives that think as we think, and speak as we speak, and vote as we vote, and will give their electoral vote for whoever we nominate as candidate for President in 1868. The power is all in our hands." *Cong. Globe*, March 15, 1867.

[4] Clanton had been a Whig, had opposed secession, made a brilliant war record, became the leader of the Democratic and Conservative party in 1866, and led the fight

white was the real friend of the negro and declaring in favor of full political and educational rights for the negro, while asserting that Wilson's plan would result in a black man's party, controlled by aliens.[1] This speech of Clanton's had the effect of rousing the people to organized resistance against the plans of the Radicals.

On May 14, Judge "Pig Iron" Kelly of Pennsylvania spoke in Mobile to an audience of one hundred respectable whites and two thousand negroes, the latter armed. His language toward the whites was violent and insulting, an invitation for trouble, which inflamed both races. A riot ensued for which he was almost solely to blame.[2] Several whites were killed or wounded and one negro. From the guarded report of General Swayne it was evident that the blame lay upon Kelly for exciting the negroes. It was a most unfortunate affair at a critical period, and the people began to understand the kind of control that would be exercised over the blacks by alien politicians.[3]

In May the *Alabama Sentinel*, a short-lived reconstructionist newspaper in Montgomery, assisted by a negro mass-meeting, nominated Grant for the presidency and Busteed for vice-president. The platform demanded that the negro have his rights at once or upon his oppressors must fall the consequences. The Republican party was indorsed as the negro party, the only party that had done anything for the negro.[4]

When the registrars were appointed it was necessary, in order to get competent men, to import both blacks and whites into some districts. The whites were brought from north Alabama or sent out from the Bureau contingents in the towns. They were members of the Union League, and it was a part of their duty to spread that organ-

---

against the carpet-bag government until his death in 1871. He was killed in Knoxville by a hireling of one of the railroad companies which had looted the state treasury and against which he was fighting. Brewer, p. 466; Garrett, pp. 632–645.

[1] See Herbert, "Solid South," p. 40; Ku Klux Rept., Ala. Test., p. 249.

[2] *N. Y. Tribune*, May 16, 1867, editorial. When the shots were fired Kelly showed the white feather, and reclined upon the platform behind and under the speaker's chair; afterwards he ran hatless to the hotel, and told the clerk to "swear he was out." A special boat at once took him from the city to Montgomery.

[3] *N. Y. Tribune*, May 16, 1767; *N. Y. Times*, May 21, 1867; *N. Y. World*, May 28, 1867; *Mobile Times*, ——, 1867; *Mobile Register*, ——, 1867; *Evening Post*, ——, 1867; Annual Cyclopædia (1867), pp. 22, 23.

[4] *N. Y. Herald*, May 26, 1867.

ization among the negroes of the Black Belt, thus carrying out that part of their instructions which directed them to instruct the negroes in their rights and privileges.[1] The Radical organization steadily progressed, but even thus early two tendencies or lines of policy appeared which were to weaken the Radicals and later to render possible their overthrow. The native white reconstructionists, living mostly in the white counties, wanted a reconstruction in which they (the native "unionists") should be the controlling element. They were in favor of negro suffrage as a necessary part of the scheme and because it would not directly interfere with them, as the negro was supposed to be content with voting. These white "scalawags" were thus to gather the fruits of reconstruction. But the "carpet-baggers," or the alien-bureau-missionary element, having worked among the negroes and learned their power over them, intended to use the negroes to secure office and power for themselves. They were less prejudiced against the negroes than were the "scalawags" and were willing to associate with them more intimately and to give them small offices when there were not enough carpet-baggers to take them. It was soon discovered that the native white "unionist" and the black "Unionist," like oil and water, would not mingle. However, all united temporarily to gain the victory for reconstruction, each faction hoping to be the greater gainer.

On June 4, 1867, a "Union Republican Convention" met in Montgomery, and at the same time the Union League held its convention. The Union League was merely a select portion of the Union Republican Convention and met at night to slate matters for the use of the convention next day. F. W. Sykes of Lawrence County[2] was chairman *pro tem.*, and William H. Smith of Randolph County was permanent chairman.[3] The delegates to the convention

---

[1] See Herbert, "Solid South," p. 43; oral accounts, etc.

[2] Sykes soon deserted the Radicals, and was a Seymour elector the next year. Later he was a candidate for the U. S. Senate against Spencer. Brewer, p. 309.

[3] He was the north Alabama candidate for appointment as provisional governor in 1865, but was defeated by Parsons, the middle Alabama candidate. Parsons made him a judge, but he resigned because the lawyers who argued before him spoke in insulting phrases concerning his war record. In 1867 Pope appointed him superintendent of registration for the state. He was a prominent member of the Union League. Brewer, p. 508; *N. Y. Herald*, June 20, 1867; Report of Joint Committee on Reconstruction, Pt. III.

consisted of a large number of office-seekers, "union" men, deserters, "scalawags," ex-Union army officers, and employees of the Freedmen's Bureau, and negroes.[1] There were one hundred negroes and fifty whites. The negroes sat on one side of the house and the whites on the other, but the committees were divided equally by color. The committee on permanent organization consisted of "three Yankees," four "palefaces," and six negroes, who nominated several negroes and Bureau men for officials.[2] The *Mail* said that the negroes presented a better appearance than the whites, that they were cleaner and better dressed. General Swayne took a prominent part in the proceedings, and with Smith and the negroes voted out Busteed.[3] Griffin (of Ohio) from Mobile offered a resolution dictated by Swayne, declaring that the recent opinions of the Attorney-General upon the registration of votes were dangerous to the restoration of the Union according to the plan of Congress.[4] The proceedings were turbulent, there was much angry discussion, and the meeting ended in a fight after

[1] *N. Y. Herald*, June 20, 1867, a northern Republican account.

[2] Nicholas Davis of Madison County and Judge Busteed were both candidates for the chairmanship. But the negroes and Union Leaguers were hostile to Davis, because he did not like negro politicians and carpet-baggers and was opposed to the Union League. Busteed was not a favorite for practically the same reasons, and because the negroes thought he was trying to "ride two horses at once." He had spoken at a meeting of moderate reconstructionists in Mobile, had presided over the Kelly meeting where the riot occurred, and was believed to be in favor of moderate measures. He wrote a letter to the president of the convention, advising moderation and criticising certain methods of the Radicals. This letter was styled the "God save the Republic" letter, and was characterized, his enemies said, by its bad taste and malignant spirit, and was a stab at his best friends. He was chosen a member of the Lowndes County delegation, but his name was erased from the list of delegates. He then asked to have the privileges of the floor as a courtesy, but his request was denied. One cause of dislike of him was that he was believed to have senatorial aspirations, and expected the support of the moderates, or "rebel" reconstructionists. But he was very unfortunate, for the "rebels" also thought he was trying to play a double game and were dropping him. Suits were pending against him charging him with malfeasance in office, fraudulent conversion of money, and corrupt abuse of the judicial office. Ex-Governor Watts, Judges S. F. Rice and Wade Keys, John A. Elmore, H. C. Semple, D. S. Troy, and R. H. Goldthwaite were the parties prosecuting him. *N. Y. Herald*, June 20, 1867; Brewer, p. 365; *Montgomery Mail*, June 5, 1867.

[3] Swayne, as well as Busteed, was an aspirant for senatorial honors. Busteed had succeeded in causing the rejection of Albert Griffin, the editor of the *Mobile Nationalist*, as register in chancery. Griffin was Swayne's friend, and now each gave the other the benefit of his influence. *N. Y. Herald*, June 20, 1867; *Montgomery Mail*, June 5, 1867.

[4] *N. Y. Herald*, June 17, 1867.

having indorsed the Radical programme and declaring against the United States cotton tax and the state poll tax,[1] and agreeing to support only "union" or "loyal" men for office.[2]

Conservative Opposition Aroused

Though the leaders complained of the "appalling apathy of the whites in political matters,"[3] a change was coming. The teachings of the Radicals were beginning to have effect on the negroes, some of whom were becoming hostile to the whites and were resisting the white officers of the civil government. Their old belief in "forty acres of land and a mule" was revived by the speeches of Thaddeus Stevens, which were widely circulated by the agents of the Union League, who were sent through the country to distribute the speeches and to organize the movement resulting from it. Many of the whites now began to believe that at last confiscation would be enforced and that the negroes and low whites of the Union League would become the landowners.[4] Clanton had been at work for two months, and on July 23, as chairman of the state committee of the Conservative party, called a convention of that party to meet in Montgomery on September 4.[5] Meetings of the Conservative party were held in the larger towns. A slight hope was entertained that the whites might be able, by uniting, to obtain some representation in the convention. At a meeting in Montgomery, in August, Joseph Hodgson[6] urged the

---

[1] The only taxes that affected these people.

[2] Annual Cyclopædia (1869), pp. 25, 26; *Montgomery Mail*, June 5, 1867; *N. Y. Herald*, June 19, 20, 1867.

[3] *Montgomery Advertiser*, July 19, 1867.

[4] Herbert, pp. 43, 44; *N. Y. Herald*, June 20 and 27, 1867. Most of the violent and radical schemes originated and were advocated by the white Radical leaders. Generally the negro leaders made moderate demands. Holland Thompson, a negro leader, in a speech at Tuskegee, advised his race not to organize a negro military company, as it would be sure to cause trouble. He said that the negro did not ask for social equality. He told the negroes to stop buying guns and whiskey and go to work. McPherson's scrapbook, "The Campaign of 1867," Vol. I, p. 107. In striking contrast were the speeches of such white men as B. W. Norris and A. C. Felder, who undertook to persuade the negroes that Reconstruction was the remedy for all the ills that affected humanity. McPherson's scrapbook, "The Fourth of July" (1867), pp. 124, 125.

[5] Herbert, p. 44.

[6] Lawyer, colonel of 7th Alabama Cavalry, superintendent of education, 1870–1872, author of "The Cradle of the Confederacy," "Alabama Manual and Statistical Register," editor *Montgomery Mail*, *Mobile Register*, etc.

people to take action and save the state from "Brownlowism,"[1] as the worst results were to be feared from inaction; the enemies of the Conservatives were making every effort to control the constitutional convention; the Conservatives were in favor of conceding every legitimate result of the war and were willing to grant suffrage to the negro by state action — the only legitimate way; at the same time the negro must assist in guaranteeing universal amnesty. The negroes were asked by the speaker to reflect and to learn for what purpose the Radical leaders were using them. The best people of the state, he said, and not the worst, ought to reconstruct the state under the Sherman law.[2]

Although strenuous efforts were made to secure a large attendance at the Conservative convention in September, there were only thirteen of the sixty-two counties represented. General M. J. Bulger was chosen to preside. Resolutions were adopted asserting the old constitutional view of the Federal government and declaring that the present state of affairs was destructive of federal government, in which each state had the absolute right to regulate the suffrage. An appeal was made to the negroes not to follow the counsels of bad men and designing strangers. The convention favored the education of the negro so as to fit him for his moral and political responsibilities.[3]

About the time of the meeting of the Conservative convention an event occurred which showed the results of the teachings of the Radical leaders. A plan was formed by the more violent blacks to prevent the meeting of the Conservatives. Some of the more sensible negroes used their influence as a "Special Committee on the Situation" to prevent the attempt to break up the convention, and L. J. Williams, a prominent negro politician, was the chairman of the committee. The white Radicals did nothing to prevent violence. Later a negro Conservative speaker was mobbed by the negroes and was rescued only by the aid of General Clanton. Other negroes who sided with the whites were expelled from their churches.[4]

The registrars continued to instruct "that part of the population

[1] A reign of terror had followed the reconstruction of Tennessee under "Parson" Brownlow.

[2] *N. Y. Times*, Aug. 19, 1867.

[3] *N. Y. Herald*, Sept. 6, 1867; Annual Cyclopædia (1867), p. 28; Herbert, p. 44.

[4] Herbert, pp. 44, 45; *N. Y. Herald*, Sept. 6, 1867.

2 L

which has heretofore been denied the right of suffrage" in the mysteries of citizenship or membership in the Union League. By the time of the election they were so effectively instructed that they were sure to vote as they were told by the League leaders. Nearly all of the respectable white members of the League in the Black Belt had fallen away, and but few remained in the white counties. Governor Patton yielded to Radical pressure, wrote Reconstruction letters, appeared at Reconstruction meetings, and deferred much to Pope and Swayne. He was harshly criticised by the Conservatives for pursuing such a course.

The Elections; the Negro's First Vote

The elections, early in October, were the most remarkable in the history of the state. For the first time the late slaves were to vote, while many of their former masters could not. Of the 65 counties in Alabama, 22 had negro majorities (according to the registration) and had 52 delegates of the 100 total, and in nearly all of the others the negro minority held the balance of power.[1] To control the negro vote the Radicals devoted all the machinery of registration and election, of the Union League, and of the Freedmen's Bureau. The chiefs of the League sent agents to the plantation negroes, who were showing some indifference to politics, with strict orders to go and vote. They were told that if they did not vote they would be reënslaved and their wives made to work the roads and quit wearing hoopskirts.[2] In Montgomery County, the day before election, the Radical agents went through the county, summoning the blacks to come and vote, saying that Swayne had ordered it and would punish them if they did not obey. The negroes came into the city by thousands in regularly organized bodies, under arms and led by the League politicians, and camped about the city waiting for the time to vote. The danger of outbreak was so great that the soldiers disarmed them. They did not know, most of them, what voting was. For what or for whom they were voting they knew not, — they were simply obeying the orders of their Bureau chiefs.[3] Likewise, at Clayton, the negroes were driven to town and camped the day before the election

---

[1] *Montgomery Sentinel*, July 3, 1867; *N. Y. Herald*, Aug. 5, 1867.

[2] Ku Klux Rept., Ala. Test., p. 357. A frequent threat.

[3] *N. Y. World*, Nov. 11, 1867; Harris, "Political Conflict in America," p. 479.

began. There was firing of guns all night. Early the next morning the local leaders formed the negroes into companies and regiments and marched them, armed with shotguns, muskets, pistols, and knives, to the court-house, where the only polling place for the county was situated. The first day there were about three thousand of them, of all ages from fifteen to eighty years of age, and no whites were allowed to approach the sacred voting place. When drawn up in line, each man was given a ticket by the League representatives, and no negro was allowed to break ranks until all were safely corralled in the court-house square. Many of the negroes had changed their names since they were registered, and their new ones were not on the books, but none lost a vote on that account.[1]

In Marengo County the Bureau and Loyal League officers lined up the negroes early in the morning and saw that each man was supplied with the proper ticket. Then the command, "Forward, March!" was given, the line filed past the polling place, and each negro deposited his ballot. About twelve o'clock a bugle blew as a signal to repeat the operation, and all the negroes present, including most of those who had voted in the morning, lined up, received tickets, and voted again. Late in the afternoon the farce was gone through the third time. Any one voted who pleased and as often as he pleased.[2]

In Dallas County the negroes were told that if they failed to vote they would be fined $50. The negroes at the polls were lined up and given tickets, which they were told to let no one see. However, in some cases the Conservatives had also given tickets to negroes, and a careful inspection was made in order to prevent the casting of such ballots. The average negro is said to have voted once for himself and once "for Jim who couldn't come." The registration lists were not referred to except when a white man offered to vote. Most of the negroes had strange ideas of what voting meant. It meant freedom, for one thing, if they voted the Radical ticket, and slavery if they did not. One negro at Selma held up a blue (Conservative) ticket and cried out, "No land! no mules! no votes! slavery again!" Then holding up a red (Radical) ticket he shouted, "Forty acres of land! a mule! freedom! votes! equal of white man!" Of course he voted the red ticket. Numbers of them brought halters

[1] *N. Y. Herald*, Oct. 13, 1867.
[2] Accounts of negroes and whites who were at the polls.

for their mules or sacks "to put it in." Some country negroes were given red tickets and told that they must not be persuaded to part with them, as each ticket was good for a piece of land. The poor negroes did not understand this figurative language and put the precious red tickets in their pockets and hurried home to locate the land. Another darky was given a ticket and told to vote — to put the ballot in the box. "Is dat votin'?" "Yes." "Nuttin' more, master?" "No." "I thought votin' was gittin' sumfin." He went home in disgust. The legend of "lands and mules" was revived during the fall and winter of 1867–1868, and many negroes were expecting a division of property. By this time they were beginning to feel that it was the fault of their leaders that the division did not take place, and there were threats against those who had made promises. However, the sellers of painted sticks again thrived — perhaps they had never ceased to thrive.[1] General Swayne reported about this time that the giving of the ballot to the negro had greatly improved his condition.[2]

The election went overwhelmingly for the convention and for the Radical candidates. The revision of the voting lists before election struck off the names of many "improper" whites and placed none on the list; with the negroes the reverse was true. The whites had no hope of carrying the elections in most of the counties, and as the negroes were intensely excited, and as trouble was sure to follow in case the whites endeavored to vote or to control the negro vote, most of the Conservatives refrained from voting. Even at this time a large number of people were unable to believe seriously that the negro voting had come to stay. To them it seemed something absurd and almost ridiculous except for the ill feelings aroused among the negroes. Such a state of affairs could not last long, they thought. Two Conservative delegates and ninety-eight Radical delegates were elected to the convention.[3]

[1] *Selma Messenger*, Oct. 10 and 12, Dec. 20 and 22, 1867, and Jan. 2, 1868; *Montgomery Mail*, Jan. 30, 1868; Ball, "Clarke County"; oral accounts.

[2] Freedmen's Bureau Report, Nov. 1, 1867.

[3] Sen. Ex. Doc., No. 53, 40th Cong., 2d Sess.; Ho. Ex. Doc., No. 238, 40th Cong., 2d Sess. The *N. Y. Tribune*, Oct. 21, 1867, gives slightly different figures. Statements of the vote do not agree. There was much confusion in the records. For statistics, see above, pp. 491, 494.

CHAPTER XIV

THE "RECONSTRUCTION" CONVENTION

Character of the Convention

THE delegates elected to the convention were a motley crew — white, yellow, and black — of northern men, Bureau officers, "loyalists," "rebels," who had aided the Confederacy and now perjured themselves by taking the oath, Confederate deserters, and negroes.[1] The Freedmen's Bureau furnished eighteen or more of the one hundred members. There were eighteen blacks.[2] Thirteen more of the members had certified, as registrars, to their own election and with six other members had certified to the election of thirty-one, nineteen of whom were on the board of registration. No pretence of residence was made by the northern men in the counties from which they were elected. Several had never seen the counties they represented, a slate being made up in Montgomery and sent to remote districts to be voted for. Of these northern men, or foreigners, there were thirty-seven or thirty-eight, from Maine, Massachusetts, Connecticut, Vermont, New York, Pennsylvania, Ohio, Iowa, New Jersey, Illinois, Ireland, Canada, and Scotland.[3] The native whites were for the most

[1] Samuel A. Hale, a dissatisfied Radical from New Hampshire, a brother of John P. Hale, wrote to Senator Henry Wilson, on Jan. 1, 1868, concerning the character of the members of the convention. He said that many were negroes, grossly ignorant; a large proportion were northern adventurers who had manipulated the negro vote; and all were "worthless vagabonds, homeless, houseless, drunken knaves." Hale had lived for several years in Alabama. Ku Klux Rept., Ala. Test., pp. 1815-1830.

[2] There is doubt about four or five men, whether they were black or white. The lists made at the time do not agree.

[3] *N. Y. World*, Nov. 11, 1867, and Feb. 22, 1868; *Selma Messenger*, Dec. 20 and 22, 1867; Annual Cyclopædia (1867), p. 30; Herbert, "Solid South," p. 45. A partial list of aliens as described by a northern correspondent: A. J. Applegate of Wisconsin; Arthur Bingham of Ohio and New York; D. H. Bingham of New York, who had lived in the state before the war, an old man, and intensely bitter in his hatred of southerners; W. H. Block of Ohio; W. T. Blackford of New York, a Bureau official, "the wearer of one of the two clean shirts visible in the whole convention"; M. D. Brainard of New York, a Bureau clerk who did not know, when elected to represent Monroe, where his

part utterly unknown and had but little share in the proceedings of the convemtion.[1] Of the negro members two could write well and were fairly well educated, half could not write a word, and the others had been taught to sign their names and that was all. There were many negroes who could read and write, but they were not sent to the convention. Perhaps the carpet-baggers feared trouble from them and wanted only those whom they could easily control.[2]

county was liocated ; Alfred E. Buck of Maine, a court clerk of Mobile appointed by Pope; Charlles W. Buckley of Massachusetts, New York, and Illinois, chaplain of a negro regimcent, later a Bureau official ; William M. Buckley of New York, his brother ; J. H. Burdiick of Iowa, extremely radical ; Pierce Burton 'of Massachusetts, who had been removceed from the Bureau for writing letters to northern papers, advocating the repeal of thie cotton tax, but now that the negroes desired the repeal of the tax, the breach was hhealed ; C. M. Cabot of (unknown), member of Convention of 1865; Datus E. Coon of Iowa ; Joseph H. Davis of (unknown), surgeon U.S.A., member of convention cof 1865; Charles H. Dustan of Illinois ; George Ely of Massachusetts and New York ; S. S. Gardner of Massachusetts, of the Freedmen's Bureau ; Albert Griffin of Ohio andl Illinois, Radical editor ; Thomas Haughey of Scotland, surgeon U.S.A.; R. M. Johnscon of Illinois, lived in Montgomery and represented Henry County; John C. Keffer of Pœnnsylvania, chairman of Radical Executive Committee, "known to malignants as the "head devil ' of the Loyal League " ; David Lore of (unknown); Charles A. Miller of Maaine, Bureau official, "wore the second clean shirt in the convention " ; A. C. Morgan of ((unknown); B. W. Norris of Maine, Commissioner of National Cemetery, 1863-1865, (Commissary and Paymaster, 1864–1866, Bureau official ; E. Woolsey Peck of New Yorlk ; R. M. Reynolds of Iowa, six months in Alabama and "knew all about it " ; J. Silsbry of Massachusetts, another Bureau reverend ; N. D. Stanwood of Massachusetts, a Bureau official who had caused several serious negro disturbances in Lowndes County; J. P. Stow of (unknown) ; Whelan of Ireland ; J. W. Wilhite of (unknown), U.S. sutler ; Benjamin Yordy of (unknown), a Bureau official and revenue official who never saw tthe county he represented ; Benjamin Rolfe, a carriage painter from New York, was tcoo drunk to sign the constitution, and was known as "the hero of two shirts," becaause when he failed to pay a hotel bill in Selma his carpet-bag was seized, and was foumd to contain nothing but two of those useful garments. Ku Klux Rept., Ala. Test., *passim* ; *N. Y. World*, Nov. 11, 1867; Herbert, p. 45.

[1] Some (of the better known were : R. Deal of Dale County, a Baptist preacher, one of those whco, in 1865, negligently reconstructed the state, and the hope was now expressed that "he has better success in reconstructing souls than sovereignties " ; W. C. Ewing of Baaine County, "one of the original Moulton Leaguers who, in 1865, first organized thie Radical party in Alabama," a bitter Radical ; W. R. Jones of Covington, had been barrbarously murdered in "a rebel outrage," but came to the convention notwithstanding;; B. F. Saffold, an officer of the Confederate army and military mayor of Selma ; Heniry C. Semple, ex-Confederate, nephew of President Tyler ; Joseph H. Speed, cousin of Atttorney-General Speed.

[2] The niegro members were : Ben Alexander of Greene, field hand ; John Caraway of Mobile, asssistant editor of the *Mobile Nationalist;* Thomas Diggs of Barbour, field hand ; Peytoon Finley, formerly doorkeeper of the House ; James K. Green of Hale, a carriage driver ; Ovid Gregory of Mobile, a barber ; Jordan Hatcher of Dallas and

Griffin of Ohio was appointed temporary chairman, and on the motion of Keffer of Pennsylvania, Robert Barbour of New York was made temporary secretary and later permanent secretary. Keffer nominated Peck, a New Yorker who had resided for some years in Alabama, for president of the convention, and he was unanimously elected.[1] There were several negro clerks in the convention. The disgusted Conservatives designated the aggregation by various epithets, such as "The Unconstitutional Convention," "Pope's Convention," "Swayne's World-renowned Menagerie," "The Circus," "Black and Tan," "Black Crook," etc. The last, which was probably given by the New York *Herald* correspondent, seems to have been the favorite name. The white people still persisted in looking upon the whole affair as a more or less irritating joke.

The carpet-baggers intended that the convention should be purged of "improper" persons, and one of them proposed that the test oath be taken. This aroused opposition on the part of the ex-"rebels," who did not care to perjure themselves more than was necessary. Coon of Iowa then proposed a simple oath to support the Constitution, which after some wrangling was taken.[2] Caraway, a negro, wanted no chaplain to officiate in the convention who had not remained loyal to the United States. Skinner of Franklin said: "Let none offer prayer who are rebels and who have not fought under the stars and stripes." This was to prevent such reverend members of the convention as Deal of Dale from officiating. Finally, the president was empowered to appoint the chaplain daily. A colored chaplain was called upon once in a while, and one of them invoked the blessings of God on "Unioners and cusses on rebels."[3]

Washington Johnson of Russell, field hands, were the blackest negroes in the convention; L. S. Latham of Bullock; Tom Lee of Perry, field hand, who had a reputation for moderation; Alfred Strother of Dallas; J. T. Rapier of Lauderdale, educated in Canada; J. W. McLeod of Marengo; B. F. Royal of Bullock; J. H. Burdick of Wilcox; H. Stokes and Jack Hatcher of Dallas; Simon Brunson and Benjamin Inge of Sumter; Samuel Blandon of Lee; Lafeyette Robinson and Columbus Jones of Madison. Beverly, "History of Alabama," p. 203; *N. Y. World*, Nov. 11, 1867; Owen, "Official and Statistical Register," p. 125.

[1] Journal Convention of 1867, pp. 3-5.

[2] Journal Convention of 1867, p. 5; *N. Y. Herald*, Nov. 13, 1867; Annual Cyclopædia (1867), p. 30.

[3] *Selma Messenger*, Dec. 22, 1867; Journal Convention of 1867, p. 6; *N. Y. World*, Nov. 11, 1867.

Another way of showing the loyalty of the body was by directing a committee to bring in an ordinance changing the names of the counties "named in honor of rebellion and in glorification of traitors." Keffer of Pennsylvania was the author of this resolution. Steed of Cleburne wanted the name of his county changed to Lincoln, and Simmons of Colbert wanted his county to be named Brownlow. The test votes on such questions were about 55 to 30 in favor of changing. Baine, Colbert, and Jones counties, established by the "Johnson" government, were abolished.[1]

The president was directed to drape his chair with two "Federal" flags. Generals Pope and Swayne, and Governor Patton, as friends of Reconstruction, were invited to seats in the convention and were asked to speak before the body. Pope was becoming somewhat nervous at the conduct of the supreme rulers of the state and in his speech counselled moderation and fairness. He also commended them for the "firmness and fearlessness with which you have conducted the late campaigns," and congratulated them upon "the success which has thus far crowned your efforts in the pacification of this state and its restoration to the Union."[2] The most radical members of the convention were bringing pressure to bear to force Pope to declare vacant at once all the offices of the provisional government and fill them with reconstructionists. In this they were aided by northern influence. Pope, however, refused to make the change, and thus displeased the Radicals, who wanted offices at once.[3]

The first ordinance of the convention reconstructed Jones County, named for a Confederate colonel, out of existence, and the second, third, and fourth arranged for the pay of the convention. The president received $10 a day and the members $8 each; the clerks from $6 to $8, and the pages $4.[4] The president and members received 40 cents as mileage for each mile travelled. To cover these expenses an additional tax of 10 per cent on taxes already assessed was levied. The comptroller refused to pay the members until ordered by Pope.

[1] Journal, pp. 69–71, 249, 251, 264; Annual Cyclopædia (1867), p. 32; N. Y. Herald, March 16, 1867.

[2] Journal, pp. 10, 12, 13; N. Y. World, Nov. 20, 1869; Annual Cyclopædia (1867), p. 30.

[3] Journal, pp. 13, 110, 111, 276; N. Y. Herald, Nov. 13, 1867.

[4] Twice the pay in the convention of 1865.

The latter hesitated to give the order, as he doubted if he had the authority. However, he finally said that he would order payment provided the compensation be fixed at reasonable rates, and that the payments be not made before the convention completed its work. He further added that the convention must be moderate in action; "I speak not more for the interests of Alabama than for the interests of the political party upon whose retention of power for several years to come the success of Reconstruction depends." When Pope urged moderation, it is likely that something serious was the matter. A proposition to reduce the pay of the members from $8 to $6 per day was lost by a vote of 35 to 57. A few days before the close of the convention, Pope ordered the payment of the *per diem* to the hungry delegates, many of whom refused to accept the state obligations called "Patton money." They were told that it was receivable for taxes, and one answered for all: "Oh, damn the taxes! We haven't got any to pay."[1]

The Race Question

The colored delegates brought up the negro question in several forms. First, Rapier of Canada wanted a declaration that negroes were entitled to all the privileges and rights of citizenship in Alabama.[2] Then Strother of Dallas demanded that the negroes be empowered to collect pay from those who held them in slavery, at the rate of $10 a month for services rendered from January 1, 1863, the date of the Emancipation Proclamation, to May 20, 1865. An ordinance to this effect was actually adopted by a vote of 53 to 31.[3] The scalawags, as a rule, wished to prohibit intermarriage of the races, and Semple of Montgomery reported an ordinance to that effect. He would prohibit intermarriage to the fourth generation. The negroes and carpet-baggers united to vote this down, which was done by a vote of 48 to 30. Caraway (negro) of Mobile wanted life imprisonment for any white man marrying or living with a black woman, but he said it was against the Civil Rights Bill to prohibit intermarriage. This seems to have irritated the scalawags. Gregory (negro) of Mobile wanted all regulations, laws, and customs wherein distinctions were

---

[1] Journal, pp. 79, 178, 249–251 ; Pope to Swayne, Nov. 20, 1867 ; *N. Y. World*, Dec. 14, 1867 ; G. O. No. 254, 3d M. D., Nov. 26, 1867.

[2] Journal, p. 57. [3] Journal, p. 61 ; *N. Y. Herald*, Nov. 15, 1867.

made on account of color or race to be abolished, and thus allow intermarriages. The convention refused to adopt the report providing against amalgamation.[1] The Mobile negroes alone seem to have been opposed to the prohibition of intermarriage. The convention of 1865 had recognized the validity of all slave marriages and had ordered that they be considered legal. During 1865 and 1866 the fickle negroes, male and female, made various experiments with new partners, and the result was that in 1867 thousands of negroes had forsaken the husband or wife of slavery times and "taken up" with others. All sorts of prosecutions were hanging over them, and an ordinance was passed for the relief of such people. It directed that marriages were to date from November 30, 1867, and not from 1865 or earlier. All who were living together in 1867 were to be considered man and wife, and all prosecutions for former misconduct were forbidden.[2]

Caraway (negro) of Mobile succeeded in having an ordinance passed directing that church property used during slavery for colored congregations be turned over to the latter.[3] Some of this property was paid for by negro slaves and held in trust for them by white trustees. Most of it, however, belonged to the planters, who erected churches for the use of their slaves.

Not much was said about separate or mixed schools for the races. There was a disposition on the part of the leaders to keep such questions in the background for a time in order to prevent irritating discussions. A proposition for separate schools was voted down on the ground that it was better for the children of both races to go to school together and wear off their prejudices. This was the carpetbaggers' view, but most of the blacks finally voted against a measure providing for mixed schools, because, they said, they did not want to send their children to school with white children. The matter was hushed up and left unsettled.[4]

In spite of efforts to keep the question in the background, the social equality of the negro race was demanded by one or two irre-

---

[1] Journal, p. 189; Herbert, "Solid South," p. 46; *N. Y. Herald*, Nov. 13, 1867; Annual Cyclopædia (1867), p. 33.
[2] Journal, pp. 262, 263.
[3] Journal, pp. 15, 212, 263; *N. Y. Herald*, Nov. 13, 1867.
[4] Annual Cyclopædia (1867), p. 33; *Selma Messenger*, Dec. 22, 1867.

pressible Mobile mulattoes, and a discussion was precipitated. The scalawags with few exceptions were opposed to admitting negroes to the same privileges as whites, — in theatres, churches, on railroads and boats, and at hotels, — though they were willing to require equal but separate accommodations for both races. Semple reported from his committee an ordinance requiring equal and separate accommodations, but declared that equality of civil rights was not affected by such a measure. By a vote of 32 to 46 this measure failed to pass.[1] Griffin[2] (white) of Ohio briefly attacked Semple for proposing such an iniquitous measure. McLeod (negro) said he did not exactly want social equality, and added "suppose one of you white gentlemen want a negro in the same car with you. The conductor would not allow it. This should be changed." Caraway (negro) objected to having his wife travel in the coach with low and obscene white men. Jim Green (negro) said it was a "common thing to put cullud folks in de same cyar wid drunk and low white folks. We want nebber be subjic to no sich disgrace," but wanted to be allowed to go among decent white people. Gregory (negro) made some scathing observations at the expense of Semple and his associates, who were hoping to make political use of the negro, yet did not want to ride in the same car with him. How could the delegates, he said, go home to their constituents, nineteen-twentieths of whom were negroes, after voting against their enjoying the same rights as the whites? Did Semple feel polluted by sitting by Finley, his colored colleague? Why then should he object to sitting in the same car with him? He (Gregory) was as good a man as Napoleon on his throne, and could not be honored by sitting by a white man, but "in de ole worl de cullud folks ride wid de whites" and so it should be here. Rapier (negro) of Canada said that the manner in which colored gentlemen and ladies were treated in America was beyond his comprehension. He (Rapier) had dined with lords in his lifetime, and though he did not feel flattered by sitting by a white man, yet he would vote for social equality. Some of the negroes feebly opposed the agitation of the question on the ground that the civil and political rights of the negro were not yet safe and should not be endangered by the agitation of the social question. Griffin

[1] Journal, p. 149; *N. Y. World*, Dec. 14, 1867.
[2] Dubbed "the incarnate fiend" by the whites because of his violent prejudice.

of Ohio and Keffer of Pennsylvania supported the negroes in all their demands. The carpet-baggers in general were in favor of social equality, but most of them thought it much more important that the spoils be secured first. The negroes were placated with numerous promises and by a special resolution opening the galleries to "their ladies" and inviting the latter to be present [1] at the sessions of the convention.

Debates on Disfranchisement

The debates on the question of suffrage were the most extended and showed the most violent spirit on the part of most of the members. Dustan of Iowa proposed that the new constitution should in no degree be proscriptive, but his resolution was voted down by a vote of 30 to 51. Some of the negroes voted for it. [2] Rapier (negro) proposed that the convention memorialize Congress to remove the political disabilities of those who might aid in reconstruction according to the plan of Congress. This was adopted and Griffin, the most radical member of the committee, was made chairman to make merciful recommendations. Gardner of Massachusetts, representing Butler County, said that there were persons in the state who should have been tried and convicted of felony and would thus have been disfranchised, but owing to fault of courts and juries they were not convicted. He wanted a special commission to disfranchise such persons. The majority report on the franchise [3] called for the disfranchisement of those who had mistreated Union prisoners, those who were disfranchised by the Reconstruction Acts, and those who had registered under the acts and had later refrained from voting. Such persons were not to be allowed to vote, register, or hold office. An oath was to be taken repudiating belief in the doctrine of secession, accepting the civil and political equality of all men, and agreeing never to attempt to limit the suffrage. "The only question is," they reported, "whether we have not been too liberal." It was necessary that all who registered be forced to vote in the election on pain of being dis-

---

[1] *N. Y. World*, Dec. 14, 1867; *Montgomery Mail*, Nov., 1867; *N. Y. Herald*, Nov. 13 and 23 and Dec. 8, 1867.

[2] Journal, pp. 8, 12, 17; *N. Y. Herald*, Nov. 13, 1867.

[3] By Griffin of Ohio, Keffer of Pennsylvania, Norris of Maine, and Davis of (?). It was said that Norris and Davis had to be influenced by Swayne to sign the majority report. *N. Y. World*, Nov. 20, 1867.

franchised, in order to get a sufficient number of voters to the polls, though the report stated that Congress was not bound by the law of March 23 to reject the constitution if a majority did not vote; the convention had the right to say that men.must vote or be disfranchised; as to the oath, any one who would refuse to take it had no faith in American principles and was hostile to the Constitution and laws of the United States.[1]

The minority report [2] objected to going beyond the acts of Congress in disfranchising whites. Lee (negro) said that such a course would endanger the ratification of the constitution and if the negroes did not get their rights now, they would never get them. He wanted his rights at the court-house and at the polls and nothing more. Charity and moderation would be better than proscription.[3] Speed said that the measure would disfranchise from 30,000 to 40,000 men beyond the acts of Congress.[4] Griffin of Ohio, speaking in favor of the majority report, said that "the infernal rebels had acted like devils turned loose from hell," and that his party could not stand against them in a fair political field; and therefore proscription was necessary. Another advocate of sweeping disfranchisement wanted all the leading whites disfranchised until 1875, in order to prevent them from regaining control of the government.[5]

Numerous amendments were offered to the majority report. Haughey of Scotland wanted to disfranchise all Confederates above the rank of captain, and all who had held any civil office anywhere, or who had voted for secession. A stringent test oath was to discover the disabilities of would-be electors. Again, he wanted every elector to prove that on November 1, 1867, he was a friend of the Reconstruction Acts. He would have voters and office-holders swear to accept the civil and political equality of all men, and to resist any change, and also swear that they had never held office, aided the Confederacy, nor given aid or comfort to Confederates.[6] Nearly all the amendments included a provision forcing the voter or office-holder to accept the political and civil equality of all men,

---

[1] Journal, pp. 30–34; *N. Y. World*, Nov. 20, 1867.
[2] By Speed of Virginia, Whelan of Ireland, and Lee (negro).
[3] Journal, pp. 36, 37; Annual Cyclopædia (1867), p. 31.
[4] Annual Cyclopædia (1867), p. 32; *N. Y. World*, Nov. 20, 1867.
[5] *N. Y. Herald*, Nov. 13, 1867; Annual Cyclopædia (1867), p. 31.
[6] Journal, pp. 42, 55, 82, 100.

and to swear never to change. Springfield of St. Clair thought that all who were opposed to Reconstruction should be disfranchised, and Russell of Barbour, with Applegate of Wisconsin, held that all Confederates should be disfranchised who had voluntarily aided the Confederacy.[1]

D. H. Bingham of New York thought that voters should swear that on March 4, 1864, they preferred the United States government to the Confederacy, and would have abandoned the latter had they had the opportunity.[2] Applegate thought that no citizen, officer, or editor who opposed congressional Reconstruction ought to be permitted to vote before 1875.[3] Silsby of Iowa would also exclude from the suffrage those who had killed negroes during the last two years, who opposed Reconstruction, or dissuaded others from attending the election.[4] Garrison of Blount wanted to disfranchise those who were in the convention of 1861 and voted for secession, Confederate members of Congress who voted for the conscription law, those disfranchised by the Reconstruction Acts, Confederates above the rank of captain, and state and Confederate officials of every kind above justice of the peace and bailiff.[5] Skinner of Franklin wanted to disfranchise enough rebels to hold the balance of power. "We have the rod over their heads and intend to keep it there." [6] The most liberal amendments were proposed by Peters of Lawrence, who would continue the disfranchisement made by Congress unless the would-be voter would swear that he was in favor of congressional Reconstruction. Rapier (negro) would have all disabilities removed by the state as soon as they were removed by Congress.[7] The price of pardon in all ordinary cases was support of congressional Reconstruction.

The debate lasted for four days, and it was all that Swayne could do to prevent a division in the Radical party. An agent was sent to Washington for instructions. The violent character of the proceedings of the convention made the northern friends of Reconstruction nervous, and Horace Greeley persuaded Senator Wilson to exert his influence to prevent the adoption of extreme measures by the convention. Wilson wrote to Swayne that the convention and especially such men as D. H. Bingham were doing much harm to Recon-

---

[1] Journal, pp. 47, 48, 54, 83.   [2] Journal, p. 47.   [3] Journal, p. 47.   [4] Journal, p. 45.
[5] Journal, p. 53.   [6] *Selma Messenger*, Dec. 22, 1867.   [7] Journal, pp. 84, 85.

struction and to the Republican party. The northern Republican press generally seemed afraid of the action of the convention, and suggested more liberal measures. So we find Pope and Swayne advocating moderation.[1] Peck, the president of the convention, still spoke out for the test oath and disfranchisement. It was necessary to secure the fruits of Reconstruction, and the test oath would keep out many; but, he said, if the old leaders, who were honorable men, should take the oath, they would abide by it,[2] and Reconstruction would then be safe. The oath finally adopted, which had to be taken by all who would vote or hold office, was the usual oath to support the Constitution and laws with the following additions: "I accept the civil and political equality of all men; and agree not to attempt to deprive any person or persons, on account of race, color or previous condition, of any political or civil right, privilege or immunity, enjoyed by any other class of men; and furthermore, that I will not in any way injure or countenance in others any attempt to injure any person or persons on account of past or present support of the government of the United States, the laws of the United States, or the principles of the political and civil equality of all men, or for affiliation with any political party."[3] It was finally settled that in addition to those disfranchised by the Reconstruction Acts others should be excluded for violation of the rules of war.[4] They could neither register, vote, nor hold office until relieved by the vote of the general assembly for aiding in Reconstruction, and until they had accepted the political equality of all men.[5] It was estimated that the suffrage clause would disfranchise from voting or holding office 40,000 white men. The oath was likely to exclude still more. Bingham thought the oath as adopted was a back-down, and demanded the iron-clad oath. The committee on the franchise wanted

---

[1] *N. Y. World,* Nov. 20 and Dec. 6 and 14, 1867.

[2] Annual Cyclopædia (1867), p. 33.

[3] Code of Alabama, 1876, p. 113. Griffin said that the oath required the voter never to favor a change in the new constitution so far as the suffrage was concerned; that "it was the determination of the committee to forever fasten this constitution on the people of Alabama. He wanted to tie the hands of rebels, so that complete political equality should be secured to the negro." Annual Cyclopædia (1867), p. 32.

[4] This was aimed at the Confederate soldiers of north Alabama, who had imprisoned and in some cases hanged the tories and outlaws of that section.

[5] Code of Alabama, 1876; Constitution of 1868, Article VII.

to prohibit the legislature from enfranchising any person unless he had aided in Reconstruction.[1]

Legislation by the Convention

The convention organized a new militia system, giving most of the companies to the black counties. All officers were to be loyal to the United States, that is, they were to be reconstructionists. No one who was disfranchised could enlist. The proceeds of the sale of contraband and captured property taken by the militia were to be used in its support.[2] Stay laws were enacted to go into force with the adoption of the constitution, also exemption laws which exempted from sale for debt more property than nineteen-twentieths of the people possessed.[3] The war debt of Alabama was again declared void, and the ordinance of secession stigmatized as "unconstitutional, null and void."[4] Contracts made during the war, when the consideration was Confederate money, were declared null and void at the option of either party, as were also notes payable in Confederate money and debts made for slaves. Bingham forced through an ordinance providing for a new settlement in United States currency of trust estates settled during the war in Confederate securities.[5] Judicial decisions in aid of the war were declared void. Defendants in civil cases against whom judgment was rendered during the war were entitled to a revision or to a new trial.[6]

The negroes were complaining about the cotton tax, and a memorial was addressed to Congress, asking for its repeal on the ground that when the tax was imposed the state had no voice in the government; that it was oppressive, amounting to 20 per cent of the gross value of the cotton crop, and fell heavily on the negroes, who were the principal producers; that for two years the tax had made cotton cultivation unprofitable, and had driven away capital.[7]

---

[1] Annual Cyclopædia (1867), pp. 34, 35; Journal, pp. 186, 187.

[2] Journal, pp. 257–262; N. Y. World, Nov. 20, 1867.

[3] Journal, pp. 265–269.   [4] Journal, pp. 255, 571.

[5] Journal, pp. 271, 272, 273; N. Y. World, Nov. 11, 1867.

[6] Journal, pp. 272, 273.

[7] Journal, p. 63. The whites had for more than two years been asking for the repeal of this unjust tax, but they were not heeded. As soon as the negroes demanded its repeal, it was repealed. That was certainly one advantage they received from the possession of political rights. One petition from the negroes asked that the tax be

A memorial to Congress was adopted by a vote of 50 to 6, asking that the part of the reconstruction law which required a majority of the registered voters to vote in the election for the adoption of the constitution be repealed. It was now seen that the Conservatives would endeavor to defeat the constitution by refraining from voting.[1]

An ordinance was passed to protect the newly enfranchised negro voters. The penalty for using "improper influence" and thereby deceiving or misleading an elector was to be not less than one nor more than ten years' imprisonment or fine of not more than $2000. The election was ordered for February 4, 1868, to be held under direction of the military commander. In order to bring out a large number of voters, elections were ordered for the same time for all state and county officers, and for members of Congress — several thousand in all. The officers thus elected were to enter at once upon their duties, and hold office for the proper term of years, dating from the legal date for the next general election after the admission of the state.[2]

Among the scalawag members of the convention, who saw that the carpet-baggers would rule the land by controlling the negro vote, there was much dissatisfaction and at length open revolt. Nine members signed a formal protest against the proposed constitution, stating that a government framed upon its provisions would entail upon the state greater evils than any that then threatened.[3] Another member protested against the test oath, against the extension of proscription, and against the absence of express provision for separate schools.[4] The constitution was adopted by a vote of 66 to 8, 26 not voting. A few days after the adjournment, 15 or 20 scalawag members united in an address to the people of Alabama, protesting against the proposed constitution because it was more proscriptive than the acts of Congress, because of the test oath, because the course of the convention had shown that the government would be in the

repealed because, in many instances, it was greater than the value of the land. If this was not done, they wanted the land taken from the owners and worked in common. *N. Y. Herald*, Nov. 13, 1867.

[1] Journal, p. 244.   [2] Journal, pp. 266, 267.

[3] Journal, p. 240; Meade, Speed, Semple, Cabot, Graves, J. L. Alexander, Ewing, Latham, and Hurst.

[4] Journal, p. 242; J. P. Stow of (?).

2 M

hands of a few adventurers under the control of the blacks, to whom
they had promised mixed schools and laws protecting the negro in his
rights of voting, eating, travelling, etc., with whites.   For these reasons
they urged that the constitution be rejected.[1]

Just before the convention adjourned, Caraway (negro) offered
a resolution, which was adopted, stating that the constitution was
founded on justice, honesty, and civilization, and that the enemies
of law and order, freedom and justice, were pledged to prevent its
adoption.   But he asserted that God would strengthen and assist
those who did right; therefore he advised that a day be set apart
"whereby the good and loyal people of Alabama can offer up their
adorations to Almighty God, and invoke His aid and assistance to
the loyal people of the state, while passing through the bitter strife
that seems to await them."[2]

A study of the votes and debates leads to the following general
conclusion: The majority of the scalawags were ready to revolt
after finding that the carpet-bag element had control of the negro
vote; the negroes with a few exceptions made no unreasonable and
violent demands unless urged by the carpet-baggers; the carpet-
baggers with a few extreme scalawags were disposed to resort to
extreme measures of proscription in order to get rid of white leaders
and white majorities, and to agitate the question of social equality
in order to secure the negroes, and to drive off the scalawags so that
there would be fewer with whom to share the spoils.[3]

[1] Address of Protesting Delegates to the People of Alabama, Dec. 10, 1867.

[2] Journal, p. 243.

[3] The Codes of Alabama for 1876 and 1896 do not recognize the validity of the
constitution of 1868.   It is listed as the "Constitution (so-called) of the State of Alabama, 1868."   The president of the convention of 1875 said, "What is called the
present constitution of the state of Alabama is a piece of unseemly mosaic, composed
of shreds and patches gathered here and there, incongruous in design, inharmonious in
action, discriminating and oppressive in the burdens it imposes, reckless in the license it
confers on unjust and wicked legislation, and utterly lacking in every element to inspire
popular confidence and the reverence and affection of the people." Journal, 1875, p. 5.

CHAPTER XV

THE "RECONSTRUCTION" COMPLETED

"Convention" Candidates

THE debates in the convention over mixed schools, proscription, militia, and representation had seemingly resulted in a division between the carpet-baggers, who controlled the negroes, and the more moderate scalawags. The carpet-baggers and extreme scalawags of the convention resolved themselves into a body for the nomination of candidates for office. This body formed the state Union League convention. Of the 101 delegates to the convention, 67 or 68 had signed the constitution, and of these at least 56 were candidates for office under it. Full tickets were nominated by the convention and by the local councils of the Union League. In the black counties only members of the League were nominated, and it was practically the same in the white counties, where the League then had but few members. Nearly all the election officials were candidates. Men represented one county in the convention, and were candidates in others for office.[1]

The state of politics in the average Black Belt county was like that in Perry or Montgomery. In Perry, the Radical nominees for probate judge, state senator, sheriff, and tax assessor were from Wisconsin; for representative, two negroes and one white from Ohio, and for tax collector, a northern man.[2] In Montgomery, for the legislature, one white from Ohio and one from Austria, and three negroes; for probate judge, clerk of circuit court, sheriff, and tax assessor, men from New York and other northern states.[3] One or two negroes ran independently in each Black Belt county. In

---

[1] Ely, a delegate from Russell, was a candidate in Montgomery; Brainard, a delegate from Monroe, was a candidate in Montgomery; R. M. Johnson, a delegate from Henry, was also a candidate in Montgomery. These men, however, lived in Montgomery and had never seen the counties they represented.

[2] *Selma Messenger*, Jan. 10, 1868.

[3] Herbert, "Solid South," p. 47 ; *N. Y. World*, Feb. 5, 1868.

"CONVENTION" CANDIDATES

NAME	NATIVITY	CANDIDATE FOR
Ben Alexander	Negro	Legislature
A. J. Applegate . . .	Ohio and Wisconsin	Lieutenant Governor
W. A. Austin	Negro	State Senate
Arthur Bingham . . .	New York	State Treasurer
W. H. Black	Ohio	Probate Judge
W. T. Blackford . . .	Illinois	Probate Judge
Samuel Blandon . . .	Negro	Legislature
Mark Brainard	New York	Clerk Circuit Court
Alfred E. Buck	Maine	Clerk Circuit Court
C. W. Buckley	New York, Mass., and Illinois	Congress
W. M. Buckley* . . .	New York and Massachusetts	State Senator
J. H. Burdick	Iowa	Probate Judge
John Caraway	Negro	Legislature
Pierce Burton	Massachusetts	Legislature
J. Collins	North	State Senate
Datus E. Coon	Iowa	State Senate
Tom Diggs	Negro	Legislature
Charles W. Dustan . .	Iowa	Major-General Militia
S. S. Gardner	Massachusetts	Legislature
George Ely	New York, Conn., and Mass.	Probate Judge
Peyton Finley	Negro	Legislature
Jim Green	Negro	Legislature
Ovide Gregory	Negro	Legislature
Thomas Haughey . . .	Scotland	Congress
G. Horton	Massachusetts	Probate Judge
Benjamin Inge	Negro	Legislature
A. W. Jones*	Alabama	Probate Judge
Columbus Jones . . .	Negro	Legislature
John C. Keffer	Pennsylvania	Supt. of Industrial Resources
S. F. Kennemer . . .	Alabama	Legislature
Tom Lee	Negro	Legislature
David Lore	Negro (?)	Legislature
J. J. Martin	Georgia	Probate Judge
B. O. Masterson . . .	Unknown	Legislature
C. A. Miller	Massachusetts and Maine	Secretary of State
Stephen Moore* . . .	Alabama (?)	Senate
A. L. Morgan	Indiana	Clerk Circuit Court
J. F. Morton*	Unknown	Senate
B. W. Norris	Maine	Congress
E. W. Peck	New York	Chief Justice
Thomas M. Peters . . .	Tennessee	Supreme Court
G. P. Plowman	Alabama	Probate Judge
R. M. Reynolds . . .	Iowa	Auditor
Benjamin Rolfe	New York	Tax Collector

"CONVENTION" CANDIDATES (continued)

NAME	NATIVITY	CANDIDATE FOR
B. F. Royal	Negro	Senate
B. F. Saffold	Alabama	Supreme Court
J. Silsby *	Massachusetts	Clerk Circuit Court
C. P. Simmons	Tennessee	Commissioner
William P. Skinner˙ . .	Alabama	Chancellor
L. R. Smith *	Massachusetts	Circuit Judge
H. J. Springfield * . . .	Alabama	Legislature
N. D. Stanwood * . . .	Maine and Massachusetts	Legislature
J. P. Stow	Connecticut	Senate
Littleberry Strange . .	Georgia	Circuit Judge
James R. Walker * . .	Georgia	Sheriff
B. L. Whelan	Georgia, Ireland, and Mich.	Circuit Judge
C. O. Whitney	North	Senate
J. A. Yordy	North	Senate[1]

the white counties the extreme scalawags had a better chance for office, and most of the moderate reconstructionists fell away at once, leaving the spoils to the Radicals. It is doubtful if there were enough white men in the state who could read and write and who supported the new constitution, to fill the offices created by that instrument. Hence the assignment of candidates to far-off counties, and the admission of negro candidates.[2] The state ticket was headed by an

[1] N. Y. World, Feb. 13 and 22, 1868; Selma Times and Messenger, Feb. 28, 1868; Cong. Globe, March 11, 1868; Herbert, " Solid South "; Beverly, "Alabama "; Owen, p. 125.

The above list is not complete, as there were undoubtedly other candidates among those who did not sign the constitution, since a number of them fell into line later. The starred names are those of candidates who were also registrars, and who not only conducted their own elections for the convention, but also for office under the new constitution. Three members of the majority who signed the report were not eligible for office when the election came off, two being in jail, — one for stealing and the other for fraud, — while a third "had been betrayed into an act of virtue by dying." N. Y. World, Feb. 13, 1868.

[2] After the election, Governor Patton, who at first had supported Reconstruction, issued an address complaining that nearly all the candidates voted for were strangers to the people ; that many were ignorant negroes, and that in one county all the commissioners-elect were negroes who were unable to read ; that unlicensed lawyers, wholly uneducated, were chosen for state solicitors ; that the strangers were too often of bad character; and that the Radical party consisted almost entirely of negroes, the native whites having forsaken the party as soon as the negroes fell under the control of the imported Radicals who ran the machine. N. Y. Times, April 23, 1868.

Alabama tory, William H. Smith, and the other candidates for state offices were from Ohio, Pennsylvania, Maine, and New York, five of them being officers of the Freedmen's Bureau.[1]   The candidates for Congress were from Massachusetts, Ohio, Michigan, New York, Maine, and Nebraska.   In several instances the candidate hailed from two or more different states.[2]

Campaign on the Constitution

The campaign in behalf of the constitution did not differ in character from that in behalf of the convention.   The Radical candidates for office, working through the Union League, drilled the negroes in the proper political faith.   Nearly all the whites having gone over to the Conservatives, or withdrawn from politics, little or no attention was paid to the white voters.   All efforts were directed toward securing the negro vote.   Agents were sent over the state by the League to organize the negroes, who were again told the old story: If the constitution is not ratified, you will be reënslaved and your wives will be beaten and your children sold; if you do not get your rights now you will never get them.   A subsidized press[3] distributed campaign stories among those negroes who could read, and they spread the news.   In this way the remotest darky heard that he was sure to return to slavery if the constitution failed of ratification.[4]   The Union League assessed its members, especially

---

[1] Herbert, p. 47.

[2] *Montgomery Mail*, July 25, 1868 ; *N. Y. World*, Sept. 22, 1868.

[3] The Radical papers in Alabama were supported almost entirely by campaign funds and by appropriations from the government for printing the session laws of the United States.   They styled themselves the "Official Journals of the United States Government."   When one offended and the Washington patronage was withdrawn, it always collapsed.   In 1867 the reconstructionist papers in the state were *Alabama State Sentinel, The Nationalist, Elmore Standard, East Alabama Monitor, Alabama Republican, The Tallapoosian, The Reconstructionist, Huntsville Advocate, Moulton Union, Livingston Messenger.*   See Journal Convention of 1867, p. 242.   The circulation of each paper was small and almost entirely among the negroes.   Special campaign editions were printed and scattered broadcast.   The constitution was printed in all of the above-named papers, and also in a Washington paper which was franked by the thousands from Congressmen through the Union League as a campaign document.   *N. Y. World*, Feb. 22, 1868.

[4] See, for example, *The Nationalist*, Feb. 4, 1868 (editorial).   On Jan. 16, 1868, an "Address to the Laboring Men of Alabama" stated in part, "If you fail to vote and the constitution fails to be ratified, your right to vote hereafter closes and all participa-

those who happened to be holding office under the military government, for money for campaign purposes.[1]

The Radicals were forced by the general denunciation of the constitution, both in the North and in the South, to make some statement in regard to the matter. So on January 2, 1868, the Radical campaign committee issued an address stating that there had been general and severe criticism of some features of the constitution, and that Congress would expect a revision, though the state would be admitted promptly even before revision. The existence of political disabilities need not fetter the party, the address stated, in the choice of a candidate. A Republican nomination was a proof that the candidate was a "proper" person, and his disabilities would be at once removed. This was a way to mitigate the proscription.[2]

From the first the Conservatives[3] had no hope of carrying the election against the reconstructionists, who had control of the machinery of election and were supported by the army and the government. There was little organized opposition to the convention election, because the people were indifferent and because the leaders feared that a contest at the polls would result in riots with the negroes. To the Conservatives the convention at first was a joke; the disposition was rather to stand off and keep quiet, and let the Radicals try their hands for a while; they could not stay in power forever. Later, the violent opinions and extreme measures of the convention excited the alarm of many of the whites; the moderate reconstructionists deserted their party; a large minority of the convention refused to sign the constitution; and a number made formal protests. The nomination of candidates by the Union League membership of the convention and the character of the nominees showed that rule by alien and negro was threatened. The Conservative party, now embracing nearly all the whites except the Radical candidates, determined to oppose the ratification of the constitution. Many of the whites,[4] now thoroughly discouraged, left the state forever — going

tion on your part in the administration of the laws of the state is at an end." *Montgomery Mail*, Jan., 1868.

[1] *Selma Messenger*, Jan. 24, 1868.

[2] *Cong. Globe*, March 28, 1868, p. 2195.

[3] Not yet called Democrats, but sometimes "Democratic and Conservative."

[4] Popular accounts say thousands, but not as many went this time as later, in the early 70's.

to the north and west, to Texas especially, and to South America and Mexico.[1]

On December 10 a number of the delegates to the convention, some of whom had signed the constitution, united in an address to the people advising against its adoption. All of them were native whites and former reconstructionists. They declared that under the proposed government designing knaves and political adventurers, who had a jealous hatred of the native whites, would use the blacks for their own selfish purposes; that this was clearly shown in the convention when the black delegation, with one honorable exception, moved like slaves at the command of their masters.[2] Several hundred citizens sent a petition to the President, setting forth that some of the delegates to the convention were not residents of the state, that others did not, and had not, resided in the counties which they pretended to represent, and that others belonged to the army or were officials of the Freedmen's Bureau, and were thus not legally qualified to sit in the convention. The petitioners asked for an investigation.[3] One of the delegates, Graves of Perry County, took the stump against the constitution framed by "strangers, deserters, bushwhackers, and perjured men," who were characterized by "a fiendish desire to disqualify all southern men from voting or holding office who are unwilling to perjure themselves with a test oath."[4]

The so-called "White Man's Movement" in Alabama is said to have been originated in 1867, by Alexander White and ex-Governor L. E. Parsons.[5] At a Conservative meeting in Dallas County, in January, 1868, the former offered a series of resolutions declaring that American institutions were the product of the wisdom of white men and were designed to preserve the ascendency of the white race in political affairs; that the United States government was a white man's government, and that white men should rule America; that the negro was not fit to take part in the government, as he had never achieved civilization nor shown himself capable of directing the affairs of a nation; that the right of suffrage was the fountain of all political power, therefore the negro should not be invested with

[1] Herbert, p. 46, and Journal Convention of 1867.
[2] *Cong. Globe*, March 12, 1868, p. 1824. [4] *Selma Messenger*, Dec. 22, 1867.
[3] *Selma Messenger*, Dec. 20, 1867. [5] Both later became Radicals.

the right. Parsons proposed the same resolutions at a Conservative conference in Montgomery in January, 1868.[1]

The Conservative executive committee decided to advise the whites to refrain from voting, and thus defeat the constitution by taking advantage of the law requiring a majority of the registered voters to vote on the question of ratification before the constitution could be ratified. No nominations for office were made for fear that some whites might thus vote on the constitution, and also for fear of conflicts between the races in case of contest at the polls. All were advised to register and to remain away from the polls on election day. It was thought that less irritation would be caused in Congress and elsewhere if the constitution failed in this way than if it were voted down directly. The whites could be more easily persuaded to remain away than to go to the polls, and fewer negroes would vote if the whites did not vote. The people were urged to form organizations to carry out this non-participating programme.[2]

In every county in the state the Conservatives held meetings, opposing the constitution and pledging all the whites to stay away from the polls. The Conservative press from day to day made known new objections to the constitution: it exempted from sale for debt $3000 worth of property, — whereas the old constitution exempted $500, — and this would exempt every Radical in the state from paying his debts; the power of taxation was in the hands of the non-taxpayers; the distribution of representation was unequal, favoring the black counties;[3] mixed schools and amalgamation of the races were not forbidden, but were encouraged by the reconstructionists; a large number of whites were disfranchised from voting or holding office,[4] while all the blacks were enfranchised; the test oath required all voters to swear that they would accept the political equality of the

---

[1] *Tuskegee News*, Oct. 1, 1874.

[2] *N. Y. Times*, Jan. 14, 1898; *Montgomery Mail*, Jan. 17, 1868; Herbert, p. 48; Annual Cyclopædia (1868), p. 15.

[3] Thirty-five white counties with a population of 393,441 — 282,282 whites and 111,159 blacks — had 135 representatives, or one representative to 11,241 of the population. Twenty-four black counties with a population of 580,717 — 252,407 whites and 328,300 blacks — had 65 representatives, or one to 8933. Three small white counties were not represented, but had to vote with others. *Selma Times and Messenger*, March 10, 1868; *Cong. Globe*, 1867–1868, pp. 2197, 2198.

[4] Variously estimated at from 10,000 to 40,000.

negro and never change their opinions; the Board of Education was given legislative power, and could pass measures over the governor's veto; an ordinance, which was kept secret, required the governor to organize at once 137 companies of militia, to be assigned almost entirely to the black counties, and under such regulations that it was certain that few whites could serve; this militia, when in service, was to be paid like the regular army, and was to get the proceeds from all property captured or confiscated by it; the government, under this constitution, would cost from one and a half to two million dollars a year.[1]

Under the proposed constitution it was certain that for a while the government would be in the hands of the extremest Radical clique. The machinery, of the Radical party, of the registration and elections and the candidates nominated by the League were of this faction. The continued rule of the military was preferred by the whites to the rule of the carpet-baggers and the negro. Another reason why the Conservatives wished to keep the state out of the Union still longer was to prevent its electoral vote from being cast for Grant in the fall of 1868. During 1865 and 1866 Grant's moderate opinions had won the regard of many of the people, but his course during the last year had caused him to be intensely disliked. Though many meetings were held in opposition to the constitution, the campaign on the Conservative side was quiet and unexciting. The thirtieth day of January was set apart as a day of fasting and prayer to deliver the people of Alabama "from the horrors of negro domination."[2]

Vote on the Constitution

The registration before the election of delegates to the convention was 165,123,[3] of whom 61,295 were whites and 104,518 were blacks. Registration continued, and all the eligible whites registered. It is probable that more whites than negroes registered during December and January. And the revision demanded by all honest people

---

[1] *Selma Times and Messenger*, March 10, 1868. The minority report, March 17, 1868, of Beck of Kentucky and Brooks of New York, on the admission of Alabama, sums up the Conservative objections to the constitution. See *Cong. Globe*, March 17, 1868, p. 1937.

[2] Annual Cyclopædia (1868), p. 15; *N. Y. Times*, Jan. 24, 1865; *Selma Times and Messenger*, March 10, 1868.

[3] *Tribune* Almanac, 1868. Pope reported 164,800; Meline, 165,000.

evidently had the effect of striking off thousands of negro names; for at the end of the year the registration stood: whites, 72,748; blacks, 88,243; total, 160,991.[1] By February 1, 1868, the registration amounted to about 170,000,[2] of whom about 75,000 were whites and 95,000 were blacks. Therefore, more than 85,000 registered voters must participate in the election, or, according to the law, the constitution would fail of adoption.[3]

The registrars were those who had been appointed by Pope in 1867. More than half of them were candidates for election to office. Meade was not favorably impressed with the character of the candidates nominated by the constitutional convention and by the local councils of the Union League, and he advised against holding the election for officers at the same time that the vote was taken on the constitution. He thought that the nominees were not such men as the friends of Reconstruction would choose if they had a free choice. He believed that the ratification would be seriously affected if these candidates were to be voted for at the same time. Swayne admitted the force of the objection, but was afraid that a revocation of the permission to elect officers at the same time would be disastrous to Reconstruction. Later he agreed that the two elections should not be held at the same time. But Grant objected to making the change, and the election went on.[4]

General Hayden, Swayne's successor, removed a dozen or more of the registrars who were candidates for important offices,[5] and in consequence was abused by the Radicals, who accused him of "hobnobbing with the rebels." He was "utterly loathed by loyal men," and they at once began to work for his removal.[6] Every

---

[1] *Tribune* Almanac, 1868. The methods of the registrars may be imagined, since Meade had more than 15,000 names of negroes struck from the lists.

[2] It is impossible to obtain exact figures of the registration; no one ever knew exactly what they were, and accounts never agree. Meade's estimate was 170,734, Report, 1868. Another estimate was 170,000, *Cong. Globe*, March 17, 1868, p. 1904; and still another 171,378, Alabama Manual and Statistical Register, p. xxiii. It is evident that the registration was about 170,000.

[3] In 1867 the vote on holding a convention had been more than a majority of registered voters.

[4] Report of Meade, 1868, published in Atlanta.

[5] For instance, William H. Smith, candidate for governor.

[6] *The Nationalist*, Aug. 24, 1868; *Mobile Register*, Feb. 6, 1868; Report of Meade, 1868.

election official was obliged to take the iron-clad test oath, and as one-third of them were negroes, it was not likely that any of them were hostile to Reconstruction, as was afterwards claimed.

The elections were to begin on February 4 and last for two days. At the suggestion of General Grant the time was extended to four days, and a storm coming on the first day, instructions were sent out to keep the polls open until the close of the 8th of February. But in the remote counties no notice of the extension of time was received. There were three voting places in each county and a person might vote at any one of them (or at all of them if he chose). Late instructions ordered election officials to receive the vote of any person who had registered anywhere in the state. Of the 62 counties, 20 voted four days; 13, two days; 27, five days; and in 2 there were no elections.[1]

Besides being told the old stories of returning to slavery, of forty acres and a mule, of social rights, etc., various new promises were made to the negroes. One was promised a divorce if he would vote for Reynolds as Auditor, and it was said that Reynolds kept his promise, and saw that the negro afterward secured it. Numerous negro politicians were, according to promise, relieved from "the pains of bigamy" by the first Reconstruction legislation. The discipline of the League was brought to bear on indifferent black citizens, and by threats of violence or of proscription many were driven to the polls. On February 3 the negroes began to flock to the voting places, each with a gun, a stick, a dog, and a bag of rations, as directed by their white leaders. It was again necessary for them to vote "early and often." The Radical candidates were desperately afraid that the constitution would fail of ratification, and every means was taken to swell the number of votes cast. Many negroes voted rolls of tickets given them by the candidates. They voted one day in one precinct, and the next day in another, or several times in the same place. Little attention was paid to the registration lists, but every negro over sixteen who presented himself was allowed to vote. Hundreds of negro boys voted; it was said that none were ever turned away. Where the whites had men at the polls to challenge voters, it was found almost impossible to follow the lists because so many of the negroes had changed their names since registration.

[1] Report of Meade, 1868.

The sick at their homes sent their proxies by their friends or relatives. In one case the Radicals voted negroes under the names of white men who were staying away. The voters migrated from one county to another during the elections and voted in each. This was especially the case in Mobile, Marengo, Montgomery, Macon, Lee, Russell, Greene, Dallas, Hale, and Barbour counties.[1] The *Mobile Register* claimed that negro women were dressed in men's clothes and voted. The Radical chairman of the Board of Registration in Perry County stated that one-third of the votes polled in that county were illegal.[2] In Mobile, when a negro man appeared whose name was not on the voting list and was challenged by the Conservatives, he was directed by a "pirate"[3] to go to one D. G. Johnson, a registrar, who would give him, not a certificate of registration, but a ballot, indorsed with the voter's name and Johnson's signature. This ballot was to serve as a certificate and was also to be voted.[4]

The Constitution fails of Adoption

The result of the voting was: for the constitution, 70,812 votes; against it, 1005. The 18,000 white votes for the convention had dwindled down to 5000 for the constitution. For ratification, 13,550 more votes were necessary, and the ratification had failed. So General Meade reported. The reasons for the falling off of the white vote have already been indicated. The black vote fell off also. One cause of this was the chilling of the negro's faith in his political leaders, who had made so many promises about farms, etc., and had broken them all. Many of the old aristocratic negroes

[1] *Montgomery Mail*, Feb. 4, 5, 12, and 19, 1868; *N. Y. World*, March 14, 1868; *Cong. Globe*, March 17, 1868, p. 1937; *Mobile Register*, Feb. 6, 1868; *Selma Times and Messenger*, Feb. 29, 1868.

[2] *Selma Times and Messenger*, Feb. 29, 1868.

[3] A political adviser at the polls.

[4] The Conservatives had challenged such voters several times and Johnson sent the following order: —

"AT OFFICE, MOBILE, Feb. 5, 1868.

"The Judges of the Election at the Mississippi Hotel will receive all ballots endorsed by the voter and my signature. The certificate of voters is in my possession.

"Respectfully,

"D. G. JOHNSON,

"Registrar District No. 1."

—*Mobile Register*, Feb. 6, 1868.

would have nothing to do with such leaders as the carpet-baggers and scalawags, and this class and many others also were influenced by the whites to stay away from the polls. The general absence of respectable whites at the elections made it easier to convince the old Conservative negroes.[1] In two white counties — Dale and Henry — no elections were held because there were not enough reconstructionists to act as election officials.[2] Some whites, probably not many, were kept away by threats of social and business ostracism. Most of the reconstructionists cared nothing for such threats, as they could not be injured.[3]

The Radicals explained the result of the election by asserting that many whites were registered illegally, foreigners, minors, etc., that the voters were intimidated by threats of violence, social ostracism, and discharge from employment; that the voting places were too few and the time too short in many of the counties; that there was a great storm and the rivers were flooded, preventing access to the polls in some places;[4] that the Conservatives interfered with the votes, and tore off that part of the ballot that contained the vote on

---

[1] *Cong. Globe*, March 17, 1868, p. 1937; Ho. Ex. Doc., No. 303, 40th Cong., 2d Sess.; *N. Y. World*, March 14, 1868.

[2] In Henry County the registrars had all forsaken the party and resigned. On the last day the United States troops opened the polls and 29 people voted. *Abbeville Register*, Feb. 16, 1868. In Dale County it was much the same way. After a careful search one John Metcalf of Skipperville was found to make complaint on behalf of the reconstructionists. It was a sad story: "We had," he said, "depended on Mr. Deal, the delegate to the convention, to bring the registration books, 'but he fused with the destructive party' and we couldn't register. On the fourth day an election was held anyway, but the Conservatives would not let us hold it on the fifth. It was the almost united wish of the voters of the county to adopt the constitution. There are about 150 in the county that are opposed to it, and they united on the fifth and broke us up. We would have polled 1400 to 1500 votes for the constitution." Ho. Mic. Doc., No. 111, 40th Cong., 2d Sess.

[3] In Montgomery 41 whites of 4200 voted. Of these 15 were carpet-baggers and nearly all were candidates for office. The *Montgomery Mail* of Feb. 11 printed the entire list, with sarcastic comments on their past history and present aspirations. The list was headed, *Our White Black List, The Roll of Dishonor*. See *Cong. Globe*, March 11, 1868, p. 1827.

[4] The storm played a very effective part in the debates in Congress later. Moving tales were told of negroes swimming the swollen streams in order to get to the polls. One instance was given where, in swimming the Alabama River, which was beyond its banks and floating with ice, a negro was drowned. *Cong. Globe*, 1867–1868, p. 2865. The river at this point when out of its banks is not less than a mile wide, and there was never any ice in it since the glacial epoch.

the constitution; that many election officials were hostile to reconstruction, and had turned off 10,000 voters because of slight defects in the registration; that there were not 170,000 voters in the state but only 160,000, as several thousand had removed from the state; that in spite of all obstructions the vote for the constitution, if properly counted, was 81,000 instead of 70,000, and that there were 120,000 "loyal" voters in the state; that the ballot-boxes in Lowndes County were stolen, and that the returns from Baine, Colbert, and Jones counties had been fraudulently thrown out;[1] that General Hayden had especially desired the defeat of Reconstruction, and that he had managed the election in such a way as to enable the "rebels" to gain an apparent victory; and that practically all the army officers were opposed to the Radical programme, which was now true; and finally, that the attendance of Conservatives as challengers at the polls in some places was "a means of preventing the full and free expression of opinion by the ballot."[2]

After a thorough investigation General Meade reported that the election had been quiet, and that there had been no disorder of any kind; that there had been no frauds in mutilating negroes' tickets by tearing off the vote for the constitution, and that the other charges of fraud would prove as illusive; that the vote for the governor and other officials was less than that for the constitution; and that a more liberal constitution would have commanded a majority of votes. He said, "I am satisfied that the constitution was lost on its merits;" that the constitution was fairly rejected by the people, under the law requiring a majority of the registered voters to cast their ballots for or against, and that this rejection was based on the merits of the constitution itself was proved by the fact that out of 19,000 white voters for the convention, there were only 5000 for

---

[1] The Conservatives claimed that the Lowndes county box was stolen by the Radicals themselves as soon as they saw the constitution had failed of ratification, in order to give point to charges of fraud. In the same way the returns from Baine, Colbert, and Jones counties were so tampered with by the Radical election officials that the military canvassers were obliged to reject them. *Montgomery Mail*, Feb. 12, 1868; *Cong. Globe*, 1867–1868, p. 2139.

[2] *The Nationalist*, Feb. 13 and 20, and Aug. 24, 1868; *N. Y. World*, March 14, 1868; *Selma Times and Messenger*, Feb. 28, 1868; *Cong. Globe*, March 11, 1868, pp. 1818, 1823. This is a statement signed by Griffin of Ohio, Keffer of Pennsylvania, Burton of Massachusetts, Hardy and Spencer of Ohio, and indorsed by Joshua Morse, who signed himself as "disfranchised rebel."

the constitution; it might also be partially explained by the fact
that the constitutional convention had made nominations to all the
state offices, which ticket was "not acceptable in all respects to the
party favoring reconstruction." [1] He recommended that Congress
reassemble the convention, which should revise the constitution,
eliminating the objectionable features, and again submit it to the
people. However, as he afterwards stated, "my advice was not followed." The tone of Meade's report showed that he did not expect
Congress to refuse to admit the state. Indeed, at times the staid
general seemed almost to approach something like disrespect toward
that highly honorable body.

When the Radicals began to make an outcry about fraud, Meade
complained that they were not specific in their charges, and told the
leaders to get their proofs ready. The state Radical Executive Committee issued instructions for all Radicals to collect affidavits concerning high water, storms, obstruction, fraud, violence, intimidation,
and discharge, and send them to the Radical agents at Washington,
who were urging the admission of the state, notwithstanding the
rejection of the constitution. They refused to send these reports
to Meade, who was not in sympathy with the Radical programme.
Many of what purported to be affidavits of men discharged from
employment for voting were printed for the use of Congress. Most
of them were signed by marks and gave no particulars. The usual
statement was "for the reason of voting at recent election." [2]

---

[1] Report of Meade, 1868. Meade made this report to Grant at the time, and at the
end of the year he made practically the same, though perhaps a little stronger. The
Nationalist (Albert Griffin of Ohio, editor) said, April 9, 1868, that the statements of
Meade, the "military saphead," were "false in letter and false in spirit."

[2] Ho. Mis. Doc., No. 111, 40th Cong., 2d Sess. The whites were complaining
loudly because of the scarcity of labor, and few would discharge a negro laborer, no
matter how often he might vote the Radical ticket. General Hayden sent a list of
eighteen questions in regard to the election to every election official. They covered
every possible point, and full answers were required. One of the questions was in
regard to the proportion of white voters. A summary of the answers is here given:
1. *Elmore County.* Intimidation and threats of discharge; of the 1000 to 1200 whites
who registered, from 12 to 15 voted. 2. *Autauga.* No intimidation, but threats of
discharge; of the 900 whites registered, 200 voted. 3. *Chambers.* Fair election, with
23 white voters of the 1400 registered. 4. *Russell.* Threats of discharge; one-thirty-
sixth of the whites voted. 5. *Tallapoosa.* "Persuasion and arguments" deterred the
blacks from voting; 20 whites voted of the 1500 who registered. 6. *Coosa.* Two
discharges; one-third of the whites voted. 7. *Montgomery.* "Ostracism," and two

The *Nationalist* gave fifteen flippant reasons why the constitution had failed, and then asserted that the state was sure to be admitted in spite of the failure of ratification. Agents were sent to discharges; 41 whites voted of the 4200 who registered. 8. *Macon.* Fair election and 4 whites voted of the 800 registered. 9. *Lee.* One discharge and threats; 30 or 40 whites voted of 1500 registered. 10. *Randolph.* Fair election. 11. *Clay.* Threats of ostracism and one discharge. 12. *Crenshaw.* Two discharges. 13. *Lowndes.* Three threats of discharge; "too much challenging;" 10 whites voted of 850 registered. 14. *Barbour.* Four threats of discharge; "whites afraid of social proscription." 15. *Bullock.* "Needless questions" to voters, and three threats of discharge; no whites voted. 16. *Pike.* One threat of discharge; one-fourth of the whites voted. 17. *Butler.* Eight threats; 3 whites of 1400 voted. 18. *Covington.* "Threats;" 225 whites voted of the 900. 19. *Coffee.* "Threats" and "proscription." 20–21. *Dale* and *Henry.* No election; no registrars; none would serve. In Dale County were a number of "outrageous acts committed by a Mr. Oats." 22–27. *Mobile, Washington, Baldwin, Clarke, Monroe,* and *Conecuh.* "Threats and social ostracism;" 125 of 3750 whites voted. 28. *Walker.* Fair election; one negro driven away; "more whites voted than were expected." 29–30. *Winston* and *Jackson.* More whites voted than were expected; one threat in Jackson. 31–32. *Madison* and *Lauderdale.* Fair elections; in Lauderdale 150 of 1500 whites voted. 33. *Lawrence.* "Persuasion;" 311 of 1400 whites voted. 34–35. *Colbert* and *Franklin.* Twenty-five per cent of the whites voted; 75 per cent "were opposed to article 7, paragraph 4, of constitution." 36–38. *Limestone, Morgan,* and *Cherokee.* Fair elections; few whites voted. 39. *Marshall.* "Threats"; one-third of the whites voted. 40. *De Kalb.* Fair; 650 of the 900 whites. 41. *Baine.* "Handbills advised people not to vote;" only one-fifth voted. 42. *Blount.* One threat; "persuasion;" one-fourth of the whites voted. 43. *St. Clair.* Threats; one-third of the whites voted. 44–45. *Marion* and *Jones.* Fair; two-sevenths of the whites voted. 46. *Fayette.* Speeches published against the constitution, three drunken men threatened the managers at one box; liquor given to negroes to "vote against their intentions," all of which "prevented full and free expression of opinion by ballot"; two-sevenths of the whites voted. 47. *Shelby.* Fair; one-fourth of the whites voted. 48. *Talladega.* Fair, though threats were heard; three-tenths of the whites voted. 49. *Perry.* Fair; 24 of the 1066 whites voted. 50. *Bibb.* Fair; 167 of the 1021 whites. 51. *Dallas.* Fair; 78 whites voted; others suffered from "want of independence." 52. *Wilcox.* Ten threats; 12 whites of 800. 53. *Tuscaloosa.* One threat; one-fifth of the whites voted. 54. *Pickens.* "Threats too numerous to mention;" 60 to 70 of the 1100 whites voted. 55. *Jefferson.* Fair; one-fifth of the whites voted. 56. *Sumter.* Threats against blacks; whites to be ostracized. 57. *Greene.* Threats, though the "Union Men" were afraid to tell who threatened them; 446 ballots had "Constitution" torn off. 58. *Marengo.* Voters were refused at one box because the names were not on the list, though the parties were willing to swear they had been registered. Threats and speeches were made at the polls and one man made 16 discharges; 16 whites of the 997 voted. 59–62. No reports from *Choctaw, Calhoun, Cleburne,* and *Hale.*

Nearly all officials reported quiet elections; the assertions about threats were almost invariably hearsay. Even the few specific instances were based on hearsay. The worst complaint was that Conservatives sometimes attended and challenged the votes of certain negroes, and made speeches or used persuasion to induce the negroes

2 N

Washington to urge the acceptance by Congress of the constitution and Radical ticket. At first all, however, were not hopeful. There was a general exodus of the less influential carpet-baggers from the state, such a marked movement that the negroes afterwards complained of it. Some returned North; others went to assist in the reconstruction of other states.[1]

C. C. Sheets, a native Radical, speaking of the failure of the ratification, declared that a year earlier the state might have been reconstructed according to the plan of Congress, but a horde of army officers sent South, followed by a train of office-seekers, went into politics, and these "with the help of a class here at home even less fit and less honest," if possible, had disgusted every one.[2]

While waiting for Congress to act, the so-called legislature met, February 17, 1868, at the office of the *Sentinel* in Montgomery. Applegate, the candidate for lieutenant-governor, called the "Senate" to order, and harangued them as follows: Congress would recognize whatever they might do; it was absolutely necessary for the assembly to act before Congress, as the life of the nation was in danger and there was a pressing "necessity for two Senators from Alabama to sit upon the trial of that renegade and traitor, Andrew Johnson"; he stated that General Meade was in consultation with them and would sustain them;[3] if protection were necessary, Major-General Dustan[4] could, at short notice, surround them with several regiments of loyal militia.[5] They attempted to transact some business, but the

---

not to vote. Much importance was attached to the ridicule and jeers of the white leaders. These reports were made by the election officials, who were thoroughgoing reconstructionists. General Meade denied the charges of fraud and intimidation.

It will be noticed that the heaviest white vote was cast in the counties where there were few negroes, and where the Peace Society had been strongest during the war. If the estimates given above by the registrars were correct, it is doubtful if 5000 whites voted in the election, as was asserted. The judges were supposed to mark "C" on the ballot of a negro and "W" on that of a white. Ho. Mis. Doc., No. 111, 40th Cong., 2d Sess.; Ho. Ex. Doc., No. 303, 40th Cong., 2d Sess.; Report of Meade, 1868; *Montgomery Mail*, Feb. 19, 1868; *N. Y. World*, March 14, 1868.

[1] Strobach, the Austrian, went so far off in the Northwest that after the state was admitted he could not return to the special session of the legislature. He drew his pay, however, the Speaker certifying that he was present. *N. Y. World*, Oct. 8, 1868; *Montgomery Mail*, April 14, 1869; *Nationalist*, Feb. 18, 1868.

[2] In *North Alabamian*, 1868.   [3] He had evidently not seen Meade's report.

[4] Dustan had been a candidate for major-general of militia.

[5] Annual Cyclopædia (1868), p. 16.

unfriendly attitude of Meade and Hayden discouraged them; and they disbanded, to await the action of Congress.

The Alabama Question in Congress

February 17, 1868, a few days after the election, Bingham of Ohio introduced a joint resolution in the House to admit Alabama with its new constitution.[1] The Radicals of Alabama assumed that it was only a question of a short time before they would be in power. On March 10, Stevens, from the Committee on Reconstruction, reported a bill for the admission of Alabama. During the lengthy debate which followed, the Radical leaders undertook to show that when Congress passed the law of March 23, it did not know what it was doing, and that therefore the law could not now be considered binding. The carpet-bag stories about frauds in the election, icy rivers, etc., were again told. During the debates it developed that Beck of Kentucky and Brooks of New York, the minority members of the Committee on Reconstruction, had not been notified of the meeting of the committee, which was called to meet at the house of Stevens, and hence knew nothing of the report until it was printed. They made strong speeches against the bill and introduced the protests of the delegates to the convention, the reports of Meade, and the petition of the whites of the state against the proposed measure, and on March 17 introduced the minority report, which had to be read as part of a speech in order to get it printed. It was a summary of the Conservative objections to the constitution. For the moment Thaddeus Stevens seemed to be convinced that it was not desirable to admit Alabama. "After a full examination," he said, "of the final returns from Alabama, which we had not got when this bill was drawn, I am satisfied, for one, that to force a vote on this bill and admit the state against our own law, when there is a majority of twenty odd thousand against the constitution, would not be doing such justice in legislation as will be expected by the people." So the measure was withdrawn.[2] But the next day Farnsworth of Illinois reported a new bill providing

---

[1] *Globe*, Feb. 17, 1868, p. 1217.

[2] *Cong. Globe*, March 10, 11, and 17, 1868, pp. 1790, 1818, 1821, 1823, 1824, 1825, 1827, 1934, 1935, 1937, 1938.

for the admission of Alabama.   He argued that 7000 whites had
voted for the constitution, and that 20,000 whites belonged to the
Union Leagues in the state,[1] and that only by fraud had the constitution been defeated.   Kelly of Pennsylvania, of "Mobile riot" fame,
said that "the letter killeth, but the spirit giveth life."   He was convinced that typographical and clerical errors in the voting lists had
turned thousands away.[2]   Spalding of Ohio proposed a substitute,
which was adopted, making the new constitution 'the fundamental
law for a provisional government, and placing in office the candidates
who were voted for.   The legislature was to be convened to adopt
amendments to the constitution and resubmit the latter to the people.
The bill passed the House, but was not taken up in the Senate.[3]   In
the debates on this bill Paine of Wisconsin said: "These men [the
whites] during the war were traitors.   They have no right to vote or
to hold office, and for the present this dangerous power is most rightfully withheld."   Williams, a Republican of Pennsylvania, objected
to accepting a negro minority government.   Stevens closed the debate, saying that Congress had passed an act "authorizing Alabama
and other waste territories of the United States to form constitutions
so as, if possible, to make them fit to associate with civilized communities"; the House had foreseen difficulties about requiring a
majority to vote, and had passed an act to remedy it, but the Senate
had let it lie for two months; he knew that he was outside the constitution, which did not provide for such a case; he wanted to shackle
the whites in order to protect the blacks.[4]

The effect of establishing a new provisional government on the
basis of the constitution just rejected would be to require a new
registration and disfranchisement according to that instrument.
The proposal pleased the local Radicals very much.   This plan was
probably preferred by all the would-be officers except those who had
been candidates for Congress and who could not sit until the state
was admitted.   The *Nationalist*[5] said: "If we can get the offices,
we, and not a 'military saphead' [Meade], can conduct the next
election; we can by the Spalding bill get the government, rule the

---

[1] Both statements were incorrect.
[2] *Globe*, March 18 and 26, 1868, pp. 1972, 2138, 2139, 2140.
[3] McPherson, "Reconstruction," p. 337; *Globe*, March 28, 1868, pp. 2193, 2216.
[4] *Globe*, March 28, 1868, pp. 2203, 2209, 2214.   [5] April 23, 1868.

state as long as we please provisionally, and, when satisfied we can hold our own against the rebels, submit the constitution to a vote. We must wait until sure of a Republican majority if we have to wait five years." [1] The carpet-baggers were in high hope. A girl applied to one of the managers of the Montgomery "soup house" for a ticket for ten days, saying that she would not need it longer, as her father by the end of that time would be a judge. [2]

The whites began to close ranks, to leave no room in their midst for the white man of the North, the ruler and ally of the black. Social and business ostracism was declared against all who should take office under the Reconstruction Acts. They were turned away from respectable hotels. [3]

The *Independent Monitor*, now the head and front of opposition to Reconstruction, gave the following advice to the white people, who, however, did not need it: "We reiterate the advice hitherto offered to those of our southern people who are not ashamed to honor the service of the 'lost cause' and the memory of their kith and kin whose lives were nobly laid down to save the survivors from a subjection incomparably more tolerable in contemplation than in realization. That advice is not to touch a loyal leaguer's hand; taste not of a loyal leaguer's hospitality; handle not a loyal leaguer's goods. Oust him socially; break him pecuniarily; ignore him politically; kick him contagiously; hang him legally; or lynch him clandestinely—provided he becomes a nuisance as Claus or Wilson." [4]

The Conservative Executive Committee addressed a memorial to Congress against the proposed measures. In conclusion the address stated: "We are beset by secret oath-bound political societies, our character and conduct are systematically misrepresented to you and in the newspapers of the North; the intelligent and impartial administration of just laws is obstructed; industry and enterprise are paralyzed by the fears of the white men and the expectation of the black that Alabama will soon be delivered over to the rule of the

---

[1] *Nationalist*, April 9, 1868.

[2] *Independent Monitor*, April 21, 1868.

[3] Yordy, a carpet-bag Bureau agent, registrar, and senator-elect from Sumter County, was turned out of a hotel at Eutaw and told to go to the negro inn. *Tuscaloosa Independent Monitor*, Sept. 1, 1868.

[4] *Globe*, March 28, 1868, p. 2140. Claus and Wilson were two carpet-baggers of Tuscaloosa.

latter; and many of our people are, for these reasons, leaving the homes they love for other and stranger lands. Continue over us, if you will, your own rule by the sword. Send down among us honorable and upright men of your own people, of the race to which you and we belong, and, ungracious, contrary to wise policy and the institutions of the country, and tyrannous as it will be, no hand will be raised among us to resist by force their authority. But do not, we implore you, abdicate your rule over us, by transferring us to the blighting brutality and unnatural dominion of an alien and inferior race." [1]

Alabama Readmitted to the Union

The proposition to establish a Radical provisional government for Alabama was forgotten in the Senate during the progress of the impeachment trial, and on May 11 Stevens introduced a bill providing for the admission of Georgia, Louisiana, North and South Carolina, and Alabama. [2] A motion by Woodbridge of Vermont to strike Alabama from the bill was lost by a vote of 60 to 74. Farnsworth said it was nonsense to make any distinction between Alabama and the other states. The bill passed the House on May 14, by a vote of 109 to 35, and went to the Senate. On June 5 Trumbull from the Judiciary Committee reported the bill with Alabama struck out because the constitution had not been ratified according to law. Wilson of Massachusetts moved to insert Alabama in the bill. Alabama, he said, was the strongest of all the states for the policy of Congress, and it would be unjust to leave her out. Sherman repeated the old charges of fraud in the elections, which had been contradicted by General Meade, from whose report Sherman quoted garbled extracts. It was absolutely necessary, he said, to admit Alabama in order to settle the Fourteenth Amendment before the presidential election. Hendricks of Indiana objected because of proscriptive clauses in the constitution, which would disfranchise from 25,000 to 30,000 men. Pomeroy of Kansas said it would be "a cruel thing" to admit the other states and leave out Alabama. Morton of Indiana was of the opinion that the bill with Alabama in it would pass over the President's veto as well as without it, and said

[1] Annual Cyclopædia (1868), p. 16; *Cong. Globe*, March 11, 1868, p. 1825.
[2] *Globe*, May 11, 1868, p. 2412.

that Congress must waive the condition and admit Alabama.[1] The Radicals of Alabama kept the wires hot sending telegrams to their agents in Washington and to Wilson and Sumner, urging the inclusion of Alabama in the bill. On June 9 the Senate in Committee of the Whole amended the bill as reported from the Committee on the Judiciary by inserting Alabama. On this the vote stood 22 to 21. The next day Senator Trumbull moved to strike out Alabama, but the motion was lost by a vote of 24 to 16. So the report of the Judiciary Committee was revised by the insertion of Alabama, and the bill passed by a vote of 31 to 5, 18 not voting.[2] The House Committee on Reconstruction recommended concurrence in certain amendments that the Senate had made, which was done by a vote of 111 to 28, 50 not voting. The bill was then signed by the Speaker and the President *pro tem.* of the Senate and sent to the President.[3] The President returned the bill with his veto on June 25. "In the case of Alabama," he said, "it violates the plighted faith of Congress by forcing upon that state a constitution which was rejected by the people, according to the express terms of an act of Congress requiring that a majority of the registered electors should vote upon the question of its ratification."[4] The bill was at once passed by both houses over the President's veto, in the Senate by a vote of 35 to 8, 13 not voting, and in the House by a vote of 108 to 31, 53 not voting.[5]

The bill as passed declared that Alabama with the other southern states had adopted by large majorities the constitutions recently framed, and that as soon as each state by its legislature should ratify the Fourteenth Amendment it should be admitted to representation upon the fundamental condition "that the constitution of neither of said states shall ever be so amended or changed as to deprive any citizen or class of citizens of the United States of the right to vote in said state who are entitled to vote by the constitution thereof herein recognized" except as a punishment for crime.[6] As soon as the

---

[1] *Cong. Globe*, June 5 and 6, 1868, pp. 2858, 2865, 2867, 2900, 2964; McPherson, "Reconstruction," p. 340; Foulke, "Life of Morton," Vol. II, p. 47.

[2] *Globe*, June 9 and 10, 1868, pp. 2965, 3017.

[3] *Globe*, June 12, 1868, pp. 3089, 3090, 3097.   [4] *Globe*, June 25, 1868, p. 3484.

[5] *Globe*, June 25, 1868, pp. 3466, 3484; McPherson, p. 338.

[6] McPherson, p. 337. The present constitution of the state, adopted in 1901, nullifies this fundamental condition. Other southern states have also disregarded this limitation.

new legislature should meet and ratify the Fourteenth Amendment, the officers of the state were to be inaugurated. No one was to hold office who was disqualified by the proposed Fourteenth Amendment.[1]

June 29, Grant wrote to Meade that to avoid question he should remove the present provisional governor and install the governor and lieutenant-governor elect, this to take effect at the date of convening the legislature. So in July, by general order, Governor Patton was removed and Smith and Applegate installed. After the ratification of the Fourteenth Amendment by the legislature, Meade directed all provisional officials to yield to their duly elected successors. The military commanders transferred state property, papers, and prisoners to the state authorities.[2] And for six years the carpet-bagger, scalawag, and negro, with the aid of the army, misruled the state.

The members of Congress returned from their migrations[3] and presented themselves with their credentials to Congress.[4] Brooks of New York objected to the admission of these men on the ground that they were there in violation of the act of Congress in force at the time of the election. But on July 21 all were admitted by a vote of 125 to 33, 52 not voting. After taking the iron-clad test oath, they took their seats among the nation's lawmakers. Spencer and Warner were admitted to the Senate on July 25, and also took the iron-clad oath.[5]

---

[1] McPherson, p. 338.   [2] G. O. No. 101, July 14, 1868.

[3] Warner, who was said to have gone to his own state — Ohio — and run for office, now returned.

[4] The credentials were signed by E. W. Peck, president of the convention of 1867, who certified to their election. *Globe*, July 24, 1868, p. 4294.

[5] *Globe*, July 17, 18, 21, and 25, 1868, pp. 4173, 4213, 4293, 4295, 4459, 4466.

SENATOR GEORGE E. SPENCER.

SENATOR WILLARD WARNER.

C. W. BUCKLEY.

JOHN B. CALLIS.

J. T. RAPIER.

CHARLES HAYS.

SOME RADICAL MEMBERS OF CONGRESS.

CHAPTER XVI

THE UNION LEAGUE OF AMERICA

Origin of the Union League

In order to understand the absolute control exercised over the blacks by the alien adventurers, as shown in the elections of 1867–1868, it will be necessary to examine the workings of the secret oath-bound society popularly known as the "Loyal League." The iron discipline of this order wielded by a few able and unscrupulous whites held together the ignorant negro masses for several years and prevented any control by the conservative whites.

The Union League movement began in the North in 1862, when the outlook for the northern cause was gloomy. The moderate policy of the Washington government had alienated the extremists; the Confederate successes in the field and Democratic successes in the elections, the active opposition of the "Copperheads" to the war policy of the administration, the rise of the secret order of the Knights of the Golden Circle in the West opposed to further continuance of the war, the strong southern sympathies of the higher classes of society, the formation of societies for the dissemination of Democratic and southern literature, the low ebb of loyalty to the government in the North, especially in the cities—all these causes resulted in the formation of Union Leagues throughout the North.[1] This movement began among those associated in the work of the United States Sanitary Commission. These people were important neither as politicians nor as warriors, and they had sufficient leisure to observe the threatening state of society about them. "Loyalty must be organized, consolidated, and made effective," they declared. The movement, first organized in Ohio, took effective form in Philadelphia in the fall of 1862, and in December of that year the Union League of Philadelphia was organized. The members were

---

[1] President Jay's Address, March 26, 1868 ; Bellows, " History Union League Club of New York," pp. 6–9 ; "Chronicle of Philadelphia Union League," pp. 5–8.

553

pledged to uncompromising and unconditional loyalty to the Union, the complete subordination of political ideas thereto, and the repudiation of any belief in states' rights. The New York Union League Club followed the example of the Philadelphia League early in 1863, and adopted, word for word, its declaration of principles.[1] Boston, Brooklyn, Chicago, Baltimore, and other cities followed suit, and soon Leagues modelled after the Philadelphia plan and connected by a loose bond of federation were formed in every part of the North. These Leagues were social as well as political in their aims. The "Loyal National League" of New York, an independent organization with thirty branches, was absorbed by the Union League, and the "Loyal Publication Society" of New York, which also came under its control, was used to disseminate the proper kind of political literature.

As the Federal armies went South, the Union League spread among the disaffected element of the southern people.[2] Much interest was taken in the negro, and negro troops were enlisted through its efforts. Teachers were sent South in the wake of the armies to teach the negroes, and to use their influence in securing negro enlistments. In this and in similar work the League acted in coöperation with the Freedmen's Aid Societies, the Department of Negro Affairs, and later with the Freedmen's Bureau. With the close of the war it did not cease to take an active interest in things political. It was one of the earliest bodies to declare for negro suffrage and white disfranchisement,[3] and this declaration was made repeatedly during the three years following the war, when it was continued as a kind of Radical bureau in the Republican party to control the negro vote in the South. Its agents were always in the lobbies of Congress, clamoring for extreme measures; the Reconstruction policy of Congress was heartily indorsed and the President condemned. Its headquarters were in New York, and it was represented in each state by "State Members." John Keffer of Pennsylvania was "State Member" for Alabama.

---

[1] "Chronicle of Philadelphia Union League," pp. 5–8; Bellows, "Union League Club," p. 9.

[2] First Annual Report of Board of Directors of Union League of Philadelphia; Bellows, pp. 9, 32; "Chronicle of Philadelphia Union League," pp. 70, 112.

[3] See Bellows, "History Union League Club."

Part of the work of the League was to distribute campaign literature, and most of the violent pamphlets on Reconstruction questions will be found to have the Union League imprint. The New York League alone circulated about 70,000 publications,[1] while the Philadelphia Union League far surpassed this record, circulating 4,500,000 political pamphlets[2] within eight years. The literature printed consisted largely of accounts of "southern atrocities." The conclusions of Carl Schurz's report on the condition of the South justified, the League historian claims, the publication and dissemination of such choice stories as these: A preacher in Bladon (Springs), Alabama, said that the woods in Choctaw County stunk with dead negroes. Some were hanged to trees and left to rot; others were burned alive.

It is quite likely that such Leagues as those in New York and Philadelphia, after the first year or two of Reconstruction, grew away from the strictly political "Union League of America" and became more and more social clubs. The spiritual relationship was close, however, and in political belief they were one. The eminently respectable members of the Union Leagues of Philadelphia and New York had little in common with the southern Leagues except radicalism. Southern "Unionists" who went North were entertained by the Union League and their expenses paid. In 1866 the Philadelphia convention of southern "Unionists" was taken in hand by the League, carried to New York, and entertained at the expense of the latter. In 1867 several of the Leagues sent delegates to Virginia to reconcile the two warring factions of Radicals. The formation of the Union League among the southern "Unionists" was extended throughout the South within a few months of the close of the war, but a "discreet secrecy" was maintained. In Alabama it was easy for the disaffected whites, especially those who had been connected with the Peace Society, to join the order, which soon included Peace Society men, "loyalists," deserters, and many anti-administration Confederates. The most respectable element con-

---

[1] Bellows, p. 90.

[2] There were 144 different pamphlets published by the Philadelphia League and 44 posters; 56,380 pamphlets were issued in 1865; 867,000 pamphlets were issued in 1866; 31,906 pamphlets were issued in 1867; 1,416,906 pamphlets were issued in 1868; 4,500,000 pamphlets were issued in eight years. "Chronicle of Philadelphia Union League," pp. 106, 107, 145.

sisted of a few old Whigs who had an intense hatred of the Democrats, and who wanted to crush them by any means. In this stage the League was strongest in the white counties of the hill and mountain country.[1]

Extension to the South

Even before the end of the war the Federal officials had established the organization in Huntsville, Athens, Florence, and other places in north Alabama. It was understood to be a very respectable order in the North, and General Burke, and later General Crawford, with other Federal officers and a few of the so-called "Union" men of north Alabama, formed lodges of what was called indiscriminately the Union or Loyal League. At first but few native whites were members, as the native "unionist" was not exactly the kind of person the Federal officers cared to associate with more than was necessary. But with the close of hostilities and the establishment of army posts over the state, the League grew rapidly. The civilians who followed the army, the Bureau agents, the missionaries, and the northern school-teachers were gradually admitted. The native "unionists" came in as the bars were lowered, and with them that element of the population which, during the war, especially in the white counties, had become hostile to the Confederate administration. The disaffected politicians saw in the organization an instrument which might be used against the politicians of the central counties, who seemed likely to remain in control of affairs. At this time there were no negro members, but it has been estimated that in 1865, 40 per cent of the white voting population in north Alabama joined the order, and that for a year or more there was an average of half a dozen "lodges" in each county north of the Black Belt. Later, the local chapters were called "councils." There was a State Grand Council with headquarters at Montgomery, and a Grand National Council with headquarters in New York. The Union League of America was the proper designation for the entire organization.

The white members were few in the Black Belt counties and

---

[1] "Chronicle of Philadelphia Union League," p. 169; Bellows, pp. 90, 99, 100, 102; Reports of the Executive Committee, Union League Club of N. Y., 1865–1866; *Century Magazine*, Vol. VI, pp. 404, 949; oral accounts.

even in the white counties of south Alabama, where one would expect to find them. In south Alabama it was disgraceful for a person to have any connection with the Union League; and if a man was a member, he kept it secret. To this day no one will admit that he belonged to that organization. So far as the native members were concerned, they cared little about the original purposes of the order, but hoped to make it the nucleus of a political organization; and the northern civilian membership, the Bureau agents, preachers, and teachers, and other adventurers, soon began to see other possibilities in the organization.[1]

From the very beginning the preachers, teachers, and Bureau agents had been accustomed to hold regular meetings of the negroes and to make speeches to them. Not a few of these whites expected confiscation, or some such procedure, and wanted a share in the division of the spoils. Some began to talk of political power for the negro. For various purposes, good and bad, the negroes were, by the spring of 1866, widely organized by their would-be leaders, who, as controllers of rations, religion, and schools, had great influence over them. It was but a slight change to convert these informal gatherings into lodges, or councils, of the Union League. After the refusal of Congress to recognize the Restoration as effected by the President, the guardians of the negro in the state began to lay their plans for the future. Negro councils were organized, and negroes were even admitted to some of the white councils which were under control of the northerners. The Bureau gathering of Colonel John B. Callis of Huntsville was transformed into a League. Such men as the Rev. A. S. Lakin, Colonel Callis, D. H. Bingham, Norris, Keffer, and Strobach, all aliens of questionable character from the North, went about organizing the negroes during 1866 and 1867. Nearly all of them were elected to office by the support of the League. The Bureau agents were the directors of the work, and in the immediate vicinity of the Bureau offices they themselves organized the councils. To distant plantations and to country districts agents were sent to gather in the embryo citizens.[2] In

[1] I am especially indebted to Professor L. D. Miller, Jacksonville, Ala., for many details concerning the Loyal Leagues. He made inquiries for me of people who knew the facts. I have also had other oral accounts. See also Ku Klux Rept., Ala. Test. (Pierce), p. 305 ; (Lowe), p. 894 ; (Forney), p. 487.

[2] Ku Klux Rept., Ala. Test. (Sayre), p. 357 ; (Governor Lindsay), p. 170 ; (Nicholas

every community in the state where there was a sufficient number of negroes the League was organized, sooner or later.[1] In north Alabama the work was done before the spring of 1867; in the Black Belt and in south Alabama it was not until the end of 1867 that the last negroes were gathered into the fold.

The effect upon the white membership of the admission of negroes was remarkable. With the beginning of the manipulation of the negro by his northern friends, the native whites began to desert the order, and when negroes were admitted for the avowed purpose of agitating for political rights and for political organization afterwards, the native whites left in crowds. Where there were many blacks, as in Talladega, nearly all of the whites dropped out. Where the blacks were not numerous and had not been organized, more of the whites remained, but in the hill counties there was a general exodus.[2] Professor Miller estimates that five per cent of the white voters in Talladega County, where there were many negroes, and 25 per cent of those in Cleburne County, where there were few negroes, remained in the order for several years. The same proportion would be nearly correct for the other counties of north Alabama. Where there were few or no negroes, as in Winston and Walker counties, the white membership held out better, for in those counties there was no fear of negro domination, and if the negro voted, no matter what were his politics, he would be controlled by the native whites. What the negro would do in the black counties, the whites in the hill counties cared but little. The sprinkling of white members served to furnish leaders for the ignorant blacks, but the character of these men was extremely questionable. The native element has been called "low-down, trifling white men," and the alien element "itinerant, irresponsible, worthless white men from the North." Such was the opinion of the respectable white people, and the later history of the Leaguers

Davis), p. 783; (Richardson), pp. 815, 855; (Ford), p. 684; (Lowe), p. 892; (Forney), p. 487; Miller, "Alabama," p. 246; Herbert, "Solid South," pp. 36, 41; also oral accounts.

[1] There is a copy of the charter of a local council in the Alabama Testimony of the Ku Klux Report, p. 1017. The Montgomery Council was organized June 2, 1866, and three days later General Swayne, of the Freedmen's Bureau, joined it. It was charged that even thus early he was desirous of representing Alabama in the Senate. Herbert, pp. 41–43.

[2] *N. Y. Herald*, Aug. 5, 1867.

has not improved their reputation.[1]   In the black counties there were practically no white members in the rank and file.   The alien element, probably more able than the scalawag, had gained the confidence of the negroes, and soon had complete control over them. The Bureau agents saw that the Freedmen's Bureau could not survive much longer, and they were especially active in looking out for places for the future.   With the assistance of the negro they had hoped to pass into offices in the state and county governments.

The Ceremonies of the League

One thing about the League that attracted the negro was the mysterious secrecy of the meetings, the weird initiation ceremony that made him feel fearfully good from his head to his heels, the imposing ritual and the songs.   The ritual, it is said, was not used in the North; it was probably adopted for the particular benefit of the African.   The would-be Leaguer was told in the beginning of the initiation that the emblems of the order were the altar, the Bible, the Declaration of Independence, the Constitution of the United States, the flag of the Union, censer, sword, gavel, ballot-box, sickle, shuttle, anvil, and other emblems of industry.   He was told that the objects of the order were to preserve liberty, to perpetuate the Union, to maintain the laws and the Constitution, to secure the ascendency of American institutions, to protect, defend, and strengthen all loyal men and members of the Union League of America in all rights of person and property,[2] to demand the elevation of labor, to aid in the education of laboring men, and to teach the duties of American citizenship.   This sounded well and was impressive, and at this point the negro was always willing to take an oath of secrecy, after which he was asked to swear with a solemn oath to support the principles of the Declaration of Independence, to pledge himself to resist all attempts to overthrow the United States, to strive for the maintenance of liberty, elevation of labor, education of all people in the duties of

---

[1] Ku Klux Rept., Ala. Test. (Lowe), p. 872 ; (English), pp. 1437, 1438 ; (Lindsay), p. 170 ; *N. Y. Herald*, Aug. 5, 1869, and June 20, 1867 ; Professor Miller's account ; oral accounts.

[2] In Sumter County a northern teacher of a negro school informed a planter that the Leaguers were sworn to defend one another, and that he, the planter, would be punished for striking a Leaguer whom he had caught stealing and had thrashed. *Selma Times and Messenger*, July 21, 1868.

citizenship, to practise friendship and charity to all of the order, and to support for election or appointment to office only such men as were supporters of these principles and measures.[1]

The council then sang "Hail Columbia" and "The Star-Spangled Banner," after which an official harangued the candidate, saying that, though the designs of traitors had been thwarted, there were yet to be secured legislative triumphs with complete ascendency of the true principles of popular government, equal liberty, elevation and education, and the overthrow at the ballot-box of the old oligarchy of political leaders. After prayer by the chaplain, the room was darkened, the "fire of liberty"[2] lighted, the members joined hands in a circle around the candidate, who was made to place one hand on the flag and, with the other raised, swore again to support the government, to elect true Union men to office, etc. Then placing his hand on a Bible, for the third time he swore to keep his oath, and repeated after the president "the Freedman's Pledge": "To defend and perpetuate freedom and union, I pledge my life, my fortune, and my sacred honor. So help me God!" Another song was sung, the president charged the members in a long speech concerning the principles of the order, and the marshal instructed the members in the signs. To pass one's self as a Leaguer, the "Four L's" were given: (1) with right hand raised to heaven, thumb and third finger touching ends over palm, pronounce "Liberty"; (2) bring the hand down over the shoulder and say "Lincoln"; (3) drop the hand open at the side and say "Loyal"; (4) catch the thumb in the vest or in the waistband and pronounce "League."[3] This ceremony of initiation was a most effective means of impressing the negro, and of controlling him through his love and fear of the secret, mysterious, and midnight mummery. An oath taken in daylight would be forgotten

[1] The Montgomery Council, May 22, 1867, resolved "That the Union League is the right arm of the Union Republican party of the United States, and that no man should be initiated into the League who does not heartily indorse the principles and policy of the Union Republican party." Herbert, "Solid South," p. 41. A Confederate could not be admitted to the League unless he would acknowledge that during the war he had been guilty of treason.

[2] Alcohol on salt burns with a peculiar flame, making the faces of those around, especially the negroes, appear ghostly.

[3] A copy of the constitution and ritual was secured by the whites and published in the *Montgomery Advertiser*, July 24, 1867; printed also in Fleming, "Documents relating to Reconstruction," No. 3.

before the next day; not so an oath taken in the dead of night under such impressive circumstances. After passing through the ordeal, the negro usually remained faithful.

Organization and Methods

In each populous precinct there was at first one council of the League. In each town or city there were two councils, one for the whites, and another, with white officers, for the blacks.[1] The council met once a week, sometimes oftener, and nearly always at night, in the negro churches or schoolhouses.[2] Guards, armed with rifles and shotguns, were stationed about the place of meeting in order to keep away intruders, and to prevent unauthorized persons from coming within forty yards. Members of some councils made it a practice to attend the meetings armed as if for battle. In these meetings the negroes met to hear speeches by the would-be statesmen of the new régime. Much inflammatory advice was given them by the white speakers; they were drilled into the belief that their interests and those of the southern whites could not be the same, and passion, strife, and prejudice were excited in order to solidify the negro race against the white, thus preventing political control by the latter. Many of the negroes still had hopes of confiscation and division of property, and in this they were encouraged by the white leaders. Professor Miller was told[3] by respectable white men, who joined the order before the negroes were admitted and who left when they became members, that the negroes were taught in these meetings that the only way to have peace and plenty, to get "the forty acres and a mule," would be to kill some of the leading whites in each community as a warning to others. The council in Tuscumbia received advice from Memphis to use the torch, that the blacks were at war with the white race. The advice was taken. Three men went in front of the council as an advance guard, three followed with coal-

[1] The Montgomery Council was composed of white Radicals, and the Lincoln Council in the same city was for blacks. Most of the officers of the latter were whites. Herbert, p. 41.

[2] This fact will partly explain why there were burnings of negro churches and schoolhouses by the Ku Klux Klan. These were political headquarters of the Radical party in each community.

[3] See Miller, "Alabama," pp. 246, 247; Lester and Wilson, "Ku Klux Klan," pp. 45, 46.

2 O

oil and fire, and others guarded the rear.   The plan was to burn the whole town, but first one negro and then another insisted on having some white man's house spared because "he is a good man."   The result was that no residences were burned, and they compromised by burning the Female Academy.   Three of the leaders were lynched.[1] The general belief of the whites was that the objects of the order were to secure political power, to bring about on a large scale the confiscation of the property of Confederates,[2] and while waiting for this to appropriate all kinds of portable property.   Chicken-houses, pig-pens, vegetable gardens, and orchards were invariably visited by members when returning from the midnight conclaves.   This evil became so serious and so general that many believed it to be one of the principles of the order.   Everything of value had to be locked up for safe-keeping.

As soon as possible after the war each negro had supplied himself with a gun and a dog as badges of freedom.   As a usual thing, he carried them to the League meetings, and nothing was more natural than that the negroes should begin drilling at night.   Armed squads would march in military formation to the place of assemblage, there be drilled, and after the close of the meeting, would march along the roads shouting, firing their guns, making great boasts and threats against persons whom they disliked.   If the home of such a person happened to be on the roadside, the negroes usually made a practice of stopping in front of the house and treating the inmates to unlimited abuse, firing off their guns in order to waken them.   Later military parades in the daytime were much favored.   Several hundred negroes would march up and down the roads and streets, and amuse themselves by boasts, threats, and abuse of whites, and by shoving whites off the sidewalks or out of the road.   But, on the whole, there was very little actual violence done the whites, — much less than might have been expected.   That such was the case was due, not to any

---

[1] Ku Klux Rept., Ala. Test. (Lindsay), pp. 170, 179; (Nicholas Davis), p. 783; (Richardson), pp. 839, 355; (Lowe), pp. 872, 886, 907; (Pettus), p. 384; (Walker), pp. 962, 975.

[2] Thaddeus Stevens's speech on confiscation, through the Loyal League, had a wide circulation in Alabama.   Agents were sent to the state to organize new councils and to secure the benefits of the proposed confiscation; free farms were promised the negroes.   N. Y. Herald, June 20, 1867.   Many whites now believed that wholesale confiscation would take place.

sensible teachings of the leaders, but to the fundamental good nature of the blacks, who were generally content with being impudent.[1]

The relations between the races, with exceptional cases, continued to be somewhat friendly until 1867–1868. In the communities where the League and the Bureau were established, the relations were soonest strained. For a while in some localities, before the advent of the League, and in others where the Bureau was conducted by native magistrates, the negroes looked to their old masters for guidance and advice, and the latter, for the good of both races, were most eager to retain a moral control over the blacks. Barbecues and picnics were arranged by the whites for the blacks, speeches were made, good advice given, and all promised to go well. Sometimes the negroes themselves would arrange the festival and invite prominent whites to be present, for whom a separate table attended by the best waiters would be reserved; and after dinner there would be speaking by both whites and blacks. With the organization of the League, the negroes grew more reserved, and finally unfriendly to the whites. The League alone, however, was not responsible for the change. The League and the Bureau had to some extent the same personnel, and it is impossible to distinguish clearly between the work of the League and that of the Bureau. In many ways the League was simply the political side of the Bureau. The preaching and teaching missionaries were also at work. On the other hand, among the lower classes of whites, a hostile feeling quickly sprang to oppose the feeling of the blacks.

When the campaign grew exciting, the discipline of the order was used to prevent the negroes from attending Democratic meetings or hearing Democratic speakers. The League leaders even went farther and forbade the attendance of the blacks at Radical political meetings where the speakers were not indorsed by the League. Almost invariably the scalawag disliked the Leaguer, black or white, and often the League proscribed the former as political teachers. Judge Humphreys was threatened with political death unless he joined the League. This he refused to do, as did most whites where there were many negroes. All Republicans in good standing had to join the League. Judge (later Governor) D. P. Lewis was a member

[1] Ku Klux Rept., Ala. Test. (Sanders), pp. 1803, 1811; (Dox), p. 432; (Herr), pp. 1662, 1663.

for a short while, but he soon became disgusted and published a denunciation of the League. Nicholas Davis and J. C. Bradley, both
scalawags, were forbidden by the League to speak in the court-house
at Huntsville because they were not members of the order. At a
Republican mass-meeting a white republican wanted to make a speech.
The negroes voted that he should not be allowed to speak because he
was "opposed to the Loyal League." He was treated to abuse and
threats of violence. He then went to another place to speak, but was
followed by the crowd, which refused to allow him to say anything.
The League was the machine of the Radical party, and all candidates
had to be governed by its edicts. Nominations to office were usually
made in its meetings.[1]

Every negro was *ex colore* a member or under the control of the
League. In the opinion of the League, white Democrats were bad
enough, but black Democrats were not to be tolerated. The first
rule was that all blacks must support the Radical programme. It
was possible in some cases for a negro to refrain from taking an active
part in political affairs. He might even fail to vote. But it was
martyrdom for a black to be a Democrat; that is, try to follow his
old master in politics. The whites, in many cases, were forced to
advise their faithful black friends to vote the Radical ticket that they
might escape mistreatment. There were numbers of negroes, as late
as 1868, who were inclined to vote with the whites, and to bring them
into line all the forces of the League were brought to bear. They
were proscribed in negro society, and expelled from negro churches,
nor would the women "proshay" (appreciate) a black Democrat.
The negro man who had Democratic inclinations was sure to find
that influence was being brought to bear upon his dusky sweetheart
or wife to cause him to see the error of his ways, and persistent adherence to the white party would result in the loss of her. The
women were converted to Radicalism long before the men, and
almost invariably used their influence strongly for the purpose of
the League. If moral suasion failed to cause the delinquent to see
the light, other methods were used. Threats were common from the
first and often sufficed, and fines were levied by the League on recalcitrant members. In case of the more stubborn, a sound beating

[1] Ku Klux Rept., Ala. Test. (Lowe), pp. 886, 887, 894, 997; (Davis), p. 783;
(Cobbs), p. 1637; (Pettus), p. 6393.

was usually effective to bring about a change of heart. The offending darky was "bucked and gagged," and the thrashing administered, the sufferer being afraid to complain of the way he was treated. There were many cases of aggravated assault, and a few instances of murder. By such methods the organization succeeded in keeping under its control almost the entire negro population.[1] The discipline over the active members was stringent. They were sworn to obey the orders of the officials. A negro near Clayton disobeyed the "Cap'en" of the League and was tied up by the thumbs; and another for a similar offence was "bucked" and whipped. A candidate having been nominated by the League, it was made the duty of every member to support him actively. Failure to do so resulted in a fine or other more severe punishment, and members that had been expelled were still under the control of the officials.[2]

The effects of the teachings of the League orators were soon seen in the increasing insolence and defiant attitude of some of the blacks, in the greater number of stealings, small and large, in the boasts, demands, and threats made by the more violent members of the order. Most of them, however, behaved remarkably well under the circumstances, but the few unbearable ones were so much more in evidence that the suffering whites were disposed to class all blacks together as unbearable. Some of the methods of the Loyal League were similar to those of the later Ku Klux Klan. Anonymous warnings were sent to the obnoxious individuals, houses were burned, notices were posted at night in public places and on the doors of persons who had incurred the hostility of the League.[3] In order to destroy the influence of the whites where kindly relations still existed, an "exodus order" was issued

[1] Ku Klux Rept., Ala. Test. (Ford), p. 684; (Herr), p. 1665; (Pettus), p. 381; (Jolly), pp. 283, 291; (Sayre), p. 357; (Pierce), p. 313; *N. Y. Herald*, Dec. 4, 1867, Oct. 2, 1868; Herbert, "Solid South," p. 45. One Wash Austin, a Democratic negro, was attacked by a mob, pursued, and when he reached home his wife called him "a damned Conservative," struck him on the head with a brick, and then left him. Norris V. Hanley, in Ho. Mis. Doc., No. 15, 41st Cong., 2d Sess.

[2] *N. Y. Herald*, Oct. 13 and Nov. 11, 1867, Eufaula correspondence; Ku Klux Rept., Ala. Test. (Sanders), p. 1812; (Pettus), p. 381; (Herr), p. 1663; (Pierce), p. 313; (Sayre), p. 357; Harris, "Political Conflict in America," p. 479.

[3] A notice posted on the door of a citizen of Dallas County was to this effect, "Irvin Hauser is the damnedest rascal in the neighborhood, and if he and three or four others don't mind they will get a ball in them." *Selma Times and Messenger*, April 21, 1868; oral accounts; see also Brown, "Lower South," Ch. IV; Herbert, pp. 3, 8.

through the League, directing all members to leave their old homes and obtain work elsewhere. This was very effective in preventing control by the better class of whites. Some of the blacks were loath to leave their old homes, but to remonstrances from the whites the usual reply was: "De word done sont to de League. We got to go." [1]

In Bullock County, near Perote, a council of the League was organized under the direction of a negro emissary, who proceeded to assume the government of the community. A list of crimes and punishments was adopted, a court with various officials established, and during the night all negroes who opposed them were arrested. But the black sheriff and his deputy were arrested by the civil authorities. The negroes then organized for resistance, flocked into Union Springs, the county seat, and threatened to exterminate the whites and take possession of the county. Their agents visited the plantations and forced the laborers to join them by showing orders purporting to be from General Swayne, giving them the authority to kill all who resisted them. Swayne sent out detachments of troops and arrested fifteen of the ringleaders, and the Perote government collapsed. [2]

When first organized in the Black Belt, and before native whites were excluded from membership, numbers of whites joined the League upon invitation in order to ascertain its objects, to see if mischief were intended toward the whites, and to control, if possible, the negroes in the organization. Most of these became disgusted and withdrew, or were expelled on account of their politics. In Marengo County several white Democrats joined the League at McKinley in order to keep down the excitement aroused by other councils, to counteract the evil influences of alien emissaries, and to protect the women of the community, in which but few men were left after the war. These men succeeded in controlling the negroes and in preventing the discussion of politics in the meetings. The League was made simply a club where the negroes met to receive advice, which was to the effect that they should attend strictly to their own affairs and vote without reference to any secret organization. Finally, they were advised to withdraw from the order. [3]

---

[1] *The Macon Telegraph*, March 12, 1905.

[2] *N. Y. Herald*, Dec. 5 and 22, 1867; *Montgomery Advertiser*, Dec. 4, 1867 (J. M. Chappell).

[3] Ku Klux Rept., Ala. Test. (Lyon), pp. 1422, 1423; (Abrahams), pp. 1382, 1384.

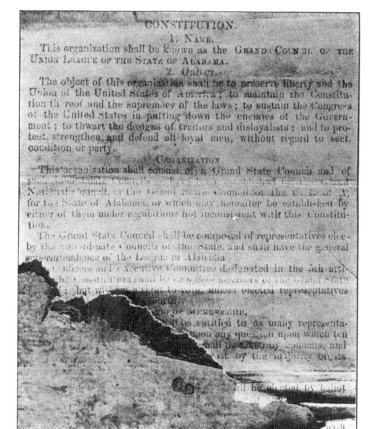

CONSTITUTION.

1. NAME.

This organization shall be known as the GRAND COUNCIL OF THE UNION LEAGUE OF THE STATE OF ALABAMA.

2. OBJECT.

The object of this organization shall be to preserve liberty and the Union of the United States of America; to maintain the Constitution thereof and the supremacy of the laws; to sustain the Congress of the United States in putting down the enemies of the Government; to thwart the designs of traitors and disloyalists; and to protect, strengthen, and defend all loyal men, without regard to sect, condition or party.

ORGANIZATION

This organization shall consist of a Grand State Council and of subordinate Councils . . . . established by the Grand National Council, or the Grand State Council of the U. L. of A, for the State of Alabama, or which may hereafter be established by either of them under regulations not inconsistent with this Constitution.

The Grand State Council shall be composed of representatives elected by the subordinate Councils of the State, and shall have the general superintendence of the League in Alabama . . . . . . officers and Executive Committee designated in the 5th arti . . . . . . the Constitution shall be ex officio members of the Grand State . . . . but will . . . . . . titled to vote, unless elected representatives . . . .

. . . OF MEMBERSHIP,

. . . entitled to as many representa . . . . . . upon any question upon which ten . . . . . . shall be taken by Councils, and . . . . st by the majority on its . . . .

. . . shall be elected by ballot . . . .

FACSIMILE OF PAGE FROM UNION LEAGUE CONSTITUTION.

For two years, 1867–1869, the League was the machine in the Radical party, and its leaders formed the "ring" that controlled party action. Nominations for office were regularly made by the local and state councils. It is said that there were stormy times in the councils when there were more carpet-baggers than offices to be filled. The defeated candidate was apt to run as an independent, and in order to be elected would sell himself to the whites. This practice resulted in a weakening of the influence of the machine, as the members were sworn to support the regular nominee, and the negroes believed that the terrible penalties would be inflicted upon the political traitor. The officers would go among the negroes and show their commissions, which they pretended were orders from General Swayne or General Grant for the negroes to vote for them.[1] A political catechism of questions and answers meant to teach loyalty to the Radical party was prepared in Washington and sent out among the councils, to be used in the instruction of negro voters.[2]

After it was seen that existing political institutions were to be overturned, the white councils and, to a certain extent, the negro councils became simply associations for those training for leadership in the new party soon to be formed in the state by act of Congress. The few whites who were in control did not care to admit more white members, as there might be too many to share in the division of the spoils. Hence we find that terms of admission were made more stringent, and, especially after the passage of the Reconstruction Acts, in March, 1867, many applicants were rejected. The alien element was in control of the League. The result was that where the blacks were numerous the largest plums fell to the carpet-baggers. The negro leaders, — politicians, preachers, and teachers, — trained in the League, acted as subordinates to the white leaders in controlling the black population, and they were sent out to drum up the country negroes when elections drew near. They were also given minor positions when offices were more plentiful than carpet-baggers. All together they received but few offices, which fact was later a cause of serious complaint.

[1] See Ku Klux Rept., Ala. Test. (Alston), p. 1017; (Herr), p. 1665; (Sayre), p. 357; (Pierce), p. 313.

[2] *Selma Messenger*, July 19, 1867; see Fleming, "Documents relating to Reconstruction," No. 3.

The largest white membership of the League was in 1865–1866, and after that date it constantly decreased. The largest negro membership was in 1867 and 1868. Only the councils in the towns remained active after the election of 1868, for after the discipline of 1867 and 1868 it was not necessary to look so closely after the plantation negro, and he became a kind of visiting member of the council in the town.[1] The League as an organization gradually died out by 1869, except in the largest towns. Many of them were transformed into political clubs, loosely organized under local political leaders. The Ku Klux Klan undoubtedly had much to do with breaking up the League as an organization. The League as the ally and successor of the Freedmen's Bureau was one of the causes of the Ku Klux movement, because it helped to create the conditions which made such a movement inevitable.[2] In 1870 the Radical leaders missed the support formerly given by the League, and an urgent appeal was sent out all over the State from headquarters in New York by John Keffer and others advocating the reëstablishment of the Union Leagues to assist in carrying the elections of 1870.[3]

However, before its dissolution, the League had served its purpose. It made it possible for a few outsiders to control the negro by alienating the races politically, as the Bureau had done socially. It enabled the negroes to vote as Radicals for several years, when without it they either would not have voted at all or they would have voted as Democrats along with their former masters. The order was necessary to the existence of the Radical party in Alabama. No ordinary political organization could have welded the blacks into a solid party. The Freedmen's Bureau, which had much influence over the negroes for demoralization, was too weak in numbers to control the negroes in politics. The League finally absorbed the personnel of the Bureau and inherited its prestige.[4]

[1] It is certain that the estimate of 18,000 white and 70,000 black members at the same time is not correct. As the latter increased in numbers the former decreased. Early in 1867 Keffer said there were 38,000 whites and 12,000 blacks in the League. *N. Y. Herald*, May 7, 1867. Perhaps he meant the total enrolment early in the year. In 1868 he claimed 20,000 whites, about 17,000 too many.

[2] Lester and Wilson, "Ku Klux Klan," p. 47 ; also Ku Klux Rept., Ala. Test., *passim*.

[3] *Montgomery Mail*, Aug. 20, 1870.

[4] In the Ku Klux Rept., Ala. Test., the Conservative and sometimes the Radical witnesses assert that the Ku Klux movement was caused partly by the workings of the Union League.

PART VI

CARPET–BAG AND NEGRO RULE

CHAPTER XVII

TAXATION AND THE PUBLIC DEBT

Taxation during Reconstruction

AFTER the war it was certain that taxation would be higher and expenditure greater, both on account of the ruin caused by the war that now had to be repaired, and because several hundred thousand negroes had been added to the civic population. Before the war the negro was no expense to the state and county treasuries; his misdemeanors were punished by his master. Yet neither the ruined court-houses, jails, bridges, roads, etc., nor the criminal negroes can account for the taxation and expenditure under the carpet-bag régime. During the three and a half years after the war, under the provisional governments, most of the burned bridges, court-houses, and other public buildings had been replaced; and there were relatively few negroes who were an expense to the carpet-bag government.

After the overthrow of Reconstruction, Governor Houston stated that the total value of all property in Alabama in 1860 was $725,000,000, and that in 1875 it was $160,000,000.[1] In 1866 the assessed valuation was $123,946,475;[2] in 1870 it was $156,770,385,[3] and in 1876, after ten years of Reconstruction, it was $135,535,792.[4] Before the war the taxes were paid on real estate and slaves. In 1860 the taxes were paid upon slave property assessed at $152,278,000, and upon real estate assessed at $155,034,000.[5]

Although there was some property left in 1865, the owners could barely pay taxes on it. The bank capital was gone, and no one had money that was receivable for taxes. Consequently, it was impossible to collect general taxes, and the state government was obliged to place temporary loans and levy license taxes. No regular taxes

---

[1] Senate Journal, 1875–1876, p. 214.   [3] Ku Klux Rept., p. 318.
[2] Ku Klux Rept., p. 171.   [4] Auditor's Report, 1902, p. 19.
[5] Ku Klux Rept., p. 170; Census of 1860. The assessed valuation of property increased 117% from 1850 to 1860. The comptroller's report of Nov. 12, 1858, states that the slave property of the state at that time paid nearly half the taxes. This was true of all ordinary taxes to 1865. See Senate Journal, 1866–1867, p. 291.

were collected during 1865 and 1866. The first regular tax was levied in 1866, and was collected in time to be spent by the Reconstruction convention.[1] For four years after the surrender the crops were bad, and when called good they were hardly more than half of the crops of 1860.[2] However, if no state taxes were paid by the impoverished farmers, there still remained the heavy Federal tax of $12.50 to $15 per bale on all cotton produced.

The rate of taxation before the war on real estate and on slaves was one-fifth of one per cent. After the war the taxes were raised by the provisional government to one-fourth of one per cent, and license taxes were added. The reconstructed government at once raised the rate to three-fourths of one per cent on property of all descriptions,[3] and added new license taxes, more than quadrupling the

[1] Journal Convention of 1867, p. 125; Patton's Report to the Convention, Nov. 11, 1867.

[2] Cotton crop, 1860 . . . . 842,729 bales
Cotton crop, 1865 . . . . 75,305 bales
Cotton crop, 1866 . . . . 429,102 bales
Cotton crop, 1867 . . . . 239,516 bales
Cotton crop, 1868 . . . . 366,193 bales

Most of the war crop was confiscated by the United States. The crops of 1866–1868 show the effects of politics among the negro laborers rather than unfavorable seasons. Hodgson, "Alabama Manual and Statistical Register," 1869.

[3] The exemption laws were so framed as to release the average negroes from paying tax, and also the class of whites that supported the Radical policy. The following list will show the incidence of taxation for 1870: —

	VALUE	TAX
Lands	$81,109,102.03	$607,979.52
Town property	36,005,780.50	268,865.89
Cattle	1,180,106.00	8,851.36
Mules	4,845,736.00	36,042.68
Horses	2,214,376.00	16,599.83
Sheep and goats	111,001.00	832.50
Hogs	277,735.50	2,083.02
Wagons, carriages, etc. . . .	131,235.00	8,480.81
Tools	237,534.50	1,769.96
Farming implements . . .	235,600.00	1,744.71
Household furniture	1,691,807.00	12,731.98
Cotton presses	41,360.00	310.30

Besides these items, heavy taxes were laid on the following: wharves, toll bridges, ferries, steamboats, and all water craft, stocks of goods, libraries, jewellery, plate and silver-

former rate. Under Lindsay, the Democratic governor in 1871–1872, the rate was lowered to one-half of one per cent. The assessment of property under Reconstruction was much more stringent than before. There were only five other states that paid a tax rate as high as three-fourths of one per cent, and four of these were southern states.[1]

Before the war the county tax was usually 60 per cent of the state tax, never more. The city and town tax was insignificant. After the war the town and city taxes were greatly increased, the county tax was invariably as much as the state tax, and many laws were passed authorizing the counties to levy additional taxes and to issue bonds. The heaviest burdens were from local taxation, not from state taxes.[2] In Montgomery County, the county taxes before the war had never been more than $30,000, and had been paid by slaveholders and owners of real estate. During Reconstruction the taxes were never less than $90,000, and every one except the negroes had to pay on everything that was property. In fact, the taxes in this county were about quadrupled.[3] In Marengo County the taxes before the war were $12,000; after 1868 they were $25,000 to $30,000, notwithstanding the fact that property had depreciated two-thirds in value since the war. Land worth formerly $50 to $60 an acre now sold for $3 to $15.[4] In Madison County, the state taxes in 1858 were $23,417.63 (gross); in 1870, $66,745.53 (net). The state land tax in 1858 in the same county was $7,213.10; in 1870, $51,445.30. Madison County taxes were: —

	STATE TAX	COUNTY TAX	TOTAL
In 1859 . . .	$26,633.71	$13,316.85	$39,950.56
In 1869 . . .	65,410.85	65,410.85	130,821.70

ware, musical instruments, pistols, guns, jacks and jennies, race-horses, watches, money in and out of the state, money loaned, credits, commercial paper, capital in incorporated companies in or out of the state, bonds except of United States and Alabama, incomes and gains over $1000, banks, poll tax, insurance companies, auction sales, lotteries, warehouses, distilleries, brokers, factors, express and telegraph companies, etc. See Ku Klux Report and Auditor's Report, 1871.

[1] Revenue Laws of Ala., 1865–1870; Report of the Debt Commission, Jan. 24, 1876; Governor Lindsay's Message, Nov. 21, 1871 ; Ku Klux Rept., Ala. Test., pp. 227, 340, 976, 1056, 1504.

[2] See Acts of Ala., 1868–1874, *passim.*

[3] Ku Klux Rept., Ala. Test., pp. 240, 360.   [4] Ala. Test., pp. 1303, 1304.

The general testimony was that the exemption laws relieved from taxation nearly all the negroes, except those who paid taxes before the war.[1]

The following table will show the taxation for 1860 and 1870: —

	CENSUS VALUATION	STATE TAX	COUNTY TAX	TOWN TAX
1860 . .	$432,198,762 [2]	$530,107	$309,474	$11,590
1870 . .	156,770,387	1,477,414	1,122,471	403,937

Administrative Expenses

TABLE OF RECEIPTS AND EXPENDITURES OF THE STATE GOVERNMENT

YEAR	RECEIPTS	EXPENDITURES	YEAR	RECEIPTS	EXPENDITURES
1860	——	$530,107.00	1871	$1,422,494.67 [9]	$1,640,116.99 [10]
1865	$1,626,782.93 [8]	2,282,355.97 [8]	1872	——	
1866	62,967.80 [4]	606,494.39 [5]	1873	2,081,649.39	2,237,822.06 [11]
1867	691,048.86	819,434.85 [6]	1874	——	
1868	724,760.56 [7]	1,066,860.24 [7]	1875	725,000.00	500,000.00 [12]
1868	1,788,982.43 [7]	2,233,781.97 [7]	1876	781,800.64	682,591.49
1869	686,451.02 [8]	1,394,960.30	1886	888,724.33	818,366.70
1870	1,283,586.52	1,336,398.85			

[1] Ala. Test., pp. 461, 963, 964.

[2] Taxes are paid on $307,312,000, slaves included ; see Census of 1860 ; Census of 1870 ; Ku Klux Rept., pp. 170, 171, 175, 317, 318.

[8] Includes receipts and disbursements in Confederate money.

[4] License taxes only.

[5] License taxes, bond issues, and temporary loans.

[6] Interest paid on the public debt with bond issues included, and expenses of the convention of 1867. The actual expenses of the state administration were $262,627.47.

[7] The first figures for 1868 include the receipts from taxes and the expenditures for state purposes only ; the other figures include the proceeds from sale of bonds used for state purposes. The Radicals always gave the first set of figures, and the Democrats the second.

[8] $620,000 should be added for the sale of bonds and state obligations.

[9] Issue of bonds to railroads included.

[10] Includes interest paid on railroad bonds.

[11] Currency had depreciated. Many claims went unpaid. The "home debt" amounted to $823,454.64. The actual state expenses were $1,384,044.46.

[12] State expenses only. Democrats in power. See Auditor's Reports, 1869–1873, 1900 ; Ku Klux Rept., pp. 170, 174, 176, 1055, 1057 ; Report of the Debt Commission, 1876 ; Journal Convention of 1867, p. 125.

The average yearly cost of state, county, and town administration from 1858 to 1860 was $800,000; from 1868 to 1870, the average cost of the state administration alone was $1,107,080, the cost of state, county, and town government being at least $3,000,000.[1] The provisional state government disbursed in the year 1866–1867, $676,476.54, of which only $262,627.47 was spent for state expenses; the remainder was used for schools.[2]

The greater expenditure of the Reconstruction government can, in small part, be explained by the greater number of officials and by the higher salaries paid.[3]

SALARIES

	BEFORE THE WAR	DURING RECONSTRUCTION
Governor	$2,000.00	$4,000.00
Governor's clerk	500.00	5,400.00, two
Secretary of State	1,200.00	2,400.00, fees and charges
Treasurer	1,800.00	2,800.00
Departmental clerks	1,000.00 each	1,500.00
Supreme Court judge	3,000.00	4,000.00
Circuit judges	13,500.00	36,000.00
Chancellors	4,500.00 three	15,000.00
Member of Legislature, per diem .	4.00	6.00
Stationery executive departments .	1,200.00	12,708.77 [4]

The administration of Lindsay to a great extent had to pay the debts of the former administration. Expenses were curtailed when possible, and notwithstanding the fact that the indorsed railroads defaulted in 1871, the business of the state was conducted much more economically, and there were fewer and smaller issues of bonds and

[1] Ku Klux Rept., pp. 170, 174, 176; Auditor's Reports, 1869–1870; Reports of the Alabama Debt Commission.

[2] Report of Governor Patton to the Convention, Nov. 11, 1867; Journal Convention of 1867, p. 125.

[3] See Tuskegee News, June 3, 1875; Auditor's Reports, 1868–1874.

[4] The average legislator in 1872–1873 was paid $904.00 and mileage. The Senate had 33 members and 44 attending officers, clerks, and secretaries; the lower house, with a membership of 100, had from 77 to 84 attending officials. Besides these there were dozens of pages, doorkeepers, firemen, assistants, etc. In 1869 there were 105 regular capitol servants who received $31,900 in wages. Auditor's Report, 1869–1873; Montgomery Mail, Dec. 31, 1870. There were about 10 in 1900.

obligations.[1] The Senate, however, had but one Democrat in it, and the House was only doubtfully Democratic, as the Democratic members were young and inexperienced men or else discontented scalawags.[2] Consequently, the tide of corruption and extravagance was merely checked, not stopped. The capitol expenses of Smith and of Lindsay for a year make an instructive comparison: —

	GOVERNOR SMITH 1869-1870	GOVERNOR LINDSAY 1871-1872
Contingent expenses	$47,197.28	$20,531.84
Stationery, fuel, etc.	24,310.07	8,847.23
Clerical services	27,883.77	21,883.03
Public printing	80,279.18	49,716.43

Other expenses, in so far as they were under the control of Lindsay, formed a like contrast.[3] The cost of holding sessions of the legislature under the provisional government was $83,856.60 in 1865–1866, and $83,852 in 1866–1867. Under Smith it was about $90,000 per session, and there were three regular sessions the first year. One session (1870–1871) under Lindsay cost $95,442.30, and two under Lewis, 1873–1874, cost $175,661.50 and $166,602.65 respectively.[4] The cost of keeping state prisoners for trial was about $50,000 a year. The Reconstruction legislature cut down expenses by passing a law to liberate criminals of a grade below that of felon, upon their own recognizance.[5]

The Democrats complained of the way the reconstructionists spent the contingent fund of the state. This abuse was never so bad as in other southern states at the time, but still there was continual stealing on a small scale. Some examples[6] may be given: Governor Lewis spent $800 on a short visit to New York and Florida;[7] the governor's private secretary received $21,000 for services rendered

---

[1] Journal of the "Capitol" Senate, 1872, p. 19–34; in Senate Journal, 1873.

[2] The older and abler men were disfranchised.

[3] *Montgomery Mail*, Sept. 22, 1872.   [4] Auditor's Reports, 1869–1873.

[5] The purpose of the act was to liberate negro prisoners and save money for the officials to spend in other ways.

[6] These items are taken from the accounts of Lewis's administration.

[7] The Investigating Committee remarked that had he chartered a parlor car and paid hotel bills at the rate of $10 a day, he would have been unable to spend $800 on that trip.

in distributing the "political" bacon in 1874;[1] the treasurer drew $1200 to pay his expenses to Mobile and New York, though he had no business to attend to in either place, and travelled on roads over which he had passes; ex-Governor W. H. Smith, when attorney for the Alabama and Chattanooga Railroad, was paid $500 by the state for services rendered in connection with his own road, and the committee was unable to discover the nature of these services; the secretary of state charged $952 for signing his name to bonds, though it was his constitutional duty to do so without charge; a bill of stationery from Benedict of New York cost $7761.58, when the bid of Joel White of Montgomery on the same order was $4336.54; $50 was allowed to John A. Bingham (presumably a relative of the treasurer) for signing enough bonds to purchase a farm for the penitentiary. Such purchases as these were common: one refrigerator, $65; one looking-glass, $5; one clothes-brush, $1.50. Very few of the small accounts against the contingent fund were itemized. In no case were any of them accounted for by proper vouchers. The private secretary of the governor was in the habit of approving and allowing accounts against the contingent fund, even going so far as to approve the governor's own accounts. The Investigating Committee said that the private secretary seemed to be the acting governor.[2]

The Florida commissioners, J. L. Pennington, C. A. Miller, and A. J. Walker, who were appointed to negotiate for the cession to Alabama of West Florida, spent $10,500, of which Walker, the Democratic member, spent $516, and Miller and Pennington spent the remainder, "according to the best judgment and discretion" of themselves. They claimed that part of it was used to entertain the Florida commissioners, and part to influence the elections in West Florida.[3]

The governor was accused of transferring appropriations. In one case, he drew out of the treasury $484,346.76, ostensibly to pay the interest on the public debt, and used it for other purposes. A committee appointed to investigate was able to trace all of it except $75,196.56, which sum could not be accounted for. The accounts

[1] See Ch. XXIV.

[2] Report of the Committee to Investigate the Contingent Fund, 1875; Senate Journal, 1874-1875, pp. 581-607.

[3] Caffey, "The Annexation of West Florida to Alabama," p. 10; Senate Journal, 1869-1870, pp. 234-244.

were carelessly kept. The auditor, treasurer, and governor never seemed to know within a million or two of dollars what the public debt was. The reports for the period from 1868 to 1875 do not show the actual condition of the finances, and the Debt Commission in 1875 was unable to get accurate information from the state records, but had to advertise for information from the creditors and debtors of the state.[1]

Effect on Property Values

The misrule of the Radicals in Alabama resulted in a general shrinkage in values after 1867, especially in the Black Belt, where financial and economic chaos reigned supreme, and where the carpetbagger flourished supported by the negro votes. Recuperation was impossible until the rule of the alien was overthrown. This was done in some of the white counties in 1870. At that date land values were still 60 per cent below those of 1860, and the numbers of live stock 40 per cent below. This was due largely to the condition of the Black Belt counties under the control of the Radicals.[2]

Thousands of landowners were unable to pay the taxes assessed, and their farms were sold by the state. The *Independent Monitor*, on March 8, 1870, advertised the sale of 1284 different lots of land (none less than forty acres) in Tuscaloosa County, and the next week 2548 more were advertised for sale, all to pay taxes Often, it was complained; the tax assessor failed to notify the people to "give in" their taxes, and thus caused them trouble. In some cases, where costs and fines were added to the original taxes, it amounted to confiscation. In 1871, F. S. Lyon exhibited before the Ku Klux Committee a copy of the *Southern Republican* containing twenty-one and a half columns of advertised sales of land lying in the rich counties of Marengo, Greene, Perry, and Choctaw.[3] One Radical declared that he wanted the taxes raised so high that the large landholders would be compelled to sell their lands, so that he, and others like him, could buy.[4] Property sold for taxes could be redeemed only by paying double the amount of the taxes plus the costs. A tax sale deed

---

[1] Report of the Committee to examine the Offices of Auditor and Treasurer, 1875 ; Report of the Debt Commission, 1875, 1876.

[2] See Edwin DeLeon, " Ruin and Reconstruction of the Southern States," in the *Southern Magazine*, Jan., 1874.

[3] Ala. Test., p. 1409.   [4] *State Journal*, April 19, 1874.

was conclusive evidence of legal sale, and was not a subject for the decision of a court.[1]

There were hundreds of mortgage sales in every county of the state during the Reconstruction period. At these sales everything from land to household furniture was sold. The court-house squares on sale days were favorite gathering places for the negroes, who came to look on, and a traveller, in 1874, states that in the immense crowds of negroes at the sales there were some who had come a distance of sixty miles.[2] Each winter, from 1869 to 1875, there was an exodus of people to Texas and to South America, driven from their homes by mortgages, taxes, the condition of labor, and corrupt government. Landowners sold their lands for what they would bring and went to the West, where there were no negroes, no scalawags, and no carpet-baggers.[3]

Most of the farmers and tenants of that period were unable to send their children to school and pay tuition. The reconstructed school system failed almost at the beginning. Consequently, tens of thousands of children grew up ignorant of schools, most of them the children of parents who had had some education. Hence the special provision for them in the constitution of 1901. The first Democratic legislature restricted taxation to three-fifths of one per cent and local taxation to one-half of one per cent. The rates were lowered gradually, until in the early nineties the rate was only two-fifths of one per cent. Since that time, the rate has again increased until in 1899 the state tax was again three-fourths of one per cent, the increase being used for Confederate pensions and for schools.

But in addition to the expenditure of the sums raised by extraordinary taxation, the Reconstruction administration greatly increased the bonded debt of the state and by mortgaging the future left a heavy burden upon the people that has as yet been but slightly lessened.

---

[1] Ala. Test., p. 1409. The Radical newspapers that had the public printing made money from the tax sale notices by dividing each lot into sixteenths of a section, advertising each, and charging for each division. The author of the tax sale law was Pierce Burton, a Radical editor.

[2] *Scribner's Monthly*, Aug., 1874 ; King, "The Great South."

[3] *Southern Argus*, Jan. 17 and Feb. 8, 1872; *Scribner's Monthly*, Aug., 1874 ; Herbert, "Solid South," pp. 64, 67. Colonel Herbert believes that during the six years of Reconstruction the state gained practically nothing by immigration, while it lost more by emigration than it had by the Civil War.

The Public Bonded Debt

After 1868 it is impossible to ascertain what the public debt of the state was at any given time until 1875, when the first Democratic legislature began to investigate the condition of the finances.

In 1860 the total debt — state bonds and trust funds — was $5,939,654.87 (and the bonded debt was $3,445,000), most of which was due to the failure of the state bank. The payment of the war debt, which amounted to $13,094,732.95, was forbidden by the Fourteenth Amendment. In 1865 the total bonded debt with three years' unpaid interest was $4,065,410, while the trust funds amounted to $2,910,000. Governor Patton reissued the bonds to the amount of $4,087,800, and the sixteenth section and the university trust funds with unpaid interest raised the total debt, in 1867, to $6,130,910. In July, 1868, when the state went into the hands of the reconstructionists, the total debt was $6,848,400. The provisional government had been increasing the debt because no taxes were collected during 1865 and 1866. Taxes were collected in 1867, but before the end of 1868 the debt amounted to $7,904,398.92, and after that date no one knew, nor did the officials seem to care, exactly how large it was.[1]

State and county and town bonds were issued in reckless haste by the plunderers, but the reports do not show the amounts issued; no correct records were kept. The acts of the legislature authorized the governor to issue about $5,000,000 state bonds, besides the direct bonds issued to railroads, which amounted to about $4,000,000 not including interest. The counties, besides being authorized to levy heavy additional taxes, were permitted to issue bonds for various purposes.[2] A number of acts gave the counties general permission

[1] Auditor's Reports, 1869–1873 ; Comptroller's Reports, 1861–1865, 1866 ; Patton's Report, 1867, to the Convention ; Journal Convention of 1867, pp. 46, 123 ; Ku Klux Rept., pp. 169, 317, 1055.

[2] The following is a partial list compiled from the session laws : —

ISSUES OF COUNTY BONDS

1868.	Walker County	$14,000.00	1869.	Pickens County	$100,000.00
1868.	Dallas County	50,000.00	1870.	Baldwin County	5,000.00
1868.	Bullock County	40,000.00	1870.	Bibb County	5,000.00
1868.	Limestone County	100,000.00	1870.	Choctaw County	(?) unlimited
1869.	Hale County	60,000.00	1870.	Crenshaw County	10,000.00
1869.	Greene County	80,000.00	1872.	Pickens County	30,000.00

to issue bonds, but there are no records accessible of the amounts raised. There were issues of town and county bonds without legislative authorization. This practice is said to have been common, but in the chaotic conditions of the time little attention was paid to such things and no records were kept.

To dispose of its bonds the state had a large number of financial agents in the North and abroad. Some of these made no reports at all; others reported as they pleased. Certain bonds were sold in 1870 by one of the financial agents, and two years later the proceeds had not reached the treasury or been accounted for. In like manner some bond sales were conducted in 1871 and in 1872.[1] Not only was no record kept of the issues of direct and indorsed bonds, but no records were kept of the payment of interest and of the domestic debts of the state. Some of the financial agents exercised the authority of auditor and treasurer and settled any claim that might be presented to them. Some agents, who paid interest on bonds, returned the cancelled coupons; others did not. In Governor Lewis's office $20,000 in coupons were found with nothing to show that they had been cancelled. One lot of bonds was received with every coupon attached, yet the interest on these had been paid regularly in New York.[2]

Provision was made for the retirement of all "state money"; but if the treasury was empty when it came in, it was apt to be reissued

ISSUES OF COUNTY BONDS (*continued*)

1873.	Butler County	. $12,000.00	(?)	Chambers County	$150,000.00
1873.	Jefferson County .	. 50,000.00	(?)	Lee County .	. 275,000.00
1873.	Montgomery County	. 130,000.00	(?)	Randolph County	. 100,000.00
1873.	Madison County .	. 130,000.00	(?)	Barbour County .	. (?)
(?)	Dallas County .	. 140,000.00	(?)	Tallapoosa County	. 125,000.00

ISSUES OF TOWN AND CITY BONDS

1868.	Troy . .	. $75,000.00	1871.	Selma . .	$500,000.00
1869.	Eutaw . .	. 20,000.00	1872.	Prattville . .	. 50,000.00
1869.	Greensboro .	. 15,000.00	1873.	Mobile . .	. 200,000.00
1871.	Mobile .	1,400,000.00		Opelika . .	. 25,000.00

And in addition each county and town had a large floating debt in "scrip" or local obligations. Speculators gathered up such obligations and sold them at reduced prices to those who had local taxes, fines, and licenses to pay.

[1] Auditor's Reports, 1871–1872; Report of Committee on Public Debt, 1876; McClure, "The South: Industrial, Financial, and Political Condition," p. 83.

[2] Report of the Committee on Public Debt, 1876; Senate Journal, 1872–1873, p. 544; Auditor's Report, 1873.

without any authority of law. A large sum was returned, but no record was made of it, and it was not destroyed. Later it was discovered among a mass of waste paper, where any thief might have taken it and put it again into circulation. One transaction may be cited as an illustration of the management of the finances: in 1873 the state owed Henry Clews & Company $299,660.20. Governor Lewis gave his notes (twelve in number) as governor, for the amount, and at the same time deposited with Clews as collateral security $650,000. in state bonds. Clews, when he failed, turned over the governor's notes to the Fourth National Bank of New York, to which he was indebted. He had already disposed of, so the state claimed, the $650,000 in bonds which he held as collateral security; and a year later, according to the Debt Commission, he still made a claim against the state for $235,039.43 as a balance due him. Thus a debt of $299,660.20 had grown in the hands of one of the state agents to $1,184,689.63, besides interest.[1]

In 1872 it was estimated that the general liabilities of the state, counties, and towns amounted to $52,762,000.[2] The country was flooded with temporary obligations receivable for public dues, and the tax collectors substituted these for any coin that might come into their hands. There was much speculation in the depreciated currency by the state and county officials. During Lewis's first year (1873), the state bonds were quoted at 60 per cent, but on November 17, 1873, he reported, "This department has been unable to sell for money any of the state bonds during the present administration." He raised money for immediate needs by hypothecation of the state securities. Thus came about the remarkable transaction with Clews. The state money went down to 60 per cent, then to 40 per cent before the elections of 1874, and at one time state bonds sold for cash at 20 and 21 cents on the dollar.[3]

---

[1] Senate Journal, 1875–1876, pp. 212, 213; Report of the Committee on the Public Debt, 1876. In his book Clews tells how he invested in the securities of the struggling southern states, being desirous of assisting them. But when the ungrateful states refused to pay the claims that he and others like him presented, he says it was because they, the creditors, were northern men. See Clews, "Twenty-eight Years in Wall Street," pp. 550, 551.

[2] DeLeon, "Ruin and Reconstruction," in the *Southern Magazine*, Jan., 1874. The state debts of the ten southern states were then estimated at $291,626,015, while the debts of the other twenty-seven states amounted to only $293,872,552.

[3] Houston's Message, 1876; Senate Journal, 1874–1875, p. 7.

The Financial Settlement

After the overthrow of the Radicals in 1874 taxation was limited, expenditures were curtailed, and the administration undertook to make some arrangement in regard to the public debt. For two years the state had been bankrupt; for nearly four years the railroads aided by the state had been bankrupt; the debt was enormous, but how large no one knew. A commission, consisting of Governor Houston, Levi W. Lawler, and T. B. Bethea, was appointed to ascertain and adjust the public debt.[1] After advertising in the United States and abroad, the commission found a debt amounting in round numbers to $30,037,563. Some claims were not ascertained; many creditors or claimants not being heard from and many fraudulent bonds not being presented. The debt was divided into four classes: (1) the *recognized* direct debt, consisting of state bonds (exclusive of bonds issued to railroads), state obligations, state certificates or "Patton money," unpaid interest and other direct debts of the state, — in all, amounting to $11,677,470; (2) the state bonds issued to railroads under the law providing for the substitution of $4000 state bonds per mile instead of $16,000 per mile in indorsed bonds, which in all amounted to $1,156,000; (3) a class of claims of doubtful character, among them that of Henry Clews & Company, amounting in all to $2,573,093; (4) the indorsed bonds of the state-aided railroads, amounting to $11,597,000 (several millions having been retired), and state bonds loaned to railroads, — which debt, with the unpaid interest on the same, amounting to $3,024,000, was in all $14,641,000.

SUMMARY OF DEBT

Class One	$11,667,470
Class Two	1,156,000[2]
Class Three	2,573,093
Class Four	14,641,000
Total	$30,037,563[3]

The interest on this debt at the legal rate of 8 per cent would be over $2,000,000, more than twice the total yearly income of the state.

[1] Act of Dec. 17, 1874. [2] Later increased to $1,192,000.

[3] Report of the Debt Commission, 1876. This was nearly half the value of the farm lands of the state, which were worth $67,700,000, and was much more than the gross value of a year's cotton crop.

The commission and the legislature declared that in the present condition of the finances the state could not pay the interest, that it would be several years before the state could pay any interest at all. Moreover, it could not recognize as valid many items in the great debt. After conference with the representatives of the more innocent creditors, the debt was thus adjusted:—

I. (a) The state proposed for the next few years to confine its attention to paying domestic claims and to retiring state obligations. (b) New bonds were issued to the amount of $7,000,000, to be exchanged for outstanding state bonds sold by the state to *bona fide* purchasers. These bonds, known as Class A, were to draw interest for five years at 2 per cent, for the next five years at 3 per cent, at 4 per cent for the next ten years, and thereafter at 5 per cent. These bonds were issued to the most innocent creditors and constituted the least questionable part of the debt.

II. On the $1,192,000 railroad debt of Class Two the state accepted a clear loss of one-half, and issued $596,000 in bonds, known as Class B, to be exchanged at the rate of one for two. These bonds drew interest at 5 per cent.

III. Class Three was the worst of all, and none of the items were at the time recognized, though the commissioners were authorized to take $310,000 of Class A bonds and distribute the amount among the innocent holders of the $650,000 bonds sold by Henry Clews when held by him as collateral. The other Clews claims were emphatically repudiated as fraudulent.

IV. Class Four was more complicated. (a) • The state gave $1,000,000 in bonds, Class C, drawing interest at 2 per cent for five years and at 4 per cent thereafter, to the holders of the Alabama and Chattanooga first mortgage indorsed bonds. The state was then relieved of further responsibility. (b) To the holders of the $2,000,000 state bonds issued to the Alabama and Chattanooga road, and which the commissioners were inclined to consider fraudulent, the state transferred its lien on the property of the Alabama and Chattanooga road, provided the bonds be returned to the governor.

The claims of the holders of the indorsed bonds of five other railroads were left for future settlement. They were declared fraudulent, and the state finally declined to recognize them. The Montgomery and Eufaula road had a loan of $300,000 in state bonds and an indorsement of $960,000. The road was sold for $2,129,000, and the state was secured against further loss.[1]

This act of settlement caused the issue of $8,596,000 in bonds. There were besides several millions more in bonds, state obligations, claims, etc. The Commission reported that the innocent holders of the bonds were very reasonable in their demands.[2] Henry Clews declined to give the Commission any information in regard to his agency for the state, but the Commission declared that he had in his possession, or had transferred improperly, coupons on which interest had been paid, and which he had not surrendered to the state. They recommended a fresh repudiation of any claim founded on Clews' securities.[3] The Commission also discovered that Josiah Morris & Company of Montgomery had possession of $650,000 in state bonds which they refused to release without legal proceedings.[4] There is not available sufficient evidence on which to base an account of the history of town and county debts. Some towns, unable to pay, gave up their charters; others still pay interest on the carpet-bag debt. For years in several counties the income was not large enough to pay the interest on its Reconstruction debt.

After the arrangement of state obligations, the state debt soon rose to par and above. The Democratic administration was economical even to stinginess. Salaries were everywhere reduced 25 per cent, the pay of the members of the legislature from $6 to $4 per day, and mileage from 40 cents to 10 cents.[5] The people of the state even complained of too much economy. It was said that a "deadhead" could not borrow a sheet of writing paper in the capitol, nor in a county court-house.

There was not an honest white person who lived in the state during Reconstruction, nor a man, woman, or child, descended from such a person, who did not then suffer or does not still suffer from the

---

[1] Report of the Debt Commission, Jan. 24, 1876; Senate Journal, 1875-1876, pp. 203-232; Report of the Joint Committee on the Public Debt, Feb. 23, 1876; Annual Cyclopædia (1875), p. 14; "Northern Alabama," p. 52; Final Report of the Committee of the Alabama and Chattanooga Bondholders, London, 1876; McClure, "The South," p. 83; Second Report of the Debt Commission, Dec. 13, 1876.

[2] Senate Journal, 1876-1876, p. 316. [3] Second Report, Dec. 13, 1876.

[4] Second Report of the Debt Commission, Dec. 13, 1876.

[5] Annual Cyclopædia (1875), p. 14; "Northern Alabama," pp. 51, 51; Acts of 1874-1875.

direct results of the carpet-bag financiering. Homes were sold or mortgaged; schools were closed, and children grew up in ignorance; the taxes for nearly twenty years were used to pay interest on the debt then piled up. Not until 1899 was there a one-mill school tax (until then the interest paid on the Reconstruction debt was larger than the school fund), and not until 1891 was the state able to care for the disabled Confederate soldiers. The debt has been slightly decreased by the retirement of state obligations, but the bonded debt remains the same. In 1902 it was $9,357,600, on which an annual interest of $448,680 was paid,[1] about one-fourth of the total income of the state.

The corrupt financiering in itself was not, by any means, the worst part of Reconstruction. It was only a phase of the general misgovernment. Though the whites were conservative and economical during the period of the provisional government and did not spend money or pledge credit recklessly, yet when the carpet-baggers began to loot the treasury, the people were not at first alarmed. Many were in sympathy with any honest scheme to aid internal improvements. Their Confederate experience made them accustomed to the appropriations of large sums — in paper.

Though from the first there were several newspapers that denounced the financial measures of the reconstructionists and warned purchasers against buying the bonds issued under doubtful authority, still it was only the thinking men who understood from the beginning the danger of financial wreck. When the railroads became bankrupt, the people began to understand, and when the state failed two years later to meet its obligations, they had learned thoroughly the condition of affairs. Extraordinary taxation had helped to teach them.

[1] Auditor's Report, 1902, p. 14.

CHAPTER XVIII

RAILROAD LEGISLATION AND FRAUDS

Federal and State Aid to Railroads before the War

For forty years before the Civil War there was a feeling on the part of many thoughtful citizens that the state should extend aid to any enterprise for connecting north and south Alabama. It was an issue in political campaigns; candidates inveighed against the political evils resulting from the unnatural union of the two sections. South Alabama was afraid that the northern section wanted connections with Charleston and the Atlantic seaboard, and not with Mobile and the Gulf; the planters of the Black Belt wanted the mineral region made accessible; the merchants of Mobile wanted all the trade from north Alabama; the Whig counties of south and central Alabama wanted closer connections with the white counties for the purpose of enlightening them and preventing the continual Democratic majorities against the Black Belt at elections.

At first it was proposed to build plank roads and turnpikes between the sections and thus bring about the desired unity. These failed, and then there was a demand for railroads. There were also other reasons for internal improvements. Not only ought the two antagonistic sections to be consolidated, but emigration to the West must be prevented, for thousands of the citizens of the state had gone to Texas during the two decades before the war. There was a general feeling that the state only needed railroads to make it immensely wealthy, and a large "western" element demanded that the state or the Federal government assist in thus developing the resources of the state and in uniting its people. During the session of 1855–1856, though the governor vetoed thirty-three bills passed in aid of railroads, still the legislature voted $500,000 to two roads.

However, conservative sentiment, strict constructionist theories, sectional jealousies, and the knowledge of the sad experience of the state in other public enterprises [1] operated against state aid to internal improvements, and before the $500,000 bonds were issued the act appropriating them was repealed, thus putting an end to the last attempt at direct state aid before the war.[2]

In 1850 Senator Douglas of Illinois began the policy of Federal aid to railroads by securing the passage of a bill in aid of the Illinois Central Railroad. The Alabama delegation was then opposed to such a measure, but Douglas visited Alabama, conferred with the directors of the Mobile Railroad, and promised to include that road in his bill in return for the support of the Representatives and Senators from Alabama and Mississippi. The directors then brought influence to bear, and the two state legislatures instructed their congressmen to support the measure, which was passed.

Thus began the Federal policy of granting alternate sections of public land along a road to the state for the corporation. Later, the grants were made directly to the corporation. Before 1857, land to the extent of 307,373 acres had been granted to Alabama railroads,[3] and liberal aid had also been given for improving the river system of the state.[4] By the act of admission to the Union in 1819, Alabama was entitled to 5 per cent of the proceeds from the sales of public lands, to be used for internal improvements. Three per cent was to be expended by the legislature, and 2 per cent by Congress. In 1841 Congress relinquished the "two per cent fund" to the state to aid railroads and other public enterprises from "east to west" and from "north to south." The State Bank failed and the "three per cent fund" was lost, but the legislature assumed it as a debt and issued state bonds to the railroads to the amount of $858,498. The "two per cent fund" was loaned before the war as follows: —

To east and west roads	.	.	.	$256,438.85
To north and south roads	.	.	.	202,551.02
Balance	.	.	.	.	.	52,246.23
Total	.	.	.	.	.	$511,236.10 [5]

---

[1] *E.g.* the State Bank.

[2] T. H. Clark, "Railroads and Navigation," in "Memorial Record of Alabama," Vol. II, pp. 322–323; Martin, "Internal Improvements in Alabama," pp. 72–77; Garrett, "Public Men," pp. 577, 580.

[3] Martin, "Internal Improvements," pp. 65–68.

[4] Martin, "Internal Improvements," p. 42 *et seq.*

[5] Martin, "Internal Improvements," pp. 68–71; Auditor's Report, Oct. 12, 1869.

In 1850 there were two railroads in the state with a total of 132.5 miles of track, which cost $1,946,209. In 1860, there were eleven roads, 743 miles long, costing $17,591,188.[1] During the Civil War the roads received much aid from the state and Confederate governments, though during this time only a few miles of track were built and some grading done. At the end of the war all were completely worn out or had been destroyed. The want of railroad communication with the armies and between the various sections of the state caused much suffering among soldiers and civilians, and after the war the people were more than ever anxious to have roads built. For two years the railway companies were busy repairing the old roads, but by 1867 popular opinion demanded new roads.

General Legislation in Aid of Railroads

The provisional legislature, on February 19, 1867, passed an act which served as a basis for all later legislation. The governor was authorized to indorse its first mortgage bonds to the extent of $12,000 per mile, when 20 miles of a new road should have been completed, and to continue the indorsement at that rate as the road was built. No indorsed bonds were to be sold by the road for less than 90 cents on the dollar, and the proceeds were to be used only for construction and equipment. The state was to have two directors, appointed by the governor, on the board of each road receiving state aid.[2] The Reconstruction Acts of Congress were passed a few days later, however, and there was no opportunity for this law to go into effect.

The first Reconstruction legislature[3] increased the endowment to $16,000 a mile, authorized the indorsement of bonds in five-mile blocks instead of twenty-mile blocks, as before, and to the roads that proposed to extend outside of the state it promised aid for 20 miles beyond the boundaries of the state.[4] The next session Governor Smith, in a message to the legislature, stated that the indorse-

---

[1] Census, 1850, 1860.   [2] Acts of Ala., 1866–1867, pp. 686–694.

[3] The constitution of 1867, Art. 13, Sec. 13, provided that the credit of the state should not be given nor loaned except in aid of railways or internal improvements, and then only by a two-thirds vote of each house.

[4] Acts of Ala., Aug. 7 and Sept. 22, 1868. The promoters of the roads claimed that the old law was useless, but that $16,000 a mile would attract northern and European capital. Herbert, "Solid South," p. 52.

ment law was defective; that he was in favor of lending the credit
of the state, but objected to a general statute requiring indorsement
of any road; that there was danger that the roads would depend
entirely upon indorsement and would have no paid-up capital;
moreover, taking advantage of the railroad fever, roads would be
built where they were not needed; that aid should be given only
to those capitalists whose enterprises promised success. Finally,
he advised that the law be repealed and aid be given only in specific
cases.[1]

The legislature responded to the Governor's message by another
general law, practically reënacting the former laws. By its provisions proof was required that the five-mile block had been built and
that the road-bed, rails, bridges, and cross-ties were in good order,
before the first issue of the bonds was made. The company was to
show what use was made of the bonds. The indorsement was to
constitute a first lien in favor of the state, and in case of default of
interest by the road, the governor was to seize and sell the road if
necessary.[2] A few days later a sweeping measure was passed, declaring that all acts and "things done in the state" for railroad purposes were ratified and made legal.[3] This was the last general
legislation enacted while the railroad boom continued. Governor
Lindsay and the pseudo-Democratic lower house stood out against
railroad legislation, and the indorsed roads were in bad condition
when the next scalawag governor was elected. Under Governor
Lewis, in 1873, an act was passed to relieve the state of some of its
obligations. Roads entitled to an indorsement might take instead a
loan of $4,000 per mile in state bonds, and roads already indorsed
might exchange indorsed bonds for state bonds at the rate of four
for one. But no state bonds were to be given for fraudulent issues
of indorsed bonds, and when exchanges were made the road was
released from all obligations to the state.[4] Had the roads accepted
this offer, the state would have suffered only a loss of $482,000 in
interest each year. However, from this time on the state authorities

---

[1] Governor's Message, Nov. 15, 1869. The carpet-bag auditor also advocated the
repeal of the law. He thought that no road should be indorsed for more than $10,000
a mile, since the average value was less than $13,000 a mile.

[2] Act of Feb. 21, 1870, Acts of Ala., 1869–1860, p. 149.

[3] Act of March 1, 1870, Acts of Ala., 1869–1870, p. 286.

[4] Act of April 21, 1873, Acts of Ala., 1872–1873, p. 45.

were busy trying to extricate the state from the bankruptcy caused by indorsing the railroad bonds.

The Alabama and Chattanooga Railroad

The Alabama and Chattanooga Railroad was the first of the roads to apply for aid under the indorsement law, and was in the worst condition. The story of this road is the story of all, only of greater length and more disgraceful. The Alabama and Chattanooga Railroad Company was made up of two older corporations, which, passing into the hands of Boston financiers, united in order to secure the spoils from the state. Before the union the officials had secured special legislation for one of the old roads, the Wills Valley. The sharpers who were engineering the scheme had agents at Montgomery when the Reconstruction legislature met, and these were instrumental in having the indorsement raised from $12,000 to $16,000 a mile. The second corporation was the Northeast and Southwest Alabama Railroad.[1] The proposed road would be 295 miles long, and when completed would be entitled to $4,720,000 from the state in indorsed bonds. The law was explicit in regard to indorsation, but Governor Smith, notwithstanding his opposition to the principle of the law, was criminally careless, if no worse, in the way he administered it. The first 20 miles were not built as required by law, but were purchased from the old Northeast and Southwest Alabama Railroad. Moreover, the road was never properly equipped, and the 20 miles from Chattanooga, on which indorsement amounting to $320,000 was secured, were only rented from another corporation (which was already indorsed to the amount of $8000 per mile by the state of Georgia), and the rent was paid from the proceeds of the indorsed bonds, which by law should have been applied only to construction and equipment. Nor was the rented road equipped.[2]

[1] Acts of Oct. 6 and Nov. 17, 1868, Acts of Ala., 1868, pp. 207, 347 ; Herbert, "Solid South," p. 52 ; Annual Cyclopædia (1871), pp. 7, 8. The railroad must have intended to profit by the indorsement, and must have paid for it, for when, a year later, ex-Governor Patton, who for the sake of respectability was made the nominal president, was in Boston, he was reproached by the Alabama and Chattanooga officials for allowing their charter to cost them $200,000. See Ku Klux Rept., Ala. Test., p. 232.

[2] Alabama vs. Burr, 115 United States Reports, p. 418. Burr, J. C. Stanton, and D. N. Stanton had been prosecuted by the state of Alabama for the fraudulent use of indorsed bonds.

The indorsed bonds of the road to November 15, 1869, amounted to $1,800,000,[1] and Auditor Reynolds reported in 1870 that the indorsement to September 30, 1870, was $3,840,000 on 240 miles.[2] These figures should have been correct, but they were not.   In fact, 240 miles had been roughly finished, but the indorsement was far above the legal limit.   On December 5, 1870, a few days before he retired from office, Smith reported to the legislature that he had indorsed the Alabama and Chattanooga road for $4,000,000 for 250 miles.[3]   The facts, as afterwards disclosed, were that only 240 miles were completed, and of these only 154 were in Alabama.   Yet he had issued bonds to the amount of $4,720,000, covering not only the whole 295 miles of the proposed road, but also including $580,000 in excess of what the law allowed to the completed road, which with equipment was worth only $4,018,388.   So here were $1,300,000 in bonds which were clearly fraudulent.   There was no further indorsement of this road.[4]

As if the enormous issue of indorsed bonds was not enough for the Stantons of Boston, who were in control of the corporation, a second descent of railroad promoters was made on the legislature in 1869–1870, and $2,000,000 in direct state bonds were obtained for the Alabama and Chattanooga Railroad.   Indorsement was not enough for them.   The act stated that the bonds were to be issued from time to time as needed for use in construction within the state, and in return the railroad lands were to be mortgaged to the state.[5]   In order to secure the passage of this act, the most shameful bribery was resorted to by the agents of the railroad and of the New York capitalists who were financing the Stantons.   One of the Stantons came to Montgomery, also an agent from the banking house of Henry Clews & Company, and agents from other houses interested in the Stanton scheme.   The Stantons themselves had no money except what they received from the state.   On February 4, 1870, the bill failed in the House; but on February 5 a reconsideration was moved and the bill was referred back to the committee with direc-

---

[1] Governor Smith's Message, Nov. 15, 1869.   [2] Auditor's Report, 1870.
[3] Message in *Independent Monitor*, Dec. 13, 1870.
[4] *Independent Monitor*, June 14, 1871; Ku Klux Rept., pp. 172, 317; Ku Klux Rept., Ala. Test., p. 193; Auditor's Report, 1871.
[5] Act of Feb. 11, 1870, Acts of Ala., 1869–1870.

tions "to report within fifteen minutes." The report was favorable, and the members having seen the light, the bill was passed by a vote of 62 to 27.[1] From the first, specific charges of bribery had been made against those who, within three days, had changed from active opposition to support of the measure.[2] A year later the House had a majority of young and inexperienced Democrats, and they ordered an investigation. The Senate, with one solitary exception, was still Radical. The investigation brought to light many unpleasant facts relating to the methods employed in securing the passage of the $2,000,000 appropriation and other railroad bills. Jerre Haralson, a negro member, told his experience. Jerre was opposing the grant and posing as a Democrat because he had not been sufficiently remembered on previous occasions when the spoils were divided. Hearing that something was to be divided, he went to Stanton's room, where, he said, there were many members. Caraway, the negro member from Mobile, told Haralson that he (Caraway) would not vote for the grant for less than $500. Stanton had four rooms at the Exchange Hotel, to which, at his invitation, all the purchasable members went. Stanton would take the members, one at a time, into the hall, after which that member would leave. Haralson, to his sorrow, was not called into the hall, but the next day he heard from the other negro members that money was to be had, so he called again. Stanton then accused Haralson of being a Democrat, but Haralson replied that he had left that party, and after receiving a "loan" of $50, he went home.[3]

George B. Holmes, of the firm of Holmes & Goldthwaite, bankers, testified that Gilmer, president of the South and North

---

[1] *Montgomery Mail*, Jan. 25, 1871 ; *Southern Argus*, Feb. 2, 1872, and Feb. 28, 1873 ; Somers, "Southern States," p. 157; Report of the House Railroad Investigation Committee, 1871 ; Herbert, "Solid South," pp. 52, 53. Colonel Herbert says that the Alabama and Chattanooga officials *demanded* the $2,000,000 and received it. "Solid South," p. 53. The legislature that voted the gift of $2,000,000 was composed as follows : Senate, 32 Radicals and 1 Democrat ; House, 85 Radicals (of whom 20 were negroes) and 15 doubtful Democrats. The carpet-bag editor of the *Demopolis Republican* said : "Men who never paid ten dollars' tax in their lives talk as flippantly as millions as the schoolboy of his marbles. Meanwhile, outsiders talk of buying and selling men at prices which would have been a disgrace to a slave before the war." *Montgomery Mail*, Jan. 25, 1871.

[2] Annual Cyclopædia (1870), p. 10.

[3] Report of the House Railroad Committee, 1871 ; Ku Klux Rept., p. 319.

2 Q

Alabama Railroad (Stanton had all the roads in need of "boodle" working with him), asked him for $25,000 to be used at the capitol. Gilmer told Holmes that the banker of the road had refused it, as had also the Farley bank. Finally, Farley and Holmes each agreed to furnish $12,000 to Gilmer. John Hardy, the chairman of the committee, had asked for $25,000 to oil the bearings of the political machine, and for that amount had agreed to have the bill passed. At the last moment Hardy demanded $10,000 more, which Holmes obtained from Josiah Morris. The committee was thus gotten into condition "to report within fifteen minutes," and the legislature made ready to accept the report.[1] Two years later, Governor Lindsay stated in his message that the Alabama and Chattanooga $2,000,000 bill had not passed the legislature by the two-thirds vote as required by law.[2] The law provided for the issue of the state bonds for $2,000,000 from time to time as the road was completed. Instead, however, they were issued in reckless haste, within a month, and hurried away to Europe for sale. The proceeds were used to build a hotel and an opera house in Chattanooga, where Stanton was accused of trying to imitate Fiske and Gould of Erie.[3]

When Governor Lindsay went into office, he could not find the "scratch of a pen" relating to railroad indorsement. Governor Smith, as later developments showed, had become careless with his

[1] Ku Klux Rept., p. 319; House Journal, 1870–1871, p. 236; Report of the House Railroad Investigating Committee, 1871; Ku Klux Rept., Ala. Test., p. 232; J. P. Stow, Radical senator from Montgomery, said that when Hardy left at the end of the session, he carried away $150,000. Not all of it was his own; some of it he had collected for others. One senator is said to have held his vote at $1000 regularly.

[2] Senate Journal, 1873; Appendix containing Journal of the Capitol Senate, 1872, pp. 19–34; Lindsay's Message, 1872, to the Capitol Legislature. Lindsay said that all the Democrats worked hard to prevent the passage of the $2,000,000 bill; that he himself worked in the lobby until three o'clock in the morning trying to defeat the thieves. Ku Klux Rept., Ala. Test., p. 199.

[3] Ku Klux Rept., p. 318; Ku Klux Rept., Ala. Test., p. 196; Report of the House Investigation Committee, p. 1871. Ex-Governor Patton testified that though president of the Alabama and Chattanooga road, he had opposed the bill and in consequence had been displaced, D. N. Stanton of Boston being elected. Patton stated that none of the capital stock had at this time been paid in by the stockholders.

In 1870–1871 "another set of financiers had made up their minds to come down South and help Alabama. Their demand was for $5,000,000 with which to set furnaces and factories going. They were too late. If they had only come the session before, there was no chance for a bill containing $5,000,000, properly pressed, to have failed." But the lower house now had a Democratic majority. Herbert, " Solid South," p. 57.

bond indorsement and kept no records, or else destroyed them or carried them away. Auditor Reynolds reported in 1871 that his office had official knowledge only of the indorsement of the Mobile and Montgomery road.[1] In his message of January 24, 1871, Lindsay said, "To what extent bonds under the various statutes have been indorsed and issued by the state it is impossible to inform you. No record can be found in any department of the action of the executive in this regard." None of the securities required by law could be found. Lindsay was unable to ascertain even the form of the indorsed bonds, except those of the Mobile and Montgomery and the Montgomery and Eufaula roads. Lindsay telegraphed to Smith's secretary, who replied that there was no record of the bond issues except the certificates of the railroad presidents. Lindsay found some of these, which were plain certificates: "This is to certify that five more miles of the (——) railroad has been finished." On each five-mile certificate, like the one above, the road drew $80,000. Yet the law was strict in requiring proof of completion, of good rails, bridges, road-bed, and equipment. At this time 45 or 50 miles of the Alabama and Chattanooga road had not been completed, and 50 miles more had only a temporary track hastily thrown together in order to get the indorsement. Governor Lindsay believed that the road as planned promised great success, and was of the opinion that had the bonds been issued according to law the road would have been completed. He had to correspond with the railroad officials in order to ascertain the amount of the bonds.[2] A few days before Smith went out of office he reported $4,000,000 indorsement on 244 miles of the Alabama and Chattanooga road. Lindsay found no record of this. Almost immediately (January, 1871) the Alabama and Chattanooga road defaulted in payment of interest, and Lindsay was authorized by the legislature to go to New York and provide for the payment of interest on 4000 bonds legally issued and held by innocent purchasers.[3] Statements were constantly appearing in the state press that fraudulent issues had been

[1] Senate Journal, 1870–1871, p. 78; Lindsay's Message, Nov. 21, 1871; Senate Journal, 1870–1871.

[2] Ku Klux Rept., Ala. Test., pp. 195, 196; Lindsay's Messages, 1871–1872; Lindsay's Statement of Facts, April 22, 1871; Report of Commissioners of the Public Debt, Jan. 24, 1876.

[3] Act of Feb. 25, 1871.

made, and the Democratic papers were warning purchasers against them, declaring that when the people of Alabama again came into power, they had no intention of paying them.

The carpet-bag régime had numerous financial agents in New York, Philadelphia, Boston, London, Germany, and elsewhere. Most of the agents in New York gave Lindsay assistance in his investigations. Souter & Company stated they had sold 4000 first mortgage Alabama and Chattanooga bonds (all that were legal), and 2000 state bonds for the Alabama and Chattanooga Company, all for more than 90 cents on the dollar. Erlanger et Cie., of Paris, had purchased the state bonds at 95 cents in gold. Lindsay soon discovered that 1300 Alabama and Chattanooga bonds in excess had been issued, 580 in excess of what the road would be entitled to when completed. Braunfels of Erlanger et Cie. testified that he had loaned $300,000 on 500 bonds numbered between 4000 and 4720. The trustees under the first deed of trust held bonds 4720 to 4800 and had refused to sell them, knowing them to be fraudulent; 344 bonds of the fraudulent excess had been partly sold and partly hypothecated to Drexel & Company of Philadelphia; thirty had been hypothecated to a firm in Boston for locomotives. Lindsay saw some of these fraudulent bonds, which were signed by Governor Smith and sealed with the seal of the state.[1] Lindsay, through the state agents, Duncan, Sherman, & Company, recognized as legal the first 4000 of these indorsed bonds and the 2000 state bonds and ordered interest to be paid on them. All the others were rejected as fraudulent.[2]

[1] Statement of Facts which influenced Governor Robert B. Lindsay in his Action in regard to the Bonds of the Alabama and Chattanooga Railroad Company, April 22, 1871; Lindsay's Message, Nov. 21, 1871. While Lindsay was in New York, Ex-Governor Smith called on him and half acknowledged the whole affair. Ala. Test., p. 199. Afterwards in a letter Smith strongly protested that some of the bonds signed and sealed by himself were fraudulent, and blamed Governor Lindsay and the legislature for recognizing them. He acknowledged that his carelessness had resulted in the present state of affairs. Somers, "Southern States," p. 158. April 3, 1871, Smith wrote, "I admit that if I had attended strictly to the indorsement and issue of these bonds, that all this never would have occurred." Herbert, "Solid South," p. 53.

[2] Statement of Facts, April 22, 1871; Ku Klux Rept., Ala. Test., pp. 198, 199. Lindsay said that since the Alabama and Chattanooga road was indorsed under the laws of 1867 and 1868, it did not come under the laws of 1870. Consequently, when the Alabama and Chattanooga defaulted, the state was not bound to pay interest on the $2,000,000 state bonds until the legislature acted in March, 1871.

In his Statement of Facts, Lindsay relates a suggestive and illuminating incident:

The acts of February 25 and March 8, 1871,[1] authorized the governor to pay interest on the Alabama and Chattanooga bonds which were in the hands of innocent purchasers on January 1, 1871. At that date at least 500 of the fraudulent issue had not been sold. The other 700 or 800 bonds numbered above 4000 were declared fraudulent by Lindsay on the ground that the part of road which called for the extra bonds simply did not exist. At this time he paid interest on the railroad bonds, amounting to $545,000,[2] and later to $834,000. No interest was paid on bonds held by the road or hypothecated by its officials. The governor was authorized to proceed against the road, and, in July 1871, Colonel John H. Gindrat, the governor's secretary, was ordered to seize the road and act as receiver. The road had ceased running two weeks before. Stanton claimed that the default had been caused by the threats of repudiation, and when Gindrat went to take charge every possible obstacle

On Dec. 13, 1870, John Demerett, an Alabama and Chattanooga bondholder, brought suit in the Superior Court of King's County, New York, against the Alabama and Chattanooga Railroad Company, the state of Alabama, and one F. B. Loomis (of the Alabama and Chattanooga Company), alleging that the said railway company was about to place on the market 500 first mortgage bonds numbered from 4800 to 5300, indorsed by the governor of Alabama in violation of the law. Demerett prayed for an injunction to restrain the company from selling the bonds. The records showed that the state of Alabama appeared by her attorney, one William D. Vieder, who declared on affidavit that he was employed by Henry Clews & Company, financial agents of Alabama. Vieder filed an answer in behalf of Alabama, stating that the bonds numbered 4801 to 5300 were properly indorsed, and were of the same class as others issued by the company, that the indorsement was in conformity to law, and that in no case would the bonds be repudiated. The injunction was dissolved and the company permitted to sell. To the Ku Klux Committee Lindsay suggested that Smith might have signed the illegal bonds after he went out of office, as they were not placed on the market until January, 1871. (See Ala. Test., p. 197.) But the Demerett case seems to disprove this and to show that the bonds were issued while Smith was governor. The House Railroad Investigation Committee, in 1871, reported that Smith asserted that the fraudulent indorsements were secured by the active coöperation of Henry Clews & Company, Souter & Company, and Braunfels of Émile Erlanger et Cie., with the Stantons. *Southern Argus*, Feb. 2, 1875. Lindsay further stated that there were evidences of collusion between Stanton and Smith to secure the election of the latter in 1870 at all hazards. They wanted to gain time in order to conceal the irregularity in the issue of bonds. Stanton furnished much money to the campaign fund, and on election day marched to the registration office at the head of 900 railroad employees, who came from the entire length of the road, had them registered, gave each of them a Radical ticket, and then voted them in a body. Ala. Test., pp. 193, 197.

[1] Acts of Alabama, 1870–1871, pp. 12, 13.

[2] Ku Klux Rept., p. 172.

and embarrassment were imposed by the company. Besides, at the Mississippi end of the line the employees had seized the road in order to secure their pay. Gindrat pacified them, and went slowly along the road toward Georgia, where he was stopped at the state line. Not only had Alabama indorsed that part of the road within Georgia and Tennessee, for $16,000 a mile, but Georgia had also indorsed it for $8000 a mile, and the part within her boundaries she seized. The governor was forced to employ a large number of attorneys and institute legal proceedings, not only in Alabama, but also in Georgia, Tennessee, Mississippi, and in the Federal courts. Bullock, the carpet-bag governor of Georgia, would not run the road in Georgia in connection with the Alabama section, and not until there was a new governor (Conley) could connections be made over the whole line.[1]

For his action in repudiating the fraudulent bonds and in seizing the road, Lindsay was much abused by all the railroad interests, by the hungry promoters who wanted more money from the state, and by a section of his own party which was influenced by prominent Democrats who were officers of the road,[2] and especially by influential Democratic lawyers. This fact was important in weakening the Democratic cause in 1872. There were some who opposed the seizure of the road because they believed that in the then unsettled condition of affairs the state would not be able to manage the road

[1] Annual Cyclopædia (1871), pp. 7, 8; Lindsay's Message, Nov. 21, 1871; Senate Journal, 1871-1872, pp. 44, 320; Report of John H. Gindrat, Receiver of the Alabama and Chattanooga Railroad, 1871.

The engineers in the employ of the state reported that to put the road in Alabama in fair condition at the time it was seized would require $507,983.74. Twenty-four miles of rails were old ones that Sherman had burned. Report of Farrand and Thom, Nov. 9, 1871; Senate Journal, 1871-1872, p. 43. To complete the road, Gindrat reported that $1,000,000 would be needed. Senate Journal, 1871-1872, p. 337. At the time the road was seized $10,500,000 from all sources had disappeared. Part of it was spent on the road, which, with all equipment, in 1871 was valued at $6,120,995. (An estimate of its value in 1873 was $4,183,388.) The capital stock authorized was $7,500,000, of which only $2,700,000 was ever paid in. Ku Klux Rept., pp. 172, 173; Auditor's Report, 1871 and 1873. The earnings of the road from November, 1872, to November, 1873, were $232,583.96. The expenses of the road from November, 1872, to November, 1873, were $1,083,851.90. Report of the Receiver of the Alabama and Chattanooga Railroad, 1873.

[2] Rice and Chilton, attorneys of the Alabama and Chattanooga road, gave the state much trouble. Rice was a scalawag, but several partners he had at that time and later were Democrats.

successfully; there were others who believed that the state should not acknowledge the legality of the indorsement by seizure of the road. The Debt Commission in 1876 reported that, although the laws were strict, yet they had been violated in letter and in spirit before indorsement. But though many (including the Debt Commission) believed the issues illegal, yet by the seizure of the road the state acknowledged the obligations.[1]

The history of the road while in the hands of the state authorities was not pleasant to Democrat or Radical. The state had first seized the section of the road that was in Alabama, and had gone into the state courts to get the remainder. The litigation promised to be endless, and the case was taken to the Federal courts. Finally the road was sold at a bankrupt sale, and Lindsay purchased it for the state, paying $312,000. The Circuit Court reversed this action, and there was a new case in which Busteed, district judge, adjudged the company bankrupt. In May, 1872, the Federal court placed the road in the hands of receivers for the first mortgage bondholders, who were to issue $1,200,000 in certificates to run the road, — this to be a *lien prior to the claim of the state.* August 24, 1874, the same court placed the road in the hands of the trustees of the first mortgage bondholders.

The road, while in the hands of the state receiver, was either badly managed or was unsuccessful because of the obstruction by the other roads and by capitalists. Several attempts were made, by Governors Lindsay, Lewis, and Houston, to sell the road, but with no success. Finally, in 1876, the Debt Commission arranged with the holders of the first mortgage bonds to turn over to them the whole claim of the state to the road, the state paying $1,000,000, besides the interest, to be out of the business.[2]

---

[1] During the whole time there was a large element in favor of not recognizing the legality of the bond issues authorized by the carpet-bag legislatures. The carpet-bag government was not a government of the people, but was imposed and upheld by military force, some said, and had no right to vote away the money of the people without their consent. The *Selma Times*, March 5, 1874, voiced this sentiment: "Alabama must and will be ruled by whites. . . . We will not pay a single dollar of the infamous debt, piled upon us by fraud, bribery, and corruption, known as the 'bond swindle' debt. Let the bondholders take the railroads." See Senate Journal, 1875–1876, pp. 213–221.

[2] Annual Cyclopædia (1871), p. 8; (1872), pp. 8, 9; Lewis's Message, Dec. 20, 1872; Senate Journal, 1872–1873, p. 43; Lewis's Message, Nov. 1874; Senate Jour-

Governor Lindsay had paid $834,000 interest on the Alabama and Chattanooga bonds, and in 1874 there were arrears amounting to $1,054,000.[1] Congress had made a grant of land, six sections per mile, amounting to 1,000,000 acres, for all the roads within the boundaries of Alabama, and the state held a mortgage on this land. Much of it was sold fraudulently by the railroad company, and titles were given where there had been no sales. One railroad agent pocketed $33,447.97 received from fraudulent sales of this land. The state never received a cent.[2]

Other Indorsed Railroads

The story of the other roads that applied for aid is similar, though shorter and of a meaner nature. The Savannah and Memphis road was the only one that failed to default.[3] It was indorsed for $640,000, but when the House committee was investigating, in 1871, as there was no record of any indorsement, the president refused to appear or to give any information.[4] Later it was ascertained that at the time that the road was worth only $263,000 it had been indorsed to the extent of $320,000.[5]

The South and North Alabama Railroad was a persistent applicant for legislative favors. On December 30, 1868, the available portion of the "two and three per cent fund," amounting to $691,789.43, was turned over to the South and North road.[6] The road secured indorsement at the rate of $16,000 a mile along with other roads, but this was not enough, and, on March 3, 1870, the legislature increased its indorsement to $22,000 a mile.[7] Governor Smith knew so little of

nal, 1874–1875; Final Report of the Committee of the Alabama and Chattanooga Bondholders, London, 1876; Acts of Ala., Dec. 21, 1872; Acts of Ala., March 20, 1875.

[1] Lewis's Message, Nov., 1874.

[2] Ku Klux Rept., p. 173; Governor Houston's Message, Dec., 1875; Senate Journal, 1875–1876.

[3] Governor Lewis's Message, Nov., 1874; Senate Journal, 1874–1875.

[4] Report of House Railroad Committee; Auditor's Report, 1873.

[5] Auditor's Report, 1871.

[6] Martin, "Internal Improvements," p. 70; Auditor's Report, 1869; Acts of Dec. 30, 1869, Acts of Ala., 1868, pp. 487, 494. The South and North road was merely an expansion of "The Mountain Railroad Company," an old corporation.

[7] Acts of 1869–1880, p. 374.

GOVERNOR L. E. PARSONS.

GOVERNOR WILLIAM H. SMITH.

GOVERNOR D. P. LEWIS.

NEGRO MEMBERS OF CONVENTION OF 1875 are on the left. The white man in the back row is Sam. Rice.

SOME RECONSTRUCTIONISTS.

what he did in regard to railroads that in his last message he stated that the South and North road was indorsed for $1,440,000, that is, for ninety miles at $16,000 a mile,[1] while he raised the indorsement of the Selma and Gulf to $22,000 a mile, thus confusing the two roads. The House Railroad Committee declared that by means of bribery the road had secured one hundred miles of indorsement, amounting to $2,200,000.[2] When Lindsay was asked to indorse more bonds for this road, he made an investigation which convinced him that too many bonds had already been issued, and he refused to sign any more. Under the law the road was entitled to 1900 one-thousand-dollar indorsed bonds, but had received 2200,[3] an indorsement of $2,200,000, while the road equipped was valued at only $1,625,200.[4] When it became known that fraudulent issues had been made, the Investigating Committee called before them the ex-treasurer of the state, Arthur Bingham, of Ohio. He claimed and was allowed the constitutional privilege of refusing to testify on the ground that his testimony would tend to incriminate himself.[5] In 1870 it was estimated that including the "three per cent" fund the road had received from the state $2,000,000 more than the cost of building it.[6] Governor Lewis, in 1873, reported that the South and North road was indorsed for $4,026,000, including $2,200,000 that was not recorded on the books of the state.[7]

The East Alabama and Cincinnati corporation consisted of Governor W. H. Smith, three senators (two of whom were J. J. Hinds and J. L. Pennington), and two members of the lower house. Stanton of the Alabama and Chattanooga was also connected with it; in fact, he was connected in some way with nearly all the schemes to secure state aid. The road was mortgaged to Henry Clews & Company for $500,000. It had no money of its own, but secured state indorsement for $400,000 and a bond issue of $25,000 from the town of Opelika. This indorsement by Governor Smith was not discovered

[1] Message, in *Independent Monitor*, Dec. 13, 1870.
[2] Report of House Railroad Inv. Com., 1871. See also Report of Auditor, 1870, which says $1,980,000 indorsement.
[3] Ku Klux Rept., Ala. Test., p. 197.
[4] Auditor's Report, 1871.
[5] Ku Klux Rept., p. 318; Report of House Railroad Inv. Com., 1871.
[6] *Montgomery Mail*, Feb. 24, 1870.
[7] Message, Nov. 17, 1874.

until 1871, when Lindsay was accused of issuing the bonds. This he flatly denied, and he was correct. The Tennessee and Coosa rivers road had $33,513.25, if no more, of the "two per cent fund." On March 2, 1870, that road was released from its indebtedness to the state (part of the "two and three per cent funds") on condition that it apply for no further aid. But now, in order to get the indorsement, a part of this road was transferred to the East Alabama and Cincinnati road, to pass as a new road. With an indorsement of $400,000 besides the $25,000 Opelika bonds, the road equipped was valued at only $264,150.[1]

The Selma and Gulf was another road without resources of its own, and, so far as it was completed, was built with state aid. Governor Smith, in clear violation of the law, the committee reported, indorsed the road for $480,000. Some one, probably Smith, though Lindsay was accused of it, raised this amount to $640,000, $160,000 of which was not recorded. At this time the road was valued at $424,900, and the company threatened to default unless further aid was extended. Smith thought that the road was indorsed for $22,000 a mile and reported $660,000 indorsement.[2]

The Mobile and Alabama Grand Trunk road, valued at $704,225, was indorsed by the state for $800,000. The city of Mobile also issued $1,000,000 in bonds for this road.[3] There was no record of an application for aid from the New Orleans and Selma Railroad. Neither Smith nor Lindsay reported it, yet its financial agent had secretly secured an indorsement of $320,000, contrary to law. The road was valued at $255,350. It had no resources except $140,000 in Dallas County bonds, and its president, Colonel William M. Byrd, resigned rather than be a party to the stealing.[4]

The promoters of the Selma, Marion, and Memphis road placed General N. B. Forrest at the head of the enterprise, and for three years he worked hard to make the road a success. Governor Smith indorsed the road for $720,000, or $18,000 a mile, when only forty

---

[1] Report of House Railroad Inv. Com., 1871; Lewis's Message, Nov. 17, 1873; Auditor's Report, 1869; Auditor's Report, 1873; House Journal, 1871–1872, pp. 305, 353; Acts of 1869–1870, p. 290.

[2] *Southern Argus*, Feb. 2, 1872; Governor Lewis's Message, Nov. 17, 1873; Auditor's Report, 1871 and 1873.

[3] Lewis's Message, Nov. 17, 1873; Auditor's Report, 1873; Act of Jan. 17, 1870.

[4] *Southern Argus*, Feb. 2, 1872; Auditor's Report, 1873; Lewis's Messages, 1873.

miles were completed. In 1873 the road was valued at $738,400. When the company failed, as was intended from the first, General Forrest gave up every dollar he could raise in order to pay debts due on contracts, and he himself was left a poor man.[1]

The Montgomery and Eufaula road obtained something over $30,000 of the "three per cent fund" from the state, and in 1868 the governor was authorized by the legislature to indorse the road, notwithstanding this debt to the state, which was considered simply as an indorsement.[2] Under this act the road was indorsed for $1,280,000, and in addition state direct bonds to the amount of $300,000 were issued to the company in 1870. For this loan there was no security. Lewis Owen, a former president, refused to answer when it was charged that bribery had been used to secure the passage of the bill. At this time the road was valued at $825,289. In 1873 capitalists offered to lease the road for enough to pay the interest on its bonds, provided the state would release the road from all claims and give to it the $330,000 already loaned. This was done. Later it was seized by the state and eventually sold for sufficient money to cover losses caused by the indorsement.[3]

The Mobile and Montgomery road secured $2,500,000 by special act of the legislature.[4] The road was valued at $2,516,250[5] and was already built, hence the indorsement was safe.

The total indorsement was about $17,000,000.

VALUE OF ALL RAILROADS IN THE STATE (FROM THE AUDITOR'S REPORTS)

1871, 1496 miles	$25,943,052.59
1872, 1629 miles	29,580,737.64
1873, 1793 miles	25,408,110.76
1874, —— miles	22,747,444.00
1875, —— miles	12,033,763.39
1875, (returns from railroad officials)	9,654,684.99

[1] *Southern Argus*, Feb. 2, 1872; Auditor's Reports, 1871 and 1873; Mathes, "General Forrest," p. 362; Wyeth, "Life of General Nathan Beford Forrest," pp. 617, 619. When Smith had indorsed this road for $720,000, he reported the amount as $640,000. *Independent Monitor*, Dec. 13, 1870.

[2] Act of Dec. 30, 1868.

[3] Senate Journal, 1872–1873, pp. 416–422; Acts of Ala., 1872–1873, p. 58; Auditor's Reports, 1871, 1873; Governor Lewis's Report, Nov. 17, 1873.

[4] Act of Feb. 25, 1870.

[5] Auditor's Report, 1873.

SUMMARY

Name of Road	Length	Value per Mile	Indorse-ment per Mile	Value of Road	Indorse-ment of Road	Present Road	Remarks
Alabama and Chattanooga	295	$15,000	$16,000	$4,018,388.00	$5,300,000 [1]	Ala. Great Southern	Seized by state. Completed.
E. Alabama and Cincinnati .	25	10,000	16,000	264,150.00	400,000	————	Never completed.
Mobile and Alabama G.T. .	50	12,000	16,000	704,225.00	880,000 [2]	Mobile and Birm'gh'm	————
Montgomery and Eufaula .	60	13,000	16,000	1,157,071.60	1,280,000 [3]	Central of Georgia	Seized and leased by the state.
Mobile and Montgomery		10,600	16,000	2,516,250.00	2,500,000 [4]	L'sville and Nashville	————
Savannah and Memphis . .	40	10,000	16,000	498,810.00	640,000	————	Did not default; never completed.
Selma and Gulf	40	10,000	16,000	424,900.00	640,000 [5]	————	Never completed.
Selma, Marion, and Memphis	45	14,000	16,000	738,400.00	765,000 [6]	————	Never completed.
New Orleans and Selma .	20	12,000	16,000	225,350.00	320,000	B'ham, Selma & N.O.	Never completed.
South and North Alabama . .	100	15,000	22,000	2,877,730.00	4,026,000 [7]	L'sville and Nashville	————

County and Town Aid to Railroads

An act of December 31, 1868, authorized the counties, towns, and cities to subscribe to railroad stock. The road corporation was to be voted on by the people. If "no subscription" was voted, a new election might be ordered within twelve months, and if again voted down, the matter was to be considered as settled. If a subscription was voted, an extra tax was to be levied to pay the interest on the bonds; the taxpayer was to be presented with a tax receipt which was good for its face value in the county or city railroad stock.[8] Several of the counties and towns issued bonds and incurred heavy debts which have burdened them for years. No one seems to have profited by

[1] $1,300,000 fraudulent indorsement; $2,000,000 in state bonds in addition.

[2] No record of $80,000 indorsement.

[3] Also "three per cent fund" amounting to $30,000+, and state bonds amounting to $300,000. No record of $720,000.

[4] No record of $1,500,000.   [5] No record of $160,000. Also a loan of $40,000.

[6] No record of $45,000.   [7] Including $2,200,000, of which no record was found.

[8] Act of Dec. 31, 1868; Acts of 1868, p. 514.

the issues except the promoters.[1] The counties that suffered worst
from Reconstruction bond issues were Randolph, Chambers, Lee,
Tallapoosa, and Pickens. These were hopelessly burdened with debt
and became known as the "strangulated" counties. There was,
after the Democrats came into power, much legislation for their
relief. The state gave them the state taxes to assist in paying off
the debt and also loaned money to them. Several cities and towns,
notably Mobile, Selma, and Opelika, were so deeply in debt that
they were unable to pay interest on their debts. They lost their
charters, ceased to be cities, and became districts under the direct
control of the governor. There are still several such districts in the
state. The constitution of 1875 forbade state, counties, or towns to
engage in works of internal improvement, or to lend money or credit
to such, or to any private or corporate enterprise.

It is impossible to secure complete statistics of the railroad bond
issues of counties and towns. Some issues were made in ignorance, without authority of law, others were made under the provisions of a general law. Naturally, the counties that suffered most
were those of the Black Belt under carpet-bag control. The following is a summary of the issues made under special acts : —

COUNTY OR TOWN	DATE	AMOUNT	ROAD AIDED	AUTHORITY	VOTE
Barbour .	—	—	Vicksburg and Brunswick	Act, Dec. 31, 1868	—
Chambers	—	$150,000	East Alabama and Cincinnati	Act, Dec. 31, 1868	—
Dallas .	—	140,000	New Orleans and Selma	Act, Dec. 31, 1868	—
Greene .	1869	80,000	Selma, Marion, and Memphis	Act, Mar. 3, 1870	1011 to 550
Hale . .	1869	60,000	Selma, Marion, and Memphis	Act, Mar. 3, 1870	2260 to 301
Lee . .	—	275,000	East Alabama and Cincinnati	Act, Dec. 31, 1868	—
Madison .	1873	130,000	Memphis and Charleston	Act, Mar. 27, 1873	Also earlier
Pickens .	1869	100,000	Selma, Marion, and Memphis	Act, Mar. 3, 1870	1212 to 607
Randolph	—	100,000		Act, Dec. 31, 1868	—
Tallapoosa	—	125,000			—
Eutaw	1869	20,000	Selma, Marion, and Memphis	Act, Mar. 2, 1870	98 to 35
Greensboro	1869	15,000	Selma, Marion, and Memphis	Act, Mar. 3, 1870	164 to 1
Mobile .	1871	1,000,000	Mobile and Northwestern	Act, Mar. 8, 1871	—
Mobile .	1873	200,000		Act, Mar. 7, 1873	—
Opelika .	—	25,000	East Alabama and Cincinnati		—
Prattville .	1872	50,000	South and North Alabama	Act, Jan. 23, 1872	—
Troy . .	1868	75,000	Mobile and Girard	Act, Oct. 8, 1868	—

[1] *Southern Argus,* June 14, 1872; Miller, "Alabama," p. 278; Acts of Ala.,
passim; "Northern Alabama," p. 737; Brown, "Alabama," p. 291; Herbert, "Solid
South," p. 53.

CHAPTER XIX

RECONSTRUCTION IN THE SCHOOLS

School System before Reconstruction

THE public school system of the state of Alabama was organized in 1854, and was an expansion of the Mobile system, which was partly native and partly modelled on the New York-New England systems.[1] By 1856 it was in good working order. The school fund for 1855 was $237,515.00; for 1856, $267,694.41, and the number of children in attendance was 100,279, which was about one-fourth of the white population. For 1857 the fund amounted to $281,874.41; for 1858, $564,210.46, with an attendance of 98,274 children.[2] The schools were not wholly free, since those parents who were able to do so paid part of the tuition.[3] In 1860 there were also 206 academies, with an enrolment of 10,778 pupils, and in the state colleges there were 2120 students.

In spite of the war the system managed to exist until 1864, and some schools were still open in 1865, at the time of surrender. Few of the private schools and colleges survived until that time, and the majority of the school buildings of all kinds were either destroyed during the war, or after its close were placed in the hands of the Freedmen's Bureau or of the army. The State Medical College was used for a negro primary school for three years, and was not given up until the reconstructionists came into power. An attempt in 1865 was made to reopen the University, although the buildings had been burned by the Federals in 1865. The trustees met, elected a president and two professors, but on the day appointed for the opening (in October) only one student appeared.[4]

---

[1] A commission from Mobile visited the schools in New York, Boston, and other cities of the North.

[2] Exclusive of Mobile County, which, as the honored pioneer, has always been outside of, and a model for, the state system.

[3] Clark, " History of Education in Alabama," pp. 221-241; Report of the United States Commissioner of Education, 1876, p. 6.

[4] The son of ex-Governor Watts. Clark, p. 94.

During the summer and fall of 1865 and during the next year the various religious denominations of the state and mass-meetings of citizens declared that the changed civil relations of the races made negro education a necessity. The. Freedmen's Bureau was established and anticipated much of the work planned by the churches and by southern leaders, but the methods employed by the alien teachers caused many whites to become prejudiced against negro education.[1]

The provisional government adopted the ante-bellum public school system and put it into operation. The schools were open to both races, from six to twenty years of age, separate schools being provided for the blacks. The greater part of the expenditure of the provisional government was for schools. Relatively few negroes attended the state schools proper, as every influence was brought to bear to make them attend the Bureau and missionary schools, and the state negro schools soon fell into the hands of the Bureau educators, who drew the state appropriation.

The colleges at Marion, Greensboro, Auburn, Florence, and other places were reopened in 1866-1867. The legislature loaned $70,000 to the University, besides paying the interest on the University fund. For three years the University was being rebuilt, and so well were its finances managed that in 1868, when the carpet-baggers came into power, the buildings were completed and the institution out of debt, although it had used only half of the loan from the state.[2]

The Reconstruction convention of 1867 was much more interested in politics than in education. The negro members demanded free schools and special advantages for the negro, and a few carpet-baggers had much to say about the malign influence of the old régime in keeping so many thousands in the darkness of ignorance. The scalawags demanded separate schools for the races, but pressure was brought to bear and most of them gave way. Sixteen of the native whites refused to sign the constitution and united in a protest against the action of the convention in refusing to provide separate schools.[3]

---

[1] See Ch. XI, Sec. 3.

[2] Clark, p. 95 *et passim.* In 1869 N. B. Cloud, the Superintendent of Public Instruction, asked the legislature to make the loan a gift, since the destruction of the buildings was "the natural fruits of secession," the fault of the "purblind leaders" who "pretended to secede." Therefore he thought the state was responsible for the damage done the University.

[3] See Journal Convention of 1867, p. 242 *et passim,* and above, Chs. XIV and XV.

The School System of Reconstruction

The new constitution placed all public instruction under the control of a Board of Education consisting of the Superintendent of Public Instruction and two members from each congressional district,[1] the latter to serve for four years, half of them being elected by the people every two years. Full legislative powers in regard to education were given to the Board. Its acts were to have the force of law, and the governor's veto could be overridden by a two-thirds vote. The legislature might repeal a school law, but otherwise it had no authority over the Board.[2] This body also acted as a board of regents for the State University. One school, at least, was to be established in every township in the state, though some townships did not have half a dozen children in them. The school income was fixed by the constitution at one-fifth of all state revenue, in addition to the income from school lands, poll tax, and taxes on railroads, navigation, banks, and insurance.[3] The legislature added another source of income by chartering several lotteries and exempted them from taxation provided they paid a certain amount to the school fund. On October 10, 1868, the Mutual Aid Association was chartered "to distribute books, paintings, works of art, scientific instruments and apparatus, lands, etc., stock and currency, awards, and prizes." For this privilege it was to give $2000 a year to the school fund.[4] Two months later the Mobile Charitable Association was formed, which paid $1000 a year to the school fund,[5] and a number of other lotteries were chartered soon after.

[1] There were four congressional districts.

[2] The supreme court decided in regard to the Board of Education : "The new system has not only administrative, but full legislative, powers concerning all matters having reference to the common school and public educational interests of the state. It cannot be destroyed nor essentially changed by legislative authority." Report of the Commissioner of Education, 1873, p. 5. But in 1873–1874 the legislature, however, by refusing appropriations, did manage to nullify the work of the Board.

[3] Constitution of 1867, Art. XI.

[4] In 1871 the legislature repealed this act, and a case that arose was carried to the United States supreme court, which, reversing a former decision of the state supreme court, held that the action of one legislature could not restrain subsequent legislatures from legislating for the public welfare by suppressing practices that tended to corrupt public morals. Besides, the court professed itself unable to find in the act any authority for a lottery. See Boyd *vs.* Alabama, 94 United States Reports, p. 645 (opinion by Justice Field).

[5] Act of Dec. 31, 1868. At the same time the office of Commissioner of Lotteries was created, with a salary of $2000 a year.

The school system, as a whole, did not differ greatly from the old, except that it was top-heavy with officials, and in that all private assistance was discouraged by a regulation forbidding the use of the public money to supplement private payments. The first Board of Education probably contained a collection of as worthless men as could be found in the state.[1] The elections had gone by default, and since only the most incompetent men had offered themselves for educational offices, the work suffered. Dr. N. B. Cloud, an incapable of ante-bellum days, was chosen Superintendent of Public Instruction. He was a man without character, without education, and entirely without administrative ability. Before the war he was known as a cruel master to his few slaves. In August, 1868, he proceeded to put the system into operation by appointing sixty-four county superintendents, of Radical politics, each of whom in turn appointed three trustees in each township. The stream rose no higher than its source, and the school officials were a forlorn lot. One of them signed for his salary by an X mark. Another, J. E. Summerford, the superintendent of Lee County, was a man of bad morals, and so incompetent that, when attempting to examine teachers for licenses, he in turn was contemptuously questioned by them on elementary subjects. In revenge for this expression of contempt, he revoked the license of every teacher in the county. One county superintendent was a preacher who had been expelled from his church for misappropriating charity funds. But Cloud paid no attention to charges made against the integrity of his school officials.

Cloud proceeded with much haste to open the schools. A year later he made a report which is an interesting document. There was little progress to be noted, but much space was devoted to an appreciation of that "glorious document," the constitution of 1867, the crowning glory of which — the article on education — should "entitle the members to the rare merit of statemen and sages." This provision for education, he said, was the first blow struck in the South,

---

[1] This is the opinion of two subsequent members — one a Democrat and one a Radical. See also Ku Klux Report, Ala. Test., p. 426. The members were G. L. Putnam, A. B. Collins (Collins was made a professor in the University, but murdered Haughey, the Radical Congressman, and fled from the state), W. D. Miller, Jesse H. Booth, Thomas A. Cook, James Nichols, William H. Clayton, Gustavus A. Smith, — four scalawags and four carpet-baggers. The first two named resigned to accept offices created by the board. See Register of the University of Alabama, 1831-1901, p. 20.

2 R

and especially in Alabama, to clear out the last vestige of ignorance with all its attendant evils; and now, in spite of the burdens imposed by the unwise legislation of the past forty years, the bosoms of the citizens expanded with a noble pride in the present system of schools.

After this he proceeds to business. He reports that in every county and in almost every township in the state his officials met with opposition, not, he confesses, on account of opposition to schools, but on account of the objectionable government and its agents. The reports from the white counties, especially, indicate opposition to the establishment of negro schools, while in the Black Belt this opposition was not so strong. Everywhere, he states, the opposition died out, more or less, in time.[1]

Before the new system went into operation, a meeting of the Board was held in Montgomery to clear away the remains of the old system. They voted to themselves a secretary, sergeant-at-arms, pages, etc., like the House of Representatives; all school offices were declared vacated and all school contracts void; separate schools were provided for the races where the parents were unwilling to send to mixed schools; eleven normal schools were provided for, with no distinction of color; and a bill was introduced by G. L. Putnam and passed into a law, the object of which was to merge the Mobile schools into the state system and also to make an office for Putnam. A sum of money had been appropriated by the previous legislatures to pay the teachers in the state schools, and now the Board declared that any association, society, or teacher in a school open to the public should have a claim for part of this money.[2] The county superintendents were made elective after 1870; coöperation with the Freedmen's Bureau was declared desirable, and the Bureau was asked to furnish or to rent houses, or to assist in building, while the aid societies were asked to send teachers who would be paid by the state, and who would be subject to the same regulations as native teachers. The "Superintendent of Education" of the Bureau was to have supervision over the Bureau schools, but he, in turn, would be under the supervision of Cloud.[3]

[1] Report, Nov. 10, 1869.

[2] This was done at the instance of the aid societies from the North which had been doing work among the negroes.

[3] Acts, Aug. 11, 1868. Public School Laws (pamphlet). See also Acts of Ala., 1868, pp. 147–160.

Reconstruction of the State University

The Board then tried to reconstruct the University. After the appearance of the lone student in 1865, the efforts of the trustees had been directed only towards completing the buildings. In 1868, after the constitution of 1867 had failed of adoption, the old trustees met, elected a president and faculty, and ordered the University to be opened in October, 1868. A few weeks later Congress imposed the constitution on the state, and the Board of Education as regents took charge of the University. Their first act was to declare null and void all acts of any pretended body of trustees since the secession of the state. This was done in order to repudiate a debt made by the University with a New York firm in 1861. No suitable candidate for the presidency was presented, and the regents chose for that position Mr. Wyman, the acting president.[1] He declined, and the position was then sought for and obtained by the Rev. A. S. Lakin, a Northern Methodist preacher, who had been sent to Alabama in 1867 by Bishop Clark of Ohio, to gather the negroes of the Southern Methodist Church into the northern fold.[2] Lakin, accompanied by Cloud, went to the University to take charge. Wyman, who was then in charge, refused to surrender the keys, and a Tuscaloosa mob, or Ku Klux Klan, serenaded Lakin and threatened to lynch him if he remained in town. It is said that he was saved from the mob by Wyman, who hid him under a bed. The next morning Lakin decided that he did not like the place and left.[3] He did not resign, however, and three years later still had a claim pending for a full year's salary. On this he collected $800 from the Board of Regents.[4]

---

[1] Clark, p. 98. [2] See Ch. XX.

[3] Nicholas Davis, a north Alabama Republican, had this to say about Lakin to the Ku Klux subcommittee : "He called on me to explain why I said unkind things about his being candidate for president of the Alabama University, and I said, 'Mr. Lakin, you and I are near neighbors, and I don't want to have much to do with you — not much ; but I think this : didn't you try to be president of the Alabama University ?' He said he did. I said, 'It would have been a disgrace to the state. You don't know an adjective from a verb, nor nothing else.' . . . He says, '. . . but I rather didn't like what you said.' I said, 'Doctor, you will have to like it or let it alone.' He let it alone." — Ku Klux Rept., Ala. Test., p. 784.

[4] Clark, p. 98, is not correct on this point ; Ku Klux Rept., Ala. Test., pp. 111, 112, 113, 114 ; account of Dr. O. D. Smith of the second Board of Education ; Independent Monitor, Aug. 9 and Sept. 1, 1868.

[From the Independent Monitor, Tuscaloosa, Alabama, September 1, 1868.]

A PROSPECTIVE SCENE IN THE CITY OF OAKS, 4TH OF MARCH, 1869.

"Hang, curs, hang!　　*　*　*　*　*　*　　*　*　*　　*　*　　*　　*　*　*　　*　　*　*　*　　*　　*　*　*　*　*　*　*　*　*　*　*　*　*　*　*　*　*　*　*

> "Hang, curs, hang!　*　*　*　*　*　　*　*　*　　*
> fate, to *their* hanging!　*　*　*　*　　*　*　*　*　*　*　*　*

The above cut represents the fate in store for those great pests of Southern society—the carpet-bagger and scalawag—if found in Dixie's land after the break of day on the 4th of March next.

The *genus* carpet-bagger is a man with a lank head of dry hair, a lank stomach, and long legs, club knees, and splay feet, dried legs, and lank jaws, with eyes like a fish and mouth like a shark. Add to this a habit of sneaking and dodging about in unknown places, habiting with negroes in dark dens and back streets, a look like a hound, and the smell of a polecat.

Words are wanting to do full justice to the *genus* scalawag. He is a cur with a contracted head, downward look, slinking and uneasy gait; sleeps in the woods, like old Crossland, at the bare idea of a Ku-Klux raid.

Our scalawag is the local leper of the community. Unlike the carpet-bagger, he is native, which is so much the worse. Once he was respected in his circle, his head was level, and he would look his neighbor in the face. Now, possessed of the itch of office and the salt rheum of radicalism, he is a mangy dog, slinking through the alleys, hunting the governor's office, defiling with tobacco juice the steps of the capitol, stretching his lazy carcass in the sun on the square or the benches of the mayor's court.

He waiteth for the troubling of the political waters, to the end that he may step in and be healed of the itch by the ointment of office. For office he "bums," as a toper "bums" for the satisfying dram. For office, yet in prospective, he hath bartered respectability; hath abandoned business and ceased to labor with his hands, but employs his feet kicking out boot-heels against lamp-post and corner-curb while discussing the question of office.

It requires no seer to foretell the inevitable events that are to result from the coming fall election throughout the Southern States.

The unprecedented reaction is moving onward with the swiftness of a velocipede, with the violence of a tornado, and with the crash of an avalanche, sweeping negroism from the face of the earth.

Woe, woe, woe to the inhabitants of Alabama who have recently become squatter-

It was in connection with Lakin's short visit that the *Independent Monitor* published the famous hanging picture of the carpet-bagger (Lakin) and the scalawag (Cloud).[1]

[1] For the picture see Ala. Test., p. 113, or the *Independent Monitor*, Sept 1, 1868. Ryland Randolph, the editor of the *Monitor* at that time, says that the picture was

The next offer of the presidency was made to R. D. Harper, a Northern Methodist Bureau minister, who at one time was the Bureau "Superintendent of Education" for the state, and who organized the Bureau schools and the Northern Methodist churches in north Alabama. He, after some consideration, declined the position, which, to an alien, was one of more danger than honor.[1]

Difficulty was also experienced in securing a faculty. Some of the faculty elected by the old board of trustees were reëlected. Geary of Ohio was given the chair of mathematics, and Goodfellow of Chicago, who had previously been a clerk of the lower house of the legislature, was elected commandant and professor of military science. The latter said that he did not know anything about his work, but that he guessed he could learn. General John H. Forney, a Confederate and native, was also elected to a chair, the Board, it is said, voting for him under a misapprehension. The native contingent refused to serve under the regents, and the vacancies had again to be filled.[2] Loomis of Illinois was elected professor of Ancient Languages; J. De F. Richards of Vermont, professor of Natural Philosophy and Astronomy, etc. W. J. Collins, who was elected professor of Oratory and Rhetoric, wrote, "I except the situation." The *Monitor* said, "We predict an uncomfortable time for the aggregation."[3] That paper chronicled all the weaknesses, peculiarities, and failings of the faculty. If one of them drank a little too much and staggered on the street, the *Monitor* informed the public.[4] Upon the arrival of an heir in the Collins family, Randolph promptly demanded that he be named for him, — Ryland Randolph Collins, — and the name stuck.

Finally, as it seemed impossible to secure a president, the regents

made from a rough woodcut, fashioned in the *Monitor* office. The *Cincinnati Commercial* published an edition of 500,000 copies of the hanging picture for distribution as a campaign document. A Columbus, Ohio, newspaper also printed for distribution a larger edition containing the famous picture. This was during the Seymour-Grant campaign, and the Democratic newspapers and leaders of the state were furious at Randolph for furnishing such excellent campaign literature to the Radicals.

[1] Clark, p. 98 ; *Independent Monitor*, Jan. 5 and March 23, 1869.

[2] *Selma Times and Messenger*, Aug. 9, 1868.

[3] Clark, pp. 98, 99. *Monitor*, Jan. 5, March 1 and 23, 1869. "The Reconstruction University," a farce, was acted at the court-house for the benefit of the brass band. There was no hope whatever that the reconstructed faculty would have a pleasant time.

[4] See the *Monitor*, March 1, 1869.

determined to open the University with Richards as acting president.[1] On April 1, 1869, the University opened with thirty students, twenty-eight of whom were beneficiaries.[2] The *Monitor* said that the members of the faculty were known as Shanghai, Cockeye, Tanglefoot, Old Dicks, etc. Another woodcut appeared in the *Monitor* — of Richards, this time.[3]

Thirty was the highest enrolment reached under the Reconstruction faculty. The number gradually dwindled away until at the end of the session there were only ten. The next session ended with only three. In October, 1870, there were ten students, four of whom were sons of professors. William R. Smith[4] was elected president during this session, but he reported that there was no prospect of success under the present conditions and resigned. By the end of the session not one student remained. The scientific apparatus was scattered and lost, as were also the museum specimens and library books, and the $2000 object-glass of the telescope had disappeared.[5]

The people of Alabama did not favor the continuance of the University under the reconstructed faculty, and were glad when the doors were closed. The Ku Klux Klan took part in the work of breaking down the venture. Notices were posted on the doors, directed to the

[1] Richards was at the same time state senator from Wilcox, sheriff of the same county, contractor to feed prisoners, and professor in the University. His income from all the offices was about $12,000, the professorship paying about $2500.

[2] Report of Cloud, Nov., 1869. Clark, p. 99.

[3] See *Monitor*, April 6, 1869. The editor of the *Monitor* finally came to grief because of his attacks on the Radical faculty. His paper had charged Professor V. H. Vaughn with drunkenness, whipping his wife, incompetence, etc. After a year of such pleasantries, Vaughn, who was a timid man, determined to secure assistance and be revenged. In the University was a student named Smith, son of a regent and nephew of the governor, who, on account of his Union record, was given the position of steward of the mess hall, after the removal of the old steward. Smith had been in trouble about abstracting stores from the University commissary, and the *Monitor* had not spared him. So he and Vaughn with their guns went after Randolph, and Smith shot him "while Vaughn stood at a respectful distance." Randolph lost his leg from the shot. Smith and Vaughn were put in jail, but through the connivance of the officials made their escape. Vaughn went to Washington and was given an office in Utah territory. See Ku Klux Rept., Ala. Test., p. 1979.

[4] He was a competent man, well educated and possessing administrative ability. In the secession convention he had led the coöperationist forces.

[5] Clark, pp. 99–101; *Monitor*, Jan. 10 and 25 and March 28, 1871. The Register of the University (p. 218) gives only thirteen names for the session 1870–1871. No record was kept at the University.

students, advising them to leave.   One sent to the son of Governor Smith read as follows: —

DAVID SMITH: You have received one notice from us, and this shall be our last.   You nor no other d—d son of a d—d radical traitor shall stay at our University.   Leave here in less than ten days, for in that time we will visit the place and it will not be well for you to be found out there.   The state is ours and so shall our University be.

WRITTEN BY THE SECRETARY BY ORDER OF THE KLAN.

Charles Muncel, son of Joel Muncel, the publisher, of Albany, New York,[1] received the following notice: —

CHARLES MUNCEL: You had better get back where you came from.   We don't want any d—d Yank at our colleges.   In less than ten days we will come to see if you obey our warning.   If not, look out for hell, for d—n you, we will show you that you shall not stay, you nor no one else, in that college.   This is your first notice; let it be your last.

THE KLAN BY THE SECRETARY.

The next warning was sent to a lone Democrat: —

HORTON: They say you are of good Democratic family.   If you are, leave the University and that quick.   We don't intend that the concern shall run any longer.   This is the second notice you have received ; you will get no other.   In less than ten days we intend to clear out the concern.   We will have good Southern men there or none.

BY ORDER OF THE K. K. K.[2]

Before the summer of 1871 the reconstructed faculty had absolutely failed; there never had been any chance for them to succeed. The regents were unfitted to manage educational affairs, and they chose men to the faculty who would have been objectionable anywhere.[3] The professors and their families were socially ostracized. Even southern men who accepted places in the Radical faculty were made to feel that they were scorned; no one would sit by them at public gatherings or in church. The men might have survived this treatment, but not so the women. In 1871 the Superintendent of Public Instruction and two members of the board of regents were

---

[1] See Register of the University of Alabama, p. 217.

[2] These notices were printed in the Ku Klux Rept., Ala. Test., p. 418.   They were fastened to the door with a dagger.   The students who were notified left at once.

[3] See Ku Klux Rept., Ala. Test., p. 426 (Speed).

Democrats. The faculty was reorganized for the eighth time since 1865, and a faculty of natives was elected. The effect upon the attendance was marked. In April, 1871, there were three students and in June none, while during the session of 1871–1872, 107 students were enrolled. In 1873 and 1874 the Radicals again had control, but they did not attempt to reconstruct the University.[1]

When the land grant college, provided for in the Morrill act of 1862, was established in 1872, there was no attempt made to appoint a reconstructed faculty or board of trustees. But there was sharp competition among the towns of the state to secure the college. The legislature was to choose the location, and many of the members let it be known that their votes were to be had only in return for material considerations. It was finally located at Auburn, in Lee County. One Auburn lobbyist went out on the floor of one of the houses and there paid a negro solon $50 to talk no more against Auburn. The next day the same negro was again speaking against the location at Auburn. His purchaser went to him and remonstrated. The negro acknowledged that he had accepted the $50 not to speak against Auburn, but said, "Dat was yistiddy, boss." Another Auburn man promised a cooking stove to a negro of more domestic inclinations, and amidst the excitement forgot all about it; but after the vote the negro came up and demanded his stove. He received it. Another was given a sewing-machine.[2]

There was no attempt to force the entrance of negroes into the State University. Some reformers wanted the test made, but too many scalawags were bitterly opposed to such a step, to say nothing of the Ku Klux Klan. In December, 1869, the Board of Education

[1] The following table gives the enrolment of students during Reconstruction : —

SESSION										STUDENTS
1868–9										
1869–70	.	.	.	.	.	.	.	.	.	.	30
1870–1	.	.	.	.	.	.	.	.	.	.	21
1871–2	.	.	.	.	.	.	.	.	.	.	107
1872–3	.	.	.	.	.	.	.	.	.	.	135
1873–4	.	.	.	.	.	.	.	.	.	.	53
1874–5	.	.	.	.	.	.	.	.	.	.	74
1875–6	.	.	.	.	.	.	.	.	.	.	111
1876–7	.	.	.	.	.	.	.	.	.	.	164

[2] I have this account from the men who furnished the bribes.

asked the legislature to provide a university for the negroes,[1] and several colored normal schools were established. In 1871, Peyton Finley, the negro member of the Board of Education,[2] introduced a series of resolutions declaring that the negro had no desire to push any claim to enter the State University, but that they wanted one of their own, and Congress was urged to grant land for that purpose.[3] But not until December, 1873, was the Lincoln school at Marion, Perry County, designated as the colored university and normal school, where a liberal education was to be given the negro.[4]

Trouble in the Mobile Schools

For more than a year Cloud had trouble in the schools of Mobile. The Mobile schools (always independent of the state system) were under the control of a school board appointed by the military authorities in 1865. When all offices and contracts were vacated, G. L. Putnam, a member of the Board of Education, and also connected with the Emerson Institute, which was conducted at Mobile by the American Missionary Association, had secured the enactment, because he wanted the position, of a school law providing for a superintendent of education for Mobile County. In August, 1868, Cloud gave him the office. The old school commissioners refused to recognize the authority of Putnam, who was unable to displace them, because he himself could not make bond. But, in order to give him some kind of office, Cloud went to Mobile and proposed a compromise, which was to appoint one of the old commissioners superintendent of education and Putnam superintendent of negro schools under the supervision of the other superintendent and the board of commissioners, which was still to exist. This was an arrangement Cloud had no lawful authority to make.

As part of the compromise the principal and teachers of the American Missionary Association were to be retained and paid by the state.

[1] Clark, p. 99.

[2] Finley had been doorkeeper for the first Board (1868–1870), and in 1870 was elected to serve four years. He was a member of the convention of 1867 and of the legislature. He had no education and no ability, but he was a sensible negro and was an improvement on the white men of the preceding Board.

[3] Journal of the Board of Education and Regents, June 20, 1871.

[4] Act of Dec. 6, 1873, School Laws.

The Emerson Institute (or "Blue College," as the negroes called it) was to remain in possession of the American Missionary Association, but the school board and county superintendent were to have control over the schools in it.   Putnam, as superintendent of the "Blue College" school, refused to allow the control of the board.   He wanted them to pay his teachers, but would have no supervision.   The general field agent of the American Missionary Association, Edward P. Smith, offered the "schools and teachers" to the school commissioners to be paid but not controlled.   "We ought now in some way," he said, "to have our teachers recognized and paid for, from the public fund, an amount equal to that paid for similar grades to other teachers in Mobile."   At the same time the state was paying $125 per month for the use of the building over which the Association and Putnam would allow no supervision.   The county superintendent and the commissioners, unable to secure any control over the Putnam schools, refused to recognize them as a part of the Mobile system.   Cloud declared all the offices vacant, but the commissioners refused to vacate.   The case was carried into court and the commissioners were put in jail.   The supreme court ordered them released. The Board of Education then met and abolished the Mobile system and merged the special and independent schools of that county into the general state system.   This was done on November 13, 1869.[1]

The judiciary committee of the legislature, consisting of three Radicals and one Democrat, was directed to investigate the conduct of Cloud in the Mobile troubles.   It was reported (1) that Cloud had appointed two superintendents in Mobile County, contrary to law; (2) that on January 29, 1869, G. L. Putnam, who was not an official of the state and who, according to the compromise, should have been

---

[1] Clark, p. 232 ; Report of Cloud, Nov., 1869; *Montgomery Mail*, Sept. 16, 1870. In connection with the act merging the Mobile schools into the state system, the Board of Education took occasion to enlarge or complete its constitutional powers.   There was no limit, according to the Constitution, to the time for the governor to retain acts of the Board.   Governor Smith had pocketed several obnoxious educational bills, and the Board now resolved "that the same rules and provisions which by law govern and define the time and manner in which the governor of the state shall approve of or object to any bill or resolution of the General Assembly shall also apply to any bill or resolution having the force of law passed by this Board of Education."   The governor approved neither resolution nor the Mobile act, but they were both declared in force.   *Montgomery Mail*, Nov. 3, 1870.

under the control of the county superintendent, drew from the state treasury with the connivance of Cloud between $5000 and $6000, with which he paid the teachers of " Blue College," who were in the employ of the American Missionary Association and not of the state of Alabama; (3) that in July, 1869, Cloud again appointed Putnam superintendent of education for Mobile County, and sixty days afterwards he made a bond which was declared worthless by the grand jury, and after that Cloud gave Putnam a warrant for $9000, which he was prevented from collecting only by an injunction; (4) that while the injunction was in force as concerned both Putnam and Cloud, the latter drew from the treasury $2000 or more of the Mobile school funds to pay lawyers' fees; (5) that while the injunction was still in force Cloud drew $3600 from the treasury for Putnam, the greater part or all of which was illegally used; (6) that Cloud again drew a warrant for $3300, which the auditor, discovering that Putnam was interested, refused to allow, and it was destroyed; (7) the committee further stated that very large salaries were paid to the teachers in " Blue College," or Emerson Institute, — that one of them (Squires) received $4000 a year. The committee went beyond the limit of the resolution and reported that county superintendents were paid too much, and recommended the abolition of the Board of Education by constitutional amendment, the reduction of the pay of all school officials who acted as a sponge to absorb all the school funds, and, finally, that no person should hold more than one school office at the same time.[1]

Later investigation showed that Putnam had made out pay-rolls for the teachers of the Emerson Institute for the last quarter of 1868 and presented them to A. H. Ryland, the county superintendent of Mobile, for his approval. This Ryland refused to give, as the compromise in regard to the Institute dated only from January 22, 1869. Putnam then went to his own American Missionary Association Negro Institute Board, had the pay-rolls approved, and then, as "county superintendent of education," drew $5327.20, Cloud certifying to the correctness of his accounts.[2] Putnam padded the pay-rolls and, in order to draw principal's wages for each teacher, divided the Institute into ten schools. As there were only ten teachers besides the principal,

[1] Senate Journal, 1869–1870, p. 419.
[2] *Montgomery Mail*, Sept. 16, 1870.

there were now eleven principals.[1] Kelsey, the principal, stated that no matter how much Putnam obtained for "Blue College," the teachers received none of it, but were paid only their regular salaries by the Association.   Kelsey himself was paid only $250 a quarter.   The teachers were under contract with the Association to teach for $15 a month and board.   Some of them testified that they had received no more.   However, a part of the appropriation was turned into the treasury of the Association, and we may well ask what became of the remainder of it.[2]

Irregularities in School Administration

Superintendent Cloud was handicapped, not only by his own incapacity, but also by the bad character of his subordinates, whom he appointed in great haste from the unpromising material that supported the Reconstruction régime.   Many of the receipts for the salaries were signed by the teachers with marks, some being unable to write their

[1] A specimen pay-roll of Emerson Institute (" Blue College ") for the quarter ending March 31, 1869 : —

	Months	Salary	Total
G. L. Putnam, Supt. of Colored Schools . . .	3	$333.33	$1000.00
H. S. Kelsey, Prin. Emerson Institute . . .	3	225.00	675.00
E. I. Ethridge, Prin. Grammar School . . .	3	200.00	600.00
Susie A. Carley, Prin. Lower School	3	180.00	540.00
A. A. Rockfellow, Prin. Intermediate School . .	3	105.00	315.00
Sarah A. Primey, Prin. Intermediate School . .	3	105.00	315.00
M. L. Harris, Prin. Intermediate School . . .	3	105.00	315.00
M. A. Cooley, Prin. Intermediate School . . .	3	105.00	315.00
M. E. F. Smith, Prin. Intermediate School. . .	3	105.00	315.00
Ruth A. Allen, Primary School	3	105.00	315.00
N. G. Lincoln, Primary School	3	105.00	315.00
M. L. Theyer, Primary School	3	105.00	315.00
Judge Rapier, legal opinion	—	—	50.00
American Missionary Association, fuel . . .	—	—	40.00
Total			$5425.00

At this time the average salary of the teacher in the state schools was $42 a month.

[2] *Montgomery Mail*, Sept. 16, 1876.   Cloud's Report, Nov., 1869, shows that $10,447.23 had been drawn out of the treasury by Putnam, and he had also drawn $2000 for his salary as county superintendent.

own names.   From the school officials he received inaccurate reports, and on these he based his apportionments, which were defective, many of the teachers not receiving their money.   The county superintendents had absolute authority over the school fund belonging to their counties, and could draw it from the treasury and use it for private purposes nearly a year before the salaries of the teachers were due.[1] Complaint was made that the black counties received more than their proper share of the school fund.   In Pickens County the superintendent neglected to draw anything but his own salary, and a north Alabama superintendent ran away with the money for his county. Other superintendents were accused of scaling down the pay of the teachers from 20 to 50 per cent, and it was estimated that in some counties two-thirds of the school money never reached the teachers.   There was no check on the county superintendent, who could expend money practically at his own discretion.[2]   Three trustees were appointed in each township by the county superintendent; these trustees, who were not paid, appointed for themselves a clerk who was paid, and these clerks met in a county convention and fixed the salary of the county superintendent.[3]

The bookkeeping in the office of State Superintendent Cloud was irregular.   Some of the accounts were kept in pencil, and for a whole year the books were not posted.   Of $235,000 paid to the county superintendents only $10,000 was accounted for by them.   In 1871, $50,000 or more was still in the hands of the ex-superintendents, and the state and the teachers were taking legal proceedings against some of them.[4]   Both sons of Cloud embezzled school money and

[1] Report of the Auditor, 1871 ; Report of the Commissioner of Education, 1871, 1876.

[2] See Act of Dec. 2, 1869 ; Somers, "Southern States," pp. 169, 170.

[3] The law stated that the trustees were to receive $2 a day, but Cloud said that it was a mistake, as it should be the clerks who were paid, and thus it was done.   There were 1485 clerks in the state; they were paid about $60,000 a year.   The county superintendents received about $65,000, an average of $1000 each, which was paid from the school fund.   Before the war the average salary of the county superintendent was $300 and was paid by the county.   In few counties was the work of the county superintendent sufficient to keep him busy more than two days in the week.   Many of the superintendents stayed in their offices only one day in the week.   The expenses of the Board of Education were from $3000 to $5000 a year, not including the salary of the state superintendent.   *Montgomery Mail*, Sept. 15 and 16, 1870.

[4] Hodgson's Report, 1871 ; Ala. Test., p. 233.

fled from the state.[1] Cloud receipted for one sum of $314 in payment for sixteenth-section lands. This he forgot to pay to the treasurer. He issued patents for 4000 acres of school land and turned into the treasury only $323. A township in Marengo County rented its sixteenth-section land; nevertheless, Cloud paid to this county its sixteenth-section funds. In 1871 an investigation of Cloud's accounts showed that a large number of his vouchers were fraudulent, hundreds being in the same handwriting. He signed the name of J. H. Fitts & Company, financial agents of the University, to a receipt by which he drew from the treasury several hundred dollars to advance to a needy professor. He said, when questioned about it, that he thought he could "draw on" Messrs. Fitts & Company. It afterwards developed that he did not know the difference between a receipt and a draft. His accounts were so confused that he often paid the same bill twice. In 1871, when he went out of office, the sum unaccounted for by vouchers amounted to $260,556.37. After two years he succeeded in getting vouchers for all but $129,595.71.[2]

In the black counties the school finances became confused, especially as the negro and carpet-bag officials tolled the funds that passed through their hands. At the end of 1870 the school funds of Selma were $40,000 short. It was found practically impossible to collect a poll tax from the negroes, the Radical collectors being afraid to insist on the negroes' paying taxes. In Dallas County the collector refused to allow the planters to pay taxes for their negro hands on the ground that it would be a relic of slavery. If the negroes refused to pay, nothing more was said about it.[3] In 1869 there were 200,000 polls

---

[1] Cloud, the state superintendent, had power of attorney to act for certain county superintendents. This he sub-delegated to his son, W. B. Cloud, who drew warrants for $8551.31, which were allowed by the auditor. This amount was the school fund for the following counties : Sumter, $1,535.59 ; Pickens, $6,423.17 ; Winston, $215.89 ; Calhoun, $176.66 ; Marshall, $200.00.

A clerk in the office of C. A. Miller, the secretary of state, forged Miller's name as attorney and drew $3,238.39 from the Etowah County fund. Miller swore that he had notified both auditor and treasurer that he would not act as attorney to draw money for any one.

John B. Cloud bought whiskey with tax stamps. See Hodgson's Report, 1871 ; Ala. Test., p. 233 ; *Montgomery Advertiser*, Sept. 27, 1872.

[2] Hodgson's Report, 1871 ; *Montgomery Advertiser*, Sept. 27, 1872 ; Report of the Commission to Examine State Offices, 1871.

[3] Somers, pp. 169, 170.

and only $66,000 poll tax was collected, which meant that only 44,000 men had paid the tax.[1] In 1870 Somers states that the insurance tax was $13,327, and the number of polls was 162,819. Yet from both sources less than $100,000 was obtained.[2]

The Board of Education, according to the constitution, was to classify by lot before the election of 1870. But in 1869, when the matter was brought up, they refused to classify. Several vacancies occurred, and these were filled by special election. Consequently the Democrats in 1870 did not get a fair representation on the board.[3]

Objections to the Reconstruction Education

The Board of Education had the power to adopt a uniform series of text-books for the public schools; Superintendent Cloud, however, assumed this authority and chose texts which were objectionable to the majority of the whites. This was especially the case with the history books, which the whites complained were insulting in their accounts of southern leaders and southern questions. Cloud was not the man to allow the southern view of controversial questions to be taught in schools under his control. About 1869 he secured a donation of several thousand copies of history books which gave the northern views of American history, and these he distributed among the teachers and the schools. But most of the literature that the whites considered objectionable did not come from Cloud's department, but from the Bureau and aid society teachers, and was used in the schools for blacks. There were several series of "Freedmen's Readers" and "Freedmen's Histories" prepared for use in negro schools. But the fact remains that for ten or fifteen years northern histories were taught in white schools and had a decided influence on the readers. It resulted in the combination often seen in the late southern writer, of northern views of history with southern prejudices; the fable of the "luxury of the aristocrats" and the numbers and wretchedness of the "mean whites" was now accepted by numerous young southerners; on such questions as slavery the northern view of the institution was accepted, but on the other hand the *tu quoque* answer was made to the North. Consequently, the task of the historian was not to explain

---

[1] *Montgomery Mail*, Sept. 15, 1870.

[2] Somers, "Southern States," p. 170; voters only counted as polls.

[3] *Montgomery Mail*, Sept. 15, 1870.

the southern civilization, but to accept it as rather bad and to prove that the North was partly responsible and equally guilty — a fruitless work.[1]

Cloud, in his first report, admitted that the opposition to schools was rather on account of the officials than because the people disliked free schools. He further stated that the opposition had ceased to a great extent. There were many whites in the Black Belt who disliked the idea of free or "pauper" schools, and to this day some of them have not overcome this feeling. They believed in education, but not in education that was given away, — at least not for the whites. Each person must make an effort to get an education. However, they, and especially the old slaveholders, were not opposd to the education of the negro, believing it to be necessary for the good of society. In the white counties of north and southeast Alabama there was less opposition to the public schools for whites. But in the same sections schools for the negroes were bitterly opposed by the uneducated whites who were in close competition with them, for they knew that the whites paid for the negro schools, and also that, having a different standard of living, it would be easier for the negroes to send their children to school than for them to send theirs. In the Black Belt there were a few of these people, who disliked to see three or four negro schools to one white school, for here the number of the negroes naturally secured for them better advantages. The whites were so few in numbers that not half of them were within easy reach of a school. Whenever the numbers of one or both races were small, it was (and has been ever since) a burden on a community to build two schoolhouses and to support two separate schools, especially where the funds provided are barely sufficient for one.[2]

The Question of Negro Education

Before the negro question in all its phases was brought directly into politics, and before the Radicals, carpet-baggers, and scalawags had caused irritation between the races, there was a determination on

[1] In recent years the people have demanded and obtained a different class of school histories, such as those of Derry, Lee, Jones, Thompson, Cooper, Estill, and Lemmon. Adams and Trent is an example of one of the compromise works that resulted from the demand of the southerners for books less tinctured with northern prejudices.

[2] Cloud's Report, Nov., 1869 ; Hodgson's Report, 1871 ; Ku Klux Rept., Ala. Test , p. 426 ; Montgomery Conference, " Race Problems," p. 107.

the part of the best whites in public and private life, as a measure of self-defence as well as a duty and as justice, to do all that lay in their power to fit the negro for citizenship. Most of the newspapers were in favor of education to fit the negro for his changed condition. Now that he had to stand alone, education was necessary to keep him from stealing, from idleness, and from a return to barbarism; in some parts of the Black Belt there was a tendency to return to African customs. It was necessary to substitute the discipline of education for the discipline of slavery.[1] The Democratic party leaders were in favor of negro education, and General Clanton, who for years was the chairman of the executive committee, repeatedly made speeches in favor of it, and attended the sessions and examinations at the negro schools, often examining the classes himself. He and General John B. Gordon spoke in Montgomery at a public meeting and declared that it was the duty of the whites to educate the negro, whose good behavior during the war entitled him to it. Their remarks were cheered by the whites.[2] Colonel Jefferson Falkner, at a Baptist Association in Pike County, advised that the negro be educated by southern men and women. Pike was a white county, and while no objection was raised to Falkner's speech, several persons told him that if he thought southern women ought to teach negroes, he had better have his own daughters do it. Falkner replied that he was willing when their services were needed.[3] White people made destitute by the war or crippled soldiers were ready to engage in the instruction of negroes; and the *Montgomery Advertiser* and other papers took the ground that they should be employed, especially the disabled soldiers.[4] General Clanton stated that many Confederate soldiers and the widows of Confederate soldiers were teaching negro schools, that he had assisted them in securing positions. Such work, he said, was indorsed by most of the prominent people.[5]

The blacks in Selma signed an appeal to the city council for their own white people to teach them, and the churches made preparations to give instruction to the freedmen.[6] The Monroe County Agricul-

[1] See Ala. Test., p. 236 (General Clanton).
[2] Ku Klux Rept., p. 53; Ku Klux Rept., Ala. Test., pp. 234, 235.
[3] Ala. Test., p. 1123.
[4] *Montgomery Advertiser*, July 30, 1866; *Selma Times*, June 30, 1866.
[5] Ala. Test., p. 236.
[6] *Selma Times*, Dec. 30, 1865; *Gulf States Hist. Mag.*, Sept., 1902.

2 S

tural Association declared it to be the duty of the whites to teach the negro, and a committee was appointed to formulate a plan for negro schools.[1] Conecuh and Wilcox counties followed with similar declarations. A public meeting in Perry County, of such men as ex-Governor A. B. Moore and J. L. M. Curry, declared that sound policy and moral obligation required that prompt efforts be made to fit the negro for his changed political condition. His education must be encouraged. The teachers, white and black, were to be chosen with a careful regard to fitness. A committee was appointed to coöperate with the negroes in building schoolhouses and in procuring teachers, whom they assured of support.[2]

Besides the purely unselfish reasons, there were other reasons why the leading whites wanted the negro educated by southern teachers. It would be a step towards securing control over the negro race by the best native whites, who have always believed and will always believe that the negro should be controlled by them. The northern school-teachers did not have an influence for good upon the relations between the races, and thus caused the southern whites to be opposed to any education of the negro by strangers, as it was felt that to allow the negro to be educated by these people and their successors would have a permanent influence for evil.[3]

The whites generally aided the negroes in their community to build schoolhouses or schoolhouses and churches combined. Schoolhouses were in the majority of cases built by the patrons of the schools; if rented, the rent was deducted from the school money; the state made no appropriation for building. In Dallas County forty negro schoolhouses were built with the assistance of the whites. This was usually done in the Black Belt, but was less general in the white counties. In Montgomery the prominent citizens gave money to help build a negro "college"; some paid the tuition of negro children at schools where charges were made. White men were often members of the board of colored schools. All this was before the negro was seen to be hopelessly in the clutches of the northerners.[4]

In spite of the fact that for several years there were southern

[1] Trowbridge, "The South," p. 431.
[2] *Marion Commonwealth;* meeting held May 17, 1866.
[3] *Montgomery Advertiser*, July 24, 1867; Ala. Test., p. 236.
[4] *Montgomery Advertiser*, July 24, 1867; Ala. Test., pp. 236, 246.

JABEZ LAMAR MONROE CURRY.

whites who taught negroes, the schools were judged by the results of the teaching of the northerners. The Freedmen's Bureau brought discredit on negro education.[1] The work of the various aid societies was little better. The personnel of both, to a great extent, passed to the new system, Bureau and Association teachers becoming state teachers; and in the transfer the teachers tried to secure a better standing for themselves than the native teachers had. Many of the northern teachers were undoubtedly good people, but all were touched with fanaticism and considered the white people hopelessly bad and by nature and training. brutal and unjust to negroes. The negro teachers who were trained by them, both in the North and in the South, and who occupied most of the subordinate positions in the schools, had caught the spirit of the teaching. The native negro teacher, however, never quite equalled his white instructor in wrong-headedness. He persisted in seeing the actual state of affairs quite often. But the results of some of the educational work done during Reconstruction for the negro was to make many white people, especially the less friendly and the careless observers, believe that education in itself was a bad thing for the negroes. It became a proverb that "schooling ruins a negro," and among the ignorant and more prejudiced whites this opinion is still firmly held. Not all of the northern teachers were of good character, and the others suffered for the sins of these. Almost from the first the doors of the southern whites were closed against the northern teacher, not only on account of the character of some and the objectionable teachings of many, but because they generally insisted on being personally unpleasant; and, had all of them been above reproach in character and training, their opinions in regard to social questions, which they expressed on every occasion, would have resulted in total exclusion from white society. They really cared little, perhaps, but they had a great deal to say on the subject, and made much trouble on account of it.[2]

At first, when they wished it, some northern teachers were able to secure board with white families. After a few weeks such was not the case, and, except in the cities where the teachers could live to-

[1] See Ch. XI, Sec. 3.
[2] For specimen letters written to their homes, see the various reports of the Freedmen's Aid Society of the Methodist Church, and the reports of other aid societies.

gether, they were obliged to live with the negroes. This could produce only bad results. It at once caused them to be excluded from
all white society, and gained for them the contempt of their white
neighbors, at the same time losing them the support and even the
respect of the negroes. For the negro always insists that a white
person to be respected must live up to a certain standard; otherwise,
he may like, or fear, or despise, but never respect. Again, some of the
doubtful characters caused scandal by their manner of life among
the negroes, and in several instances male teachers were visited by
the Ku Klux Klan because of their irregular conduct with negro
women. One in Calhoun County was killed. Negro men who lived
with white women teachers were killed, and in some cases the
women were thrashed. Others were driven away.[1] But on the
whole there was little violence, the forces of social proscription at
length sufficing to drive out the obnoxious teachers.[2]

Much was said during Reconstruction days about the burning of
negro schoolhouses by the whites. There were several such cases,
but not as many as is supposed. In the records only one instance
can be found of a school building being burned simply from opposition to negro schools. As a rule the schoolhouses (and churches
also) were burned because they were the headquarters of the Union
League and the general meeting places for Radical politicians, or
because of the character of the teacher and the results of his or her
teachings. Regular instruction of the negro had been going on for
two years or more before the Ku Klux Klan began burning schoolhouses. When one was burned, the Radical leaders used the fact
with much effect among the negroes; and in several instances it was
practically certain that the Radical leaders, when the negroes were
wavering, fired a church or a schoolhouse in order to incense them
against the whites, who were charged with the deed. When a schoolhouse was burned, the negroes were invariably assisted to rebuild by
the respectable whites. The burnings were condemned by all respect-

---

[1] The best-known instances of the killing of such negroes were in Tuscaloosa and
Chambers counties. The Ku Klux Report gives only about half a dozen cases of
outrages on teachers. See Ala. Test., pp. 52, 54, 67, 71, 140, 252, 755, 1047, 1140, 1853.
Cloud in his report made no mention of violence to teachers, nor did the governor.
Lakin said a great deal about it, but gave no instances that were not of the well-known
few. There was much less violence than is generally supposed, even in the South.

[2] Ala. Test., p. 252.

able persons, and also by the party leaders on account of the bad effect on political questions.[1]

Some teachers of negro schools fleeced their black pupils and their parents unmercifully. Teachers of private schools collected tuition in advance and then left. In Montgomery, a teacher in the Swayne school notified his pupils that they must bring him fifty cents each by a certain day, and that he, in return, would give to each a photograph of himself.[2] In Eutaw, Greene County, the Rev. J. B. F. Hill, a Northern Methodist preacher who had been expelled from the Southern Methodist Church, taught a negro school and taxed his forty little scholars twenty-five cents each to purchase a forty-cent water bucket.[3]

In the cities where there were several negro schools, it was found difficult at first to keep the small negro in attendance in the same school. A little negro would attend a school until he discovered that he did not like the teacher or the school, and then he would go to another. A rule was made against such impromptu transfers, and then the small boy changed his name when he decided to try another school. Finally, the teacher was required to ask the other children the newcomer's name before he was admitted.[4]

The negro children were poorly supplied with books, and what few they did have they promptly lost or tore up to get the pictures.

[1] See Ala. Test., pp. 236, 1889 ; Somers, " Southern States," p. 169 ; Report of the Joint Committee on Outrages, 1868. In Crenshaw, Butler, and Chambers counties some schools existed for a year or more until teachers of bad character were elected. Then the neighborhood roughs burned the school buildings. Neither Cloud nor any other official reported cases of such burnings. The legislative committee could discover but two, and in both instances the women teachers were of bad character. In the records can be found only seventeen reports of burnings, and several of these were evidently reports of the same instance ; few were specific. Lakin, who spent several years in travelling over north Alabama, and who was much addicted to fabrication and exaggeration, made a vague report of " the ruins of a dozen " schoolhouses. (Ala. Test., pp. 140, 141.) There may have been more than half a dozen burnings in north Alabama, but there is no evidence that such was the case. The majority of the reports originated outside the state through pure malice. The houses burned were principally in the white counties and were, as Lakin reports, slight affairs costing from $25 to $75. It was so evident that some of the fires were caused by the carelessness of travellers and hunters who camped in them at night, that the legislature passed a law forbidding that practice. See Acts of Ala., p. 187. About as many schoolhouses for whites were destroyed as for blacks. Some were fired by negroes for revenge, others were burned by accident.

[2] *Weekly Mail*, Aug. 18, 1869.   [3] *Demopolis New Era*, April 1, 1868.

[4] Hodgson's Report, Nov. 11, 1871.

The attendance was very irregular. For a few days there would be a great many scholars and perhaps after that almost none, for the parents were willing to send their children when there was no work for them to do, but as soon as cotton needed chopping or picking they would stop them and put them to work.[1] If the negroes suspected that the trustees, who were (later) Democrats, had appointed a Democratic teacher, they would not send their children to school to him, and in this they were upheld by their new leaders.[2]

When the public funds were exhausted, the majority of the white schools continued as pay schools, but the negro schools closed at once, for after 1868 the interest of the negro in education was no longer strong enough to induce him to pay for it. The education given the negro during this period was little suited to prepare him for the practical duties of life. The New England system was transplanted to the South, and the young negroes were forced even more than the white children. As soon as a little progress was made, the pupils were promoted into the culture studies of the whites. Those who learned anything at all had, in turn, to teach what they had learned; their education would help them very little in everyday life.[3] Negro education did not result in better relations between the races. The northern teacher believed in the utter sinfulness of slavery and in all the stories told of the cruelties then practised. The *Advertiser* gave as one reason why the southern whites should teach negro schools, that northern teachers caused trouble by using books and tracts with illustrations of slavery and stories about the persecution and cruelties of the whites against the blacks.[4] General Clanton stated that in the school in which he had often attended the exercises and examined the classes, and where he had paid the tuition of negro children, the teachers ceased to ask him to make visits; that the school-books had "Radical pictures" of the persecuted slaves and the freedman; that Radical speeches were made by the scholars, reciting the wrongs done the negro race; finally, that the school was a political nursery of race

[1] Hodgson's Report, Nov. 15, 1871.   [2] Hodgson's Report, Nov. 15, 1871.

[3] For opinions in regard to the value of the early education among the negroes, see Washington's "Future of the American Negro" and "Up from Slavery"; W. H. Thomas's "American Negro"; P. A. Bruce's "Plantation Negro as a Freeman"; J. L. M. Curry, in Montgomery Conference.

[4] *Montgomery Advertiser*, July 24, 1867.

prejudice, and that where the negroes were greatly in excess of the whites, it was a serious matter.[1] He also said that the teachers from the North were responsible for the prejudice of the whites against negro schools. The native whites soon refused to teach, and if they had wished to do so, they probably could have gotten no pupils. The primary education of the negro was left to the northern teachers and to incompetent negroes ; higher education was altogether under the control of the alien. It was most unfortunate in every way, he added, that the southern white had had no part in the education of the negro.[2] The higher education of the negroes in the state continued to be directed by northerners. Washington and Councill have done much toward changing the nature of the education given the negro; they have also educated many whites from opposition to friendliness to negro schools.

The Failure of the Educational System

In 1870 Cloud was a candidate for reëlection, but was defeated by Colonel Joseph Hodgson, the Democratic candidate.[3] When

[1] Ala. Test., p. 236.

[2] Ku Klux Rept., Ala. Test. Dr. J. L. M. Curry, who, in 1865, began his work for the education of the negro, has thus expressed his opinion of the early attempts to educate the blacks: "The education was unsettling, demoralizing, pandered to a wild frenzy for schooling as the quick method of reversing social and political conditions. Nothing could have been better devised for deluding the poor negro, and making him the tool, the slave, of corrupt taskmasters. . . . With deliberate purpose to subject the southern states to negro domination and secure the states permanently for partisan ends, the education adopted was contrary to common sense, to human experience, to all noble purposes. The aptitude and capabilities and needs of the negro were wholly disregarded. Especial stress was laid on classics and liberal culture to bring the race *per saltum* to the same plane with their former masters, and realize the theory of social and political equality. Colleges and universities, established and conducted by the Freedmen's Bureau and northern churches and societies, sprang up like mushrooms, and the teachers, ignorant and fanatical, without self-poise, proceeded to make all possible mischief." Montgomery Conference, "Race Problems," p. 109. See also the papers of Rev. D. Clay Lilly and Dr. P. B. Barringer in Montgomery Conference, "Race Problems," p. 130; William H. Baldwin and Dr. Curry in Second Capon Springs Conference; Barringer, "The American Negro: His Past and Future"; Barringer, W. T. Harris, and J. D. Dreher in Proceedings Southern Education Association, 1900; Haygood, "Pleas for Progress" and "Our Brother in Black"; Abbott, "Rights of Man," pp. 225–226.

[3] The United States Commissioner of Education, in his report for that year, made before the elections, stated that in educational matters the state of Alabama was about

Hodgson appeared as president of the Board, Cloud refused to yield on the ground that Hodgson was not eligible to the office, having once challenged a man to a duel. The Board, however, refused to recognize Cloud, and he was obliged to retire.[1]

The first year of the reform administration was a successful one in spite of the fact that the state was bankrupt and the treasury ceased to make cash payments to county superintendents early in 1872.[2] The second year was a fair one, although the treasury could not pay the teachers, for the Radical senate refused to make the appropriations for which their own constitution provided. However, the attendance of both whites and blacks increased, notwithstanding the fact that the United States Commissioner of Education reported that Alabama had retrograded in educational matters.[3] The school officials elected in 1870 were much superior to their predecessors in every way. A state teachers' association was organized, and institutes were frequently held. Four normal schools were established for black teachers and four for whites. Private assistance for public schools was now sought and obtained, and hundreds of the schools continued after the public money was exhausted.[4]

Hodgson did valuable service to his party and to the state in exposing the corrupt and irregular practices of the preceding administration. His own administration was much more

to take a " backward step," meaning that it was about to become Democratic. Report, 1870, p. 15. Later he made similar remarks, much to the disgust of Hodgson, who was an enthusiast in educational matters.

[1] Journal of the Board of Education and Regents, 1870. Dr. O. D. Smith, who was one of the newly elected Democratic members of the Board, says that Cloud refused to inform the Board of the contents of Hodgson's communications. Thereupon Hodgson addressed one to the Board directly and not to Cloud. When it came in through the mail, Cloud took possession of it, but Dr. Smith, who ,was on the lookout, called his attention to the fact that it was addressed to the Board and reminded him of the penalties for tampering with the mail of another person. The secretary read Hodgson's communication, and the Board was then free to act. The Democratic members convinced the Radicals that if Cloud continued in office they would not be able to draw their *per diem*, so Cloud was compelled to vacate at once. When he left he had his buggy brought to the door, and into it he loaded all the government coal that was in his office and carried it away.

[2] Hodgson's Report, 1872.

[3] See Hodgson's Report, 1871.

[4] Hodgson's Report, 1871 ; Report of the Commissioner of Education, 1876, p. 7 ; Journal of the Board of Education and Regents, 1871 ; Acts of the Board of Education, pamphlet.

economical than that of his predecessor, as the following figures will show:—

	1870	1871	DECREASE
Salaries of county superintendents . .	$57,776.50	$34,259.50	$23,517.00
Expenses of county superintendents . .	21,202.86	4,752.00	16,450.86
Expenses of disbursement . . .	78,979.36	39,009.50	39,969.86
Clerical expenses (at Montgomery) . .	3,544.46	1,978.71	1,565.75
Cost of administration	86,123.82	44,588.21	41,535.61[1]

In the fall of 1872, owing to the operation of the Enforcement Acts, the elections went against the Democrats. The Radicals filled all the offices, and Joseph H. Speed was elected Superintendent of Public Instruction.[2] Speed was not wholly unfitted for the position, and did the best he could under the circumstances. But nowhere in the Radical administration did he find any sympathy with his department, not even a disposition to comply with the direct provisions of the constitution in regard to school funds. So low had the credit of the state fallen that the administration could no longer sell the state bonds to raise money. The taxes were the only resources, and the office-holding adventurers, feeling that never again could they have an opportunity at the spoils, could spare none of the money for schools. Practically all of the negro schools and many of the white ones were forced to close, and the teachers, when paid at all by the state, were paid in depreciated state obligations.

The constitution required that one-fifth of all state revenue in addition to certain other funds be appropriated for the use of schools. Yet year by year an increasing amount was diverted to other uses. The poll tax and the insurance tax were used for other purposes. At the end of 1869, $187,872.49, which should have been appropriated for schools, had been diverted. In 1872, $330,036.93 was lost to

---

[1] And this was the case notwithstanding the fact that the county superintendents were now allowed mileage at the rate of eight cents a mile in order to get them to come to Montgomery for their money and thus to decrease the chances of corrupt practices of the attorneys. Hodgson complained that many old claims which should have been settled by Cloud were presented during his administration.

[2] Speed was a southern Radical. During the war he was a state salt agent at the salt works in Virginia. He was a member of the Board of Education from 1870 to 1872, and was far above the average Radical office-holder in both character and ability.

the schools by failure to appropriate, and in 1873, $456,138.47 was lost in the same way. By the end of 1873 the shortage was $1,260,511.92, and a year later it was nearly two million dollars. During 1873 and 1874 schools were taught only where there were local funds to support them. The carpet-bag system had failed completely.[1]

The new constitution made by the Democrats in 1875 abolished the Board of Education, and returned to the ante-bellum system. Separate schools were ordered; the administrative expenses could not amount to more than 4 per cent of the school fund;[2] no money was to be paid to any denominational or private school;[3] the constitutional provision of one-fifth of the state revenue for school use was abolished;[4] and the legislature was ordered to appropriate to schools at least $100,000 a year besides the poll taxes, license taxes, and the income from trust funds. The schools began to improve at once, and the net income was never again as small as under the carpet-bag régime.

Neither of the Reconstruction superintendents, Cloud or Speed, furnished full statistics of the schools. It appears that the average enrolment of students under Cloud was, in 1870, 35,963 whites and

[1] Report of the Commissioner of Education, 1873, 1874, 1876; Speed's Report, 1873. Speed was ill much of the time, and his bookkeeping was little better than Cloud's. Two clerks, who, a committee of investigation stated, were distinguished by a "total want of capacity and want of integrity," managed the department with "such a want of system . . . as most necessarily kept it involved in inextricable confusion." Money was received and not entered on the books. A sum of money in coin was received in June, 1873, and six months later was paid into the treasury in depreciated paper. Vouchers were stolen and used again. Bradshaw, a county superintendent, died, leaving a shortage of $10,019.06 in his accounts. A large number of vouchers were abstracted from the office of Speed by some one and used again by Bradshaw's administrator, who was no other than Dr. N. B. Cloud, who made a settlement with Speed's clerks, and when the shortage was thus made good, the administrator still had many vouchers to spare. This seems to have been Cloud's last raid on the treasury. *Montgomery Advertiser*, Dec. 18, 1873; Report of the Joint Committee on Irregularities in the Department of Education, 1873.

[2] Under the Reconstruction administrative expenses amounted to 16 per cent, and even more.

[3] The experiences with the American Missionary Association, etc., made this provision necessary.

[4] The United States Commissioner of Education gave a disapproving account of these changes. It was exchanging "a certainty for an uncertainty," he said. Speed had not found it a "certainty" by any means.

16,097 blacks; under his Democratic successor the average enrolment, in spite of lack of appropriations, was 66,358 whites and 41,308 blacks in 1871, and 61,942 whites and 41,673 blacks in 1872. Speed evidently kept no records of attendance. In 1875, after the Democrats came into power, the attendance was 91,202 whites and 54,595 blacks. The average number of days taught in a year under Cloud was 49 days in white schools and the same in black; under Hodgson the average length of term was 68.5 days and 64.33 days respectively. Theoretically the salaries of teachers under Cloud should have been about $75 per month, but they received increasingly less each year as the legislature refused to appropriate the school money. The following table will show what the school funds should have been, as provided for by the constitution; the sums actually received were smaller each successive year. In no case was the appropriation as great as in the year 1858, nor was the attendance of black and white together much larger in any year than the attendance of whites alone in 1858 or 1859.

SCHOOL FUND, 1868–1875

1868	
1869	$524,621.68 [1]
1870	500,409.18 [2]
1871	581,389.29 [3]
1872	604,978.50 [4]
1873	524,452.40 [5]
1874	474,346.52 [6]
1875	565,042.94 [7]

[1] Plus the poll tax, which was not appropriated as required by the constitution, but diverted to other uses.

[2] There was a shortage of $187,872.49, diverted to other uses.

[3] Shortage unknown; teachers were paid in depreciated state obligations.

[4] Shortage was $330,036.93.

[5] Only $68,313.93 was paid, the rest diverted; shortage now was $1,260,511.92.

[6] None was paid, all diverted; shortage nearly two millions.

[7] All was paid (by Democrats, who were now in power).

CHAPTER XX

RECONSTRUCTION IN THE CHURCHES

SEC. 1. THE "DISINTEGRATION AND ABSORPTION" POLICY AND ITS FAILURE

THE close of the war found the southern church organizations in a more or less demoralized condition. Their property was destroyed, their buildings were burned or badly in need of repair, and the church treasuries were empty. It was doubtful whether some of them could survive the terrible exhaustion that followed the war. The northern churches, "coming down to divide the spoils," acted upon the principle that the question of separate churches had been settled by the war along with that of state sovereignty, and that it was now the right and the duty of the northern churches to reconstruct the churches in the South. So preparations were made to "disintegrate and absorb" the "schismatical" southern religious bodies.[1]

The Methodists

In 1864 the Northern Methodist Church declared the South a proper field for mission work, and made preparations to enter it. None were to be admitted to membership in the church who were slaveholders or who were "tainted with treason."[2] In 1865 the bishops of the northern organization resolved that "we will occupy so far as practicable those fields in the southern states which may be open to us . . . for black and white alike."[3] The General Missionary Committee of the northern church divided the South into departments for missionary work, and Alabama was in the Middle Department. Bishop Clark of Ohio was sent (1886) to take charge of the Georgia and Alabama Mission District. The declared pur-

---

[1] McTyeire, "A History of Methodism," p. 670; Smith, "Life and Times of George F. Pierce"; *Southern Review*, April, 1872.

[2] Buckley, "History of Methodism in the United States," pp. 516, 517.

[3] Matlack, "Anti-Slavery Struggle and Triumph in the Methodist Episcopal Church," p. 339; Smith, "Life and Times of George F. Pierce," p. 530.

pose of this mission work was to "disintegrate and absorb" the southern church, the organization of which was generally believed to have been destroyed by the war.[1]

In August, 1865, three Southern Methodist bishops met at Columbus, Georgia, to repair the shattered organization of the church and to infuse new life into it. They stated that the questions of 1844 were not settled by the war; that, "A large portion of the Northern Methodists has become incurably radical. . . . They have incorporated social dogmas and political tests into their church creeds." They condemned the northern church for its action during the war in taking possession of southern church property against the wishes of the people and retaining it as their own after the war, and for its more recent attempts to destroy the southern church.[2]

In the confusion following the war, before the church administration was again in working order, the Protestant Episcopal Church, especially the northern section, attempted to secure the Southern Methodists. Some Methodists wanted to go over in a body to the Episcopalians. The great majority, however, were strongly opposed to such action, and the attempt only caused more ill feeling against the North.[3]

At the time there was a belief among the Northern Methodists that in 1845 thousands of members had been carried against their will into the southern church, and that they would now gladly seize the opportunity to join the northern body, which claimed to be the only Methodist Episcopal Church. Those thousands proved to be as disappointing as the "southern loyalists" had been, both in character and in numbers. The greatest gains were among the negroes, and to the negroes the few whites secured were intensely hostile. In 1866, A. S. Lakin was sent to Alabama to organize the Northern Methodist Church.[4] After two years' work the Alabama Conference

[1] Annual Cyclopædia (1865), p. 552; Caldwell, "Reconstruction of Church and State in Georgia" (pamphlet).

[2] Annual Cyclopædia (1865), p. 552.

[3] "The schismatical plans of the Northern Methodists and the subtle proselytism of the Episcopalians" (Pierce). See Smith, "Life and Times of George F. Pierce," pp. 491, 499, 505, 530; West, "History of Methodism in Alabama," p. 717; McTyeire, "A History of Methodism," p. 673.

[4] A Federal official in north Alabama who had known of Lakin in the North testified that he had had a bad reputation in New York and in Illinois and had been sent

was organized, with 9431 members, black and white.[1] In 1871, Lakin reported 15,000 members, black and white.[2] The whites were from the "loyal" element of the population. There was great opposition by the white people to the establishment of the northern church. Lakin and his associates excited the negroes against the whites and kept both races in a continual state of irritation. Governor Lindsay stated before the Ku Klux Committee that in his opinion the people bore with Lakin and his church with a remarkable degree of patience; that Lakin encouraged the negroes to force themselves into congregations where they did not belong and to obstruct the services; and that they also made attempts to get control of church property belonging to the southern churches.[3] No progress was made among the whites, except in the white counties among the hills of north Alabama and in the pine barrens of the southeast. The congregations were small and were served by missionaries. Lakin and his assistants had a political as well as a religious mission — General Clanton said that they were "emissaries of Christ and of the Radical party." They claimed, nevertheless, that they never talked politics in the pulpit. Lakin once preached in Blountsville, and when he opened the doors of the church to new members, he said that there was no northern church, no southern church, there was only the Methodist Episcopal Church.[4] But every member of this

South as a means of discipline. See Ku Klux Rept., Ala. Test., p. 619 (L. W. Day, United States Commissioner). Governor Lindsay said that Lakin was a shrewd, cunning, strong-willed man, given to exaggeration and lying, — one who had a "jaundiced eye," "a magnifying eye," and who among the blacks was a power for evil. Ala. Test., p. 180.

[1] N. Y. Herald, May 10, 1868; Buckley, "History of Methodism," Vol. II, p. 191.

[2] In 1871, Lakin stated that of his 15,000 members, three-fourths were whites of the poorer classes; that there were under his charge 6 presiding elders' districts with 70 circuits and stations, and 70 ministers and 150 local preachers; and that he had been assisted in securing the "loyal" element by several ministers who had been expelled by the Southern Methodists during the war as traitors. Ala. Test., pp. 124, 130. Governor Lindsay stated that some of the whites of Lakin's church were to be found in the counties of Walker, Winston, and Blount; that there were few such white congregations, and that some of these afterward severed their connection with the northern church, and by 1872 there were only two or three in the state. Lakin worked among the negro population almost entirely, and his statement that three-fourths of his members were whites was not correct. See Ala. Test., pp. 180, 208.

[3] Ku Klux Rept., Ala. Test., pp. 111, 112, 124, 180, 623, 957. Lakin secured all church property formerly used by the southern church for negro congregations.

[4] Lakin never acknowledged the present existence of the southern church.

church, he added, must be loyal, and therefore no secessionist could join. He said that he had been ordered by his conference not to receive "disloyal" men into the church.[1]

The political activity of these missionaries resulted in visits from the Ku Klux Klan. Some of the most violent ones were whipped or were warned to moderate their sermons. Political camp-meetings were sometimes broken up, and two or three church buildings used as Radical headquarters were burned.[2] Every Northern Methodist was a Republican; and to-day in some sections of the state the Northern Methodists are known as "Republican" Methodists, as distinguished from "Democratic" or Southern Methodists.

The Baptists

The organization of the Baptist church into separate congregations saved it from much of the annoyance suffered by such churches as the Methodist and the Episcopal, with their more elaborate systems of government. Yet in north Alabama, there was trouble when the negro members were encouraged by political and ecclesiastical emissaries to assert their rights under the democratic form of government by taking part in all church affairs, in the election of pastors and other officers. Often there were more negro members than white, and under the guidance of a missionary from the North these could elect their own candidate for pastor, regardless of the wishes of the whites and of the character of the would-be pastor. This danger, however, was soon avoided by the organization of separate negro congregations.[3]

The Southern Baptist Convention, organized in 1845, continued its separate existence. The northern Baptists demanded, as a pre-

---

[1] Ala. Test., pp. 238, 758.

[2] One of Lakin's relations was that while he was conducting a great revival meeting among the hills of north Alabama, Governor Smith and other prominent and sinful scalawag politicians were under conviction and were about to become converted. But in came the Klan and the congregation scattered. Smith and the others were so angry and frightened that their good feelings were dissipated, and the devil reëntered them, so that he (Lakin) was never able to get a hold on them again. Consequently, the Klan was responsible for the souls lost that night. Lakin told a dozen or more marvellous stories of his hairbreadth escapes from death by assassination, — enough, if true, to ruin the reputation of north Alabama men for marksmanship.

[3] Shackleford, "History of the Muscle Shoals Baptist Association," p. 84.

requisite to coöperation and fellowship, a profession of loyalty to the government. During 1865 the southern associations expressed themselves in favor of continuing the former separate societies, and severely censured the northern Baptists for their action in obtaining authority from the Federal government to take possession of southern church property against the wishes of the owners and trustees, and for trying to organize independent churches within the bounds of southern associations. They were not in favor of fraternal relations with the northern Baptist societies.[1]

The Presbyterians

In May, 1865, the Presbyterian General Assembly (New School) voted to place on probation the southern ministers of the United Synod South who had supported the Confederacy.[2] Few, if any, offered themselves for probation, while as a body the United Synod joined the Southern Presbyterians (Old School). The General Assembly (O. S.) of the northern church in 1865 stigmatized "secession as a crime and the withdrawal of the southern churches as a schism." The South, the Assembly decided, was to be treated as a missionary field, and loyal ministers to be employed without presbyterial recommendation. Southern ministers and members were offered restoration if they would apply for it, and submit to certain tests, namely, proof of loyalty or a profession of repentance for disloyalty to the government, and a repudiation of former opinions concerning slavery.[3] Naturally this policy was not very successful in reconstructing their organization in the South. The General Assembly (O. S.) of the Presbyterian Church in the South met in the fall of 1865 at Macon, Georgia, and warned the churches against the efforts of the northern Presbyterians to sow seeds of dissension and strife in their congregations.[4] A union was formed with the United Synod South (N. S.), and the "Presbyterian Church in the United States," popularly known as the Southern

---

[1] Annual Cyclopædia (1865), p. 106. In 1905 there is a much better spirit, and the churches of the two sections are on good terms, though not united.

[2] Annual Cyclopædia (1865), p. 705. See p. 23 and Ch. IV, Sec. 7, above.

[3] Thompson, "History of the Presbyterian Churches," p. 167.

[4] Annual Cyclopædia (1865), p. 706.

Presbyterian Church, was formed. To this acceded in 1867 the Associate Reformed Church of Alabama.[1]

The Episcopal Church in the United States during the war had held consistently to the same theory in regard to the withdrawal of the southern dioceses that the Washington administration held in regard to the secession of the southern states. There was no recognition of a withdrawal, nor of a southern organization. The Confederate church was called a schismatic body, and its actions considered as illegal. The roll in the General Convention was called as usual, beginning with Alabama.[2] But after the war a generous policy of conciliation was pursued; the southern churchmen were asked to come back; no tests or conditions were imposed; the House of Bishops of the northern church upheld Wilmer in his trouble with the military authorities. The acts of the southern church during the war were recognized and accepted as valid by the northern church. Such a policy easily resulted in reunion.

The attempt at Reconstruction in the churches had practically failed. Only the Episcopal Church, one of the weakest in numbers, had reunited.[3] The others seemed farther apart than ever.

The other denominations had recognized the legal division of their churches before the war. Now they acted on the principle that territory conquered for the United States was also conquered for the northern churches. Southern ministers and members were asked to submit to degrading conditions in order to be restored to good standing. They must repudiate their former opinions, and renouncing their sins, ask for pardon and restoration. Naturally no reunion resulted.

SEC. 2. THE CHURCHES AND THE NEGRO DURING RECONSTRUCTION

At the end of the war nearly every congregation had black members as well as white, the blacks often being the more numerous. With the changed conditions, the various denominations felt it necessary to make declarations of policy in regard to the former slaves.

---

[1] Carroll, " Religious Forces," p. 281 ; Thompson, " History of the Presbyterian Churches," pp. 163, 171 ; Johnson, " History of the Southern Presbyterian Churches," pp. 333, 339.

[2] Perry, p. 328 *et seq.*

[3] Later the northern congregations of the Methodist Protestant Church rejoined the main body, which was southern.

2 T

General Swayne, Assistant Commissioner of the Freedmen's Bureau in Alabama, in his report for 1866, stated that at an early date the several denominations expressed themselves as being strongly in favor of the education of the negro. "The principal argument," he said, "was an appeal to sectional and sectarian prejudice, lest, the work being inevitable, the influence which must come from it be realized by others; but it is believed that this was the shield and weapon which men of unselfish principle found necessary at first." [1]

The Baptists and the Negroes

The Alabama Baptist Convention, in 1865, passed the following resolution in regard to the relations between the white and black members : —

"*Resolved,* That the changed civil status of our late slaves does not necessitate any change in their relations to our churches; and while we recognize their right to withdraw from our churches and form organizations of their own, we nevertheless believe that their highest good will be subserved by their retaining their present relation to those who know them, who love them, and who will labor for the promotion of their welfare."

The Convention also ordered renewed exertions in the work among the negroes by means of lectures, private instruction, and Sunday-schools.[2] In 1866 the North Alabama Baptist Association directed that provision be made for the religious welfare of the negroes and for their education in the common schools. The negroes were to be allowed to choose their own pastors and teachers from among the whites.[3] But soon the results of the work of the northern missionaries and political emissaries were seen in the separation of the two races in religious matters. The negroes were taught that the whites were their enemies, and that they must have their own separate churches. They were encouraged to assert their rights by obstructing in all the affairs of the churches, and in the north Alabama Baptist churches, where they were in the majority, there was danger

---

[1] Sen. Ex. Doc., No. 6, 39th Cong., 2d Sess.

[2] Riley, " History of the Baptists in Alabama," p. 310 ; *Montgomery Advertiser*, Oct. 15, 1865; *N. Y. Times,* Oct. 22, 1865 ; George Brewer, "History of the Central Association," pp. 46, 49.

[3] *Huntsville Advocate,* May 16, 1866.

that they would take advantage of the democratic system of the church government and, prompted by emissaries from the North, control the administration. They were, therefore, assisted by the whites to form separate congregations and associations.[1]

The principal work of the northern Baptists in central and south Alabama was to separate the blacks into independent churches, and the second Colored Baptist Convention in the United States was organized in Alabama in 1867. The free form of government of this church attracted both ministers and members. In 1868 Bethel Association (white) reported that a large number of the negroes desired no religious instruction from the whites, although they were in great need of it, and that this opposition was caused by ignorance and prejudice. But, the report stated, there should be no relaxation in the effort to impart to them a knowledge of the Gospel; that the first duty of the church was to instruct the ignorant and superstitious at home before sending missionaries to the far-off heathen; that all self-constituted negro preachers who claimed personal interviews with God and personal instruction from Him should be discouraged, and only the best men selected as pastors. Advice and assistance were now given to the negro congregations, which were organized into associations as soon as possible. In 1872 three negro churches with a white pastor applied for admission to Bethel Association. But it was thought best to maintain separate associations.[2] For years the white Baptists of Alabama exercised a watchful care over the colored Baptists, whom they assisted in the work of organizing congregations and associations, and in the erection of schoolhouses and churches. Church and school buildings destroyed by the Ku

[1] Shackleford, "History of the Muscle Shoals Baptist Association," p. 84.

The Radical missionaries, in order to further their own plans, encouraged the negroes to assert their equality by forcing themselves into the congregations of the various denominations. Governor Lindsay related an incident of a negro woman who went alone into a white church, selected a good pew, and calmly appropriated it. No one molested her, of course. Ku Klux Rept., Ala. Test., p. 208.

America Trammell, a negro preacher of east Alabama, before the war and afterward as late as 1870 preached to mixed congregations of blacks and whites. A part of the church building was set apart for the whites and a part for the blacks. Later he became affected by the work of the missionaries, and in 1871 began to preach that "Christ never died for the southern people at all ; that he died only for the northern people." A white woman teacher lived in his house, and he was killed by the Ku Klux Klan. Ku Klux Rept., Ala. Test., p. 1119.

[2] Ball, "History of Clarke County," pp. 591, 630 ; Statistics of Churches, p. 171.

Klux Klan were rebuilt by the whites, even when the colored congregation was only moderately well behaved. The whites in Montgomery contributed to build the first negro Baptist church in that city, and a white minister preached the sermon when the church was dedicated and turned over to the blacks. A number of white ladies were present at the services.[1] For fifteen years Dr. I. T. Tichenor was pastor of the First Baptist Church in Montgomery. During that time he baptized over 500 negroes into its fellowship. At the end of the war there were 300 white and 600 negro members. Dr. Tichenor tells the story of the separation as follows: "When a separation of the two bodies was deemed desirable, it was done by the colored brethren, in conference assembled, passing a resolution, couched in the kindliest terms, suggesting the wisdom of the division, and asking the concurrence of the white church in such action. The white church cordially approved the movement, and the two bodies united in erecting a suitable house of worship for the colored brethren. Until it was finished they continued to occupy jointly with the white brethren their house of worship, as they had done previous to this action. The new house was paid for in large measure by the white members of the church and individuals in the community. As soon as it was completed the colored church moved into it with its organization all perfected, their pastor, board of deacons, committees of all sorts; and the whole machinery of church life went into action without a jar. Similar things occurred in all the states of the South."[2]

The old plantation preachers were ordained and others called and regularly ordained to the ministry by the whites. But good negro preachers were overwhelmed by an influx of "self-called" pastors who were often incompetent and often immoral. At last the whites seem to have given up as hopeless their work for the negroes. In 1885 an urgent appeal from the Colored Baptist Convention for advice and assistance met with no response from the white convention. Politics and prejudice, imprudent and immoral leaders, had completed the work of separation. Still something was done by the Home Mission Board towards instructing negro preachers and deacons, and in 1895 this Board and the Home Mission Board of the northern Baptists agreed to coöperate and aid such negro con-

[1] Ku Klux Rept., Ala. Test., pp. 236, 1067.
[2] "The Work of the Southern Baptists among the Negroes" (pamphlet).

ventions as might desire it. But the Alabama negro convention has not yet asked for assistance.[1]

The Presbyterians and the Negroes

In 1869, encouraged by the white members, the negro members of the Cumberland Presbyterian Church in Tennessee and north Alabama asked for and received separate organization and were henceforth known as the African Cumberland Presbyterian Church.[2]

It is this division of the Cumberland Presbyterians that is now (1905) hindering somewhat the union of the Cumberland Presbyterian with the Northern Presbyterian organization. The blacks demanded the separation of the races; the whites now demand that it be continued.

Various branches of the Northern Presbyterian organizations worked in Alabama among the negroes. The principal result of their work was the separation of the blacks into independent churches. The Southern Presbyterian Church (Presbyterian Church in the United States) made earnest efforts for the negro after the war, and with some success. The Institute at Tuscaloosa for the education of colored Presbyterian ministers is now the only school in the South for negroes which is conducted entirely by southern white teachers.[3] The work of the Presbyterians among the negroes has continued to the present day, though in 1898 a movement was started to separate the blacks of the Southern Presbyterian Church into an independent church. This movement was not successful, as not a majority of the negro preachers desired separation. But the number of colored Presbyterians has always been small.[4]

[1] See the *Southern Baptist Convention Advanced Quarterly*, p. 30, "Missionary Lesson, The Negroes," March 29, 1903, which is a most interesting, artless, southern lesson. The northern Baptists also have a mission lesson on the negroes which is distinctly of the abolitionist spirit. The average student will get about the same amount of prepared information from each. See "Home Mission Lesson No. 3, The Negroes."

[2] Foster, "Sketch of History of the Cumberland Presbyterian Church," p. 300; Carroll, "Religious Forces," p. 294; Thompson, "History of the Presbyterian Churches," p. 193.

[3] Thompson, "History of the Presbyterian Churches," p. 193; Scouller, "History of the United Presbyterian Church of North America," p. 246.

[4] Montgomery Conference, "Race Problems," p. 114.

The Roman Catholics

The Roman Catholic Church did much work among the negroes in the cities and at first with a fair degree of success. It was strongly opposed by all Protestant denominations, both northern and southern, and especially by the Northern Methodist Church. It seemed to be dreadful news to the Methodists when it was reported that the Catholic Church was about to open fifteen schools in Alabama for the negro, where free board and tuition would be given.[1] The American Missionary Association, supported in Alabama mainly by money from the Freedmen's Bureau, used its influence among the negroes against the Catholic Church, which, the Association stated in a report, "was making extraordinary efforts to enshroud forever this class of the unfortunate race in Popish superstition and darkness."[2]

But the Catholic Church had no place for the negro preacher of little education and less character who desired to hold a high position in the negro church. There was better prospect for promotion in the Baptist and Methodist churches, and to those churches went the would-be negro preacher and, through his influence, the majority of his people.[3]

The Episcopalians

The Protestant Episcopal Church did nearly all of its work among the negroes in the cities and among the negroes on the large plantations of the Black Belt. This church offered little more hope of advancement to the average negro preacher than the Roman Catholic, and the hostility of the military authorities to this church in 1865 and 1866 and the efforts of the missionaries and politicians caused a loss of most of the negro members that it had. In 1866 the laity of the State Convention seemed rather unenthusiastic in regard to work among the negroes, and left it to be managed by the bishop and clergy. The General Convention established the "Freedmen's Commission" to assist in the work, which was not to be under the jurisdiction of the bishop. Bishop Wilmer stated that he was un-

---

[1] Eighth Annual Report of the Freedmen's Aid Society.

[2] House Rept., No. 121, 41st Cong., 2d Sess.

[3] See " Race Problems," p. 139, for a statement of the work now being done among the negroes in Alabama by the Catholic Church.

willing to accept this "schism-breeding proposition," but would be glad of assistance which would be under his direction as bishop. No such aid was forthcoming. In 1867 only two congregations of negroes were left, one in Mobile and one in Marengo County. A few solitary blacks were to be found in the white congregations, and during Reconstruction these suffered real martyrdom on account of their loyalty to their old churches. They were ostracized by the other negroes, were called heathen and traitors, and were left alone in sickness and death. Under such treatment, the majority of the negro members were forced to withdraw from the Episcopal churches.[1]

The Methodists and the Negroes

In 1861 the Methodist Episcopal Church South had more than 200,000 colored members and 180,000 children under instruction. One year after the surrender of Lee only 78,000 remained.[2] The Montgomery Conference, in November, 1865, decided that there was no necessity for a change in the church relations of white and black; that in the church there should be no distinction on account of color and race; and that the negro had special claims on the whites. Presiding elders and preachers were directed to do all that lay in their power for the colored congregations, and establish Sunday-schools and day schools for them when practicable.[3] The Methodist Protestants announced a similar policy.[4] General Swayne of the Freedmen's Bureau reported that he received much assistance toward negro education from the Southern Methodist Church, and especially from Reverend H. N. McTyeire (afterwards bishop).[5]

The Southern Methodist congregations lost their negro members from the same causes that brought about the separation of the races in other churches. The negroes were told by their new leaders that for their safety they must consider the southerners as their natural

---

[1] Whitaker, "The Church in Alabama," pp. 193, 205, 206–212. The work of the Episcopal Church among the negroes is more promising in later years. See "Race Problems," pp. 126–131. It is not a sectional church, with a northern section hindering the work of a southern section among the negroes, as is the Methodist Episcopal Church.

[2] Carroll, "Religious Forces," p. 263.

[3] *Montgomery Advertiser*, Nov. 24, 1865.

[4] *Montgomery Advertiser*, Nov. 11, 1865.

[5] Report for 1866, Sen. Ex. Doc., No. 6, 39th Cong., 2d Sess.

enemies;[1] they were convinced that there was spiritual safety only in the northern or in independent churches. All the forces of social ostracism were employed against those who chose to remain in the old churches. The southern planter was not able to support the missionary who formerly preached to his slaves, the negroes would not pay; and the church treasury was empty.[2] In 1866 the General Conference directed that the colored members be organized as separate charges when they so desired; that colored preachers and presiding elders be appointed by the bishop, annual conferences organized when necessary, and especial attention be directed towards Sunday-schools for the negroes.[3]

Against all efforts of the Southern Methodists to work among the negroes, the Northern Methodists struggled with a persistence worthy of a better cause. Missionaries were sent South, narrow and prejudiced, though sincere, men and women, who were possessed with the fixed conviction that no good could come to the negro except from the North; in this conviction schools were established and churches organized. The injudicious and violent methods of these

[1] Lakin fomented disturbances between the races. His daughter wrote slanderous letters to northern papers, which were reprinted by the Alabama papers. Lakin told the negroes that the whites, if in power, would reëstablish slavery, and advised them, as a measure of safety, physical as well as religious, to unite with the northern church. The scalawags did not like Lakin, and one of them (Nicholas Davis) gave his opinion of him and his talks to the Ku Klux Committee as follows: "The character of his [Lakin's] speech was this: to teach the negroes that every man that was born and raised in the southern country was their enemy, that there was no use trusting them, no matter what they said, — if they said they were for the Union or anything else. 'No use talking, they are your enemies.' And he made a pretty good speech, too; awful; a hell of a one; . . . inflammatory and game, too, . . . it was enough to provoke the devil. Did all the mischief he could. . . . I tell you, that old fellow is a hell of an old rascal." Ala. Test., pp. 784, 791. One of Lakin's negro congregations complained that they paid for their church and the lot on which it stood, and that Lakin had the deed made out in his name.

[2] In the Black Belt and in the cities the slaveholders often erected churches or chapels for the use of the negroes, and paid the salary of the white preacher who was detailed by conference, convention, association, or presbytery to look after the religious instruction of the blacks. Nearly always the negro slaves contributed in work or money towards building these houses of worship, and the Reconstruction convention in 1867 passed an ordinance which transferred such property to the negroes whenever they made any claim to it. See Ordinance No. 25, Dec. 2, 1867. See also Acts of 1868, pp. 176–177; Governor Lindsay in Ku Klux Rept., Ala. Test., p. 180; *Montgomery Advertiser*, Nov. 24, 1865.

[3] *Huntsville Advocate*, May 5, 1865; Carroll, "Religious Forces," p. 263.

persons and their bitter prejudices caused their exclusion from all desirable society, and naturally they became more violent and prejudiced than ever. Their letters written to their homes showed that they believed the native white to be possessed by an inhuman hatred of the blacks, and that on the slightest provocation the whites would slaughter the entire negro population.[1] They favored at least a partial confiscation in behalf of the negro. Through the Freedmen's Aid Society the northern church entered upon work among the whites also, opposing the southern church on the ground that it was sectional and condemning all its efforts among the blacks as useless and harmful. For years there was not a word of recognition of the work done by the southern churches among the slaves.[2] The missionaries were afraid of "the old feudal forces" which were still working, they thought, under various disguises such as "Historical Societies, Memorial Days, and monuments to the Confederate dead."[3] Their work was thoroughly done. Two negro Methodist churches, organized in the North, secured the greater part of the negroes.[4] Some joined the Northern Methodist Church, "which also came down to divide the spoils."[5]

[1] Reports of the Freedmen's Aid Society, 1866–1874.

[2] The first recognition of such work, I find, is in the Report of the Freedmen's Aid Society in 1878.

[3] Tenth and Eleventh Reports of the Freedmen's Aid Society.

[4] These religious bodies were the African Methodist Episcopal and the African Methodist Episcopal Zion. The former was organized in Philadelphia in 1816, and the latter in New York in 1820. Both were secessions from the Methodist Episcopal Church. See Statistics of Churches, pp. 543, 559. At first there were bitter feuds between the blacks who wished to join the northern churches and those who wished to remain in the southern churches, but the latter were in the minority and they had to go. See Ala. Test., p. 180; Smith, "History of Methodism in Georgia and Florida"; "Life and Times of George F. Pierce," p. 491.

The main difference between the A. M. E. and the A. M. E. Zion Church, according to a member of the latter, is that in one the dues are 25 cents a week and in the other 20 cents.

[5] McTyeire, "History of Methodism," pp. 670–673. A Southern Methodist negro preacher in north Alabama was trying to reorganize his church and was driven away by Lakin, who told his flock that there was a wolf in the fold. See Ala. Test , p. 430. The statements of several of the negro ministers would seem to indicate that Lakin took possession of a number of negro congregations and united them with the Cincinnati Conference without their knowledge. Few of the negroes knew of the divisions in the Methodist Episcopal Church, and most of them thought that Lakin's course was merely some authorized reorganization after the destruction of war. One witness who knew Lakin in the North said that he was an original secessionist, since, in Peru, Indiana, he

After 1866 the colored congregations still adhering to the Southern Methodists had been divided into circuits, districts, and conferences. By 1870 political differences and the efforts of other churches had so alienated the races that it was thought best to set up an independent organization for the negroes, for their own protection. This was done in 1870 by the General Conference. Two negro bishops were ordained, and all church property that had ever been used for negro congregations was turned over to the new organization, which was called the Colored Methodist Episcopal Church. A few negroes refused to leave the white church, and in 1892 there were still 357 colored members on its rolls.[1] Until recently there has been strong opposition on the part of the other African churches to the Colored Methodist Episcopal Church because of its relations to the Southern Methodist Church. The latter has continued to aid and direct its protégé, and the opposition is gradually subsiding.[2]

After thirty years' experience, most people who have knowledge

broke up a church and organized a secession congregation because he was opposed to men and women sitting together. The same person testified that once in north Alabama Lakin asked for lodging one night at a white man's house. The host was treated to a lecture by Lakin on the equality of the races, and thereupon sent out and got a negro and put him in a bed to which Lakin was directed at bedtime. He hesitated, but slept with the negro. Ala. Test., pp. 791-794. Lakin was a strange character, and for several years was a powerful influence among the Radicals and negroes of north Alabama. See Ala. Test., p. 959. A Northern Methodist leader among the negroes of Coosa County was the Rev. —— Dorman, who had formerly belonged to the southern church, but had been expelled for immorality. He lived with the negroes and led a lewd life. He advised the negroes to arm themselves and assert their rights, and required them to go armed to church. See Ala. Test., pp. 164, 230. Rev. J. B. F. Hill of Eutaw was another ex-Southern Methodist who taught a negro school and preached to the negroes. He had been expelled from the Alabama Conference (Southern) for stealing money from the church, and it was charged that he tried to sell a coffin which had been sent him and in which he was to send to Ohio the body of a Federal soldier who had died in Eutaw. See Demopolis New Era, April 1, 1868. During the worst days of Reconstruction a number of negro churches which were used as Radical headquarters were burned by the Ku Klux Klan. The Northern Methodist Church is the weakest of the three negro churches; mountaineers and negroes do not mix well. The church is not favored by the whites, and there is opposition to the establishment of a negro university at Anniston by the Freedmen's Aid Society of this church, on the ground that socially, commercially, and educationally the interests of the white race suffer where an institution is located by this society. See Brundidge (Ala.) News, Aug. 22, 1903.

[1] McTyeire, "A History of Southern Methodism," p. 670; Carroll, "Religious Forces," p. 263; Alexander, "Methodist Episcopal Church South," pp. 91-133.

[2] Carroll, "Religious Forces," p. 263; Bishop Halsey in the N. Y. Independent, March 5, 1891; Statistics of Churches, p. 604.

of the subject agree that the religious interests of the negro have suffered from the separation of the races in the churches and from the enforced withdrawal of the native whites from religious work among the blacks. The influence of the master's family is no longer felt, and instead of the white minister came the negro preacher, with "ninety-five superstitions to five eternal truths,"—superstitions, many of them reminiscences from Africa.[1] There have been too many negro churches; every one who could read and write wanted to preach,[2] and many of them claimed direct communication with the Supreme Being; every one who applied was admitted to the churches; morality and religion were only remotely connected; leaders of the *demi-monde* were stout pillars of the church. A Presbyterian minister in charge of negro interests has stated that in his church the personnel of the independent negro congregations is inferior in character and morality to the congregations under the supervision of the whites. In the colored Baptist associations it is reported that frequent and radical changes have been the custom. Discontented churches secede and form new associations, which exist for a short while, and are then absorbed by other associations. The boundaries of the associations also change frequently; the church government seems to be in a kind of fluid state. Thoughtful religious leaders now believe that the southern white, for the good of both races, should again take part in the religious training of the negro.[3] But the difficulties in the way of such a course are almost insurmountable and date back to forced separation of the races in the churches.

An editorial in the *Nation* in 1866 expressed the situation from one point of view very clearly and forcibly: The northern churches claim that the South is determined to make the religious division permanent, though "slavery no longer furnishes a pretext for separation." Too much pains are taken to bring about an ecclesiastical reunion,

---

[1] W. T. Harris, Richmond Meeting, Southern Educational Association (1900), p. 100.

[2] See Washington, "Up from Slavery." One church with two hundred members had eighteen preachers. Exhorters or "zorters" and "pot liquor" preachers were still more numerous.

[3] "Race Problems," pp. 114, 120, 123, 126, 130, 131, 135; Haygood, "Our Brother in Black," *passim;* Statistics of Churches, p. 171.

and irritating offers of reconciliation are made by the northern churches, all based on the assumption that the South has not only sinned, but sinned knowingly, in slavery and in war. We expect them to be penitent and to gladly accept our offers of forgiveness. But the southern people look upon a "loyal" missionary as a political emissary, and "loyal" men do not at present possess the necessary qualifications for evangelizing the southerners or softening their hearts, and are sure not to succeed in doing so. We look upon their defeat as retribution and expect them to do the same. It will do no good if we tell the southerners that "we will forgive them if they will confess that they are criminals, offer to pray with them, preach with them, and labor with them over their hideous sins."[1]

"Reconstruction" in the church was closely related to "Reconstruction" in the state, and was so considered at the time by the reconstructionists of both.[2] The same mistaken, intolerant policy was followed, on the theory that the southern whites were as incapable of good action in church as in state. Irritating and impossible tests and conditions of readmission were proposed before reconciliation. Later the efforts to weaken and destroy the southern churches after attempts at reunion had failed completed the alienation, which in several organizations seems to be permanent. There was a Solid South in church as well as in politics.

[1] *The Nation*, July 12, 1866, condensed.

[2] Caldwell, " Reconstruction of Church and State in Georgia " (pamphlet). The circulars of advice to the blacks by the Freedmen's Bureau officials repeatedly mention the advisability of the separation of the races in religious matters. But this was less the case in Alabama than in other southern states.

CHAPTER XXI

THE KU KLUX REVOLUTION

THE Ku Klux movement was an understanding among southern whites, brought about by the chaotic condition of social and political institutions between 1865 and 1876. It resulted in a partial destruction of the Reconstruction and a return, as near as might be, to ante-bellum conditions. This understanding or state of mind took many forms and was called by many names. The purpose was everywhere and always the same: to recover for the white race control of society, and destroy the baleful influence of the alien among the blacks.[1]

Causes of the Ku Klux Movement

When the surviving soldiers of the Confederate army returned home in the spring and summer of 1865, they found a land in which political institutions had been destroyed and in which a radical social revolution was taking place — an old order, the growth of hundreds of years, seemed to be breaking up, and the new one had not yet taken shape; all was confusion and disorder. At this time began a movement which under different forms has lasted until the present day — an effort on the part of the defeated population to restore affairs to a state which could be endurable, to reconstruct southern society. This movement, a few years later, was in one of its phases known as the Ku Klux movement. For the peculiar aspects of this secret revolutionary movement many causes are suggested.

For several months before the close of the war the state government was powerless except in the vicinity of the larger towns, the country districts being practically without government. After the surrender there was an interval of four months during which there was no pretence of government except in the immediate vicinity

[1] See Testimony of Minnis in Ku Klux Rept., Ala. Test.; Brown, "Lower South," Ch. IV.

of the points garrisoned by the Federal army. The people were forbidden to take steps toward setting up any kind of government.[1] From one end of the state to the other the land was infested by a vicious element left by the war, — Federal and Confederate deserters, and bushwhackers and outlaws of every description. These were especially troublesome in the counties north of the Black Belt. The old tory class in the mountain counties was troublesome.[2] Of the little property surviving the wreck of war, none was safe from thievery. The worst class of the negroes — not numerous at this time — were insolent and violent in their new-found freedom. Murders were frequent, and outrages upon women were beginning to be heard of.[3] The whites, especially the more ignorant ones, were afraid of the effects of preaching of the doctrines of equality, amalgamation, etc., to the blacks. There were soon signs to show that some negroes would endeavor to put the theories they had heard of into practice.[4]

There was much talk of confiscation of property and division of land among the blacks. The negroes believed that they were going to be rewarded at the expense of the whites, and many of the latter began to fear that such might be the case. The Freedmen's Bureau early began its most successful career in alienating the races, by teaching the black that the southern white was naturally unfriendly to him. In this work it was ably assisted by the preaching and teaching missionaries sent out from the North, who taught the negro to beware of the southern white in church and in school. The Bureau broke up the labor system that had been patched up in the summer and fall of 1865, and people in the Black Belt felt that labor must be regulated in some way.[5] In the white counties the poorer whites, who had been the strongest supporters of the secession movement, not because they liked slavery, but because they were afraid of the competition of free negroes, began to show signs of a desire to drive the negro tenants from the rich lands which they wanted for them-

[1] See above, Ch. VIII, Sec. 2.

[2] Saunders, " Early Settlers " ; Miller, " Alabama " ; Ku Klux Rept., Ala. Test., p. 394 (General Pettus); Somers, " Southern States," p. 153.

[3] Ku Klux Rept., pp. 80–81; Ku Klux Rept., Ala. Test., p. 170 (Governor Lindsay).

[4] Ala. Test., pp. 433, 459 (P. M. Dox, M.C.); p. 1749 (W. S. Mudd); p. 476 (William H. Forney); Beard, " Ku Klux Sketches."

[5] Somers, p. 153 ; Birmingham Age-Herald, May 19, 1901 (J. W. DuBose); Ala. Test., p. 487 (Gen. William H. Forney).

selves.[1] For years after the war it was almost impossible for the farmer or planter to raise cows, hogs, poultry, etc., on account of the thieving propensities of the negroes.[2] Houses, mills, gins, cotton pens, and corn-cribs were frequently burned.[3] The Union League was believed by many to be an organization for the purpose of plundering the whites and for the division of property when the confiscation should take place.[4] It was also an active political machine. Nearly all the witnesses before the Ku Klux Committee who stated the causes of the rise of Ku Klux said that the League was the principal one. The whites soon came to believe that they were persecuted by the Washington government. The cotton frauds in 1865; the cotton tax, 1865–1868; the refusal to admit the southern states to representation in Congress, though they were heavily taxed; the passage of the Reconstruction Acts, by which the governments in the South were overturned, the negroes enfranchised, and all the prominent whites disfranchised, — all combined to make the white people believe that the North was seeking to humiliate them, to punish them when they were weak. They did not contemplate such treatment when they laid down their arms. As one soldier expressed it: the treatment received was in violation of the terms of surrender as expressed in their paroles; the southern soldiers could have carried on a guerilla warfare for years; the United States had made terms with men who had arms in their hands; they had laid them down, and the United States had violated these terms and punished individuals for alleged crime without trial; yet their paroles stated that they were not to be disturbed as long as they were law-abiding; the whole Reconstruction was a violation of the terms of surrender as the southern

---

[1] Ala. Test., p. 230 (General Clanton); pp. 1751, 1758, 1765 (W. S. Mudd).

[2] Planters who before the war were able to raise their own bacon at a cost of 5 cents a pound now had to kill all the hogs to keep the negroes from stealing them, and then pay 20 to 28 cents a pound for bacon. The farmer dared not turn out his stock. Ala. Test., pp. 230, 247 (Clanton).

[3] *N. Y. World*, April 11, 1868 (*Montgomery Advertiser*). There was a plot to burn Selma and Tuscumbia; Talladega was almost destroyed; the court-house of Greene County was burned and that of Hale set on fire. In Perry County a young man had a difficulty with a carpet-bag official and slapped his face. That night the carpet-bagger's agents burned the young man's barn and stables with horses in them. It was generally believed that the penalty for a dispute with a carpet-bagger was the burning of a barn, gin, or stable. See also Brown, "Lower South," Ch. IV.

[4] Ala. Test., p. 487 (Gen. William H. Forney).

soldiers understood it; it was punishment of a whole people by legislative enactment, and contrary to the spirit of American institutions. It was not a matter of law, but of common honesty.[1]

General Clanton complained that the southern people passed out of the hands of warriors into the hands of squaws.[2] The government imposed upon Alabama after the voters had fairly rejected it according to act of Congress was administered by the most worthless and incompetent of whites — alien and native — and negroes. Heavy taxes were laid; the public debt was rapidly increased; the treasury was looted; public office was treated as private property. The government was weak and vicious; it gave no protection to person or property ; it was powerless, or perhaps unwilling, to repress disorder; and was held in general contempt. The officials were notoriously corrupt and unjust in administration. There were many disorders which the people believed the state and Federal governments could not or would not regulate.[3] There was a general feeling of insecurity, in some sections a reign of terror. Innumerable humiliations were inflicted on the former political people of the state by carpet-bagger and scalawag, using the former slave as an instrument. Negro policemen stood on the street corners annoying the whites, making a great parade of all arrests, sometimes even of white women. The elections were corrupt, and the law was deliberately framed to protect ballot-box frauds.[4] The highest officers of the judiciary, Federal and state, took an active interest in politics, contrary to judicial traditions. Justice, so called, was bought and sold. The most thoroughly political people of the world, the proudest people of the English race, were the political inferiors of their former slaves, and the newcomers from the North never failed to make this fact as irritating as possible, by speech and print and action.[5]

In short, there was anarchy, social and political and economic. As the negro said, "The bottom rail is on top." The strenuous

---

[1] Ku Klux Rept., Ala. Test., pp. 377, 381, 382, 400, statement of General Pettus, the present junior Senator from Alabama. Pope and Grant continually reminded the old soldiers that their paroles were still in force. Also Beard, "Ku Klux Sketches"; testimony of John D. Minnis, a carpet-bag official, in Ku Klux Rept., Ala. Test., pp. 527-571.

[2] Ala. Test., p. 224.

[3] Ala. Test., p. 873 (William M. Lowe).   [4] See Ch. XXIII.

[5] For general accounts: Lester and Wilson, "Ku Klux Klan"; Beard, "Ku Klux Sketches"; Brown, "The Lower South in American History," Ch. IV ; Nordhoff,

editor Randolph said, "The origin of Ku Klux Klan is in the galling despotism that broods like a nightmare over these southern states, — a fungus growth of military tyranny superinduced by the fostering of Loyal Leagues, the abrogation of our civil laws, the habitual violation of our national constitution, and a persistent prostitution of all government, all resources, and all powers, to degrade the white man by the establishment of negro supremacy."[1]

Secret Societies of Regulators, before Ku Klux Klan

On account of the disordered condition of the state in 1865, some kind of a police power was necessary, the Federal garrisons being but few and weak. The minds of all men turned at once to the old ante-bellum neighborhood police patrol.[2] This patrol had consisted of men usually selected by the justice of the peace to patrol the entire community once a week or once a month, usually at night. The duty was compulsory, and every able-bodied white was subject to it, though there was sometimes commutation of service. The principal need for this patrol was to keep the black population in order, and to this end the patrollers were invested with the authority to inflict corporal punishment in summary fashion. There were about two companies, of six men and a captain each, to every township where there was a dense negro population. The attentions of the patrol were not confined to negroes alone, but now and then a white man was thrashed for some misdemeanor.[3] In this respect the patrol was a body for the regulation of society, so far as petty misdemeanors were concerned, and every respectable white man was by virtue of his color a member of this police guard. He had the right, whether in active patrol or not, to question any strange negro found abroad, or any negro travelling without a pass, or any white man found tampering with the negroes. It was to some extent a military organization of society. Much of this was simply custom, the development of hundreds of years, not a statute regulation, for that was a recent

"Cotton States in 1875"; Somers, "The Southern States." For documents, see Fleming, "Docs. relating to Reconstruction." For innumerable details, see the Ku Klux testimony and the testimony taken by the Coburn investigating committee.

[1] *Independent Monitor* (Tuscaloosa), April 14, 1868.
[2] The negroes called them "paterollers."
[3] Ala. Test., p. 490 (William H. Forney).

2 U

thing in the history of slavery.   It was the old English neighborhood
police system become a part of the customary law of slavery.   After
the war some regulation was necessary; the whites were accustomed
to settling such matters outside of law or court; it was bred into
their nature, and they returned perhaps unconsciously to the old
system.[1]

But now, under the régime of the Freedmen's Bureau backed
by the army, the old way of dealing with refractory blacks was
illegal.   As a matter of fact there was no legal way to control them.
The result was natural — the movement to regulate society became a
secret one.   The white men of each community had a general understanding that they would assist one another to protect women, children,
and property.   They had a system of signals for communication,
but no disguises, and the organization was not kept secret except from
the negroes.   In one locality the young men alone were united into
a committee for the regulation of the conduct of negroes.   They
requested the women who lived alone on the plantations, the old
men, and others who were likely to be unable to control the negroes,
to inform the committee of instances of misconduct on the part of
the blacks.   When such information came, it was immediately
acted upon, and the next day there were sadder and better negroes
on some one's plantation.[2]   As a rule one thrashing in a community
lasted a long time.   In Hale County a vigilance committee was
formed to protect the women and children in a section of the black
country where there were few white men, most having been killed in
the war.   They had a system of signals by means of plantation bells.
There were no disguises, and there was a public place of meeting.[3]
In the same county, in the fall of 1865, the whites near Newberne
asked General Hardee, then living on his plantation, to take command
of their patrol.   His answer was: "No, gentlemen, I want you to
enroll my name for service, but put a younger man in command.
I have served my day as commander.   I will be ready to respond

---

[1] Ala. Test., p. 873 (William M. Lowe); p. 443 (P. M. Dox); oral accounts.   It
must be remembered that, so far as numbers of whites are considered, the Black Belt
has always been as a thinly populated frontier region, where every white must care
for himself.

[2] Rev. W. E. Lloyd and Mr. R. W. Burton, both of Auburn, Ala., and numerous
negroes have given me accounts of the policy of the black districts soon after the war.

[3] Ala. Test., p. 1487 (J. J. Garrett).

when called upon for active duty. I want to advise you to get ready for what may come. We are standing over a sleeping volcano." [1] In Limestone County a similar organization was composed of peaceable citizens united to disperse or crush out bands of thieves.[2] This was in a white county in the northern section of the state, where the people had suffered during the war, and were still suffering, from the depredations of the tories. In Winston and Walker counties the returning Confederate soldiers banded together and drove many of the tories from the country, hanging several of the worst characters.[3] In central and southern Alabama the citizens resolved themselves into vigilance committees and hanged horse thieves and other outlaws who were raiding the country, some of them disguised in the uniforms of Federal soldiers.[4]

. In Marengo County while negro insurrection was feared a secret organization was formed for the protection of the whites. The members were initiated in a Masonic hall. Regular meetings were held, and each member reported on the conduct of the negroes in his community. There were no whippings necessary in this section, and after a few night rides the society dissolved. The Bureau and Union League were never successful in getting absolute control over the "Cane Brake" region, and therefore the negroes were better behaved and there was less disorder.[5]

Before Christmas, 1865, when there seemed to be danger of outbreaks of that part of the negro population who were disappointed in regard to the division of property, there was a disposition among the whites in some counties, especially in the eastern Black Belt, to form militia companies, though this was forbidden by the Washington authorities. Some of these companies regularly patrolled their neighborhoods. Others undertook to disarm the freedmen, who were purchasing arms of every description, and in order to do this searched the negro houses at night. General Swayne, recognizing the dangerous situation of the whites, forbore to interfere with these militia companies until after Christmas, when, the negroes

---

[1] *Birmingham Age-Herald*, May 19, 1901 (J. W. DuBose).

[2] Ala. Test., p. 592 (L. W. Day).

[3] Saunders, " Early Settlers " ; oral accounts.

[4] Ala. Test., p. 445 (P. M. Dox); Miller, " Alabama." The negroes still point out and avoid the trees on which these outlaws were hanged.

[5] J. W. DuBose and accounts of other members.

remaining peaceable, he issued an order forbidding further inter-ference;[1] but the militia organizations persisted in some shape until the Reconstruction Acts were passed.

In the eastern counties of the state there was in 1865 and 1866 an organization, preceding the Ku Klux, called the "Black Cavalry." It was a secret, oath-bound, night-riding order. Its greatest strength was in Tallapoosa County, where it was said to have 200 to 300 members. It was not only a band to regulate the conduct of the negroes, but there was a large element in it of the poorer whites, who wanted to drive the negro from the rich lands upon which slavery had settled them, in order to get them for themselves. This was generally true of all secret orders of regulators in the white counties from 1865 to 1875, and exactly the opposite was the case in the Black Belt, where the planters preferred the negro labor, and never drove out the blacks. The "Black Cavalry," it is said, drove more negroes from east Alabama than the Ku Klux did.[2]

There were local bands of regulators policing nearly every dis-trict in Alabama. Few of them had formal organizations or rose to the dignity of having officers or names, but there were the "Men of Justice," in north Alabama, principally in Limestone County, and the "Order of Peace," partially organized in Huntsville early in 1868,[3] and many other local orders.

The Origin and Growth of Ku Klux Klan

The local bands of regulators in existence immediately after the war were a necessary outcome of the disordered conditions pre-vailing at the time, and would have disappeared with a return to normal conditions under a strong government which had the respect of the people. But during the excitement over the action of the Reconstruction convention in the fall of 1867 and the elections of February, 1868, a new secret order became prominent in Ala-bama; and when, after the people had defeated the constitution, Congress showed a disposition to disregard the popular will as ex-pressed in the result of the election, this order — Ku Klux Klan —

---

[1] Report of the Joint Committee on Reconstruction, 1866, Pt. III, p. 140 (Swayne).
[2] Ala. Test., pp. 1125, 1126 (Daniel Taylor); pp. 1136, 1142 (Col. John J. Holley).
[3] Ala. Test., p. 877 (Wm. M. Lowe); p. 664 (Daniel Coleman).

sprang into activity in widely separated localities. The campaign of the previous six months had made the people desperate when they contemplated what was in store for them under the rule of carpet-bagger, scalawag, and negro. The counter-revolution was beginning.

The Ku Klux Klan originated in Pulaski, Tennessee, in the fall of 1865.[1] The founders were James R. Crowe, Richard R. Reed, Calvin Jones, John C. Lester, Frank O. McCord, and John Kennedy. Some were Alabamians and some Tennesseeans. Lester and Crowe lived later in Sheffield, Alabama. Crowe and Kennedy are the only survivors. It was a club of young men who had served in the Confederate army, who united for purposes of fun and mischief, pretty much as college boys in secret fraternities or country boys as "snipe hunters." The name was an accidental corruption of the Greek word *kuklos*, a circle, and had no meaning.[2] The officers had outlandish titles, and fancy disguises were adopted. The regalia or uniform consisted of a tall cardboard hat covered with cloth, on which were pasted red spangles and stars; there was a face covering, with openings for nose, mouth, and ears; and a long robe coming nearly to the heels, made of any kind of cloth — white, black, or red — often fancy colored calico. A whistle was used as a signal.[3]

This scheme for amusement was successful, and there were plenty of applications for admission. Members went away to other towns, and under the direction of the Pulaski Club, or "Den" as it was called, other Dens were formed. The Pulaski Den was in the habit of parading in full uniform at social gatherings of the whites at night, much to the delight of the small boys and girls. Pulaski was near the Alabama line, and many Alabama young men saw these parades or heard of them, and Dens were organized over north

---

[1] "The so-called Ku Klux organizations were formed in this state (Alabama) very soon after the return of our soldiers to their homes, following the surrender. To the best of my recollection, it was during the winter of 1866 that I first heard of the Klan in Alabama." — Ryland Randolph. The quotations from Randolph are taken from his letters, unless his paper, the *Independent Monitor*, is referred to.

[2] "This fellow Jones up at Pulaski got up a piece of Greek and originated it, and then General Forrest took hold of it." — Nicholas Davis, in Ala. Test., p. 783.

[3] Lester and Wilson, "Ku Klux Klan," p. 17; Ala. Test., pp. 660, 661, 1282; accounts of members.

Alabama in the towns. Nothing but horse-play and tomfoolery took place in the meetings. In 1867 and 1868 the order appeared in parade in the north Alabama towns and "cut up curious gyrations" on the public squares.[1] The Klan had not long been in existence and was still in this first stage, and was rapidly speeding, when a pretty general discovery of its power over the negro was made. The weird night riders in ghostly disguises frightened the superstitious negroes, who were told that the spirits of dead Confederates were abroad.[2] There was a general belief outside the order that there was a purpose behind all the ceremonial and frolic of the Dens; many joined the order convinced that its object was serious; others saw the possibilities in it and joined in order to make use of it. After discovering the power of the Klan over the negroes, there was a general tendency, owing to the disordered conditions of the time, to go into the business of a police patrol and hold in check the thieving negroes, the Union League, and the "loyalists." From being a series of social clubs the Dens swiftly became bands of regulators, adding many fantastic qualities to their original outfit. All this time the Pulaski organization exercised a loose control over a federation of Dens. There was danger, as the Dens became more and more police bodies, of some of the more ardent spirits going to excess, and in several instances Dens went far in the direction of violence and outrage. Attempts were made by the parent Den to regulate the conduct of the Dens, but owing to the loose organization, they met with little success. Some of the Dens lost all connection with the original order.

Early in 1867 the Grand Cyclops of the Pulaski Den sent requests to the various Dens in the southern states to send delegates to a convention in Nashville. This convention met in May, 1867. Delegates from all of the Gulf states and from several others were present, and the order of Ku Klux Klan was reorganized. There were at

[1] Ala. Test., p. 660.

[2] "It [the Klan] originated with the returned soldiers for the purpose of punishing those negroes who had become notoriously and offensively insolent to white people, and, in some cases, to chastise those white-skinned men who, at that particular time, showed a disposition to affiliate socially with negroes. The impression sought to be made was that these white-robed night prowlers were the ghosts of the Confederate dead, who had arisen from their graves in order to wreak vengeance upon an undesirable class of white and black men." — Randolph.

this time Dens in all the southern states, and even in Illinois and Pennsylvania.[1] A constitution called the "Prescript" was here adopted for the entire order. The administration was centralized, and the entire South was placed under the jurisdiction of its officials. The former slave states except Delaware constituted the Empire, which was ruled by the Grand Wizard[2] with a staff of ten Genii; each state was a realm under a Grand Dragon and eight Hydras; the next subdivision was the Dominion, consisting of several counties,[3] ruled by a Grand Titan and six Furies; the county as a Province was governed by a Grand Giant[4] and four Goblins; the unit was the Den or community organization. There might be several in each county, each under a Grand Cyclops and two Night Hawks. The Genii, Hydras, Furies, Goblins, and Night Hawks were staff officers. Each of the above divisions was called a Grand *. The order had no name, and at first was designated by two **, later by three ***. The private members were called Ghouls. The Grand Magi and the Grand Monk were the second and third officers of the Den, and had the authority of the Grand Cyclops when the latter was absent. The Grand Sentinel was in charge of the guard of the Den, and the Grand Ensign carried its banner on the night rides.[5] Every division had a Grand Exchequer, whose duty it was to look after the revenue,[6] and a Grand Scribe, or secretary, who called the roll, made reports, and kept lists of members (without anything to show what the list meant), usually in Arabic figures,

[1] Lester and Wilson, Ch. I; Ala. Test., p. 1283 (Blackford); Somers, p. 152; oral accounts.

[2] General Forrest was the first and only Grand Wizard.

[3] There could not be more than two Dominions in a single congressional district.

[4] There might be two Grand Giants in a province.

[5] The office of Grand Ensign was abolished by the Revised and Amended Prescript, adopted in 1868. The banner was in the shape of an isosceles triangle, five feet by three, of yellow cloth with a three-inch red border. Painted on it in black was a *Draco volans*, or Flying Dragon, and this motto, "Quod semper, quod umbique, quod ab omnibus." This, in a note to the Prescript, was translated, "What always, what everywhere, what by all is held to be true."

[6] Sources of revenue: (1) sale of the Prescript to Dens for $10 a copy, of which the treasuries of Province, Dominion, and Realm each received $2 and the treasury of the Empire $4; (2) a tax levied by each division on the next lower one, amounting to 10% of the revenue of the subordinate division; (3) a special tax, unlimited, might be levied in a similar manner, when absolutely necessary; (4) the Dens raised money by initiation fees ($1 each), fines, and a poll tax levied when the Grand Cyclops saw fit.

1, 2, 3, etc. The Grand Turk was the adjutant of the Grand Cyclops, and gave notice of meetings, executed orders, received candidates, and administered the preliminary oaths. The officers of the Den were elected semiannually by the Ghouls; the highest officers of the other divisions were elected biannually by the officers of the next lower rank. The first Grand Wizard was to serve three years from May, 1867.[1] Each superior officer could appoint special deputies to assist him and to extend the order. Every division made quarterly reports to the next higher headquarters. In case a question of paramount importance should arise, the Grand Wizard was invested with absolute authority.[2]

The Tribunal of Justice consisted of a Grand Council of Yahoos for the trial of all elected officers, and was composed of those of equal rank with the accused, presided over by one of the next higher rank; and for the trial of Ghouls and non-elective officers, the Grand Council of Centaurs, which consisted of six Ghouls appointed by the Grand Cyclops, who presided.[3]

A person was admitted to the Den after nomination by a member and strict investigation by a committee. No one under eighteen was admitted. The oath taken was one of obedience and secrecy. The Dens governed themselves by the ordinary rules of deliberative bodies. The penalty for betrayal of secret was "the extreme penalty of the Law."[4] None of the secrets was to be written. There was a Register of alarming adjectives used in dating the wonderful Ku Klux orders.[5]

In the original Prescript no mention was made of the peculiar objects of the order. The Creed acknowledged the supremacy of

---

[1] The Revised Prescript made all officers appointive except the Grand Wizard, who was elected by the Grand Dragons, — a long step toward centralization.

[2] It was by virtue of this authority that the order was disbanded in 1869.

[3] The judiciary was abolished by the Revised Prescript.

[4] "We had a regular system of by-laws, one or two of which only do I distinctly remember. One was, that should any member reveal the names or acts of the Klan, he should suffer the full penalty of the identical treatment inflicted upon our white and black enemies. Another was that in case any member of the Klan should become involved in a personal difficulty with a Radical (white or black), in the presence of any other member or members, he or they were bound to take the part of the member, even to the death, if necessary." — Randolph.

[5] "Terrible, horrible, furious, doleful, bloody, appalling, frightful, gloomy," etc. The Register was changed in the Revised Prescript. It was simply a cipher code.

the Divine Being, and the Preamble the supremacy of the laws of the United States.[1] The Revised and Amended Prescript sets forth the character and objects of the order: (1) To protect the weak, the innocent, and the defenceless from the indignities, wrongs, and

CHARACTER AND OBJECTS OF THE ORDER.

THIS is an institution of Chivalry, Humanity, Mercy, and Patriotism; embodying in its genius and its principles all that is chivalric in conduct, noble in sentiment, generous in manhood, and patriotic in purpose; its peculiar objects being

First: To protect the weak, the innocent, and the defenceless, from the indignities, wrongs, and outrages of the lawless, the violent, and the brutal; to relieve the injured and oppressed; to succor the suffering and unfortunate, and especially the widows and orphans of Confederate soldiers.

Second: To protect and defend the Constitution of the United States, and all laws passed in conformity thereto, and to protect the States and the people thereof from all invasion from any source whatever.

Third: To aid and assist in the execution of all constitutional laws, and to protect the people from unlawful seizure, and from trial except by their peers in conformity to the laws of the land,

ARTICLE I.
TITLES.

SECTION 1. The officers of this Order shall consist of a Grand Wizard of the Empire, and his ten Genii; a Grand Dragon of the Realm,

3

Facsimile of Page 3 of the Revised and Amended Prescript of Ku Klux Klan.

outrages of the lawless, the violent, and the brutal;[2] to relieve the injured and oppressed; to succor the suffering and unfortunate, and

[1] The Revised Prescript says "the constitutional laws." Lester and Wilson, p. 54.

[2] Compare with the declaration of similar illegal societies, — the "Confréries" of France in the Middle Ages, — which sprang into existence under similar conditions seven hundred years before, "pour defendre les innocents et réprimer les violences iniques." See Lavisse et Rambaud, "Histoire Générale," Vol. II, p. 466.

especially the widows and orphans of Confederate soldiers. (2) To protect and defend the Constitution of the United States and all laws passed in conformity thereto, and to protect the states and people thereof from all invasion from any source whatever. (3) To aid and assist in the execution of all "constitutional" laws, and to protect the people from unlawful arrest, and from trial except by their peers according to the laws of the land.[1]

The questions asked of the candidate constituted a test sufficient to exclude all except the most friendly whites. The applicant for admission was asked if he belonged to the Federal army or the Radical party, Union League, or Grand Army of the Republic, and if he was opposed to the principles of those organizations. He was asked if he was opposed to negro equality, political and social, and was in favor of a white man's government, of constitutional liberty and equitable laws. He was asked if he was in favor of reënfranchisement and emancipation of the southern whites, and the restoration to the southern people of their rights, — property, civil, and political, — and of maintaining the constitutional rights of the South, and if he believed in the inalienable right of self-preservation of the people against the exercise of arbitrary and unlicensed power.

The Revised and Amended Prescript, made in 1868, was an attempt to give more power of control to the central authorities in order to enable them to regulate the obstreperous Dens. The purposes of the order, omitted in the first Prescript, was clearly declared in the revision. Little change was made in the administration of the order.[2]

---

[1] See also Lester and Wilson, pp. 55, 56.

[2] I have before me the original Prescript, a small brown pamphlet about three inches by five, of sixteen pages. The title-page has a quotation from "Hamlet" and one from Burns. At the top and bottom of each page are single-line Latin quotations: "Damnant quod non intelligunt"; "Amici humani generis"; "Magna est veritas, et prevalebit"; "Hic manent vestigia morientis libertatis"; "Cessante causa, cessat effectus"; "Dormitur aliquando jus, moritur nunquam"; "Deo adjuvante, non timendum"; "Nemo nos impune lacessit," etc. This Prescript belonged to the Grand Giant of the Province of Tuscaloosa County, the late Ryland Randolph, formerly editor of the *Independent Monitor*, and was given to me by him. It is the only copy known to be in existence. He called it the "Ku Klux Guide Book," and states that it was sent to him from headquarters at Memphis. An imperfect copy of the original Prescript was captured in 1868, and printed in Ho. Mis. Doc., No. 53, pp. 315–321, 41st Cong., 2d Sess., and again in the Ku Klux Rept., Vol. XIII, pp. 35–41.

There is a copy of the Revised and Amended Prescript in Columbia University Library, the only copy known to be in existence. No committee of Congress ever dis-

The order continued to spread after the reorganization in 1867. There were scattered Dens over north Alabama and as far south as Tuscaloosa, Selma, and Montgomery. It came first to the towns and then spread into the country. It was less and less an obscure organization, and more and more a band of regulators, using mystery, disguise, and secrecy to terrify the blacks into good behavior. It was in many ways a military organization, the shadowy ghost of the Confederate armies.[1] The whites were all well-trained military men; they looked to their military chieftains to lead them. The best men were members,[2] though the prominent politicians as a rule did not belong to the order. They fought the fight against the Radicals on the other side of the field.[3]

After the elections in February, 1868, the Ku Klux came into greater prominence in Alabama, especially in the northern and western portions, while south Alabama was still quiet.[4]

The counties of north Alabama infested were Lauderdale, Limestone, Madison, Jackson, Morgan, Lawrence, Franklin, Madison, Winston, Walker, Fayette, and Blount. In central Alabama, Montgomery, Greene, Pickens, Tuscaloosa, Calhoun, Talladega, Randolph, Chambers, Coosa, and Tallapoosa.[5] There were bands in most of the other counties, and in the counties of the Black Belt. The order seldom extended to the lower edge of the Black Belt. In the Black

covered this Prescript, and when the Klan disbanded, in March, 1869, it was strictly ordered that all papers be destroyed. A few Prescripts escaped destruction, and years afterward one of these was given to the Southern Society of New York by a Nashville lady. The Southern Society gave it to Columbia University Library. It was printed in the office of the *Pulaski Citizen* in 1868. The Revised and Amended Prescript is reproduced in facsimile as No. 2 of the W. Va. Univ. " Docs. relating to Reconstruction." Lester and Wilson use it incorrectly (p. 54) as the one adopted in Nashville in 1867. At this time General Forrest is said to have assumed the leadership. See Wyeth, " Life of Forrest," p. 619 ; Mathes, " General Forrest," pp. 371–373 ; Ku Klux Rept., Vol. XIII, Forrest's testimony.

[1] Somers, p. 153.

[2] " Breckenridge Democrats, Douglas Democrats, Watts State Rights Whigs, Langdon Consolidation Know-Nothings," united in Ku Klux. *Birmingham Age-Herald,* May 19, 1901 ; Ala. Test., p. 323 (Busteed) *et passim.*

[3] But some survivors are now inclined to remember all opposition to the Radical programme as Ku Klux, that is, to have been a Democrat then was to have been a member of Ku Klux.

[4] General Terry, in Report of Sec. of War, 1869–1870, Vol. II, p. 88.

[5] "The Ku Klux organizations flourished chiefly in middle and southern Alabama ; notably in Montgomery, Greene, Tuscaloosa, and Pickens counties." — Randolph.

Belt it met the Knights of the White Camelia, the White Brotherhood, and later the White League, and in a way absorbed them all.[1]

The actual number of the men in regular organized Dens cannot be ascertained. It was estimated that there were 800 in Madison County, and 10,000 in the state.[2] Others said that it included all Confederate soldiers.[3] The actual number regularly enrolled was much less than the number who acted as Ku Klux when they considered it necessary. In one sense practically all able-bodied native white men belonged to the order, and if social and business ostracism be considered as a manifestation of the Ku Klux spirit, then the women and children also were Ku Klux.

It is the nature and vice of secret societies of regulators to degenerate, and the Ku Klux Klan was no exception to the rule. By 1869 the order had fallen largely under control of a low class of men who used it to further their own personal aims, to wreak revenge on their enemies and gratify personal animosities. Outrages became frequent, and the order was dangerous even to those who founded it.[4] It had done its work. The negroes had been in a measure controlled, and society had been held together during the revolution of 1865–1869. The people were still harassed by many irritations and persecutions, but while almost unbearable, they were mostly of a nature to disappear in time as the carpet-bag governments collapsed. The most material evil at present was the misgovernment of the Radicals, and this could not last always. But though the organized Ku Klux Klan was disbanded, the spirit of resistance was higher than ever; and as each community had problems to deal with they were met in the old manner — a sporadic uprising of a local Klan.

[1] Ku Klux Rept., p. 21; Ala. Test., pp. 67, 68 (B. W. Norris); pp. 364, 395 (Swayne); p. 443 (P. M. Dox); p. 385 (General Pettus); p. 462 (William H. Forney); p. 77 (Parsons); pp. 1282, 1283 (Blackford); p. 547 (Minnis); p. 660 (Daniel Coleman); p. 323 (Busteed).

[2] Ala. Test., p. 785 (Nicholas Davis); pp. 79, 80 (Governor Parsons).

[3] Ala. Test., p. 1282.

[4] "Had these organizations confined their operations to their legitimate objects, then their performances would have effected only good. Unfortunately the Klan began to degenerate into a vile means of wreaking revenge for personal dislikes or personal animosities, and in this way many outrages were perpetrated, ultimately resulting in casting so much odium on the whole concern that about the year 1870 there was an almost universal collapse, all the good and brave men abandoning it in disgust. Many outrages were committed in the name of Ku Klux that really were done by irresponsible parties who never belonged to the Klan." — Randolph.

As long as a carpet-bagger was in power, the principles of the Klan were asserted.

The Knights of the White Camelia

The order known as the Knights of the White Camelia originated in Louisiana in 1867,[1] and spread from thence through the Gulf states. In Alabama it was well organized in the southwestern counties, and to some extent throughout the lower Black Belt. It probably did not exist in the southeastern white counties.[2] The former local vigilance committees, neighborhood patrol parties, and disbanded militia were absorbed into the order, which gave them a uniform organization and a certain loose union, and left them pretty much as independent as before. There was a closer sympathy between southwest Alabama and Louisiana than between the two sections of Alabama, which perhaps will account for the failure of Ku Klux Klan to organize in the southern counties. The White Camelia came to Alabama from New Orleans *via* Mobile, and also through southern Mississippi to southwestern Alabama. Later the White League came the same way.

In June 1868 a convention of the Knights of the White Camelia was held in New Orleans, and a constitution was adopted for the order.[3] The preamble stated that Radical legislation was subversive of the principles of government adopted by the fathers, and in order to secure safety and prosperity the order was founded for the preservation of those principles. The order consisted of a Supreme Council of the United States, and of Grand, Central, and Subordinate councils. The Supreme Council with headquarters in New Orleans consisted of five delegates from each Grand Council. It was the

---

[1] It was evidently organized May 23, 1867, since the constitution directed that all orders and correspondence should be dated with "the year of the B. — computing from the 23d of May, 1867. . . . Thursday the 20th of July, 1868, shall be the 20th day of the 7th month of the 2d year of the B. of the ——." Constitution, Title VIII, Article 77.

[2] Ala. Test., pp. 1282–1283 (Blackford); p. 9 (William Miller); accounts of former members. P. J. Glover testified in the Coburn-Buckner Report, pp. 882–883 (1875), that in 1867–1868 he was a member of the order of the White Camelia in Marengo County, and that it coöperated with a similar order in Sumter County. The Ku Klux testimony relating to Alabama (p. 1338) shows that in 1871 Glover had denied any knowledge of such secret orders.

[3] W. Va. Univ. Docs., No. 1 ; Brown, "Lower South," Ch. IV.

general legislative body of the order, and maintained communication within the order by means of passwords and cipher correspondence. Communication between and with the lowest organizations was verbal only. All officers were designated by initials.[1]

In each state the Grand Council[2] was the highest body, and held its sessions at the state capital. The membership consisted of delegates from the Central Councils — one delegate for one thousand members. The Grand Council had the power of legislation for the state, subject to the constitution of the order and the laws of the Supreme Council. In each county or parish there was a Central Council of delegates from Subordinate Councils.[3] It was charged with the duty of collecting the revenue and extending the order within its limits. The lowest organization was the Council (or Subordinate Council) in a community. This body had sole authority to initiate members. In each county the Subordinate Councils were designated by numbers. Each was composed of several Circles (each under a Grand Chief); each Circle of five Groups (each under a Chief); and each Group of ten Brothers. Officials of the order were elected by indirect methods. An ex-member states that "during the three years of its existence here [Perry County] I believe its organization and discipline were as perfect as human ingenuity could have made it."[4]

The constitution prohibited the order as a body from nominating or supporting any candidate or set of candidates for public office. Each subordinate rank had the right of local legislation. Quarterly reports were made by each division. The officers of the higher councils were known only to their immediate subordinates. When

---

[1] The officers of the Supreme Council were: (1) Supreme Commander, (2) Supreme Lieutenant Commander, (3) Supreme Sentinel, (4) Supreme Corresponding Secretary, (5) Supreme Treasurer.

[2] The officers were Grand Commander, Grand Lieutenant Commander, etc.

[3] The officers of a Central Council were Eminent Commander, etc.; of a Subordinate Council, Commander, etc.

[4] Dr. G. P. L. Reid, Marion, Alabama, formerly an official in the order. Mr. William Garrott Brown gives the statement of one of the leaders of the order: "The authority of the commander [this office I held] was *absolute*. All were sworn to obey his orders. There was an inner circle in each circle, to which was committed any particular work; its movements were not known to other members of the order. This was necessary because, in our neighborhood, almost every southern man was a member." "Lower South," p. 212.

a question came up that could not be settled it was referred to the next higher council.

Only whites [1] over eighteen were admitted to membership, after election by the order in which no adverse vote was cast. Each council acted as a court when charges were brought against its members. Punishment was by removal or suspension from office; there was no expulsion from the order; punishment was simply a reducing to ranks. The candidate for membership into the order was required first to take the oath of secrecy, which was administered by a subordinate official, who then announced him to the next higher official.[2] By the latter the candidate was presented to the commander of the Council, and in answer to his interrogations made solemn declaration that he had not married and would never marry a woman not of the white race, and that he believed in the superiority of the white race. He promised never to vote for any except a white man, and never to refrain from voting at any election in which a negro candidate should oppose a white. He further declared that he would devote his intelligence, energy, and influence to prevent political affairs from falling into the hands of the African race, and that he would protect persons of the white race in their lives, rights, and property against encroachments from any inferior race, especially the African. After the candidate had made the proper declarations the final oath was administered,[3] after which he was pronounced a "Knight of the ——."

[1] It is said that the Ku Klux Klan had a number of negro members.

[2] In making the presentation the following dialogue took place: *Q.* Who comes there ? *Ans.* A son of your race. *Q.* What does he wish ? *Ans.* Peace and order ; the observance of the laws of God ; the maintenance of the laws and Constitution as established by the Patriots of 1776. *Q.* To obtain this, what must be done ? *Ans.* The cause of our race must triumph. *Q.* And to secure its triumph, what must we do ? *Ans.* We must be united as are the flowers that grow on the same stem, and, under all circumstances, band ourselves together as brethren. *Q.* Will he join us ? *Ans.* He is prepared to answer for himself, and under oath.

[3] The oath: "I do solemnly swear, in the presence of these witnesses, never to reveal, without authority, the existence of this Order, its objects, its acts, and signs of recognition ; never to reveal or publish, in any manner whatsoever, what I shall see or hear in this Council ; never to divulge the names of the members of the Order, or their acts done in connection therewith ; I swear to maintain and defend the social and political superiority of the White Race on this continent ; always and in all places to observe a marked distinction between the White and African races ; to vote for none but white men for any office of honor, profit, or trust ; to devote my intelligence, energy,

The Commander next instructed the new members in the principles of the order, which he declared was destined to regenerate the unfortunate country, and to relieve the white race from its humiliating condition. Its fundamental object was the "MAINTENANCE OF THE SUPREMACY OF THE WHITE RACE."[1] History and physiology were called upon to show that the Caucasian race had always been superior to, and had always exercised dominion over, inferior races. No human laws could permanently change the great laws of nature. The white race alone had achieved enduring civilization, and of all subordinate races, the most imperfect was the African. The government of the Republic was established by white men for white men. It was never intended by its founders that it should fall into the hands of an inferior race. Consequently, any attempt to transfer the government to the blacks was an invasion of the sacred rights guaranteed by the Constitution, as well as a violation of the laws established by God himself, and no member of the white race could submit, without humiliation and shame, to the subversion of the established institutions of the Republic. It was the duty of white men to resist attempts against their natural and legal rights in order to maintain the supremacy of the Caucasian race and restrain the "African race to that condition of social and political inferiority for which God has destined it." There was to be no infringement of laws, no violations of right, no force employed, except for purposes of legitimate and necessary defence.

As an essential condition of success, the Order proscribed absolutely any social equality between the races. If any degree of social equality should be granted, there would be no end to it; political equality was necessarily involved. Social equality meant finally intermarriage and a degraded and ignoble population. The white blood must be kept pure to preserve the natural superiority of the

and influence to instil these principles in the minds and hearts of others; and to protect and defend persons of the White Race, in their lives, rights, and property, against the encroachments and aggressions of persons of any inferior race. I swear, moreover, to unite myself in heart, soul, and body with those who compose this Order; to aid, protect, and defend them in all places; to obey the orders of those who, by our statutes, will have the right of giving those orders; to respond at the peril of my life, to a call, sign, or cry coming from a fellow-member whose rights are violated; and to do everything in my power to assist him through life. And to the faithful performance of this Oath I pledge my life and sacred honor."

[1] The motto is printed in large capitals in the original text.

race. The obligation was therefore taken "To OBSERVE A MARKED DISTINCTION BETWEEN THE TWO RACES," [1] in public and in private life.

One of the most important duties of the members was to respect the rights of the negroes, and in every instance give them their lawful dues. It was only simple justice to deny them none of their legitimate privileges. There was no better way to show the inherent superiority of the white race, than by dealing with the blacks in that spirit of firmness, liberality, and impartiality which characterizes all superior organizations. It would be ungenerous to restrict them in the exercise of certain privileges, without conceding to them at the same time the fullest measure of their legitimate rights. A fair construction of the white man's duty to the black would be, not only to respect and observe their acknowledged rights, but also to see that they were respected and observed by others.

These declarations give a good idea of what was in the minds of the southern whites in 1867 and 1868, and later.[2]

Like the Ku Klux Klan, the Knights of the White Camelia disbanded when the objects of the order were accomplished, or were in a fair way toward accomplishment. In some counties it lived a year or two longer than in others. In certain counties, by order of its authorities, it was never organized. It did not extend north of the Black Belt, though it existed in close proximity to the more southerly of the Klans. As the oldest of the large secret orders, the name of Ku Klux Klan was more widely known than the others, and hence the name was applied indiscriminately to all. A local body would assume the name of a large one when there was no direct connection. The other organizations similar to Ku Klux in objects and methods [3] did not have a strong membership in Alabama.

[1] Large capitals in the original text.

[2] The Constitution and the Ritual of the Knights of the White Camelia are reprinted in W. Va. Univ. Docs., No. 1. They were preserved by Dr. G. P. L. Reid of Perry County, Alabama, who buried his papers when the order was disbanded, and years afterward dug them up. The secrets of the Knights of the White Camelia were more closely kept than those of the Ku Klux Klan, and the Federal officials were unable to find out anything about the order.

[3] Constitutional Union Guards, Sons of '76, The '76 Association, Pale Faces, White Boys, White Brotherhood, Regulators, White League, White Rose, etc. Sumarez de Haviland, in an article on "Ku Klux Klan" in the *Gentleman's Magazine*, Vol. XL, 1888 (evidently based on Lester and Wilson), gives the names of a number of secret

2 X

The Work of the Secret Orders

The task before the secret orders was to regulate the conduct of the blacks and their leaders, in order that honor, life, and property might be made secure. They planned to do this by playing upon the fears, superstitions, and cowardice of the black race; by creating a white terror to offset the black one. To this end they made use of strange and horrible disguises, mysterious and fearful conversation, midnight rides and drills, and silent parades.

The costume varied with the locality, often with the individual.[1] The Tennessee regalia was too fine for the backwoods Ku Klux to duplicate. The cardboard hat was generally worn. It was funnel-shaped, eighteen inches to two feet high, covered with white cloth, and often ornamented with stars of gold, or by pictures of animals. The mask over the face was sometimes white, with holes cut for eyes, mouth, and nose. These holes were bound around with red braid so as to give a horrible appearance. Other eyes, nose, and mouth were painted higher up on the hat. Black cloth with white or red braid was also used for the mask. Sometimes simply a woman's veil was worn over the head and held down by an ordinary woollen hat. The "hill billy" Ku Kluxes did not adorn themselves very much. To the sides of the cardboard hats horns were sometimes attached, and to the mask a fringe of quills, which looked like enormous teeth and made a peculiar noise. The mask and the robe were usually of different colors. Sometimes a black sack was drawn

societies, which he says were connected in some way; the first group was absorbed into Ku Klux Klan ; the second consisted of opposing societies ; they existed before, during, and after the Civil War. 1. The Lost Clan of Cocletz, Knights of the Golden Circle, Knights of the White Camelia, Centaurs of Caucasian Civilization, Angels of Avenging Justice, etc. 2. The Underground Railroad, The Red String Band, The Union League, The Black Avengers of Justice, etc.

"The generic name of Ku Klux was applied to all secret organizations in the South composed of white natives and having for their object the execution of the 'first law of nature.' There were many organizations (principally of local origin) which had no connection one with another ; others, again, were more extended in their influence and operations. The one numerically the largest and which embraced the most territory was the White Camelia." — Dr. G. P. L. Reid.

[1] "Their robes used in these nocturnal campaigns consisted simply of sheets wrapped around their bodies and belted around the waist. The lower portion reached to the heels, whilst the upper had eyeholes through which to see, and mouth holes through which to breathe. Of course, every man so caparisoned had one or more pistols in holsters buckled to his waist." — Randolph.

over the head, and eyes, mouth, and nose holes cut in it. False or painted beards were often worn. The robe consisted of a white or colored gown, reaching nearly to the heels, and held by a belt around the waist; it was usually made of fancy calico; white gowns were sometimes striped with red or black. As long as the negro went into spasms of fear at the sight of a Ku Klux, the usual costume

KU KLUX COSTUMES.
Worn in Western Alabama.

seems to have been white; but after the negro became somewhat accustomed to the Ku Klux, and learned that there were human beings behind the robes, the regalia became only a disguise, and less attention was devoted to making fearful costumes. As a rule the ordinary clothes worn were underneath, but in Madison County the Ghouls sported fancy red flannel trousers with white stripes, while the west Alabama spirits were content with wearing ordinary dark trousers, and shirts slashed with red. The white robe was often a bed sheet held on by a belt. After a night ride the disguise could be taken off and stowed about the person. The horses were covered with sheets or white cloth, held on by the saddle and by belts. There was, at times, a disguise which fitted the horse's head, and the horses were sometimes painted. Skeleton sheep's heads or cows' heads, or even human skulls, were frequently carried on the saddle-bows. A framework was sometimes made to fit the shoulders of a Ghoul and caused him to appear twelve feet high. A skeleton wooden hand at the end of a stick served to greet negroes at midnight. Every man had a small whistle. The costume was completed by a brace of pistols worn under the robe.[1]

The trembling negro who ran into the Ku Klux on his return from the love-feasts at the Loyal League meetings was informed that the white-robed figures he saw were the spirits of the Confederate dead, killed at Chickamauga or Shiloh, and that they were unable to rest in their graves because of the conduct of the negroes. He was told in a sepulchral voice of the necessity for his remaining at home more and taking a less active part in various predatory excursions. In the middle of the night the sleeping negro would wake to find his house surrounded by the ghostly company, or find several standing by his bedside, ready, as soon as he woke, to inform him that they were the ghosts of men whom he had formerly known, killed at Shiloh. They had scratched through from Hell to warn the negroes of the consequences of their misconduct. Hell was a dry and thirsty land; they asked him for water. Buckets of water went sizzling into a sack of leather, rawhide, or rubber, concealed within the flowing robe. At other times, Hell froze over to give passage to the spirits who were returning to earth. It was seldom necessary at this early stage to use violence. The black population was in an ecstacy of fear. A silent host of white-sheeted horsemen parad-

---

[1] Ala. Test., pp. 149–152, 275, 452, 453, 535, 574, 579, 597, 668, 707, 919, 1048, 1553; Somers, "Southern States," p. 152; Report of Joint Committee, Alabama Legislature, 1868; oral accounts. The Ku Klux costumes represented in Wilson's "History of the American People," Vol. V, Ch. I, were captured after a Ku Klux parade in Huntsville, Ala. When costumes were to be made, the materials were sometimes sent secretly to the women, who made them according to directions and returned them secretly.

ing the country roads at night was sufficient to reduce the black to good behavior for weeks or months. One silent Ghoul, posted near a League meeting place, would be the cause of the dissolution of that club. Cow bones in a sack were rattled. A horrible being, fifteen feet tall, walking through the night toward a place of congregation, was pretty apt to find that every one vacated .the place before he arrived. A few figures, wrapped in bed sheets and sitting on tombstones in a graveyard near which negroes passed, would serve to keep the immediate community quiet for weeks, and give it a reputation for "hants" which lasts perhaps until to-day. At times the Klan paraded the streets of the towns, men and horses perfectly disguised. The parades were always silent, and so conducted as to give the impression of very large numbers. Regular drills were held in town and country, and the men showed that they had not forgotten their training in the Confederate army. There were no commands unless in a very low tone or in a mysterious language; usually they drilled by signs or by whistle signals.[1]

For a year or more, — until the spring of 1868, — the Klan was successful so far as the negro was concerned, through its mysterious methods. The carpet-bagger and the scalawag were harder problems. They understood the nature of the secret order and knew its objects. As long as the order did not use violence they were not to be moved to any great extent. Then, too, the negro lost some of his fear of the supernatural beings. Different methods were now used. In March and April, 1868, there was an outbreak of Ku Kluxism over a large part of the state.[2] For the first time the newspapers were filled with Ku Klux orders and warnings. The warnings were found posted on the premises of obnoxious negroes or white Radicals. The newspapers sometimes published them for the benefit of all who might be interested. One warning was supposed to be suffi-

---

[1] Ala. Test., pp. 352, 452, 453, 490, 533, 534 ; Beard, "Ku Klux Sketches"; Brown, "Lower South," Ch. IV ; Lester and Wilson, Ch. III ; Weir, "Old Times in Georgia," p. 32 ; accounts of former members.

[2] "Concerning any elaborate organization, I am unable to state from any personal experience. There were certain heads of departments or organizations, under heads or chiefs bearing titles intended to strike awe into the minds of the ignorant. In some instances organizers were sent to towns to establish the Klans. These latter were formed into companies officered somewhat in military style. In (1868) I was honored by being chosen leader of the Tuscaloosa Klan, and even at this late day I am gratified to be able to say that my company did good service to Tuscaloosa." — Randolph.

cient to cause the erring to mend their ways.[1] If still obstinate in their evil courses, a writ from the Klan followed and punishment was inflicted. Warnings were sent to all whom the Klan thought should be regulated—white or black. The warnings were written in disguised handwriting and sometimes purposely misspelled. The following warning was sent to I. D. Sibley, a carpetbagger in Huntsville: —

"Dam Your Soul. The Horrible Sepulchre and Bloody Moon has at last arrived. Some live to-day to-morrow "Die." We the undersigned understand through our Grand "Cyclops" that you have recommended a big Black Nigger for Male agent on our rc rode ; wel, sir, Jest you understand in time if he gets on the rode you can make up your mind to pull roape. If you have any thing to say in regard to the Matter, meet the Grand Cyclops and Conclave at Den No. 4 at 12 o'clock midnight, Oct. 1st, 1871.

" When you are in Calera we warn you to hold your toungo and not speak so much with your mouth or otherwise you will be taken on supprise and led out by the Klan and learnt to stretch hemp. Beware. Beware. Beware. Beware.

(Signed)   "PHILLIP ISENBAUM,
                              " Grand Cyclops.
          "JOHN BANKSTOWN.
          "ESAU DAVES.
          "MARCUS THOMAS.
          "BLOODY BONES.

" You know who. And all others of the Klan."

KU KLUX WARNING.

Mr. Selblys you had better leave here.   You are a thief and you know it. If you don't leave in ten days, we will cut your throat.   We aint after the negroes ; but we intend for you damn carpet bag men to go back to your homes.   You are stealing everything you can find.   We mean what we say.   *Mind your eye.*

JAMES HOWSYN.
WILLIAM WHEREATNEHR.
[Rude drawing of coffin.]   JOHN MIXEMUHH.
SOLIMAN WILSON.
P. J. SOLON.

Get away!
We ant no cu-cluxes but if you dont go we will make you.[2]

---

[1] "We had regular meetings about once a week, at which the conduct of certain offensive characters would be discussed, and if the majority voted to punish such, it would be done accordingly on certain prescribed nights.   Sometimes it was deemed necessary only to post notices of warning, which, in some cases, were sufficient to alarm the victims and to induce them to reform in their behavior.   To the best of my recollection, our company consisted of about sixty members.   As soon as our object was effected, viz., got the negroes to behave themselves, we disbanded.   I well remember those notices in *The Monitor*, for they were concocted and posted by my own hand — disguised of course." — Randolph.

[2] Printed in Report of Joint Committee, Alabama Legislature, 1868.   The warning is not in the ordinary Ku Klux form.   The purpose is clear, however.   The illiteracy is probably assumed, though not necessarily.

The published orders of the Klan served a double purpose —
to notify the members of contemplated movements, and to frighten
the Radicals, white or black, who had made themselves offensive.
The newspapers usually published these orders with the remark
that the order had been found or had been sent to them with a request
for publication.[1] Each Cyclops composed his own orders, but there
was a marked resemblance between the various decrees. The most
interesting and lively orders were concocted by the Cyclops editor of
the *Tuscaloosa Independent Monitor*.[2] Some specimens are given below.

A Black Belt warning was in this shape: —

K. K. K.

Friday, April 3rd, 1868

Warning — For one who understands.

26 / 3 / 68   No. 5 — 116

Recorded 8th / 16 / 24 — B.

K. K. K.

[1] HEADQUARTERS S. V. W.,

ANCIENT COMMANDERY,

Mother Earth.

1st Quarter New Moon.

1st year of Revenge.

Special Order :

The worldly medium for the expression of SOUTHERN OPINION is notified to
publish for the eyes of humanity the orders of the offended Ghosts. Failing to do so,
let him prepare his soul for travelling beyond the limits of his corporosity.

Cyclops warns it — print it well,

Or glide instanter down to h—l!

By order of the Great

BLUFUSTIN

The Mighty Chief.   HOBGOBLIN.

True Copy,   PETERLOO.

S. K. K. K.

— *Independent Monitor*, April 1, 1868.

[2] "They [Ku Klux orders] had this meaning : the very night of the day on which
said notices made their appearance, three notably offensive negro men were dragged out
of their beds, escorted to the old boneyard (¼ mile from Tuscaloosa) and thrashed in
the regular ante-bellum style, until their unnatural nigger pride had a tumble, and
humbleness to the white man reigned supreme." — Randolph.

The following order was posted in Tuscaloosa : —

KU KLUX.

> Hell-a-Bulloo Hole — Den of Skulls.
> Bloody Bones, Headquarters of the
> Great Ku Klux Klan, No. 1000
> Windy Month — New Moon.
> Cloudy Night — Thirteenth Hour.

General Orders, No. 2.

The great chief Simulacre summons you!
Be ready! Crawl slowly! Strike hard!
Fire around the pot!

> Sweltered venom, sleeping got
> Boil thou first i' the charmed pot!

Like a hell broth boil and bubble!
The Great High Priest Cyclops! C. J. F. Y.
Grim Death calls for one, two, three!
Varnish, Tar, and Turpentine!
The fifth Ghost sounds his Trumpet!
The mighty Genii wants two black wethers!
Make them, make them, make them! Presto!
The Great Giantess must have a white barrow.   Make him, make him, make him!
Presto!

Meet at once — the den of Shakes — the Giant's jungles — the hole of Hell! The second hobgoblin will be there, a mighty Ghost of valor.   His eyes of fire, his voice of thunder!   Clean the streets — clean the serpents' dens.

Red hot pincers! Bastinado!! Cut clean!!! No more to be born.   Fire and brimstone.

Leave us, leave us, leave us!   One, two, and three to-night!   Others soon!

Hell freezes!   On with skates — glide on.   Twenty from Atlanta.   Call the roll. *Bene dicte !*   The Great Ogre orders it!

> By order of the Great
> BLUFUSTIN.

G. S.   K. K. K.

A true copy,

PETERLOO.

P. S.   K. K. K.

The following was circulated around Montgomery in April, 1868 : —

K. K. K.

CLAN OF VEGA.

> HDQR'S K. K. K. HOSPITALLERS.
> *Vega Clan,* New Moon.
> 3rd Month, Anno K. K. K. 1.

Order No. K. K.

Clansmen — Meet at the Trysting Spot when Orion Kisses the Zenith.   The doom of treason is Death.   *Dies Iræ.*   The wolf is on his walk — the serpent coils to strike. Action!   Action!!   Action!!!   By midnight and the Tomb ; by Sword and Torch and the Sacred Oath at Forrester's Altar, I bid you come! The clansmen of Glen Iran and Alpine will greet you at the new-made grave.

Remember the Ides of April.

By command of the Grand D. I. H.

CHEG. V.

The military authorities forbade the newspapers to publish Ku Klux orders,[1] and the Klan had to trust to messengers. Verbal orders and warnings became the rule. The Den met and discussed the condition of affairs in the community. The cases of violent whites and negroes were brought up, one by one, and the Den decided what was to be done. Except in the meeting the authority of the Cyclops was absolute.

C. C. Sheets, a prominent scalawag, had been making speeches to the negroes against the whites. The Klan visited him at his hotel at Florence, caught him as he was trying to escape over the roof, brought him back, and severely lectured him in regard to his conduct. They explained to him that the Klan was a conservative organization to hold society together. A promise was required of Sheets to be more guarded in his language for the future. He saw the light and became a changed man.[2] When a carpet-bagger became unbearable, he would be notified that he must go home, and he usually went. If an official, he resigned or sold his office; the people of the community would purchase a $100 lot from him for $2500 in order to pay for the office. The office was not always paid for; a particularly bad man was lucky to get off safe and sound.[3] Objectionable candidates were forced to withdraw, or to take a conservation bondsman, who conducted the office.[4]

Before the close of 1868 the mysterious element in the power of Ku Klux Klan ceased to be so effective. The negroes were learning. Most of the mummery now was dropped. The Klan became purely a body of regulators, wearing disguises. It was said that in order

[1] Report of Meade, 1868.

[2] Report of Joint Committee, 1868 ; Ala. Test., p. 876 (William M. Lowe).

[3] In 1869–1870 there was an epidemic of resignations in the Black Belt. It was in the rich Black Belt that the carpet-bagger flourished. The departing Radical could always sell his property at a high price, the whites often uniting to purchase it. In Perry, Pickens, Choctaw, Marengo, Hale, and other Black Belt counties the carpet-baggers resigned and left. Ala. Test., pp. 103, 104.

[4] The case of W. B. Jones of Marengo County was well known. See Ala. Test., p. 1455 *et passim.*

to have time to work for themselves, and in order not to frighten away negro laborers, the Klan became accustomed to making its rounds in the summer after the crops were laid by, and in the winter after they were gathered.[1]

The activities of the Klan were all-embracing. From regulating bad negroes and their leaders they undertook a general supervision of the morals of the community. Houses of ill-fame were visited, the inmates, white or black, warned and sometimes whipped. Men who frequented such places were thrashed. A white man living with a negro woman was whipped, and a negro man living with a white woman would be killed.[2] A negro who aired his opinion in regard to social equality was sure to be punished. One negro in north Alabama served in the Union army and, returning to Alabama, boasted that he had a white wife up North and expected to see the custom of mixed marriages grow down South. He was whipped and allowed a short time in which to return North.[3] White men who were too lazy to support their families, or who drank too much whiskey, or were cruel to their families, were visited and disciplined. Such men were not always Radicals — not by any means.[4] Special attention was paid to the insolent and dangerous negro soldiers who were mustered out in the state. As a rule they had imbibed too many notions of liberty, equality, and fraternity ever to become peaceable citizens. They brought their arms back with them, made much display of them, talked largely, drilled squads of blacks, fired their hearts with tales of the North, and headed much of the deviltry. The Klan visited such characters, warned them, thrashed them, and disarmed them. Over north Alabama there was a general disarming of negroes.[5]

---

[1] Ala. Test., p. 935 (a Bureau agent). It is more likely that this was when the Klan was dying out and the class of men composing it had no time to go on night rides while the crops were needing their attention. During the leisure seasons time would hang heavy on their hands, and they would begin their deviltry again.

[2] I have learned of only two such cases ; one was in Tuscaloosa County. The woman was a Bureau school-teacher from the North. *Independent Monitor*, May 24, 1871. The other was the case of America Trammell in east Alabama. Ala. Test., p. 1119.

[3] Ala. Test., pp. 166, 433, 459, 462, 476, 1125, 1126, 1749.

[4] Ala. Test., pp. 476, 1125, 1126.

[5] Ala. Test., pp. 922, 923, *et passim*. I have been told that in one place 2000 muskets were collected, taken from negroes.

The tories or "unionists," who had never ceased to commit depredations on their Confederate neighbors, were taken in hand by the Klan. In parts of the white counties where there were neither negroes nor carpet-baggers the Klan's excuse for existence was to hold in check the white outlaws. For years after the war the lives and property of ex-Confederates were not safe. A smouldering civil war existed for several years, and the Klan was only the ex-Confederate side of it.

During the administration of Governor Smith there was no organized militia. The militia laws favored the black counties at the expense of the white ones, and Smith was afraid to organize negro militia; he shared the dislike of his class for negroes. There were not enough white reconstructionists to organize into militia companies. The governor was afraid to accept organizations of Conservatives; they might overthrow his administration. So he relied entirely upon the small force of the Federal troops stationed in the state to assist the state officials in preserving order. The Conservative companies, after their services were rejected, sometimes proceeded to drill without authority, and became a kind of extra-legal militia. In this they were not secret. But the drills had a quieting effect on marauders of all kinds, and the extra-legal militia of the daytime easily became the illegal night riders of the Klan.[1]

The operations of the Klan, especially in the white counties which had large negro populations, were sometimes directed against negro churches and schoolhouses, and a number of these were burned.[2] This hostility may be explained in several ways: The element of poor whites in the Klan did not approve of negro education; all negro churches and schoolhouses were used as meeting places for Union Leagues, political gatherings, etc.; they were the political headquarters of the Radical Party;[3] again, the bad character of some of the white teachers of negro schools or the incendiary teachings of others was excuse for burning the schoolhouses. The burning of school and church buildings took place almost exclusively in the white counties of northern and eastern Alabama. The school and church

[1] Ala. Test., p. 1179. The legal militia consisted of Major-General Dustan only.
[2] Not nearly so many as is usually supposed. Lakin, who never underestimated anything, could think of only *six* in all north Alabama.
[3] Ala. Test., 1138; Coburn-Buckner Report.

buildings of the whites were also burned.[1] The negroes were invariably assisted by the whites in rebuilding the houses. Most of the burnings were probably done by the so-called spurious Ku Klux. The teachers of negro schools who taught revolutionary doctrines or who became too intimate with the negroes with whom they had to board were disciplined, and the negroes also with whom they offended.[2] It was likewise the case with the northern missionaries, especially the Northern Methodist preachers who were seeking to disrupt the Southern Methodist Church. Parson Lakin when elected president of the State University was chased away by the Ku Klux, and life was made miserable for the Radical faculty.[3] Thieves, black and white, and those peculiar clandestine night traders who purchased corn and cotton from the negroes after dark were punished.[4]

The quietest and most effective work was done in the Black Belt principally by the Knights of the White Camelia. Nothing was attempted beyond restraining the negroes and driving out the carpetbaggers when they became unbearable. There were few cases of violence, fewer still of riots or operations on a large scale.[5] In northern and western Alabama were the most disordered conditions.[6] The question was complicated in these latter regions by the presence

---

[1] Several southern churches seized by Lakin for the northern church were burned.

[2] Report of Joint Committee, 1868 ; Ala. Test., p. 1138.

[3] Ala. Test., pp. 126, 127, 230, 418. See above, p. 612.

[4] Ala. Test., p. 1983.

[5] "Of the acts of this Order much has been written which is untrue ; every disturbance between the races was laid at its door ; every act of violence, in which the negro or the northern man was the victim, it was charged with. I do not deny that extreme measures were sometimes resorted to, but of such I have no personal knowledge. . . . Four hours would have been in [Perry County] ample time to secure the assembly, at any central point, of a thousand resolute men who would have done the bidding of their commander whatever it might have been, yet in this time [three years] no single act of violence was committed on the person or property of a negro or alien by its order or which received its sanction or indorsement." — Dr. G. P. L. Reid.

[6] However, in 1871 Governor Lindsay stated that there were in the state fewer feuds, crimes, difficulties, etc., than since 1819, when the state was admitted. This was especially the case, he said, in northern Alabama, for this reason : the people of the mountain and hill county were now prosperous ; cotton was selling for $100 to $150 a bale ; these white mountaineers by their own labor were doing well. Such was not the case with the planter who had to hire negro labor and pay high prices for provisions, farming implements, and mules. Meat that cost the planter 22 cents a pound was raised by the mountain people. Outrages against negroes were now very rare. Ala. Test., pp. 206–207. It is certain that the prosperity of the white counties which in 1870 got rid of the alien local officials had much to do with allaying disorder.

of poor whites and planters, negroes, Radicals and Democrats, Confederates and Unionists. Tuscaloosa County, the location of the State University, is said to have suffered worst of all. A strong organization of Ku Klux cleared it out. In the northern and western sections of the state politics were more likely to enter into the quarrels. The Radicals — white and black — were more apt to be disciplined because of politics than in the Black Belt. Negroes and offensive whites were warned not to vote the Radical ticket. There was a disposition to suppress, not to control, the negro vote as the Black Belt wanted to do. There were more frequent collisions, more instances of violence.

The most famous parade and riot of the Ku Klux Klan occurred in Huntsville, in 1868, before the presidential election. A band of 1500 Ku Klux[1] rode into the city and paraded the streets. Both men and horses were covered with sheets and masks. The drill was silent; the evolutions were executed with a skill that called forth praise from some United States army officers who were looking on. The negroes were in a frenzy of fear, and one of them fired a shot. Immediately a riot was on. The negroes fired indiscriminately at themselves and at the undisguised whites who were standing around. The latter returned the fire; the Ku Klux fired no shots, but formed a line and looked on. Several negroes were wounded, and Judge Thurlow, a scalawag, of Limestone County, was accidentally killed by a chance shot from a negro's gun. The whites who took part received only slight wounds. Some of the Ghouls were arrested by the military authorities, but were released.[2] This was, in the annals of the Radical party, a great Ku Klux outrage.

Another widely heralded Ku Klux outrage was the Patona or Cross Plains affair, in Calhoun County, in 1870. It seems that at Cross Plains a negro boy was hired to hold a horse for a white man. He turned the horse loose, and was slapped by the white fellow. Then the negro hit the white on the head with a brick. Other whites came up and cuffed the negro, who went to Patona, a negro railway

[1] The estimate is Lakin's.
[2] Report Joint Committee of 1868 ; Ala. Test., p. 115 *et passim*. The *N. Y. Tribune,* Nov. 14, 1868, states that Gustavus Horton, the first Radical mayor of Mobile, was killed in this riot. After the riot was over the United States troops appeared too late, as they usually were in such cases.

village a mile away, and told his story. William Luke, a white Canadian, who was teaching a negro school at Patona, advised the negroes to arm themselves and go burn Cross Plains in revenge and for protection. Thirty or forty went, under the leadership of Luke, and made night hideous with threats of violence and burning, but finally went away without harming any one. The next night Luke and his negroes returned, and fired into a congregation of whites just dismissed from church. None were injured, but Luke and several negroes were arrested. There were signs of premeditated delay on the part of some of the civil authorities, so the Ku Klux came and took the Canadian and four negroes from the officers, carried them to a lonely spot, and hanged some and shot the rest.[1]

In Greene County the county solicitor, Alexander Boyd, an ex-convict, claimed to have evidence against members of the Ku Klux organization. He boasted about his plans, and the Ku Klux, hearing of it, went to his hotel in Eutaw and shot him to death.[2]

Another famous outrage was the Eutaw riot in 1870. Both Democrats and Radicals had advertised political meetings for the same time and place. The Radicals, who seem to have been the latest comers, asked the Democrats for a division of time. The latter answered that the issues as to men or measures were not debatable. So the Democrats and Radicals held their meetings on opposite sides of the court-house. The Democrats' meeting ended first, and they stood at the edge of the crowd to hear the Radical speakers. Some of the hot bloods came near the stand and made sarcastic remarks. One man who was to speak, Charles Hays, was so obnoxious to the whites that even the Radicals were unwilling for him to speak. He persisted, and some one, presumably a Conservative, pulled his feet out from under him, and he fell off the table from which he was speaking. The negroes, seeing his fall, rushed forward with knives and pistols to protect him. A shot was fired, which struck Major Pierce, a Democrat, in the pocket. Then the whites began

---

[1] Ala. Test., pp. 77, 429 *et passim*; *Montgomery Mail*, July 16, 1870. The mountain people had another grudge against Luke. He associated constantly with negroes and was said to be a miscegenationist. The mountain farmers had the greatest horror of such.

[2] Ala. Test., pp. 257, 266, 275, *et passim*. Boyd had many private enemies, among them relatives of a man he had killed, and it was charged that they killed him. He was a man of low character, and his own party was not sorry to lose him.

firing, principally into the air. The negroes tore down the fence in their haste to get away. After the whites had chased the negroes out of town the military came leisurely in and quelled the riot.[1] The campaign report of casualties was five killed and fifty-four wounded. As a matter of fact only one wounded negro was ever found, and no dead ones.[2]

A common kind of outrage was that on James Alston, the negro representative in the legislature from Macon County in 1870. Alston was shot by negro political rivals just after a League meeting in Tuskegee. They were arrested, and Alston asked the whites to protect him. The Democratic white citizens of Tuskegee guarded him. The carpet-bag postmaster in Tuskegee saw the possibilities of the situation and sent word to the country negroes to come in armed, that Alston had been shot. They swarmed into Tuskegee, and, thinking the whites had shot Alston, were about to burn the town. The white women and children were sent to Montgomery for safety. About the same time the negroes murdered three white men. The excitement reached Montgomery, and a negro militia company was hastily organized to go to the aid of the Tuskegee negroes. General Clanton got hold of the sheriff, and they succeeded in turning back the negro volunteer company. The affair passed off without further bloodshed, and Alston was notified to leave Tuskegee.[3]

There were no collisions between the United States soldiers and the night riders. At first they were on pretty good terms with one another. The soldiers admired their drills and parades and the way they scared the negroes. One impudent Cyclops rode his band into Athens, and told the commanding officer that they were there to assist in preserving order, and, if he needed them, would come if he scratched on the ground with a stick.[4]

---

[1] It was a marked fact that no resistance to the United States soldiers was ever attempted. When the soldiers appeared, all violence ceased. The soldiers were as a rule in favor of the whites and sometimes took a hand in the Ku Kluxing. They usually appeared after the row was over.

[2] Ala. Test., pp. 81, 221, *et passim*; *Eutaw Whig*, Oct. 27, 1870.

[3] Ala. Test., p. 229 *et passim*. When he testified before the Ku Klux Committee, Alston swore that it was the men whom he had asked to protect him that had shot him, — such men as General Cullen A. Battle.

[4] Ala. Test., p. 723.

While there was not much dependence upon central authority,[1] there was a loose bond of federation between the Dens. They coöperated in their work; a Den from Pickens County would operate in Tuscaloosa or Greene and *vice versa*. Alabama Ku Kluxes went into Mississippi and Tennessee, and those states returned such favors. When the spurious organizations began to commit outrages, each state claimed that the other one furnished the men.[2]

The oath taken by the Ku Klux demanded supreme allegiance to the order so far as related to the problems before the South. Members of the order sat on juries and refused to convict; were summoned as witnesses and denied all knowledge of the order; were members of the legislature, lawyers, etc. It is claimed that no genuine members of the order were ever caught and convicted.[3]

Though the Klan was almost wholly a Democratic organization,[4] it took little share in the ordinary activities of politics, more perhaps in the northern counties than elsewhere. In Fayette County, in 1870, the Klan went on a raid, and when returning stopped in the court-house, took off disguises, resolved themselves into a convention, and nominated a county ticket.[5] Nothing of the kind was done in south Alabama; indeed, the constitution of the White Camelias forbade interference in politics.[6] The Union League meetings were broken up only when they were sources of disorder, thievery, etc. When cases of outrage were investigated, it was almost invariably found that they had no political significance. Governor Lindsay sent an agent into every community where an outrage was reported, and in not a single instance was a case of outrage by Ku Klux discovered.

It is probably true that few, if any, of the leading Democratic politicians were members of the Klan or of any similar organization. Under certain conditions they might be driven by force of circum-

---

[1] "The company of K. K. K.'s which was organized in Tuscaloosa, was an independent organization, *i.e.* it was altogether a local affair, having no connection with any general Klan." — Randolph.

[2] Miss. Test., pp. 60, 223, 249; Ala. Test., pp. 213, 1822–1824 ; Garner, "Reconstruction in Mississippi," pp. 345, 346.

[3] Ala. Test., p. 942 ; Lester and Wilson, p. 78.

[4] The anti-negro bands of the hills and mountains were rather of the spurious Ku Klux and were largely composed of tories and Radicals.

[5] Ala. Test., p. 1763.

[6] Constitution, Article 76; Brown, "Ku Klux Movement," *Atlantic Monthly*, May, 1901.

stances to join in local uprisings against the rule of the Radicals. But as a rule they knew little of the secret orders. There were various reasons for this. The Conservative leaders saw the danger in such an organization, though recognizing the value of its services. It was sure to degenerate. It might become too powerful. It would have a bad influence on politics and would furnish too much campaign literature for the Radicals. It would result in harsh legislation against the South. The testimony of General Clanton [1] and Governor Lindsay [2] shows just what the party leaders knew of the order and what they thought of it. The Ku Klux leaders were not the political leaders.[3] The newspapers of importance opposed the order. The opposition of the political leaders to the Klan in its early stages was not because of any wrong done by it to the Radicals, but because of fear of its acting as a boomerang and injuring the white party. It was the middle classes, so to speak, and later the lower classes, who felt more severely the tyranny of the carpet-bag rule, who formed and led the Klan. The political leaders thought that in a few years political victories would give relief; the people who suffered were unable to wait, and threw off the revolutionary government by revolutionary means.[4]

The work of the secret orders was successful. It kept the negroes quiet and freed them to some extent from the baleful influence of alien leaders; the burning of houses, gins, mills, and stores ceased; property was more secure; people slept safely at night; women and children were again somewhat safe when walking abroad, — they had faith in the honor and protection of the Klan; the incendiary agents who had worked among the negroes left the country, and agitators, political, educational, and religious, became more moderate; "bad niggers" ceased to be bad; labor was less disorganized; the carpet-baggers and scalawags ceased to batten on the southern communities, and the worst ones were driven from the country.[5] It

---

[1] Ala. Test., pp. 226–257.   [2] Ala. Test., pp. 159–225.

[3] With the White Camelia in south Alabama the case was somewhat different.

[4] See Testimony of Lindsay and Clanton, cited above ; also Ala. Test., p. 376 (Pettus); p. 896 (Lowe).

[5] Somers, "Southern States," pp. 4, 15, 21 ; Lester and Wilson, Chs. III, IV, V; Sanders, "Early Settlers," p. 31. "The peaceful citizen knew that a faithful patrol had guarded his premises while he slept." — Mrs. Stubbs. Brown, "Lower South," Ch. IV ; Ala. Test., pp. 432, 1520, 1532, 1803.

2 Y

was not so much a revolution as a conquest of revolution.[1] Society was bent back into the old historic grooves from which war and Reconstruction had jarred it.

Spurious Ku Klux Organizations

After an existence of two or three years the Ku Klux Klan was disbanded in March, 1869, by order of the Grand Wizard. It was at that time illegal to print Ku Klux notices and orders in the newspapers. It is probable, therefore, that the order to disband never reached many Dens. However, one or two papers in north Alabama did publish the order of dissolution, and in this way the news obtained a wider circulation.[2] Many Dens disbanded simply because their work was done. Otherwise the order of the Grand Wizard would have had no effect. Numbers of Dens had fallen into the hands of lawless men who used the name and disguise for lawless purposes. Private quarrels were fought out between armed bands of disguised men. Negroes made use of Ku Klux methods and disguises when punishing their Democratic colored brethren and when on marauding expeditions.[3] This, however, was not usual except where the negroes were led by whites. Horse thieves in northern and western Alabama, and thieves of every kind everywhere, began to wear disguises and to announce themselves as Ku Klux. All their proceedings were heralded abroad as Ku Klux outrages.[4]

In Morgan County a neighborhood feud was resolved into two parties calling themselves Ku Klux and Anti Ku Klux, and frequently fights resulted. In Blount and Morgan counties (1869) former members of the Ku Klux organized the Anti Ku Klux along the lines of the Ku Klux, held regular meetings, and continued their

---

[1] Throughout the pages of the Ku Klux Testimony are found assertions that Ku Klux was not an organization, but merely the understanding of the southern people, the spirit of the community, the concert of feeling of the whites, a state of mind in the population.

[2] Ala. Test., pp. 165, 380, 649, 724 ; Somers, " Southern States," p. 154. Governor Lindsay said that the so-called Ku Klux who went over to Mississippi were roughs and that the people were glad when they heard that one of them had been shot. In 1870-1871, while living in Alabama, General Forrest, the reputed Grand Wizard, repeatedly condemned in the strongest terms the conduct of the so-called Ku Klux. Ala. Test., pp. 212, 213.

[3] Ala. Test., pp. 162, 376.   [4] Ala. Test., p. 719.

midnight deviltry as before.   It was composed largely of Union men
who had been Federal soldiers.[1]   In Fayette County the Anti Ku
Klux order was styled, by themselves and others, "Mossy Backs"
or "Moss Backs," in allusion to their war record.   They were regularly organized and had several collisions with another organization
which they called the Ku Klux.   The Radical sheriff summoned
the "Moss Backs" as a *posse* to assist in the arrest of the Ku Klux,
as they called the ex-Confederates.[2]   As long as the Federal troops
were in the state it was the practice of bands of thieves to dress in
the army uniform and go on raids.

The Radicals took care that all lawlessness was charged to the
account of Ku Klux.   It was to their interest that the outrages continue and furnish political capital.   Governor Smith accused Senator
Spencer and Hinds and Sibley, of Huntsville, of fostering Ku Klux
outrages for political purposes.[3]

The disordered condition of the country during and after the war
led to a general habit among the whites of carrying arms.   This
fact and the drinking of bad whiskey accounts for much of the shooting in quarrels during the decade following the war.   Few of these
quarrels had any connection with politics until they were catalogued
in the Ku Klux Report as Democratic outrages.   As a matter of fact,
nearly all the whites killed by whites or by blacks were Democrats.
The white Radicals were too few in number to furnish many martyrs.[4]
The anti-negro feeling of the poorer whites found expression after
the war in movements against the blacks, called Ku Klux outrages.
In Winston County, a Republican stronghold, the white mountaineers

---

[1] Ala. Test., pp. 610, 778.

[2] Ala. Test., pp. 559, 560, 1229.

[3] Ala. Test., p. 679.   Governor Smith, a Radical, said in regard to the motives of
Senator George E. Spencer, I. D. Sibley, and J. J. Hinds, carpet-baggers : " My candid
opinion is that Sibley does not want the law executed, because that would put down
crime and crime is his life's bread.   He would like very much to have a Ku Klux
outrage every week to assist him in keeping up strife between the whites and blacks,
that he might be more certain of the votes of the latter.   He would like to have a few
colored men killed every week to furnish semblance of truth to Spencer's libels upon
the people of the state generally.   It is but proper in this connection that I should
speak in strong terms of condemnation of the conduct of two white men in Tuskegee a
few days ago, in advising the colored men to resist the authority of the sheriff ; these
men were not Ku Klux, but Republicans." Letter in *Huntsville Advocate*, June 25,
1870. See also Herbert, " Solid South," p. 55.

[4] See Ala. Test., p. 433.

met and passed resolutions that no negro be allowed in the county. General Clanton stated that he found a similar prejudice in all the hill counties.[1]

In the Tennessee valley the planters found difficulty in securing negro labor because of the operations of the spurious Ku Klux. In Limestone, Madison, and Lauderdale counties the tory element hated the negroes, who lived on the best land, and attempts were made to drive them off. The tories were incensed against the planters because they preferred negro labor.[2] Judge W. S. Mudd of Jefferson County testified that the anti-negro outrages in Walker and Fayette counties were committed by the poorer whites, who did not like negroes and wanted a purely white population there. In the white counties generally the negro held no political power and hence the outrages were not political, but because of racial prejudice. In the north Alabama mountain counties the majority of the whites were in favor of deportation and colonization of the blacks. But in nearly every county there was also the large landholder, formerly a slaveholder, who wanted the negro to stay and work, and who treated the ex-slave kindly. The poorer whites who had never owned slaves nor much property wanted the negro out of the way.[3] As a general rule, where the population was exclusively white, the people disliked the negro and wanted no contact with the black race. They wanted a white society, and all lands for the whites. In one precinct in Jefferson County, where all the whites were Republican, an organization of boys and young men was formed to drive out the negroes and keep the precinct white. In the black counties exactly the opposite was true. The secret orders merely wanted to control negro labor and keep it, regulate society, and protect property. General Forney stated that in Calhoun the small mountain farmers, non-slavehold-ing, poorer whites, were intensely afraid of social equality and hated the negroes, who called them "poor white trash." The feeling was cordially returned by the negroes.[4]

From Tallapoosa County and from eastern Alabama generally,

[1] Ala. Test., p. 230. In some communities a negro is still told that he must not let the sun go down on him before leaving.

[2] Ala. Test., pp. 944, 947, 948.

[3] Ala. Test., pp. 1757, 1758, 1764, 1765, 1768. Judge Mudd was by no means a representative of the old slaveholding element, but rather of the white county people.

[4] Ala. Test., p. 492.

where the Black Cavalry and its successors flourished, there was a general exodus of negroes who had lived on the richer lands of the larger farms and plantations. The white renters and small farmers were afraid, after slavery was abolished and the negroes were free, that the latter would drag all others down to negro level. The planters preferred negro labor. Therefore the poorer whites united to drive out the negro. This was called Ku Kluxism. The whites wanted higher pay.[1] Wage-earners felt that they could not compete with the negro, who could work for lower wages. General Crawford, who commanded the United States troops in Alabama, stated that the planter bore no antagonism toward the negro at all, but he wanted his labor; that at present he saw the uselessness of interfering with the negro's politics and was indifferent about whether the negro voted or not; he looked forward to the time when the black voters would fall away from their alien leaders and would vote according to the advice of their old masters; on the other hand, the poorer whites, many of them from the hill country, were hostile to the negroes; they disliked to see them at work building the new railroads, and on all the rich lands, and possessed of political privileges. If rid of the negro, they could be more prosperous and divide the political spoils now shared by the adventurers who controlled the black vote. In north Alabama the negro was more generally kept away from the polls.[2] This feeling on the part of the poor whites was not new, but had survived from slavery days, and its manifestations were now called Ku Kluxism. The negro was no longer under the protection of a master, and the former master was no longer able to protect the negro. However, there was a general movement among the ex-slaves, under the pressure, to return to their old masters.

Attempts to suppress the Ku Klux Movement

In March and April, 1868, the operations of the Ku Klux Klan came to the notice of General Meade, who was then in command of the Third Military District. By his direction General Shepherd issued an order from Montgomery, requiring sheriffs, mayors, police, constables, magistrates, marshals, etc., under penalty of being held responsible, to suppress the "iniquitous" organization and appre-

---

[1] Ala. Test., pp. 1127, 1128, 1139. [2] Ala. Test., pp. 1175, 1179.

hend its members. The expenses of *posses* were to be charged against the county. If the code of Alabama was silent on the subject of the offence, the prisoners were to be turned over to the military authorities for trial by military commission. The state officers were reminded that the code of Alabama derived its vitality from the commanding general of the Third Military District, and in case of a conflict between the code and military orders, the latter were paramount. The posting of placards and the printing in newspapers of orders, warnings, and notices of Ku Klux Klans was forbidden. In no case would ignorance be considered as an excuse. Citizens who were not officers would not be held guiltless in case of outrage in their community.[1] This was a revival of the method of holding a community responsible for the misdeeds of individuals.

Troops were shifted about over northern and central Alabama in an endeavor to suppress Ku Klux. Several arrests were made, but there were no trials. There was much parade and night riding, but as yet little violence. The soldiers could do nothing.

When the carpet-bag government was installed, the military forces of the United States remained to support it. Every one called upon the military commands for aid—governor, sheriffs, judges, members of Congress, justices of the peace, and prominent politicians. No request from official sources was ever refused, and they were frequent. From October 31, 1868, to October 31, 1869, there were fifteen different shiftings of bodies of troops for the purpose of checking the Ku Klux movement. This does not include the movements made in individual cases, but only changes of headquarters. These were principally in northern and western Alabama—at Huntsville, Livingston, Guntersville, Lebanon, Edwardsville, Alpine, Summerfield, Decatur, Marysville, Vienna, and Tuscaloosa.[2]

After a few months' experience of the carpet-bag government, the bands of Ku Klux were excited to renewed activity. The legislature which met in September, 1868, memorialized the President to send an armed force to Alabama to execute the laws, and to preserve order, etc., during the approaching presidential election. Governor Smith with two members of the Senate and three of the lower house were

---

[1] G. O. No. 11, Sub-Dist. Ala., April 4, 1868; *Selma Times and Messenger*, April 9, 1868; *N. Y. Herald*, April 7, 1868.

[2] Report of the Secretary of War, 1869, p. 83 *et seq.*; Report of Meade, 1868.

appointed to bear the application to the President.[1] In December an act was passed authorizing any justice of the peace to issue warrants running in any part of the state, and authorizing any sheriff or constable to go into any county to execute such process.[2] This enabled a sheriff of proper politics to enter counties where the officials were not of the proper faith, and arrest prisoners.

One of the members of the general assembly, M. T. Crossland, was killed by the Klan, it was alleged. The legislature offered a reward of $5000 for his slayers, and authorized the appointment of a committee to investigate the recent alleged outrages and to report by bill.[3] The committee,[4] after pretence of an examination of about a dozen witnesses, all Radicals, some by affidavit only, reported that there was in many portions of Alabama a secret organization, purely political, known as Ku Klux Klan, and that Union men and Republicans were the sole objects of its abuse, none of the opposite politics being interfered with. It worked by means of threatening letters, warnings, and beatings; by intimidation and threats negroes were driven from the polls; negro schoolhouses were burned; teachers were threatened, ostracized, and driven from employment; officers of the law were obstructed in the discharge of their duty and driven away. In some parts of the state, the report declared, it was impossible for the civil authorities to maintain order. The governor was authorized and advised to declare martial law in the counties of Madison, Lauderdale, Butler, Tuscaloosa, and Pickens.[5] The committee reported a bill, which was passed, with a preamble of twenty-two lines reciting the terrible condition of the state. To appear away from home in

---

[1] Joint Resolution, Sept. 22, 1868, in Acts of Ala., p. 292. The delegation to Washington did not provide themselves with an authenticated copy of the resolution and had to wait for it. Governor Smith, who was with the delegation, spoiled everything by declaring that there was no disorder except along the Tennessee River and in southwestern Alabama and that troops were not needed. No officials had been resisted, he said, and it would be imprudent to send troops. *N. Y. Herald*, Sept. 27, 1868. The citizens of Montgomery held a mass-meeting and denied *in toto* the allegations of the memorial, denouncing it as a move of partisan politics. The strangers were sure to fall from power unless upheld by outside force. *N. Y. Herald*, Sept. 25, 1868.

[2] Act of Dec. 24, 1868; Acts of Ala., p. 439.

[3] Joint Resolutions, Nov. 14 and Dec. 8, 1868; Acts of Ala., pp. 593, 594.

[4] J. DeF. Richards and G. R. McAfee of the Senate, and E. F. Jennings, W. R. Chisholm, and G. W. Malone of the House.

[5] Report of Joint Committee on Outrages, 1868.

mask or disguise was made a misdemeanor, punishable by a fine of $100 and imprisonment from six months to one year. For a disguised person to commit an assault was made a felony, and punishment was fixed at a fine of $1000, and imprisonment from five to twenty years. Any one might kill a person in disguise. The penalty for destruction of property by disguised persons — burning a schoolhouse or church — was imprisonment from ten to twenty years. A warrant might be issued by any magistrate directed to any lawful officer of the state to arrest disguised offenders, and in case of refusal or neglect to perform his duty, the official was to forfeit his office and be fined $500.[1]

Two days later it was enacted that in case a person were killed by an outlaw, or by a mob, or by disguised persons, or for political opinion, the widow or next of kin should be entitled to recover of the county in which the killing occurred the sum of $5000. The claimants should bring action in the circuit court, and in case judgment were rendered in favor of the claimants, the county commissioners should assess an additional tax sufficient to pay damages and costs. Failure of any official to perform his duty in such cases was punishable by a fine of $100 or imprisonment for twelve months for every thirty days of neglect or failure. In case of whipping the amount of damages collectible from the county was $1000. But if the offenders were arrested and punished, there could be no claim for damages. And if the offenders were arrested during the pendency of the suit for damages, the presiding judge might suspend proceedings in the damage suit until the result of the trial of the offenders was known. It was made the duty of the solicitor to prosecute the claim for the relatives, and his fee was fixed at 10 per cent of the amount recovered; and if the relatives failed to sue within twelve months, the solicitor was to prosecute in the name of the state, and the damages were to go to the asylums for the insane, deaf, dumb, and blind.[2]

---

[1] Act Dec. 26, 1868; Acts of Ala., 444-446. A supplementary act had to be passed allowing the probate judges to license *for one dollar* the wearing of masks or disguises at balls, theatres, and circuses and other places of amusement, public and private. Application had to be made at least three days beforehand by "three responsible persons of established character and reputation." Act Dec. 31, 1868; Acts of Ala., p. 521.

[2] Act of Dec. 28, 1868; Acts of Ala., pp. 452-454.

A number of arrests were made under these acts, but only one or two convictions were secured. It resulted that most of the arrests were of ignorant and penniless negroes, who were unable to pay any fine whatever. Governor Lindsay defended several such cases. The laws were so severe that the officials were unwilling to prosecute under them, but always prosecuted under the ordinary laws.

After 1868 there was no further anti-Ku-Klux legislation by the state government, but in 1869–1870 some of the southern states, Alabama among them, began to show signs of going Democratic. Virginia, Georgia, Mississippi, and Texas had been forced to ratify the Fifteenth Amendment in order to secure the requisite number for its adoption.[1] President Grant then sent in a message announcing the ratification as "the most important event that has occurred since the nation came into life."[2] Congress responded to the hint in the message by passing the first of the Enforcement Acts, which had been hanging fire for nearly two years. The excuse for its passage was that the Ku Klux organizations would prevent the blacks from voting in the fall elections of 1870.[3] The act, as approved on May 31, 1870, declared that all citizens were entitled to vote in all elections without regard to color or race and provided that officials should be held personally responsible that all citizens should have equal opportunity to perform all tests or prerequisites to registration or voting; election officials were held responsible for fair elections; any person who hindered another in voting might be fined $500, to go to the party aggrieved, and persons in disguise might be fined $5000 or imprisoned for ten years, or both, and should be disfranchised besides. Federal courts were to have exclusive jurisdiction over cases arising under this law, and Federal officials were to see to its execution; the penalty for obstructing an official or assisting an escape might be $500 fine and six months' imprisonment;

---

[1] See Dunning, "Essays," pp. 243–246.

[2] Messages and Papers, Vol. VII, pp. 55, 56, March 30, 1871.

[3] *The Nation*, Feb. 4, 1875, in regard to the "Force" legislation: "It would not have been possible for the most ingenious enemy of the blacks to draw up a code better calculated to keep up and fan the spirit of strife and contention between the races." James L. Pugh, later United States Senator from Alabama: The people were tired of being reconstructed by President and by Congress. Now the Enforcement Laws punish all for the crime of a few. They are an insult to a whole people, assuming them incorrigible. Alabama Testimony, pp. 407, 408, 411.

the President was given authority to use the army and navy to enforce the law; the district attorneys of the United States were to proceed by *quo warranto* against disfranchised persons who were holding office, and such persons might be fined $1000 and imprisonment for one year, — such cases were to have precedence on the docket; the same penalties were visited upon those who under color of any law deprived a citizen of any right under this law; the Civil Rights Bill of 1866, April 9, was reënacted;[1] fraud, bribery, intimidation, or undue influence or violation of any election law at Congressional elections might be punished by a fine of $500 and imprisonment for three years; registrations — congressional, state, county, school, or town — came under the same regulation, and officials of all degrees who failed in their duty were liable to the same penalties; a defeated candidate might contest the election in the Federal courts when there were cases of the negro having been hindered from voting.[2]

This act marked the arrival of the most ruthless period of Reconstruction. Endowing the negro with full political rights had not sufficed to overcome the white political people. Disappointed in that, an attempt was now to be made so to regulate southern elections as to put the mass of the white population permanently under the control of the negroes and their white leaders, and to secure the permanent control of those states to the Republican party. Tennessee had already escaped from the Radical rule, and stringent measures were necessary to prevent like action in the other states. Notwithstanding the Enforcement Act, Alabama, in the election of 1870, went partially Democratic, which was to the Radical leaders *prima facie* evidence of the grossest frauds in elections. Other states were in a similarly bad condition.

The supplementary Enforcement Act of February 28, 1871, provided for the appointment of two supervisors to each precinct by

---

[1] See Burgess, "Reconstruction," pp. 69–73.

[2] Text of act in McPherson, pp. 549–550. This act was ostensibly to provide for the enforcement of the Fourteenth and Fifteenth amendments. Its constitutionality has been criticised on these grounds: (1) the amendments were directed against *states*, not *persons*; (2) the law enacted penalties not only against state officers, but also against any *person* who might offend against the election laws of the state or against this act; (3) it is entirely out of the question to claim that the amendments protect the right of a person within a state against infringement by other persons, or even against the state itself unless on account of race, color, or previous condition. See Burgess, pp. 253–255.

the Federal circuit judge upon the application of two persons; the Federal courts were to be in session during elections for business arising under this act; the supervisors were to have full authority around the polls, and were to certify and send in the returns, and report irregularities, which were to be investigated by the chief supervisor, who was to keep all records; the supervisors were to be assisted in each precinct by two special deputy marshals appointed by the United States marshal for that district. These deputies and also the supervisors had full power to arrest any person and to summon a *posse* if necessary. Offenders were haled at once before the Federal court. Any election offence was punishable by a fine of $3000 and imprisonment of two years, with costs. To refuse to give information in an investigation subjected the person to a fine of $100 and thirty days' imprisonment and costs. State courts were forbidden to try cases coming under the act, and proceedings after warning, by state officials, resulted in imprisonment and fine amounting to one year and $500 to $1000, plus costs.[1]

It was feared that these acts might prove insufficient to carry the southern states for the Republican party in 1872. Grant was becoming more and more radical as the Republican nominating convention and the elections drew nearer. Under the influence of the Radical leaders, he sent, on March 23, 1871, a message [2] to Congress, declaring that in some of the states a condition of affairs existed rendering life and property insecure, and the carrying of mails and collection of revenue dangerous; the state governments were unable to control these evils; and it was doubtful if the President had the authority to interfere. He therefore asked for legislation to secure life, property, and the enforcement of law.[3]

Congress came to the rescue with the Ku Klux Act of April 20,

---

[1] Text of act in McPherson, "Handbook of Politics," 1872, pp. 3–8. While only the congressional elections and all the registrations were to be guarded, the chief purpose of the act was to control state elections, which were held at the same time and place. See Burgess, "Reconstruction," pp. 256–257. This was so clearly the purpose that after the rescue of the state government from carpet-bag rule the time of the state and local elections was changed from November to August in order to escape Federal espionage.

[2] "Upon the basis of information which turned out to be very insufficient and unreliable." — Burgess, p. 257.

[3] Messages and Papers, Vol. VII, pp. 127–128.

1871, "in which Congress simply threw to the winds the constitutional distribution of powers between the states and the United States government in respect to civil liberty, crime, and punishment, and assumed to legislate freely and without limitation for the preservation of civil and political rights within the state." [1]

It gave the President authority to declare the southern states in rebellion and to suspend the writ of *habeas corpus* — after a proclamation against insurrection, domestic violence, unlawful combinations, and conspiracies. Such a state of affairs was declared a rebellion, and the President was authorized to use the army and navy to suppress it. Heavy penalties were denounced ($500 to $5000 fine, and six months' to six years' imprisonment) against persons who conspired to overthrow or destroy the United States government or to levy war against the United States; or who hindered the execution of the laws of the United States, seized its property, prevented any one from accepting or holding office or discharging official duties, drove away or injured, in person or property, any official or any witness in court, went in disguise on highway or on the premises of others, and hindered voting or office-holding. Any person injured in person, property, or privilege had the right to sue the conspirators for damages under the Civil Rights Bill. In Federal courts the jurors had to take oath that they were not in any way connected with such conspiracies, and the judges were empowered to exclude suspected persons from the jury. Persons not connected with such conspiracies, yet having knowledge of such things, were liable to the injured party for all damages. [2]

On May 3, 1871, Grant issued a proclamation calling attention to the fact that the law was one of "extraordinary public importance" and, while of general application, was directed at the southern states, and stating that when necessary he would not hesitate to exhaust the powers vested by the act in the executive. The failure of local communities to protect all citizens would make it necessary for the national government to interfere. [3]

---

[1] Burgess, pp. 257, 258.

[2] Text in McPherson, "Handbook," 1872, pp. 85–87. For criticism, Burgess, pp. 257, 259.

[3] Messages and Papers, Vol. VII, pp. 134, 135.

Ku Klux Investigation

In order to justify the passage of the Enforcement Acts and to obtain material for campaign use the next year, Congress appointed a committee, which was organized on the day the Ku Klux Act was approved, to investigate the condition of affairs in the southern states.[1] From June to August, 1871, the committee took testimony in Washington. In the fall subcommittees visited the various southern states selected for the inquisition. About one-fourth of the Alabama testimony was taken in Washington, the rest was taken by the subcommittee in Alabama.

The members of the subcommittee that took testimony in Alabama were Senators Pratt and Rice, and Messrs. Blair, Beck, and Buckley of the House. Blair and Beck, the Democratic members, were never present together. So the subcommittee consisted of three Republicans and one Democrat. C. W. Buckley was a Radical Representative from Alabama, a former Bureau reverend, who worked hard to convict the white people of the state of general wickedness. The subcommittee held sessions in Huntsville, October 6-14; Montgomery, October 17-20; Demopolis, October 23-28; Livingston, October 30 to November 3; and in Columbus, Mississippi, for west Alabama, November 11. All these places were in black counties. Sessions were held only at easily accessible places, and where scalawag, carpet-bag, and negro witnesses could easily be secured. Testimony was also taken by the committee in Washington from June to August, 1871.

It is generally believed that the examination of witnesses by the Ku Klux committees of Congress was a very one-sided affair, and that the testimony is practically without value for the historian, on account of the immense proportion of hearsay reports and manufactured tales embraced in it. Of course there is much that is worthless because untrue, and much that may be true but cannot be regarded because of the character of the witnesses, whose statements are unsupported. But, nevertheless, the 2008 pages of testimony taken in Alabama furnish a mine of information concerning the social, religious, educational, political, legal, administrative, agricultural, and financial conditions in Alabama from 1865 to 1871. The report

[1] Report of the Committee, pp. 1, 2.

itself, of 632 pages, contains much that is not in the testimony, especially as regards railroad and cotton frauds, taxation, and the public debt, and much of this information can be secured nowhere else.

The minority members of the subcommittee which took testimony in Alabama, General Frank P. Blair and later Mr. Beck of New York, caused to be summoned before the committee at Washington, and before the subcommittee in Alabama, the most prominent men of the state — men who, on account of their positions, were intimately acquainted with the condition of affairs. They took care that the examination covered everything that had occurred since the war. The Republican members often protested against the evidence that Blair proposed to introduce, and ruled it out. He took exceptions, and sometimes the committee at Washington admitted it; sometimes he smuggled it in by means of cross-questioning, or else he incorporated it into the minority report. On the other hand, the Republican members of the subcommittee seem to have felt that the object of the investigation was only to get campaign material for the use of the Radical party in the coming elections. They summoned a poor class of witnesses, a large proportion of whom were ignorant negroes who could only tell what they had heard or had feared. The more respectable of the Radicals were not summoned, unless by the Democrats. In several instances the Democrats caused to be summoned the prominent scalawags and carpet-baggers, who usually gave testimony damaging to the Radical cause.

An examination of the testimony shows that sixty-four Democrats and Conservatives were called before the committee and subcommittee. Of these, fifty-seven were southern men, five were northern men residing in the state, and two were negroes. The Democrats testified at great length, often twenty to fifty pages. Blair and Beck tried to bring out everything concerning the character of carpet-bag rule.[1]

[1] Some of the Conservatives who testified were Gen. Cullen A. Battle, R. H. Abercrombie, Gen. James H. Clanton, P. M. Dox, Gov. Robert B. Lindsay, Reuben Chapman, Thomas Cobbs, Daniel Coleman, Jefferson M. Falkner, William H. Forney, William M. Lowe, William Richardson, Francis S. Lyon, William S. Mudd, Gen. Edmund W. Pettus, Turner Reavis, James L. Pugh, P. T. Sayre, R. W. Walker, — all prominent men of high character.

Thirty-four scalawags, fifteen carpet-baggers, and forty-one negro Radicals came before the committee and subcommittee. Some of these were summoned by Blair or Beck, and a number of them disappointed the Republican members of the committee by giving Democratic testimony.[1] The Radicals could only repeat, with variations, the story of the Eutaw riot, the Patona affair, the Huntsville parade, etc. Of the prominent carpet-baggers and scalawags whose testimony was anti-Democratic, most were men of clouded character.[2] The testimony of the higher Federal officials was mostly in favor of the Democratic contention.[3] The negro testimony, however worthless it may appear at first sight, becomes clear to any one who, knowing the negro mind, remembers the influences then operating upon it. From this class of testimony one gets valuable hints and suggestions. The character of the white scalawag and carpet-bag testimony is more complex, but if one has the history of the witness, the testimony usually becomes intelligible. In many instances the testimony gives a short history of the witness.

The material collected by the Ku Klux Committee, and other committees that investigated affairs in the South after the war, can be used with profit only by one who will go to the biographical books and learn the social and political history of each person who testified. When the personal history of an important witness is known, many obscure things become plain. Unless this is known, one cannot safely accept or reject any specific testimony. To one who works in Alabama Reconstruction, Brewer's "Alabama," Garrett's "Reminiscences," the "Memorial Record," old newspaper files, and the memories of old citizens are indispensable.

There is in the first volume of the Alabama Testimony a delightfully partisan index of seventy-five pages. In it the summary of Democratic testimony shows up almost as Radical as the most partisan on the other side. It is meant only to bring out the violence in the testimony. According to it, one would think all those killed

---

[1] Some of those who gave, willingly or unwillingly, Democratic testimony: W. T. Blackford (c.), Judge Busteed (c.), General Crawford, Nicholas Davis (s.), L. W. Day (c.), Samuel A. Hale (c.), J. H. Speed (s.), Senator Willard Warner (c.), N. L. Whitfield (s.). (c.) = carpet-bagger; (s.) = scalawag.

[2] Charles Hays (s.), W. B. Jones (s.), S. F. Rice (s.), John A. Minnis (c.), A. S. Lakin (c.), B. W. Norris (c.), L. E. Parsons (s.), E. W. Peck (s.), and L. R. Smith (c.).

[3] Day, Busteed, Van Valkenburg, General Crawford, etc.

or mistreated were Radicals. The same man frequently figures in three situations, as "shot," "outraged," and "killed." General Clanton's testimony of thirty pages gets a summary of four inches, which tells nothing; that of Wager, a Bureau agent, gets as much for twelve pages, which tells something; and that of Minnis, a scalawag, twice as much. There is very little to be found in the testimony that relates directly to the Ku Klux Klan and similar organizations. Had the sessions of the subcommittee been held in the white counties of north and southwest Alabama, where the Klans had flourished, probably they might have found out something about the organization. But the minority members were determined to expose the actual condition of affairs in the state from 1865 to 1871. No matter how much the Radicals might discover concerning unlawful organizations, the Democrats stood ready with an immense deal of facts concerning Radical misgovernment to show cause why such organizations should arise. Consequently the three volumes of testimony relating to Alabama are by no means pro-Radical, except in the attitude of the majority of the examiners.[1]

Below is given a table of alleged Ku Klux outrages, compiled from the testimony taken. The Ku Klux report classifies all violence under the four heads: killing, shooting, outrage, whipping. The same case frequently figures in two or more classes. Practically every case of violence, whether political or not, is brought into the testimony. The period covered is from 1865 to 1871. Radical outrages as well as Democratic are listed in the report as Ku Klux outrages. In a number of cases Radical outrages are made to appear as Democratic. Many of the cases are simply hearsay. It is not likely that many instances of outrage escaped notice, for every case of actual outrage was proven by many witnesses. Every violent death of man, woman, or child, white or black, Democratic or Radical, occurring between 1865 and 1871, appears in the list as a Ku Klux outrage. Evidently careful search had been made, and certain witnesses had informed themselves about every actual deed of violence. There were then sixty-four counties in the state, and in only twenty-nine of them were there alleged instances of Ku Klux outrage.

[1] Senate Report, No. 48, 42d Cong., 2d Sess., Pts. 8, 9, and 10, and House Report, No. 22, 42d Cong., 2d Sess., Pts. 8, 9, and 10, contain the Alabama Testimony.

TABLE OF ALLEGED OUTRAGES COMPILED FROM THE KU KLUX TESTIMONY

COUNTY	KILLINGS	OUTRAGES	SHOOTINGS	WHIPPINGS	TOTAL	COUNTY	KILLINGS	OUTRAGES	SHOOTINGS	WHIPPINGS	TOTAL
Autauga	—	1	—	—	1	Limestone (k)	7	1	—	1	9
Blount (k)	2	3	—	6	11	Macon (x)	1	4	1	1	7
Calhoun	6	1	1	1	9	Madison (x)	6	19	5	19	49
Chambers (k)	1	—	1	—	2	Marshall (k)	1	—	1	1	3
Cherokee (k)	—	2	—	1	3	Marengo (x)	1	6	—	4	11
Choctaw (x)	11	1	3	—	15	Montgomery (x)	—	1	—	—	1
Coosa	—	—	1	12	13	Morgan (k)	4	2	1	3	10
Colbert (k)	1	1	—	1	3	Perry (x)	2	—	2	2	6
Dallas (x)	1	1	—	—	2	Pickens (x)	—	—	—	9	9
Fayette (k)	1	—	—	3	4	Sumter (x)	21	4	9	4	38
Greene (x)	11	4	1	3	19	St. Clair	1	1	1	—	3
Hale (x)	1	3	2	1	7	Tallapoosa (k)	—	—	—	1	1
Jackson	4	2	2	2	10	Tuscaloosa (k)	8	—	—	—	8
Lauderdale	—	—	—	1	1	Walker (k)	—	—	—	1	1
Lawrence (k)	2	—	—	—	2	Total					258

(x) = black counties, and (k) = white counties, where Ku Klux Klan operated.

The Ku Klux Committee reported a bill[1] providing for the execution of the Ku Klux Act until the close of the next session of Congress. It passed the Senate May 21, 1872, and failed in the House on June 6.[2] The act of February 28, 1871, was amended by extending the Federal supervision of elections from towns to all election districts on application of ten persons. Other unimportant amendments were made.[3]

The passage of these laws had no effect on the Ku Klux Klan proper, which had died out in 1869-1870. Nor did they have any effect in decreasing violence. It is quite likely that there was more violence toward the negro in 1871 and 1872 than in 1869-1870. But the laws did affect the elections. The entire machinery of elections was again under Radical control, and in 1872 the state again sank back into Radicalism. But it was the last Republican majority the

[1] Feb. 17, 1872; Report of Committee, p. 626.
[2] McPherson, " Handbook," 1872, pp. 89, 90.
[3] McPherson, " Handbook," 1872, pp. 90, 91. These provisions had to be inserted in the Sundry Civil Bill, which was approved June 10, 1872. Kellogg of Louisiana introduced the " rider."

2 Z

state ever cast. The execution of these laws did much to hasten the union of the whites against negro rule.

Few cases were tried under the Enforcement Acts, though District Attorney Minnis and United States Marshal Healy were very active.[1] Busteed, in 1871, testified that at Huntsville he had tried several persons for an outrage upon a negro, and that there were still untried two indictments under the Act of 1870. He stated that his jurors and witnesses were never interfered with. One of his grand juries, in 1871, encouraged by the attitude of Congress, reported that while there was no organized conspiracy throughout the middle district, there was such a thing in Macon, Coosa, and Tallapoosa. Two of the jurors — Benjamin F. Noble and Ex-Governor William H. Smith — objected to the report, and Busteed, the Federal judge, condemned it as unwarranted by the facts.[2]

Nearly all of the carpet-bag and scalawag witnesses who testified on the Radical side before the Ku Klux Committee complained that the courts would not punish Ku Klux when they were arrested, and that juries would not indict them.[3]

In 1872 a gang of men·in eastern Alabama, the home of the Black Cavalry and the spurious Ku Klux Klan, burned a negro meeting-house where political meetings were held. They were arrested and tried under the Ku Klux Act. Four of them, R. G. Young, S. D. Young, R. S. Gray, and Neil Hawkins, were fined $5000 each and sentenced to ten years' imprisonment in the penitentiary at Albany, New York. Ringold Young was fined $2000

[1] For instances of petty annoyances to the people from marshals, deputy marshals, and supervisors, see Sen. Ex. Doc., No. 119, 47th Cong. 1st Sess., and Ho. Ex. Doc., No. 246, 48th Cong., 2d Sess. These annoyances lasted for several years.

[2] Ku Klux Rept., pp. 320, 330.

[3] In his Message, Nov. 15, 1869, Smith stated : "Nowhere have the courts been interrupted. No resistance has been encountered by the officers of courts in their effort to discharge the duties imposed upon them by law." Smith was criticised by the carpet-baggers for not calling out the negro militia to "enforce the laws." He stood out against them, and on July 25, 1870, he replied to their criticisms, denouncing George E. Spencer (United States Senator), J. D. Sibley, J. J. Hinds, and others as systematically uttering every conceivable falsehood. "During my entire administration of the state government," he said, "but one officer had certified to me that he was unable, on account of lawlessness, to execute his official duties. That officer was the sheriff of Morgan County. I immediately made application to General Crawford for troops. They were sent and the said sheriff refused their assistance." "Solid South," p. 55.

and sent to prison for seven years. —— Blanks and —— Howard were each fined $100 and imprisoned for five years. The prisoners were taken from state officers by force, and during the trial there was much parade by a guard of United States troops. There was complaint that the evidence was insufficient, and the punishment disproportionate to the offence even if proven.[1]

In the elections of 1872 and 1874 there were numerous arrests of Democrats by the deputy marshals, who often made their arrests before election day and paraded the prisoners about the country for the information of the voters. I have been unable to find record of any convictions.[2]

[1] *Montgomery Mail*, July 3, 1872. The Black Cavalry and its spurious Ku Klux successors infested those parts of eastern Alabama where, in 1903, the existence of a system of peonage was discovered.

[2] *Tuskegee News*, Sept. 3, 1874; Report of Joint Committee on Election of George Spencer. During the remainder of Reconstruction under the Enforcement Acts, the Federal government exercised supervision over all elections. Election outrages by the Democrats probably decreased, while outrages by the Radicals tended to increase. The Democrats put in their work of influence and intimidation in the summer and early fall, and when the elections came were quiet, trusting to the influence brought to bear some months previously. After the carpet-bag government collapsed, the Federal Enforcement Acts still gave supervision of elections to the Washington government. The Democrats in Congress were unable to secure the repeal of the force legislation. "We do not expect to repeal any of the recent enactments [Force Laws]. They may stand forever, but we intend by superior intelligence, stronger muscle, and greater energy, to make them dead letter upon the statute books." *Birmingham News*, quoted in the *State Journal*, June 24, 1874. But in 1880 no appropriation was made for the pay of the deputy marshals and supervisors.

In 1875 the supreme court in the case of United States *vs.* Reese declared the two most important sections of the Enforcement Act of 1870 unconstitutional. In 1883, in the case of the United States *vs.* Harris, the Ku Klux Act of April 20, 1871, was declared unconstitutional. In 1888, when House, Senate, and President were Republican, an attempt was made by Mr. McKinley (afterward President) to pass a Force Bill to enforce the old election laws, which were still on the statute book. The measure failed to pass. It was in opposition to this Force Bill that Colonel Hilary A. Herbert of Alabama and other southern congressmen wrote the work called "Why the Solid South? or Reconstruction and its Results." It is said that this book had some influence in causing a halt in force legislation. It was the first attempt to write the history of the Reconstruction period, and is still the best general account. In 1894, when House, Senate, and President were Democratic, the remnants of the Enforcement Acts were repealed, and thus was swept away the last of the Radical system. See Dunning, "The Undoing of Reconstruction," in the *Atlantic Monthly*, Oct., 1901.

Later Organizations

While the Ku Klux Klan was disbanded by order in 1869, it is not likely that the order of the White Camelia disbanded except when there was no longer any necessity for it. In one county it might disband; in another it might survive several years longer. It is said that its operations were by order suspended in counties when conditions improved.

The White Brotherhood was a later organization, but had only a limited extension over south Alabama. The most widely spread of the later organizations was the White League, which in some form seems to have spread over the entire state from 1872 to 1874. The close connection between southwestern Alabama and Louisiana accounts for the introduction of both the White Camelia and the White League. In 1875 Arthur Bingham, the ex-carpet-bag-treasurer of the state, stated that he had secured a copy of the constitution of the White League and had published it in the *State Journal*. Its members were sworn not to regard obligations taken in courts, and to clear one another by all means.[1]

The White League in Barbour and Mobile, in 1874, declared that no employment should be given to negro Radicals and no business done with white Radicals, and in Sumter County they were said to have gone on raids like the Ku Klux of former days. Military organizations of whites were enrolled and applications made to the Radical Governor Lewis for arms. He rejected the services of these companies, but they remained in organization and drilled. The Confederate gray uniforms were worn. In Tuskegee arms were purchased for the company by private subscription. By 1874 the white people of the state had become thoroughly united in the White Man's Party. There had been no compromises. The color and race line had been sharply drawn by the white counties, and the black counties later fell into line. The campaign of 1874 was the most serious of all. The whites intended to live no longer under Radical rule, and the whole state was practically a great Klan. There was but little violence, but there was a stern determination to defeat the Radicals at any cost; and if necessary, violence would have been used. At the inauguration of Governor Houston, in 1874, several of

---

[1] Coburn-Buckner Report, p. 238. The constitution is not in the *Journal*, however.

the gray-coated White League companies appeared from different parts of the state.[1]

In several later elections the old Ku Klux methods were used, and there was much mysterious talk of "dark rainy nights and bloody moons." The "Barbour County Fever" was prevalent for many years: young men and boys would serenade the Radicals of the community and mortify them in every possible way, and their families would refuse to recognize socially the families of carpet-baggers and scalawags. They would not sit by them in church. The children at school imitated their elders.[2]

The Ku Klux method of regulating society was nothing new; it was as old as history; it had often been used before; it may be used again; when a people find themselves persecuted by aliens or by the law, they will find some means outside the law for protecting themselves; it is certain also that such experiences will result in a great weakening of respect for law and in a return to more primitive methods of justice.

[1] Coburn-Buckner Report, pp. 7, 12, 19, 702, 882, 883.
[2] Cameron Report, 1876, pp. 53, 108; oral accounts.

CHAPTER XXII

REORGANIZATION OF THE INDUSTRIAL SYSTEM

Break-up of the Ante-bellum System

THE cotton planter of the South, the master of many negro slaves, organized a very efficient slave labor system. Each plantation was an industrial community almost independent of the outside world; the division of labor was minute, each servant being assigned a task suited to his or her strength and training. Nothing but the most skilful management could save a planter from ruin, for, though the labor was efficient, it was very costly. The value of an overseer was judged by the general condition, health, appearance, and manners of the slaves; the amount of work done with the least punishment; the condition of stock, buildings, and plantation; and the size of the crops. All supplies were raised on the plantation, — corn, bacon, beef, and other food-stuffs; farm implements and harness were made and repaired by the skilled negroes in rainy weather when no outdoor work could be done; clothes were cut out in the "big house" and made by the negro women under the direction of the mistress. The skilled laborers were blacks. Work was usually done by tasks, and industrious negroes were able to complete their daily allotment and have three or four hours a day to work in their own gardens and "patches." They often earned money at odd jobs, and the church records show that they contributed regularly. Negro children were trained in the arts of industry and in sobriety by elderly negroes of good judgment and firm character, usually women.[1] Children too young to work were cared for by a competent mammy in the plantation nursery while their parents were in the fields.

In the Black Belt there was little hiring of extra labor and less renting of land. Except on the borders, nearly all whites were of the

[1] The accounts of the wild and idle negro children of the rice and tobacco districts are not true of those in the Cotton Belt. The smallest tot could do a little in a cotton field.

planting class. Their greater wealth had enabled them to outbid the average farmer and secure the rich lands of the black prairies, cane-brakes, and river bottoms. The small farmer who secured a foothold in the Black Belt would find himself in a situation not altogether pleasant, and, selling out to the nearest planter, would go to poorer and cheaper land in the hills and pine woods, where most of the people were white.

In the Black Belt cotton was largely a surplus money crop, and once the labor was paid for, the planter was a very rich man.[1] In the white counties of the cotton states about the same crops were raised as in the Black Belt, but the land was less fertile and the methods of cultivation less skilful. In the richer parts of these white counties there was something of the plantation system with some negro labor. But slavery gradually drove white labor to the hill and mountain country, the sand and pine barrens. No matter how poor a white man was, he was excessively independent in spirit and wanted to work only his own farm. This will account for the lack of renters and hired white laborers in black or in white districts, and also for the fact that the less fertile land was taken up by the whites who desired to be their own employers. . Land was cheap, and any man could purchase it. There was some renting of land in the white counties, and the form it took was that now known as "third and fourth."[2] It was then called "shares." There was little or no tenancy "on halves" or "standing rent." But the average farmer worked his own land, often with the help of from three to ten slaves.

[1] See *Birmingham Age-Herald*, March 31 and April 7, 1901 (J. W. DuBose); *Review of Reviews*, Sept., 1903, on "The Cotton Crop of To-day," by R. H. Edmonds; Ingle, "Southern Sidelights," p. 271; Address of President Thach, Alabama Polytechnic Institute, before the American Economic Association, 1903; Tillinghast, "Negro in Africa and America," pp. 126, 143; Mallard, "Plantation Life before Emancipation"; Washington, "Up from Slavery," and "The Future of the American Negro," *passim*. The immense cost of slave labor is seen when the value of the slaves is compared with the value of the lands cultivated by their labor. In 1859 the cash value of the lands in Alabama was $175,824,622, and that of the slaves was $215,540,000. The larger portion of this land had not a negro on it, and if cultivated, was cultivated exclusively by whites. See Census of 1860. The effect of the loss of slaves on the welfare of a planter is shown in the case of William L. Yancey. His slaves were accidentally poisoned and died. The loss ruined him, and he was forced to sell his plantation and engage in a profession. A farmer in a white county employing white labor would have been injured only temporarily by such a loss of labor.

[2] The tenant furnished labor, supplies, and teams, and paid the landlord a fourth of the cotton and a third of the corn produced.

On the borders of the Black Belt in Alabama dwelt a peculiar class called "squatters." They settled down with or without permission on lots of poor and waste land, built cabins, cleared "patches," and made a precarious living by their little crops, by working as carpenters, blacksmiths, etc. Some bought small lots of land on long-time payments and never paid for them, but simply stayed where they were. In the edge of the Black Belt in the busy season were found numbers of white hired men working alongside of negro slaves,[1] for there was no prejudice against manual labor, that is, no more than anywhere else in the world.[2]

As soon as the war was over the first concern of the returning soldiers was to obtain food to relieve present wants and to secure supplies to last until a crop could be made. In the white counties of the state the situation was much worse than in the Black Belt. The soil of the white counties was less fertile; the people were not wealthy before the war, and during the war they had suffered from the depredations of the enemy and from the operation of the tax-in-kind, which bore heavily upon them when they had nothing to spare. The white men went to the war and there were only women, children, and old men to work the fields. The heaviest losses among the Alabama Confederate troops were from the ranks of the white county soldiers. In these districts there was destitution after the first year of the war, and after 1862 from one-fourth to one-half of the soldiers' families

[1] There was usually good feeling between the whites and blacks at work together; but the negroes, at heart, scorned the poor whites, and had to be closely watched to keep them from insulting or abusing them. The negro had little respect for the man who owned no slaves or who owned but few and worked with them in the fields. To protect the slaves against outsiders was one reason why discipline was strict, supervision close, passes required, etc. When both white and black were allowed to go at will over the plantation and community, trouble was sure to result from the impudent behavior of the negro to "white trash" and the consequent retaliation of the latter. The whites often came to the master and wanted him to whip his best slaves for impudence to them. The master, to prevent this, regulated the liberty of the slave by passes, etc., and the whites, especially strangers, were expected not to trespass on a plantation where slaves were.

[2] The idea of the so-called "prejudice" against manual labor is perhaps due largely to abolitionist theories and arguments, which have been partially accepted since the war by some southerners who think it due to the old system to show its lofty attitude toward the common things of life. But the negro had, and still has, a contempt for a white who works as he does. And it has always been a custom of mankind, — white, yellow, or black, — to get out of doing manual labor if there was anything else to do.

received aid from the state. The bountiful Black Belt furnished enough for all, but transportation facilities were lacking. At the close of hostilities the condition of the people in the poorer regions was pitiable. Stock, fences, barns, and in many cases dwellings had disappeared; the fields were grown up in weeds; and no supplies were available. How the people managed to live was a mystery. Some walked twenty miles to get food, and there were cases of starvation. No seeds and no farm implements were to be had. The best work of the Freedmen's Bureau was done in relieving these people from want until they could make a crop.

The Black Belt was the richest as well as the least exposed section of the state and fared well until the end of the war. The laborers were negroes, and these worked as well in war time as in peace. Immense food crops were made in 1863 and 1864, and there was no suffering among whites or blacks. Until 1865 there was no loss from Federal invasion, but with the spring of 1865 misfortune came. Four large armies marched through the central portions of the state, burning, destroying, and confiscating. In June, 1865, the Black Belt was in almost as bad condition as the white counties. All buildings in the track of the armies had disappeared; the stores of provisions were confiscated; gin-houses and mills were burned; cattle and horses and mules were carried away; and nothing much was left except the negroes and the fertile land. The returning planter, like the farmer, found his agricultural implements worn out and broken, and in all the land there was no money to purchase the necessaries of life. But in the portions of the black counties untouched by the armies there were supplies sufficient to last the people for a few months. A few fortunate individuals had cotton, which was now bringing fabulous prices, and it was the high price received for the few bales not confiscated by the government that saved the Black Belt from suffering as did the other counties.

Neither master nor slave knew exactly how to begin anew, and for a while things simply drifted. Now that the question of slavery was settled, many of the former masters felt a great relief from responsibility, though for their former slaves they felt a profound pity. The majority of them had no faith in free negro labor, yet all were willing to give it a trial, and a few of the more strenuous ones said that the energy and strength of the white man that had made the savage negro an efficient laborer could make the free negro work fairly well; and if the free negro would work, they were willing to admit that the change might be beneficial to both races.

During the spring and summer and fall the masters came straggling home, and were met by friendly servants who gave them cordial welcome. Each one called up his servants and told them that they were free; and that they might stay with him and work for wages, or find other homes. Except in the vicinity of the towns and army posts the negroes usually chose to stay and work; and in the remote districts of the Black Belt affairs were little changed for several weeks after the surrender, which there hardly caused a ripple on the surface of society. Life and work went on as before. The staid negro coachmen sat upon their boxes on Sunday as of old; the field hands went regularly about their appointed tasks. Labor was cheerful, and the negroes went singing to the fields. "The negro knew no Appomattox. The Revolution sat lightly, — save in the presence of vacant seats at home and silent graves in the churchyard, in the memorials of destructive raids, in the wonder on the faces of a people once free, now ruled, where ruled at all, by a Bureau agent." Here it was that the master race believed that after all freedom of the negro might be well.[1] In other sections, where the negro was more exposed to outside influences, people were not hopeful. The common opinion was that with free negro labor cotton could not be cultivated with success. The northerner often thought that it was a crop made by forced labor and that no freeman would willingly perform such labor; the southerner believed that the negro would neglect the crop too much when not under strict supervision. Yet later years have shown that free white labor is most successful in the cultivation of cotton because of the care the whites expend upon their farms; while cotton is the only crop that the free negro has cultivated with any degree of success, because some kind of a crop can be made by the most careless cultivation.

At first no one knew just how to work the free negro; innumerable plans were formed and many were tried. The old patriarchal relations were preserved as far as possible. Truman,[2] who made a long stay in Alabama, reported that in most cases there was a genuine attachment between masters and negroes; that the masters were

---

[1] Accounts from old citizens, former planters.   [2] The agent of President Johnson.

the best friends the negroes had; and that, though they regarded the blacks with much commiseration, they were inclined to encourage them to collect around the big house on the old slavery terms, giving food, clothes, quarters, medical attendance, and a little pay.[1] At that time no one could understand the freedom of the negro.[2] As one old master expressed it, he saw no "free negroes"[3] until the fall of 1865, when the Bureau began to influence the blacks. But with the extension of the Bureau and the spread of army posts, the negroes became idle, neglected the crops that had been planted in the spring, moved from their old homes and went to town to the Bureau, or went wandering about the country. The house servants and the artisans, who were the best and most intelligent of the negroes, also began to go to the towns. Negro women desiring to be as white ladies, refused to work in the fields, to cook, to wash, or to perform other menial duties. It was years before this "freedom" prejudice of the negro women against domestic service died out.[4] The negro would work one or two days in the week, go to town two days, and wander about the rest of the time. Under such conditions there was no hope of continuing the old patriarchal system, and new plans, modelled on what they had heard of free labor, were tried by the planters. In the white counties the ex-soldiers went to work as before the war, but they had come home from the army too late to plant full crops, and few had supplies enough to last until the crops should be gathered. In most of the white counties the negroes were so few as to escape the serious attention of the Bureau, and consequently they worked fairly well at what they could get to do.[5]

---

[1] Report to President, April 9, 1866.

[2] Colonel Saunders, a noted slaveholder in one of the white counties in north Alabama, established a patriarchal protectorate over his former slaves. He built a church for them, and organized a monthly court, presided over by himself, in which the old negro men tried delinquents. It is said that the findings of this court were often ludicrous in the extreme, but order was preserved, and for a long while there was no resort to the Bureau. Saunders, "Early Settlers," p. 31. Many similar protectorates were established in the remote districts, but the policy of the Bureau was to break them up.

[3] A term of contempt.

[4] See *Sewanee Review*, Jan., 1905, article on "Servant Problem in a Black Belt Village."

[5] *N. Y. Herald*, July 17, 1865; Reid, "After the War," pp. 211, 218, 219; Tillet, in *Century Magazine*, Vol. XI; Reports of General Swayne, 1865, 1866; Van de Graaf, in *Forum*, Vol. XXI, pp. 330, 339; *DeBow's Review*, Feb., 1866, p. 220; oral accounts,

The first work of the Bureau was to break up the labor system that had been partially constructed, and to endeavor to establish a new system based on the northern free labor system and the old slave-hiring system with the addition of a good deal of pure theory. The Bureau was to act as a labor clearing-house; it was to have entire control of labor; contracts must be written in accordance with the minute regulations of the Bureau, and must be registered by the agent, who charged large fees.[1]

The result of these regulations was to destroy industry where an alien Bureau agent was stationed, for the planters could not afford to have their land worked on such terms. In some of the counties, where the native magistrates served as Bureau agents, no attention was paid to the rules of the Bureau, and the people floundered along, trying to develop a workable basis of existence. In the districts infested by the Bureau agents the negroes had fantastic notions of what freedom meant. On one plantation they demanded that the plantation bell be no longer rung to summon the hands to and from work, because it was too much like slavery.[2] In various places they refused to work and congregated about the Bureau offices, awaiting the expected division of property, when they would get the "forty acres and one old gray mule." When wages were paid they believed that each should receive the same amount, whether his labor had been good or bad, whether the laborer was present or absent, sick or well. In one instance a planter was paying his men in corn according to the time each had worked. The negroes objected and got an order from the Bureau agent that the division should be made equally. The planter read the order (which the negroes could not read), and at once directed the division as before. The negroes, thinking that the Bureau had so ordered, were satisfied. In the cane-brake region the agents were afraid of the great planters and did not interfere with the negroes except to organize them into Union Leagues;

---

[1] For a description of the Bureau labor regulations, see Chapter XI, Sec. 1. Also *Montgomery Mail*, May 12, 1865; Howard's Circular, May 30, 1865; Circular No. 11, War Department, July 12, 1865; *Huntsville Advocate*, July 26, 1865; Swayne's Reports, 1865, 1866; G. O. No. 12, Dept. Ala., Aug. 30, 1865; G. O. No. 13, Dept. Ala., Sept., 1865; *Selma Times*, Dec. 4, 1865. The so-called "Black Laws" passed by the legislature in 1865–1866 to regulate labor were scarcely heard of by the people who hired negroes.

[2] Somers, "Southern States," 130.

but elsewhere in the Black Belt the planter could not afford to hire negroes on the terms fixed by the Bureau.[1]

Northern and Foreign Immigration

With the break-up of the slave system the planter found himself with much more land than he knew what to do with. He could get no reliable labor, he had no cash capital, so in many cases he offered his best lands for sale at low prices.   The planters wanted to attract northern and foreign immigration and capital into the country; the cotton planter sought for a northern partner who could furnish the capital.   Owing to the almost religious regard of the negro for his northern deliverers, many white landlords thought that northern men, especially former soldiers, might be better able than southern men to control negro labor.   General Swayne, the head of the Bureau, said that the negroes had more confidence in a "bluecoat" than in a native, and that among the larger planters northern men as partners or overseers were in great demand.[2]

For a short time after the close of the war northern men in considerable numbers planned to go into the business of cotton raising. DeBow[3] gives a description of the would-be cotton planters who came from the North to show the southern people how to raise cotton with free negro labor.   They had note-books and guide-books full of close and exact tables of costs and profits, and from them figured out vast returns.   They acknowledged that the negro might not work for the southern man, but they were sure that he would work for them.   They were very self-confident, and would listen to no advice from experienced planters, whom they laughed at as old fogies, but from their note-books and tables they gave one another much information about the new machinery useful in cotton culture, about rules for cultivation, how to control labor, etc.   They estimated that each laborer's family would make $1000 clear gain each year.   DeBow

[1] *Southern Magazine*, Jan., 1874 ; *Selma Messenger*, Nov. 15, 1865 ; *Harper's Monthly Magazine*, Jan., 1874 ; *Selma Times*, Dec. 4, 1865 ; oral accounts ; *DeBow's Review*, Feb., 1866.

[2] Swayne to A. F. Perry, *N. Y. Herald*, Aug. 28, 1865 ; *N. Y. Herald*, July 17, 1865 ; Reid, "After the War," pp. 211–219 ; *DeBow's Review*, 1866, pp. 213, 220 ; Somers, "Southern States," p. 131.

[3] *DeBow's Review*, Feb., 1866.

would not say they were wrong, but he said that he thought that they should hasten a little more slowly. Northern energy and capitol flowed in; plantations were bought, and the various industries of plantation life started; and mills and factories were established. Because of the paralyzed condition of industry the southern people welcomed these enterprises, but they were very sceptical of their final success. The northern settler had confidence in the negro and gave him unlimited credit or supplies; consequently, in a few years the former was financially ruined and had to turn his attention to politics, and to exploiting the negro in that field in order to make a living.[1] Both as employer and as manager the northern men failed to control negro labor. They expected the negro to be the equal of the Yankee white. The negroes themselves were disgusted with northern employers. Truman reported, after an experience of one season, that "it is the almost universal testimony of the negroes themselves, who have been under the supervision of both classes, — and I have talked with many with a view to this point, — that they prefer to labor for a southern employer."[2]

Northern capital came in after the war, but northern labor did not, though the planters offered every inducement. Land was offered to white purchasers at ridiculously low rates, but the northern white laborer did not come. He was afraid of the South with its planters and negroes. The poorer classes of native whites, however, profited by the low prices and secured a foothold on the better lands. So general was the unbelief in the value of the free negro as a laborer, especially in the Bureau districts, and so signally had all inducements failed to bring native white laborers from the North, that determined efforts were made to obtain white labor from abroad. Immigration societies were formed with officers in the state and headquarters in the northern cities. These societies undertook to send to the South laboring people, principally German, in families at so much per head.

[1] Many of the carpet-bag politicians were northern men who had failed at cotton planting.
[2] Report to the President, April 9, 1866; "Ten Years in a Georgia Plantation," by the Hon. Mrs. Leigh; oral accounts. On account of the general failure of the northern men who invested capital in the South in 1865 and 1866, there grew up in the business world an unfavorable feeling against the South, and for the remainder of Reconstruction days that section had to struggle against adverse business opinion. *Harper's Magazine*, Jan., 1874.

The planter turned with hope to white labor, of the superiority of which he had so long been hearing, and he wished very much to give it a trial. The advertisements in the newspapers read much like the old slave advertisements: so many head of healthy, industrious Germans of good character delivered f.o.b. New York, at so much per head. One of the white labor agencies in Alabama undertook to furnish "immigrants of any nativity and in any quantity" to take the place of negroes. Children were priced at the rate of $50 a year; women, $100; men, $150, — they themselves providing board and clothes. One of every six Germans was warranted to speak English.[1] Most of these agencies were frauds and only wanted an advance payment on a car load of Germans who did not exist. In a few instances some laborers were actually shipped in; but they at once demanded an advance of pay, and then deserted. Like the bounty jumpers, they played the game time and time again. The influence of the Radical press of the North was also used to discourage emigration to the South;[2] consequently white immigration into the state did not amount to anything,[3] and the Black Belt received no help from the North or from abroad, and had to fall back upon the free negro.

In the white counties there had been little hope or desire for alien immigration. The people and the country were so desperately poor that the stranger would never think of settling there. Many of the whites in moderate circumstances, living near the Black Belt, took advantage of the low price of rich lands, and acquired small farms in the prairies, but there was no influx of white labor to the Black Belt from the white counties.[4] Nearly every man, woman, and child in the white districts had to go to work to earn a living. Many persons — lawyers, public men, teachers, ministers,

---

[1] *Selma Times*, Dec. 4, 1865. Nearly all the newspapers printed advertisements of the immigration societies.

[2] "Northern Alabama Illustrated," p. 378.

[3] *Selma Times*, Dec. 4, 1865 ; *N. Y. Times*, July 2, 1866.

[4] The great evil of slavery was its tendency to drive the whites who were in moderate circumstances away from the more fertile lands of the prairie and cane-brake and river bottoms, leaving them to the few slaveholders and the immense number of slaves. Emancipation thus left on the finest lands of the state a shiftless laboring population, which still retains possession. Now, as in slavery times, the white prefers not to work as a field hand in the Black Belt when he can get more independent work elsewhere. And besides, he does not wish to live among the negroes. Slavery kept white farmers from settling on the fertile lands ; the negro keeps whites from taking possession now.

physicians, merchants, overseers, managers, and even women—who had never before worked in the fields or at manual occupations, were now forced to do so because of losses of property, or because they could not live by their former occupations.[1]

While the number of white laborers had increased somewhat, negro labor had decreased. Several thousand negro men had gone with the armies; for various reasons thousands had drifted to the towns, where large numbers died in 1865–1866. The rural negro had a promising outlook, for at any time he could get more work than he could do; the city negro found work scarce even when he wanted it.[2]

Attempts to organize a New System

Several attempts were made by the negroes in 1865 and 1866 to work farms and plantations on the coöperative system, that is, to club work, but with no success. They were not accustomed to independent labor, their faculty for organization had not been sufficiently developed, and the dishonesty of their leading men sometimes caused failures of the schemes.[3]

[1] *Mobile Daily Times*, Oct. 21, 1860; *Montgomery Advertiser*, March 21, 1866; *DeBow's Review*, March 18, 1866.

Several young women of Montgomery, who were once wealthy, worked in the printing-office of the *Advertiser*. One of them was a daughter of a former President of the United States. Many women became teachers, displacing men, who then went to the fields. Disabled soldiers generally tried teaching.

There seems to be a belief that emancipation had a good effect in driving to work a certain "gentleman of leisure" class, who had been supported by the work of slaves and who had scorned labor. (See W. B. Tillett, in the *Century Magazine*, Vol. XI, p. 769.) It is a mistake to regard the slaveholding, planting class as, in any degree, idle, unless from the point of view of the negro or the ignorant white, who believed that any man who did not work with his hands was a gentleman of leisure. The Alabama planter was and had to be a man of great energy, good judgment, and diligence. It was a belief that a man who could not manage a plantation or other business should not be intrusted with an official position. One of the most serious objections made by the cotton planters to Jefferson Davis as President was that he had failed to manage his plantation with success. See also Somers, "Southern States," p. 127.

[2] *DeBow's Review*, Feb. and March, 1866; *Montgomery Advertiser*, March 21, 1866; *N. Y. Herald*, July 17, 1866. It was estimated that in the fall of 1865 the negro male population of the state was reduced by 50,000 able-bodied men, who were hanging around the cities and towns, doing nothing. At Mobile there were 10,000; at Meridian, Miss., 5000; at Montgomery, 10,000; at Selma, 5000; and at various smaller points, 20,000. *Mobile Times*, Oct. 21, 1865.

[3] See also Reid, "After the War," p. 221.

In the summer of 1865 the Monroe County Agricultural Association was formed to regulate labor, and to protect the interests of both employer and laborer. It was the duty of the executive committee to look after the welfare of the freedmen, to see that contracts were carried out and the freedmen protected in them, and, in cases of dispute, to act as arbitrator. The members of the association pledged themselves to see that the freedman received his wages, and to aid him in case his employer refused to pay. They were also to see that the freedman fulfilled his contract, unless there was good reason why he should not. Homes and the necessaries of life were to be provided by the association for the aged and helpless negroes, of whom there were several on every plantation. The planters declared themselves in favor of schools for the negro children, and a committee was appointed to devise a plan for their education. Every planter in Monroe County belonged to the association.[1] An organization in Conecuh County adopted, word for word, the constitution of the Monroe County association. In Clarke and Wilcox counties similar organizations were formed, and in all counties where negro labor was the main dependence some such plans were devised.[2] But it is noticeable that in those counties where the planters first undertook to reorganize the labor system, there were no regular agents of the Freedmen's Bureau and no garrisons.

The average negro quite naturally had little or no sense of the obligation of contracts. He would leave a growing crop at the most critical period, and move into another county, or, working his own crop "on shares," would leave it in the grass and go to work for some one else in order to get small "change" for tobacco, snuff, and whiskey. After three years of experience of such conduct, a meeting of citizens at Summerfield, Dallas County, decided that laborers ought to be impressed with the necessity of complying with contracts. They agreed that no laborers discharged for failure to keep contracts would be hired again by other employers. They declared it to be the duty of the whites to act in perfect good faith

[1] Trowbridge, "The South," p. 431 *et seq.*

[2] Trowbridge, "The South," p. 431; Reports of General Swayne, Dec. 26, 1865, and Jan., 1866, in Ho. Ex. Doc., No. 70, 39th Cong., 1st Sess. General Swayne strongly approved the objects of these societies. He said there was not and never had been any question of the right of the negro to hold property. Free negroes had held property before the war.

3 A

in their relations with freedmen, to respect and uphold their rights, and to promote good feeling.[1]

Development of the Share System

At first the planters had demanded a system of contracts, thinking that by law they might hold the negro to his agreements. But the Bureau contracts were one-sided, and the planters could not afford to enter into them. General Swayne early reported[2] a general breakdown of the contract system, though he told the planters that in case of dispute, where no contract was signed, he would exact payment for the negro at the highest rates. The "share" system was discouraged, but where there were no Bureau agents it was developing. And so bad was the wage system, that even in the Bureau districts, share hiring was done. The object of "share" renting was to cause the laborer to take an interest in his crop and to relieve the planter of disputes about loss of time, etc. Some of the negroes also decided that the share system was the proper one. On the plantations near Selma the negroes demanded "shares," threatening to leave in case of refusal. General Hardee, who was living near, proposed a plan for a verbal contract; wages should be one-fourth of all crops, meat and bread to be furnished to the laborer, and his share of crop to be paid to him in kind, or the net proceeds in cash; the planter to furnish land, teams, wagons, implements, and seed to the laborer, who, in addition, had all the slavery privileges of free wood, water, and pasturage, garden lot and truck patch, teams to use on Sundays and for going to town. The absolute right of management was reserved to the planter, it being understood that this was no copartnership, but that the negro was hired for a share of the crop; consequently he had no right to interfere in the management.[3]

On another plantation, where a share system similar to Hardee's was in operation, the planter divided the workers into squads of four men each. To each squad he assigned a hundred acres of cotton and corn, in the proportion of five acres of cotton to three of corn, and forty acres of cotton for the women and children of the four families. The squads were united to hoe and plough and

---

[1] *DeBow's Review*, Feb., 1868.   [2] Jan. 31, 1866.
[3] I have this account from a planter of the district.

to pick the cotton, because they worked better in gangs. Wage laborers were kept to look after fences and ditches, and to perform odd jobs. A frequent source of trouble was the custom of allowing the negro, as part of his pay, several acres of "outside crop," to be worked on certain days of the week, as Fridays and Saturdays. The planter was supposed to settle disputes among the negroes, give them advice on every subject except politics and religion, on which they had other advisers, pay their fines and get them out of jail when arrested, and sometimes to thrash the recalcitrant.[1]

Several kinds of share systems were finally evolved from the industrial chaos. They were much the same in black or white districts, and the usual designations were "on halves," "third and fourth," and "standing rent." The tenant "on halves" received one-half the crop, did all the work, and furnished his own provisions. The planter furnished land, houses to live in, seed, ploughs, hoes, teams, wagons, ginned the cotton, paid for half the fertilizer, and "went security" for the negro for a year's credit at the supply store in town, or he furnished the supplies himself, and charged them against the negro's share of the crop. The "third and fourth" plan varied according to locality and time, and depended upon what the tenant furnished. Sometimes the planter furnished everything, while the negro gave only his labor and received one-fourth of the crop; again, the planter furnished all except provisions and labor, and gave the negro one-third of the crop. In such cases "third and fourth" was a lower grade of tenancy than "on halves." Later it developed to a higher grade: the tenant furnished teams and farming implements, and the planter the rest, in which case the planter received a third of the cotton, and a fourth of the corn raised. "Standing rent" was the highest form of tenancy, and only responsible persons, white or black, could rent under that system. It called

---

[1] Somers, an English traveller, thought that the economic relations of planter and negro were startling, and that anywhere else they would be considered absurd. The tenant, he said, was sure of a support, and did not much care if the crop failed. Even his taxes, when he condescended to pay any, were paid by his master. For all work outside of his crop he had to be paid, and often he went away and worked for some one else for cash. And his privileges were innumerable. "The soul is often crushed out of labor by penury and oppression. Here a soul cannot begin to be infused into it through the sheer excess of privilege and license with which it is surrounded." "Southern States since the War," pp. 128, 129.

for a fixed or "standing" rent for each acre or farm, to be paid in money or in cotton. The unit of value in cotton was a 500-pound bale of middling grade on October 1st. Tenants who had farm stock, farming implements, and supplies or good credit would nearly always cultivate for "standing rent." The planter exercised a controlling direction over the labor and cultivation of a crop worked "on halves"; he exercised less direction over "third and fourth" tenants, and was supposed to exercise no control over tenants who paid "standing rent." In all cases the planter furnished a dwelling-house free, wood and water (paid for digging wells), and pasture for the pigs and cows of the tenants. In all cases the renter had a plot of ground of from one to three acres, rent free, for a vegetable garden and "truck patch." Here could be raised watermelons, sugar-cane, potatoes, sorghum, cabbage, and other vegetables. Every tenant could keep a few pigs and a cow, chickens, turkeys, and guineas, and especially dogs, and could hunt in all the woods around and fish in all the waters. "On halves" was considered the safest form of tenancy for both planter and tenant, for the latter was only an average man, and this method allowed the superior direction of the planter.[1] Many negroes worked for wages; the less intelligent and the unreliable could find no other way to work; and some of the best of them preferred to work for wages paid at the end of each week or month. Wage laborers worked under the immediate oversight of the farmer or tenant who hired them. They received $8 to $12 a month and were "found," that is, furnished with rations. In the white counties the negro hired man was often fed in the farmer's kitchen. The laborer, if hired by the year, had a house,

[1] My father's tenants, white and black, rented on all systems. The negroes usually began as wage laborers or as tenants " on halves," for they had no supplies when they came. Then the more industrious and thrifty would save and rent farms for " third and fourth " or for "standing rent." The whites usually obtained the highest grade, and the average white man would save enough of his earnings to purchase a team, wagon, buggy, farm implements, and a year's supply and spend all else, though some saved enough to buy land of their own in cheaper districts or to support themselves for a year or two while opening up a homestead in the pine woods. The negro, as a rule, rented " on halves," for he spent all his earnings and required supervision. The average negro stays only a year or two at one place before he longs for change and removes to another farm. About Christmas, or just before, the negroes and many of the whites begin to move to new homes. For a description of conditions in Mississippi, where the negro has somewhat better opportunities than in Alabama, see Mr. A. H. Stone's article in the *Quarterly Journal of Economics*, Feb., 1905.

vegetable garden, truck patch, chickens, a pig perhaps, always a dog, and he could hunt and fish anywhere in the vicinity. Sometimes he was "found"; sometimes he "found" himself. When he was "found," the allowance for a week was three and a half pounds of bacon, a peck of meal, half a gallon of syrup, and a plug of tobacco; his garden and truck patch furnished vegetables. This allowance could be varied and commuted. The system was worked out in the few years immediately following the war, and has lasted almost without change. Where the negroes are found, the larger plantations have not been broken up into small farms, the census statistics to the contrary notwithstanding.[1] The negro tenant or laborer had too many privileges for his own good and for the good of the planter. The negro should have been paid more money or given a larger proportion of the crop, and fewer privileges. He needed more control and supervision, and the result of giving him a vegetable garden, a truck patch, a pasture, and the right of hunting and fishing, was that the negro took less interest in the crop; the privileges were about all he wanted. Agricultural industry was never brought to a real business basis.[2]

An essential part of the share system was the custom of advancing supplies to the tenant with the future crop as security. The universal lack of capital after the war forced an extension of the old ante-bellum credit or supply system. The merchant, who was also a cotton buyer, advanced money or supplies until the crop was gathered. Before the war his security was crop, land, and slaves; after the war the crop was the principal security, for land was a drug in the market. Consequently, the crop was more important to the creditor. Cotton was the only good cash staple, and the high prices encouraged all to raise it. It was to the interest of the merchant, even when prices were low, to insist that his debtors raise cotton to the exclusion of food crops, since much of his money was made by selling food supplies to them. Before the war the planter alone had much credit, and a successful one did not make use of

---

[1] In the census each person cultivating a crop is counted as a farmer and the land he cultivates as a farm. Thus a plantation might be represented in the census statistics by from five to twenty-five farms.

[2] See also Otken, "Ills of the South"; Somers, "South since the War," p. 281; *Harper's Monthly*, Jan., 1874; *DeBow's Review*, Feb., 1868.

the system; but after the war all classes of cotton raisers had to have advances of supplies. The credit or crop lien system was good to put an ambitious farmer on the way to independence, but it was no incentive to the shiftless. Cotton became the universal crop under the credit system, and even when the farmer became independent, he seldom planted less of his staple crop, or raised more supplies at home.

Negro Farmers and White Farmers

At the end of the war everything was in favor of the negro cotton raiser; and everything except the high price of cotton was against the white farmer in the poorer counties. The soil had been used most destructively in the white districts, and it had to be improved before cotton could be raised successfully.[1] The high price of cotton caused the white farmer, who had formerly had only small cotton patches, to plant large fields, and for several years the negro was not a serious competitor. The building of railroads through the mineral regions afforded transportation to the white farmer for crops and fertilizers, — an advantage that before this time had been enjoyed only by the Black Belt, — and improved methods gradually supplanted the wasteful frontier system of cultivation. The gradual increase[2] of the cotton production after 1869 was due entirely to white labor in the white counties, the black counties never again reaching their former production, though the population of those counties has doubled. Governor Lindsay said, in 1871, that the white people

[1] Any stick is good enough to beat slavery with, so it is usually stated that slavery was responsible for the wasteful methods of cultivation that prevailed in the South before the war. That can be true only indirectly, for the soil always received the worst treatment in the white counties. Like frontiersmen everywhere, the Alabama white farmers found it easier to clear new land or to move West than to fertilize worn-out soils. The lack of transportation facilities in the white districts made it almost impossible to bring in commercial fertilizers or to move the crops when made. The railroads had opened up only the rich slave districts. If there had not been a negro in the state, the frontier methods would have prevailed, as they still do among the farmers in some parts of the West. On the other hand, the rich lands worked by slave labor under intelligent direction were kept in good condition. Under free negro labor they are in the worst possible condition. Experience, necessity, the disappearance of free land, and the increase of transportation facilities have caused the white county farmer to employ better methods, and to keep up and increase the fertility of the land by using fertilizers.

[2] But it was nearly forty years before the entire cotton crop of the state was as large as in 1859.

of north Alabama, where but little had been produced before the war, were becoming prosperous by raising cotton, and at the same time raising supplies that the planter on the rich lands with negro labor had to buy from the West. This prosperity, he thought, had done more than anything else to put an end to Ku Klux disturbances. Somers reported, as early as 1871, that the bulk of the cotton crop in the Tennessee valley was made by white labor, not by black.[1] As long as there was plenty of cheap, thin land to be had, the poor but independent white would not work the fertile land belonging to some one else; and before and long after the war there was plenty of practically free land.[2] Therefore the tendency of the whites was to remain on the less fertile land. Dr. E. A. Smith, in the Alabama Geological Survey of 1881-1882, and in the Report on Cotton Production in Alabama (1884), shows the relation between race and cotton production, and race location, with respect to fertility of soil: (1) On the most fertile lands the laboring population was black; the farmers were shiftless, and no fertilizers were used; there the credit evil was worse, and the yield per acre was less than on the poorest soils cultivated by whites. (2) Where the races were about equal the best system was found; the soils were medium, the farms were small but well cultivated, and fertilizers were used. (3) On the poorest soils only whites were found. These by industry and use of fertilizers could produce about as much as the blacks on the rich soils.

The average product per acre of the fertile Black Belt is lower than the lowest in the poorest white counties. Only the best of

[1] *Southern Magazine*, Jan., 1874; Ku Klux Rept., Ala. Test., pp. 206, 207; Somers, "Southern States," p. 117. In 1860 it was estimated that of the whole cotton crop 10 to 12 per cent was produced by white labor; in 1876 the proportion of whites to blacks in the cotton fields was 30 to 51; in 1883 white labor produced 44 per cent of the cotton crop; in 1884, 48 per cent; in 1885, 50 per cent; in 1893, 70 per cent. And this was done by the whites on inferior lands. See W. B. Tillett, in *Century Magazine*, Vol. XI, p. 771; Hammond, "The Cotton Industry," pp. 129, 130, 132.

[2] DeBow estimated that the entire acreage of the cotton crop was as follows:—

1836.	2,000,000 acres	1850.	5,000,000 acres
1840.	4,500,000 acres	1860.	6,968,000 acres

The Commissioner of Agriculture in 1876 estimated that the acreage in 1860 was 13,000,000. Taking this estimate, which, while probably too large, is more nearly correct, only 4 per cent of the arable land was planted in cotton — the staple crop. Hammond, "The Cotton Industry," p. 74.

soil, as in Clarke, Monroe, and Wilcox counties, is able to overcome the bad labor system, and produce an average equal to that made by the whites in Winston, the least fertile county in the state. In white counties, where the average product per acre falls below the average for the surrounding region, the fact is always explained by the presence of blacks, segregated on the best soils, keeping down the average product. For example, Madison County in 1880 had a majority of blacks, and the average product per acre was 0.28 bale, as compared with 0.32 bale for the Tennessee valley, of which Madison was the richest county; in Talledega, the most fertile county of the Coosa valley, the average production per acre was 0.32, as compared with 0.40 for the rest of the valley; in Autauga, where the blacks outnumbered the whites two to one, the average fell below that of the country around, though the Autauga soil was the best in the region. The average product of the rich prairie region cultivated by the blacks was 0.27 bale per acre; the average product in the poor mineral region cultivated by the whites was 0.26 to 0.28; in the short-leaf pine region the whites outnumber the blacks two to one, and the average production is 0.34 bale, while in the gravelly hill region, where the blacks are twice as numerous as the whites, the production is 0.30, the soil in the two sections being about equal. In general, the fertility of the soil being equal, the production varies inversely as the proportion of colored population to white. Density of colored population is a sure sign of fertile soil; predominance of white a sign of medium or poor soil. Outside of the Black Belt, white owners cultivate small farms, looking closely after them. The negro seldom owns the land he cultivates, and is more efficient when working under direction on the small farm in the white county. In the Black Belt, nearly all land is fertile and capable of cultivation, but in the white counties a large percentage is rocky, in hills, forests, mountains, etc. Many soils in southeast and in north Alabama, formerly considered unproductive, have been brought into cultivation by the use of fertilizers, hauled in wagons, in many cases, from twenty to a hundred miles. Fertilizers have not yet come into general use in the Black Belt. In the negro districts are still found horse-power gins and old wooden cotton presses; in the white counties, steam and water power and the latest machinery. In the white counties it has always been a general custom to raise a part of the supplies on the farm; in the Black Belt this has not been done since the war.[1] Though many of the white farmers remained under the crop lien bondage, there was a steady gain toward independence on the part of the more industrious and economical. But not until toward the close of the century did emancipation come for many of the struggling whites.

In other directions the whites did better. They opened the mines of north Alabama, cut the timber of south Alabama, built the railroads and factories, and to some extent engaged in commerce.[2] Market gardening became a common occupation. Negro labor in factories failed. It was the negro rather than slavery that prevented and still prevents the establishment of manufactures.[3] The development of manufactures in recent years has benefited principally the poor people of the white counties. "For this mill people is not drawn from foreign immigrants, nor from distant states, but it is drawn from the native-born white population, the poor whites, that belated hill-folk from the ridges and hollows and coves of the silent hills."[4] The negro artisan is giving way to the white; even in the towns of the Black Belt, the occupations once securely held by the negro are passing into the hands of the whites.

In the white counties, during Reconstruction, the relations between the races became more strained than in the Black Belt. One of the manifestations of the Ku Klux movement in the white counties was the driving away of negro tenants from the more fertile districts by the poorer classes of whites who wanted these lands. For years immigration was discouraged by the northern press. Foreigners were afraid to come to the "benighted and savage South."[5]

[1] Smith, "Cotton Production in Alabama" (1884); Census, 1880; Smith in Ala. Geolog. Survey, 1881–1882; Kelsey, "The Negro Farmer"; oral accounts and personal observation.

[2] So poor were the people after the war that, even though the value of the mineral and timber lands was well known, there was no native capital to develop them, and the lion's share went to outsiders, who bought the lands at tax and mortgage sales during and after the carpet-bag régime.

[3] Slavery or negroes prevented the establishment of manufactures by crowding out a white population capable of carrying on manufactures. The census shows that in 1860 the white districts had a fair proportion of manufactures for a state less than forty years old.

[4] Address of President C. C. Thach, Dec. 29, 1903.

[5] "Northern Alabama Illustrated," p. 378; see article on "Immigration to the Southern States" in the *Political Science Quarterly*, June, 1905.

But in the '80's the railroad companies began to induce Germans to settle on their lands in the poorest of the white counties. Later there has been a slow movement from the Northwest. As a rule, where the northerners and the Germans settle the wilderness blossoms, and the negro leaves.

After ploughing their hilltops until the soil was exhausted, the whites, even before the war, decided that only by clearing the swamps in the poorer districts could they get land worth cultivating. This required much labor and money. After the war, with the increase of transportation facilities, fertilizers came into use, the swamps were deserted, and the farmers went back to the uplands. "By the use of commercial fertilizers, vast regions once considered barren have been brought into profitable cultivation, and really afford a more reliable and constant crop than the rich alluvial lands of the old slave plantations. In nearly every agricultural county in the South there is to be observed, on the one hand, this section of fertile soils, once the heart of the old civilization, now largely abandoned by the whites, held in tenantry by a dense negro population, full of dilapidation and ruin; while on the other hand, there is the region of light, thin soils, occupied by the small white freeholder, filled with schools, churches, and good roads, and all the elements of a happy, enlightened country life." [1]

The Decadence of the Black Belt

The patriarchal system failed in the Black Belt, the Bureau system of contracts and prescribed wages failed, the planter's own wage system failed,[2] and finally all settled down to the share system.

[1] Address of President C. C. Thach, Dec. 29, 1903.

[2] The decreasing value of the wage laborer is shown by the following table of wages :

YEAR	MEN	WOMEN	YOUTHS, 14-20
1860	$138	$89	$66
1865–1866 . .	150–200	100–150	75–100
1867	117	71	52
1868	87	50	40
1890	150	100	60–75

The figures of 1860 are based on the wages of an able-bodied negro. The statistics of 1865–1866 are taken from tables of wages prescribed by the Freedmen's Bureau ;

In this there was some encouragement to effort on the part of the laborer, and in case of failure of the crop he bore a share of the loss. After a few years' experience, the negroes were ready to go back to the wage system, and labor conventions were held demanding a return to that system.[1] But whatever system was adopted, the work of the negro was unsatisfactory. The skilled laborer left the plantation, and the new generation knew nothing of the arts of industry. Labor became migratory, and the negro farmer wanted to change his location every year.[2] Regular work was a thing of the past. In two or three days each week a negro could work enough to live, and the remainder of the time he rested from his labors, often leaving much cotton in the fields to rot.[3] He went to the field when it suited him to go, gazed frequently at the sun to see if it was time to stop for meals, went often to the spring for water, and spent much time adjusting his plough or knocking the soil and pebbles from his shoes. The negro women refused to work in the fields, and yet did nothing to better the home life; the style of living was "from hand to mouth." Extra money went for whiskey, snuff, tobacco, and finery, while the standard of living was not raised.[4] The laborer would always stop to go to a circus, election, political meeting, revival, or camp-meeting. A great desolation seemed to rest upon the Black Belt country.[5]

In the interior of the state, the negroes worked better during

those for 1867 and 1868 show the decline caused by the inefficiency of the free negro laborer. Yet the demand for labor was always greater than the supply. In 1860 clothing and rations were also given; in 1866–1868 rations and no clothing. In 1890 nothing was furnished. In 1866–1868 the currency was inflated, and the wages for 1868 were really much lower. Hammond, "The Cotton Industry," p. 124; *Montgomery Mail*, May 16, 1865; Freedmen's Bureau Reports, 1865–1870.

[1] A convention held in Montgomery, in 1873, recommended that the share system be abolished and a contract wage system be inaugurated; wages should be secured by a lien on the employer's crop; separate contracts should be made with each laborer, and the "squad" system abolished. In this way the laborer would not be responsible for bad crops. To aid the laborers, Congress was asked to pass the Sumner Civil Rights Bill, providing for the recognition of certain social rights for negroes, to exempt homesteads from tax action, and to increase the tax on property held by speculators. And the President was asked to supply bread and meat to the negro farmers. Annual Cyclopædia (1873), p. 19; *Tuscaloosa Blade*, Nov. 30, 1873.

[2] See Willet, "Workers of the Nation," Vol. II, pp. 701, 702.

[3] Willet, Vol. II, p. 714.

[4] Washington, in *Atlantic Monthly*, Vol. LXXVIII, pp. 324–326.

[5] Somers, p. 166.

and after Reconstruction than where they were exposed to the ministrations of the various kinds of carpet-baggers.[1] In the Tennessee valley, where the negroes had taken a prominent part in politics, and had not only seen much of the war, but many of them had enlisted in the Federal army, cotton raising almost ceased for several years. The only crops made were made by whites.[2] In Sumter County, where the black population was dense, it was, in 1870, almost impossible to secure labor; those negroes who wished to work went to the railways.[3] A description of a "model negro farm" in 1874 was as follows: The farmer purchased an old mule on credit and rented land on shares, or for so many bales of cotton; any old tools were used; corn, bacon, and other supplies were bought on credit, and a lien given on the crop; a month later, corn and cotton were planted on soil not well broken up; the negro "would not pay for no guano," to put on other people's land; by turns the farmer planted and fished, ploughed and hunted, hoed and frolicked, or went to "meeting." At the end of the year he sold his cotton, paid part of his rent, and some of his debt, returned the mule to its owner, and sang: —

> " Nigger work hard all de year,
> White man tote de money."[4]

If the negro made anything, his fellows were likely to steal it. Somers said, "There can be no doubt that the negroes first steal one another's share of the crop, and next the planter's, by way of general redress."[5] Crop stealing was usually done at night. Stolen cotton, corn, pork, etc., was carried to the doggeries kept on the outskirts of the plantation by low white men, and there exchanged for bad whiskey, tobacco, and cheap stuff of various kinds. These doggeries were called "deadfalls," and their proprietors often became rich.[6] So serious did the theft of crops become, that the legislature passed a "sunset" law, making it a penal offence to purchase farm produce

---

[1] *Southern Magazine*, Jan., 1874.

[2] Somers, p. 117.

[3] Somers, p. 159.

[4] *Southern Magazine*, March, 1874.

[5] "Southern States," p. 131.

[6] The prosperity of several large commercial houses in Alabama is said to date from the corner groceries of the '70's.

after nightfall. Poultry, hogs, corn, mules, and horses were stolen when left in the open.

Emancipation destroyed the agricultural supremacy of the Black Belt. The uncertain returns from the plantations caused an exodus of planters and their families to the cities, and formerly well-kept plantations were divided into one- and two-house farms for negro tenants, who allowed everything to go to ruin. The negro tenant system was much more ruinous than the worst of the slavery system, and none of the plantations ever again reached their former state of productiveness. Ditches choked up, fences down, large stretches of fertile fields growing up in weeds and bushes, cabins tumbling in and negro quarters deserted, corn choked by grass and weeds, cotton not half as good as under slavery, — these were the reports from travellers in the Black Belt, towards the close of Reconstruction.[1] Other plantations were leased to managers, who also kept plantation stores whence the negroes were furnished with supplies. The money lenders came into possession of many plantations. By the crop lien and blanket mortgage, the negro became an industrial serf. The "big house" fell into decay. For these and other reasons, the former masters, who were the most useful friends of the negro, left the Black Belt, and the black steadily declined.[2] The unaided negro has steadily grown worse; but Tuskegee, Normal, Calhoun, and similar bodies are endeavoring to assist the negro of the black counties to become an efficient member of society. In the success

[1] Somers, "Southern States," pp. 159, 272; *Harper's Monthly Magazine*, Jan., 1874; King, "The Great South"; C. C. Smith, "Colonization of Negroes in Central Alabama"; *Southern Magazine*, Jan., 1874; *The Forum*, Vol. XXI, p. 341; Hoffman, p. 261; Hammond, p. 191. See also Appendix II.

[2] A northern traveller in the Alabama Black Belt in recent years says of it: "The white population is rapidly on the decrease and the negro population on the increase. . . . There are hundreds of the 'old mansion houses' going to decay, the glass broken in the windows, the doors off the hinges, the siding long unused to paint, the columns of the verandas rotting away, and the bramble thickets encroaching to the very doors. The people have sold their land for what little they could get and moved to the cities and towns, that they may educate their children and escape the intolerable conditions surrounding them at their old beloved homes. . . . These friends have largely gone from the negro's life, and he is left alone in the wilderness, held down by crop liens and mortgages given to the alien. Land rent is half its value; the tenant must purchase from the creditor's store and raise cotton to pay for what he has already eaten and worn." C. C. Smith, "Colonization of Negroes in Central Alabama," published by the Christian Women's Board of Missions, Indianapolis, Ind.

of such efforts lies the only hope of the negro, and also of the white of the Black Belt, if the negro is to continue to exclude white immigration.[1]

[1] See also Edmunds, in *Review of Reviews*, Sept., 1900; Dillingham, in *Yale Review*, Vol. V, p. 190; Stone, "The Negro in the Yazoo-Mississippi Delta"; Stone, in *Quarterly Journal of Economics*, Feb., 1905; *Gunton's Magazine*, Sept., 1902 (Dowd); Brown, in *North American Review*, Dec., 1904; Census 1900, Vol. VI, Pt. II, pp. 406–416; *Harper's Monthly Magazine*, Jan., 1874, and Jan., 1881; Stone, in *South Atlantic Quarterly*, Jan., 1905; Kelsey, "The Negro Farmer"; Hammond, "The Cotton Industry."

Another solution of the problem is often suggested, viz. the crowding out of the blacks from the Black Belt by the whites — especially northerners and Germans — who want to cultivate the Black Belt lands, who settle in colonies, and who have no place for the negro in their plans of industrial society. The Black Belt landlords are becoming weary of negro labor, and some are disposed to make special inducements to get whites to settle in the Black Belt. In Louisiana and Mississippi, Italians have replaced negroes on many sugar and cotton plantations. Georgia and Alabama, in order to make the negro work, have recently passed stringent vagrancy laws, and the planters are talking of Chinese labor. For the opinions of those who favor white immigration to the South, see the *Manufacturers Record*, the *Atlanta Constitution*, and the *Montgomery Advertiser*, during recent years. There is a general demand for foreigners who will perform agricultural labor.

CHAPTER XXIII

POLITICAL AND SOCIAL CONDITIONS DURING RECONSTRUCTION

SEC. I. POLITICS AND POLITICAL METHODS

DURING the war the administration of the state government gradually fell into the hands of officials elected by people more or less disaffected toward the Confederacy. Provisional Governor Parsons, who had been secretly disloyal to the Confederacy, retained in office many of the old Confederate local officials, and appointed to other offices men who had not strongly supported the Confederacy. In the fall of 1865 and the spring of 1866 elections under the provisional government placed in office a more energetic class of second and third rate men who had had little experience and who were not strong Confederates. Men who had opposed secession and who had done little to support the war were, as a rule, sent to Congress and placed in the higher offices of state. The ablest men were not available, being disfranchised by the President's plan.

In 1868, with the establishment of the reconstructed government, an entirely new class of officials secured control. Less than 5000 white voters, of more than 100,000 of voting age, supported the Radical programme, and, as more than 3000 officials were to be chosen, the field for choice was limited. The elections having gone by default, the Radicals met with no opposition, except in three counties. In all the other counties the entire Radical ticket was declared elected, even though in several of them no formal elections had been held.

William H. Smith, who was made governor under the Reconstruction Acts, was a native of Georgia, a lawyer, formerly a Douglas Democrat, and had opposed secession, but was a candidate for the Confederate Congress. Defeated, he consoled himself by going over to the Federals in 1862. Smith was a man of no executive ability, careless of the duties of his office, and in few respects a fit person to be governor. He disliked the Confederate element and also the carpet-baggers, but as long as the latter would not ask for high offices, he was at peace with them. It was his plan to carry on the state government with the 2000 or 3000 "unionists" and the United States troops. He did not like the negroes, but could endure them as long as they lived in a different part of the state and voted for him. In personal and private matters he was thoroughly honest, but his course in regard to the issue of bonds showed that in public affairs he could be influenced to doubtful conduct. It is certain that he never profited by any of the stealing that was carried on; he merely made it easy for others to steal; the dishonest ones were his friends, and his enemies paid the taxes. As governor he had the respect of neither party. He went too far to please the Democrats, and not far enough to please the Radicals. He exercised no sort of control over his local officials and shut his eyes to the plundering of the Black Belt. He was emphatically governor of his small following of whites, not of all the people, not even of the blacks. During his administration the whites complained that he was very active in protecting Radicals from outrage, but paid no attention to the troubles of his political enemies. His government did not give adequate protection to life and property.

His lieutenant-governor, A. J. Applegate of Ohio and Wisconsin, was an illiterate Federal soldier left stranded in Alabama by the surrender. During the war he was taken ill in Mississippi and was cared for by Mrs. Thompson, wife of a former Secretary of the Treasury. Upon leaving the Thompson house he carried some valuable papers with him, which, after the war, he tried to sell to Mrs. Thompson for $10,000. Lowe, Walker, & Company, a firm of lawyers in Alabama, gave Applegate $300, made him sign a statement as to how he obtained the papers, and then published all the correspondence.[1] The charge of thievery did not injure his candidacy. Before election he had been an *attaché* of the Freedmen's Bureau. After the constitution had been rejected in 1868, Applegate went North, so far that he could not get back in time for the first session of the legislature. A special act, however,

---

[1] Ku Klux Rept., Ala. Test., p. 879 (Lowe); *N. Y. World*, Dec. 14, 1867, Aug. 15, 1868.

authorized him to draw his pay as having been present. In a letter written for the Associated Press, which was secured by the Democrats, there were thirty-nine mistakes in spelling. As a presiding officer over the Senate, he was vulgar and undignified. His speeches were ludicrous. When the conduct of the Radical senators pleased him, he made known his pleasure by shouting, "Bully for Alabama!"

The secretary of state, Charles A. Miller, was a Bureau agent from Maine; Bingham, the treasurer, was from New York; Reynolds, the auditor, from Wisconsin; Keffer, the superintendent of industrial resources, from Pennsylvania. Two natives of indifferent reputation — Morse and Cloud — were, respectively, attorney-general and superintendent of public instruction. Morse was under indictment for murder and had to be relieved by special act of the legislature. The chief justice, Peck, was from New York; Saffold and Peters were southern men; the senators and all of the representatives in Congress were carpet-baggers. There were six candidates for the short-term senatorship — all of them carpet-baggers. Willard Warner of Ohio, who was elected, was probably the most respectable of all the carpet-baggers, and was soon discarded by the party. He had served in the Federal army and after the war was elected to the Ohio Senate. His term expired in January, 1868; in July, 1868, he was elected to the United States Senate from Alabama. George E. Spencer was elected to the United States Senate for the long term. He was from Massachusetts, Ohio, Iowa, and Nebraska. In Iowa he had been clerk of the Senate, and in Nebraska, secretary to the governor. He entered the army as sutler of the First Nebraska Infantry. Later he assisted in raising the First Union Alabama Cavalry and was made its colonel. Spencer was shrewd, coarse, and unscrupulous, and soon secured control of Federal patronage for Alabama. He attacked his colleague, Warner, as being lukewarm.

The representatives and their records were as follows: F. W. Kellogg of Massachusetts and Michigan represented the latter state in Congress from 1859 to 1865, when he was appointed collector of internal revenue at Mobile. C. W. Buckley of New York and Illinois was a Presbyterian preacher who had come to Alabama as chaplain of a negro regiment. For two years he was a Bureau official and an active agitator. He was a leading member in the

3 B

convention of 1867. B. W. Norris of Skowhegan, Maine, was an oil-cloth maker and a land agent for Maine, a commissary, contractor, cemetery commissioner, and paymaster during the war. After the war he came South with C. A. Miller, his brother-in-law, and both became Bureau agents. C. W. Pierce of Massachusetts and Illinois was a Bureau official. Nothing more is known of him. John B. Callis of Wisconsin had served in the Federal army and later in the Veteran Reserve Corps. After the war he became a Bureau agent in Alabama, and when elected he was not a citizen of the state, but was an army officer stationed in Mississippi. Thomas Haughey of Scotland was a Confederate recruiting officer in 1861-1862 and later a surgeon in the Union army. He was killed in 1869 by Collins, a member of the Radical Board of Education. It was said that he was without race prejudice and consorted with negroes, but he was the only one of the Alabama delegation whom Governor Smith liked. The latter wrote that "our whole set of representatives in Congress, with the exception of Haughey, are . . . unprincipled scoundrels having no regard for the state of the people." [1]

In the first Reconstruction legislature, which lasted for three years, there were in the Senate 32 Radicals and 1 Democrat. In the House there were 97 Radicals (only 94 served) and 3 Democrats. The lone Democrat in the Senate was Worthy of Pike, and to prevent him from engaging in debate, Applegate often retired from his seat and called upon him to preside; the Democrats in the House were Hubbard of Pike, Howard of Crenshaw, and Reeves of Cherokee.[2] In the Senate there was only 1 negro; in the House there were 26, several of whom could not sign their names. In the apportionment of representatives there was a difference of 40 per cent in favor of the black counties. Hundreds of negroes swarmed in to see the legislature begin, filling the galleries, the windows, and the vacant seats, and crowding the aisles. They were invited by resolution to fill the galleries and from that place they took part in the affairs of the House, voting on every

---

[1] For information in regard to the Radical congressmen: Barnes, "History of the 40th Congress," Index; Ku Klux Rept., Ala. Test. (Clanton, Lowe, Lindsay); *Harper's Weekly*, May 1, 1869 (picture of Spencer); *Elyton Herald*, ——, 1868; *Montgomery Mail*, July 25, 1868; *N. Y. World*, Feb. 15 and Sept. 22, 1868; *Alabama Manual* (1869), p. 32; *N. Y. Herald*, ——, 1868.

[2] Pike was the only county that never fell completely into the hands of the Radicals.

SCENES IN THE FIRST RECONSTRUCTED LEGISLATURE.

(Cartoons from "The Loil Legislature," by Captain B. H. Screws.)

measure with loud shouts. A scalawag from north Alabama wanted the negroes to sit on one side of the House and the whites on the other, but he was not listened to. The doorkeepers, sergeant-at-arms, and other employees were usually negroes. The negro members watched their white leaders and voted *aye* or *no* as they voted. When tired they went to sleep and often had to be wakened to vote. Both houses were usually opened with prayer by northern Methodist ministers or by negro ministers. None but "loyal" ministers were asked to officiate. Strobach, the Austrian member, wearied of much political prayer, moved that the chaplain cut short his devotions.

The whites in the legislature were for the most part carpet-baggers or unknown native whites. The entire taxes paid by the members of the legislature were, it is said, less than $100. Applegate, the lieutenant-governor, did not own a dollar's worth of property in the state. Most of the carpet-bag members lived in Montgomery; the rest of them lived in Mobile, Selma, and Huntsville. Few of them saw the districts they represented after election; some did not see them before or after the election. The representative from Jackson County lived in Chattanooga, Tennessee. The state constitution prohibited United States officials from holding state offices, but nearly all Federal officers in the state also held state offices. This was particularly the case in the southwestern counties, which were represented by revenue and custom-house officials. from Mobile. Some of them were absent most of the time, but all drew pay; one of the negro members, instead of attending, went regularly to school after the roll was called. No less than twenty members had been indicted or convicted, or were indicted during the session, of various crimes, from adultery and stealing to murder. The legislature passed special acts to relieve members from the penalties for stealing, adultery, bigamy, arson, riot, illegal voting, assault, bribery, and murder.[1]

Bribery was common in the legislature. By custom a room in the capitol was set apart for the accommodation of those who wished

---

[1] "North Alabama Illustrated," p. 50; *Montgomery Advertiser*, July 13, 1866; *N. Y. World*, April 11 and July 23, 1868; Ku Klux Rept., Ala. Test., pp. 187, 188, 881, 1815, 1956; Acts of Ala. (1868), p. 414; (1869–1870), pp. 157, 336; Beverly, "Alabama," p. 203. A vivid description of the first session of the reconstructed legislature was published by Capt. B. H. Screws, "The Loil Legislature."

to "interview" negro members.[1] There the agents of railroad companies distributed conscience money in the form of loans which were never to be paid back. Harrington, the speaker, boasted that he received $1700 for engineering a bill through the House. A lottery promoter said that it cost him only $600 to get his charter through the legislature, and that no Radical, except one negro, refused the small bribe he offered. Senator Sibley held his vote on railroad measures at $500; Pennington, at $1000; W. B. Jones, at $500. Hardy of Dallas received $35,000 to ease the passage of a railroad bond issue, and kept most of it for himself; another received enough to start a bank; still another was given 640 acres of land, a steam mill, and a side track on a railroad near his mill. Negro members, as a rule, sold out very cheaply, and probably most often to Democrats who wanted some minor measures passed to which the Radical leaders would pay no attention. It was found best not to pay the larger sums until the governor had signed the bill. A member accepted a gift as a matter of course, and no attention was paid to charges of bribery.[2]

The election of February 4 and 5, 1868, at which the constitution was rejected on account of the whites' refraining from voting, was in many counties a farce. The legislature, in order to remedy any defects in the credentials of the Radical candidates, passed a number of general and special acts legalizing the "informal" elections of February 4 and 5, and declaring the Radical candidates elected. In seven counties no votes had been counted, but this made no difference.[3]

The presiding officers addressed the members as "Captain, John, Mr. Jones," etc. Quarrels and fights were frequent. One member chased another to the secretary's desk, trying to kill him, but was prevented by the secretary. In the cloak-rooms and halls were fruit and peanut stands, whiskey shops, and lunch counters. Legislative action did not avail to clear out the sovereign negroes and

---

[1] Tradition says that what is now known as the Davis Memorial Room was the one thus used.

[2] Ku Klux Rept., Ala. Test., pp. 231, 881, 1411, 1424, 1468; *Weekly Mail*, March 24, 1869; *Independent Monitor*, Jan. 11, 1870; Report of Investigating Committee; Miller, "Alabama," p. 254; "Northern Alabama," p. 50; oral accounts of former members.

[3] Acts of Ala. (1868), pp. 67, 71, 79, 212, 305, 352.

keep the halls clean. Political meetings were held in the capitol, much to the damage of the furniture.[1]

The only measures that excited general interest among the members were the bond-issue bills. Other legislation was generally purely perfunctory, except in case an election law or a Ku Klux law was to be passed. There was much special legislation on account of individual members, such as granting divorces, ordering release from jail, relieving from the "pains" of marriage with more than one woman, trick legislation, vacating offices, etc. When, as in Mobile, the Democrats controlled too many minor offices, the legislature remedied the wrong by declaring the offices vacant and giving the governor authority to make appointments to the vacancies. The Mobile offices were vacated three times in this way. In connection with the Mobile bill it was found that fraudulent interpolations were sometimes made in a bill after its passage. It would be taken from the clerk's desk, changed, and then returned for printing.[2]

Some of the laws passed failed of their object because of mistakes in spelling. A committee was finally appointed to correct mistakes in orthography. The House and Senate constantly returned engrossed bills to one another for correction. A joint committee to investigate the education of the clerks reported that they were unable to ascertain which of the clerks was illiterate, though they discharged one of them. The minority report declared that the fault was not with the clerks, but with the members, many of whom could not write. Finally a spelling clerk was employed to rewrite the bills submitted by the members.[3] For making fun of the ignorance of the Radical members, Ryland Randolph, a Democratic member, elected in a by-election, was expelled from the House.

In 1868 the Radicals, fearing the result of the presidential election and afraid of the Ku Klux movement which was beginning to be felt, passed a bill giving to itself the power to choose presidential

[1] Senate Journal (1868), pp. 168, 176, 297.
[2] Acts of Ala. (1868), pp. 113, 129, 133, 350, 407, 414, 421; (1869–1870), p. 451; *Montgomery Mail*, Feb. 24, 1870; Annual Cyclopædia (1870), p. 12.
[3] Annual Cyclopædia (1870), p. 13; Journal (1869–1870), *passim*; Brown, "Alabama," p. 268.

electors. The negroes were aroused by the Radical leaders who were not in the legislature, and sufficient pressure was brought to bear on the governor to induce him to veto the measure.[1]

According to the constitution, the Senate was to classify at once after organization, so that·half should serve two years and half four years. No one was willing to take the short term and lose the $8 *per diem* and other privileges. So in 1868 the Senate refused to classify. Again in 1870 it refused to classify. The Radicals permitted the usurpation because it was known that the Democrats would carry the white counties in case the classification were made and elections held. Then, too, it was feared that in 1870 the Democrats would have a majority in the lower house; hence a Radical Senate would be necessary to prevent the repudiation of the railroad indorsation. So all senators held over until 1872, and by shrewd manipulation and the use of Federal troops the Senate kept a Radical majority until 1874.[2]

County and other local officials were incompetent and corrupt. The policy of the whites in abstaining from voting on the constitution (1868) gave nearly every office in the state to incompetent men. In the white counties it was as bad as in the black, because the Radicals there despaired of carrying the elections and put up no regular candidates. However, in every county some freaks offered themselves as candidates, and at "informal" elections received, or said they received, a few votes. After the state was admitted in spite of the rejection of the constitution, these people were put in office by the legislature. Had the white people taken part in the elections instead of relying upon the law of Congress in regard to ratification and not refrained from voting, they could have secured nearly all the local offices in the white counties. No other state had such an experience; no other state had such a low class of officials in the beginning of Reconstruction. But the very incapacity of them worked in favor of better government, for they had to be gotten rid of and others appointed. Not a single Bureau agent whose name is on record failed to get some kind of an office. In Perry County most of the officials were soldiers of a Wisconsin regiment discharged in the South; the circuit clerk was under indictment for horse stealing. In Greene

[1] Annual Cyclopædia (1870), p. 19; *N. Y. Herald*, Aug. 17, 1868.
[2] Ku Klux Rept., Ala. Test., pp. 90, 91, 187; Senate Journals (1868–1874).

County a superintendent of education had to be imported under contract from Massachusetts, there being no competent Radical. In Sumter County one Price, who had a negro wife, was registrar, superintendent of education, postmaster, and circuit clerk. A carpetbagger, elected probate judge, went home to Ohio, after the supposed rejection of the constitution, and never returned. The sheriff and the soliciter were negroes who could not read. Another Radical was at once circuit clerk, register in chancery, notary public, justice of the peace, keeper of the county poorhouse, and guardian *ad litem*. In Elmore County the probate judge was under indictment for murder. In Montgomery, Brainard, the circuit clerk, killed his brother-in-law and tried to kill Widmer, the collector of internal revenue. The Radical chancellor and marshal were scalawags — one a former slave trader, the other a former divine-right slave owner. The sheriff of Madison could not write. In Dallas the illiterate negro commissioners voted for a higher rate of taxation, though their names were not on the tax books; their scalawag associates voted for the lower rate. Thus it was all over Alabama.

In July, 1868, the Reconstruction legislature continued in force the code of Alabama, which provided for heavy official bonds. But the adventurers could not make bond. So a special law was passed authorizing the supreme court, chancellors, and circuit judges to "fix and prescribe" the bonds of all "judicial and county officials." Later the suspended code went into effect, and the Democrats succeeded in turning out many newly elected Radicals who could not make bond. Almost at the beginning the Democrats began the plan of refusing to make bond for Radicals, and thus made it almost impossible for the latter to hold office until the legislature again came to their relief.

There were many vacancies and few white Radicals to fill them; the scalawags thought that the negro ought to be content with voting. Smith had many vacancies to fill by appointment. Most of the paying ones were given to Radicals, and many of the others were given to Democrats, whom he preferred to negroes. In the black counties the property owners and the Ku Klux began to make the most obnoxious officials sell out and leave, and Governor Smith would, by agreement, appoint some Democrat to such vacancies. This custom became frequent, and, in spite of himself, Smith's "lily white" sentiments were undermining the rule of his party.[1] An argument used by the more liberal of the Radicals in favor of removal of disabilities was that in some counties the local offices could not be filled on account of the operation of the disfranchising laws.[2]

The Federal judiciary was represented by Richard Busteed, an Irishman, who was made Federal judge in 1864. He came South in 1865 with bloodthirsty threats and at once began prosecutions for treason. More than 900 cases were brought before him. There were no convictions, but a rich harvest of costs. He was ignorant of law, and in the court room was arbitrary and tyrannical to lawyers, witnesses, and prisoners. It was charged that he was in partnership with the district attorney. Bribery was proven against him. The leading lawyers, both Radical and Democratic, asked Congress to impeach him, but to no effect. It was his custom to solicit men to bring causes before him. A Selma editor was brought before him and severely lectured for writing a disrespectful article about Busteed's grand jury. There was one Democratic lawyer whom Busteed feared — General James H. Clanton. Clanton paid no attention to Busteed's vagaries, but sat on the bench with him, advised him and made him take his advice, won all his cases, and bullied Busteed unrebuked. The latter was afraid he would be killed if he angered Clanton, and Clanton played upon his fears. At first a great negrophile, Busteed became more and more obnoxious to the Radical party, and was soon accused of being a Democrat and removed. Another Federal officer, Wells, the United States district attorney, had been discharged from the Union army on the ground of insanity.[3]

The new constitution made all judgeships elective and also provided for the election of a solicitor in each county. The result was seen in the number of incapable judges and illiterate solicitors. The probate judge of Madison was "a common jack-plane carpenter from Oregon," and his sheriff could not write. Many of the judges had never studied law and had never practised. Public meetings

---

[1] Ku Klux Rept., Ala. Test., pp. 189, 239, 240, 324, 435, 523, 962, 1421, 1590, 1816, 1819, 1820, 1957; Herbert, "Solid South," p. 53; Coburn Report, p. 256; *N. Y. World*, April 11, 1868; *Montgomery Mail*, April 21, 1870.

[2] Annual Cyclopædia (1870), p. 13.

[3] Ku Klux Rept., Ala. Test., p. 510; *Augusta Chronicle and Sentinel*, June 13, 1866; *Selma Times and Messenger*, June 9, 1868.

were held to protest against incompetent judges and to demand their resignations. Governor Smith usually appointed better men, and not always those of his own party, to the places vacated by resignation, sale, or otherwise. Before the war the state judiciary had stood high in the estimation of the people, and judicial officers were forbidden by public opinion to take part in party politics. Under the Reconstruction government the judicial officials took an active part in political campaigns, every one of them, from Busteed and the supreme court to a county judge, making political speeches and holding office in the party organization. From a party point of view the scarcity of white Radicals made this necessary. Notaries public, who also had the powers of justices of the peace, were appointed by the governor. Their powers were great and indefinite, and in consequence they almost drove the justices out of activity. Some of them issued warrants running into all parts of the state, causing men to be brought forty to fifty miles to appear before them on trifling charges.

The Reconstruction judiciary generally held that a jury without a negro on it was not legal. In the white counties such juries were hard to form. Northern newspaper correspondents wrote of the ludicrous appearance of Busteed's half negro jury struggling with intricate points of maritime law, insurance, constitutional questions, exchange, and the relative value of a Prussian guilder to a pound sterling. When they were bored they went to sleep. The negro jurors recognized their own incompetence and usually agreed to any verdict decided upon by the white jurors. Had the latter been respectable men, no harm would have been done, but usually they were not. A negro jury would not convict a member of the Union League — he had only to give the sign — nor a negro prosecuted by a white man or indicted by a jury; but many negroes prosecuted by their own race were convicted by black juries. For many years it was impossible to secure a respectable Federal jury on account of the test oath required, which excluded nearly all Confederates of ability. As an example of the working of a local court, the criminal court of Dallas may be taken. The jurisdiction extended to capital offences. Corbin, the judge, was an old Virginian who had never read law. He refused to allow one Roderick Thomas, colored, to be tried by a mixed jury, demanding a full negro jury. The prosecution was

then dropped because all twelve negroes drawn were of bad character. Corbin then entered on the record that Thomas was "acquitted." Thomas had stolen cotton, and the fact had been proven;
but he soon became clerk of Corbin's court and later took Corbin's
place as judge, with another negro for clerk. Nearly every Radical
official in Dallas County was indicted for corruption in office by a
Radical or mixed jury, but negro juries refused to convict them.[1]

An elaborate militia system was provided for by the carpet-baggers, with General Dustin of Iowa, a carpet-bagger, as major-general.
The strength of organization was to be in the black counties, but
Governor Smith persistently refused to organize the negro militia.
He was afraid of the effect on his slender white following, and he did
not think that the negro ought to do anything but vote. He was
also afraid of Democratic militia, afraid that it would overturn the
hated state government. He tried to get several friendly white
companies to organize, but failed, and during the rest of his term
relied exclusively upon Federal troops. Even before the Reconstruction government was set going it was seen that the whites would be
restless. Forcing the rejected constitution and the low-class state
government upon the people against the will of the majority had a
very bad effect. They recognized it as the government *de facto* only,
and they so considered it all during the Reconstruction. Then the
Ku Klux movement began, and north Alabama especially was disturbed for several years. Smith sometimes threatened to call out the
militia, but never did so. However, he kept the Federal troops busy
answering his calls. After the election of Grant the army was always at the service of the state officials, who used detachments as
police, marshals, and *posses*. The government had not the respect
of its own party, and had to be upheld by military force. It was a
fixed custom to call in the military when the law was to be enforced
— governor, congressmen, marshals, sheriff, judge, justice of peace,
politicians, all calling for and obtaining troops. It was distasteful
duty to the Federal officers and soldiers. Though the people knew
that only the soldiers upheld the state government, yet they were
not, as a rule, sorry to see the soldiers come in. The military rule
was preferable to the civil rule, and acted as a check on Radical

---

[1] Ku Klux Rept., Ala. Test., pp. 93, 103, 104, 358, 435, 1878; *N. Y. World*,
Nov. 3, 1868; Coburn Report, p. 512; Herbert, "Solid South," p. 60.

misgovernment. The whites were often sorry to see the soldiers leave, even though they were instruments of oppression. Wholesale arrests by the army were not as frequent during Smith's administration as later.[1]

The state government was shaken to its foundations by the presidential campaign and election of 1868. The whites had waked up and gone to work in earnest. It was the first election in which the races voted against one another. Busteed, Strobach, and other carpet-baggers toured the North, predicting chains and slavery for the blacks and butchery for the "loyal" whites in case Seymour were elected. The Union League whipped the negroes into line. Brass bands lent enthusiasm to Radical parades. The negroes were afraid that they would "lose their rights " and be reënslaved, that their wives would have to work the roads and not be allowed to wear hoopskirts. The Radicals urged upon the Democrats the view that those

ELECTION FOR PRESIDENT, 1868.
- Democratic majority
- Republican majority
- About evenly divided, electing some candidates on each ticket.
- O Black counties.

Grant, Republican 76,366.
Seymour, Democrat 72,086.

who did not believe in negro suffrage could not take the voter's oath. Many Democrats refused to register because of the oath. There were numbers who would not vote against Grant because they believed that he was the only possible check against Congress. Others felt that so far as Alabama was concerned the

---

[1] Annual Cyclopædia (1870), p. 14; Ku Klux Rept., Ala. Test., pp. 91, 1177, 1178, 1179, 1242; N. Y. Herald, Sept. 27 and Oct. 26, 1868; Report of Sec. of War, 1869, vol. I, p. 88.

election was cut and dried for Grant. But nevertheless a majority of the whites determined to resist further Africanization in government. Their natural leaders were disfranchised, but a strong compaign was made. The hope was held out of overthrowing the irregular revolutionary state government and driving out the carpet-baggers in case Seymour became President. North Alabama declared that a vote for Grant was a vote against the whites and formed a boycott of all Radicals. The south Alabama leaders tried to secure a part of the negro vote, and urged that imprudent talk be avoided and that carpet-baggers and scalawags be let alone, and the negroes be treated kindly as being responsible for none of the evils. Orders purporting to be signed by General Grant were sent out among the negroes, bidding them to beware of the promises of the whites and directing them to vote for him. Some rascally whites made large sums of money by selling Grant badges to the blacks. They had been sent down for free distribution; but the negroes, ordered, as they believed, by the general, purchased his pictures at $2 each, or less. The carpet-baggers were afraid of losing the state. Some left and went home. Others wanted the legislature to choose electors. Still others wanted to have no election at all, preferring to let it go by default; but the higher military commanders, Terry and Grant, were sympathetic and troops were so distributed over the state as to bring out the negro vote. Army officers assisted at Radical political meetings, and the negro was informed by his advisers that General Grant had sent the troops to see that they voted properly. The result was that the state went for Grant by a safe majority.[1]

During the administration of Smith the incompatibility of the elements of the Radical party began to show more clearly. The native whites began to desert as soon as the convention of 1867 showed that the negro vote would be controlled by the carpet-baggers. The genuine Unionist voters resented the leadership of renegade secessionists. The carpet-baggers demanded the lion's share of the spoils and were angered because Smith vetoed some of their

---

[1] McPherson's scrap-book, "Campaign of 1868," Vol. I, p. 156; Vol. V, pp. 43, 45, 46, 48, 49; Ku Klux Rept., Ala. Test., pp. 95, 360, 502, 1956; *N. Y. World*, Sept. 12, 1868; G. O. No. 27, Dept. of the South, Oct. 8, 1868; G. O. No. 38, Dept. of the South, Nov. 10, 1868; *Tuskegee News*, July 29, 1876.

measures; the scalawags upheld him. The carpet-baggers felt that since they controlled the negro voters they were entitled to the greater consideration. Their manipulation of the Union League alarmed the native Radicals.

The negroes were becoming conscious of their power and were inclined to demand a larger share of the offices than the carpet-baggers wanted to give them. Some of the negroes were desirous of voting with the whites. Negro leaders were aspiring to judge-ships, to the state Senate, to be postmasters, to go to Congress. Even now the party was held together only by the knowledge that it would be destroyed if divided.[1]

In 1868 Governor Smith and other Radical leaders, convinced that they were permanently in power, secured the passage of a law providing for the gradual removal of disabilities imposed by state law. The same year a complete registration had been made for the purpose of excluding the leading whites. After disabilities were removed, so far as state action was concerned there was no advan-tage to Radicals in a registration of voters. On the other hand, it threatened to become a powerful aid to the Democrats, who began to attend the polls and demand that only registered voters be allowed to cast ballots, thus preventing repeating. Consequently, as a prepa-ration for the first general election in the fall of 1870, the legislature passed a law forbidding the use of registration lists by any official at any election. No one was to be asked if he were registered. No one was to be required to show a registration certificate. The as-sertion of the would-be voter was to be taken as sufficient. And it was made a misdemeanor to challenge a voter, thus interfering with the freedom of elections. After this a negro might vote under any name he pleased as often as he pleased. This election system was in force until 1874, when the Democrats came into power.[2]

To the Forty-first Congress in 1869 returned only one of the former carpet-bag delegation, C. W. Buckley. Two so-called Demo-crats were chosen, two scalawags, and a new carpet-bagger. P. M. Dox, one of the Democrats, was a northern man who had lived in the South before the war, who was neutral during the war; and after the

[1] N. Y. Times, Sept. 7, 1868 (speech of Judge T. M. Peters).

[2] Nordhoff, "Cotton States in 1870," pp. 85, 86; Ku Klux Rept., Ala. Test., pp. 185, 209, 210, 434, 435, 1879.

war he posed as a "Unionist." Congressional timber was scarce on account of the test oath and the Fourteenth Amendment, so Dox secured a nomination. His opponent was a negro, which helped him in north Alabama. The other Democrat, W. C. Sherrod, who was also from north Alabama, had served in the Confederate army. His opponent was J. J. Hinds, one of the most disliked of the carpet-baggers.

ELECTION OF 1870 FOR GOVERNOR.

☐ Democratic Majority
▨ Radical Majority   ○ Black Counties.
▤ Nearly evenly divided
Lindsay (Dem), 77,721; Smith, (Rep.), 76,292

Robert S. Heflin, one of the scalawags, was from that section where the Peace Society flourished during the war. At first a Confederate, in 1864 he deserted and went within the Federal lines. Charles Hays, the other scalawag, became the most notorious of the Reconstruction representatives in Congress. He was a cotton planter in one of the densest black districts and managed to stay in Congress for four years. He is chiefly remembered because of the Hays-Hawley correspondence in 1874. Alfred E. Buck of Maine had been an officer of negro troops. He served only one term and after defeat passed into the Federal service. He died as minister to Japan in 1902. This delegation was weaker in ability and in morals than the carpet-bag delegation to the Fortieth Congress.

In the fall of 1870 Governor Smith was a candidate for reëlection against Robert Burns Lindsay, Democrat. The hostility of Smith to carpet-baggers weakened the party. The ticket was not acceptable to the whites because Rapier, a negro, was candidate for secretary of state. The genuine Unionists were becoming ultra Democrats, because of the prominence given in their party to former secessionists like Parsons, Sam Rice, and Hays, and to negroes and carpet-baggers. Lindsay was from north Alabama, which supported him as a "white man's candidate." The negroes had been taught to distrust scalawags, as being little better than Democrats. Smith was asked why he ran on a ticket with a negro. He replied that now that was the only way to get office. He also called attention to the fact that in north Alabama the Democrats drew the color line, and called themselves the "white man's party," while in the black counties they made an earnest effort to secure the negro vote. The Union League, through Keffer, sent out warning that whatever would suit "Rebels" would not suit "union men," who must treat their "fine professions as coming from the Prince of Darkness himself," and that if Lindsay were elected, the "condition of union men would be like unto hell itself." Smith and Senator Warner said that the Democrats would repudiate railroad bonds, destroy the schools, and repeal the Amendments and the Reconstruction Acts. In the white counties the Radical speakers were generally insulted, and soon the white districts were given up as permanently lost. The Black Belt alone was now the stronghold of the Radicals. Strict inspection here prevented the negroes from voting Democratic, as some were disposed to do. Negroes in the white counties voted for Democrats with many misgivings. An old man told a candidate, "I intend to vote for you; I liked your speech; but if you put me back into slavery, I'll never forgive you." Federal troops were again judiciously distributed in the Black Belt and in the white counties when there was a large negro vote. As a result the election was very close, Lindsay winning by a vote of 76,977 to 75,568.

Ex-Governor Parsons, who had now become a Radical, advised Smith not to submit to the seating of Lindsay, but to force a contest, and meanwhile to prevent the vote from being counted by the legislature. So, by injunction from the supreme court, the Radical president of the Senate, Barr, was forbidden to count the votes for governor. But the houses in joint session counted the rest of the votes, and E. H. Moren, Democrat, was declared elected lieutenant-governor. A majority of the House was anti-Radical. The old

Senate, refusing to classify, held over.   As soon as Moren was declared elected, Barr arose and left, followed by most of the Radical senators, saying that he was forbidden to count the vote for governor. Moren at once appeared, took the oath, and the joint meeting not having been regularly adjourned, he ordered the count for governor to proceed.   A few Radical senators had lingered out of curiosity, and were retained.   Thus Lindsay was counted in, and at once took the oath of office.   By the advice of Parsons, Smith, though willing to retire, refused to give place to Lindsay.   The Radical senators recognized Smith; the House recognized Lindsay.   Smith brought Federal troops into the state-house to keep Lindsay out, and for two or three weeks there were rival governors.   Finally Smith was forced to retire by a writ from the carpet-bag circuit court of Montgomery.[1]

Lindsay was born in Scotland and educated at the University of St. Andrews.   He lived in Alabama for fifteen years before the war, opposed secession, and gave only a half-hearted support to the Confederacy.   As he said: "I would rather not tell my military history, for there was very little glory in it. . . . I do not know that I can say much about my soldiering." [2]   Lindsay was a scholar, a good lawyer, and a pure man, but a weak executive.   In this respect he was better than Smith, however, who was supported by a unanimous Radical legislature.   Under Lindsay the Senate was Radical and the House doubtful.   The Radical auditor held over; Democrats were elected to the offices of treasurer, secretary of state, attorney-general, and superintendent of public instruction.   W. W. Allen, a Confederate major-general, was placed in command of the militia and organized some white companies.

The Democratic and independent majority of the House had some able leaders, but many of the rank and file were timid and inexperienced.   Several thousand of the best citizens were still disfranchised.   There were too many young men in public office, half-educated and inexperienced.   In the House there were only fourteen ne-

---

[1] Miller, "Alabama," p. 256; Ku Klux Rept., Ala. Test., pp. 84, 182, 183, 216, 232, 311, 356, 357, 378, 379, 512, 531, 1038, 1625; McPherson's scrap-book, "Campaign of 1870," Vol. I, pp. 55, 61: Annual Cyclopædia (1870), pp. 16, 17; "Northern Alabama," p. 50; *Montgomery Mail*, Aug. 20, 1870 (Union League Appeal).

[2] Somers, "Southern States," p. 132; Ku Klux Rept., Ala. Test., p. 225; Miller, "Alabama," p. 256.

groes. So far as the legislature was concerned, there would be a deadlock for two years. The Radicals would consent to no repeal of injurious legislation, and thus the evil effects of the laws relating to schools, railroads, and elections continued. Governor Lindsay tried to bring some order into the state finances, but the Democrats were divided on the subject of repudiating the fraudulent bond issues, while the Radicals upheld all of the bond stealing. Lindsay was blamed by the people for not dealing more firmly with the question, but, as a matter of fact, he did as well as any man in his position could do.

One cause of weakness to the administration was the fact that some of the attorneys for the railroads were prominent Democrats who insisted upon the recognition of the fraudulent bonds. These attorneys were few in number, but they caused a division among the leaders. The selfish motive was very evident, though for the sake of appearance they talked of "upholding the state's credit," "the fair name of Alabama," etc. It is difficult to see that their conduct was in any way on a higher plane than that of the carpet-baggers, who issued the bonds with intent to defraud. In order to protect themselves they mercilessly criticised Lindsay.

Most of the local officials held over from 1868 to 1872; in by-elections it was clearly shown that the Radicals had lost all except the Black Belt, where they continued to roll up large majorities, but even here they were losing by resignation, sale of offices, Ku Kluxing, and removal. The more decent carpet-baggers were leaving for the North; the white Radicals were distinctly lower in character than before, having been joined by the dregs of the Democrats while losing their best white county men. Lindsay made many appointments, thus gradually changing for the better the local administration. Owing to the peculiar methods by which the first set of officials got into office, the local administration was never again as bad, except in some of the black counties, as it was in 1868-1869. As the personnel of the Radical party ran lower and lower, more and more Democrats entered into the local administration. But in spite of the fact that they secured representation in the state government, they were unable to make any important reforms until they gained control of all departments. The results of one or two local elections may be noticed. In Mobile, which had a white majority, the carpet-bag and negro

3 C

government was overthrown in 1870. Though prohibited by law from challenging fraudulent voters, the Democrats intimidated the negroes by standing near the polls and fastening a fish-hook into the coat of each negro who voted. The negroes were frightened. Rumor said that those who were hooked were marked for jail. Repeating was thus prevented; many of them did not vote at all. In Selma the Democrats came into power. Property was then made safe, the streets were cleaned, and the negroes found out that they would not be reënslaved. Governor Lindsay endeavored to reform the local judicial administration by getting rid of worthless young solicitors and incompetent judges, but the Radical Senate defeated his efforts. He was unable to secure any good legislation during his term, and all reform was limited to the reduction of administration expenses, the checking of bad legislation, and the appointment of better men to fill vacancies.[1]

To the Forty-second Congress Buckley, Hays, and Dox were reëlected. The new congressmen were Turner, negro, Handley, Democrat, and Sloss, Independent. Turner had been a slave in North Carolina and Alabama and had secured a fair education before the war. He had at first entered politics as a Democrat, and advised the negroes against alien leaders. To succeed Warner, George Goldthwaite, Democrat, was chosen to the United States Senate.

In 1872 the Democrats nominated for governor, Thomas H. Herndon of Mobile, who was in favor of a more aggressive policy than Lindsay. He was a south Alabama man and hence lost votes in north Alabama. David P. Lewis, the Radical nominee, was from north Alabama and in politics a turncoat. Opposed to secession in 1861, he nevertheless signed the ordinance and was chosen to the Confederate Congress; later he was a Confederate judge; in 1864 he went within the Federal lines; in 1867–1868 he was a Democrat, but changed about 1870. He was victorious for several reasons: the administration was blamed for the division in the party and for not reforming abuses; Herndon did not draw out the full north Alabama vote; the presidential election was held at the same time and

---

[1] Somers, "Southern States," pp. 167, 186; Ku Klux Rept., Ala. Test., 214, 232, 381, 423, 1299, 1371, 1558–1561 (see also the whole of Lindsay's testimony); "Northern Alabama," p. 50; Annual Cyclopædia (1871), p. 11; Miller, "Alabama," pp. 259–261; Beverly, "Alabama," p. 204.

the Democrats were disgusted at the nomination of Horace Greeley; Federal troops were distributed over the state for months before the election, and the Enforcement Acts were so executed as to intimidate many white voters. The full Radical ticket was elected. All were scalawags, except the treasurer. In a speech, C. C. Sheets said of the Radical candidates, "Fellow-citizens, they are as pure, as spotless, as stainless, as the immaculate Son of God." [1]

In both houses of the legislature the Democrats had by the returns a majority at last. The Radicals were in a desperate position. A United States Senator was to be elected, and Spencer wanted to succeed himself. He had spent thousands of dollars to secure the support of the Radicals, and a majority of the Radical members were devoted to him. Most scalawags were opposed to his reëlection, but it was known that he controlled the

ELECTION OF 1872 FOR GOVERNOR.

☐ Democratic Majority.
☐ Radical Majority.
▨ Nearly evenly divided.
○ Black Counties.

Herndon (Dem), 81,371; Lewis, (Rad), 89,878

negro members, and to prevent division all agreed to support him. But how to overcome the Democratic majorities in both houses? Parsons was equal to the occasion. He advised that the Radical members refuse to meet with the Democrats and instead organize separately. So the Democrats met in the capitol and the Radicals in the United States court-house, as had been previously arranged. The Senate consisted of 33 members and the House of 100. The

[1] *Montgomery Advertiser*, Sept. 23, 1872.

Democrats organized with 19 senators and 54 members in the House, all bearing proper certificates of election, and each house having more than a quorum.   At the court-house the Radicals had 14 senators and 45 or 46 representatives who had certificates of election. There were 4 negroes in the Senate and 27 in the House.   In neither Radical house was there a quorum; so each body summoned 5 Radicals who had been candidates, to make up a quorum.   It was hard to find enough, and some custom-house officials from Mobile had to secure leave of absence and come to Montgomery to complete the quorum.

The regular (Democratic) organization at the capitol counted the votes and declared all the Radical state officials elected.   Lewis and McKinstry, lieutenant-governor, accepted the count and took the oath and at once recognized the court-house body as the general assembly.   Lindsay had recognized the regular organization, but had taken no steps to protect it from the Radical schemes.   The militia was ready to support the regular body, but Lewis was more energetic than Lindsay.   He telegraphed to the nearest Federal troops, at Opelika, to come; when they came, he stationed them on the capitol grounds.   He proposed to the Democrats that they admit the entire Radical body, expelling enough Democrats to put the latter in a minority.   Upon their refusal, he told the court-house body to go ahead with legislation.   Some of the Radicals — one or two whites and four or five negroes — were dubious about the security of their *per diem* and showed signs of a desire to go to the capitol.   These were guarded to keep them in line, and were also paid in money and promises of Federal offices.   The weak-kneed negroes were shut up in a room and guarded, to keep them from going to the capitol.

Spencer was determined to be elected and would not wait for the trouble to be settled.   On December 3, 1872, the court-house Radicals chose him to succeed himself.   The next thing was to prevent the regular assembly from electing a Senator who might contest.   Two of that body had died; one or two were indifferent and easily kept away from a joint session; others were called away by telegrams (forged by the Radicals) about illness in their families; three members were arrested before reaching the city; one member was drugged and nearly killed.   By such methods a quorum was defeated in both houses at the capitol until December 10, when the absent members came in, and F. W. Sykes was chosen to the United States Senate.

Meanwhile Lewis and the Radical members had appealed to President Grant to be sustained. By his direction United States Attorney-General Williams prepared a plan of compromise skilfully designed to destroy the Democratic majority in the House and produce a tie in the Senate. Lewis was assured that the plan would be supported by the Federal authorities. The plan was as follows: (1) Both bodies were to continue separate organizations until a fusion was effected. (2) On a certain day, both parties of the House were to meet in the capitol, and in the usual manner form a temporary organization — but the Democrats whose seats were contested but who had certificates of election were to be excluded, while the Radical contestants were to be seated. This would give a Radical majority. Then the contests were to be decided and a permanent organization formed. (3) In the same way the Senate was to be temporarily organized, the regularly elected Democrats being excluded, while their contestants were seated, except in the case of the Democratic senator from Conecuh and Butler, who was to sit but not to vote. By this arrangement there was a bare chance that the Democrats might secure a majority of one in the Senate. (4) As soon as the fusion was thus made, the permanent organization was to be effected. Nothing was said about the legality of past legislation by each body, but the understanding was that all was to be considered void.

Meanwhile Lewis had tried to obtain forcible possession of the capitol, but Strobach, the sheriff whom he sent, was arrested by order of the House and imprisoned until he apologized. The Democrats were plainly informed that the "gentle intimations of the convictions of the law officer of the United States" would be enforced by the use of Federal troops, and there was nothing to do but give way. The plan was put into operation on December 17.

In the House contests the Democrats lost their majority, as was intended. In the Senate they lost all except one by the plan itself. To unseat Senator Martin from Conecuh would be a flagrant outrage. So his case went over until after Christmas. The Democrats elected the clerks, doorkeepers, and pages. The Radicals still kept up their separate organization, not meaning to abide by the fusion unless they could gain the entire legislature. During the vacation Lieutenant-

Governor McKinstry wrote to Attorney-General Williams asking if the Federal government would support him in case he himself should decide as to the rightful senator from Conecuh. He explained that a majority of the committee on elections was going to report in favor of Martin, Democrat, who held the certificate of election. Further, he said that if the Senate were allowed to vote on the question, the Democratic senator would remain seated. He proposed to decide the contest himself upon the report made, and not allow the Senate to vote. Williams was now becoming weary of the conduct of the Radicals; he told McKinstry that the course proposed was contrary to both parliamentary and statute law, and said that Federal troops would not be furnished to support such a ruling. Moreover, he expressed strong disapproval of the course of the Radicals in keeping up their separate organization contrary to the plan of compromise. He ordered the marshal not to allow the Federal court-house to be used by the Radicals, but the marshal paid no attention to the order.

After the holidays the Democrats and anti-Spencer Radicals hoped to bring about a new election for Senator. On February 11, 1873, Hunter of Lowndes, a Radical member of the House, proposed that the legislature proceed to the election of a Senator. Parsons, the speaker, refused to entertain the motion and ordered Hunter under arrest. McKinstry refused to consider the Senate as permanently organized until Martin was disposed of, fearing a joint session. The Radical solicitor of Montgomery secured several indictments against Spencer's agents for bribery, and summoned several members of the legislature as witnesses. Parsons ordered Knox, the solicitor, and Strobach, the sheriff, to be arrested for invading the privileges of the House. Next, Hunter, who had been arrested for proposing to elect a Senator, had Parsons arrested for violation of the Enforcement Acts in preventing the election of a Senator. Busteed, Federal judge, discharged Parsons "for lack of evidence."

In the Senate the Radicals matured a plan to get rid of Martin. A caucus decided to sustain McKinstry in all his rulings. It was known that Edwards, a Democratic senator, wanted to visit his home. So Glass, a Radical senator, proposed to pair with him, and at the same time both get leave of absence for ten days. Edwards and Glass went off at the same time, in different directions. A mile outside of town, Glass left the train, returned to Montgomery, and went into hiding. Now was the time. The reports on the Martin contest were called up. A Democrat moved the adoption of the majority report in favor of Martin; a Radical moved that the minority report be substituted in the motion. The Democrats were voting under protest because they wanted debate and wanted Edwards, one of the writers of the majority report, to return. In order to move a reconsideration, Cobb, a Democrat, fearing treachery, voted with the Radicals; Glass appeared before his name was reached, broke his pair, and voted; McKinstry refused to entertain Cobb's motion for a reconsideration, and though the effect of the voting was only to put the minority report before the Senate to be voted upon, McKinstry declared that Martin by the vote was unseated and Miller admitted. The temporary Radical majority sustained him in all his rulings, and thus the Democrats lost their majority in the Senate. The whole thing had been planned beforehand; McKinstry had arms in his desk; the cloak-rooms were filled with roughs to support the Radicals in case the Democrats made a fight; the Federal troops were at the doors in spite of what Williams had said. McKinstry now announced that the Senate was permanently organized and the schism healed. Glass was expelled by the Masonic order for breaking the pair. Spencer was safe, since the Republican Senate at Washington was sure to admit him.

In the course of the contest Spencer had spent many thousands of dollars in defeating dissatisfied Radical candidates for the legislature and in purchasing voters. The money he used came from the National Republican executive committee, from the state committee, and from the government funds of the post-office at Mobile and the internal revenue offices in Mobile and Montgomery. More than $20,000 of United States funds were used for Spencer, who, after his election, refused to reimburse the postmaster and the two collectors, who were prosecuted and ruined. Every Federal office-holder was assessed from one-fifth to one-third of his pay during the fall months for campaign expenses. They were notified that unless they paid the assessments their resignations would be accepted. Spencer refused to pay the bills of a negro saloon-keeper who had, at his orders, "refreshed" the negro members of the legislature. But of those who voted for Spencer in the Radical "legislature" more than thirty secured Federal appointments. Of other agents about twenty secured Federal appointments. One of them, Robert Barbour, was given a position in the custom-house at Mobile with the understanding that he would not have to go there. His pay was sent to him at Montgomery.

As a preparation for the autumn presidential contest, Spencer worked upon the fears of Grant and secured the promise of troops, though he had some difficulty. His letters are not at all complimentary to Grant. Finally he wrote, "Grant is scared and will do what we want." The deputy marshals manufactured Ku Klux outrages and planned the arrest of Democratic politicians, of whom scores were gotten out of the way, for a week or two, but none were prosecuted. There was no election of Senator other than that of Spencer by the irregular body and that of Sykes by the regular organization at the capitol, neither of which took place on the day appointed by law. The Senate admitted Spencer on the ground that Governor Lewis had recognized the court-house aggregation. Sykes contested and of course failed; the Senate refused for several years to vote his expenses, as was customary. In 1885, Senator Hoar secured $7,132 for Spencer as expenses in the contest. In 1875 the Alabama legislature, Radical and Democratic, united in an address to the United States Senate, asking that Spencer's seat be declared vacant.[1]

Under Lewis the Radical administration went to pieces. The enormous issues of bonds, fraudulent and otherwise, by Smith and Lewis which destroyed the credit of the state; ignorant negroes in public office; drunken judges on the benches; convicts as officials; teachers and school officers unable to read; intermarriage of whites and blacks declared legal by the supreme court; the low character of the Federal officials; constant arrests of respectable whites for political purposes; use of Federal troops; packed juries; purchase and sale of offices; defaulters in every Radical county; riots instigated

---

[1] Report of Joint Committee in regard to election of George E. Spencer; Taft, "Senate Election Cases," pp. 558, 562, 574–578; Annual Cyclopædia (1872), pp. 11, 12; (1873), 16–18; Memorial of General Assembly (Radical) to President, November, 1872; Coburn Report, p. 716; Senate Journal (1872–1873), pp. 15–86 ("Court-House Senate"); Senate Journal, 1871 ("Capitol Senate"), Appendix; McPherson, "Handbook of Politics" (1874), pp. 85, 86; Acts of Ala. (1872–1873), p. 532; Acts of Ala., 1873, p. 156; *Montgomery Advertiser*, Nov. 12 and 24, 1872; Jan. 4, Feb. 22 and 23, 1873; *Southern Argus*, Nov. 22, 1872; Jan. 10, 1873; Herbert, "Solid South," pp. 57–59; Miller, "Alabama," p. 261.

GOVERNOR R. M. PATTON.

GENERAL JAMES H. CLANTON,
Organizer of the present Democratic Party in Alabama.

GOVERNOR GEORGE S. HOUSTON.

GOVERNOR R. B. LINDSAY.

MAJOR J. R. CROWE, now of Sheffield,
Ala., one of the founders of the Ku
Klux Klan at Pulaski, Tenn.

DEMOCRATIC AND CONSERVATIVE LEADERS.

by the Radical leaders; heavy taxes, — all these burdens bore to the ground the Lewis administration before the end of its term. The last year was simply a standstill while the whites were preparing to overthrow the Radical government, which was demoralized and disabled also by constant aid and interference from the Federal administration.

Lewis appointed a lower class of officials than Smith had appointed, among them many ignorant negroes for minor offices. Carpet-baggers and scalawags were becoming scarce. The white counties under their own local government were slowly recovering; the formerly wealthy Black Belt counties were being ruined under the burden of local, state, and municipal taxation.[1]

To the Forty-second Congress Alabama, now entitled to eight representatives, sent four scalawags, Pelham, Hays, White, and Sheets; one negro, Rapier; and three Democrats or Independents, Bromberg, Caldwell, and Glass; carpet-baggers were now at a discount; scalawags and negroes wanted all the spoils.

In the spring of 1874 the whites began to organize to overthrow Radical rule. They were firmly determined that there should not be another Radical administration. In the Radical party only a few whites were left to hold the negroes together. Some of the negroes were disgusted because of promises unfulfilled; others were grasping at office; the Union League discipline was missed; "outrages" were no longer so effective. The Radicals had no new issues to present. The state credit was destroyed; the negroes no longer believed so seriously the stories of reënslavement; the northern public was becoming more indifferent, or more sympathetic toward the whites. The time for the overthrow of Radical rule was at hand.

Sec. 2. Social Conditions during Reconstruction

In previous chapters something has been said of social and economic matters, especially concerning labor, education, religion, and race relations. Some supplementary facts and observations may be of use.

The central figure of Reconstruction was the negro. How was his life affected by the conditions of Reconstruction? In the first

[1] Coburn Report, pp. 230, 262, 267, 271, 274, 280, 525, 528, 529; "Northern Alabama," p. 51; *Tuscaloosa Blade*, Nov. 27, 1873; *Montgomery Advertiser*, Sept. 27, 1872.

place, crime among the blacks increased, as was to be expected. Removed from the restraints and punishments of slavery, with criminal leaders, the negro, even under the most African of governments, became the chief criminal. The crime of rape became common, caused largely, the whites believed, by the social equality theories of the reconstructionists. Personal conflicts among blacks and between blacks and whites were common, though probably decreasing for a time in the early '70's. Stealing was the most frequent crime, with murder a close second. During the last year of negro rule the report of the penitentiary inspectors gave the following statistics: —

CRIMES	WHITES	NEGROES
Murder	11	43
Assault	2	21
Burglary and grand larceny	15	199
Arson	1	4
Rape	0	6
Other felonies	2	14
Total	31	287

Thus 1 white to 16,936 of population was in prison for felony; 1 black to 2294; felonies, 1 white to 8 blacks; misdemeanors, 1 white to 64 blacks. In Montgomery jail were confined about 12 blacks to 1 white. These statistics do not show the real state of affairs, since most convictions of blacks were in cases prosecuted by blacks. To be prosecuted by a white was equivalent to persecution — so reasoned the negro jury in the Black Belt. Under the instigation of low white leaders, the negroes frequently burned the houses and other property of whites who were disliked by the Radical leaders. Several attempts, more or less successful, were made to burn the white villages in the Black Belt; hardly a single one wholly escaped. For several years the whites had to picket the towns in time of political excitement. The worst negro criminals were the discharged negro soldiers, who sometimes settled in gangs together in the Black Belt. More charges were made of crimes by blacks against whites, than by whites against blacks. Most criminals did not go to prison after conviction. The Radical legislature passed a law allowing the sale of the convict's labor to relatives. A good old negro could buy the time of a worthless son for ten cents a day and have him released.

The marriage relations of the negroes were hardly satisfactory, judged by white standards. The white legislatures in 1865-1866 had declared slave marriages binding. The reconstructionists denounced this as a great cruelty and repealed the law. Marriages were then made to date from the passage of the Reconstruction Acts. Many negro men had had several wives before that date. They were relieved from the various penalties of desertion, bigamy, adultery, etc. And after the passage of these laws, numerous prominent negroes were relieved of the penalties for promiscuous marriages. Divorces became common among the negroes who were in politics. During one session of the legislature seventy-five divorces were granted. This was cheaper than going through the courts, and more certain. The average negro divorced himself or herself without formality; some of them were divorced by their churches, as in slavery.

Upon the negro woman fell the burden of supporting the children. Her husband or husbands had other duties. Children then began to be unwelcome and fœticide and child murder were common crimes. The small number of negro children during the decade of Reconstruction was generally remarked. Negro women began to flock to towns; how they lived no one can tell; immorality was general among them. The conditions of Reconstruction were unfavorable to honesty and morality among the negroes, both male and female. The health of the negroes was injured during the period 1865-1875. In the towns the standard of living was low; sanitary arrangements were bad; disease, especially consumption and venereal diseases, killed large numbers and permanently injured the negro constitution.

Negro women took freedom even more seriously than the men. It was considered slavery by many of them to work in the fields; domestic service was beneath the freedwomen — especially were washing and milking the cows tabooed. To live like their former mistresses, to wear fine clothes and go often to church, was the ambition of a negro lady. After Reconstruction was fully established the negro women were a strong support to the Union League, and took a leading part in the prosecution of negro Democrats. Negro women never were as well-mannered, nor, on the whole, as good-tempered and cheerful, as the negro men. Both sexes during Reconstruction lost much of their cheerfulness; the men gradually ceased to go "holloing" to the fields; some of the blacks, especially the women, became impudent and insulting toward the whites. While many of the negroes for a time seemed to consider it a mark of servility to behave decently to the whites, toward the close of Reconstruction and later conditions changed, and the negro men especially were in general well-behaved and well-mannered in their relations with whites except in time of political excitement.

The entire black race was wild for education in 1865 and 1866, but most of them found that the necessary work — which they had not expected — was too hard, and by the close of Reconstruction they were becoming indifferent. The education acquired was of doubtful value. There was in 1865–1867 a religious furor among the negroes, and several negro denominations were organized. The chief result, as stated at length elsewhere, was to separate from the white churches, discard the old conservative black preachers, and take up the smooth-tongued, ranting, emotional, immoral preachers who could stir congregations. The negro church has not yet recovered from the damage done by these ministers. Negro health was affected by the night meetings and religious debauches. In general it may be said that the negro speech grew more like that of the whites, on account of schools, speeches, much travel, and contact with white leaders. The negro leaders acquired much superficial civilization, and very quickly mastered the art of political intrigue.

A very delicate question to both races was that of the exact position of the negro in the social system. The convention of 1867 had contained a number of equal-rights members, and there had been much discussion. A proposition to have separate schools was not made obligatory. A measure to prevent the intermarriage of the races was lost, and the supreme court of the state declared that marriages between whites and blacks were lawful. Laws were passed to prevent the separation of the races on street cars, steamers, and railway cars, but the whites always resisted the enforcement of such laws. Some negroes, especially the mulattoes, dreamed of having white wives, but the average pure negro was not moved by such a desire. When the Coburn investigation was being made, Coburn, the chairman, was trying to convince a negro who had declared against the policy and the necessity of the Civil Rights Bill. The negro retorted by asking how he would like to see him sitting by his (Coburn's) daughter's side. The black declared that he would not like to be sitting by Miss Coburn and have some young man who was courting her come along and knock over the big black negro; further he did not want to eat at the table nor sit in cars with the whites, preferring to sit by his own color. Some of the negroes were displeased at the proposed Civil Rights Bill, thinking that it was meant to force the negro to go among the whites.[1] There were negro police in the larger towns, Selma, Montgomery, and Mobile, who irritated the whites by their arrests and by discrimination in favor of blacks. The negroes, in many cases, had ceased to care for the good opinion of the whites and, following disreputable leaders, suffered morally. The color line began to be strictly drawn in politics, which increased the estrangement of the races, though individuals were getting along better together.[2]

The white carpet-baggers and scalawags never formed a large section of the Radical party and constantly decreased in numbers, — the natives returning to the white party, the aliens returning to the North. The native Radicals were found principally in the cities and holding Federal offices, and in the white counties were still a few genuine Republican Unionist voters. The carpet-baggers were found almost entirely in the Black Belt and in Federal offices. As their numbers decreased the general character was lowered. Some of the white Radicals were sincere and honest men, but none of this sort stood any chance for office. If they themselves would not steal, they must arrange for others to steal. The most respectable of the Radicals were a few old Whigs who had always disliked Democrats and who preferred to vote with the negroes. Such a man was Benjamin Gardner, who became attorney-general in 1872.

All white Radicals suffered the most bitter ostracism — in business, in society, in church; their children in the schools were persecuted by other children because of their fathers' sins. The scalawag, being a renegade, was scorned more than a carpet-bagger. In every possible

[1] See Coburn Report, pp. 154, 161.

[2] *Montgomery Advertiser*, March, 1870; Report of Inspector of Penitentiary, 1873-1874; Ku Klux Rept., Ala. Test., pp. 230, 244, 1220, 1380, 1384; Acts of Ala. (1869-1870), p. 28; Washington, "Up from Slavery," pp. 83-90; *N. Y. World*, Feb. 22 and April 11, 1868; *Tuscaloosa Monitor*, Dec. 18, 1867; Coburn Report, pp. 108, 110, 161, 203, 204, 295; Clowes, "Black America," pp. 131, 140; Herbert, "Solid South," p. 59.

way they were made to feel the weight of the displeasure of the whites. Small boys were unchecked when badgering a white Radical. One Radical complained that the youngsters would come near him to hold a spelling class. The word would be given out: "Spell *damned rascal.*" It would be spelled. "Spell *damned Radical.*" That would be spelled. "They are nearly alike, aren't they?"

The blacks always felt that the carpet-bagger was more friendly to them than the scalawag was, for the carpet-baggers associated more closely with the negroes. The alien white teachers boarded with negroes; some of the politicians made it a practice to live among the negroes in order to get their votes. The candidates for sheriff and tax collector in Montgomery went to negro picnics, baptizings, and church services, drank from the same bottle of whiskey with negroes, had the negro leaders to visit their homes, where they dined together, and the white women furnished music. The carpet-baggers seldom had families with them, and, excluded from white society, began to contract unofficial alliances among the blacks. Scarcely an alien office-holder in the Black Belt but was charged with immorality and the charges proven. Numbers were relieved by the legislature of the penalties for adultery. The average Radical politician was in time quite thoroughly Africanized. They spoke of "us niggers," "we niggers," at first from policy, later from habit. When Lewis was elected, in 1872, a white Radical cried out in his joy, "We niggers have beat 'em." Two years later white Radicals marched with negro processions and sang the song: —

> "The white man's day has passed;
> The negro's day has come at last."[1]

One effect of Reconstruction was to fuse the whites into a single homogeneous party. Before the war political divisions were sharply drawn and feeling often bitter, so also in 1865–1867 and to a certain extent during the early period of Reconstruction. At first there was no "Solid South"; within the white man's party there were grave differences between old Whig and old Democrat, Radical and Conservative. There were different local problems before the whites of

---

[1] Ku Klux Rept., Ala. Test., pp. 71, 233, 390, 391, 881, 1815, 1816; Coburn Report, p. 861; *Huntsville Democrat*, 1872; Straker, "The New South Investigated," pp. 24, 41, 57; *Ala. State Journal*, May 20, 1874; McPherson's Scrap-book, "Campaign of 1869," Vol. I, p. 57.

the various sections that for a while prevented the formation of a unanimous white man's party. There were the whites of the Black Belt, the former slaveholders, who wished well to the negro, favored negro education, and looked upon his political activity as a joke, but who came nearer than any other white people to recognizing the possibility of permanent political privileges for the black. They believed that they could sooner or later regain moral control over their former slaves and thus do away with the evils of carpet-bag government.

It must be said that the former slaveholding class had more consideration, then, before, and since, for the poor negro than for the poor white, probably because the negroes only were always with them. The poorest whites felt that the negro was not only their social but also their economic enemy, and, the protection of the owner removed, the blacks suffered more from these people than ever before. The negro in school, the negro in politics, the negro on the best lands — all this was not liked by the poorest white people, whose opportunities were not as good as those of the blacks. Between these two extremes was the mass of the whites, displeased at the way negro suffrage, education, etc., was imposed, but willing to put up with the results if good. The later years of Reconstruction found the temper of the whites more and more exasperated. They were tired of Reconstruction, new amendments, force bills, Federal troops, and of being ruled as a conquered province by the least fit. Every measure aimed at the South seemed to them to mean that they were considered incorrigible, not worthy of trust, and when necessary to punish some whites, all were punished. And strong opposition to proscriptive measures was called fresh rebellion. "When the Jacobins say and do low and bitter things, their charge of want of loyalty in the South because our people grumble back a little seems to me as unreasonable as the complaint of the little boy: 'Mamma, make Bob 'have hisself. He makes mouths at me every time I hit him with my stick.'" Probably the grind was harder on the young men, who had all life before them and who were growing up with slight opportunities in any line of activity. Sidney Lanier, then an Alabama school-teacher, wrote to Bayard Taylor, "Perhaps you know that with us of the young generation in the South, since the war, pretty much the whole of life has been merely not dying." Negro and alien rule was a constant insult to the intelligence of the country. The taxpayers were non-participants. Some people withdrew entirely from public life, went to their farms or plantations, kept away from towns and from speech-making, waiting for the end to come. I know old men who refused for several years to read the newspapers, so unpleasant was the news. The good feeling produced by the magnanimity of Grant at Appomattox was destroyed by his southern policy when President. There was no gratitude for any so-called leniency of the North, no repentance for the war, no desire for humiliation, for sackcloth and ashes and confession of wrong. The insistence of the Radicals upon a confession of depravity only made things much worse. There was not a single measure of Congress during Reconstruction designed or received in a conciliatory spirit.

Under the Reconstruction régime the political, and to some extent the social, morality of the whites declined. Constant fighting fire with fire scorched all. While in one way the bitter discipline of Reconstruction was not lost, yet with it the pleasantest of southern life went out. During the war and Reconstruction there was a radical change in southern temperament toward the severe. Hospitality has declined; old southern life was never on a strictly business basis, the new southern life is more so; the old individuality is partially lost; class distinctions are less felt. The white people, by the fires of Reconstruction, have been welded into a homogeneous society.[1] The material evils of Reconstruction are by no means the more lasting : the state debt may be paid and wasted resources renewed; but the moral and intellectual results will be the permanent ones.

In spite of the misgovernment during the Reconstruction, there was in most of the white counties a slow movement toward industrial development. All over the state in 1865–1868 and 1871–1874 there were poor crops. The white counties gradually found themselves better able to stand bad seasons. The decadence of the Black Belt gave the white farmer an opportunity. The railroads now began to open up the mineral and timber districts, rather than the cotton counties. During the last four years of negro rule the coal and iron of the northern part of the state began to attract northern capital and rapid development began. The timber of the white counties now began

---

[1] *International Monthly*, Vol. V, p. 220; Coburn Report, p. 527; "The Land We Love," Vol. I, p. 446; Ku Klux Rept., Ala. Test., pp. 390, 391, 405, 411, 926; Riley, "Baptists of Alabama," pp. 321, 322, 329; Clowes, "Black America," pp. 53, 131, 140, 144; Murphy, "The Present South."

to be cut. In the mines, on the railroads, and in the forests many whites were profitably employed. Farmers in the white counties, having thrown off the local Reconstruction government, began to organize agricultural societies, Patrons of Husbandry, Grangers, etc., and to hold county fairs. The Radicals maintained that this granger movement was only another manifestation of Ku Klux, and it was, in a way.[1]

Immigration from the North or from abroad amounted to nothing; disturbed political conditions and the presence of the negroes prevented it. Nor did the Reconstruction rulers desire immigration; their rule would be the sooner overthrown. There were two movements of emigration from the state — culminating in 1869 and in 1873–1874. Those were the gloomiest periods of Reconstruction, especially for the white man in the Black Belt. Most of the emigrants went to Texas, others to Mexico, to Brazil, to the North, and to Tennessee and Georgia, where the whites were in power. It was estimated that in this emigration the state lost more of its population than by war.

In the Black Belt the condition of the whites grew worse. Frequent elections demoralized negro labor, and crops often failed for lack of laborers. The more skilful negroes went to the towns, railroads, mines, and lumber mills. On account of this migration and the gradual dying off of slavery-trained negroes, negro agricultural labor was less and less satisfactory. The negro woman often refused to work in the fields. The white population of the Black Belt decreased in comparison with the numbers of blacks. The whites deserted the plantations, going to the towns or gathering in villages. Taxation was heavy, tax sales became frequent. One of the worst evils that afflicted the Black Belt was the so-called "deadfall." A "deadfall" was a low shop or store where a white thief encouraged black people to steal all kinds of farm produce and exchange it with him for bad whiskey, bad candy, brass jewellery, etc. This evil was found all over the state where there were negroes. Whites and industrious blacks lost hogs, poultry, cattle, corn in the fields, cotton in the fields and in the gin. The business of the "deadfall" was usually done at night. The thirsty negro would go into a cotton field and pick a sack of cotton worth a dollar, or take a bushel of corn from

[1] See also Ch. XXII.

3 D

the nearest field, and exchange it at a "deadfall" for a glass of whiskey, a plug of tobacco, or a dime. These "deadfalls" were in the woods or swamps on the edges of the large plantations. It was not possible to guard against them. The "deadfall" keepers often became rich, the harvests of some amounting to 30 to 80 bales of cotton for each, besides farm produce. Careful estimates by grand juries and business men placed the average annual loss at one-fifth of the crop. A bill was introduced into the legislature to prohibit the purchase after dark of farm produce from any one but the producer. The measure was unanimously opposed by the Radicals, on the ground that it was class legislation aimed at the negroes. The debates show that some of them considered it proper for a negro to steal from his employer. After the Democratic victory in 1874 a law was passed abolishing "deadfalls." [1]

[1] Charge of Judge H. D. Clayton to Barbour County grand jury in Coburn Report, p. 839; Report of Montgomery grand jury in *Advertiser*, Oct. 20, 1871; *Tuskegee News*, March 16, 1876; Little, "History of Butler County," p. 111; *Tuscaloosa Blade*, Nov. 19, 1874; Coburn Report, pp. 524, 1219; *Montgomery Advertiser*, Nov. 27, 1873; Ku Klux Rept., Ala. Test., pp. 230, 1175, 1179; *Scribner's Monthly*, Sept., 1874; Herbert, "Solid South," pp. 63, 67.

CHAPTER XXIV

THE OVERTHROW OF RECONSTRUCTION

The Republican Party in 1874

THE Republican party of Alabama went into the campaign of 1874 weakened by dissensions within its own ranks and by the lessening of the sympathy of the northern Radicals. During the previous six years the opposition to the radical Reconstruction policy had gradually gained strength. The industrial expansion that followed the war, the dissatisfaction with the administration of Grant, the disclosure of serious corruption on the part of public officials, and the revelations of the real conditions in the South — these had resulted in the formation of a party of opposition to the administration, which called itself the "Liberal Republican" party and which advocated home rule for the southern states. The Democratic party, somewhat discredited by its course during the war, had now regained the confidence of its former members by accepting as final the decisions of the war on the questions involved and by bringing out conservative candidates on practical platforms. By 1874 nine northern states had gone Democratic in the elections; from 1869 to 1872, five southern states returned to the Democratic columns. The lower house of Congress was soon to be safely Democratic and no more radical legislation was to be expected; the executive department of the government alone was in active sympathy with the Reconstruction régime in the southern states.

The divisions within the party in the state were due to various causes. In the first place, the action of the more respectable of the whites in deserting the party left it with too few able men to hold the organization well together. By 1874 all but about 4000 whites had forsaken the Republicans and returned to the Democrats. These whites were mainly in north Alabama, though there were some few in the Black Belt, — five, for instance, in Marengo County, and fifty in Dallas. A further source of weakness was the disposition of the black politician to demand more consideration than had hitherto been accorded to him. The blacks had received much political training of a certain kind since 1867, and the negro leaders were no longer the helpless dupes of the carpet-bagger and the scalawag. A meeting of the negro politicians, called the "Equal Rights Union," was held in Montgomery in January, 1874. The resolutions adopted demanded that the blacks have first choice of the nominations in black counties and a proportional share in all other counties. They expressed themselves as opposed to the efforts of the carpet-baggers to organize new secret political societies, "having found no good to result from such since the disbursement [sic] of the Union League." [1] If the negroes should be able to obtain these demands, nothing would be left for the white members of the party. The rank and file of the blacks had lost much of their faith in their white leaders and were disposed to listen to candidates of their own color. Closely connected with the negroes' demands for office were their demands for social rights. The state supreme court had decided that whites and blacks might lawfully intermarry, and there had been several instances of such marriages between low persons of each race. [2] Noisy negro speakers were demanding the passage of the Civil Rights Bill then pending in Congress. A Mobile negro declared that he wanted to drink in white men's saloons, ride in cars with whites, and go to the same balls. The white Radicals in convention and legislature were disposed to avoid the subject when the blacks brought up the question of "mixed accommodations." The negroes constantly reminded the white Radicals that the latter were very willing to associate with them in the legislature and in political meetings. The speeches of Boutwell of Massachusetts and Morton of Indiana in favor of mixed schools were quoted by the negro speakers, who now became impatient of the constant request of their leaders not to offend north Alabama and drive out of the party the whites of that region. Lewis, a negro member of the legislature, declared that they were weary of waiting for their rights; that the state would not grant them, but the United States would; and then they would take their proper places alongside the whites, and "we intend to do it in defiance of the immaculate

[1] *Ala. State Journal*, Jan. 14, 1874.

[2] *State Journal*, March 10, 1874. The justice who performed the ceremony in one case gave as his excuse that the woman was so bad that nothing she could do would make her worse.

white people of north Alabama. . . . Hereafter we intend to demand [our rights] and we are going to press them on every occasion, and preserve them inviolate if we can. The day is not far distant when you will find on the bench of the supreme court of the state a man as black as I am, and north Alabama may help herself if she can." [1] An "Equal Rights Convention," from which white Radicals were excluded, met in Montgomery in June, 1874. The various speakers demanded that colored youths be admitted to the State University, to the Agricultural and Mechanical College, and to all other schools on an equal footing with the whites, "in order that the idea of the inferiority of the negro might be broken up." Several delegates expressed themselves as in favor of mixed schools, but advised delay in order not to drive out the white members of the party. A negro preacher from Jackson County said that he wanted to hold on to the north Alabama whites "until their stomachs grew strong enough to take Civil Rights straight." [2] In 1867 and 1868 there had been some blacks who had opposed the agitation of social matters on the ground that their civil and political rights would be endangered, but these were no longer in politics. The result of the agitation in 1874 was to irritate the whites generally and to cause the defection of north Alabama Republicans.

Another cause of weakness in the Radical party was the quarrel among the Reconstruction newspapers of the state over the distribution of the money for printing the session laws of Congress. The *State Journal* and the *Mountain Home* lost the printing, which, by direction of the Alabama delegation in Congress, was given to the *Huntsville Advocate* and the *National Republican*, "to aid needy newspapers in other localities for the benefit of the Republican party." The result was discord among the editors and a lukewarm support of the party from those dissatisfied. [3]

In 1874 in each county where there was a strong Republican vote discord arose among those who wanted office. Every white Radical wanted a nomination and the negroes also wanted a share. The results were temporary splits everywhere in the county organiza-

---

[1] *Montgomery Advertiser* and other Montgomery papers of March 5, 1873.

[2] Coburn Report on Affairs in Alabama, 1874, pp. xiv, 341, 519, 520, 521, 743; *Montgomery Advertiser*, Oct. 23, 1902.

[3] See *State Journal*, Jan. 10 and Feb. 1, 1874.

tions, which were usually mended before the elections, but which seriously weakened the party. The Strobach-Robinson division in Montgomery County may be taken as typical. Strobach was the carpet-bag sheriff of Montgomery County, which was overwhelmingly black. There was reason to believe that Strobach was being purchased by the Democrats.[1] The stalwarts accused him of conspiring with the Democrats to sell the administration to them. They charged that he would not allow the negroes to use the court-house for political meetings, that entirely too many Republicans were indicted at his instance, and that he summoned as jurors too many Democrats and "Strobach traitors" and too few Republicans. As leader of the regular organization Strobach had considerable influence in spite of these charges, and his enemies undertook to form a new organization. The leaders of the bolters, known as the Robinson faction, were Busteed, Buckley, Barbour, and Robinson. They made the fairest promises and secured the support of the majority of the negroes, though Strobach still controlled many. Between the two factions there was practically civil war during 1874. The bolters organized their negroes in the "National Guards," a semi-military society — 5000 or 6000 strong. This body broke up the Strobach meetings, and serious disturbances occurred at Wilson's Station, Elam Church, and at Union Springs. At the latter place the bolters attempted to take forcible possession of the congressional nominating convention. The negroes, led by a few whites, invaded the town, firing guns and pistols and making threats until it seemed as if a three-cornered fight would result between the whites and the two factions of the blacks. Rapier, the negro congressman, made peace by agreeing to support the Robinson-Buckley faction provided they kept the peace and allowed him to receive the nomination for Congress from the other faction. They forced him to sign an agreement to that effect, which he repudiated a few days later. The bolters were not admitted to the state convention in 1874, and thus weakness resulted. During the summer and fall of 1874, ten or twelve negroes were killed and numbers injured in the fights between the factions.[2]

---

[1] A few years ago Strobach offered to tell me all about his political career in exchange for $50, but died before he could begin the account.

[2] Coburn Report, pp. 225, 230, 272, 280–282; *State Journal*, May 20 and 27, 1874; *Montgomery Advertiser*, Oct. 23, 1902.

The Democrats naturally did all that was possible to encourage such division in the ranks of the enemy. Bolting candidates and independent candidates, especially negroes, were secretly supported by advice and funds. Carpet-bag and scalawag leaders were purchased, and agreed to use their influence to divide their party. To some of them it was clear that the whites would soon be in control, and meanwhile they were willing to profit by selling out their party.[1] For two or three years it had been a practice in the Black Belt for the Radical office-holders to farm out their offices to the Democrats, who appointed deputies to conduct such offices. The stalwarts now endeavored to cast these men out of the party, but only succeeded in weakening it.

The Negroes in 1874

In spite of all adverse influence, however, the great majority of the negroes remained faithful to the Republican party and voted for Governor Lewis in the fall elections. They missed the rigid organization of former years, and many of them were greatly dissatisfied because of unfulfilled promises made by their leaders; but the Radical office-holders, realizing clearly the desperate situation, made strong efforts to bring out the entire negro vote. The Union League methods were again used to drive negro men into line. They were again promised that if their party succeeded in the elections, there would be a division of property. Some believed that equal rights in cars, hotels, theatres, and churches would be obtained. Clothes, bacon and flour, free homes, mixed schools, and public office were offered as inducements to voters. In Opelika, A. B. Griffin told the negroes that after the election all things would be divided and that each Lee County negro would receive a house in Opelika. To one man he promised "forty acres and an old gray horse." Heyman, a Radical leader of Opelika, told the blacks that if the elections resulted properly, the land would be taxed so heavily that the owners would be obliged to leave the state, and then the negroes and northerners would get the land.[2]

---

[1] See Coburn Report, pp. 225, 282–288.

[2] Coburn Report, pp. 118, 135, 145, 151, 279. When the Coburn Committee was in Opelika, Washington Jones, colored, appeared before it and demanded that the promises made to him be fulfilled. He wanted the mule, the land, " overflow " bacon, etc. The committee got rid of him in a hurry. See Coburn Report, p. 135.

Promises of good not being sufficient to hold the blacks in line, threats of evil were added.   Circulars were sent out, purporting to be signed by General Grant, threatening the blacks with reënslavement unless they voted for him.   The United States deputy marshals informed the blacks of Marengo County that if they voted for W. B. Jones, a scalawag candidate who had been purchased by the whites, they would be reënslaved.   Heyman of Opelika declared that defeat would result in the negroes' having their ears cut off, in whipping posts and slavery.   Pelham, a white congressman, told the blacks that if the Democrats carried the elections, Jefferson Davis would come to Montgomery and reorganize the Confederate government. So industriously were such tales told that many of the negroes became genuinely alarmed, and it was asserted that negro women began to hide their children as the election approached.[1]

The negro women and the negro preachers were more enthusiastic than the negro men, and through clubs and churches brought considerable pressure to bear on the doubtful and indifferent.   They agreed that negro children should not go to schools where the teachers were Democrats.   In Opelika a negro women's club was formed of those whose husbands were Democrats or were about to be.   The initiate swore to leave her husband if he voted for a Democrat.   This club was formed by a white Radical, John O. D. Smith, and the negroes were made to believe that General Grant ordered it.   A similar organization in Chambers County had a printed constitution by which a member, if married, was made to promise to desert her husband should he vote for a Democrat, and a single woman promised not to marry a Democratic negro or to have anything to do with one. The negro women were used as agents to distribute tickets to voters. These tickets had Spencer's picture on them, which they believed was Grant's.[2]

In the negro churches to be a Democrat was to become liable to discipline.   Some preachers preferred regular charges against those members who were suspected of Democracy.   The average negro still believed that it was a crime "to vote against their race" and offenders were sure of expulsion from church unless, as happened

---

[1] Coburn Report, pp. 59, 63, 106, 118, 122, 142, 181, 641 ; *State Journal*, June 10, 1874.

[2] Coburn Report, pp. 58, 59, 92, 106, 136, 275, 295, 296, 416, 641.

sometimes, the bolters were strong enough to turn the Republicans out. Nearly every church had its political club to which the men belonged and sometimes the women. Robert Bennett of Lee County related his experience to the Coburn Committee. He wanted to vote the Democratic ticket, he said, and for that offence was put on trial in his church. The "ministers and exhorters" told him that he must not do so, saying, "We had rather you wouldn't vote at all; if you won't go with us to vote with us, you are against us; the Bible says so. . . . We can have you arrested. We have got you; if you won't say you won't vote or will vote with us, we will have you arrested. . . . All who won't vote with us we will kick out of the society — and turn them out of church;" and so it happened to Robert Bennett.[1]

The efforts made to hold the negroes under control indicate that numbers of them were becoming restless and desirous of change. This was especially the case with the former house-servant class and those who owned property. One negro, in accounting for his change of politics, said, "Honestly, I love my race, but the way the colored people have taken a stand against the white people . . . will not do." Of the white Radicals he said, "They know that we are a parcel of poor ignorant people, and I think it is a bad thing for them to take advantage of a poor ignorant person, and I do not think they are honest men; they cannot be." He said that the Radicals promised much and gave little; that they never helped him. The Democrats gave him credit and paid his doctor's bills; so that it was to his interest to vote for the Democrats — "I done it because it was to my interest. I wanted a change." Another negro explained his change of politics by saying that bad government kept up the price of pork, and allowed sorry negroes to steal what industrious negroes made and saved — eggs, chickens, and cotton. When Adam Kirk, of Chambers County, was asked why be belonged to the "white man's party," he answered: "I was raised in the house of old man Billy Kirk. He raised me as a body servant. The class that he belongs to feels nearer to me than the northern white man, and actually, since the war, everything that I have got is by their aid and assistance. They have helped me raise up my family and have stood by me, and whenever I want a doctor, no matter what hour of the day or

[1] Coburn Report, pp. 58, 59, 106, 203, 204.

night, he is called in whether I have got a cent or not. I think they have got better principles and better character than the Republicans." [1] There is no doubt that these represented the sentiments of several thousand negroes who had mustered up courage to remain away from the polls or perhaps to vote for the Democrats. And while in white counties the campaign was made on the race issue, in the Black Belt the whites, as Strobach said, "were more than kind" to negro bolters. They encouraged and paid the expenses of negro Democratic speakers, and gave barbecues to the blacks who would promise to vote for the "white man's party." Numerous Democratic clubs were formed for the negroes and financed by the whites. Of these there were several in each black county, but none in the white counties. Though safer than ever before since enfranchisement, negro Democrats still received rather harsh treatment from those of their color who sincerely believed that a negro Democrat was a traitor and an enemy to his race. Negro Democratic speakers were insulted, stoned, and sometimes killed. At night they had to hide out. Their political meetings were broken up; their houses were shot into; their families were ostracized in negro society, churches, and schools. One negro complained that his children were beaten by other children at school, and that the teacher explained to him that nothing better could be expected as long as he, the father, remained a Democrat. Some negro Democrats were driven away from home and others were whipped. Most of them found it necessary to keep quiet about politics; and the members of Democratic clubs were usually sworn to secrecy. [2] The colored Methodist Episcopal Church, which was under the guardianship of the white Methodist Church, suffered from negro persecution; several of its buildings were burned and its ministers insulted.

The Democratic and Conservative Party in 1874

If the Republican party was weaker in this campaign than ever before, the Democrats, on the other hand, were more united and more firmly determined to carry the elections, peaceably if possible, by force if necessary. There are evidences that the state government

---

[1] Coburn Report, pp. 59, 63, 109, 118, 119. See also Ku Klux Rept., Ala. Test., pp. 1072–1075.

[2] Coburn Report, pp. 58, 59, 61, 118, 278, 280, 308, 317, 320, 446.

in Alabama would have been overthrown early in 1874 if the Louisiana revolution of that year had not been crushed by the Federal government. The different sections of the state were now more closely united than ever before, owing to the completion of two of the railroads which had cost the state treasury so much. The people of the northern white counties now came down into central Alabama and learned what negro government really was, and it was now made clear to the Unionist Republican element of the mountain counties that while they had local white government they were supporting a state government by the negro and the alien, both of whom they disliked. In order to gain the support of north Alabama, the opposition of the whites in the Black Belt to a campaign on the race issue was disregarded, and the campaign, especially in the white counties, was made on the simple issue — Shall black or white rule the state?

It may be of interest here to examine the attitude of the whites toward the blacks since the war. In 1865, the whites would grant civil rights to the negro, but would have special legislation for the race on the theory that it needed a period of guardianship; by 1866, many far-sighted men were willing to think of political rights for the negro after the proper preparation; by 1867, there was serious thought of an immediate qualified suffrage for the black, the object being to increase the representation in Congress, to disarm the Radicals, — the native whites believing that they could control the negro vote. This shifting of position was checked by the grant of suffrage to the negroes by Congress, and during the campaigns of 1867 and 1868 the whites held aloof, meaning to try to influence the negro vote later, when the opportunity offered. From 1869 to 1872 there was an increasing tendency, especially in the Black Belt, to appeal to the negro for political support, but, though the former personal relations were to some extent resumed, the effort always ended in practical failure. The result was that by 1873–1874, the whites despaired of dividing the black vote and many of the Black Belt whites were willing to join those of the white counties in drawing the color line in politics.[1]

The Democrats were aided in presenting the race issue to north Alabama by the attitude, above referred to, of the negroes in de-

[1] The *State Journal* of Aug. 1, 1874, has a list of extracts from Democratic papers from 1868 to 1874, showing the change of attitude in regard to the negro.

manding office and social privileges and by the fact that a strong effort had been made in Congress and would again be made to enact a stringent civil rights law securing equal rights to negroes in cars, theatres, hotels, schools, etc. The Alabama members of Congress, who were Republicans, had voted for such a bill. The Democrats made the most of the issue. The speeches of Boutwell, Morton, and Sumner were circulated among the whites as campaign documents, and were most effective in securing the unionists and independents of north Alabama.[1]

The following extracts from state papers will indicate the state of mind of the whites. The *Montgomery Advertiser* of February 19, 1874, declared that "the great struggle in the South is the race struggle of white against black for political supremacy. It is all in vain to protest that the southern wing of the Radical party is not essentially a party of black men arrayed against their white neighbors in a close and bitter struggle for power. The struggle going on around us is not a mere contest for the triumph of this or that platform of party principles. It is a contest between antagonistic races and for that which is held dearer than life by the white race. If the negro must rule Alabama permanently, whether in person or by proxy, the white man must ultimately leave the state." "Old Whig" protested in the *Opelika Daily Times* of June 6, 1874, against the rule of the mob of 80,000 yelling negroes who, at scalawag mandate, and in the name of liberty, deposited ballots against southern white men. Another writer declared that "all of the good men of Alabama are for the white man's party. Outcasts, libellers, liars, handcuffers, and traitors to blood are for the negro party." Pinned down by bayonets and bound by tyranny, the whites had been forced to silence and expedients and humiliation until wrath burned "like a seven-fold furnace in the bosom of the people." The negro must be expelled from the government. The white was a God-made prince; the black, a God-made subordinate. "What right hath Dahomey to give laws to Runnymede, or Bosworth Field to take a lesson from Congo-Ashan? Shall Bill Turner give laws to Watts, Elmore, Barnes, Morgan, and the many mighty men of the South?" "When

---

[1] *Tuskegee News*, June 4, and Aug. 20, and Sept. 10, 1874; Coburn Report, pp. 120, 860, 861, 1231, 1232, *et passim*; *Eufaula Times*, July 30, 1874, quoting from the *Birmingham News*, *Shelby Guide*, and *Eutaw Whig*; *State Journal*, June 24, 1874.

Alabama goes down the white men of Alabama will go with her." [1]

The whites who still remained with the negro party were subjected to more merciless ostracism than ever before. No one would have business relations with a Republican; no one believed in his honor or honesty; his children were taunted by their schoolmates; his family were socially ostracized; no one would sit by them at church or in public gatherings. [2] In the white counties numerous conventions adopted a series of resolutions in regard to ostracism, known as the "Pike County Platform," which first was adopted in June, 1874, by the Democratic convention in Pike County. It read in part as follows: "Resolved that nothing is left to the white man's party but social ostracism of all those who act, sympathize, or side with the negro party, or who support or advocate the odious, unjust, and unreasonable measure known as the Civil Rights Bill; and that henceforth we will hold all such persons as the enemies of our race, and will not for the future have intercourse with them in any of the social relations of life." [3]

With the changed conditions in 1874 appeared a considerable number of "independent" candidates and voters. These were (1) those whites who had wearied of radicalism, and, foreseeing defeat, had left their party, yet were unwilling to join the Democrats; (2) certain half-hearted Democrats who did not want to see the old Democratic leaders come back to power; (3) disappointed politicians, especially old Whigs of strong prejudices, who disliked the Democrats from ante-bellum days. These people, foreseeing the defeat of the Radicals, hastened to offer themselves as independent candidates and voters. They hoped to get the votes of the bulk of the Radicals and many Democrats and thus get into power. The Radicals, otherwise certain of defeat, showed some disposition to meet those people halfway, and a partial success was possible if the Demo-

---

[1] *Opelika Times*, Aug. 22, 1874, condensed; Coburn Report, pp. 97, 100, 104.

[2] See testimony of Dunbar and Gardner in Coburn Report, pp. 101, 209, 210, 300, 302; *Opelika Daily Times*, Sept. 30, 1874.

[3] *State Journal*, June 16, 1874. For a typical readoption of this platform see the resolutions of the Tuscaloosa County Democrats in *State Journal*, June 24, 1874. "Old Whig" in the *Opelika Daily Times*, Sept. 30, 1874, proposed that the whites "fall back upon the old Wesleyan doctrine 'to prefer one another in business';" "Give the Radicals no support;" "The adder that stings should find no warmth in the bosom of the dying victim."

crats could not whip the "independents" into line. This was successfully done. The following dissertation on "independents" is offered as typical: The independent is the Brutus of the South, "the protégé of radicalism, the spawn of corruption or poverty, or passion, or ignorance, come forth as leaders of ignorant or deluded blacks, to attack and plunder for avarice. There may be no God to avenge the South, but there is a devil to punish independents." The independents are only the tools of the Radicals, they are like bloodhounds, — to be used and then killed, for no sooner than their work is done the Radicals will knife them. "Satan hath been in the Democratic camp and, taking these independents from guard duty, led them up into the mountains and shown them the kingdoms of Radicalism, his silver and gold, storehouses and bacon, and all these promised to give if they would fall down and worship him; and they worshipped him, throwing down the altars of their fathers and trampling them under their feet." [1]

The Campaign of 1874

The Democrats nominated for governor George S. Houston of north Alabama, a "Union" man whose "unionism" had not been very strong, and the Republicans renominated Governor D. P. Lewis, also of north Alabama. The Democratic convention met in July, 1874, and put forth a declaration and a platform declaring that the Radicals had for years inflamed the passions and prejudices of the races until it was now necessary for the whites to unite in self-defence. The convention denied the power of Congress to legislate for the social equality of the races and denounced the Civil Rights Bill then pending in Congress as an attempt to force social union. Legislation on social matters was condemned as unnecessary and criminal. The Radical state administration was blamed for extravagance and corruption, and a declaration was made that fraudulent state debts would not be paid if the Democrats were successful. [2]

The fact that the race issue was the principal one is borne out by the county platforms. In Barbour County the "white man's

---

[1] *Opelika Times*, Oct. 14, 1874; Coburn Report, pp. 97, 103-104.

[2] Coburn Report, p. 856; Annual Cyclopædia (1874), p. 15.

party" declared that the issue was "white *vs.* black"; that if the whites were defeated, the county would no longer be endurable and would be abandoned to the blacks; that a conflict of races would be deplorable, but that the whites must protect themselves, and that though in the past some had stayed away from the polls through disgust, those who did not vote would be reckoned as of the negro party; that the whites would be ready to protect themselves and their ballots by force if necessary. In Lee County the convention declared that the Democrats had long avoided the race issue, but that now it had been forced upon them by the Radicals; that "this county is the white man's and the white man must rule over it," and that whites or blacks who aid the negro party "are the political and social enemies of the white race." In the same county a local club declared that peace was wanted, but not peace purchased by "unconditional surrender of every freeman's privilege to fraud, Federal bayonets, and intimidation." [1]

The Republican state convention in August pronounced itself in favor of the Civil Rights Bill and the civil and political equality of all men without regard to race, declared that the race issue was an invention of the Democrats which would result in war with the United States, and accused the Democrats of being responsible for the bad condition of the state finances. The Equal Rights convention and the Union Labor convention declared for the Civil Rights Bill and indorsed Charles Sumner and J. T. Rapier, the negro congressman. [2]

In preparation for the fall elections the Radical members of Congress had secured the passage of a resolution by Congress appropriating money for the relief of the sufferers from floods on the Alabama, Warrior, and Tombigbee rivers. The floods occurred in the early spring; the appropriation became available in May, but as late as July the governor had not appointed agents to distribute the bacon which had been purchased with the appropriation. The members of Congress from the state met and agreed upon a division of the bacon without reference to flooded districts, but with reference

---

[1] Coburn Report, pp. 99, 101, 856, 859; *Opelika Daily Times,* June 29 and Oct. 3, 1874; *Montgomery Advertiser,* Oct. 23, 1902.

[2] *State Journal,* June 4 and 27, 1874; Coburn Report, p. 881; Annual Cyclopædia (1874), pp. 15, 16; *Tuskegee News,* July 2, 1874.

to the political conditions in the various counties.[1] Their agents were to distribute the bacon, but the governor was unable to get their names until August. The purpose was to hold the bacon until near the election. The governor and other Republican leaders were opposed to the use of bacon in the campaign, and the state refused to pay transportation; so the agents had to sell part of the bacon to pay expenses. In Lewis's last message to the legislature, he said pointedly, "Our beloved state has been free from pestilence, floods, and extensive disasters to labor."[2] As a matter of fact, there had been the regular spring freshets, but there were no sufferers. The loss fell upon the planters, who were under contract to furnish food, stock, and implements to their tenants. In August, Captain Gentry of the Nineteenth Infantry was sent by the War Department, which was supplying the bacon, to investigate the matter of the "political" bacon. He found no suffering, and no one was able to tell him where the suffering was, though the members of Congress were positive that there was suffering. The crops were doing well. In Montgomery Captain Gentry found that the agents in charge of Congressman Rapier's share of the bacon were J. C. Hendrix and Holland Thompson (colored), both active politicians. Distribution had been delayed because Rapier thought that he had not received his share. Congressman Hays had bacon sent to Calera, Brierfield, and Marion, none of the places being near flowing water. He sent quantities to Perry, Shelby, and Bibb counties, but none to Fayette and Baker (Chilton). As he wrote to his agent, "Of course the overflowed districts will need more than those not overflowed." When the War Department discovered the use that had been made of the bacon, Captain Gentry was directed to seize the bacon in dry districts that

[1] The division was as follows : —

DISTRICT	DISTRIBUTING POINTS	POUNDS
First	Mobile, Selma, Camden	55,851
Second	Montgomery	44,402
Third	Opelika, Talladega, Seale	41,802
Fourth	Demopolis	53,663
Fifth and sixth	Decatur	31,278

[2] Senate Journal, 1874–1875, p. 7.

was being held until the election. At Eufaula, 80 miles from the nearest flooded district, he seized 5348 pounds that Rapier had stored there; at Seale, 7638 pounds were seized; and at Opelika, 9792 pounds; but not all was discovered at either place.[1]

An Opelika negro thus described the method of using the bacon: It was understood that only the faithful could get any of it. This negro was considered doubtful, but was told, "If you will come along and do right, you will get two or three shoulders." Bacon suppers were held at negro churches, to which only those were admitted who promised to vote the Republican ticket.[2]

The use of bacon in the campaign injured the Republican cause more than it aided it; the supply of bacon was too small to go around, and the whites were infuriated because the negroes stopped work so long while trying to get some of it.

In previous campaigns the Republicans had used with success the "southern outrage" issue; stories of murder, cruelty, and fraud by the whites were carried to Washington and found ready believers, and Federal troops and deputy marshals were sent to assist the southern Republicans in the elections by making arrests, thus intimidating the whites and encouraging the blacks. In the campaign of 1874 such assistance was more than ever necessary to the black man's party in Alabama. The race line was now distinctly drawn and most

[1] For full account of the bacon question see Ho. Doc., No. 110, 43d Cong., 2d Sess.; also *Tuskegee News*, June 4, Aug. 27, and Sept. 24, 1874 ; Coburn Report, pp. 36, 50, 69, 207, 241.

The following list shows how one distribution was made in October, just before the elections : —

COUNTY	POUNDS	COUNTY	POUNDS
Montgomery	14,151	Randolph	2,000
Lowndes	8,283	Coosa	3,000
Butler	4,235	Elmore	3,500
Dale (to P. King, Haw Ridge)	2,482	Talladega	7,500
Barbour	4,527	Lee (to W. H. Betts) . .	9,792
Bullock	5,169	Russell (to W. H. Betts) .	2,390
Pike (to Gardner and Wiley)	2,066	Walker	2,178
Henry	1,036	"To G. P. Plowman, by order	
Clay	3,000	of Charles Pelham, M. C." .	1,000

[2] Coburn Report, pp. 59, 60.

3 E

of the whites had forsaken the black man's party. The blacks, many of them, were indifferent; the whites were determined to overthrow the Reconstruction rule.

The leaders of the whites were confident of success and strongly advised against every appearance of violence, since it would work to the advantage of the hostile party. There were some, however, who did not object to the tales of outrage, since they would cause investigation and the sending of Federal troops. These would, in the black districts, really protect the whites, and any kind of an investigation would result in damage to the Radical party.

Pursuing its plan of a peaceable campaign, the Democratic executive committee, on August 29, 1874, issued an address as follows: "We especially urge upon you carefully to avoid all injuries to others while you are attempting to preserve your own rights. Let our people avoid all just causes of complaint. Turmoil and strife with those who oppose us in this contest will only weaken the moral force of our efforts. Let us avoid personal conflicts; and if these should be forced upon us, let us only act in that line of just self-defence which is recognized and provided for by the laws of the land. We could not please our enemies better than by becoming parties to conflicts of violence, and thus furnish them plausible pretext for asking the interference of Federal power in our domestic affairs. Let us so act that all shall see and that all whose opinions are entitled to any respect shall admit that ours is a party of peace, and that we only seek to preserve our rights and liberties by the peaceful but efficient power of the ballot-box." [1] There is no doubt but that the whites engaged in less violence in this campaign than in former election years and less than was to be expected considering their temper in 1874. But there is also no doubt that very little incentive would have been necessary to have precipitated serious conflict. The whites were determined to win, peaceably if possible, forcibly if necessary. This very determination made them inclined to peace as long as possible and made the opposite party cautious about giving causes for conflict.

The Republican leaders industriously circulated in the North stories of "outrages" in Alabama. The most comprehensive "outrage" story was that of Charles Hays, member of Congress, published

[1] Annual Cyclopædia (1874), p. 13; Coburn Report, pp. 247–254.

in the famous "Hays-Hawley letter" of September 7, 1874. Hays had borne a bad character in Alabama while a slaveholder and had been ostracized for being cruel to his slaves, and as a Confederate soldier he had a doubtful record. Naturally, in Reconstruction he had sided against the whites, and the negroes, with few exceptions, forgot his past history. In order to get campaign material, Senator Joseph Hawley of Connecticut wrote to Hays to get facts for publication, — "I want to publish it at home and give it to my neighbors and constituents as the account of a gentleman of unimpeachable honor." Hays responded in a long letter, filled with minute details of horrible outrages that occurred within his personal observation. The spirit of rebellion still exists, he said; riots, murders, assassinations, torturings, are more common than ever; the half cannot be told; unless the Federal government interposes there is no hope for loyal men. The letter created a sensation. Senator Hawley sent it out with his indorsement of Hays as a gentleman. The *New York Tribune*, then "Liberal" in politics, sent "a thoroughly competent and trustworthy correspondent who is a lifelong Republican" to investigate the charges made by Hays. The charges of Hays were as follows: (1) for political reasons, one Allen was beaten nearly to death with pistols; (2) five negroes were brutally murdered in Sumter County, for no reason; (3) "No white man in Pickens County ever cast a Republican vote and lived after;" (4) in Hale County a negro benevolent society was ordered to meet no more; (5) masked men drove James Bliss, a negro, from Hale County; (6) J. G. Stokes, a Republican speaker, was warned by armed ruffians not to make another Radical speech in Hale County; (7) in Choctaw County 10 negroes had been killed and 13 wounded by whites in ambuscade; (8) in Marengo County W. A. Lipscomb was killed for being a Republican; (9) "Simon Edward and Monroe Keeton were killed in Sumter County for political effect;" (10) in Pickens County negroes were killed, tied to logs, and sent floating down the river with the following inscription, "To Mobile with the compliments of Pickens;" (11) W. P. Billings, a northern Republican, was killed in Sumter County on account of his politics, and Ivey, a negro mail agent, was also killed for his politics in Sumter; (12) there were numerous outrages in Coffee, Macon, and Russell counties; (13) near Carrollton, two negro speakers were hanged. Hays also declared that "only an occasional murder leaks out;" Republican speakers were always "rotten-egged" or shot at, while not a single Democrat was injured; the Associated Press agents were all "rebels and Democrats," and systematically misrepresented the Radical party to the North.

The *Tribune* after investigation pronounced the Hays-Hawley letter "a tissue of lies from beginning to end." The correspondent sent to Alabama investigated each reported outrage and found that the facts were as follows: (1) Allen said that he was beaten for private reasons by one person with the weapons of nature; (2) three negroes were killed by negroes and two were shot while stealing corn; (3) since 1867 there had been white Republican voters and officials in Sumter County; (4) the negro societies in Hale County denied that any of them had been ordered to disband; (5) James Bliss himself denied that he had been driven from Hale County; (6) affidavits of the Republican officials of Hale County denied the Stokes story; (7) in regard to the "10 killed and 13 wounded" outrage, affidavits were obtained from the "killed and wounded" denying that the reported outrage had occurred (the truth was, a negro was beaten by other negroes, and when the sheriff had attempted to arrest them, they resisted and one shot was fired; the negroes swore that they had told Hays that none was injured); (8) Lipscomb in person denied that he had been murdered or injured; (9) Edward and Keeton lived in Mississippi and there was no evidence that either had been murdered; (10) the story of the dead negroes tied to floating logs was not heard in Pickens County before Hays published it, and no foundation for it could be discovered; (11) Billings was killed by unknown persons for purposes of robbery, and Republican officials testified that the killing of Ivey was not political; (12) nothing could be found to support the statement about outrages in Coffee, Macon, and Russell counties; (13) the hanging of the two negroes near Carrollton was denied by the Republicans of that district. The *Tribune* correspondent asserted that Hays "knew that his statements were lies when he made them"; that the whites were exercising remarkable restraint; that they were trying hard to keep the peace; that counties in Hays's district were showing signs of going Democratic, and since his was the strongest Republican district, desperate measures were necessary to hold the Republicans in line; and that the administration press "had grossly slandered the people of the state."

Governor Lewis and a few of the Republicans had opposed the "outrage" issue, and though troops were sent to the state it was against the wishes of Lewis.[1]

The Washington administration readily listened to the "outrage" stories and prepared to interfere in Alabama affairs, though Governor Lewis could not be persuaded to ask for troops. President Grant wrote, on September 3, 1874, to Belknap, Secretary of War, directing him to hold troops in readiness to suppress the "atrocities" in Alabama, Georgia, and South Carolina. Early in September Attorney-General Williams began to encourage United States Marshal Healy to make arrests under the Enforcement Acts, and on September 29, 1874, he instructed Healy to appoint special deputies at all points where troops were to be stationed. He promised that the deputies would be supported by the infantry and cavalry. During October the state was filled with deputy marshals, agents of the Department of Justice and of the Post-office Department, and Secret Service men, most of them in disguise, searching for opportunities to arrest whites. Most of these men were of the lowest class, since only men of that kind would do the work required of them. The deputies were appointed, ten to twenty-five in each county, by Marshal Healy on the recommendation of the officials of the Republican party. Charles E. Mayer of Mobile, chairman of the Republican executive committee, nominated and secured the appointment of 217 deputy marshals, vouching for them as good Republicans, all except four Democrats who were warranted to be "mild, i.e. honest." Robert Barbour of Montgomery and Isaac Heyman of Opelika also nominated deputies.[2]

The marshals did some effective work during October. In Dallas County, where the Democrats had encouraged a bolting negro candidate with the intention of purchasing his office from him, the negro bolter and General John T. Morgan were arrested for violation of the Enforcement Acts.[3] In Sumter County, John Little, a negro

---

[1] *The Tribune*, Oct. 7, 8, and 12, 1874; *The Nation*, Aug. 27, and Oct. 15 and 27, 1874; Annual Cyclopædia (1874), p. 12; Foulke, "Life of O. P. Morton," Vol. II, p. 350. The Hays-Hawley letter was first published in the *Hartford Courant* and in the *Boston Daily Advertiser*. It is also in the Coburn Report, pp. 1254-1260.

[2] *N. Y. Tribune*, Oct. 7, 1874; Coburn Report, pp. 244, 245, 1221, 1226, 1241, 1247, 1264, 1266.

[3] Coburn Report, p. 512.

who had started a negro Democratic club called the "Independent Thinkers," was arrested and the club was broken up.[1] From Eufaula several prominent whites were taken, among them General Alpheus Baker, J. M. Buford, G. L. Comer, W. H. Courtney, and E. J. Black.[2]

In Livingston, where a Democratic convention was being held in the court-house, the deputy marshals came in, pretended to search through the whole room, and finally arrested Renfroe and Bullock, whom, with Chiles, they handcuffed and paraded about the county, exposing them to insult from gangs of negroes. The jailer in Sumter County refused to give up the jail to the use of the deputy marshals and was imprisoned in his own jail.[3] About the same time Colonel Wedmore, chairman of the Democratic county executive committee, was arrested with forty-two other prominent Democrats, thus almost destroying the party organization in Sumter County. Though there were three United States commissioners in Sumter County, Wedmore and others were carried to Mobile for trial before a United States commissioner there, and, instead of being carried by the shortest route, they were for political effect taken on a long détour via Demopolis, Selma, and Montgomery. Those arrested were never tried, but were released just before or soon after the election.[4] The whites were thoroughly intimidated in the black districts, but were not seriously molested in the white counties. The houses of nearly all the Democrats in the Black Belt were searched by the deputies and soldiers, and the women frightened and insulted. The officers of the army were disgusted with the nature of the work.[5]

Such was the intimidation practised by the officials of the Federal government. The Republican state administration took little part in the persecutions, because it was weak, because it was not desirous of being held responsible, and because some of the prominent officials were certain that the intimidation policy would injure their party. In the white counties there was considerably less effort to influence the elections. But by no means was all of the intimidation on the Repub-

---

[1] Coburn Report, p. 931.

[2] *Eufaula News*, Sept. 3, 1874; Coburn Report, p. 855.

[3] Coburn Report, pp. 679, 681, 746.

[4] Coburn Report, pp. 514, 515, 681, 1239.

[5] Coburn Report, pp. 680, 682; "An appeal to Governor Lewis from the People of Sumter."

lican side. In the counties where the whites were numerous the determination was freely expressed that the elections were to be carried by the whites. There were few open threats, very little violence, and none of the kind of persecution employed by the other side. But the whites had made up their minds, and the other side knew it, or rather felt it in the air, and were thereby intimidated. Besides the silent forces of ostracism, etc., already described, the whites found many other means of influencing the voters on both sides. Where Radical posters were put up announcing speakers and principles, the Democrats would tear them down and post instead caricatures of Spencer, Lewis, Hays, or Rapier, or declarations against "social equality enforced by law." In white districts some obnoxious speakers were "rotten-egged," others forbidden to speak and asked to leave. One Radical speaker complained that whites in numbers came to hear him, sat on the front seats with guns across their knees, blew tin horns, and asked him embarrassing questions about "political bacon" and race equality under the Civil Rights Bill. "Blacklists" of active negro politicians were kept and the whites warned against employing them; "pledge meetings" were held in some counties and negroes strenuously advised to sign the "pledge" to vote for the white man's party. "The Barbour County Fever" spread over the state. This was a term used for any process for making life miserable for white Radicals. There was something like a revival of the Ku Klux Klan in the White Leagues or clubs whose members were sworn to uphold "white" principles. In many towns these clubs were organized as military companies. Some of them applied to Governor Lewis for arms and for enrolment as militia. But he was afraid to organize any white militia because it might overthrow his administration, and, on the other hand, he also refused to give arms to negro militia because he feared race conflicts. By private subscription, often with money from the North, the white companies were armed and equipped. They drilled regularly and made long practice marches through the country. They kept the peace, they made no threats, but their influence was none the less forcible. The Democratic politicians were opposed to these organizations, but the latter persisted and several companies went in uniform to Houston's inauguration. The Republicans found cause for anxiety in the increasing frequency of Confederate veterans' reunions, and it is said that cavalry companies and squadrons of ex-Confederates began to drill again, much to the alarm of the blacks.[1] In truth, some of the whites were exasperated to the point where they were about ready to fight again. As one man expressed it: "The attempt to force upon the country this social equality, miscalled Civil Rights Bill, may result in another war. The southern people do not desire to take up arms again, but may be driven to desperation."[2]

The feelings of the poorer whites and those who had suffered most from Radical rule are reflected in the following speeches. A negro who was canvassing for Rapier, the negro congressman, was told by a white: "You might as well quit. We have made up our minds to carry the state or kill half of you negroes on election day. We begged you long enough and have persuaded you, but you will vote for the Radical party." Another white man said to negro Republicans, "God damn you, you have voted my land down to half a dollar an acre, and I wish the last one of you was down in the bottom of hell."[3]

The Democratic campaign was managed by W. L. Bragg, an able organizer, assisted by a competent staff. The state had not been so thoroughly canvassed since 1861. The campaign fund was the largest in the history of the state; every man who was able, and many who were not, contributed; assistance also came from northern Democrats, and northern capitalists who had investments in the South or who owned part of the legal bonds of the state. The election officials were all Radicals and with Federal aid had absolute control over the election. If inclined to fraud, as in 1868–1872, they could easily count themselves in, but they clearly understood that no fraud would be tolerated. To prevent the importation of negroes from Georgia and Mississippi guards were stationed all around the state. To prevent "repeating," which had formerly been done by massing the negroes at the county seat for their first vote and then sending them home to vote again, the whites made lists of all voters, white and black, kept an accurate account of all Democratic votes cast, and demanded that the votes be thus counted. So well did the Democrats know their resources that a week before the election an estimate of the vote was made that turned out to be almost exactly correct. In Randolph

County, several days before the election, the Democratic manager reported a certain number of votes for the Democrats; on election day two votes more than he estimated were cast.

Tons of campaign literature were distributed mainly by freight, express, and messengers, the mails having proved unsafe, being in the hands of the Radicals. For the same reason political messages were sent by telegraph. Every man who could speak had to "go on the stump." Toward the close of the campaign a hundred speeches a day were made by speakers sent out from headquarters. The lawyers did little or no business during October; it is said that of seventy-five lawyers in Montgomery all but ten were usually out of the city making speeches.[1]

The Election of 1874

The election of 1874 passed off with less violence than was expected; in fact, it was quieter than any previous campaign. The Democrats were assured of success and had no desire to lose the fruits of victory on account of riots and disorder. So the responsible people strained every nerve to preserve the peace. A regiment of soldiers was scattered throughout the Black Belt and showed a disposition to neglect the affairs of the blacks. But here, in the counties where the numerous arrests had been made, the blacks voted in full strength. In fact, with few exceptions, both parties voted in full strength, and, as regards the counting of the votes, it was the fairest election since the negroes began to vote. There were instances in white counties of negroes being forced to vote for the Democrats, while in the Black Belt negro Democrats were mobbed and driven from the polls. But the negro Democrats resorted to expedients to get in their tickets. In one county where the Democratic tickets were smooth at the top and the negro tickets perforated, the Democrats prepared perforated tickets for negro Democrats which went unquestioned. In other places special tickets were printed for the use of negro Democrats with the picture of General Grant or of Spencer on them and these passed the hurried Radical inspection and were cast for the Democrats. In Marengo County the Democrats purchased a Republican candidate,

[1] For information in regard to the campaign of 1874 I am indebted to several of those who took part in it, and especially to Mr. T. J. Rutledge, now state bank examiner, who was then secretary of the Democratic campaign committee.

who agreed for $300 that he would not be elected. By his "sign of the button," sent out among the negroes, the latter were instructed to vote a certain colored ticket which did not conform to law and hence was not counted. Other candidates agreed not to qualify after election, thus leaving the appointment to the governor.

In the Black Belt, now as before, the negroes were marshalled in regiments of 300 to 1500 under men who wrote orders purporting to be signed by General Grant, directing the negroes to vote for him. In Greene County 1400 uniformed negroes took possession of the polls, and excluded the few whites.[1] A riot in Mobile was brought on by the close supervision over election affairs, which was objected to by a drunken negro who wanted to vote twice, and who declared that he wanted "to wade in blood up to his boot tops." The negro was killed. A conflict at Belmont, where a negro was killed, and another at Gainesville were probably caused by the endeavor of the whites to exclude negroes who had been imported from Mississippi. By rioting the Republicans had everything to gain and the Democrats everything to lose, and while it is impossible in most cases to ascertain which party fired the first shot or struck the first blow, the evidence is clear that the desperate Radical whites encouraged the blacks to violent conduct in order to cause collisions between the races and thus secure Federal interference. In Eufaula occurred the most serious riot of the Reconstruction period that occurred in Alabama. The negroes came armed and threatening to the polls, which were held by a Republican sheriff and forty Republican deputies. Judge Keils, a carpet-bagger, had advised the blacks to come to Eufaula to vote: "You go to town; there are several troops of Yankees there; these damned Democrats won't shoot a frog. You come armed and do as you please." The Democrats were glad to have the troops, who were disgusted with the intimidation work of the previous month. Order was kept until a negro tried to vote the Democratic ticket and was discovered and mobbed by other blacks. The whites tried to protect him and some negro fired a shot. Then the riot began. The few whites were heavily armed and the negroes also. The deputies, it was said, lost their heads and fired indiscriminately. When the fight was over it was found that ten whites were wounded, and four negroes killed and sixty wounded. The Federal troops came leisurely in after

[1] Coburn Report, pp. 125, 530.

it was over, and surrounded the polls. The course of the Federal troops in Eufaula was much as it was elsewhere. They camped some distance from the polls, and when their aid was demanded by the Republicans the captain either directly refused to interfere, or consulted his orders or his telegrams or his law dictionary. At last he offered to *notify* the white men wanted by the marshal to meet the latter and be arrested.

Another commander, who took possession of the polls in Opelika in order to prevent a riot, was censured by General McDowell, the department commander. The troops were weary of such work, and their orders from General McDowell were very vague.[1] After the election, as was to be expected, an outcry arose from the Radicals that the troops had in every case failed to do their duty.

When the votes were counted, it appeared that the Democrats had triumphed. Houston had 107,118

ELECTION OF 1874 FOR GOVERNOR.

☐ Democratic Majority.
▨ Radical Majority, Houston, (Dem). 107,118.
▨ Nearly evenly divided, Lewis, (Rad). 93,928.
○ Black Counties.
⊗ U.S. Troops posted.

votes to 93,928 for Lewis. Two years before Herndon (Democrat) had received 81,371 votes to 89,868 for Lewis. The presidential campaign in 1872 had assisted Lewis. Grant ran far ahead of the Radical state ticket. The legislature of 1874–1875 was to be composed as follows: Senate, 13 Republicans (of whom 6 were negroes)

[1] Coburn Report, pp. xix, 43, 80–84, 427, 434, 476, 794, 850, 851, 949, 1200–1204; *Tuskegee News*, Nov. 5, 1874; *State Journal*, Oct. and Nov., 1874.

and 20 Democrats; House, 40 Republicans (of whom 29 were negroes) and 60 Democrats.[1]

The whites were exceedingly pleased with their victory, while the Republicans took defeat as something expected. There were, of course, the usual charges of outrage, Ku Kluxism, and the intimidation of the negro vote, but these were fewer than ever before.

ELECTION OF 1876 FOR GOVERNOR.

○ Black Counties
☐ Democratic Majority.
▨ Republican Majority.
═══ underscoring lines, a heavy minority vote, 25% to 49%.
Houston (Dem). 99,255, Woodruff (Rep), 55,582.
No Republican vote in 1878.

There was considerable complaint that the Federal troops had sided always with the whites in the election troubles. The Republican leaders knew, of course, that for their own time at least Alabama was to remain in the hands of the whites. The blacks were surprisingly indifferent after they discovered that there was to be no return to slavery, so much so that many whites feared that their indifference masked some deep-laid scheme against the victors.

The heart of the Black Belt still remained under the rule of the carpet-bagger and the black. The Democratic state executive Committee considered that enough had been gained for one election, so it ordered that no whites should contest on technical grounds alone the offices in those black counties. Other methods gradually gave the Black Belt to the whites. No Democrat would now go on the bond of a Republican official and numbers were unable to make

---

[1] Annual Cyclopædia (1874), p. 17; *Tribune* Almanac, 1875.

bond; their offices thus becoming vacant, the governor appointed Democrats. Others sold out to the whites, or neglected to make bond, or made bonds which were later condemned by grand juries. This resulted in many offices going to the whites, though most of them were still in the hands of the Republicans.[1]

Houston's two terms were devoted to setting affairs in order. The administration was painfully economical. Not a cent was spent beyond what was absolutely necessary. Numerous superfluous offices were cut off at once and salaries reduced. The question of the public debt was settled. To prevent future interference by Federal authorities the time for state elections was changed from November, the time of the Federal elections, to August, and this separation is still in force. The whites now demanded a new constitution. Their objections to the constitution of 1868 were numerous: it was forced upon the whites, who had no voice in framing it; it "reminds us of unparalleled wrongs"; it had not secured good government; it was a patchwork unsuited to the needs of the state; it had wrecked the credit of the state by allowing the indorsement of private corporations; it provided for a costly administration, especially for a complicated and unworkable school system which had destroyed the schools; there was no power of expansion for the judiciary; and above all, it was not legally adopted.[2]

The Republicans declared against a new constitution as meant to destroy the school system, provide imprisonment for debt, abolish exemption from taxation, disfranchise and otherwise degrade the blacks. By a vote of 77,763 to 59,928, a convention was ordered by the people, and to it were elected 80 Democrats, 12 Republicans, and 7 Independents. A new constitution was framed and adopted in 1875.[3]

---

[1] Coburn Report, pp. 239, 253, 701, 703; *The Nation*, Nov. 30, 1874; *Tuskegee News*, Dec. 10, 1874.

[2] In the code of Alabama (1876), pp. 100–120, is printed the "Constitution (so-called) of the State of Alabama, 1868," as the code terms it. The last three amendments are thus noted, "Adoption proclaimed by the Secretary of State, Dec. 18, 1865" (or July 20, 1868, or March 30, 1870). The other amendments have notes stating date of submission and date of ratification by the state. See code of 1876, pp. 27, 28; also code of 1896.

[3] The negroes voted against it. Some of them were told that, if adopted, a war with Spain would result and that the blacks, being the "only truly loyal," would have to do most of the fighting against the Spanish, who would land at Apalachicola, Milton,

Later Phases of State Politics

From 1875 to 1889 neither national party was able to control both houses of Congress. Consequently no "force" legislation could be directed against the white people of Alabama, who had control and were making secure their control of the state administration.

ELECTION OF 1880 FOR GOVERNOR
☐ Democratic majority ○ Black Co's
▨ Republican - Greenback majority.
Dem. = 133,878 to 42,363 Rep.
═ Underscoring lines, a heavy minority
vote, 25% to 49%

The black vote was not eliminated, but gradually fell under the control of the native whites when the carpet-bagger and scalawag left the Black Belt. In order to gain control of the black vote, carpet-bag methods were sometimes resorted to, though there was not as much fraud and violence used as is believed, for the simple reason that it was not necessary; it was little more difficult now to make the blacks vote for the Democrats than it had been to make Republicans of them; the mass of them voted, in both cases, as the stronger power willed it.

The Black Belt came finally into Democratic control in 1880, when the party leaders ordered the Alabama Republicans to vote the Greenback ticket. The negroes did not understand the meaning of the manœuvre, did not vote in force, and lost their last stronghold. A few white Republicans and a few black leaders united to maintain the Republican state organization in order that they

and Eufaula. See *Tuskegee News*, Dec. 9, 1875. See also in regard to the new constitution, *Tuskegee News*, June 3, 1875; "Northern Alabama Illustrated," pp. 51, 52; Annual Cyclopædia (1875), p. 14; Ho. Ex. Doc., No. 46, 43d Cong., 2d Sess.; "Report of the Joint Committee in regard to the Amendment of the Constitution."

might control the division of spoils coming from the Republican administration at Washington. Most of them were or became Federal officials within the state. It was not to their interest that their numbers should increase, for the shares in the spoils would then be smaller. Success in the elections was now the last thing desired.

This clique of office-holders was almost destroyed by the two Democratic administrations under Cleveland, and has been unhappy under later Republican administrations; but the Federal administration in the state is not yet respectable. Dissatisfaction on the part of the genuine Republicans in the northern counties resulted in the formation of a "Lily White" faction which demanded that the negro be dropped as a campaign issue and that an attempt be made to build up a decent white Republican party. The opposing faction has been called "The Black and Tans," and has held to the negro. The national party organization and the administration have refused to recognize the

ELECTION OF 1890 FOR GOVERNOR

O Black Counties.
☐ Dem. majority, vote = 139.910
▨ Rep. majority, vote = 42,440
══ Underscoring lines, a heavy minority
     vote, 25 % to 49 %.

demands of the "Lily Whites"; and it would be exceedingly embarrassing to go back on the record of the past in regard to the negro as the basis of the Republican party in the South. In consequence the growth of a reputable white party has been hindered.

The Populist movement promised to cause a healthy division of the whites into two parties. But the tactics of the national Republican organization in trying to profit by this division, by running in the negroes, resulted in a close reunion of the discordant whites, the Populists furnishing to the reunited party some new principles and many new leaders, while the Democrats furnished the name, traditions, and organization.

To make possible some sort of division and debate among the whites the system of primary elections was adopted. In these elections the whites were able to decide according to the merits of the candidate and the issues involved. The candidate of the whites chosen in the primaries was easily elected. This plan had the merit of placing the real contest among the whites, and there was no danger of race troubles in elections. In the Black Belt the primary system was legalized and served by its regulations to confine the election contests to regularly nominated candidates, and hence to whites, the blacks having lost their organization.

ELECTION FOR GOVERNOR 1902,
UNDER NEW CONSTITUTION

The Fourteenth and Fifteenth amendments in their operation gave undue political influence to the whites of the Black Belt, and this was opposed by whites of other districts. It also resulted in serious corruption in elections. There was always danger in the Black Belt that the Republicans, taking advantage of divisions among the whites, would run in the negroes again. There were instances when the whites simply counted out the negro vote or used "shotgun" methods to prevent a return to the intolerable conditions of Reconstruction. The people grew weary of the eternal "negro in the woodpile," and a demand arose for a revision of the constitution in order to eliminate the mass of the negro voters, to do away with corruption in the elections and to leave the whites free. The conservative leaders, like Governors Jones and Oates, were rather opposed to a disfranchising movement. The Black Belt whites were somewhat doubtful, but the mass of the whites were determined, and the work was done; the stamp of legality was thus placed upon the long-finished work of necessity, and the "white man's movement" had reached its logical end.[1]

The mistakes and failures of Reconstruction are clear to all. Whether any successes were achieved by the Congressional plan has been a matter for debate. It has been strongly asserted that Reconstruction, though failing in many important particulars, succeeded in others. The successes claimed may be summarized as follows: (1) there was no more legislation for the negro similar to that of 1865–66, that following the Reconstruction being "infinitely milder"; (2) Reconstruction gave the negroes a civil status that a century of "restoration" would not have accomplished, for though the right to vote is a nullity, other undisputed rights of the black are due to the Reconstruction;. the unchangeable organic laws of the state and of the United States favor negro suffrage, which will come the sooner for being thus theoretically made possible; (3) Reconstruction prevented the southern leaders from returning to Washington as irreconcilables, and gave them troubles enough to keep them busy until a new generation grew up which accepted the results of war; (4) by organizing the blacks it made them independent of white control in politics; (5) it gave the negro an independent church; (6) it gave the negro a right to education and gave to both races the public school system; (7) it made the negro economically free and showed that free labor was better than slave labor; (8) it destroyed the former

---

[1] Most whites believe that eliminating the negro has solved the problem of the negro in politics. It seems to me that this is a superficial view. The black counties are still represented in party conventions and legislature in proportion to population. The white counties are jealous of this undue influence and would like to reduce this representation. The party leaders have been able to repress this jealousy, but it is not forgotten. Before it will submit to loss of representation the Black Belt, it is believed, will gradually admit to the franchise those negroes who have been excluded, and they will vote with the whites. Such a course will undoubtedly cause political realignments. Notice on the maps that the Republican strongholds are now in the white counties. The "Lily Whites" are increasing in numbers.

3 F

leaders of the whites and "freed them from the baleful influence of old political leaders"; in general, as Sumner said, the ballot to the negro was "a peacemaker, a schoolmaster, a protector," soon making him a fairly good citizen, and secured peace and order — the "political hell" through which the whites passed being a necessary discipline which secured the greatest good to the greatest number.[1]

On the other hand, it may be maintained (1) that the intent of the legislation of 1865–1866 has been entirely misunderstood, that it was intended on the whole for the benefit of the negro as well as of the white, and that it has been left permanently off the statute book, not because the whites have been taught better by Reconstruction, but because of the amendments which prohibit in theory what has all along been practised (hence the gross abuses of peonage); (2) that the theoretical rights of the negro have been no inducement to grant him actual privileges, and that these theoretical rights have not proven so permanent as was supposed before the disfranchising movement spread through the South; (3) that the generation after Reconstruction is more irreconcilable than the conservative leaders who were put out of politics in 1865–1867 — that the latter were willing to give the negro a chance, while the former, able, radical, and supported by the people, find less and less place for the negro; (4) that if the blacks were united, so were the whites, and in each case the advantage may be questioned; (5) that the value of the negro church is doubtful; (6) that as in politics, so in education, the negro has no opportunities now that were not freely offered him in 1865–1866, and the school system is not a product of Reconstruction, but came near being destroyed by it; (7) that negro free labor is not as efficient as slave labor was, and the negro as a cotton producer has lost his supremacy and his economic position is not at all assured; (8) that the whites have acquired new leaders, but the change has been on the whole from conservatives to radicals, from friends of the negro to those indifferent to him. In short, a careful study of conditions in Alabama since 1865 will not lead one to the conclusion that the

---

[1] These views are set forth most clearly by Alexander Johnston in Lalor's "Cyclopædia of Political Science," Vol. III, p. 556. See also McCall, "Thaddeus Stevens," and his article in the *Atlantic Monthly*, June, 1901; Blaine, "Twenty Years"; Schurz, in *McClure's Magazine*, Jan., 1905; Grosvenor, in *Forum*, Aug., 1900.

black race in that state has any rights or privileges or advantages that were not offered by the native whites in 1865–1866.

For the misgovernment of Reconstruction, the negro, who was in no way to blame, has been made to suffer, since those who were really responsible could not be reached; so politically the races are hostile; the Black Belt has had, until recently, an undue and disturbing influence in white politics; the Federal official body and the Republican organization in the state have not been respectable, and the growth of a white Republican party has been prevented; the whites have for thirty-five years distrusted and disliked the Federal administration which, until recent years, showed little disposition to treat them with any consideration;[1] the rule of the carpet-bagger, scalawag, and negro, and the methods used to overthrow that rule, weakened the respect of the people for the ballot, for law, for government; the estrangement of the races and the social-equality teachings of the reconstructionists have made it much less safe than in slavery for whites to reside near negro communities, and the negro is more exposed to imposition by low whites.

In recent years there have been many signs of improvement, but only in proportion as the principles and practices that the white people of the state understand are those of Reconstruction are rejected or superseded. To the northern man Reconstruction probably meant and still means something quite different from what the white man of Alabama understands by the term. But as the latter understands it, he has accepted none of its essential principles and intends to accept none of its so-called successes.

In destroying all that was old, Reconstruction probably removed some abuses; from the new order some permanent good must have resulted. But credit for neither can rightfully be claimed until it can be shown that those results were impossible under the régime destroyed.

[1] For a belated recognition of the reasons for this, see H. L. Nelson, "Three Months of Roosevelt," in the *Atlantic Monthly*, Feb., 1902.

APPENDIX I

PRODUCTION OF COTTON IN ALABAMA. 1860-1900

(a) Typical black counties with boundaries unchanged.   (b) Typical white counties.

County	1860	1870	1880	1890	1900
	bales	bales	bales	bales	bales
Autauga . . .	17,329	7,965	7,944	10,431	14,348
Baker (Chilton) . .	—	1,360	3,534	6,233	9,932
Baldwin . . .	2,172	87	638	1,663	531
Barbour (a) . .	44,518	17,011	26,063	33,440	29,395
Bibb	8,303	3,973	4,843	5,216	6,535
Blount (b) . . .	1,071	950	4,442	9,748	11,449
Bullock . . .	—	17,972	22,578	30,547	31,774
Butler . . .	13,489	5,854	11,895	18,200	21,147
Calhoun . . .	11,573	3,038	10,848	11,504	11,554
Chambers . .	24,589	7,868	19,476	27,276	30,676
Cherokee (b) . .	10,562	1,807	10,777	11,870	12,767
Choctaw (a) . .	17,252	6,439	9,054	13,586	13,091
Clarke (a) . .	16,225	5,713	11,097	16,380	16,594
Clay (b) . . .	—	1,143	4,973	8,250	10,459
Cleburne (b) . .	—	873	3,600	5,389	5,035
Coffee (b) . .	5,294	2,004	4,788	11,791	16,747
Colbert . . .	—	3,936	9,012	3,956	9,234
Conecuh (b) . .	6,850	1,539	4,633	8,167	9,801
Coosa . . .	13,990	3,893	8,411	10,141	11,370
Covington (b) . .	2,021	689	1,158	2,740	5,969
Crenshaw (b) . .	—	4,638	8,173	13,442	18,909
Cullman (b) . .	—	—	378	5,268	9,374
Dale (b) . . .	7,836	4,273	6,224	16,259	17,868
Dallas (a) . .	63,410	24,819	33,534	42,819	48,273
De Kalb (b) . .	1,498	205	2,859	4,573	9,860
Elmore (b) . .	—	7,295	9,771	16,871	18,458
Escambia . . .	—	605	94	462	1,131
Etowah (b) . .	—	1,383	6,571	8,482	11,651
Fayette (b) . .	5,462	1,909	4,268	6,141	9,128
Franklin . . .	15,592	2,072	3,603	2,669	6,047
Geneva (b) . .	—	420	1,112	7,158	9,813

County	1860	1870	1880	1890	1900
	bales	bales	bales	bales	bales
Greene (a) . . .	57,858	9,910	15,811	20,901	23,681
Hale	—	18,573	18,093	28,973	28,645
Henry (b) . . .	13,034	7,127	12,573	23,738	27,281
Jackson (b) . .	2,713	2,339	6,235	5,358	5,602
Jefferson (b) . .	4,940	1,470	5,333	4,829	7,044
Lamar (Sanford) (b) .	—	1,825	5,015	6,998	10,118
Lauderdale . . .	11,050	5,457	9,270	5,156	9,708
Lawrence . . .	15,434	9,243	13,791	9,248	12,541
Lee	—	11,591	13,189	18,332	22,431
Limestone . . .	15,115	7,319	15,724	8,093	14,887
Lowndes (a) . .	53,664	18,369	29,356	40,388	39,839
Macon (a) . . .	41,119	11,872	14,580	19,099	20,434
Madison . . .	22,119	12,180	20,679	13,150	20,842
Marengo (a) . .	62,428	23,614	23,481	31,651	38,392
Marion (b) . .	4,285	463	2,240	4,454	6,309
Marshall (b) . .	4,931	2,340	5,358	8,118	13,318
Mobile . . .	440	317	1	24	116
Monroe (a) . .	18,226	6,172	10,421	15,919	17,101
Montgomery (a) . .	58,880	25,517	31,732	45,827	39,202
Morgan (b) . .	6,326	4,389	6,133	6,227	9,313
Perry (a) . . .	44,603	13,449	21,627	24,873	29,690
Pickens (a) . .	29,843	8,263	17,283	18,904	21,485
Pike (b) . . .	24,527	7,192	15,136	25,879	34,757
Randolph (b) . .	6,427	2,246	7,475	10,348	17,148
Russell (a) . . .	38,728	20,796	19,442	20,521	21,174
Shelby (b) . . .	6,463	2,194	6,643	7,308	10,193
St. Clair (b) . .	4,189	1,244	6,028	7,136	9,411
Sumter (a) . . .	36,584	11,647	22,211	25,768	31,906
Talladega . . .	18,243	5,697	11,832	15,686	21,563
Tallapoosa (b) . .	17,399	5,446	14,161	20,337	24,955
Tuscaloosa . . .	26,035	6,458	11,137	13,008	20,041
Walker (b) . . .	2,766	928	2,754	3,211	4,746
Washington . .	3,449	1,803	1,246	2,030	2,213
Wilcox (a) . . .	48,749	20,095	26,745	32,582	35,005
Winston (b) . .	352	205	568	1,464	3,686
Totals . . .	989,955	429,482	699,654	915,219	1,093,697

APPENDIX II

REGISTRATION OF VOTERS UNDER THE NEW CONSTITUTION

COUNTY	MALES OF VOTING AGE IN 1900		REGISTERED VOTERS IN 1905	
	White	Black	White	Black
Autauga	1,524	2,311	1,554	35
Baldwin	2,096	991	1,390	206
Barbour	2,889	4,201	2,846	46
Bibb	2,701	1,598	2,725	59
Blount	4,401	417	3,182	—
Bullock	1,415	5,168	1,291	14
Butler	2,766	2,617	2,739	2
Calhoun	5,390	2,380	4,892	130
Chambers	3,441	3,380	3,098	28
Cherokee	3,896	702	3,004	27
Chilton	2,852	707	2,970	1
Choctaw	1,697	1,929	1,496	29
Clarke	2,652	3,103	2,485	158
Clay	3,220	393	3,501	—
Cleburne	2,565	181	2,280	—
Coffee	3,508	996	3,334	—
Colbert	2,927	2,030	2,233	22
Conecuh	2,110	1,608	2,079	7
Coosa	2,338	942	2,134	—
Covington	2,803	786	2,857	3
Crenshaw	3,062	1,156	2,982	—
Cullman	3,359	5	4,641	4
Dale	3,492	1,002	3,021	11
Dallas	2,360	9,871	2,419	52
De Kalb	4,819	226	4,388	—
Elmore	3,202	2,758	3,030	54
Escambia	1,628	821	1,676	46
Etowah	5,140	1,031	4,186	39
Fayette	2,698	338	2,563	7
Franklin	2,989	634	2,600	12
Geneva	3,355	981	2,873	30
Greene	852	4,344	739	104

County	Males of Voting Age in 1900		Registered Voters in 1905	
	White	Black	White	Black
Hale	1,358	5,370	1,362	92
Henry }	4,904	2,933	2,072	—
Houston }	(new	county)	2,757	—
Jackson	5,939	731	4,704	73
Jefferson	21,036	18,472	18,315	352
Lamar	2,715	592	2,356	7
Lauderdale	4,235	1,586	3,305	76
Lawrence	2,761	1,426	2,367	49
Lee	2,988	3,472	2,652	12
Limestone	2,832	2,050	2,722	28
Lowndes	1,121	6,455	1,085	57
Macon	1,042	3,782	917	65
Madison	5,788	4,397	4,479	112
Marengo	2,095	6,143	2,043	302
Marion	2,735	144	2,698	25
Marshall	4,595	333	4,251	—
Mobile	7,934	7,371	7,295	193
Monroe	2,307	2,570	2,178	40
Montgomery . . .	5,087	11,429	4,995	53
Morgan	4,987	1,713	4,506	60
Perry	1,574	5,028	1,659	90
Pickens	2,408	2,846	2,217	111
Pike	3,598	2,611	3,126	26
Randolph	3,457	978	3,363	13
Russell	1,433	3,961	1,170	191
Shelby	3,611	1,672	3,712	19
St. Clair	3,777	712	3,340	50
Sumter	1,391	5,304	1,244	57
Talladega	3,934	3,814	3,303	81
Tallapoosa	4,185	2,056	4,166	33
Tuscaloosa	5,100	3,413	4,153	165
Walker	4,582	1,351	4,894	1
Washington . . .	1,386	1,179	1,339	53
Wilcox	1,686	5,967	1,522	41
Winston	1,884	3	1,833	1
Totals	224,212	181,471	205,278	3,654

Number of whites of voting age not registered, estimated at 45,000.
Number of blacks of voting age not registered, estimated at 190,000.
Foreign whites of voting age, 8082.
Number of whites registered but unable to comply with other requirements for voting,
estimated at 60,000.

INDEX

VITA

WALTER LYNWOOD FLEMING, born April 8, 1874, at Brundidge, Pike County, Alabama. Prepared for college in the public schools of Alabama; pursued college course at the Alabama Polytechnic Institute (Alabama State College), and graduate work in the School of Political Science, Columbia University. Degrees: B.S., Alabama Polytechnic Institute, 1896; M.S., *ibid.*, 1897; A.M., Columbia University, 1901; Ph.D., *ibid.*, 1904. Taught in the public schools of Alabama, 1894–1895; assistant in History, English, and Mathematics, and assistant librarian, Alabama Polytechnic Institute, 1896–1898; officer, United States Army, 1898–1899; instructor in English and assistant librarian, Alabama Polytechnic Institute, 1899–1900; lecturer in History, Columbia University, 1902–1903; associate professor of History, West Virginia University, 1903–1904; professor of History, *ibid.*, since 1904. Editor of "Documents relating to Reconstruction" (1904), and of Lester and Wilson's "History of Ku Klux Klan" (1905); author of "The Reconstruction of the Seceded States" (1905).

PUBLICATIONS OF THE

COLUMBIA UNIVERSITY PRESS

The Macmillan Company, Agents, 64-66 Fifth Avenue, New York

Books published at net prices are sold by booksellers everywhere at the advertised net prices. When delivered from the publishers, carriage, either postage or expressage, is an extra charge.

SCIENCE OF STATISTICS. By RICHMOND MAYO-SMITH, Ph.D., Professor of Political Economy and Social Science, Columbia University.
Part I. **STATISTICS AND SOCIOLOGY.** 8vo, cloth, pp. xvi + 399. Price, $3.00 *net*.
Part II. **STATISTICS AND ECONOMICS.** 8vo, cloth, pp. xiii + 467. Price, $3.00 *net*.

ESSAYS IN TAXATION. By EDWIN R. A. SELIGMAN, Professor of Political Economy and Finance, Columbia University. 8vo, cloth, pp. x + 434. Price, $3.00 *net*.

THE SHIFTING AND INCIDENCE OF TAXATION. By EDWIN R. A. SELIGMAN, Professor of Political Economy and Finance, Columbia University. Second Edition, completely revised and enlarged. 8vo, cloth, pp. xii + 337. Price, $3.00 *net*.

THE ECONOMIC INTERPRETATION OF HISTORY. By EDWIN R. A. SELIGMAN, Professor of Political Economy and Finance, Columbia University. 12mo, cloth, pp. ix + 166. Price, $1.50 *net*.

THE PROBLEM OF MONOPOLY. By JOHN BATES CLARK, LL.D., Professor of Political Economy, Columbia University. 12mo, cloth, pp. vi + 128. Price, $1.25 *net*.

THE GOVERNMENT OF MUNICIPALITIES. By DORMAN B. EATON. 8vo, cloth, pp. x + 498 + 28. Price, $4.00 *net*.

MUNICIPAL HOME RULE. A Study in Administration. By FRANK J. GOODNOW, A.M., LL.D., Professor of Administrative Law, Columbia University. 12mo, cloth, pp. xxiv + 283. Price, $1.50 *net*.

MUNICIPAL PROBLEMS. By FRANK J. GOODNOW, A.M., LL.D., Professor of Administrative Law, Columbia University. 12mo, cloth, pp. xiii + 321. Price, $1.50 *net*.

THE PRINCIPLES OF SOCIOLOGY. An Analysis of the Phenomena of Association and of Social Organization. By FRANKLIN HENRY GIDDINGS, M.A., Professor of Sociology, Columbia University. 8vo, cloth, pp. xxvi + 476. Price, $3.00 *net*.

CRIME IN ITS RELATION TO SOCIAL PROGRESS. By ARTHUR CLEVELAND HALL, Ph.D. 8vo, pp. 427. Price, paper, $3.00 *net*; in cloth, $3.50 *net*.